Sociology of Families

SECOND EDITION

David M. Newman

DePauw University

Liz Grauerholz

Purdue University

PINE FORGE PRESS
An Imprint of Sage Publications, Inc.
Thousand Oaks • London • New Delhi

To my family

— David

To David F.,
Emma, and Lara

— Liz

For information:

Pine Forge Press
An imprint of Sage Publications, Inc.
2455 Teller Road
Thousand Oaks, California 91320
(805) 499-4224
E-mail: order@pfp.sagepub.com

Sage Publications Ltd.
6 Bonhill Street
London EC2A 4PU
United Kingdom

Sage Publications India Pvt. Ltd.
M-32 Market
Greater Kailash I
New Delhi 110 048 India

Printed in the United States of America

Library of Congress Cataloging-in-Publication Data
Newman, David M., 1958–
    Sociology of families / David M. Newman, Elizabeth Grauerholz. — 2nd.
  ed.
        p.   cm.
    Includes bibliographical references and index.
    ISBN 978-0-7619-8749-9 (cloth)
      1. Family—United States. 2. Family—United States—Public opinion
  3. Social problems—United States. 4. Public opinion—United States.
  5. United States—Social conditions. I. Grauerholz, Elizabeth, 1958–
  II. Title.
    HQ536 .N523   2002
    306.85'0973—dc21

                                                    2001007232

This book is printed on acid-free paper.

10 11 12 13 14   9 8 7 6 5 4 3

Production Management: *Scratchgravel Publishing Services*
Copy Editor: *Linda Purrington*
Typesetter: *Scratchgravel Publishing Services*
Indexer: *James Minkin*
Cover Designer: *Michelle Lee*

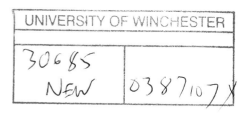

ABOUT THE AUTHORS

David M. Newman (Ph.D., University of Washington) is Associate Professor of Sociology at DePauw University. He teaches courses in introductory sociology, research methods, family, social psychology, and deviance. He has won teaching awards at both the University of Washington and DePauw University.

Liz Grauerholz (Ph.D., Indiana University) is Associate Professor of Sociology at Purdue University. Her research and teaching focus on gender, families, and power. She has been the recipient of Purdue's Outstanding Undergraduate Teaching Award, Teaching for Tomorrow Award, and the School of Liberal Arts' Educational Excellence Award. She is also a fellow in Purdue's Teaching Academy.

ABOUT THE PUBLISHER

Pine Forge Press is an educational publisher, dedicated to publishing innovative books and software throughout the social sciences. On this and any other of our publications, we welcome your comments.

Please write to:

Pine Forge Press
An imprint of Sage Publications, Inc.
2455 Teller Road
Thousand Oaks, CA 91320-2218
(805) 499-0871
E-mail: info.pineforge@sagepub.com

Visit our World Wide Web site, your direct link to a multitude of online resources:

www.pineforge.com

Titles of Related Interest from Pine Forge Press

Social Statistics for a Diverse Society, Third Edition,
by Chava Frankfort-Nachmias and Anna Leon-Guerrero

Investigating the Social World: The Process and Practice of Research, Third Edition,
by Russell K. Schutt

Sociology for a New Century
by York Bradshaw, Joseph F. Healey, and Rebecca Smith

Race, Ethnicity, Gender, and Class: The Sociology of Group Conflict and Change, Third Edition,
by Joseph F. Healey

Illuminating Social Life: Classical and Contemporary Theory, Second Edition,
by Peter Kivisto

Sociology in Action: Cases for Critical and Sociological Thinking
by David Hachen

Aging: The Social Context, Second Edition,
by Leslie Morgan and Suzanne Kunkel

The Production of Reality: Essays and Readings on Social Interaction, Third Edition,
by Jodi O'Brien and Peter Kollock

The Social Worlds of Higher Education: Handbook for Teaching in a New Century
by Bernice Pescosolido and Ronald Aminzade

Designing Families: The Search for Self and Community in the Information Age
by John Scanzoni

Worlds of Difference: Inequality in the Aging Experience, Third Edition,
by Eleanor Palo Stoller and Rose Campbell Gibson

Families in Later Life
by Alexis Walker, Margaret Manoogian-O'Dell, Lori McGraw, and Diana White

Sociology: Exploring The Architecture of Everyday Life, Fourth Edition,
by David M. Newman

Sociology: Exploring the Architecture of Everyday Life, Readings, Fourth Edition,
by David M. Newman and Jodi A. O'Brien

Brief Contents

Detailed Contents

PART I   Examining Family Issues and Controversies   1

ISSUE 1   What Is a Family? / 2

ISSUE 2   Is the Institution of Family Breaking Down— and Society with It? / 18

CHAPTER 3   Race, Ethnicity, and Families / 141

CHAPTER 4   Wealth, Poverty, and Families / 165

CHAPTER 7   Work Life and Family Life / 277

CHAPTER 8   Parenthood and Parenting / 321

CHAPTER 9   ## Childhood and Child Rearing / 357

CHAPTER 10   ## Intimate Violence / 395

CHAPTER 11 ## Divorce and Remarriage / 437

CHAPTER 12 ## Family Transitions in Adulthood / 479

CHAPTER 13   ## Families in a Changing Society / 517

Preface

You'd be hard pressed to find a topic as emotionally compelling and as personally interesting to people as family. Tell people you're writing a book about families, and you're sure to hear some anecdote that they thought should be included ("You want to know about families? Just ask me. I'll tell you about *families*. Mine's a doozy!"); or an opinion about society-wide family problems ("Parents aren't disciplining their kids enough, and *that's* why there's so much violence in schools!"); or a request for advice on some difficulty they're having ("How can I get my teenage daughter to listen to me?!").

Everybody, it seems, has something to say or some strong feeling about families. Type the word *families* into an Internet search engine, and you'll discover hundreds of categories and thousands of sites devoted to different aspects of families. Most sites highlight academic research on various aspects of family life (marriage, divorce, children, and so on), the positions of political interest groups devoted to some family-related issue, or services provided by nonprofit family organizations.

If you move beyond those types of sites, you'll find something even more interesting: thousands of *personal* family home pages—individual families simply presenting information about, well, themselves. Some of these pages are temporary postings that people use to provide relatives with information about specific upcoming events such as family reunions. But most of these sites go much further, conveying the sort of information you typically find in those letters people stuff in Christmas cards: "Fred finally passed the CPA exam." "Suzie loves her new position as goalkeeper on the travel soccer team." "Our trip to China was simply breathtaking." "We're thinking of planting cherry tomatoes instead of Romas this year." Many Web pages contain elaborate digital family photo albums with pictures of weddings, christenings, children through various stages of growth and development, beloved pets, redecorated houses, cruise trips, and so on. Some offer even deeper peeks into private lives by providing detailed family trees, religious testimonials, wedding vows, favorite cookie recipes, opinions on controversial issues such as home schooling or gay marriage, and space to submit suggestions for baby names. A few years back, one woman even broadcast the birth of her child, live, over the Internet.

What do you suppose would motivate people to expose the private details of their families to the vast, anonymous world of cyberspace? It's not as if there's a critical mass of people out there dying to know right away about Joe and Martha Klotzman's fondness for Tupperware parties. Instead, people like the Klotzmans are taking this technological opportunity to make a public statement about their commitment to and pride in their families. And they're not the only ones.

Lately a parade of high-profile people have publicly declared their commitment to their families and their willingness to sacrifice for them. In the span of just two months during the summer of 2001, newspaper stories described how the following people retired or left their jobs because they wanted to spend more time with their families: a San Jose,

California, newspaper executive; a Los Angeles newspaper publisher; the chairman of the CNN newsgroup; a real estate developer in Marina del Rey, California; the founder of an educational consulting firm in Iowa City; an all-star hockey player; a future Hall of Fame baseball player; the founder of a vending machine company in Seattle; an actor on the hit TV series *NYPD Blue;* the president of the Chicago Board of Education; the founder of the Home Depot retail chain; the Chamber of Commerce president in Paso Robles, California; the owner of a famous clothing store in Boulder, Colorado. And these are just the people who are famous enough or rich enough to be newsworthy. Devotion to family has certainly become fashionable at the dawn of the twenty-first century.

A topic so central and so deeply interesting to so many people should be the easiest thing to write about, right? Not necessarily. For as long as people have pondered the human condition, scholars, poets, novelists, musicians, and clergy have examined, studied, celebrated, bemoaned, made predictions about, and written about every conceivable aspect of family life. There is no shortage of contemporary "experts" who are willing to offer their 2 cents about the joys and sorrows of families. So how does one write about something so eternally important without trodding over well-worn ground?

We knew from the beginning that we didn't want this book simply to be an encyclopedia of information useful only in the context of a college course and easily discarded at the end of the semester. We wanted it to be something of a guide as well—not only *informative* in terms of current sociological knowledge of families, but *meaningful* in terms of contemporary family debates and *applicable* to your own family life. In other words, we wanted the book to connect to your personal experiences while, at the same time, showing you how sociologists understand and explain families.

One of the difficulties in accomplishing this goal is that a student's first course or first textbook on family is never his or her introduction to the topic of family. Everybody has grown up in one type of family or another. Consequently, all students bring with them to these courses a lifetime's worth of personal information, data, values, expectations, and assumptions about family life. Many have seen their parents divorce and remarry. Most have siblings or grandparents or cousins. Some have even formed their own families. Indeed, it's often said that when it comes to a topic like family, everyone is a potential expert.

With this direct knowledge comes some deeply held beliefs about what a family is and how it should work. Such preconceived notions present special challenges to instructors—and, by extension, to textbook authors. Certainly we want our students to be able to apply the course material directly to their own lived experiences. We've discovered in our own classes that students are more attentive and learn more when they find the subject matter immediately relevant to their lives.

But at the same time we want our classes and our textbooks to be more than just an album of personally familiar snippets of family life. The "it-happens-to-me-therefore-it-must-be-true-for-everyone" approach to family-related topics can be a serious obstacle to learning. Classroom discussions that stay at this level become mere exchanges of personal anecdotes, and students learn little about understanding the subject sociologically.

So a course—and a textbook—on family must go beyond simply telling stories you can relate to. It must show how professional scholars go about understanding the social patterns that underlie those family matters that everyone seems to have some experience with or some opinion about. A textbook must therefore provide you with the intellectual tools you need to *understand* the broader social implications of your own family experiences, *appreciate* the applicability of the sociological perspective to your own life, and critically *evaluate* the social information about families that bombards you every day. In short, it must strike a balance between the personal and emotional relevance of the material on the one hand and the scholarly understanding of it on the other.

One way to accomplish this goal is to teach (and write) "deductively"—starting with an examination of sociological theory and research and then "working down" to the level of personally relevant examples, "real-world" experiences, and controversial issues. This style of teaching often relies on a traditional lecture-style format and an authoritative textbook. Unfortunately such an approach—especially with a topic such as family—runs the serious risk of "losing" you early on. Certainly you should understand the sociological perspective on family. But a perspective that sounds technical and seems scientifically disconnected runs the risk of robbing personally meaningful topics of all their flavor and interest. Many very good, informative textbooks today that aim to be rigorous, scholarly, and thoroughly sociological turn students off before the end of the first chapter. As we've seen in our own teaching, students want the knowledge they acquire in college to be intellectually stimulating, but they also want it to be pertinent, provocative, and timely.

Thus, we've organized this textbook on family around an "inductive" style of learning, the sort of "active" approach that more and more instructors are using these days. The book begins at the level of personal relevance and controversy with an examination of some familiar contemporary issues—topics you are likely to know or feel strongly about. Once this personal connection has been made, we "work up" to the deeper and more detailed sociological understanding of the issues at hand. First we examine the relationship between people's family experiences and key sociological theories and concepts. From there we focus on family experiences through the life course, using the theories and the data of social science to understand the meaning and broader relevance of those experiences.

The Design of This Book

Because this book is based on an inductive style of learning, it is organized very differently from most family textbooks. It's divided into three parts that are distinct from one another in style, content, and purpose.

Part I, *Examining Family Issues and Controversies,* contains five relatively short essays—which we call "issues"—that focus on various controversial topics and questions pertaining to family life. Our purpose in these essays is to highlight some crucial and sometimes emotional questions that bear on contemporary family experiences: Who gets to be called a family? Has family as an institution lost its influence over people's lives? How private should families be? Are people's personal desires incompatible with their obligations to family members? How does religion influence family life? These essays are meant to provoke critical thought and debate. To that end, each issue concludes with a set of discussion questions. These questions are designed not to gauge your ability to recall facts from these essays but to spur classroom debate on the societal and personal implications of the material.

The ultimate teaching value of the issues lies in their connection to subsequent chapters. In Part II, *Thinking Sociologically About Families,* we discuss the sociological concepts and theories that can help you understand your family experiences. Chapter 1 is an overview of how sociologists think about and study families. Chapters 2, 3, and 4 look at families through the lens of key sociological concepts: gender, race and ethnicity, and social class. These concepts are crucial to the sociological study of any phenomenon in society. When applied to the study of families, they are particularly important.

The chapters in Part III, *Investigating Families over the Life Course,* closely resemble those you'd find in most family textbooks: attraction and love, marriage, work, parenting, child rearing, intimate violence, divorce and remarriage, old age and death, and the future of families. But our goal here is to move beyond simple descriptions of these phenomena to an intellectually challenging (and, we hope, personally relevant) examination of the relationship between social structural forces and private family experiences. These chapters build on the issues presented in Part I and the sociological methods and concepts presented in Part II. You will therefore see many discussions in this section of the book that incorporate history, culture, economics, politics, and religion in family experiences. You'll also see that discussions of race, social class, gender, and sexual orientation are woven throughout these chapters.

You will quickly notice that all three parts are interrelated. One of the greatest difficulties in writing a book on family is that family matters don't align neatly in distinct and conceptually independent chapters. For instance, you can't talk about relationship formation, the dynamics of marriage, the balance of work and family, children and child rearing, and so on without taking gender into consideration. A topic such as divorce is closely related to economics, child rearing, work, social policy, perhaps even intimate violence. To help you see these connections, the chapters in Parts II and III contain brief margin notes referring you back to the issues in Part I that contain information pertinent to the passage you're reading.

Other Helpful Features

This book contains several other features that are designed to provide useful information and make teaching more effective. For instance, each Part I issue contains a set of discussion questions designed to help you think about some of the important controversies raised in that issue. At the end of each issue is a table linking material to topics covered in Part II and III.

Each chapter in Parts II and III begins with a photographic essay called *Windows on Family*. If you thumb through most family textbooks, you'll see an abundance of photographs. But those images often seem to be simply filling up space. The visual aspects of this book convey important information by painting vivid sociological portraits of family life. Each multipage *Windows on Family* photo essay will help you "see" many of the concepts and ideas that you will read about in that chapter. A series of questions embedded in each essay will draw your attention to some of the most important issues that the essay raises. As you study these visual essays, you will be practicing the skills of observation that can make you a more astute participant in your family and in your social world.

Each chapter in Parts II and III also contains a feature called *Demo•Graphics.* These special sections include graphs and charts to present statistical information on various aspects of families in a way that is easy to understand and visually appealing. The topic of family has been the subject of a vast amount of quantitative research, but a barrage of individual graphs, tables, and charts—such as what you see in a typical textbook—can obscure the overall picture painted by the research. Each *Demo•Graphics* feature in this book is self-contained, with explanatory text and thought-provoking questions, but is also tied conceptually to the chapter in which it appears. The purpose of the *Demo•Graphics* is not only to provide statistical support for the points made in the text but also to help you learn how to think critically about statistical information.

Each chapter in Parts II and III ends with a short list of *Chapter Highlights,* which clarify the important concepts, and a section called *Your Turn.* The *Your Turn* section encourages you to study the "real world," much as professional sociologists do, to get a better understanding of the similarities and differences among families.

Changes in the Second Edition

This book has undergone a dramatic renovation since the first edition was published in 1999. The three-part organizational strategy replaces a two-part layout used in the first edition. This new organization provides more thorough coverage of important sociological ideas and concepts. We have added a new issue on the relationship between religion and family life in Part I and a new chapter on couplehood and married life in Part III.

These major changes are accompanied by a comprehensive updating of information in existing issues and chapters. As in the first edition, the book is peppered with anecdotes, personal observations, and accounts of contemporary events. Many of the examples you will read are taken from today's news headlines; others are taken from incidents in our own lives. All these examples are meant to show you the pervasiveness and applicability of sociology in our everyday experiences in a way that, we hope, rings familiar with you.

Throughout the book we've also tried to provide the most up-to-date statistical information possible. So we've updated all of the graphics and, in the process, changed many from statistical tables to more readable charts, making trends and relationships more obvious. Much of the new statistical data are drawn from the 2000 Census.

A Word About Words

As sociologists, we know the power of language in shaping ideas, values, and attitudes. We have tried to be very careful in our choice of terminology. Consider, for instance, the title of this book: *Sociology of Families.* You will notice that we use the word *Families* and not *the Family.* One of the key themes of this book is that families are extremely diverse in form and function. No single family structure can serve as a prototype for all Americans. Hence in the title we have avoided using the term *the Family.* In fact, throughout the book we have opted for the more inclusive (and more accurate) term *families.* Only when referring to the *institution* of family or referring to a specific family (for example, "When she became the head of the family . . .") do we use *the family.*

A Final Thought

As you've probably noticed, few subjects in today's society carry as much social, political, and emotional freight as "family." Whether spoken of reverently as the moral foundation of society or referred to disparagingly by some rebellious teenager as the greatest obstacle to happiness and freedom, "family" permeates our lives and defines who we are as a culture like no other institution.

Sociologists may have many things in common, but our assumptions, perspectives, and attitudes can be quite different. Some sociologists focus on broad demographic information about large groups of people; others concentrate on the everyday interpersonal experiences of individuals. Some write from a specific political position or theoretical perspective; others are more pluralistic in the ideologies and theories they use. This book reflects our sociological perspective—one that draws heavily on the interrelationship between the everyday experiences of individuals and the society in which they live. We believe that family is both an individually lived experience and a systematic social institution. So our private lives are always a combination of the idiosyncrasies of the family to which we belong and the broader social rules and expectations associated with families in general. In that sense, our families are strongly influenced by large-scale social forces, including culture, history, economics, politics, religion, the media, and so on. At the same time, however, we as individuals are vital contributors to our social structure. As individuals or in groups, we can, through our actions, change, modify, or reinforce existing elements of family life.

We hope you will find the unique organization of this book both informative and provocative. Above all, we hope you will find it useful in helping you understand why and how families have such great significance for all of us.

Good luck,

David M. Newman
Department of Sociology and Anthropology
DePauw University
Greencastle, IN 46135
E-mail: DNEWMAN@DEPAUW.EDU

Liz Grauerholz
Department of Sociology and Anthropology
Purdue University
West Lafayette, IN 47907
E-mail: GRAUER@SRI.SOC.PURDUE.EDU

Acknowledgments

> My 9-year old son, Seth, helped me when I packed up the last chapters of this book to send to the publisher. "Wow," he said as he looked at the imposing stack of paper, "it must have taken you *a whole month* to write this book!" I smiled at his naïveté. "Well," I said in that condescending, fatherly tone that we use when we're convinced we know more than the child we're speaking to, "it actually took a *little* longer than that." "What, like two months?" he suggested. "More like two *years*," I replied. He looked astonished. "Two years!?! Boy, you're not very good at this, are you?" (David Newman, from the Preface to the first edition)

Seth may or may not have been right, but we do know that writing a book like this one is an enormously time-consuming endeavor that simultaneously requires total seclusion and utter dependence on others' expertise, guidance, and good will. Although our names appear on the cover, many people contributed their time, suggestions, opinions, emotional support, and sometimes simply a well-timed meal to bring this project to fruition.

First, we'd like to express our heartfelt appreciation to Steve Rutter, former publisher and president of Pine Forge Press, for his vision and his wisdom. He pushed hard and demanded a lot, and there were times when we were convinced that he believed there were 36 hours in a day. But he never wavered from his goal of publishing a book that is useful and unique. For that, we will always be grateful.

As always, Becky Smith provided impeccable editorial guidance during various stages of cutting, revising, polishing, and, in this edition, constructing the photo essays that appear in the book. If not for Becky, this book simply could not have been written.

The staff at Pine Forge—Sherith Pankratz, Jean Skeels, Kirsten Stoller, and Windy Just—were invaluable in guiding us through the obstacles that inevitably arose from time to time. Our gratitude also goes to Anne and Greg Draus at Scratchgravel Publishing Services for their efficiency and attention to detail in producing this book. And Linda Purrington did a wonderful job copy editing the final version of the manuscript.

We also appreciate the numerous helpful comments offered by our many reviewers:

Joan Alway, University of Miami
Trudy Anderson, Texas A&M University, Kingsville
Judith Barker, Ithaca College
Richard E. Barrett, University of Illinois–Chicago
Kristin Bates, California State University, San Marcos
Dianne Carmody, Old Dominion University
Wanda Clark, South Plains College
June Ellestad, Washington State University
Cheryl Elman, University of Akron
Kristin Esterberg, University of Massachusetts, Lowell

Betty Farrell, Pitzer College
Carol Gardner, Indiana University–Purdue University, Indianapolis
Becky Glass, State University of New York, Geneseo
Christine L. Himes, Syracuse University
Erin L. Kelly, University of Minnesota
Ginger Macheski, Valdosta State University
Martha Terrie Mazzarella, Bowling Green State University
Jane Nielsen, State University of New York, Oneonta
James M. Raymo, University of Wisconsin–Madison
Susan Roxburgh, Kent State University
Georganne Rundblad, Illinois Wesleyan University
Laura Sanchez, Tulane University
Scott Sernau, Indiana University, South Bend
Linda Stephens, Clemson University
Dianne Sykes, Marian College
Elaine Wethington, Cornell University

We especially want to express our sincere gratitude to the many colleagues and friends who offered cherished bits and pieces of assistance along the way. In particular, we'd like to thank Meryl Altman, Srimati Basu, Istvan Csicsery-Ronay, Nancy Davis, Rachel Einwohner, Jodi O'Brien, Eric Silverman, Bruce Stinebrickner, Andrew Williams, Janet Wilmoth, Maggie Snow, Carol Jones, and Bizz Steele.

Finally, we want to thank our families (Elizabeth, Zachary, and Seth Newman; David Fisher and Emma and Lara Grauerholz-Fisher) for their patience and understanding. We know that our frequent bouts with self-doubt, grumpiness, and frustration over deadlines took an enormous toll on them, yet they always remained steadfast in their support.

Examining Family Issues and Controversies

Part I of this book examines several controversial issues that provide the backdrop against which people experience their own families and form opinions and beliefs about families in general. In this section you will probe questions such as, Which arrangements get to be called a "family"? Is the institution of family breaking down? Should families be completely private? How do people balance personal interests and needs with family obligations? Do families need religion to thrive? The information presented in response to these questions is designed to provoke personal reflection, critical thought, and impassioned discussion.

What is a family?

Hours after the terrorist attack on the Pentagon and New York's World Trade Center on September 11, 2001, a major network newscaster completed his report by saying, "It's in times like these that all Americans become a *family*." Several days later, a member of the New York Mets baseball team said, "In New York, everybody's a *family* right now."

In the film *Fried Green Tomatoes,* Evelyn Couch—a character played by actress Kathy Bates—becomes quite fond of an old woman named Ninny Threadgoode, whom she meets while visiting a nursing home. Ninny—played by the late Jessica Tandy—inspires Evelyn to take control of her own life. Evelyn decides she would like Ninny to live in her house with her and her husband, Ed. But Ed is unwilling to have a stranger live in their house, and he forcefully shouts, "She's not even *family!*" to which Evelyn quickly replies, "Well, she's *family* to me!"

In a video exhibit in the U.S. Holocaust Memorial Museum in Washington, DC, one Holocaust survivor after another offers moving testimony of their experiences in German concentration camps during World War II. The survivors reminisce frequently and with great emotion about their *camp families*—those fellow inmates with whom they formed immensely important and powerful relationships in the face of what they perceived as certain death. Before imprisonment, the people who would become these survivors' "parents," "children," "brothers," and "sisters" were complete strangers; many came from different countries and spoke different languages.

In 2000, the Olive Garden Italian restaurant chain began a new television advertising campaign that featured the tag line "When you're here, you're *family.*" This image pervades the company's Web site: "Olive Garden is a *family* of local restaurants focused on delighting every guest with a genuine Italian dining experience. . . . We offer a comfortable, home-like setting where guests are welcomed like *family.*"

It seems that nothing is more obvious and commonplace than the concept of family. Family is something that everyone can relate to. We're all born into a family of one sort or another and will spend at least part of our lives inside one. Ideas about what families look like are so clear that if someone asked you to pick out families strolling through a large shopping mall, you'd probably have no trouble doing so.

Yet all these examples illustrate the varied, fluid, and somewhat unexpected ways people use the term *family* and its powerful connotations. In all these

What makes a family a family? Why are some groups granted family status and others not? What does a family do for its members that other groups can't?

Certain holidays, rituals, and other celebrations invite or even require family participation. The people at this backyard barbecue seem to be close knit and genuinely happy. Do you think they are a family? What features in this photo are you using as evidence of family relationships? Is more than one family present at the cookout? How can you tell? If no children were present, would you be less inclined to consider this group of people a family?

examples, only the word *family* was forceful enough to describe the strength of people's feelings and sense of connection to others. As a symbolic marker of the depth of affection and obligation, the vocabulary of *family* is unparalleled in the English language. No other term would do. Notice how much weaker the message would have been if, say, the newscaster or the baseball player had referred to the shock and grief of *U.S. citizens*, or if Evelyn Couch had tried to make her point by saying, "Well, she's *a real companion* to me!" or if the concentration camp survivors referred to fellow inmates who saved their lives as *good friends*. Could Olive Garden inspire feelings of comfort in potential customers if their advertisements read, "When you're here, you're *an important customer*"? Certainly not.

The really curious thing, though, is that in none of these examples was the word *family* used to describe the relationships most people usually think of as family—husbands and wives, parents and children, brothers and sisters, grandparents, aunts, uncles, cousins, and so on. Instead, it was used to describe real and imagined relationships based on love, commitment, sacrifice, and obligation.

Obviously, as familiar and recognizable as it is, *family* is also a remarkably elusive term that defies agreement or consistent application. Coming up with a universal definition of the family that everyone everywhere would agree on is a little like trying to nail pudding to a wall.

Indeed, a nationwide poll conducted by the Roper Organization found wide variation in what people consider a family. Although 98 percent of the respondents identified a married couple living with their children as a family, 53 percent also identified an unmarried man and woman who've lived together for a long time as a family; 27 percent felt a lesbian couple raising children was a family; and 20 percent felt two gay men committed to each other and living together constituted a family (cited in Gelles, 1995).

These statistics and examples point up one of the most fundamental and deceptively simple questions facing people who study family: Just exactly what is a family? Which groups of people get to be called a family? Conversely, which groups of people *can't* claim to be families? Far from being an ob-

scure issue of linguistic and philosophical debate argued in the hallowed halls of academia, the definition of *family* has very real and very critical consequences for us all. A family may be in line to receive such benefits as housing, health care, and sick leave, not to mention legitimate recognition within the community (Popenoe, 1993). People who fall outside the definition of *family,* however, not only are ineligible for such benefits, but their relationships may also be considered illegitimate, inappropriate, or immoral (Hartman, 1994). Ideas about which family forms are acceptable, normal, desirable, and praiseworthy determine which forms are considered abnormal, problematic, and in need of repair or condemnation.

Images of Family

Our ideas about what families are come to us partly from the people around us. From the time we are small, we are exposed to ideas about what families ought to look like and how they ought to function. Our immediate family is an obvious model, and older relatives can provide images of past families. We are even exposed to alternative images as we become acquainted with the different family structures of neighbors and friends. But these personal experiences are not the only source of information we have on the definition of family.

Many of our ideas about families come from the media: books, newspapers, magazines, films, and especially, television. For 50 years, television has served as a high-powered cultural lens on U.S. families (Stacey, 1996b). Between 1946 and 1990, close to 400 fictional families appeared on prime-time network programming alone (Moore, 1992). Add commercials, daytime soap operas and talk shows, and news stories into the mix, and you get a sense of how pervasive television images of families have been throughout the years. For the most part, these images have tended to be conventional and narrow in scope, fostering a largely inaccurate version of family reality.

One study of all long-running prime-time families since the 1950s found that on TV the traditional nuclear family predominates. Two-thirds of these shows depicted "conventional" families—families that consist of married couples living together with their children or nuclear families sharing a household with one or more members of their extended families (Moore, 1992). The overwhelming majority of families (88 percent) were middle class or higher. Ninety-four percent of the shows featured white families. Interestingly, at the time of this study there were more white TV families with black members (usually adopted children) than there were black families. Only 14 percent of the programs featured childless couples.

A more recent study found that prime-time, entertainment TV still presents a distorted view of family life: Most adults are men, almost no one is over 50, child care is almost never a problem, and elder care comes up even less (National Partnership for Women and Families, 1998). After analyzing 150 episodes of 92 different programs, the researchers discovered that adult TV characters are disproportionately male, young, and free of family obligations as compared to real adults. Not surprisingly, this study found that 45 percent of U.S. adults say no TV families are like theirs, and another 39 percent say they can find "only a few" families like theirs.

In some ways, however, media images of families have changed dramatically over the years. In the 1950s and early 1960s, shows like *Leave It to Beaver*, *Ozzie and Harriet*, *Make Room for Daddy*, *Father Knows Best*, *The Donna Reed Show*, and *The Dick Van Dyke Show* provided optimistic, homogeneous images of U.S. families. With some notable exceptions—such as the childless, working-class Kramdens in *The Honeymooners* or the urban, interethnic Ricardos in *I Love Lucy*—these early television families were happy, prosperous, suburban, and white. They consisted of husband-father breadwinners and nurturing wife/mothers whose primary task was to look good in an apron and keep peace among the children. In the 1950s a viewer would have been hard pressed to find on television the sorts of people and families that, in reality, characterized much of U.S. society at the time: the old, the nonwhite, those not in the middle class, or people in nontraditional households (Coontz, 1992). Instead, the viewing audience was presented with nuclear families without serious economic problems or embarrassing histo-

ries. The most pressing problems could be solved in 30 minutes with a few sage words from Dad or a plate of Mom's chocolate chip cookies. No wonder when people today look back on families of the past, they gravitate toward these blissful "good old days" TV images. To this day, reruns of these old shows remain a popular fixture on nightly cable TV.

- -

In the 1960s and 1970s television families began making small but significant forays into the uncharted territory of social problems such as poverty, violence, drugs, and racism. TV families were even becoming a little less traditional in their structure.

- -

The social upheavals of the late 1960s and early 1970s motivated networks to create shows that were more "relevant" and "realistic." The working-class families on *All in the Family* and *Good Times* demonstrated that family life wasn't always a middle-class haven. Conflict was a part of their day-to-day existence. Television families began making small but significant forays into the uncharted territory of social problems such as poverty, violence, drugs, and racism. TV families were even becoming a little less traditional in their structure. *The Brady Bunch* featured a sugar-coated white, middle-class, suburban family, but the Bradys were a blended family that sometimes had to deal—albeit cheerily—with dilemmas posed by step-siblings and stepparents. The show *One Day at a Time* featured a divorced woman raising two children alone. *Three's Company* consisted of three single adults—one man and two women—living in the same household. Popular shows such as *The Mary Tyler Moore Show* and *Laverne and Shirley* featured single women whose emotional nurturing came primarily from close friends rather than family. These characters enjoyed freedoms that had previously been taboo for women on television.

During the 1980s and 1990s, a time when conservative politics and "family values" became more popular, the traditional television family reasserted its dominance—most notably through shows such as

The Cosby Show, Family Ties, and *Home Improvement*—even though the number of people living in intact families in the real world continued to decline. Although many popular shows—such as *Roseanne, The Simpsons,* and *Married with Children*—were offering an unsparing portrayal of the ugly side of family life, the tone was humorous and the generally positive emotional interactions that we associate with family relationships remained. These families may have been flawed, but they were still cohesive, especially in the face of crisis.

In the early 2000s, the television portrayal of families has become more diverse. The theme of the dysfunctional yet intact family can still be seen in sitcoms such as *Malcolm in the Middle, That 70s Show,* and *Grounded for Life.* Other shows—such as *Queer as Folk, The Sopranos, Once and Again, The Fighting Fitzgeralds, Frazier, Judging Amy, Everybody Loves Raymond,* and *Providence*—explore various extended, blended, single-parent, and even more nontraditional family arrangements.

In recent years, some of the most popular television shows—most notably *Seinfeld, Friends, Ed, Sex and the City, Will and Grace,* and *Ally McBeal*—have drifted away from examining family groups to focus primarily on the lives of single people. However, these shows are not "antifamily" by any stretch of the imagination. In fact, many of the anxieties and travails that characters on these shows experience stem from a gap between their present singlehood and their desire for traditional family life—getting married, having children, and so on.

Television images of families have obviously changed over the years: Women now play a more dominant role than they once did in family shows, gay characters as well as single-parent and minority families are more common, and both mothers and fathers are more frequently seen outside the home (Cantor, 1991; Douglas & Olsen, 1996). However, television still tends to portray traditional gender roles within families. In television commercials, for instance, men (compared to women) are less often shown doing housework and spending time with children. When they are shown with children, men are more likely to be shown outdoors, with boys, and not with infants. Interestingly, men are rarely shown caring for daughters (G. Kaufman, 1999). Other discrepancies between TV life and real life exist. One study reports that of all the "nonconventional" families on television, 79 percent feature single-parent households. But unlike real-life parents, most single parents on TV had suffered the death of a spouse and not divorce. In only 9 percent of cases was single parenthood the result of divorce (Moore, 1992).

In addition, the formulas of contemporary family programs remain quite similar to those aired in the 1950s (Cantor, 1991). The stories often revolve around teen and preteen mischief or parent–child conflict. The content of the conflict has, of course, changed. The 1950s argument over kissing and wearing too much makeup has evolved, in the 2000s, into an argument over sleeping with a boyfriend or purchasing contraceptives. But the dynamics of the situations portrayed remain remarkably similar, and parents and children almost always resolve their differences by the end of the show. No matter how "nontraditional" the lifestyle, the central virtue of family togetherness is still depicted as the main source of individual happiness and well-being for adults and children alike.

And rarely do television programs reflect the larger social and political contexts in which most U.S. residents live. Contemporary programs have addressed the tough problems of everyday life: drugs, poverty, unwanted pregnancy, and so forth. But for most of their history, television families have rarely tackled big problems such as the changing economy or ethnic conflict and political unrest abroad. Rather, these fictional families act out morality plays about appropriate and inappropriate beliefs and behaviors. The majority of TV programs teach correct (and ideal) social and sexual relationships (Cantor, 1991).

The significance of these trends in television programming is that they are far more than entertainment; they shape our ideas about what a family is and is not, how its members should relate to one another, and how a family should relate to the world. But television viewers (and readers of other mass media) are hardly passive recipients who absorb every message uncritically. Even young viewers actively watch and make judgments about characters based on their own personal experience. For example, 9- to 13-year-old girls in one recent study tended to dismiss as unrealistic families that did not look and act like their own. These girls did, however, accept the family-oriented values they saw on television, probably because they were consistent with those they received at home (Fingerson, 1999). In short, people learn from others in their lives, as well as from the media, to dismiss and discount alternative forms of families and to laugh at or dislike unconventional characters who challenge accepted notions about family life (Currie, 1997).

The "Official" U.S. Definition of Family

With so much flux and variation in images of family, is it possible or even desirable to come up with a single definition? In fact, it *is* necessary if you are faced with the task, as the U.S. federal government is, of managing certain programs for families and providing certain benefits only to families.

The official definition of *family* comes from the U.S. Census Bureau, the government agency responsible for determining how many families there are in the United States. In compiling these statistics, this agency distinguishes between *households* and *families.* Households are defined as all persons or groups of persons who occupy a dwelling such as a house, apartment, single room, or other space intended to be living quarters. Households can consist of one person who lives alone or several people living together. A family, in contrast, is defined as two or more persons who are related by blood, marriage, or adoption and who live together as one household (U.S. Bureau of the Census, 2000a).

· ·

The official definition of *family* comes from the U.S. Census Bureau . . . two or more persons who are related by blood, marriage, or adoption and who live together as one household.

· ·

Right away you can see this definition limits who may be considered family. Grown children who no longer live with their parents are not part of their parents' families. And what about other relatives—grandparents, aunts, uncles, and cousins? Most of us would consider them to be part of our family as well, even though they don't live with us. For the most part, what social scientists call the *nuclear family*—the small unit consisting of a married couple with or without children or at least one parent and his or her children—is what gets all the attention.

How useful is this official definition of family? What does it imply about the nature of people's relationships and responsibilities within families? To address these questions, let's break down the official definition of *family* and examine its component parts.

"Two or More People": Family as Social Group

Sociologically speaking, families contain not only individuals but relationships: husband–wife, parent–child, sister–brother, and so on. These relationships imply connections, bonds, attachments, and obligations *among people,* which is a key characteristic of any type of social group.

The groups called families differ from other types of social groups, however, such as friendship groups, social clubs, church groups, and so on (Beutler, Burr, Bahr, & Herrin, 1989). For one thing, involvement between family members is more intense than in other groups. The range of activities shared with family members is much broader than contacts with friends, co-workers, or other people in groups to which you belong. People do pretty much everything with fellow family members: eating, sleeping, playing, punishing, fighting, convalescing from illness, having sex, and so on. Such close involvement adds a unique emotional element to family relationships.

Another big difference is that families tend to last for a considerably longer period of time than do most other social groups (Klein & White, 1996). We're born into a family that already exists, and it endures for our lifetime. Even after we become adults and start our own families, our parents are still our parents and our siblings are still our siblings no matter what we think of them. During the 1997

NCAA Men's Basketball Championships, a great deal of media attention focused on the strained relationship between Mike Bibby, a star player for the University of Arizona Wildcats, and his estranged father, former NBA player and current University of Southern California coach Henry Bibby. Henry had divorced Mike's mother when Mike was quite young and played only a minor role in his upbringing. Mike clearly bore some animosity toward his father and wanted to downplay the influence his father had had on his life. But he could not escape the immutable fact that Henry is, and will always be, his father. People can certainly have lifelong relationships with close friends, but families are the only groups that virtually require lifetime membership.

The strong prospect for continuing interaction gives families a history and tradition rarely found in other groups. Relationships between parents and their children, whether biological or adopted, are not easily severed. Given how common divorce is now—nearly one of every two marriages that begins this year is projected to end in divorce sometime in the future (Cherlin, 1992)—this idea of permanence applied to families may seem hopelessly outdated. However, people still assume that those involved don't enter such relationships as temporary arrangements with a foreseeable, predetermined end.

Unlike most other social groups, the family is also considered a social institution within the larger society. To be a member of a family group means more than simply being connected to other individuals. It also means having certain legal and culturally recognizable rights and responsibilities, which are spelled out in the formal laws of the state and the informal norms of custom and tradition. Parents, for instance, have legal obligations to provide basic necessities—food, shelter, clothing, nurturance—for their children. If they fail to meet these obligations, they may face legal charges of negligence or abuse.

Along with spelling out obligations, the institution of family makes some assumptions about authority—about who has the legitimate right to control or influence the lives of others (Hunter, 1991). In other societies, such authority may be granted to someone outside the nuclear family, such as the father's brother or the community at large. In U.S. society, parents have the legal right to control their children. However, in cases of multiple parents (birth parents, adoptive parents, stepparents, foster parents, and so on) the lines of authority may be murky. Courts must sometimes determine who has legitimate authority over children, as in custody cases where biological parents have attempted to regain custody of children who had been previously put up for adoption.

"Living Together": Family as Household

Another implication of the official U.S. definition of family is that the family group share a common residence. Indeed, for many social scientists common residence is *the* defining characteristic of family (for example, Murdock, 1949). This reflects the view that individuals who make up a family constitute a single identifiable entity located in a common space.

The belief that members of a nuclear family ought to live together is common but not universal. Among the Kipsigis of Kenya, for instance, the mother and children live in one house while the father lives in another (Stephens, 1963). Once they stop breastfeeding, Thonga children of southern Africa go to live with their grandmothers. They remain there for several years and are then returned to their parents. On the traditional Israeli kibbutz, or commune, children are raised not in the home of their biological parents but in an "infants' house," where a trained nurse cares for them (Nanda, 1994). Wealthy European families may send their children away to boarding schools where they spend most of their childhood.

In U.S. society, there are situations in which members of nuclear families do not occupy a common household. Consider, for instance, the "commuter marriage." A commuter marriage is one in which spouses spend at least several nights a week in separate residences yet are still married and intend to remain so (Gertsel & Gross, 1984). Marriages in which spouses live apart much of the time have always existed. Careers such as the military, the merchant marine, professional sports, and entertainment often require spouses to travel for long periods. Today, however, commuter marriages are likely to result from both husband and wife having careers that involve commitments to different locations. Although the difficulties of such arrangements are substantial, no one would deny that the people involved in them are families.

It's also true that common household residence does not, in and of itself, determine whether a unit is a family. Perhaps you are currently living with a roommate. Not only do you share an address, but you are likely to share domestic chores and household expenses as well. You may even feel very close to each other, sharing personal experiences, helping out in times of need, and so on. Yet most people wouldn't consider roommates family. Your common residence is assumed to be the result of economic convenience rather than emotional commitment.

. . . .

In 1960, 15 percent of all households were nonfamily; today the figure has more than doubled, rising to over 32 percent.

. . . .

It's often unclear exactly why some household arrangements are considered family and others not. Several years ago, for instance, a Cleveland woman was convicted and sentenced to five days in jail for failing to comply with the city's local residential zoning laws. Her crime? She resided in a "nonfamily" household in a neighborhood zoned for "families." The ordinance defined family as "a number of individuals related to the nominal head of the household or to the spouse of the nominal head of the household living as a single housekeeping unit in a single dwelling" (Minow, 1993). The woman lived with her son and two grandsons, but because the two boys were first cousins rather than brothers, the arrangement was not considered a family.

Yet around the same time, the New Jersey Supreme Court ruled that a group of ten male college students living in a home in a residential district in the borough of Glassboro could be considered a family. Under a zoning ordinance that limited residence in this area to stable and permanent "traditional family units" or their "functional equivalent,"

the borough had sought an injunction to prevent the students from using or occupying the home. The students shared the kitchen as well as household chores, grocery shopping, and yard work. They maintained a common checking account to pay for food and other household bills. They all intended to live there as long as they were enrolled at a nearby college (they were sophomores at the time). The court ruled that these facts reflected a plan by the students to live together for three years under conditions that met the requirement of a "stable and permanent living unit" (Thoresen, 1991).

The growth of "nonfamily households" over the past several decades has been dramatic (elderly people living with friends, roommates sharing an apartment, cohabiting couples, young single people, and so on). In 1960, 15 percent of all households were nonfamily; today the figure has more than doubled, rising to over 32 percent (U.S. Bureau of the Census, 2001d).

"Related by Marriage": Family as Legal Entity

Marriage is the legal cornerstone of the official definition of family. Most people take for granted that *monogamy*, the marriage of one man and one woman, is the fundamental building block of family. Reproduction remains more socially acceptable when it occurs inside a marriage than outside. Some people may have several spouses over their lifetime, but in the United States they are allowed only one at a time (a phenomenon known as *serial monogamy*). And some families do exist without a married couple. But monogamous marriage continues to be the only adult intimate relationship that is legally recognized, culturally approved, and endorsed by the U.S. Internal Revenue Service. It is still the one relationship in which sexual activity is not only acceptable but expected.

Monogamous marriage, like the family in general, is an institution, a patterned way of life that includes a set of commonly known roles, statuses, and expectations. Although the expectations of husbands and wives are always changing, and will differ from one couple to the next, the expectations people have for spouses are far more culturally understood than for any other type of relationship, such as a "significant other" or "girlfriend." Furthermore, no other intimate relationship has achieved such status or is privileged as highly as marriage. Despite public concern with its disintegration, monogamous marriage remains the cultural standard against which all other types of intimate relationships are judged.

Even though marriage is undeniably important, not all states agree as to who can and can't marry. Today, some states (such as Pennsylvania) still recognize common-law marriage. These marriages are agreements by which couples who have not had their relationships validated religiously or civilly are considered legally married if they've lived together long enough. Some states allow first cousins to marry, others don't; the minimum legal age for marriage varies from state to state, as does recognition of such contracts across state lines (F. Johnson, 1996).

Despite these variations, it's hard to imagine a society that is not structured around the assumption that the vast majority of adults will live in a monogamous marriage. Yet many cultures around the world allow an individual to have several spouses at the same time (an arrangement known as *polygamy*). Some anthropologists have estimated that about 75 percent of the world's societies accept some type of polygamy (usually *polygyny*—the marriage of one man to multiple wives), although few members within those societies actually have the resources to afford more than one spouse (Murdock, 1957; Nanda, 1994). In some parts of northern India, a woman sometimes has more than one husband (marriage of one woman to multiple husbands is known as *polyandry*). The husbands are always brothers. The practice stems from economic pressures. This area's terrain is rugged—steep forests and mountains leave only about a quarter of the land suitable for farming. With so little land to support a larger population, having all sons in one family marry the same woman ensures the control of childbirth and keeps the family wealth under one roof (Fan, 1996). It's estimated that roughly 10 out of 100 families in this region still practice polyandry.

Even in the United States, certain groups practice polygyny. Between 30,000 and 50,000 members of a dissident Mormon sect in Utah live in polygynous households (McCarthy, 2001). Although these marriages are technically illegal—Utah outlawed it as a condition of statehood in 1896—few polygynists are ever prosecuted. In fact, 2001 marked the first time in 50 years that a person was convicted on polygyny charges. However, this case shouldn't be taken as an indicator that Utah is cracking down on polygyny. It involved a man—with five wives and twenty-five children—who decided to discuss his polygynous marriage openly on national talk shows, violating an unspoken rule that such arrangements would be quietly tolerated if the participants didn't speak publicly about them.

"Related by Blood or Adoption": Family as Kinship Group

No matter what form it takes, marriage is important in all societies because it serves as the legally sanctioned setting for reproduction. Although not all sexual activity in marriage leads to the birth of children and not all children are born to married couples, sexual reproduction in families is the core mechanism of *kinship*—who is related to whom across generations (Schneider, 1980).

Even adoption is based symbolically on the biological model of kinship. Once adopted, children are treated and raised just as if they had been produced biologically by the adoptive parents. In fact, laws in some states keep adoption records sealed and refuse adoptees access to information about their birth parents and their biological relatives. Such laws were established to protect biological parents' rights to privacy, but they also demonstrate that birth ties may be no more powerful or enduring than the kinship ties established by adoption. Thus adoption presents no challenge to the image of family assembled around a biological core of parent(s) and children (Weston, 1991).

At birth everyone inherits two separate bloodlines, raising the question of which bloodline—the mother's or the father's—is to be more important for an individual's heredity. These designations are vital because they determine not only names but also authority, ownership of property, and inheritance. However, kinship has as much to do with social norms as with genetic facts. Definitions of kinship vary from culture to culture.

In some societies, kin are connected by father–child links (a system called *patrilineal* descent). In such societies, a woman typically takes her husband's name. Children downplay or ignore their connections with members of their mother's family, showing allegiance and loyalty to kin on the father's side of the family. So, for instance, a mother's sister—whom we'd call an "aunt"—has no culturally recognized role in the family.

In other societies, the family group is made up of people connected by mother–child links (*matrilineal* descent). Here a child's status and heritage are traced through his or her mother's lineage, and the father's kin are not considered part of the family. For instance, the Hopi, a Pueblo group in the U.S. Southwest, are a matrilineal community. The relationship a Hopi child maintains with his or her father's relatives may be affectionate, but it involves little direct cooperation or recognized authority.

· ·

Who people consider "family" is increasingly a matter of choice rather than legal obligation or biological connection.

· ·

Finally, in some societies (such as the United States) children trace their descent and define their family relationships through both parents' bloodlines (*bilateral* descent). Although U.S. women typically take their husbands' names when they marry and children take their fathers' names, descent and inheritance are linked to both parents. We may distinguish between our *paternal* and *maternal* grandparents and even favor one set over the other, but both are equally recognized as kin. Neither side of the family is expected to exert special influence and power over the children.

In bilateral descent societies, the potential for kin relationships can be quite extensive. If you were to map out a family chart of kin on both sides of your family, the size and complexity of your family tree could be immense. But at some point we all stop counting distant kin—for instance, fourth cousins—as family.

Blood Families and Chosen Families

The official, broad definition of family is not as straightforward or helpful as you might expect. In everyday usage, *family* is a significantly more elastic term than implied by the U.S. Bureau of the Census definition: two or more people, living together, who are related by marriage, blood, or adoption.

Moreover, it seems that today, compared with the 1950s and 1960s, who people consider "family" is increasingly a matter of choice rather than legal obligation or biological connection. Families can now consist of people who are tied to one another not by law, birth, or blood but by commitments, love, and ability to confide in one another (Settles, 1987). These relationships form a safety net of significant connections to choose from in case of need. Hence, people today are likely to use the word *family* to describe a group of individuals who have achieved a significant degree of emotional closeness and sharing, even if they're not related by blood, marriage, or adoption. In a national survey, 75 percent of respondents, when asked to define *family,* chose, "a group of people who love and care for each other" (Scanzoni & Marsiglio, 1991).

An approach to defining family that relies more on feelings and less on formal structure appeals to many family scholars. Compare the following definition from the American Home Economics Association (AHEA) to the Census Bureau definition we examined earlier:

> AHEA defines the family unit as two or more persons who share resources, share responsibility for decisions, share values and goals, and have commitment to one another over time. The family is that climate that one "comes home to" and it is this network of sharing and commitments that most accurately describes the family unit, regardless of blood, legal ties, adoption or marriage. (quoted in Christensen, 1990, p. 36)

Notice that the AHEA definition emphasizes emotional ties, commitment, and cooperation, not formally recognized relationships. One prominent sociologist defines family as "a unit comprising two or more persons who live together for an extended period of time, and who share in one or more of the following: work (for wages and house), sex, care and feeding of children, and intellectual, spiritual, and recreational activities (D'Antonio, 1983, p. 92). Another author argues that the concept of family should apply to "people who have shared history, who have loved each other . . . lived through major parts of each other's lives together, [and] who share professional interests, economic needs, political views or sexual preference" (Lindsey, 1981, pp. 179–188).

· ·

In practice, family is rarely limited to formally recognized kin relations.

· ·

Structural changes in society and changes in contemporary lifestyles compel many people to seek from other groups the kinds of satisfactions that are typically sought from kin (Marciano, 1988). We all know of situations in which *fictive kin*—people other than legal or biological relatives—play the family's role in providing for the emotional and other needs of its members. Sometimes roommates play this role. As life expectancy increases, some elderly people whose children are unable or unwilling to take care of them are also turning to longtime friends for companionship, emotional support, and practical assistance. Or perhaps you have a close family friend whom you've referred to for years as "Uncle So-and-So" or "Aunt So-and-So" even though he or she isn't a sibling of either parent. In some situations, which people you choose to identify as family is left to your discretion. The family status of in-laws and step-relatives, for instance, is often left to the judgment of individual families. The powerful emotional connections people can form with these "chosen relatives" show that, in practice, family is rarely limited to formally recognized kin relations.

Fictive kin have historically played an important role in some African-American communities. In her book *All Our Kin*, anthropologist Carol Stack (1974) describes "family" relationships in a midwestern black neighborhood called "the Flats." The people in this community used many kinship terms to celebrate relationships based on caring, loving, and close friendship. These "kin" felt the sort of obligations, responsibilities, and loyalties typically associated with blood relations. Consider the family meanings that one resident bestowed on the people in her life:

> Billy, a young black woman in the Flats, was raised by her mother and her mother's "old man." She has three children of her own by different fathers. Billy says, "Most people kin to me are in this neighborhood, right here in the Flats, but I got people in the South, in Chicago, and in Ohio, too. I couldn't tell most of their names and most of them aren't really kinfolk to me. Starting down the street from here, take my father, he ain't my daddy, he's no father to me. I ain't got but one daddy and that's Jason. The one who raised me. My kids' daddies, that's something else, all their daddies' people really take to them—they always doing things and making a fuss about them. We help each other out and that's what kinfolks are all about. (Stack, 1974, p. 4)

Stack found that the community's informal system of parental rights and duties determines who is eligible to be a member of a child's "family." This system often doesn't coincide with the official law of the state concerning parenthood. For instance, a girl who gives birth as a teenager may not raise and nurture the child. Although she may live in the same house as the baby, an "othermother"—her mother, aunt, older sister, cousin, or family friend—may do the actual child rearing. Young mothers and their first-born daughters are often raised as sisters. This sort of acquired parenthood lasts throughout the child's lifetime. The child learns to distinguish his or her "mother" and "father" (the biological parents) from his or her "mama" and "daddy" (the people who raised him or her). Most of the time—Stack estimates about 80 percent—the mother and the "mama" are the same person. But in those other cases, the "mama" can be a grandmother, an aunt, or someone else, when relatives conclude that the mother is not emotionally ready to nurture the child and fulfill her parental duties. The "mama's" relatives and their husbands and wives also become a part of the child's extended family.

In sum, Stack found that the people she studied clearly operate within two different family systems: the folk system of their community and the legal system of the courts and welfare offices. People are recognized as family not because they have biological ties but because they assume the recognized responsibilities of kin—they "help each other out." Given the pressures of the economy in these communities, this expanded definition of family and the respect afforded to "othermothers" served a critical role in people's lives, providing much-needed support.

The Controversy over Gay Families

One of the most contentious debates concerning how elastic the definition of family ought to be is whether gay and lesbian couples should be granted the right to marry and thereby create culturally and legally "legitimate" families. Traditional heterosexual marriages have long benefited from legal and social recognition. Marriage partners can take part in a spouse's health insurance plan and pension program, share the rights of inheritance and community property, claim a spouse's rent-controlled apartment, receive Social Security and veterans' benefits, including medical and educational services, file joint tax returns, determine the spouse's medical and burial arrangements, and receive crime victims' recovery benefits (Hunter, 1991; Sherman, 1992). In addition, spouses cannot be forced to testify in court against a partner and are granted visitation rights when the partner or his or her children are in an intensive care unit or prison (reported in Ingraham, 1999). These legal, social, and economic advantages encourage the stability and interdependence of the traditional family unit. Such benefits have historically been denied to cohabiting heterosexual couples, long-term platonic roommates, and homosexual couples—all of whom may

nevertheless have the same degree of economic and emotional interdependence found in heterosexual marriages.

Historically, gay and lesbian couples either had to live with their legally unrecognized status or find ways other than marriage to establish such recognition. One rather creative method of approximating a legal relationship was adoption. In one case, a 22-year-old New York man petitioned to adopt his 26-year-old male partner. The parties testified that "they wish[ed] to establish a legally cognizable relationship in order to facilitate inheritance, the handling of their insurance policies and pension plans, and the acquisition of suitable housing" (quoted in Anderson, 1988, p. 360). They contended that they wanted a "more permanent legal bond" that would provide their relationship with some security. The court approved the petition. This arrangement automatically created certain legal rights and duties for both partners (Anderson, 1988).

In 1999, the Canadian Supreme Court took a huge step toward legally recognizing homosexual unions when it struck down a heterosexual definition of the word *spouse*. The court ruled that Canada's Family Law Act was unconstitutional because it limited to married or common-law heterosexual couples the right to claim alimony. The result of this ruling may be far-reaching, because laws governing adoption, marriage, pensions, and taxes also contain hundreds of references to spouses ("Canada overturns definition," 1999).

The steps toward legally recognizing homosexual unions have usually been less dramatic. In 1999, France created a new form of legal partnership called a "civil solidarity pact," which grants homosexual couples—as well as heterosexual cohabiting couples—some of the benefits and responsibilities of marriage. Under this law, couples are responsible for financially supporting each other. They can file joint income tax returns and are eligible for the other partner's work benefits (Daley, 2000).

In 2000, Vermont became the first state to approve "civil unions," legally recognized relationships that give gay couples all the benefits of marriage. Couples officially register their relationships and in so doing formally declare that they have "an intimate, committed relationship of mutual caring," that they live together, and that they agree to be responsible for each other's basic living expenses.

Similar laws have been enacted at the local level in cities such as San Francisco and West Hollywood, California; Ithaca, New York; Minneapolis, Minnesota; Washington, DC; Seattle, Washington; and Madison, Wisconsin. These laws usually extend to the domestic partners of city workers full spousal rights such as health insurance, life insurance, pension benefits, employee discounts, and health club membership. In addition, thousands of employers—including over 100 Fortune 500 companies—now grant the partners of homosexual employees some of the same benefits traditionally granted to spouses ("Employers offer gays more benefits," 2000).

The Push to Legalize Gay Marriage

Although domestic partnership laws and policies go a long way in legally recognizing gay and lesbian relationships, many people feel such changes are inadequate. Many elements of society still discriminate against homosexual relationships. For instance, in 1991 and again in 2000, the governing body of the Presbyterian Church ruled that same-sex union ceremonies could be performed in the denomination's churches by ordained pastors—but only so long as the ceremonies were not considered marriages (Sherman, 1992; Stammer, 2000). The Vermont law stopped short of calling same-sex unions *marriages*. In fact, it defines a marriage as an arrangement between a man and a woman. To many, domestic partnerships are still "not quite" marriages and therefore not quite families. Consequently, homosexual partnerships remain culturally and legally second-class.

Advocates of gay marriage argue that allowing gay and lesbian individuals to legally marry would result in a more secure, stable, and protective relationship. Without legal status, such relationships can sometimes be difficult to preserve. For instance, in 1999, Samer Yahya, an Italian man attending college in Hartford, Connecticut, was attempting to return from a month-long visit with relatives in Rome. He never made it on the flight. Immigration agents determined that he had a flawed visa. He was strip-

searched and shackled to a bench overnight at the airport. The U.S. embassy in Rome denied him a new visa, saying that although he was a legitimate student, it was likely that he would stay in the country illegally after graduation because of a long-term relationship with a U.S. man. But this relationship was not a legal marriage, and so it gave Mr. Yahya no protection against deportation. Had they been a heterosexual married couple, Mr. Yahya would have automatically gained residency rights as the spouse of a U.S. citizen. U.S. immigration law considers foreign nationals whose work or student visas have expired to be "illegal immigrants," even though they and their partners may share mortgages, businesses, homes, and even children. Immigration lawyers estimate that tens of thousands of relationships have been broken apart by this law (Jacobs, 1999).

· ·

Advocates of gay marriage argue that allowing gay and lesbian individuals to legally marry would result in a more secure, stable, and protective relationship.

· ·

In addition to citing these sorts of practical problems, some advocates of gay marriage argue that legalizing it would lead to greater public acceptance of homosexual people in general. Having the right to legally marry and start families would combat the all-too-common belief that gay relationships are solely about sexual activity and would force heterosexuals to acknowledge that gay couples can be seriously committed to each other and can take on traditional family responsibilities. Far from being a repudiation of family, then, the desire to legally marry acknowledges the ideal of family.

Opposition to Legalizing Gay Marriage

Opposition to gay marriage nevertheless remains strong. According to a recent poll, nearly 50 percent of U.S. Americans oppose homosexual marriages (Lester, 2000). Gay and lesbian partners are typically thought of as individuals, not as family members, reflecting a pervasive belief that homosexuality and family are mutually exclusive concepts (reported in Allen & Demo, 1995). Indeed, claiming a gay or lesbian identity has typically been considered a rejection of family (reported in Weston, 1991).

To many people, the power and significance of marriage as an institution rest on its uniqueness—the belief that it is not one lifestyle among many but the fundamental intimate arrangement in society. The U.S. Supreme Court once declared that marriage is "noble" and "intimate to the degree of being sacred" (Stoddard, 1992, p. 17). Its concern is that when relationships that aren't marriages start being treated as if they are, marriage loses its power and significance. One U.S. congressman called homosexual relationships "the most vicious attack on traditional family values that our society has seen in the history of our republic" (quoted in Hunter, 1991, p. 189).

Currently, no state legally recognizes same-sex marriage. To date, 30 states have enacted laws explicitly defining as valid only marriages between a man and a woman. In 1996, President Clinton signed the Defense of Marriage Act, which formally reaffirmed the federal government's definition of marriage as the union of one man and one woman, authorized all states to refuse to accept same-sex marriages from other states (if they ever became legal at the state level), and denied federal pension, health, and other benefits to same-sex couples. In 2001, the Alliance for Marriage, an organization of legal experts, scholars, and religious leaders proposed a federal amendment to the U.S. Constitution that would wipe out legal protections and benefits for same-sex couples.

It's important to note that opposition to gay marriage comes not only from people who disapprove of homosexuality and perceive it as a threat to traditional definitions of family but also from a small number of gays and lesbians. These opponents argue that legalizing gay marriage would be a civil rights victory but would render gays and lesbians even more invisible to the larger society and undermine the movement to establish a separate and unique gay culture and identity (Ettelbrick, 1992; F. Johnson, 1996). Furthermore, some fear that homosexual married couples would be expected to behave just

like heterosexual married couples, amounting to an acceptance of a heterosexual standard for what a successful intimate relationship should look like (Lewin, 1996). This sort of arrangement would subsequently diminish the notion that valid and committed relationships can exist outside traditional marriage. In fact, some gay opponents of homosexual marriage argue that the absence of marriage as a dominant, regulating institution in their intimate lives actually gives them the space to define their families in richer ways, to include friends, neighbors, and community (F. Johnson, 1996). Some gay and lesbian activists take the argument further, contending that having no "marriage" or even "family" should constitute a point of pride for homosexual people (Stacey, 2001). Indeed, some gay people look down on homosexual parents for having failed to "escape" the family and for trying to gain acceptance in mainstream society by approximating the "traditional" family (Lynch, 1982).

In sum, more is at stake in this debate than the emotional rewards of formalizing shared commitment in a loving relationship and the practical rewards of legal recognition of gay and lesbian marriage. This issue is fundamentally about what arrangements we believe deserve the label "family." These beliefs can ultimately shape the law, public policy, and the contours of our everyday lives.

The Symbolism of Family

Judging from the strong emotions evoked by debates over the definition of family, it's clear that family is important not just for what it looks like but for what it symbolizes. Many people fervently believe that as the family goes, so goes the country. It stands for what people, as a culture, hold dear. Hence,

> the task of defining what the American family *is* [is] integral to the very task of defining America itself. . . . Obviously more is at stake than a dictionary definition of "the family." The debate actually takes form as a political judgment about the fate of *one particular conception of the family and family life* [emphases in original]. (Hunter, 1991, pp. 177, 180)

In U.S. society the idea of family has become a powerful symbol of decency. Disneyland and Disneyworld, for instance, are considered "family" theme parks because they supposedly emphasize the wholesomeness of the recreational activities they provide. You'll find no bars, strip clubs, or gambling halls there. Likewise, every video rental store has a "family movie" section. But the films you'll find in this section aren't necessarily about families. Instead, the label "family" presumably identifies films that are devoid of graphic sex and violence, whose themes children and adults can enjoy together.

Politicians looking for a convenient way to whip up public sentiment often rail against policies and practices considered "antifamily" (read "indecent" and "immoral"), signal their support for "family values," and espouse the view that the U.S. family is being attacked and threatened by dangerous forces of change. Today political candidates try to situate themselves as more "profamily" than their rivals. Having a smiling spouse and children displayed prominently in photos and television coverage is practically a prerequisite for getting elected.

Such positions reflect a belief, held by many, that an expanded definition of family demeans the family's symbolic importance. From this perspective, "family" is a sacred label that should be applied only to the most traditional type of family: married parents and their children. To those who ascribe to this position, family is the very foundation of society and therefore shouldn't be taken lightly. People should not have the right to define themselves as family however they see fit. Those who seek to expand the definition of family to apply to all sorts of relationships are believed to be emptying it of its symbolic meaning and power (Gellott, 1985).

But to many others, the rhetoric of family values is little more than a thin cover for a particular political agenda. According to these skeptics, those who deplore the greater visibility of cohabiting and homosexual couples, the increasing numbers of single and working mothers, and the high rates of divorce are making a rather explicit judgment about the sorts of human relationships people ought to define as "appropriate." Many believe that the shape and configuration of a family are less important than the emotional bonds and the feelings of mutual obligation that can exist between people. It doesn't matter so much whether a child has two biological parents or lives in some other arrangement as long as that child has someone to take care of him or her. It doesn't matter so much whether a couple is married as long as they, too, have a committed and caring relationship.

The point here is that there is no agreement among the media, society, and academia about what families are, what they should be, or what the implications of recent social changes will be. These disagreements aren't always politically motivated. They can arise simply and earnestly from people's different perspectives, values, beliefs, and desires.

Something to Think About

One of the issues that most deeply divides U.S. society today is the definition of the term *family* and the valuing of particular family forms over others. You've seen that there's more to family than meets the eye. Some cultures have ideas very different from ours about what sorts of family arrangements are normal and natural. And in this society, most people's lives depart in some way from the traditional nuclear family depicted in the official definition and in popular images of family. This diversity raises some interesting questions:

1. On prime-time television today, what family form predominates? Have you noticed significant social class or racial variation in TV families? How are "nontraditional" family arrangements handled (for example, single-parent households, divorce, gay families, interracial marriage)? What sorts of issues do TV families deal with? How do they solve problems? Make decisions? Deal with crises?

2. How do media images of family affect people's own family experiences? Do the media (television, in particular) *create* images of family that viewers then use to form their own attitudes about family, or do they simply *reflect* the reality of family life as people experience it?

3. Should the societal recognition of family be limited to blood and legal relations, or should people be

able to choose whomever they want to be their family? What is society's interest in controlling which arrangements people call family?

4. In the near future, do you think the concept of family will expand to acknowledge the validity of

many diverse relationships and living arrangements, or will it contract, reinforcing the legitimacy and desirability of the "traditional" family? Explain.

5. Which definition of family do you think ought to provide the basis for official family policy? Explain.

For More On . . .	See . . .
Family as household	"Coping Strategies of Dual-Earner Couples" in Chapter 7
Family as kinship	"Adoption and the Primacy of Genetic Parenthood" in Chapter 8
Gay families	"Sexuality" in Chapter 5

Is the institution of family breaking down— and society with it? _____

On May 19, 1992, then Vice President Dan Quayle gave a speech at the Commonwealth Club in San Francisco, California. Although the speech began as an assessment of United States–Japan relations and trade, it quickly turned to the topic of street riots that had occurred in Los Angeles about 2½ weeks earlier, following the not-guilty verdicts in a famous police brutality case. In trying to make sense out of the violence many people had witnessed on television, the vice president minced no words. He placed blame for the riots squarely at the doorstep of troubled families:

> I believe the lawless social anarchy which we saw is directly related to the breakdown of family structure, personal responsibility, and social order in too many areas of our society. For the poor the situation is compounded by a welfare ethos that impedes individual efforts to move ahead in society. . . .
>
> The failure of our families is hurting America deeply. When families fail, society fails. The . . . lack of structure in our inner cities [is] testament to how quickly civilization falls apart when the family foundation cracks. Children need love and discipline. They need mothers and fathers. A welfare check is not a husband.

> The state is not a father. It is from parents that children learn how to behave in society; it is from parents above all that children come to understand values and themselves as men and women, mothers and fathers. And for those concerned about children growing up in poverty, we should know this: marriage is probably the best anti-poverty program of all. . . . Where there are no mature, responsible men around to teach boys how to be good men, gangs serve in their place. . . . Marriage is a moral issue that requires cultural consensus, and the use of social sanctions. Bearing babies irresponsibly is, simply, wrong. Failing to support children one has fathered is wrong. . . . It doesn't help matters when prime time TV has Murphy Brown— a character who supposedly epitomizes today's intelligent, highly paid, professional woman— mocking the importance of fathers by bearing a child alone, and calling it just another "lifestyle choice." . . . It's time to talk again about family, hard work, integrity and personal responsibility. We cannot be embarrassed out of our belief that two parents, married to each other, are better in most cases for children than one. (Quayle, 1992, pp. 517–519)

Do recent changes in the structure of American families signal their decline or their ability to adapt to changing social circumstances?

This young girl is about to board an airplane by herself. Children today are more likely than ever to find themselves traveling as "unaccompanied minors," often because of their parents' divorce. Notice the "intact" family with a baby in the background. If the baby's family remains intact, how might its childhood, and its future life, differ from the young girl's? How might those differences affect society as a whole?

Such concerns have not fallen out of favor. About a decade later, former Vice President Quayle had this to say about families:

> There is extraordinary turmoil and dysfunction in families today. What has caused this? Time pressure is one reason. . . . Time formerly spent in family activities is now spent on the computer, in front of the television, on the phone, in the car and at the mall. We are a harried society. . . . Our mobile society has caused more families to live far away from the support system of their extended families. Add to this the fact that pop culture focuses too much on tearing down institutions that give us a sense of stability, and it is no wonder the traditional family structure is in decline. (Quayle, 2001, p. 52)

Many U.S. residents today believe that "alarming" changes in the institution of family have robbed it of its traditional influence over people's everyday lives and its importance in society. Disturbing media stories about violent crime, school shootings, drugs, poverty, homelessness, and domestic abuse symbolize the fraying of U.S. social fiber. Journalists, politicians, and social commentators assessing the current health and future prospects of U.S. families often use Quayle-like rhetoric of "moral panic" (Stacey, 1996b): words such as *endangered, vulnerable, dying, disappearing, declining,* and *doomed.* An organization comprising well-known sociologists and other family experts has this to say about the state of U.S. families:

> [We wish to focus attention] on a problem of enormous scope and consequence. Simply stated, the problem is this: marriage is declining as an institution for childbearing and child rearing, with devastating consequences for millions of children. (National Marriage Project, 2001)

As popular as these sentiments seem to be, not everyone agrees that families are in such dire straits. Some scholars argue that as an institution, the family is as strong as ever. Consider its ability to change form and process in response to shifting economic, political, and cultural forces. As one prominent historian notes, "For at least 150 years there have been

periods of fear that 'the family'—meaning a popular image of what families were supposed to be like, by no means a correct recollection of any actual 'traditional' family—was in decline; and these fears tended to escalate in periods of social stress" (Gordon, 1988, p. 3). Although many of today's families may bear little resemblance to the traditional families of our nostalgic past, these scholars believe that families still work for the most part and hence are here to stay.

Who's right? Is the institution of family weak and on the verge of collapse, or is it strong and adaptable to changing social circumstances? Does family "breakdown" cause the problems that plague society today, or is it a consequence of those problems? Let's see if we can get past the rhetoric to examine a variety of facts about the current state of U.S. families and then try to assess just how much trouble they really are in.

The Family Decline Perspective

Many people believe, as Dan Quayle does, that the U.S. family's overall importance as a social institution is eroding (Benokraitis, 2000). Such a view reflects what we can call the *family decline perspective.* Supporters of this perspective point to the strong movement in recent years, in the United States and other Western societies, toward a strange assortment of households claiming to be families. They link these changes to what they see as widespread cultural and moral weakening, a demise of "family values," and increasing sexual promiscuity among young people. They argue that the institution of family has lost many, if not all, of its traditional functions.

The Declining Institutional Influence of Family

Throughout history, the institution of family has been the center of many important activities. In the family, children have received most of their education and religious training, both children and adults could expect emotional nurturing and support, and sexual activity and reproduction have been regulated. And the family has also been the economic center of society, where family members worked together to earn a living and support one another financially.

• •

More recently, the family's role as a source of emotional security and nurturing has disappeared as it has become less able to shield its members from the harsh realities of modern life.

• •

But as the economy has shifted, so too has the role of family. In the nineteenth century, when economic production moved from the home to the factory, the teaching of skills and values that was once a part of everyday home life began to take place in schools. Much of the history of childhood and adolescence in the twentieth century was marked by a steady decline of parental authority and influence and an accompanying increase in the influence of educators, peer groups, and the mass media.

Families have also lost much of their ability to regulate members' sexual behavior, as witnessed by today's high rates of premarital and extramarital sex. And more recently, the family's role as a source of emotional security and nurturing has disappeared as it has become less able to shield its members from the harsh realities of modern life (Lasch, 1977). The absenteeism rate of fathers, the decline in the amount of time parents spend with their children, and the increasing proportion of a child's life spent alone, with peers, or in day care attest to the loss of this function (Popenoe, 1993).

The strength (or weakness) of family as an institution can also be measured not just in how well (or poorly) it performs important social functions but in the hold it has over its individual members. Strong families are those that maintain close ties among members and direct their activities toward collective goals. But today individuals have become increasingly more autonomous, less bound by their sense of obligation to family, and less committed to

its norms and values (Popenoe, 1993). Further signs that the family may be in steep decline include the steady erosion of people's belief in an obligation for mutual assistance among family members, of family loyalty, of concern for perpetuating the family as a unit, and of subordination of individual interests to the interests and welfare of the family as a group (Popenoe, 1993).

The past several decades have also seen a dramatic and pervasive weakening of the expectation that people will marry, remain married, have children, restrict intimate relations to marriage, and maintain separate roles within families for men and women. The transition from singlehood to marriage no longer carries the strong sense of obligation and commitment it once did. The blurring of rights and duties has destroyed the boundaries among childhood, adolescence, adulthood, and old age; between parents and children; and between male and female (Farber, 1987).

Social Change and Family Structure

In addition to believing that the family is weakening as a social institution, people who subscribe to the family decline perspective note that its fundamental form—the traditional nuclear family—is becoming less common. Family structure in modern industrialized societies has indeed undergone greater change in the past several decades, and at a more accelerated rate, than in any previous period of human history (Popenoe, 1988, 1993). According to a report by the Population Council, similar trends are occurring worldwide (Lewin, 1995a). For instance, in many industrialized countries (including Canada, France, the United States, and Denmark) divorce rates doubled between 1970 and the mid-1980s and have remained high ever since. In less developed countries, about 25 percent of first marriages end by the time women are in their 40s.

Likewise, unwed motherhood is increasing everywhere. In northern Europe, for example, as many as a third of all births occur to unwed mothers. Mothers worldwide are carrying increasing economic responsibility for their children, too.

We should note that since the beginning of recorded history, family has always been changing. But according to family decline theorists, these recent changes—beginning in the 1960s—have been unique and much more serious. Consequently, they believe that something can and should be done to restore family to its natural state and its rightful place in social life (Glenn, 2000).

The "Shrinking" U.S. Family.

One of the chief concerns of the family decline perspective is that people are having fewer children than they did a half century ago. In the early 1960s, the average U.S. woman had 3.5 children over the span of her life. By 1998, it was closer to 2.0 (Bianchi & Casper, 2000). Having fewer children suggests that people are less committed to the traditional ideals of family (Popenoe, 1993).

Why are people having fewer children? Certainly economic pressures and concerns about overpopulation have convinced many married couples to limit the number of children they produce. But equally important are changes in the timing of marriage and childbearing. Increasing numbers of women are getting married later and delaying childbearing until after they've graduated from college and established careers. For example, in 2000, Massachusetts became the first state where more babies were born to women over 30 than under 30 (Goldberg, 2000). When couples wait to marry and begin childbearing, they are bound to have fewer children.

. . . .

The U.S. birth rate is currently at about the level necessary to replace the current population in the next generation.

. . . .

Moreover, some married couples are choosing not to have children at all. Sociologists Tim Heaton, Cardell Jacobson, and Kimberlee Holland (1999) studied patterns of childlessness and parenthood among a group of individuals surveyed initially in 1988 and again in 1994 as part of the National Survey of Families and Households. Overall, about 20 percent of respondents were what we would call "voluntarily childless." Among this group, about 13 percent of respondents had intended to have a child when surveyed in 1988 but changed their minds or were undecided six years later, and 7 percent had originally intended to be childless and still were by the time of the second survey. However, the largest proportion of surveyed couples (45 percent) were simply "postponers"—they said in 1988 and again in 1994 that they intended to have children but had not yet done so.

A reduction in the size of families is not proof, in and of itself, of family decline. Strength is not always in numbers. But according to the family decline perspective, small families can cause problems. The U.S. birth rate is currently at about the level necessary to replace the current population in the next generation. In parts of western Europe and Scandinavia the birth rates are actually below this level. Many people fear the economy will decline if society fails to produce ever-increasing numbers of consumers. Some fear that other cultures with larger populations will render their culture obsolete. And there's also concern that declining numbers of entry-level workers will not be able to make up for the larger number of retiring workers.

Some countries have taken an active role in trying to get their citizens to have more children. In Italy, which has the world's lowest birth rate, alarmed government officials are looking for ways to make it easier for women to have careers and children simultaneously. In Japan, a country with a similarly low birth rate, some companies will pay their employees bonuses—as much as $10,000—for each child they have (Sims, 2000).

A decrease in the number of children being born can have long-term consequences for individual families as well, especially in their ability to care for needy members. The past several decades have witnessed a dramatic shift in the age structure of U.S. society. More people are living into their 80s and 90s than ever before. Hence, families are expanding *vertically* (more generations living per family) at the same time that they're shrinking *horizontally* (fewer individuals per generation). The consequence may be a shortage of family members to share in caring for elderly parents in the future (Sherman, Ward, & LaGory, 1988). With few or no siblings to help them, many people—particularly women—in their 40s, 50s, and 60s will have to cope with the burden of caring for elderly parents on their own in addition to the usual demands of work and family, further straining family relationships.

Changing Family Roles. Other changes having a powerful impact on family are those that break down traditional separations between male and female family roles (Goldscheider & Waite, 1991). In the past several decades, the women's movement has encouraged large numbers of women to reject the idea that motherhood and family are their primary destiny and to strive for success, independence, and occupational achievement (Nock, 1987). Today mothers participate in the paid labor force almost as much as nonmothers, averaging about 34 hours per week on the job (Cohen & Bianchi, 1999). In fact, the fastest increase in female labor force participation has been among mothers of children under age 2 (Bianchi & Casper, 2000).

Similar changes in the gender-based division of labor are occurring worldwide. In the Philippines, for instance, a country that retains many traditional views on gender, women contribute 55 percent of the household finances (Lewin, 1995b). Although the reasons for entering the paid labor force vary from country to country and from family to family within the same country, women worldwide are finding that to provide their children an adequate life they must earn more money (Lewin, 1995b). In short, women are working more and contributing more to the economic well-being of their families than ever before.

With more women entering the paid labor force, wives are becoming less dependent on their husbands for economic support. Indeed, the higher a wife's income relative to her husband's, the greater the likelihood of separation or divorce (Cherlin, 1992). Furthermore, families in which both parents work for pay can experience conflict over the balance between work and family responsibilities. Many working women have come to expect complete equality in their relationships and therefore feel disillusioned when they face the day-to-day task of juggling household chores, child care and spousal responsibilities, and career. Given these forces, the concern is that husbands and children will cease being the most important part of women's lives and that the family will relinquish even more of its nurturing functions to day care centers and others outside the family.

Equally disturbing to some is the effect that women's paid labor force participation has on society at large. There is evidence that as women's labor force participation increases, so does the demand for public funding and public delivery of social services (Huber & Stephens, 2000). Working women need relief from traditional caregiving responsibilities, and they tend to look to the government for that relief in the form of better health, education, and welfare services. As their numbers grow, working women become more successful at pressuring the government to spend more on such services.

Some observers also see a link between a lack of parental presence at home—especially mothers'—and rising rates of teenage suicide, growing juvenile arrest rates, more and earlier drug use and sexual activity, and falling SAT scores. A 2001 study of more than 1,100 children in ten U.S. cities found that children who spend a lot of their time in child care are more likely than children cared for primarily at home to be aggressive, defiant, and disobedient (reported in Stolberg, 2001). Another researcher has found that so-called latchkey children—those unsupervised by adults after school—suffer from heightened rates of psychological disturbance, delinquency, and drug use (Galambos & Maggs, 1991).

Burgeoning Divorce Rates and the Erosion of the Two-Parent Family. For much of the history of human civilization, the death of a parent was the most common form of family disruption. Separation and divorce were kept rare by social, religious, and legal restrictions. But separation and divorce have become increasingly common experiences for U.S. families. Consequently, a growing number of children are experiencing a significant period with only one parent present (usually the mother). In

1960, 9 percent of children under 18 lived with a single parent; by 1998, the figure had increased to 32 percent for all U.S. children. The rate is higher for African-American children (around 64 percent) and Hispanic children (36 percent) (U.S. Bureau of the Census, 2000a).

The causes of the high divorce rate include things such as weakening of the family's traditional economic bonds, higher expectations for marriage, reduced influence of religion, and the stress of shifting gender roles (Popenoe, 1993). Moreover, divorce tends to feed on itself. The more common it is, the more "normal" and less stigmatizing it becomes.

Although divorce can be traumatic for adults, most recover and are able to get on with their lives after a while. Children have a more difficult time adjusting. For them, divorce sets a series of changes in motion, each with the potential to disrupt their lives. They may have to move to a new home in a new neighborhood, make new friends, and go to a new school. Because the overwhelming majority of children of divorce live with their mothers, their standard of living may also decline because of the lower earning capacity of women in general and the all-too-common failure of noncustodial fathers to pay child support.

In addition, the relationship children have with their noncustodial parent diminishes over time. One study found that 23 percent of children living with their mothers had not seen their fathers in the past five years. Another 20 percent had not seen their fathers within the past year. In addition, 60 percent of the mothers had received no financial assistance from the fathers during the previous year (Furstenberg, Morgan, & Allison, 1987). To some sociologists, the disappearance of fathers is one of the most serious changes that has taken place in U.S. families. Several sociologists (McLanahan & Booth, 1991; McLanahan & Sandefur, 1994; Popenoe, 1996) have found that children who grow up in divorced, fatherless households are more likely than other children to

- Earn poorer grades in school and perform worse on standardized tests
- Be absent from school
- Drop out of school
- Commit violent crime and engage in drug and alcohol abuse
- Become victims of child abuse and neglect
- Suffer from eating disorders and depression
- Be poor and, when they reach adulthood, have lower earnings
- Marry early, have children early, and divorce

Once considered an event to avoid unless absolutely necessary, marital separation has come to be seen as morally neutral or even positive in some cases. Few people today feel that a couple in a troubled marriage should stay together "for the sake of the children" (Adelson, 1996). Given these prevailing societal attitudes, couples have increasing difficulty committing themselves wholeheartedly to their marriage. As a result, many couples take protective steps, such as prenuptial agreements, that may undermine the quality of the relationship and predispose it to failure (Gill, 1991). Not surprisingly, there has been a steady erosion of the expectation that marriage is permanent. Furthermore, children of divorce may grow up expecting that their own future marriages will not last. A high divorce rate, therefore, can have cumulative and long-lasting effects on cultural perceptions of marriage.

The "Flight" from Marriage. Traditionally, marriage has been perceived as a *social obligation*—a relationship designed to strengthen society by promoting economic security and procreation. But today people are likely to see marriage as more flexible and as a path toward self-fulfillment, a voluntary relationship that people can make or break at will (Popenoe, 1993). In 1999, a study published by the National Marriage Project at Rutgers University claimed that marriage rates had dropped 43 percent over the last four decades to their lowest point ever ("The institution of marriage," 1999). Even for couples who do get and remain married, marital quality has taken a turn for the worse. The Rutgers study found that fewer people than in the past claim that they are "very happy" in their marriages.

The past several decades have witnessed a dramatic increase in nonmarital cohabitation. Between 1970 and 2000 the number of cohabiting couples increased by over 1,000 percent, growing from

523,000 to 5.5 million (U.S. Bureau of the Census, 2001d). They now comprise over 5 percent of all U.S. households, up from 3 percent in 1990. In the past, cohabiting couples were likely to be poor people who couldn't afford to get married. Today, cohabiting couples come from all classes and all age, ethnic, and racial groups. Cohabitation is also common among divorced individuals, many of whom have children. It is estimated that at some point during their childhood, one in four children are likely to live in a family headed by a cohabiting couple (Graefe & Lichter, 1999).

Social policies may be motivating many people's decision to "live together" rather than marry (Waite & Gallagher, 2000). For instance, marriage reduces welfare eligibility for individuals. Also, the standard income tax deduction is often lower for working married couples than for two singles. Unwed couples who become pregnant may forgo or delay marriage, because insurance companies usually won't cover such "preexisting conditions." Domestic partnership policies of private companies, cities, or even states—designed to grant cohabiting couples many of the same benefits that married couples receive—may also deter marriage if couples believe they can gain the same benefits whether they're married or not.

Despite its growing popularity, cohabitation has some built-in difficulties. For one thing, it lacks the predictability, cultural support, and social recognition of marriage. This lack of institutionalization may explain why cohabitors report less commitment to their relationships, less happiness, and poorer relationships with their parents than do married individuals (Nock, 1995). Most research shows that people who cohabit before marriage actually have higher divorce rates—regardless of whether they marry their cohabiting partner or somebody else—than people who don't cohabit before marriage (DeMaris & Rao, 1992).

Furthermore, although the public seems to have grown more tolerant of unmarried adults living together, the law sometimes has been slower to adjust. In New Mexico, for example, "unlawful cohabitation" is a crime punishable by up to six months in jail. In 2000, efforts in Arizona to repeal that state's 80-year-old anticohabitation law failed. Massachusetts did repeal a 1784 law that banned "lewdly and lasciviously

associating and cohabitating without the benefit of marriage"—but not until 1987 (Yardley, 2000).

Another oft-cited sign of the reduced importance of marriage in people's lives is the increasing number of women who are bearing children while unmarried (Cherlin, 1992). In 1980, 18 percent of all births in the United States were to single women. By 1998, the proportion had increased to 33 percent (U.S. Bureau of the Census, 2000b). In fact, in 1998, for the first time on record, the majority of first children (53 percent) were born to or conceived by unmarried women. In the 1940s, that figure was 18 percent (cited in Eckel, 1999). Contrary to popular belief, these single mothers aren't just teenagers. Only about one-third of out-of-wedlock births occur to women under the age of 20 (U.S. Bureau of the Census, 2000a). In fact, between 1980 and 1998, births to teenage mothers as a percentage of all births actually decreased, from 15.6 percent to 12.5 percent (U.S. Bureau of the Census, 2000a). And over the past five years, the teenage birth rate has decreased substantially for all racial groups (Lewin, 1998a).

· ·

Despite its growing popularity, cohabitation has some built-in difficulties. For one thing, it lacks the predictability, cultural support, and social recognition of marriage.

· ·

At the same time there has been a dramatic increase in the number of older, never-married single mothers (Gringlas & Weinraub, 1995). Between 1982 and 1992, the birth rate doubled among never-married, college-educated women and almost tripled among never-married women who work in a professional or managerial capacity (Siegel, 1995). These figures remain high today. Like married mothers, these women accept motherhood as a fundamental part of their womanhood. However, they don't feel the need to become a spouse in order to become a parent.

This so-called flight from marriage is troubling to family decline theorists, because they believe that marriage can provide people—and ultimately the larger society—with significant benefits. For instance, some evidence suggests that married individuals—especially men—are physically healthier, live longer, show higher rates of overall satisfaction, and have more money than single or cohabiting individuals (Waite, 1995). Hence, a decline in marriage rates could possibly create an overall drop in people's well-being.

The Family Transformation Perspective

These trends are understandably cause for concern. But many social scientists oppose the notion that the institution of family is in steep, perhaps irreversible, decline. They disagree that a family's structure is more important than the relationships and processes that take place within it. So, for instance, parental supervision, control, involvement, and sensitivity to the needs of children are better predictors of a child's well-being than whether the child lives with one parent or two, whether the child's mother works or not, or whether the parents are biological parents or stepparents (Acock & Demo, 1994). In addition, they say, by accepting the notion that the idealized, "traditional" family is something to be preserved, the family decline perspective misses the crucial sociological point that historical changes influence family structures and create new arrangements.

This perspective—what we'll call the *family transformation perspective*—maintains that the family—both as a living arrangement and as a social institution—is not disappearing at all but instead is becoming more diverse and complex as it adapts to changing social and economic circumstances (Kain, 1990). Although changes in work, family, and sexual opportunities for men and women can create significant instability and uncertainty in people's lives, these changes also have the potential of introducing greater democracy, equality, and choice into our family relationships (Stacey, 1996b). In short, just because many families today aren't "traditional" in form doesn't mean that the institution of family itself is disappearing or in some sort of danger.

Supporters of the family transformation perspective ask people to rethink traditional ideas about what family is or should be (Sjoberg, Williams, Gill, & Himmel, 1995; Stacey, 1994). "Nontraditional" family forms such as dual-earner families, childless couples, single-parent families, and heterosexual and homosexual cohabiting couples are viable alternatives. The difficulties that all families face today may be as much a matter of rapid demographic, economic, and political change as a matter of family decline, more a failure of social policy than a failure of individual families (Elkind, 1994).

Those who support the notion of family transformation also take issue with the argument that the collapse of the traditional family is the prime cause of social decay. The losses in real earnings and high-paying jobs caused by the decline in industrial manufacturing, the ghettoization of women in low-wage work, and global restructuring that exports jobs to other countries have wreaked far more havoc on families and on society than the effects of feminism, sexual revolution, divorce, cohabitation, and individualism. When significant economic changes take place, it's inevitable that families will feel their effects. For instance, competitive pressures of the international capitalist marketplace have forced many businesses and industries to make greater use of so-called disposable workers—those who work part time or on temporary contract—to maintain profits. These jobs offer no benefits and no security and therefore import instability directly into family life (Kilborn, 1993; Uchitelle, 1993).

· ·

The family—both as a living arrangement and as a social institution—is not disappearing at all but instead is becoming more diverse and complex as it adapts to changing social and economic circumstances.

· ·

In short, the belief that we just need to return to the good old nuclear family and everything will be fine allows the public and the government to avoid responsibility for intervening in destitute neighborhoods, creating affordable housing, ensuring that all young people have access to quality education, and creating needed jobs. According to family transformation theorists, as a society, we have two choices:

> We can come to grips with the [contemporary] family condition by accepting the end of a singular ideal family and begin to promote better living and spiritual conditions for the diverse array of real families we actually inhabit and desire. Or we can continue to engage in denial, resistance, displacement, and bad faith, by cleaving to a moralistic ideology of *the family* at the same time that we fail to provide social and economic conditions that make life for the modern family or any other kind of family viable, let alone dignified and secure. (Stacey, 1996b, p. 11)

Focusing on the personal and moral failings of individuals as the source of family and social problems keeps people from trying to improve other social institutions so life in all kinds of families would be more workable.

Taking a Long-Term, Historical View

Supporters of the family transformation perspective argue that many claims of family decline are based on a flawed, somewhat nostalgic belief that family life in the past was more harmonious and more stable than today:

> It is a pretty picture of life down on grandma's farm. There are lots of happy children, and many kinfolk live together in a large rambling house. Everyone works hard. Most of the food to be eaten during the winter is grown, preserved, and stored on the farm. . . . The family has many functions; it is the source of economic stability and religious, educational, and vocational training. Father is stern and reserved and has the final decision in all important matters. . . .
>
> All boys and girls marry, and marry young. . . . After marriage, the couple lives harmoniously, either near the boy's parents or with them. . . . No one divorces. (Goode, 1971, p. 624)

But this nostalgic image is distorted. The family transformation perspective points out that the traditional U.S. family of the past never really existed in the form it takes in our collective imagination. In truth, from the time of the Puritans to the twenty-first century, each succeeding generation has been concerned about some crisis of the family (Hareven, 1992; Skolnick, 1991). Families have always been diverse in structure and have always had trouble protecting members from economic hardship, internal violence, political upheaval, and social change. Glorifying a mythical past fosters artificial or limited standards of a "normal" family and, in the process, ignores the potential value of other family forms.

Colonial Families. It's common when describing life in colonial North America for people to focus exclusively on families of European origin. But we must remember that several different types of families coexisted during this period. The Iroquois in the Northeast, for instance, lived in longhouses that accommodated large, extended families. In some colonies, contact between Europeans and Native Americans was typically violent. But that wasn't the case in other areas. In the Carolinas and Georgia, for instance, there were many mixed marriages as Native American women often voluntarily married Englishmen (Berkin, 1996). African-American slaves—whose nuclear families were routinely and purposely torn apart by their owners—secretly built extended-family networks through co-parenting and the adoption of orphans (Coontz, 1996).

What seems consistent across all types of families during this era was that death was a common occurrence of everyday family life. Almost half of all children died before reaching adulthood; half of those who survived didn't reach 50. Short life expectancies meant that most children spent time in a single-parent family or stepfamily. The average length of an eighteenth-century marriage was less than 12 years (Skolnick, 1991). Even children fortunate enough to come from intact families usually left home well before puberty to work as servants or apprentices in other people's homes. Mothers were much less involved in the care of their children than the busiest of working mothers today. And because it was common to send children away from home to work or learn a trade, many children depended more on siblings, neighbors, and masters for their upbringing than on their parents.

Male authority was taken for granted, and slight disobediences by women and children were considered punishable forms of treason. Children were not protected from sexuality, either in action or in discussion. Indeed, many parents at the time believed that children were inherently corrupt beings. So a key task of parents and other caretakers was to "break the will" of children and conquer their naturally evil tendencies (Skolnick, 1991). Harsh physical punishment and humiliation were considered legitimate forms of parental authority. Complete obedience and submission were demanded of children:

> In some households [children] were made to stand through meals, eating whatever was handed to them. They were taught it was sinful to complain about food, clothing, or their lot in life. Courtesy of a formal sort was insisted upon. Corporal punishment seems to have been liberally employed. Use was made of birchrods, canes, and [leather straps], and at school dunce stools and caps and placards bearing humiliating names. (Queen & Habenstein, 1974, p. 306)

Nineteenth-Century Families. At the beginning of the Revolutionary War, small family farms and shops flourished and a wife's work was valued as highly as her husband's. But by the middle of the nineteenth century, industrialization and wage labor took work (and husbands) away from small family farms and businesses, leaving wives without their former economic partners. For the first time, men became known as the family breadwinners. By the post–Civil War era, the participation of women in the paid labor force was at an all-time low (Coontz, 1996).

But as middle-class women left the workforce, working-class children entered it by the thousands, often toiling in horrible conditions for 10 hours or more a day. In the North, they worked in factories, tenement workshops, and mines. It was estimated that in the early part of the nineteenth century, half the workers in northern factories were children under 11 (Coontz, 1992). In the South, they worked in the fields. Slave children were not exempt from field labor unless they were infants, and even then their mothers were not allowed time off to nurture them.

At the same time, self-styled "child savers" were defining parents from the "wrong" religion, race, ethnic group, or social class as unfit, thereby justifying the removal of children from their families. These "orphans" were frequently sent to live with farmers in the West who needed extra hands, or they were simply dumped in another town.

People who lived during this period were quite aware that U.S. households were not always particularly nice places. Critics of the time talked about the "great neglect in many parents and masters in training up their children" and expressed grief over the "rising generation" of Americans. Yet when nineteenth-century middle-class families began to withdraw their children from the harsh and dangerous work world, observers were quick to criticize them for raising children who were "too sheltered" (Coontz, 1992).

As is always the case, children were the ones most likely to suffer. Because nineteenth-century adults had a short life expectancy, children at that time were actually more likely to live in a single-parent home, because of the death of a parent, than are children today (Kain, 1990). Although close to 20 percent of U.S. children live in poverty today, about the same proportion lived in orphanages at the turn of the century, and not just because their parents had died. Many were there because their parents simply couldn't afford to raise them. Rates of alcohol abuse, school dropout, and child abuse were all higher a century ago than they are today (Coontz, 1992).

One of the most pervasive myths of nineteenth-century U.S. families is that they were usually large and extended, with a massive and perpetually available support network of grandparents, aunts, uncles, and other relatives living together. Historical research shows, however, that U.S. families have always been fairly small (Goode, 1971; Hareven, 1992). There is no strong tradition in this country of large extended families. In fact, the highest proportion of extended-family households ever recorded in this country was only around 20 percent, and it occurred between 1850 and 1885 (Hareven, 1978). Even then, these families were large for economic reasons, not emotional ones. "Producing" families depended on the labor of children and others for their survival.

Early and Mid-Twentieth-Century Families. The early twentieth century brought more challenges to U.S. families. Concerned that longer life spans would put a strain on marriages, experts and clergy encouraged people to direct their emotional, nurturing, and sensual energy into their marriages. Although this change introduced new intimacy into marriages, it also created a disturbing trend. People's expectations about what they should get out of their marriages increased, leading more and more married couples to express dissatisfaction over what they weren't getting. Not surprisingly, in the early twentieth century the United States had the highest divorce rate in the world. Social commentators bemoaned the fragility of the nuclear family and pined for the "good old days." Birth rates among highly educated U.S. residents dropped, prompting some state legislatures to pass laws prohibiting abortion, to boost the nation's birth rate.

The Great Depression of the 1930s brought further turmoil to U.S. families. Contrary to nostalgic images, the poverty brought about by the Depression didn't bring families closer together. It's true that divorce rates fell during this decade, but they didn't fall because of spouses' strong emotional commitment to each other. With jobs and housing scarce, many couples simply couldn't afford to divorce. Hence, marital unhappiness, domestic violence, and desertion increased dramatically. Economic stress often led to harsh parenting practices, which left many children with emotional as well as physical scars. Murder rates were higher in 1933 than in the 1980s (Coontz, 1997). Marriage rates and birth rates plummeted.

The divorce rate rose sharply again right after World War II. In 1946 one out of every three marriages ended in divorce. Such a high rate most likely resulted from the briefness of the courtships before the young men shipped out and from the stress of separation when the men were overseas. When the soldiers returned home, the disruption of relationships that had occurred during the war was made official. In one study of fathers who returned from the war, four times as many men reported unhappy, even traumatic, reunions as remembered happy ones (Tuttle, 1993).

The Baby Boom of the 1950s. By the time the 1950s rolled around, Americans were hungry for financial security and family stability. For people who could recall their family's struggle to make ends meet during the Depression and who had experienced instability and family separation during World War II, the opportunity to buy a home and have a big family represented an attractive promise of security and fulfillment (Acock & Demo, 1994; Mintz & Kellogg, 1988). The result was the "baby boom": Births rose from 18.4 per 1,000 women during the Depression to 25.3 per 1,000 in 1957 (Mintz & Kellogg, 1988). For many U.S. residents the 1950s still stand out as the "glory days" of families, a reference point against which recent changes in family life can be measured and interpreted. It was the most family-oriented period in U.S. history, dramatically reversing what had been occurring in this country since the turn of the century. For example, half of all women in the 1950s married while they were still teenagers. And the divorce rate steeply declined, to about half what it is today.

· ·

For many U.S. residents the 1950s still stand out as the "glory days" of families.

· ·

For the first time in history the vast majority of U.S. children could expect to live with married biological parents throughout childhood. Although society had some serious problems to deal with—poverty, racial discrimination, lack of educational opportunity—the lives of many white middle- and working-class children were markedly better than they were in the past:

No longer did children have to be haunted by fears . . . that their parents would die, that they would have to live with a stepparent and stepsiblings, or that they would be abandoned. These were the years when the nation confidently boarded up orphanages and closed foundling hospitals, certain that such institutions would never again be needed. In movie theaters across the country parents and children could watch the drama of parental separation and death in the great Disney classics, secure in the knowledge that such nightmare visions as the death of Bambi's mother and the wrenching separation of Dumbo from his mother were only make-believe. (Whitehead, 1993a, p. 50)

Economic prosperity further bolstered the pro-family features of this era. Per capita income rose by 35 percent between 1945 and 1960. The increase in ownership of single-family homes between 1946 and 1956 was larger than the increase during the entire preceding 150 years. Of new homes, 85 percent were built in the suburbs, away from the turmoil of growing cities (Coontz, 1992).

New values regarding families also developed in the 1950s. The belief that all the satisfaction and amusement one needed could be found within the nuclear family had no precedent in history. According to one popular magazine of the time, the defining characteristic of the ideal family was "togetherness," a "new and warmer way of life" in which men and women sought fulfillment not alone, isolated from one another, but as a family sharing a common experience (Mintz & Kellogg, 1988). U.S. residents consistently reported in surveys that home and family were the primary source of their happiness and esteem. Fewer than one in ten believed an unmarried person could ever be truly happy. Indeed, people who didn't marry were thought to suffer from "emotional immaturity and infantile fixations," "unwillingness to assume responsibility," the selfish "pursuit of career ambitions," and "deviant physical characteristics" (Ehrenreich, 1983).

It certainly appears as if families of this era were strong, stable, and culturally valued. Unfortunately,

the reality of family life was far more painful and complex than television reruns and nostalgic memories of the baby boom era would suggest. Twenty-five percent of U.S. residents were officially poor, and in the absence of food stamps, housing programs, and other forms of government aid, this poverty could literally be deadly. Even at the end of the decade, a third of U.S. children were poor, a figure higher than today's. High school graduation rates were also lower in the 1950s than they are today. Minority families were almost entirely excluded from the gains enjoyed by white middle-class families. Although the vast majority of white middle-class mothers were housewives, close to half of all black women with small children had to work outside the home to support their families (Coontz, 1992).

Other mythical ideas about the nuclear families of the 1950s don't hold up under close scrutiny. By 1960, for instance, less than half of U.S. families consisted of traditional single-earner married couples, and nearly one-fourth were dual-earner couples (Masnick & Bane, 1980). Unmarried people were hardly sexually abstinent in the 1950s, either. Between 1940 and 1958, the nonmarital birth rate tripled (Coontz, 1997).

Even among those families that approximated the middle-class ideal, life was not always so joyous. Beneath the idyllic image of family was an undercurrent of anxiety. Concerns about children's health, safety, and happiness pervaded child care manuals of the 1950s. These fears were very real. Before the Salk vaccine was introduced in 1955, polio crippled tens of thousands of children each year. Because of the risk that a minor ailment could grow into a more serious disease, parents were told to watch out for the tiniest symptoms, such as a sore throat, headache, stomach cramps, fever, neck stiffness, and so on (Mintz & Kellogg, 1988).

Also lurking in the shadows were considerable violence, terror, and misery. Although people in white, middle-class suburbs could effectively ignore conflict and turmoil, elsewhere there was tremendous hostility toward people who were defined as somehow different: Jews, African Americans, Puerto Ricans, the poor, homosexuals, and so on. Blacks in the South faced legally sanctioned segregation and pervasive brutality. Those in the North were systematically excluded from the benefits of economic expansion that their labor helped to create. Harassment and violence awaited blacks who tried to participate in the U.S. family dream. When a black man attempted to move his family into Cicero, Illinois, in 1951, a mob of 4,000 whites spent four days tearing his apartment apart while police stood by and joked with them (Coontz, 1992).

Alcoholism, battering, and incest were rampant among all classes during the 1950s, but more often than not were swept under the rug. Researchers in Colorado found 302 battered-child cases in a single year, although virtually none of them was publicized (cited in Mintz & Kellogg, 1988). When girls or women reported being victimized by incest or sexual abuse, they were frequently told they were "fantasizing" their unconscious desires.

Less dramatic, but perhaps more widespread, was a high level of marital unhappiness. Despite the images of family warmth and togetherness, a significant number of people were dissatisfied with their family life. One researcher at the time found that less than a third of the couples she interviewed were happily married (Komarovsky, 1962).

. . . .

Despite the images of family warmth and togetherness, a significant number of people were dissatisfied with their family life.

. . . .

Women who wanted to work—or had to work—outside the home were attacked in books and newspapers as seriously ill people or as symbolic castrators of men. Those who didn't want to have children were considered perverted. *Esquire* magazine called working wives a "menace"; *Life* magazine called female employment a "disease" (cited in Coontz, 1992).

The frustration many women felt from being forced into tightly defined domestic roles led to a soaring increase in the incidence of mental illness and the use of tranquilizers and alcohol (Warren,

1987). Ironically, at the same time women were being labeled as "unnatural" if they didn't seek fulfillment in motherhood and housework, psychologists and psychiatrists were writing that most psychological problems people had could be traced to domineering mothers who spent too much time doting over them as children.

Men were also pressured into accepting family roles. They sometimes lost jobs or promotions because they weren't married. Bachelors were considered "immature," "infantile," or deviant. Those who were married and did have children often resented the long, sometimes mindless hours they had to spend at work to support their families.

These stirrings planted the seeds of discontent that drove much of the tumult that characterized the following decade, the 1960s. Many U.S. residents had buried themselves in the private concerns of family, home, and career. Now there were signs of restlessness and change (Skolnick, 1991).

The Sixties and Beyond. People who came of age in the 1940s and 1950s played out a pretty clear life script that escorted them into adulthood rather quickly: They married, had children, and settled into careers, all in their early 20s. But by the 1960s it was becoming increasingly apparent that this life pattern was a poor fit with social reality. The rising educational demands of modern society were keeping young people in school longer and prolonging adolescence (Skolnick, 1991). People were being forced to reexamine the previously taken-for-granted foundation of family: sexual norms, gender roles, and marital patterns.

Consequently, since 1960 U.S. families have undergone changes as dramatic and far-reaching as those that took place at the turn of the century. In the 1960s more people began postponing marriage or choosing not to marry at all. Birth rates plummeted, as they had during the Depression. The number of divorces in 1966 rose three times higher than the number in 1950 (Mintz & Kellogg, 1988). This trend sharply increased the number of female-headed households. New sexual norms let people improvise and experiment with new forms of family, such as cohabitation.

To observers in the 1960s and 1970s, the institution of family seemed under fierce attack. But, in many ways, the 1960s merely resumed cultural trends that had been put aside since the 1920s. Issues such as sexual codes, women's rights, household division of labor, child care, sexual satisfaction in marriage, and so on were reemerging.

In part because women were increasingly dissatisfied with and actively protesting against limited roles as housewives and mothers, new family issues began to appear in the 1960s and 1970s that have continued through the 1980s and 1990s and into the 2000s: demand for equal responsibilities for both spouses in work, household, and child care; liberalization of divorce laws; paternal rights and joint custody arrangements after divorce; premarital contracts spelling out marital and economic rights and obligations; cohabitation and singlehood as viable living arrangements; the right of unmarried women to bear and retain custody of their children and the right of married couples not to have children at all; legitimacy of homosexual relationships; and so on.

Although many of these specific changes are unique to the past few decades, family life has experienced serious and sometimes fearsome change throughout U.S. history. From the family transformation perspective, when social commentators lament the decline of the traditional family, they are invariably referring to a romanticized and idealized image. Calls for a return to the good old days are, in fact, calls to return to something that has never truly existed.

Rebutting the Notion of Family Decline

The current statistics on family problems are compelling signs that all may not be well. But is it possible that a high divorce rate, falling marriage rate, low birth rate, and so on are not as harmful as the family decline perspective leads us to believe? Let's take another look at the evidence—this time from the family transformation perspective.

Marriage and Divorce. Although family expectations have shifted somewhat over the past three decades, overall people's feelings about intimacy and family seem to be quite stable. Most people who live in the United States still want the love, affection, companionship, and emotional security that go with long-term relationships. The number of teenagers who think a good marriage and family life are important has increased since the mid-1970s ("The institution of marriage," 1999). And most U.S. residents who marry are still committed to the idea of having healthy and happy children (Barich & Bielby, 1996). Such feelings suggest that family expectations are embedded in the culture.

For instance, even though cohabitation has become more popular in recent years, it does not seem to threaten marriage. Most cohabiting relationships either end or evolve into legal marriage within a few years (Brien, Lillard, & Waite, 1999). And among never-married women who have cohabited, the vast majority have had only one cohabiting partner (U.S. Bureau of the Census, 2000b). Hence the most notable effect of cohabitation is that it delays marriage for people who live together first. Also, the older people are prior to marriage, the less likely they are to divorce, so cohabitation, for some, may actually have a stabilizing effect on marriage.

What about divorce? Divorce undeniably creates serious problems for families and for society. But some social scientists argue that the negative impact of divorce has been exaggerated. Throughout history, significant numbers of people have been involved in intact but miserable marriages. Just because people weren't divorcing in large numbers—for religious or social or financial reasons—didn't mean their marriages were solid and satisfying. Indeed, many of those intact families of the past were filled with emotional and physical abuse or irresponsible behavior (Coontz, 1992). Moreover, separation and desertion were common alternatives to legal divorce.

Despite the high rate of divorce—and growing rates of cohabitation and voluntary singlehood—marriage still remains the living arrangement of choice for the overwhelming majority of U.S. adults. In 1990, for example, 95.5 percent of women and 94 percent of men aged 45 to 54 had been married at some point in their lives (U.S. Bureau of the Census, 2000b). Over the past several decades a consistent 96 percent of the U.S. population has expressed a personal desire for marriage. Even individuals whose own parents had divorced show a rather strong commitment to marriage (Landis-Kleine, Foley, Nall, Padgett, & Walters-Palmer, 1995).

Divorce itself doesn't seem to diminish people's desire to marry again, either. Nearly half of all marriages today involve at least one partner who was previously married (U.S. Bureau of the Census, 2000b). Overall, about 70 percent of divorced individuals in this country are likely to remarry, and many others will enter cohabiting relationships (Cherlin & Furstenberg, 1994). Many remarried couples feel that their second marriages are happier and more satisfying than their first (Kain, 1990). The high rate of remarriage indicates that people who are unhappy with their spouses do not necessarily become disillusioned with the institution of marriage. People still value marriage and will seek long-term, fulfilling relationships with others in the aftermath of divorce.

. . . .

The high rate of remarriage indicates that people who are unhappy with their spouses do not necessarily become disillusioned with the institution of marriage.

. . . .

Another concern raised by divorce is the effect it has on children. The problems that children with divorced parents experience are typically attributed to factors such as the absence of a father, increased strain on the custodial parent to keep the household running, or the emotional stress and anger associated with the separation. But some researchers have found that children's academic or psychological well-being doesn't suffer that much when they have little contact with their noncustodial fathers (Furstenberg et al.,

1987). Indeed, many of the factors that create the most serious problems for children can also be found in two-parent, "intact" families: low income, poor living conditions, and lack of parental supervision (Cherlin, 1992). Most problems experienced by children living in single-parent households can be traced to financial insecurity (Gerson, 2000).

Furthermore, some research suggests that children's behavioral problems—particularly those of younger children—stem not from the divorce itself but from exposure to conflict between parents, both before and after the divorce (Stewart, Copeland, Chester, Malley, & Barenbaum, 1997). If you look at kids whose parents are unhappily married or display a great deal of conflict, differences in frequency of problems between children of divorce and children in intact families virtually disappear (Furstenberg & Cherlin, 1991). In fact, children who grow up in intact families where there is frequent parental conflict may actually have *more* problems. In short, the simple fact of being exposed to a breakup may not be as important in a child's development as the way parents relate to each other and to the child. It seems that a stable, conflict-free family with at least one responsible, caring, nurturing adult is a child's best path to becoming a well-rounded adult (Furstenberg & Cherlin, 1991).

From the family transformation perspective, single-parent families—whether the result of divorce or nonmarital birth—may even have some benefits. Children in these settings tend to have more autonomy, make more decisions, and have more control over their lives than children in two-parent families. In addition, children in single-parent families tend to be less stereotypically masculine or feminine than children in two-parent households (Amato, 1987). Boys learn to cook and do laundry; girls learn to do household repairs.

In sum, even though single-parent families have been vilified in the media and by politicians, the problems children experience in them cannot all be attributed to "poor" child-rearing values, lack of rules, or low expectations for children. Instead, the disadvantages of single-parent families tend to stem from sustained economic hardship—a factor that can just as easily impede children's development in two-parent households (Acock & Demo, 1994).

Family Roles. Some feminist sociologists (for example, Stacey, 1994) have argued for years that the traditional breadwinner/homemaker marriage makes women economically dependent, reduces their influence in the family, and makes their survival in the case of divorce more difficult. Thus, family transformation theorists would argue that the dual-earner family is an important development in making marriages more equitable. Furthermore, they would point out, the family decline argument that parents' (particularly mothers') decision to enter the paid labor force is motivated by the selfish pursuit of career ambitions ignores the economic realities facing many families, which require both parents to work to support the household.

Yet an important question remains: Is mothers' employment outside the home in fact detrimental to the well-being of children? Although working women spend less time with their children than nonemployed women, research suggests that working women may be more involved in their children's lives than critics would have us believe. Only about 12 to 14 percent of children between the ages of 5 and 12 spend some time home alone after school, and the average amount of time they spend without adult supervision is only about an hour a day (Berger, 2000).

. . . .

Is mothers' employment outside the home in fact detrimental to the well-being of children?

. . . .

Moreover, although stress on the job can sometimes spill over into family relations, maternal employment itself has few adverse effects (Acock & Demo, 1994; Bianchi & Spain, 1986; Gottfried, 1991; Rodman, Pratto, & Nelson, 1985). In fact, maternal employment may even have positive consequences. For instance, daughters of employed mothers show greater independence and more egalitarian attitudes toward the roles of men and women than daughters of nonemployed women do (Spitze, 1988). One study found that children who have mothers with high-paying, complex jobs have greater verbal and cognitive abilities than other children (Parcel & Menaghan, 1990).

Some social scientists also argue that *more* time together is not always *better* time together. A recent nationwide study of children found that although children feel time with their parents is important, the vast majority don't want to spend more time with their parents (Galinsky, 1999). In some cases, higher levels of interaction between nonemployed mothers and their children become stressful. Indeed, rates of child abuse are higher among housewives who spend all day with preschool children than among mothers employed full time, who see their children less frequently (Gelles, 1987).

The belief that employed mothers create problems for their children is thus not so much a conclusion based on a body of research as a function of broader cultural attitudes. Children's well-being doesn't depend solely on whether a mother works outside the home or not but rather on her satisfaction with work and family, the availability of quality child care, and the active participation of fathers (Gerson, 2000).

According to several prominent sociologists who fall into the family transformation camp, our society could easily solve the "problems" created by working mothers if it had the will to provide more government-supported child care services, workplace day care, after-school programs, longer school days, and flexible work schedules for parents (Gerson, 1985; Skolnick, 1991). To that end, in 1998 President Clinton proposed a $21 billion package of federal grants and tax breaks to address the shortage of qualified and affordable child care. Among other things, the money was to be used to increase the number of licensed child care centers, boost wages of child care workers, and improve safety and training (Schmitt, 1998).

Family Size and Children's Well-Being. The contention that U.S. families are dangerously small and that this size can adversely affect the institution of family may also be overstated, according to the family transformation perspective. And with all the talk we hear these days about the perils of overpopulation, it would seem that smaller families would be beneficial to society. A smaller population would put less pressure on limited resources.

· ·

Some scholars have argued that when children began to be seen for their emotional value and not so much for their economic contributions, families began to do more emotionally for each child.

· ·

It's also important to note that compared to the 1950s, U.S. families today are quite small. But the 1950s was a decade of abnormally large families (Cherlin, 1992). People were having more babies then than at any period in the past 100 years. Aside from this anomalous era, the size of U.S. families has been declining since around 1800. In the latter half of the nineteenth century, urbanization and industrialization combined to reduce the size of nuclear families rather dramatically.

In any case, the sheer number of people in a family cannot be used as a barometer of its quality. Some scholars have argued that when children began to be seen for their emotional value and not so much for their economic contributions, families began to do more emotionally for each child (Zelizer, 1985). With fewer children, parents could invest more time, energy, supervision, and enrichment in each child. In fact, some have suggested that today is a "golden age for America's children" (Recer, 2000b, p. A1). Although current rates of drug use, smoking, and drinking among children continue to concern many, children today are healthier, better nourished, and more likely to survive into adulthood than those in previous generations. In this regard too, then, the family transformation perspective allows people to see the positive aspects of the changes that so distress those taking the family decline perspective.

Examining Cross-Cultural Evidence of Family Change

Many studies have attempted to link specific indicators of family decline (increasing incidence of divorce, single-parent households, stepfamilies, and so on) to negative well-being in children, but few social scientists have attempted to examine the issue by comparing societies. An exception is a study by sociologists Sharon Houseknecht and Jaya Sastry (1996). They ranked four countries (Sweden, United States, Germany, and Italy) on several indicators that might reflect family decline: rising median age at first marriage, increasing percentage of the population never married, lower marital birth rates and higher nonmarital birth rates, increasing divorce rate, increasing percentage of single-parent households, increasing percentage of working mothers, and declining average household size. They found that Sweden, by far, ranked highest in overall "family decline" based on these factors, followed, in order, by the United States, Germany, and Italy. They then compared these countries on various measures that are typically associated with the well-being of children: average reading and writing proficiency, percentage of children in poverty, rate of child abuse deaths, teen suicide rates, juvenile crime rates, and rates of juvenile drug offenses.

The comparisons across countries did not clearly support either the family decline or family transformation perspective. On the one hand, the data from Italy supports the family decline perspective. This country showed the lowest levels of family decline and the most positive levels of child well-being on four indicators (lowest child abuse death rate, teen suicide rate, juvenile crime rate, and drug offense rate). And children in the United States—second only to Sweden in the severity of family decline—were the least well off of the four countries on four of the six indicators of well-being (highest percentage of children in poverty, and highest rates of child abuse death, teen suicide, and juvenile drug offenses).

However, Sweden represents an interesting exception that lends support to the family transformation perspective. One sociologist has described Sweden as the world leader in family decline (Popenoe, 1988). But Swedes take pride in the fact that they are a nation of individuals, and their family policies reflect that attitude. Married couples receive no tax benefits and cannot file joint income tax returns. There is no tax deduction for children. Swedes aren't particularly religious, and without financial incentives, it's not surprising that many couples don't bother to marry. About half the babies in Sweden are born to unwed mothers, though very few are born to teenagers. Half of Swedish marriages end in divorce, and unmarried parents separate three times as often as married ones. Approximately one in five Swedish families is a single-parent family ("Home sweet home," 1995).

Despite all these "problems," the Swedish birth rate has increased steadily since 1970 ("Home sweet home," 1995), and children rarely suffer. Sweden has several generous state-supported policies that assist children—such as parental leave, subsidized day care, and leave for taking care of sick children. Fewer than 7 percent of Swedish children live in families with less than half the average income. Perhaps as a result, Swedish children showed the highest educational performance of the four groups in the study, the lowest percentage in poverty, and nearly the lowest child abuse death rate.

These findings may alarm some, but they are also cause for hope. It's hard to imagine a society without some form of family. As long as society finds a way to support the types of long-term, committed, interdependent relationships that people actually create, there will always be family. It may not look much like a family looked 30 years ago, and it may have vocal detractors with very real and legitimate concerns, but it will still be a family to those within it.

Something to Think About

You can see there is no clear answer to the question of whether the institution of family is falling apart or undergoing a metamorphosis. What some consider a loss of stability, others see as an expansion of freedom. Both sides of the issue have compelling arguments. And scholars on both sides genuinely care about the state of U.S. families.

Certainly, people shouldn't ignore or trivialize the very real problems that things such as unwed parenthood or divorce can create. On the whole, children usually do better with two parents than one. And many people suffer from the breakdown of their families. But at the same time, people shouldn't condemn single mothers, divorced parents, or voluntarily childless couples as the culprits behind the destruction of society. Some unwed parents shirk their parental responsibilities, but others do a splendid job in raising their children. Some divorces do irrevocable harm, but others create better situations for everyone involved. Some married couples do decide not to have children for selfish reasons, but others are motivated by a real concern for society and find other ways to contribute to its perpetuation. In short, there is no formula that can predict which family forms are most likely to keep society functioning smoothly.

1. Do you think that U.S. families are in decline, or are they simply adjusting to shifting social circumstances? Explain.

2. Why do you think there's such a pervasive tendency in the media to focus only on the problems facing U.S. families?

3. How useful in the search for an accurate image of contemporary U.S. families is information about families of the past? What is the connection, if any, between families of the past and current family forms?

4. Do you believe that voluntary childlessness, cohabitation, working mothers, divorce, and so on are dangerous trends in U.S. society? Explain your position.

5. Imagine that you've been given the responsibility of designing a set of government policies that will help families in the twenty-first century. What would be your top two or three priorities? Why?

For More On . . .	See . . .
Work–family balance	Chapter 7
Effects of divorce on children	"Divorce and Children" in Chapter 11
Shrinking American families	"The Stigma of Voluntary Childlessness" in Chapter 8
The flight from marriage	"Unique Aspects of Marriage" in Chapter 6

How private should family life be?

On the evening of October 8, 1977, a 17-year-old St. Paul, Minnesota, high school track star and straight-*A* student was driving his parents' station wagon when it skidded on some wet leaves and crashed into a tree. The young man was severely injured, went into a coma, and was placed on life-support systems and a feeding tube. For several years after the accident, his parents hoped he would someday regain consciousness. They consulted various specialists and considered taking their son to Japan for special treatment.

Eventually the parents made a decision: They wouldn't let their son live longer in his "vegetative" state than he had in his active life. So they elected to disconnect his life-support equipment in 1994, on his thirty-fourth birthday.

But when word of their plans became public, an advocacy group representing disabled people claimed that the young man's rights weren't being adequately represented and filed a last-minute motion to stop his parents from carrying out their wishes. Believing that the parents weren't acting in the best interests of their son, the group contended that he should have a legally appointed guardian before such a life-and-death decision could be made for him. They proposed that a local registered nurse—a woman who did not know the family but who was morally opposed to removing patients from life-support equipment—be appointed the young man's legal guardian.

The parents fought the group in court for close to a year to retain the right to make decisions concerning their son. A judge eventually ruled in favor of the family, and their son was taken off the machinery ("Family wins right," 1994).

Dennis and Lorie Nixon had twelve children. Dennis is the pastor of the Faith Tabernacle Congregation in Altoona, Pennsylvania. In 1991 their 8-year-old son died of dehydration and malnutrition when an untreated inner ear infection became worse. The parents did not seek medical attention for the boy. They believe that the Bible is opposed to all means of healing apart from God's intervention and do not use any medical or surgical practices whatsoever when they or their children become ill. They pleaded no contest to a charge of involuntary manslaughter and received probation.

In 1996 a second child—a 16-year-old daughter—died of complications resulting from untreated diabetes. She lapsed into a coma after 4 days of severe nausea and dry mouth. Her father attempted to cure her by praying and anointing her head with oil. This time the Nixons were convicted of involuntary manslaughter and child endangerment and sentenced to $2\frac{1}{2}$ to 5 years in a state prison, far longer

Family is both a public and a private institution. How can we balance a family's need for privacy with the public's need to ensure the well-being of those within it?

As children get older, their need for privacy increases. Bedrooms become well-guarded fortresses. If you were this teen's parent, would you worry about the barrier being erected between him or her and the rest of the family? Would you worry about the attitudes and behaviors that your teen might be developing behind closed doors? Families themselves seek privacy and protection from the larger community and from society as a whole. But where do we draw the line? How much privacy is too much?

than the 1-year sentence the district attorney had recommended. The court also ordered social workers to visit the Nixon home every 30 days and instructed County Children and Youth Services to have blood tests performed on the surviving children to see if any of them suffer from diabetes (Mellot, 1997).

Both of these events revolve around the rights of parents to determine the course of their children's lives without any outside intervention. In each case the parents believed they were acting in the best interests of their children; and in each case the timing and appropriateness of outsiders' involvement in the private domain of the family became a source of controversy and debate.

In the first instance, a group with no personal ties to the family tried to prevent parents from taking their child off artificial life support. Seeing the issue more as a right-to-life case than a private family matter, they felt it was their duty to step in on behalf of the young man and protect his rights and interests. To most people, however, this group's attempt was insensitive and wrongheaded. Families, they believe, and not some outside agency, should make such life-and-death decisions. These parents were not acting frivolously. They had agonized over their son's condition for 17 years.

· ·

When is it appropriate for others to intervene in a family's business? Should there be legal limitations on how family members ought to treat one another?

· ·

Similarly, in the second case the privacy rights of a family came into conflict with the physical well-being of their child. These parents, too, would no doubt claim that they would never do anything to harm their child. But, because the family's religious practices and beliefs were not mainstream, most observers felt when the parents placed their children's lives in danger they sacrificed the right to privately practice their religion.

As you can see, the issue of family privacy, the focus of this section, is a knotty one. When is it appropriate for others to intervene in a family's business? Should there be legal limitations on how family members ought to treat one another? Whether we're talking about children's rights to privacy from their parents, the family's rights to privacy from the larger community, or the state's compelling interest to dictate how families should operate, privacy is one of the most crucial and controversial elements of contemporary family life.

The Ideal of Family Privacy

One of the most powerful values regarding family in U.S. society today is that it is, or should be, a private institution. Within its zone of privacy, a family can exercise its liberty and discretion and be protected from unwanted outside interference. The private family is assumed to be the best judge and guardian of its own interests and needs. Privacy is usually linked to *autonomy,* another important concept, which refers to the family's independence from outside control and its right to make its own decisions about its future or about treatment of its members.

There is nothing "natural" about family privacy. It is created when there is widespread agreement in a society that certain aspects of family life are legitimately off limits to the scrutiny of others (Nock, 1998b). In general, people in the United States include in this category such matters as sexuality and other displays of affection, grieving, failure to maintain family roles as in the loss of a job or the end of a marriage, and family conflict (Fox, 1999).

Family privacy is maintained by powerful social norms. For instance, people are advised to "keep their noses out" of other people's family affairs. The violation of this norm—when someone feels compelled to discipline another parent's child, for example—can create profound discomfort in that person and extreme anger in others. Such norms, of course, vary from society to society. In many African cultures, community members are expected to discipline any child who is misbehaving.

To protect crucially important intimate relationships, decision making within families is often protected by laws and customs. For instance, in some right-to-die cases, such as the one described earlier, courts have ruled that the family should have the right to make such ultimate decisions because it is in the best position to interpret the probable wishes and best interests of a patient in a "persistent vegetative state" (Arras, 1991).

At first glance the question of whether or not family life is—or should be—private and autonomous appears obvious and simple. After all, you decide with whom you will form relationships, what those relationships will look like, if and when to have children, how you will treat other members of your family, and so on. Indeed, few would question that these decisions ought to be solely your responsibility.

Many people today feel that what goes on in a family should always be protected from community interference, public scrutiny, and state regulation. Family life, they believe, is best left to families—not the government, courts, or other public agencies (Gubrium & Holstein, 1990). Such privacy is essential to the development of liberty and freedom (Feshbach & Feshbach, 1978; Fraser, 1987).

In 1928 U.S. Supreme Court Justice Louis Brandeis stated that privacy is "the most comprehensive of rights, and the right most valued by civilized" people (quoted in Gleick, 1996, p. 130). Justice Brandeis was talking about *individuals'* rights to privacy. But these sentiments are just as powerful when applied to the rights of families. We resent the thought of other people or our government telling us how to run a household, how to treat our partners, or how to raise our children.

Some sociologists also argue that privacy contributes to family stability. Once marital problems are made public, the marriage may start falling apart at an accelerated rate; the couple may have a better chance of working out their problems if outsiders minded their own business. In addition, family privacy can help its members develop a feeling of being a unified, cohesive group, which is healthy for that family as well as for the larger society (Berardo, 1998).

Unfortunately, the high value this society places on family privacy has made it difficult for people to recognize the problems that privacy can cause. For instance, when couples don't have access to information about what goes on in other relationships, they often look to TV and film couples for role models, which may be far from realistic (Berardo, 1998). More seriously, the private nature of family often hides domestic violence and shields it from intervention. When the violence remains hidden, violent family members feel less pressure to stop, and their victims have a harder time seeking outside help.

The Location of Privacy

Although not every family consists of members who live in the same household, the home provides the symbolic as well as the physical boundaries between private and public, between family and nonfamily. Homes are the places where people most expect to be left alone or to deal with others if and as they choose. Home denotes a place where they can relax, express themselves candidly, show affection, enjoy sexuality, and reinforce family ties (Allen, 1988).

Home Sweet Home. The privacy of the home is protected by a number of legal provisions. The Third Amendment to the U.S. Constitution prohibits the quartering of soldiers in private homes during peacetime, reflecting the notion of home as a place where people are entitled to undisturbed seclusion. The Fourth Amendment guarantees individuals the right to be secure in their houses against unreasonable searches and seizures. The Omnibus Crime Control and Safe Streets Act of 1986 protects the privacy of the home by placing federal limits on wiretapping and surveillance (Allen, 1988).

To be sure, friends, neighbors, distant relatives, strangers, people selling things or soliciting donations, and various others breach the privacy of homes from time to time. But allowing their presence is clearly a courtesy people in the household extend. They are visitors, and they are expected to behave as such. Unlike household members, who can use the phone, check what's in the refrigerator, or turn on the TV whenever they want, visitors must seek and receive permission to do these things. Even people who have known their in-laws for years, sleeping and eating in their home many times, may be somewhat reluctant to shed the visitor role and really make themselves "at home" by entering without knocking or taking food from the refrigerator without asking. Much of the humor of a character such as Kramer on the popular 1990s television show *Seinfeld* derived from his wanton disregard for this norm when he barged into his neighbor's apartment.

In everyday life, the privacy of the home is useful and valuable in that it gives people a place where they can behave in ways that might be discouraged if such behavior were constantly being watched and evaluated by outsiders. As you're well aware, all people do and say things in the privacy of their own homes and in the company of family members that they wouldn't dream of doing or saying in front of strangers or even close friends.

Front Stage and Backstage. To some sociologists—most notably Erving Goffman (1959)—the distinction between private and public behavior is crucial to understanding family life. Goffman argues that social life often requires that people be like actors on a theatrical stage, performing so that others will see them in a particular way. Think of these people who observe your behavior as the "audience." The "roles" you play are the images of yourself you are trying to project. And the "dialogue" consists of your communications with others. The overarching goal is to enact a performance that is believable to a particular audience and that allows you to achieve the goals you desire.

Different locations require different sorts of performances. An important consideration is the distinction between public, front stage interaction and private, backstage interaction. In the theater, *front stage* is where performances take place. These performances are presented for the eyes and ears of the audience and are meant to convey a believable image. The most skilled actors are the ones who portray characters so credibly that you forget you're watching actors playing roles. When applied to everyday social interaction, "front stage" is where people carry out interaction performances and maintain appropriate appearances in front of others. For restaurant workers, for instance, front stage would be the dining room where the customers (the audience) are present. Here the servers (the actors) are expected to present themselves as upbeat, happy, competent, and courteous.

. . . .

To some sociologists, the distinction between private and public behavior is crucial to understanding family life.

. . . .

In contrast, theatrical *backstage* refers to the wings and to the dressing rooms where people remove makeup, rehearse lines, rehash performances, and slip "out of character." In social life, "backstage" is synonymous with privacy. It's where people can prepare for upcoming front stage encounters or comment on those just completed. It's also where people can knowingly and sometimes cynically violate their front stage performances. Going back to the restaurant example, backstage would be the kitchen area where the once-friendly, courteous servers now shout, shove dishes, and even complain about or make fun of the customers.

The distinction between front stage and backstage is crucial to family life. Much of the time people spend with their family members is spent in front of others—at supermarkets, Little League games, front porches, school plays, neighborhood parties, and so on—where audiences expect families to present a cohesive and consistent image of themselves. If you've ever witnessed a married couple fighting in a shopping mall or a parent screaming at a child in a store, you know how disturbing such scenes can be. They violate the unspoken norm that families not "air their dirty laundry" in public. Hence, family members—especially spouses—often feel compelled to hide conflict and criticism of each other when they are on front stage, even if they're in the middle of an ongoing, bitter feud.

Fortunately for society, however, most families do have access to a backstage area in their private households. We all need a place to relax, where we need not be concerned with how our looks, actions, or statements are received by others. Karen Fowler, one of the individuals who spent nearly 6 weeks living under constant camera surveillance for the television show *Big Brother*, claimed that the stress of having no privacy and constantly being watched nearly caused her to have a nervous breakdown ("Indiana woman says 'Big Brother' made her unwelcome at home," 2000).

The problems caused by violating backstage privacy needn't be as blatant as having surveillance cameras watching your every move. If you've ever had guests stay at your house for a long time, you know how disruptive they can be to family life. It's not just that they represent an extra mouth to feed or an extra set of interests and desires that must be taken into account when decisions are made. It's that their presence robs the family of the ability to "go backstage" in its own home.

But the importance of backstage and, more generally, family privacy goes beyond individuals' ability to act comfortably without worrying about the images they present to others. Underlying the distinction between front stage and backstage family behavior is the belief that the most authentic family experiences occur in the privacy of the home (Gubrium & Holstein, 1987). This is where a family's *true* feelings and characteristics emerge. It is widely presumed that the *real* family can only be seen in its private moments, "behind closed doors."

The assumption here is that the public, front stage family is often motivated to conceal its flaws and shortcomings. For example, parents who are harsh and abusive to their children in private may work hard to appear loving and gentle in public. Likewise, the incompatible married couple may maintain a façade of cordiality when with friends. Thus, the backstage aspect of the household is not only intrinsic to family life but is also, at times, camouflaged, hidden, or protected (Gubrium & Holstein, 1990).

This notion has implications for a real understanding of families. We know what our own families are really like because we've seen them backstage. However, despite our curiosity about other people's family relationships, we usually don't have access to their backstage, so we can only know them in terms of their public presentations and discourse. The gap between public images and private realities may be quite wide (Skolnick, 1979). If, in fact, the "true" nature of family interaction remains hidden from public view, others' understanding of families may be inaccurate or incomplete. It's ironic that privacy, so essential to family life, is also a cultural value that can obscure our understanding of it.

The History of Privacy

Privacy and autonomy, in recent years, have come to symbolize many of the political and cultural struggles over "family values." In U.S. society, people tend to take for granted that the family is and always was a private, autonomous institution. But according to many family historians, only since the latter part of the nineteenth century and early twentieth century have we begun to perceive family privacy as a basic, inalienable right and made it a rallying cry in political disputes and debates (Laslett, 1973).

Community and the Open Door. Despite beliefs about the rugged, independent families of U.S. history, families have never been completely self-sufficient and autonomous. In the small, preindustrial societies of the distant past, family privacy was a foreign concept. Every person had to perform essential tasks to ensure community survival. One person's actions had significance for everyone. Such societies depended on close monitoring and supervision to enforce conformity (Nock, 1998b). Farm households may have been far apart, but people still had a lot of contact with their neighbors. And more affluent people living in towns and villages frequently interacted with one another as they conducted their business.

Furthermore, many people considered privacy a threat to families and ultimately to society. In colonial North America, for instance, church attendance was practically mandatory, and ministers believed it was their duty to watch the behaviors of their congregants both in and out of church (Nock, 1998b). As one social historian put it, at this time "there was no such thing as private life, no refuge from the public gaze and its ceaseless criticism" (quoted in Gleick, 1996, p. 130). Indeed, it was not uncommon for city officials, church elders, and prying neighbors to regularly enter people's homes and tell them with whom to associate, what to wear, and what to teach their children. Families that didn't comply were sometimes punished, or worse, forcibly separated.

In addition, early industrial households typically contained a variety of residents. In working-class homes, the boarding and lodging of strangers and the "doubling up" of families under one roof were common means of helping with expenses (Gubrium & Holstein, 1990; Hareven, 1992). Upper-class families could afford to bring servants, distant kin (extended family), and sometimes even employees into the household. Obviously the presence of these other people greatly reduced the degree of privacy that could exist in a home. By just being around, they limited what spouses or parents and children could do without detection. In fact, in eighteenth-century adultery trials the key witnesses were typically servants or other boarders whose curiosity, close proximity, and willingness to peep through keyholes made sexual privacy nearly impossible (Stone, 1979).

Although people today may blanch at the thought of such a lack of privacy in everyday family life, it did have a positive effect: It held social groups together and stabilized society. There was a wholeness and certainty to life that people today no longer have. In the past, people lived without privacy, to be sure, but they also lived without the sort of social isolation and alienation that characterize contemporary society: "We seek more and more privacy, and feel more and more alienated and lonely when we get it. What accidental contacts we do have, furthermore, seem more intrusive, not only because they are unsought but because they are unconnected with any familiar pattern of interdependence" (quoted in Berardo, 1998, p. 12).

By the mid-nineteenth century, things began to change. New forms of technology and the promise of new financial opportunities and a good living drew people (particularly men) away from the farms and into city factories. For the first time in U.S. history, the family economy was based primarily outside the household. The increasing population density brought about by urbanization and industrialization increased the contact people had with strangers. Fur-

thermore, immigrants at the turn of the century, for whom family privacy was likely an alien concept, settled in the close quarters of growing urban areas.

Amid the clamor of rapidly growing cities, middle-class, urban families began to look to their homes for solace and privacy (Laslett, 1973). An expanding economy eventually gave them the means to move into residences all their own. Domesticity, intimacy, and privacy became desirable characteristics of middle-class family life (Hareven, 1992). Consequently people's family activities became visible to fewer and fewer outsiders (Vanek, 1980). By the end of the nineteenth century, middle-class families were less often taking in boarders and lodgers or joining forces with relatives and more often seeking their own private residence (Hareven, 1992). Married couples were having fewer children. Single-family detached houses became more popular, eventually becoming the ideal setting for U.S. domestic life.

Technology and Family Privacy. The gradual shift toward family self-sufficiency that continues today was helped along by technological developments (Skolnick, 1987). In small, preindustrial towns and villages, the layout of houses made privacy difficult. Most homes built in the seventeenth century consisted of a single room. Eating, sleeping, recreating, and procreating all took place in the same area, usually in the company of others. In many cases family members slept in the same bed (Shorter, 1975). Even the great houses of the upper classes were constructed of interlocking suites of rooms without corridors, so that the only way of moving about was by passing through other people's rooms (Stone, 1979). Given such architectural constraints, privacy as we know it today was an idea most people wouldn't have comprehended (Gelles & Straus, 1988).

This architecture began to change as society became more industrial and urban. Even in middle-class homes, the trend toward inside doors and a central hallway, with rooms opening to it, permitted a degree of family privacy not previously available (Laslett, 1973). Today we take for granted a home consisting of separate rooms that accommodate separate functions, freeing family members from even one another's watchful gaze. Indeed, many luxurious homes being built today include a secluded "couple's suite" and a children's area in a totally separate floor or "wing" of the house.

Innovations in the amenities available within the home (refrigerators, telephones, indoor plumbing, radios, and, more recently, central heating, air conditioning, backyard swimming pools, televisions, and computers) have all contributed to increasing family privacy, by bringing family activities from more visible, more public locations into the home. Refrigerators, for instance, make it unnecessary to visit the market every day. Air conditioning allows people to spend hot, stuffy summer evenings inside instead of on the front porch or at the local ice cream parlor. Today, with the Internet, fax machines, and home shopping cable networks, a family can practically survive without *ever* leaving the privacy of its home.

Ironically, however, technology also poses one of the greatest challenges to family privacy in contemporary society. When you surf the Internet, for instance, you leave a record of the Web sites you've visited that is accessible to businesses and marketers. In addition, the media increasingly expose private family matters to public scrutiny. Sometimes the exposure is voluntary, as when family members appear on "shock TV" talk shows to "tattle and battle" with family members; sometimes it is involuntary, as when a family tragedy occurs and TV provides up-close footage of the grieving relatives (Fox, 1999). Either way, the media increasingly offer people opportunities to scrutinize other families' private behaviors.

· ·

Ironically, however, technology also poses one of the greatest challenges to family privacy in contemporary society.

· ·

As in earlier times, when lack of family privacy served to stabilize families and societies, such public scrutiny can serve some useful social functions (Fox, 1999). For one thing, it can teach about the boundaries of what is acceptable and what is not. In addition, publicly exposing the moral indiscretions or illegal activities of community members not only

embarrasses the transgressors but can also control their future behavior and that of others, who are reminded of what can happen when private matters are aired in public. Finally, public scrutiny can be helpful. Sometimes the airing of personal troubles and woes is met not with censure and ridicule but with compassion and support (Fox, 1999).

Social Institutions and the Paradox of Family Privacy

As you can see, the shift from public to private has not been complete. Although the constant, personal surveillance that characterized small, tight-knit communities of the past has largely disappeared, people still face a form of family surveillance. It is simply more abstract than before and likely to be carried out by large organizations such as schools, employers, courts, hospitals, credit agencies, and so on. To some extent, people still trade privacy for a sense of security and stability.

Although it may sometimes seem as if institutional interference in family life were on the rise, keep in mind that U.S. families have always depended on the government and other social institutions for their survival. Colonial families, for instance, relied on a large network of neighbors, churches, courts, and government officials. Later, prairie farmers and other pioneer families were able to exist because of massive federal land grants, government-funded military expeditions that made land available to them (by forcing Native Americans off their ancestral land and confiscating half of Mexico), and government-sponsored investment into new territories (Coontz, 1992).

Working-class and minority families have always found it difficult to survive without assistance beyond family. Immigrants founded lodges to provide material aid and foster cooperation. Laborers formed funeral aid societies and associations that provided death or sick benefits; they held balls and picnics to raise money for injured workers, widows, or orphans and took collections at the mills or plant gates nearly every payday (Coontz, 1992, p. 71).

Even in the 1950s, which some consider the golden age of the self-sufficient nuclear family, suburban families owed much of their good fortune to government-subsidized programs such as the GI Bill, which permitted a whole generation of men to expand their education, improve their job prospects, and own their own homes.

More recently, the conservative George W. Bush administration—despite the traditional Republican opposition to government intrusion into people's private lives—devised policy initiatives to strengthen U.S. families, such as tax credits to promote two-parent homes, federally funded programs to promote "responsible fatherhood," marriage counseling to prevent divorce, and character education for children (Milbank, 2001). Such reliance on outside social institutions makes complete family privacy and autonomy impossible.

In addition, family life always exists within the structure of statutory regulations. Parents must vaccinate their children and provide proper medical attention; they have to send their children to school and provide adequate shelter and nutrition (Bollenbacher & Burtt, 1997). There are also laws—such as murder laws—that all people must abide by, even in the privacy of their families. The state cannot be neutral or remain uninvolved in this regard, nor would anyone want it to do so (Olsen, 1993). And even the staunchest supporters of a family's right to privacy insist that the state needs to reinforce parents' authority over their children from time to time. People may justify state officials returning runaway children to their parents or courts ordering incorrigible children to obey their parents as proper efforts to keep families together. But keep in mind that even in these cases the state is venturing deep into the private matters of families.

Most people would also agree that the state has the right to intervene in family life to protect family members when others threaten to interfere. Imagine your reaction if state agencies did nothing to prevent doctors from performing nonemergency surgery on a child without the parents' permission or to prevent neighbors from trying to take a child on their vacation against the parents' wishes. Imagine if the state refused to get involved in nasty child custody battles between divorced parents. Such state intervention is bound to affect other decisions people make, such as how families ought to be formed, how power in

families ought to be distributed, and how roles ought to be assigned (Olsen, 1993).

The state also routinely nullifies privacy rights in situations where behavior is deemed "immoral." In 1986 the U.S. Supreme Court ruled constitutional a Georgia law forbidding married couples, unmarried heterosexual couples, and homosexual couples from participating in oral or anal sex. Such a law may be difficult to enforce, but its existence represents a "moral" symbol of what some people in this society will and won't tolerate within other people's private lives.

• •

Most people would also agree that the state has the right to intervene in family life to protect family members when others threaten to interfere.

• •

The legal system, however, is not the main source of outside intervention in private families in today's society. Organizations such as the Internal Revenue Service, the Social Security Administration, credit card and credit rating companies, and local utility companies routinely invade the privacy of families through their access to intimate information. Commercial interests also impinge on family privacy. For example, data sellers market to insurance companies lists of families who have filed medical malpractice suits or workers' compensation claims. Some of these organizations sell lists of renters who have sued landlords.

The workplace can also disturb the privacy of families. Employment actions and policies—such as work schedules, health benefits, forced overtime, transfers, pay cuts, and layoffs—regulate family life far more intimately than the state does.

School officials, too, are beginning to realize that in order to provide an environment conducive to learning, they sometimes must delve into the private lives of their students. For instance, many schools across the country have codes of conduct that control students' off-campus behavior, such as smoking or using drugs in their homes (Lewin, 1998d).

In an even more direct sense, some individuals seem to care very much about what goes on in others' private lives. If you've ever been the sole single person in a group of couples, you've no doubt felt the subtle, perhaps blatant, pressures people exert on you to "settle down and find someone." Few young married couples are able to escape probing questions from parents and others about if and when they're going to have children. Many divorcing couples find they must cope with friends and family who demand explanations for the breakup.

Consider also a common family event everyone is familiar with: the wedding ceremony. If you've ever been married or been to a wedding, you know these ceremonies are not private affairs designed solely for the bride and groom; they also exist for the benefit of relatives, friends, and the community. Weddings are traditionally considered the formal beginning of a family—the public, legal, and sometimes religious recognition of a couple's new status. Two people traditionally can't declare on their own that they're married, without some sort of public ratification.

So, although people typically think of family as the most private and most intimate of social institutions, complete family privacy is an illusion. Private family decisions are always made within larger societal and cultural boundaries (Burtt, 1994). And although many people may espouse family privacy, families never really belong exclusively to their members. People may resent intrusions into family life, but no family can exist in a vacuum, completely free of external demands and expectations.

Parents and Children

The paradox of family privacy is striking when it comes to the relationship between parents and their children. As noted earlier, U.S. society has a strong belief in parents' rights to raise their children as they see fit. However, people also consider the institution of family essential to society because of its role in teaching habits, patterns, lessons, and values that will eventually make children good citizens. At some point, then, we adults also expect children to inherit certain privacy rights themselves. The basic conflict between the privacy rights of parents and children is complicated further by society's ambivalence toward unfettered individuality, especially when it challenges important social values.

Parental Rights

To exist at all, society needs loyalty, stability, and achievement from its members—all qualities that families are able to foster (Yoest, 1997). Given the role families play in the very survival of society, it's not surprising that intervening in family life would be considered appropriate, even necessary, under certain conditions. In one sense, then, parents are never allowed to do whatever they want with the children under their care. In earlier times, community elders ensured that children would be raised "properly." Today the less personal, more bureaucratic institution of the state sets standards and rules about parental choices in all areas of child rearing (Burtt, 1994).

But there is a growing sentiment that too much state involvement compromises parental authority and family stability. In 1995 a bill was introduced in Congress that would have forbidden state and local governments to interfere with the right of parents to direct the upbringing and education of their children ("The new 'parental rights' crusade," 1996). This bill would have allowed parents to sue teachers, librarians, school counselors, police officers, and social workers for interfering with parents' ability to control the education, health, discipline, and religious teaching of their children. The bill did not receive full committee approval and never came to the floor of Congress for a vote. Nevertheless, it and similar bills introduced in various states since then signal a growing concern among some legislators that parents' ability to raise their children as they see fit is being eroded.

Increasingly, as definitions of family shift and expand, courts are being asked to balance parents' rights to privacy and autonomy against the claims of others seeking ongoing connections with their children. For instance, should a man who helped raise his lover's son for all the years he lived with her have the right to keep seeing the child even after the mother's new husband adopts him? In one case, grandparents won the right to continue seeing their granddaughters after their son committed suicide. However, the girls' mother, now married to a man who adopted the girls, opposed court-ordered visitation as a violation of her parental autonomy (Lewin, 1999a). She appealed the decision and in 2000 the U.S. Supreme Court ruled that the law, in fact, violated parents' rights to privacy. In doing so, it reinforced the legal notion that parents alone should be the ones to choose whether to expose their children to certain people.

· ·

In one sense, then, parents are never allowed to do whatever they want with the children under their care.

· ·

Yet when parental behavior clearly violates popular notions of appropriate child rearing, the winds of public opinion can shift toward allowing greater intervention and sanctioning. Parents have been tried and convicted of crimes for not exercising appropriate control over their children. In other cases, parents have lost custody of their children for engaging in activities considered inappropriate by the general public. In 2000, a 32-year-old mother in Champaign, Illinois, lost custody of her 5-year-old son after a babysitter called a local child abuse hotline and reported that the mother was still breastfeeding the boy. A County Circuit Judge in the case ruled that breastfeeding a child this old created a situation with "enormous potential for emotional harm" (quoted in Lewin, 2001a).

Sometimes state involvement in the private lives of families is influenced by broader political concerns. Consider, for example, the highly publicized case of the 6-year-old Cuban boy, Elián Gonzalez. In November 1999, Elián and his mother were attempting to flee Cuba for the United States. The boat they

were on capsized, drowning the mother. Elián survived and was taken in by relatives living in Florida. Although his father in Cuba wanted him returned, Elián's relatives in the United States felt he would be better off living in the democratic United States than in Communist Cuba and kept him here despite court orders to relinquish him. To these relatives, the desire to prevent Elián from being raised under communism outweighed the parental rights of his father. In April 2000, U.S. officials removed Elián at gunpoint from his uncle's home in Miami and returned him to his father, who had come to the United States to get him. Although the images of armed officials pointing weapons at a frightened boy were upsetting, most U.S. residents thought the state did the right thing by stepping in to reunite the boy with his father.

Children's Rights

The controversy over privacy in parent–child relationships is also apparent when we look at the extent to which children have rights to privacy *from* their parents. Whether a child is granted privacy in any sense—privacy of quarters, of possessions, of thoughts and behaviors, of relationships with others—or whether these things are thought to be open to parents' inspection depends on how parents define themselves and their children (Hess & Handel, 1985). As children mature, they begin to demand increasing privacy in their personal lives, something most child development experts agree is important if children are to develop individual autonomy and a sense of personal dignity (cited in McKinney, 1998). As you well know, many adolescents consider their bedrooms their impenetrable sanctuaries (Fiene, 1995). It's not uncommon for a teenager today to post a "Keep Out" sign on his or her door or otherwise make it clear to the rest of the family that his or her domain is off limits.

Yet many parents express little interest in protecting their children's privacy needs. In fact, one study found that parents are likely to be more concerned about their own privacy than that of their children (McKinney, 1998). Most parents in this study approved of going through children's belongings to obtain more information about them if they feel their children aren't disclosing enough. Furthermore, parents are more willing to honor their children's need for spatial privacy (for example, to have their own bedrooms) than for body privacy or emotional privacy. For instance, parents frequently compel their children to give or receive physical affection from relatives or friends (a violation of body privacy) and feel it's appropriate to pressure them into disclosing their feelings and emotions (a violation of emotional privacy).

Historically, parents have enjoyed wide discretionary authority over their children's upbringing. But over the past few decades, the nation's courts have held that children do have independent rights that can override parental authority. Some states have struck down laws that give parents an absolute veto over whether a minor girl can obtain an abortion, for instance. Other states have greatly expanded minors' rights, permitting them, in some cases, to seek temporary placement in another home if they have conflicts with their parents (Mintz, 1989).

At the same time, however, there seems to be heightened concern about the problems teenagers are getting into and an increased desire to give parents help in monitoring their behavior. Consider these recent innovations:

- Many communities are now forming parenting networks, which often include telephone trees and neighborhood watches, so that parents can help one another keep tabs on their kids.
- Teen curfews have been imposed in cities all across the country.
- Adults can use computer chips and television rating systems to prevent children from accessing Internet sites or watching TV programs that parents find objectionable.
- You can now see bumper stickers all across the country that read, "Is my teenager driving safely?" with a toll-free number for anonymous observers to report careless driving (Diamond, 1996).
- A device called DriveRight monitors the speed at which a teenager drives a car. Parents can download data from the device into their home computer and print out driving speeds and rates of acceleration and deceleration.

One aspect of teen life that many parents worry about is drug use. A growing number of companies around the country are marketing drug-testing kits to parents. Some kits, such as the Parents Alert Home Drug Test Service, provide parents with the necessary materials so they can have their child's urine tested for the presence of drugs. Others, like the one marketed by the Psychemedics Corporation of Cambridge, Massachusetts, provide parents with instructions on how to clip a small lock of their child's hair, deposit it in a company-supplied envelope, and send it to the company's chemical lab for drug analysis (Stolberg, 1998b). Concerned parents who don't feel comfortable asking their children for a urine sample or cutting their hair can purchase a kit called DrugAlert, manufactured by Barringer Technologies in New Jersey, which detects traces of up to thirty illicit drugs from a child's room or belongings ("New kit can help," 1995). One company encourages parents to start a "family drug policy":

> Start when they are 11 or 12. Say that part of the family drug policy is that there is going to be random drug testing. That doesn't mean I don't love you and I don't trust you. It means that the thing is too serious to take a chance. (quoted in Stolberg, 1998b, p. D7)

These companies all advocate that children's rights to privacy can and should be violated when parents suspect them of behavior contrary to the parents' values. At the same time, most of these parents would vigorously defend their own right to privacy within the boundaries of their family. Relationships between parents and children offer a prime example of the paradox of family privacy.

Variations in Family Privacy

Every society has some norms protecting family privacy. But the extent and manifestation of these norms vary from culture to culture. In traditional Samoa, for instance, there were no walls in the houses, and only thin mosquito netting separated the sleeping rooms of the married couples, children, and old folks. The processes of birth and death were not hidden from public view; even children were allowed to watch these moments of intimacy. As the famous anthropologist Margaret Mead put it, in the Samoa she studied in the 1930s, "Little is mysterious . . . little forbidden" (quoted in Westin, 1984, p. 60).

But even societies where household entry is fairly free and open typically have rules limiting what a nonfamily visitor can touch or where she or he may go within the house. There may also be norms limiting family acts or topics of conversation while outsiders are present.

In societies that have a tradition of large, extended families and where lots of people live in small, single-room dwellings, privacy is likely to be accomplished through rules of avoidance rather than through architecture. These rules, such as covering the face, averting the eyes, going to one's sleeping mat, or facing the wall, have the effect of ensuring a certain amount of psychological privacy even though actual physical privacy is impossible (Westin, 1984). In Java, for instance, virtually all aspects of everyday life occur in the presence of others. But the Javanese are able to "shut people out" with highly developed patterns of etiquette, emotional restraint, and a general lack of openness in speech and behavior.

· ·

Every society has some norms protecting family privacy. But the extent and manifestation of these norms vary from culture to culture.

· ·

Families and individuals within the same culture may have different expectations regarding privacy as well. I (David Newman) have firsthand experience with the problems that can arise. When I first began living with my wife, I quickly became aware of a glaring difference in our respective families' attitudes toward privacy. In my family, the bathroom was a place where one was granted automatic, total, and unquestionable privacy. Even though these norms were strong and no one would purposely violate them,

locked doors were common. My wife's experiences were quite different. For her family, bathroom doors—indeed, all doors within the house—remained not only unlocked but wide open. Imagine my surprise the first time she barged in on me while I was using the bathroom. I simply assumed she'd apologize for not knowing it was occupied, show an acceptable amount of repentance, and leave. It soon became clear, though, that she had no intention of leaving and, in fact, intended to stay and chat. Little did I know at the time that, in her family, the bathroom was the preferred location for deep conversations. There one faced few distractions and had, as it were, a captive audience.

Within U.S. society, privacy is a privilege that not everyone can enjoy equally. For example, in households where one or more members are disabled, privacy may be difficult or impossible to honor, although the perceived need for privacy is no less. For instance, parents of a child with some kind of physical disability may arrange the child's room so that the child can spend time alone—although, for safety reasons, an adult may always need to be within "earshot" (Weigel-Garrey, Cook, & Brotherson, 1998). Toileting and bathing—two functions most Americans accomplish in private—can be particularly difficult for disabled children and adults. One mother reported that when bathing her disabled daughter: "I will allow her a few minutes where I go out and come back, but it's not more than a few seconds at a time. She would like to be in there by herself and she tells you to go away, but I'm just too nervous about leaving her in water" (quoted in Weigel-Garrey et al., 1998, p. 58).

A family's class standing also has a substantial impact on how much privacy its members are accorded. Prior to the mid-nineteenth century, slave families were entitled to no privacy whatsoever. Because slaves were considered property, they had no legal right to make a contract, including a marriage contract. Hence they could not legally marry. The slave owner could decide who lived with whom. Slaves lived in constant fear that their families would be separated (Aulette, 1994).

In today's poor households, dwellings are smaller and more crowded than are those of more affluent households, making privacy structurally difficult to obtain. Thin walls separating cramped apartments hide few secrets. Under such conditions it's hard for family members to have any semblance of privacy—whether from one another or from neighbors. Privacy is further diminished by mandatory inspections by welfare caseworkers and housing authorities. In addition, poor people must often use public facilities (health clinics, laundromats, public transportation, and so on) to carry out day-to-day tasks that wealthier people can carry out privately. In effect, the need for such facilities forces poor people to share their privacy with strangers.

Social class also influences broader societal perceptions of "appropriate" environments for children, thereby increasing the state's willingness to step into private matters of poor (and usually minority) families. In 1967, for instance, welfare workers were given the power to remove children from their poor, unmarried mothers on the grounds that poverty and lack of marriage, in and of themselves, constituted a potentially harmful environment for children (Coontz, 1992).

In sum, the ideal of family privacy rarely applies to everyday life in its pure form. Furthermore, it is not something that is available equally to all families.

Something to Think About

One of the most compelling sociological paradoxes is that family is the most private and protected of all social institutions yet one whose cultural, political, and personal importance provokes unparalleled public attention and scrutiny. Family is both autonomous and regulated, private and public. Most intimate and family behavior occurs away from the watchful eyes of others, and only its members have access to their thoughts, desires, and feelings regarding the people with whom they are intimately involved. But whether they like it or not, others do care about what goes on in families. The people around the family, the government, even society as a whole, will always have a keen interest in what happens in a family's intimate life.

1. When and under what conditions should a family's privacy and autonomy be tolerated and protected by society? When should it be breached? Explain.

2. How can people balance an individual's right to physical and emotional well-being against a family's right to be free from outside intrusion and to make its own decisions? Which of these values should be given top priority? Why?

3. Should children have rights to privacy that protect them from parental intrusion? Explain.

4. If family activities are more "honest" when they occur in private, how can sociologists ever accurately study families scientifically? If you were given the task of studying "intimate family communication" or "parental discipline tactics," how would you do so?

For More On . . .	See . . .
Privacy and research	"Family Privacy and Research Ethics" in Chapter 1
Privacy and child abuse	"Parental Rights and State Intervention" in Chapter 10
Parenting	Chapter 8
Children's rights	"The Historical Construction of Childhood" in Chapter 9

How should individual rights and family obligations be balanced?

The 1996 hit film *Shine* is based on the life story of a wildly eccentric but highly talented Australian pianist named David Helfgott, who overcame extreme personal trauma and mental problems to become a successful concert performer. In his early teens, David attracted the attention of a well-known international musician, who offered him a scholarship to study piano in the United States. David was thrilled. But his strict and domineering father couldn't bear the thought of losing David and forbade him to go. In no uncertain terms he told David that his primary loyalty and responsibility must always be to the family:

> David, if you go you will never come back to this house again. You will never be anybody's son. The girls will lose their brother. Is that what you want? . . . You want to destroy the family . . . if you love me you will stop this nonsense.

David grudgingly relented to his father's demands and turned down the scholarship.

Several years later, another opportunity to study abroad arose—this time at the Royal College of Music in London. David finally defied his father's brutal authority and accepted the offer. In doing so, however, he was banished from his home. His father cut off all communication with David while he was in London. David couldn't cope with the separation from his family and the feeling that he had betrayed his father. After one stirring, virtuoso concert performance, he suffered a nervous breakdown and returned to Australia, where for a decade he lived in and out of psychiatric institutions.

The film has a happy ending, though. As an adult, David developed an unlikely romance with a woman who brought stability to his chaotic world. The film concludes with his return to the concert stage in triumph.

Although *Shine* portrays an example of an extreme conflict between individual desire and family obligation, and is somewhat fictionalized, it nonetheless raises an important point about the role family loyalty and obligation ought to play in individual lives. People every day face the dilemma of how to balance the pursuit of their personal desires with their responsibilities to their loved ones. Consider the 18-year-old college student who wants desperately to be an actress but whose parents are counting on her to take over the family dry-cleaning business after graduation. Or what about the 50-year-old son who must turn down a promotion in a different state because he needs to live close to his elderly, ailing parent? When a deep sense of duty and obligation butts up against personal wishes, significant pain and hard feelings can result.

What do we do when the cornerstones of family life—duty, responsibility, commitment to others—conflict with our personal needs and desires?

This woman's napping elderly father, newspaper-reading husband, and uninterested daughter seem oblivious to her work on their behalf. Balancing family obligations with personal needs has been especially difficult for women in U.S. society. Are women expected to devote too much of their lives to the service of their families? What obligations do men have? Should they take more responsibility? How should men and women adjust the balance between individual rights and obligations to family?

These types of situations raise interesting questions about how family obligations are balanced with individual interests. More specifically, what should be more important, your personal rights or your obligations based on the family roles you occupy? What do people owe one another as members of the same family? Do people need to return to traditional role obligations—parent and child, husband and wife—to maintain committed family relationships? These are the topics explored here.

Rights and Responsibilities

The tension between individual interests and the collective interests of family can be understood as a difference between personal rights and group responsibilities. *Rights* are individual entitlements or privileges, which are often protected by law. The right to free speech, to a fair and speedy trial, and to police protection are the sorts of things to which all U.S. citizens are entitled.

Individual rights lie at the very core of U.S. culture. The Declaration of Independence, the Constitution, and the Bill of Rights all declare individual rights to be "inalienable." U.S. children learn that you have the right to "life, liberty and the pursuit of happiness." The belief that public policies ought to emphasize individual rights is deeply ingrained in the collective U.S. psyche:

> We believe in the dignity, indeed the sacredness, of the individual. Anything that would violate our right to think for ourselves, judge for ourselves, make our own decisions, live our lives as we see fit, is not only morally wrong, it is sacrilegious. Our highest and noblest aspirations, not only for ourselves, but for those we care about, for our society and for the world, are closely linked to our individualism. (Bellah, Madsen, Sullivan, Swidler, & Tipton, 1985, p. 142)

In contrast, people in the United States are not so deeply committed as a culture to *responsibilities*—their duties and obligations to others. It's true that parents have an abiding responsibility to provide food, clothing, and shelter for their children. And

there are norms that govern relationships among other family members across a wide range of circumstances, influencing, for example, how obligated you feel to attend your niece's first birthday party or to provide shelter and financial aid to other relatives in times of need (Rossi & Rossi, 1990). Certainly these responsibilities are necessary for a society to exist, and they deserve respect. But we usually don't stand up and cheer for them or fight for their protection as we do for individual rights (Oaks, 1995). Whereas laws exist to protect our rights, they exist to enforce our responsibilities.

Nevertheless, as the famous sociologist Émile Durkheim (1915/1965) argued, people need clearly defined responsibilities to bind them together in a moral community. He believed people are inherently selfish and therefore can form lasting relationships with others only if society's rules keep their natural feelings and desires in check. Clearly defined family roles and responsibilities thus play a key part in society: They not only sustain the institution of family, they also ensure stable attachments throughout society.

It's worth noting that rights and responsibilities aren't always dissimilar. Parents, for example, may fight for the *right* to child custody, but that right also includes clear responsibilities. Adult children can both be responsible for the care of their elderly parents and, at the same time, exercise their right to protect their parents from unwanted medical care. Our purpose in discussing rights and responsibilities as distinct is to allow you to see how much of the tension people experience in their family lives can result from conflict between what they feel entitled to as individuals and what they feel obligated to do as members of a family.

Culture and Family Obligation

The balance between rights and responsibilities varies from society to society. Scholars often distinguish between collectivist and individualist cultures. *Collectivist* cultures are those in which individual goals are subordinated to the goals of the larger group, and obligation to others is emphasized over personal freedom. In contrast, *individualist* cultures are those in which individual rights, self-realization, personal autonomy, and personal identity take precedence (Dion & Dion, 1996).

Collectivist Cultures

In collectivist cultures, such as those in most Asian countries, people assume that family members are interdependent and highly involved in one another's lives. Duty, sacrifice, and compromise are considered desirable. Collectivism doesn't mean complete negation of the individual's well-being or interest, however. Instead, people in such cultures assume that maintaining the group's well-being is ultimately the best guarantee of the individual's well-being (Hofstede, 1984).

Shame is a powerful means of social control in collectivist cultures. Because one person is seen as a reflection of the entire group, his or her individual actions can disgrace everyone in that group. Thus family members have a great stake in the behavior of other family members. And shame is not limited to living relatives. In China, for instance, an individual's present misbehaviors can dishonor all ancestors as well as all future generations.

In collectivist cultures, personal identity is often subsumed within the family. In India, for instance, feelings of status and prestige derive more from strong identification with the family's reputation and honor than from individual achievements (Roland, 1988). The tradition of arranged marriages in India fits this orientation: Personal well-being in marriage is not as much a matter of emotional intimacy as in individualistic societies, where people assume marriages are based on personal feelings of romantic love (Dion & Dion, 1996).

Traditional Japan offers another good example of collectivist family ideology. Until the last decade or so, the sense of familial responsibility was quite strong in Japan. When Japanese men and women reached their mid-twenties, pressure to marry—to please parents and peers and to fulfill one's social obligations—tended to mount rapidly. As recently as a decade ago, between 25 and 30 percent of Japanese marriages were arranged (Applbaum, 1995). In addition, most people had a strong, lifelong commitment to their relatives. Most Japanese elderly lived with one of their children.

But things in Japan are changing. Arranged marriage is becoming less and less popular, although young people in metropolitan areas are increasingly seeking the services of professional matchmakers to find them a suitable spouse (Applbaum, 1995). The Japanese emphasis on family responsibility now plays against a societal backdrop of an intense desire for individual social mobility. Workplace pressures are strong, and long hours away from family are the norm—especially for men. On average, Japanese workers put in about 4 more hours a week on the job than their U.S. counterparts, amounting to about 200 more work hours per year ("Length of workweek," 2001).

Perhaps it is not surprising, then, that collectivism appears to be losing some of its influence among younger Japanese. In one study of Japanese attitudes, older people were more likely to hold traditionally collectivist attitudes toward their families and their place in society than were younger people, who were more dedicated to improving their own lives and valued their own achievements rather than collective achievements (Ishii-Kuntz, 1989). Even though their primary loyalty is still to their families, many young Japanese report resentment at being forced to subordinate their personal interests to a tightly organized educational and employment system. Not coincidentally, over the past several decades the number of three-generation Japanese families living in the same household has steadily declined (cited in Strom, 2001).

Individualist Cultures

In sharp contrast, cultures such as those of western Europe, the United States, Canada, and Australia tend to value individual freedom, autonomy, personal development, and gratification over group obligation and duty. Interestingly, in some individualist societies family obligation is written into the law, perhaps to ensure that individuals, who otherwise may feel little moral obligation to assist family members in need, do so. In France, for instance, a law known as *obligation alimentaire* spells out which family members are required to give support to others and under what circumstances. The first priority is to spouses. The second is to ascendants and descendants (parents, grandparents, children, grandchildren, and beyond—without limit). The third priority is to in-laws, unless a divorce occurs. But even if an individual's spouse dies, the individual's obligation to in-laws persists as long as there are surviving children (Twigg & Grand, 1998).

- -

Individualism is not valued equally among different segments of U.S. society.

- -

In the United States, people have always admired independent people whose success—usually measured in financial terms—rests on their individual achievement and self-reliance (Bellah et al., 1985). A key task in "normal" self-development in such an environment is the eventual separation from one's family. People take for granted that some day they will leave their parents' home and start their own families, where they will be expected to devote most of their emotional and economic attention. Childhood is sometimes seen chiefly as preparation for the crucial event of leaving home. Some people can't wait to "get out of the house" and begin an independent life. Even those who experience significant pain and sadness at the thought of breaking these ties accept that it is a necessary step in growing up. Few Americans in their 40s or 50s see living with their parents as an attractive option.

However, individualism is not valued equally among different segments of U.S. society. A recent survey of 2,352 Americans between the ages of 45 and 55 found that fewer than 20 percent of whites care for or provide financial support for their parents or in-laws, compared to 28 percent of African Americans, 34 percent of Hispanic Americans, and 42 percent of Asian Americans (American Association of Retired Persons, 2001). People born outside the United States are much more likely to provide such care (43 percent) than those born in the United States (20 percent). Ironically, this study also found that although Asian-American adults provide the most care to their elderly parents, they are also the most likely to feel guilt over not doing enough, reflecting a powerful sense of collectivist obligation.

Also, in poor communities throughout the United States, many people are very loyal to close-knit kinship networks that support members in times of need. Research suggests that adult children in working-class families provide more assistance to their elderly parents and interact with them more than do middle-class children and that they feel less burdened by their parents (Kulis, 1991). Intergenerational bonds tend to grow stronger when parents help their grown children with resources such as hand-me-down furniture or money for a car and then, later in life, the children return the favor by helping their parents pay for things such as trips to visit the grandchildren.

Cultural Conflict

The differences between collectivist and individualist cultures are all too obvious to individuals who move from one type of culture to the other. In the United States, where social mobility across generations is likely (Kulis, 1991), conflict can arise when adult children move into a higher (or lower) social class and come to embrace a different understanding of family obligation. Or they may find themselves less able to offer support because of a job transfer to a faraway locale. Such conflict is especially likely to occur among recent immigrants, who often expend a great deal of energy trying to maintain their original family ideology in the face of contradictory forces in their new culture.

Vietnamese immigrants, for instance, come from a culture solidly structured around family collectivism (Kibria, 1994a). To them the family is always more important than the individual. It is the center of the individual's life and activities (Tran, 1998). The common practice of ancestor worship among the Vietnamese affirms the sacredness, unity, and permanence of the family group. The individual is transient, but the family is permanent.

At the same time, traditional Vietnamese believe that family is a person's most reliable source of support—something that can always be counted on for help no matter what the circumstances. As an old Vietnamese proverb states, "If your father leaves you, you still have your uncle; if your mother leaves you, you can nurse on your aunt's milk" (quoted in Kibria, 1994b, p. 91).

Vietnamese collectivism encourages cooperative economic behavior, which is essential to the survival of new refugees. The resources potentially available from any one person are limited and unreliable. Pooling wages from several members helps protect the family against economic instability.

The education of young people in Vietnamese families is a collective goal of all members of the household. Schooling is seen as the most effective path by which the whole family can achieve economic mobility in the future, and the academic achievements of young people are a source of family prestige within the ethnic community. Children frequently study together and assist one another with school-related problems. Older siblings play a major role in tutoring younger brothers and sisters.

Not surprisingly, many young Vietnamese Americans feel pressure to sacrifice their true interests—in, say, art or music—to focus on fields of study that will allow them to more effectively meet their economic obligations to the family. Weak students may be persuaded by their families to give up pursuing a college degree and to find a job that makes immediate financial contributions so the family can channel its grander aspirations into a sibling who shows more academic promise.

The challenges of migration and adaptation to U.S. culture have threatened this ideology, however. Immigrant families fear that young people will become "Americanized," favoring an individualist rather than a collectivist approach to their future. Indeed, more and more young people are rebelling against the tight constraints family obligation places on them. Consequently, many Vietnamese families are concerned that the "payback" they expect to receive from their investments in the education of the young may never materialize.

Nevertheless, family collectivism among Vietnamese Americans in general remains strong. In a sense, the poverty and uncertainty that often accompany migration actually reinforce traditional beliefs about the importance of family. Ironically, however, economic success consistent with the American Dream may end up weakening the family's influence on individuals' actions.

Gender and Family Obligation

In the United States, the value of individualism has always varied along gender lines as well as ethnic lines. Independence and self-reliance have traditionally been thought more appropriate for males than females. For instance, research on play patterns shows that girls are rewarded more for remaining close to their parents and that boys are encouraged to explore the limits of their play areas (Beal, 1994).

As they get older, men are expected to pursue self-fulfillment, individual achievement, and autonomy. Separation from others (particularly their mothers) is critically tied to their self-image as men (Chodorow, 1986). In other words, cutting attachments is considered normal and necessary for male development.

In contrast, girls and women have traditionally been encouraged to emphasize relationships, responsibilities, and caring for others, particularly spouses and children, as the key to their identity (Allen, 1988; Dalley, 1988). The self-sacrificing woman who subordinates her own desires for the sake of the family has long been the prototype of the ideal wife and mother. However, the women's movement of the 1960s and 1970s made women aware that they were all too often sacrificing themselves to the demands of family. Today, more women than ever before are striving for independence and economic self-reliance.

But the cultural messages women receive still convey the idea that they should be responsible for the well-being of other family members. The women's movement is often criticized for putting too much emphasis on self-development and for encouraging women to place their own interests ahead of their family's. Those who believe women's individualism hurts society cite a variety of distressing trends.

For instance, the fact that couples are having fewer children is often blamed on work life replacing family life as a primary source of self-fulfillment for women. To some people, this trend suggests that U.S. women are less willing than ever before to invest time, money, and energy in their families, with the inevitable result that families and thus society will be less stable.

To others, however, women's increasing independence and self-reliance will, in the end, strengthen families. For instance, a mother's career success may serve as a positive model for her own daughters. Furthermore, there is little evidence to suggest that self-reliant women have totally abandoned their family obligations. For instance, daughters who have successful careers continue to offer assistance to their elderly parents, although they seem to feel more resentment about doing so than do less financially successful daughters or sons (Kulis, 1991). Thus, although working women may struggle for a sustainable balance between career and family demands, it seems highly unlikely that they will, in the foreseeable future, sacrifice either.

Costs, Benefits, and Family Decisions

Some critics of individualism note that it creates an economic, cost-versus-benefit, "What's in it for me?" approach to intimacy and family. As in an economic transaction, people are initially attracted to and are more likely to stay with others they think can provide them with the highest "payoff" at the lowest cost. Obligations and responsibilities are often not part of the equation. When people ask themselves questions such as "Am I getting what I want from this relationship?" "Am I getting as much as my partner is getting?" or "Would I be more satisfied with someone else?" they are implicitly applying an individualistic calculus to their intimate lives (Bellah, 1995). These questions, critics argue, replace other questions such as "Didn't my marriage vows commit me to try to make this relationship work?" and "What can I do to make my partner feel happy and fulfilled?"

Individualist thinking is quite common in U.S. society and can pervade all stages of family life. Arguments over distribution of housework chores or imbalances in expression of affection, for instance, often boil down to one person feeling he or she is doing too much and the partner is doing too little. Consider also couples' decision making regarding whether or not to have children. The wide availability of contraceptives means that children can be the end result of deliberate planning on the part of parents (Popenoe, 1988). Instead of seeing childbearing as an unquestioned and "natural" family obligation, some married individuals today, when making childbearing decisions, ask themselves whether children will facilitate or inconvenience *their* personal fulfillment, achievement, and success (Nock, 1987). If young married couples view children as costly—that is, as expensive luxuries or a downright intrusion—they are likely to delay parenthood or avoid it altogether, ultimately creating ambivalence or indifference toward the very idea of having children (Acock & Demo, 1994).

• •

Some critics of individualism note that it creates an economic, cost-versus-benefit, "What's in it for me?" approach to intimacy and family.

• •

Although some degree of cost-benefit thinking in intimacy is inevitable—after all, you're not likely to form a relationship with someone who provides you with no desirable or satisfying outcomes—relationships formed only in terms of personal gratification may fail to fulfill their traditional function of providing people with stable relationships that tie them to the larger community (Bellah et al., 1985). Take, for instance, the phenomenon of interracial or interfaith marriage. In a culture that prides itself on the ideal of individual rights and freedom, marriages between people of different racial, ethnic, or religious backgrounds ought to be perceived as little more than individual people acting on their right to fall in love with whomever they want. However, for groups whose numbers are declining or are already small, such marriages can be perceived as threats to an entire culture and heritage. Individual decisions to marry outside the faith may have a far-reaching effect on an entire community. The personal cost-benefit calculus, critics of individualism note, is insufficient to protect broader, collective interests.

Family Obligation and Social Policy

When individual self-interest replaces duty as the guiding principle of life, some people may be inclined to reject the burdens of responsibility not only to the community but even, perhaps, to their own families. Indeed, according to some sociologists, people who live independently before marriage or who were raised by parents who lived independently are less oriented toward family living and are poorly prepared for adult family obligations (Nock, 1998b).

As a society becomes more individualistic in general, things such as strong emotional interdependence, mutual caring, and a high degree of sensitivity to others' needs and desires can begin to crumble. From this perspective, the positive effects of recent societal changes—increasing individual autonomy, choice of lifestyles, material affluence, social power for women as well as men, tolerance of individual and cultural diversity—are far outweighed by the heavy toll they have taken on both family and society (Popenoe, 1995).

Some contemporary family scholars believe that U.S. society will suffer unless family obligation—in particular, parents' obligation to their children—becomes the guiding force in public policy (Bellah et al., 1985; Etzioni, 1993). In families without children, an emphasis on the individual rights of the adults involved may be appropriate. But families with children are engaged in activities with vital social consequences. When people have children, they enter into an unspoken social contract with the larger society. Hence many people feel that individual freedoms may need to be restrained in the

interests of family obligation (Galston, 1995a).

This controversy is illustrated in the debate over existing divorce laws. Critics have argued that the liberalization of divorce laws in the 1970s made it too easy for married couples to abandon their family obligations. As one columnist put it, "You can divorce someone easier than you can fire a secretary" (quoted in Clark, 1996, p. 416). They feel it may be naïve or old-fashioned to celebrate the virtues of individual freedom in the face of the continuing increase in single-parent families or the evidence of the harm to children of "broken" marriages:

> I think we may do more for children by trying to reinforce the responsibilities of parents, natural and adoptive, even when those responsibilities are not legally enforceable. We might start by reducing our enthusiasm for "no-fault" divorces in the case of marriage partners who are parents. In many such cases, we should encourage the parents to keep their marriage together for the sake of interests larger than their own rights, convenience, and desires. (Oaks, 1995, p. 39)

In the interests of protecting children's well-being, some critics feel it would be reasonable to require parents contemplating divorce to at least pause for reflection before proceeding. One survey found that 55 percent of U.S. Americans favor making it harder to leave a marriage when one partner wants to stay (cited in Leland & Rhodes, 1996). In some states legal measures are being debated that would impose mandatory waiting periods for couples contemplating divorce or restore the old requirement of proving fault in cases where only one spouse is seeking divorce. Such measures are designed to make it more difficult for couples with children to divorce (D. Johnson, 1996).

Such policies reflect a preference for intact, two-parent families. People who support these policies don't necessarily believe that all single-parent families are somehow "dysfunctional" or that all parents seeking divorce are selfish. After all, millions of single parents successfully provide good homes for their children. Nor does the endorsement of two-parent families necessarily imply nostalgia for the traditional male-breadwinner families of the 1950s. Many supporters of divorce law reform simply want to point out that, on balance and all else being equal, two-parent families are best suited to the task of raising children, and that family policy therefore ought to focus on strengthening two-parent families (Galston, 1995a).

Some social scientists fear that contemporary marriage has become a "disposable relationship"—much like a rental agreement in which tenants have an escape clause should they desire to move out and seek housing elsewhere (Etzioni, 1994). To protect the integrity of marriage, one sociologist suggests something called Super Vows (Etzioni, 1993). These would be, in essence, premarital contracts in which those about to be married declare that they are committing more to their marriage than the law requires. They can choose from a menu of items what they wish to include in their voluntary marriage agreement. For instance, the couple may agree that if one partner asks for a divorce, he or she must promise to wait 6 months to see if differences can be worked out. Once the couple arrives at an agreement, the Super Vows would become legal commitments between the spouses. Already, church and synagogue programs are fulfilling a similar social need by encouraging (sometimes requiring) couples to discuss, before they marry, such issues as who will take care of the children and who will control the family finances.

The crusade to heighten the value of marriage in U.S. society by suggesting programs designed to make people think more about the dynamics of their marriages is an idea few would argue with. The risk, however, is that in trying to promote marriage, more specifically traditional marriage, people will stigmatize other family forms.

A Balance of Individualism and Family Obligation

The suggestion that people should take family obligations more seriously than they presently do may sound rather simplistic, but it strikes a responsive chord among those who feel the family is in trouble.

Given all the negative press about the "decline" of U.S. families, more and more people are buying that argument. The idea that all people have to do to save the institution of family is to return to a bygone sense of responsibility and sacrifice sounds appealing. But such a position does overlook the historical, social, cultural, and institutional forces that have put the society where it is today.

Historically, the sacrifice of individuals' rights in favor of family obligations has had a dark side. It gave some members (usually husbands) power over others (usually wives and children), leading to severe forms of exploitation and inequality (Cancian, 1987). Marriage manuals once advised couples that the path to successful marriage was to shed their independent identities and "become one"—a "we" instead of two "I's." Such a perceptual shift, it was believed, was necessary to get people to think of the good of the family first and their personal needs second. Unfortunately for a woman, "becoming one" usually meant subordinating her interests to her husband's and taking on his identity—being known, for instance, as Mrs. John Doe instead of Mary Doe and becoming, say, the wife of an engineer instead of an engineer in her own right. The husband's life, his interests, and his identity were dominant. The idealized, "collective" marriage of the 1950s often made women totally economically dependent on their husbands and rendered them incapable of escaping from abusive relationships.

More recent marriage manuals have emphasized the importance of two partners giving each other the breathing room to retain their own personalities and some measure of independence. Replacing the old norms of self-sacrifice and rigid gender roles are the new ideals of self-development and more flexible roles (Cancian & Gordon, 1988).

What the critics also need to realize is that, just like the work of husbands and fathers, the entry of wives and mothers into the paid labor force is likely to be "for the good of the family." When women who have been homemakers enter the paid labor force, they usually do so to provide better living conditions and opportunities for their children and families. It's rather startling that women's work outside the home is often decried as selfish, whereas their husbands' work outside the home is perceived as the normal fulfillment of family duties.

Furthermore, women's growing presence in the paid workforce is a trend that shows no sign of reversing. It is extremely unlikely that society will soon see a massive exodus of mothers—or for that matter, fathers—from the workplace. In a volatile, market-driven economy, few individuals earn enough on their own to support a spouse and children.

. . . .

Perhaps self-fulfillment isn't necessarily incompatible with family. . . . Family obligations are difficult to satisfy unless a person is first personally fulfilled.

. . . .

Whether people realize it or not, the pursuit of individual interests has become an acceptable part of family life. As one author puts it, "We marry to make ourselves happy" (Smiley, 2000, p. 62). Even the staunchest critic of individualism would have trouble congratulating a woman who stays with a man who beats her because she agreed to stay married "for better or worse." Few people want to return to an age when it was nearly impossible for women to earn enough money to support themselves or for them to divorce their husbands. And few of us feel that parents should sacrifice all their worldly pleasures and personal happiness so that their children or their elderly parents can live a little better (Schwartz, 1987).

So perhaps self-fulfillment isn't necessarily incompatible with family. If you think about it, family obligations are difficult to satisfy unless a person is first personally fulfilled. Can an unhappy person ever be a good, thoughtful spouse? Can a person in a miserable marriage ever be a complete and effective parent to his or her children? Research continually shows that people who are personally satisfied and gratified with their relationships are more committed to seeing them work. In other words, it's easier to remain in a relationship when you're happy

than when you're unhappy (Cox, Wexler, Rusbult, & Gaines, 1997).

If all this is true, legal reforms, such as those making it more difficult for unhappy spouses to divorce, may in the end do more harm than good. Sixty-five percent of U.S. respondents in one survey disagreed with the notion that parents should stay together even if they don't get along (cited in Clark, 1996). People forced to stay in failed marriages against their will often sabotage their relationships, either consciously or unconsciously, through adultery, abuse, or withdrawal. Remaining in loveless or conflict-ridden marriages often costs both the spouses and their children dearly (Riley, 1991).

And what about the argument that parents who devote significant time and energy to their jobs are neglecting their familial obligations? Ironically, such an argument rests on the individualistic assumption that parents alone raise their children. But all people have a stake in the successful development of children, and all people ought to be committed to ensuring their well-being. Other societies protect children not by punishing working parents but by changing the social structure to provide adequate institutional support for children. Sweden, for instance, shows a societal commitment to children through prenatal and postnatal medical care and liberal parental leave policies, childhood immunization, adequate nutrition, access to preschool programs and well-funded schools, elimination of child poverty, safe neighborhoods, and the prevention of unwanted pregnancies through sex education and the availability of contraceptives.

Hence, instead of decrying the reliance on professional day care as the archenemy of family and condemning parents who use it, people could, as a society, work to improve its quality, affordability, and availability:

> The time has come for this nation to regard child care as an infrastructure issue and make the same kind of investment in it that we talk about making in our bridges and roads. . . .
> To gain insight into the costs, specifically foregone opportunity costs of not endeavoring to improve child care and increase options for

families, imagine for a moment an America with the automobile but without paved roads. (Belsky, 1990, p. 11)

Finally, the contention that people in the United States have completely abandoned all their social, familial obligations and commitments in the pursuit of unbridled self-fulfillment is most certainly an overstatement. After all, family—with its enduring emphasis on interdependence and attachment—has survived despite an enormous cultural emphasis on individualism and self-reliance. Couples are still marrying, interest in having and raising children remains high, and the vast majority of elderly who need care receive it from their families.

Research evidence also suggests that people haven't become a society of individuals totally isolated from their families. For instance, more Americans than ever have grandparents alive, and the ties between grandparents and grandchildren may be stronger than ever (Bengtson, 2001). Today most adults see or talk to a parent on the phone at least once a week (Coontz, 1992), more than half see them at least once a month, and a similar proportion believe that aging parents ought to live with or near their adult children (Orthner, 1990). Most Americans stay in contact with family and provide advice, emotional support, and financial help when needed. Close ties between siblings and with an extended network of aunts and uncles, cousins, and other kin often persist over the life course, providing a critical source of support (Horwitz, 1994). So even against a cultural backdrop of extreme individualism, collective interests remain strong in U.S. families.

Indeed, some social observers are starting to see an increasing commitment to family among some segments of the population (Whitehead, 1993b). Ironically, this apparent change is strong among baby boomers, the generation that first defined independent singlehood as a lifestyle. They were at the cutting edge of increasing rates of cohabitation and sexual experimentation. They delayed marriage longer and had fewer children than any previous generation. But once this generation matured, many discovered that family relationships are a source of fulfillment.

Furthermore, the generation of individuals born between 1979 and 1994 seems even more committed to traditional family obligations. For instance, according to the General Social Survey, over 80 percent of 18- to 24-year-olds said they'd get married if they found the right person, compared to 69 percent of 25- to 34-year-olds. Young people today are significantly more likely to think that premarital sex is wrong than their counterparts a decade or two ago (cited in Stapinski, 1999).

It would be naïve, though, to think that the United States is on its way toward becoming a collectivist culture. Few want a society of isolated individuals who don't know and don't want to know their neighbors and feel no abiding interest in the lives of their fellow citizens or even their fellow family members. However, most people don't want to sacrifice individual freedoms and return to an era of constraining and oppressive social roles. Furthermore, human beings can never fully ignore their personal needs and well-being.

Something to Think About

Being a member of society and a member of a family requires a delicate balance between freedom and belonging. Part of being a fully functioning citizen is the ability to choose or guide your own destiny. Part of being a fully functioning family member is the sense that you belong to a group of significant others and matter to them. The problem is that it is difficult to achieve self-fulfillment and, at the same time, meet familial obligations. All people struggle, walking the fine line between what they want to do for themselves and what they feel they should do for their families.

1. Do you think individual self-fulfillment is incompatible with family responsibility? Would it be possible or desirable to abandon the current U.S. cultural emphasis on individual achievement in favor of a more collectivist approach to everyday life? Explain.

2. To what extent should society limit individuals' freedom to divorce? What about their freedom to bear or not to bear children?

3. At what point do individual choices about inter-racial or interfaith marriage conflict with or even threaten the groups to which people belong? Do people have any compelling obligation to ignore their personal interests and desires and marry only people from similar racial, ethnic, or religious backgrounds? Why or why not?

4. How far should family obligation extend? Most people agree that they have some obligation to help parents, but what sort of help should they feel obligated to offer siblings? And at what point should maturing children be forced to fend for themselves instead of relying on their parents? Explain your position.

5. Who do you think feels the power of family obligations more strongly, men or women? Explain.

For More On . . .	See . . .
Collectivism and individualism	"The Cultural Context of Intimacy" in Chapter 5
Immigrant families	"Asian-American Families" and "Hispanic Families" in Chapter 3
Gender and family obligation	Chapter 2 and "Gender and Parenthood" in Chapter 8
Family obligation and social policy	"Changes in Divorce Laws" in Chapter 11

Does religion help or hurt families?

When a writer for the *New York Times* visited the home of Stephen and Megan Scheibner in the hills outside Allentown, Pennsylvania, the couple's seven children ranged in age from 20 months to 12 years. The Scheibners are well off by contemporary standards, yet their house is unique not for what it contains but for what's missing:

> There is no Pokemon or "Star Wars" paraphernalia. There are no Britney Spears or Ricky Martin tapes. There are no posters of Leonardo DiCaprio or Michael Jordan taped to the walls, no pots of lip gloss or bottles of metallic nail polish scattered around. No Mortal Kombat, no "Goosebumps." No broadcast TV—though the family does watch carefully selected videos . . . from the 1940s and 50s. . . . There is no giggling about . . . cute guys and girls. . . . There is little sign of eye-rolling pre-teen rebellion. . . . There is no sports gear lying around. . . . The Scheibners don't celebrate Halloween. . . . At Christmas, they decorate the house . . . but they don't indulge in a buy-fest. (Talbot, 2000, p. 34)

The Scheibners are not evil parents bent on punishing their children by denying them access to the things that are popular among young people today. Instead they are what Stephen Scheibner calls "selective separatists"—people who vote, pay taxes, and have regular jobs but who deliberately choose not to participate in those parts of the culture they find offensive and godless. The Scheibners are fundamentalist Christians who believe the United States has become morally corrupt and has lost its spiritual way. But instead of trying to change mainstream society through political activism—a task they consider futile—they've decided, like a growing number of fundamentalist families, simply to drop out and create what they consider a righteous and godly life for their children within the protective confines of their own home. Parent-sanctioned courtship (the Scheibners don't believe in dating, which they consider "practice for divorce"), the restriction of peer-group contacts, the emphasis on thrift and moderation, and a relentless adherence to biblical teaching are all ideals that infuse everyday life in the Scheibner household.

What is especially striking about the Scheibners is the degree to which the parents surround their children with a culture over which they (the adults) have almost complete control. Turning the spiritual development of the children over to others would be an intolerable betrayal. As Megan Scheibner puts it, "We didn't want to lose our children to other people's ideas and ideologies. We wanted our children's hearts, and we really feel we have them" (quoted in Talbot, 2000, p. 37).

What role should religion play in family life? Do families require some sort of spiritual component to be stable and successful?

People often turn to religion for guidance and support in times of need—such as a major national tragedy or the death of a loved one. Although religious organizations welcome traditional families with open arms, they tend to marginalize nontraditional families. We can't be sure whether this pregnant woman is a recent widow or a single mother—but how might her relationship with her church change with these different statuses? How accommodating should religious organizations be to nontraditional family arrangements?

The children therefore learn only the values Stephen and Megan want them to learn. They are home-schooled to ensure they get a biblical education, and they even conduct their own Sunday School, under the direction of their father. All their toys, books, computer games, and music have Christian themes. Every aspect of their lives is structured to remind them of God's power or their parents' unquestioned authority. For instance, when asked about his strict opposition to casual dating, Stephen explained,

> If a girl dates 100 guys before she gets married, she's given her heart away 100 times but every time she gets it back, it's a little more scarred. So when I took Katie [the 12-year-old] out, I had bought this cheap little wedding ring in my size, and I gave it to her and I said, "This is yours and what it represents is your heart. Go ahead and try it on." Well, of course it was about as big as three of her fingers. So I said, "See, it doesn't fit you, but it does fit Daddy, so if you don't mind, I want you to give Daddy your heart and let him hold on to it until the appropriate time when I will give it back to you and you in turn will give it to the man you marry. (quoted in Talbot, 2000, p. 38)

Have the children suffered under the weight of such control? By outward appearances, they seem fine. They are nice, polite, caring individuals who are genuinely happy. But under the surface lies something else. They spend so much of their lives under the vigilant eyes of their parents that they rarely, if ever, express an original thought or opinion. Certainly the likelihood of defiance or rebellion once these children hit the teen years seems remote. And that's just fine with the Scheibners. According to the author of the article, stunted creativity and a loss of independence is the price they're willing to pay to save the souls of their children.

In this family you can see a vivid illustration of an important sociological question: What role does and should religion play in contemporary family life? Do families need religion? Such a question, if posed to the Scheibners, would be like asking them if they need oxygen to survive. Their answer would obviously be a resounding yes. But does religion always strengthen families? Is a family such as the Scheibners' doing more harm than good by embracing religious ideals so fervently?

Spirituality in Contemporary Life

Although the Scheibners have gone further than most to protect their children, many parents would agree that raising children today is an enormous challenge. Many people concerned about the future of society are especially distressed by the glorification of sex, violence, and the latest brand-name fad that pervades U.S. culture. In their longing for something more—for children and for themselves—many people these days turn to spiritual pursuits.

Spirituality encompasses a lot of things: morality, soulfulness, intellectualism, philosophy, and religion, among other things. Often it is considered the opposite of materialism and consumerism. So instead of trying to earn and spend more—which usually requires working more—some Americans have begun to simplify their lives. They are giving up promotions and raises so they can spend more time at home with family. They are taking leisurely walks in the woods instead of frantic sprints in the shopping mall. They are thinking about how to get more out of life instead of the best way to get ahead.

As you can see, it's possible to be spiritual without being religious. However, the social institution that has developed most thoroughly to tend to the spiritual needs of individuals is *religion,* a system of beliefs about the purpose of the universe and the intervention of God (or some other divine force) in human lives. Often parents who feel powerless in the face of materialism turn to religion in an attempt to instill a different set of values in their children:

> Children these days have no concept of life or death, no concept of respect, no concept of God. . . . There's so much going on, particularly in the high schools now, particularly from the standpoint of morality and looseness of charac-

ter and drugs and all that sort of thing. . . .
That's gotta make it tougher for parents than it
was. . . . [I tell my children,] "I want to see a recognition of a power greater than you. Now you
do it any way you want to do it, but you better
understand that something greater . . . something made you, and it wasn't Mom and Dad."
(quoted in Wolfe, 1998, pp. 122, 123)

The institution of religion consists of a network
of large and small organizations and specialized
roles for individuals. It serves as a major source of
cultural knowledge. It plays a key role in the development of people's ideas about right and wrong. It
also helps form people's identities by providing coherence and continuity to the episodes that make
up each individual's life (Kearl, 1980). Religious
rites of passage—such as baptisms, bar and bat
mitzvah ceremonies, confirmations, and weddings—reaffirm an individual's religious identity
while impressing on her or him the rights and obligations attached to a new status within a particular
community (Turner, 1972).

• •

**Belonging to an organized religion is not
necessarily synonymous with being religious
or even spiritual.**

• •

How do you determine if someone is religious?
For many people, being religious means having a *religious affiliation*—identifying oneself as a member
of some organized religion. But belonging to an organized religion is not necessarily synonymous with
being religious or even spiritual. For instance, many
people may belong to a church for primarily social
reasons rather than their deep religious faith. In contrast, among those who do not identify with an organized religious group, many firmly and devoutly believe in God or try to invest their lives with spiritual
meaning. Many consider spirituality private and
something that can only be developed in its purest
form outside of any structured religious context
(Wuthnow, 1998).

Furthermore, membership in a particular religion doesn't ensure adherence to all that religion's
teachings. For example, the Catholic Church has
clear positions on many controversial issues, including opposition to artificial birth control, divorce and
remarriage, abortion, and support for priest celibacy
and papal authority. But Catholics themselves widely
disagree on these issues—many favor allowing marriage for priests, ordination of women, legalized
abortion under some circumstances, and remarriage
after divorce. Close to 3 decades ago, sociologists
documented that Catholic women were just as likely
as non-Catholic women to use artificial birth control
(Westoff & Jones, 1977), a trend that continues today. As one person stated, "I'm comfortable being a
Catholic, but I have my own mind and I don't
believe in everything the Catholic Church does"
(quoted in Davidson et al., 1997, p. 41).

Thus specific religious affiliation may tell others
something about a person's beliefs, values, and practices but is probably not a very good measure of how
religious or spiritual that person is. Many sociologists therefore argue that *religiosity*—how conscien-
tiously devout and faithful one is—is more important than religious affiliation in analyzing the effects
of religion on family life. Religiosity can be expressed
behaviorally (for example, attending religious services) as well as experienced subjectively (for instance, feeling the presence of God in one's life)
(Peterson, 1986).

Religion in America

According to some social observers, people in the
United States have turned away from religion over
the last half of the twentieth century. For instance,
people are now less likely to marry someone of the
same religion than they once were.

To some, this de-emphasis on religion is responsible for moral breakdown in U.S. society. Consider
this response to the mass killings at Columbine High
School by two young men in 1999:

Those two young men are, to put it bluntly,
savages. They are completely incapable of recognizing and refraining from an act of absolute

evil. . . . Those two young men were the hapless victims of their country's default in its most fundamental obligation to its children. . . . Until World War II . . . the standards of acceptable behavior, largely drawn from the Ten Commandments, were inculcated into the young people, starting at an early age, by the churches, the schools . . . and the families. And this was not an uphill struggle because most of the society was in agreement about these standards. . . . As you know all this has changed. . . . All the concepts of right and wrong have been banished. . . . And God, once held to be sovereign over all peoples, . . . has been sidelined. (Howard, 2000, p. 301)

Many believe that growing secularism, or a decline in the importance of religion in families, is at the root of many contemporary social problems, such as high rates of divorce, cohabitation, premarital sexuality, AIDS, and violence.

Religious Roots

In the nineteenth and early twentieth centuries, religion did appear to be a stronger presence in people's lives. One study of family rituals, based on 100 autobiographies written between 1880 and 1950, found that religious ceremonies were performed frequently in families: parents read spiritual or religious texts to children (especially before the advent of radio), prayers were spoken aloud when one woke up in the morning and went to bed in the evening, and grace before meals was common practice (cited in Wuthnow, 1998). According to sociologist Robert Wuthnow (1998), in the early twentieth century families placed "increasing emphasis on spirituality within the household, thus heightening the sense that sacredness and familial space went hand in hand. Parents were expected to nurture the spiritual development of their children and to set an example for them by praying and reading sacred texts in their presence" (p. 27).

In one national survey, 80 percent of people born before 1940 recalled that they had been sent to Sunday school as children; 60 percent claimed that

when they were growing up, religion was very important in their families; half said their parents read the Bible to them; and nearly a third said they had had daily "family devotions" (cited in Wuthnow, 1998). Indeed, during the 1950s the saying, "one nation under God" was added to the Pledge of Allegiance to the United States and the statement "In God we trust" was engraved on U.S. currency (Wuthnow, 1998). If you compare these practices to contemporary social life, you might well conclude that religion played a far more prominent and observable role in the lives of Americans in the past than it does now.

Contemporary Signs of Religiosity

Although today most people in the United States claim some religious affiliation (U.S. Bureau of the Census, 2000b), far fewer attend religious services regularly or are active members of a particular religious organization than in the past (Sherkat & Ellison, 1999). Nonetheless, U.S. residents stand out for the depth of their religious beliefs compared to most other Western democracies, such as Great Britain and Germany (Kelley & DeGraaf, 1997). Religion remains a significant and influential force in people's everyday lives. Consider these facts:

- Seventy percent of Americans belong to a church, mosque, or synagogue.
- Sixty-two percent of Americans have no doubts that God exists; only 2 percent express outright disbelief.
- Forty-seven percent of Americans believe that God created human beings.
- Nine out of every ten homes contain at least one Bible. About one-third of Americans believe the Bible is the actual word of God, and more than 80 percent believe it was divinely inspired.
- Ninety percent of Americans believe in heaven, 65 percent believe in the devil, and 75 percent believe that angels exist and affect human lives. A greater percentage of American adults, no matter what their religious affiliation, believe in life after death today than in the 1970s.

- More and more states are considering measures that would require the posting of the Ten Commandments in all public school classrooms.
- Sales of Christian books, computer games, videos, and toys increase each year. The contemporary Christian music industry alone is a $1 billion-a-year business.
- Enrollment in evangelical colleges grew 24 percent between 1990 and 1996.
- The number of families choosing to homeschool their children for religious reasons has increased at an annual rate of 15 to 20 percent since 1985. (Greeley & Hout, 1999; Moore, 1999; Niebuhr, 1996; Sherkat & Ellison, 1999; Shorto, 1997; Talbot, 2000; U.S. Bureau of the Census, 2000b)

Perhaps what has given some commentators cause for alarm is the declining numbers of Americans belonging to mainstream religious denominations since the 1980s. For instance, between 1980 and 1999, the proportion of Americans identifying themselves as Protestant decreased from 61 percent to 55 percent (U.S. Bureau of the Census, 2000b). The waning influence of this denomination has been largely offset, however, by interest in newer religious organizations. During this same period, the number of people identifying their religions as something other than Catholicism, Protestantism, or Judaism increased from 2 to 6 percent. Sociologists Roger Finke and Rod Stark (1992) studied trends in church membership between 1776 and 1990. They found that whenever membership in "mainline" religious denominations declines, membership in religious sects grows.

Even with these changes in religious affiliation, what comes to mind when Americans talk about "religion" is a fairly traditional image stemming from the dominant Judeo-Christian heritage. Nontraditional religions are often dismissed as cults. For instance, early in his presidency, George W. Bush proposed a series of "faith-based initiatives" that would allow religious organizations to compete for federal funding to administer their programs. He assumed that these initiatives would be popular among his conservative Christian supporters. However, many of them opposed the idea once they realized that non–Judeo-Christian organizations would also be included.

Indeed, although they claim to constitute a country of religious diversity, most people in the United States identify with a Christian-based religion. Currently, about 28 percent of Americans claim to be Catholics and 55 percent identify themselves as Protestant. Two percent report themselves to be Jewish, and 6 percent consider themselves members of some other non-Christian religion. About 8 percent claim no religious affiliation (U.S. Bureau of the Census, 2000b). Keep in mind also that about 30 percent of Americans switch religions at some point in their adult lives, and a third of those switch more than once (Roof, 1989).

• •

About 30 percent of Americans switch religions at some point in their adult lives, and a third of those switch more than once.

• •

In short, despite public outcry about the diminishing importance of religion in people's lives, most Americans continue to be religiously or spiritually oriented. After all, they still consider themselves to be "one nation under God." Today, religion can be found in every corner of social life. It's virtually impossible to watch a sporting event these days without seeing a baseball player cross himself before batting, a football player point to the heavens after scoring a touchdown, or a basketball player thanking God for a victory in a postgame interview.

How Religion Strengthens Families

A key aspect of religion is that it constrains human behavior or at the very least encourages members to act in certain ways. This normative aspect of religion has important consequences for people's family experiences. Religious beliefs can play a role in virtually every stage of family life: dating, marriage, sexuality, childbearing decisions, parenting techniques, responses to illness and death, household division of labor, divorce, and so on. For instance, in recent years, more and more churches have begun requiring engaged couples to participate in premarital counseling and religious education programs before the wedding. In highly religious families, the Bible or the Koran or the Talmud may serve not only as a source of faith and inspiration but as a literal guidebook for every aspect of family life.

Given the influential role religion can play in everyday life, it's not surprising that higher levels of religiosity tend to be associated with aspects of family life that many people would consider "positive": higher levels of marital commitment (Larson & Goltz, 1989), more positive parent–child relationships (Pearce & Axinn, 1998), less permissive sexual attitudes (Thornton & Camburn, 1989), lower rates of cohabitation (Thornton, Axinn, & Hill, 1992), and lower rates of voluntary childlessness (Heaton, Jacobson, & Fu, 1992). Religion can protect and nurture family life in a variety of ways.

Keeping Marriages Intact

One area of family life that has received substantial scholarly attention is the intersection of religiosity and divorce. Prohibitions against divorce still exist among some American religious groups. Catholics, Jews, and fundamentalist Christians have historically been stricter about marital dissolution than mainstream Protestants. And in fact, the divorce rate tends to be highest among couples who are unaffiliated with any religious organization, perhaps because they are less bound by social conventions and face fewer sanctions than those actively involved with their faith (Call & Heaton, 1997). In addition, interfaith marriages tend to be less stable than marriages between people of the same religion.

It is commonly argued that religion acts as a buffer against divorce. Ending a marriage is much more difficult within a religious community not only because of obvious constraints against divorce but also because such communities offer so much support for staying together (Larson & Goltz, 1989). For instance, in their analysis of seven national surveys,

sociologists Norval Glenn and Michael Supancic (1984) found that people who claim never to attend religious services are three times more likely than those who attend services at least two or three times a month to have divorced or separated. In another study of people in long-term marriages (married, on average 40 years), most respondents said that religious faith was one of the most important factors enhancing their marriages (Robinson, 1994).

· ·

In fact, the divorce rate tends to be highest among couples who are unaffiliated with any religious organization.

· ·

But no religious group, even one that actively forbids divorce, is completely immune to members wanting to end their marriages. For instance, despite the Catholic Church's clear and strong opposition to divorce, practicing Catholics are just as likely as non-Catholics to divorce (cited in Coontz, 1997).

Furthermore, means other than divorce exist to accommodate people who are unhappy in their marriages but whose religious beliefs are strong enough to prevent them from divorcing. Every year in the United States, over 50,000 Catholic marriages are annulled (cited in Woodward, Quade, & Kantrowitz, 1995). An annulment is a church declaration that a marriage was invalid from the beginning and therefore never existed in the eyes of God or the church. Because the church does not recognize divorce, the only way for devout Catholics to dissolve a marriage and be free to marry again in the church or to receive communion and other church sacraments is to have their marriage declared "null and invalid."

Promoting a Spiritual Outlook

Religion can also strengthen family life by providing a shared system of spiritual beliefs that reinforces family bonds and supports family members through difficult times. Belief systems are important because they shape convictions, attitudes, biases, values, and assumptions. They trigger emotional responses, guide actions, and inform decisions (Walsh, 1998). For example, virtually every religion—from Christianity to Zoroastrianism, Judaism, and Islam to Taoism—promotes some version of "the Golden Rule" ("Do unto others as you would have them do unto you") and encourages its members to subordinate their selfish, personal desires in the interests of their family (Vela, 1996). Such principles can inspire commitment, tolerance, and unconditional love.

It's not difficult to imagine such rules fostering positive interactions. For instance, one study found that parents with conservative religious ideologies are more likely to praise and hug their children and are less likely to yell at their children than are parents with less conservative beliefs (Wilcox, 1998, 2000). Consider how this 8-year-old girl, raised in a strict Catholic family, describes what such rules mean to her and her family:

> One way religion is used in our family is that Jesus told us to worship Him and serve Him. We also read our Bible in school, church, and home. Mother reads it to us at night or sometimes in the afternoon. We go to church and communion every Sunday. We also serve Jesus by the way we treat each other at home. We treat each other nicely. If someone falls down, we help them up. When my little baby sister cries, I give her the pacifier. (quoted in Vela, 1996, p. 166)

Active commitment to religious or spiritual belief systems—often through participation in religious rituals—can elicit loyalty and provide family members with a sense of purpose (Durkheim, 1915/ 1965). Note how this Irish Catholic father explains the role religious beliefs play in his family:

> It seems that our religion provides a superstructure, a whole framework upon which to hang our beliefs and values. They are based on the authority of God. They serve as a guideline for living. Many different religions teach basic truths, such as how to trust people, how you

should interact, and about being fair. (quoted in Vela, 1996, p. 244)

In some religions, informal religious rituals often promote family togetherness, as this Seventh Day Adventist explains:

> Ritual gives you a sense that all is well. . . . That is the wholesome service of family ritual. One ritual that I have found to be valuable is the candle light supper on Friday evening to welcome the Sabbath. . . . Hopefully the house is clean and the chaos is over. Many times on Friday evening I will sit on the sofa and read. Often my two oldest daughters will snuggle up beside me and talk. We can talk about anything they want to talk about. . . . Another is I kneel by the children's beds, put my arms around them, and pray with them. I will thank Jesus for the incredible, awesome child. (quoted in Vela, 1996, pp. 154–155)

Specific religious beliefs can also help families weather adversity. In times of stress, which can be potentially disruptive to families, a dominant religious or sacred belief system often provides "answers" to difficult questions and serves as a guide for behavior. Through such beliefs, family members can begin to understand painful, uncertain, and frightening events, making them less vulnerable to hopelessness and despair (Walsh, 1998). Here's one man's explanation of how strong religious beliefs helped him and his wife deal with the death of their child:

> You could almost get bitter when you have a child die. . . . If you didn't have a faith that is taught by the teaching of God for the future, eternal life, it would be easy to get pretty bitter. And I don't think that either one of us did, and we were able to face it and without too much difficulty. (quoted in Robinson, 1994, p. 213)

Providing Support Services

Another mechanism through which religion can strengthen family bonds has to do with the more formal types of support that religious organizations can offer. One of the most obvious is regular religious services. Some couples who have not participated much in religious activities before decide to start attending services once their children reach a certain age. There is indeed some evidence that the arrival of children increases church membership and attendance among young families (Stolzenberg, Blair-Loy, & Waite, 1995).

Frequent attendance also increases contact with religious messages that may subtly encourage family bonds (Thornton, Axinn, & Hill, 1992). Clergy often preach the importance of positive relationships among family members, thereby validating people's commitments to their spouses and their children (Pearce & Axinn, 1998; Sherkat & Ellison, 1999).

In most religions, people are reminded regularly of the value of marriage and family through activities primarily aimed at families and married couples and not the solitary individual (Wilson & Musick, 1996). Some church-based educational programs teach communication skills to engaged or recently married couples so they will be better equipped to handle problems and disagreements when they arise. Others provide specific child-rearing instruction, as when conservative Protestant churches emphasize children's strict obedience to their parents and the use of corporal punishment.

Religious organizations and families are often strongly interdependent (Call & Heaton, 1997) and mutually reinforcing (Roof, 1999). In some cases, religious organizations and families draw on the same emotional bonds and symbols. So intertwined are some families with their religious communities that people view their place of worship as a second home and the members of the congregation as a second family (Wuthnow, 1998). For others, church and family are virtually indistinguishable. The common use of terms such as "father," "mother," "brother," and "sister" in churches of various sorts reinforces the connection between religious organizations and family.

Religious organizations can create strong social ties by linking friends and family members in the same social group. From time to time they also offer more formal support for families (Pearce & Axinn, 1998). For example, many African-American churches have long-standing traditions of providing support and financial assistance to needy families. These churches can draw on their preexisting organizational skills and spiritual traditions to mobilize their better-off members in the service of those in the community who lack the resources to help themselves (Chatters, Taylor, & Jayakody, 1994).

How Religion Creates Stress

For families that are fairly traditional (married, with children, and heterosexual), religion often has a positive, reinforcing effect. For families that don't fit this mold, however, religion may create considerable stress. Problems can arise when the nature of a family or its practices don't coincide with religious doctrines—as is often true of cohabiting families, single-parent families, childless couples, homosexual couples and families with homosexual members, and any other families that do not fit the nuclear model. These types of families represent a growing percentage of U.S. households. Of course, the more rigid a religion's belief system, the harder it is to live up to these expectations and the more serious the consequences, both psychological and social, for not doing so.

Rejecting Nontraditional Values and Practices

A wide range of actions that many people find necessary or desirable for their own circumstances—such as abortion, cohabitation, divorce, female labor force participation, egalitarian decision making by couples, voluntary childlessness, and homosexual and nonmarital sexual activity—may contradict religious communities' principles, especially the more conservative ones. The conflict between religious rules and one's own actions can be intense and have serious implications. When religious organizations take unambiguous, categorical stands on issues such as sexual behavior, divorce, and gender roles, families with different values or ways of doing things will receive little comfort. For instance, many divorced or remarried individuals feel that their churches no longer regard them as members (Aldous, 1983).

Sociologist Nancy Tatom Ammerman (1987) interviewed 62 adult members of a conservative, fundamentalist church she called the "Southside Gospel Church." She found that the prohibition against divorce is so strong among fundamentalists that many unsatisfying marriages are preserved because the couples see no option. Only if one partner commits adultery or abandons the family entirely can the remaining partner feel innocent in seeking a divorce. Even then, divorced individuals may change churches to avoid facing their old friends.

This tendency for people to turn away from their churches when they violate religious doctrine shows us that the relationship between religion and family ties is a complicated one. As we mentioned earlier, most people assume that low levels of religiosity cause a variety of family-related problems. However, the relationship may work in the other direction as well: People who engage in what their religious organization defines as problematic behavior withdraw from the congregation and become less religious as a result. In fact, some evidence suggests that divorced or separated individuals quit attending services because they feel rejected, or were rejected, by clergy or others in the organization (Glenn & Supancic, 1984).

. . . .

Most people assume that low levels of religiosity cause a variety of family-related problems. However, the relationship may work in the other direction as well.

. . . .

Similarly, in those religious groups that are most opposed to sex outside of marriage, the decision to cohabit or engage in premarital sex leads young people to reduce their religious participation. Such withdrawal is especially likely among those who were originally the most religious (Thornton & Camburn, 1989; Thornton et al., 1992). It is very difficult to commit yourself to a group that believes your actions have reserved you an eternal spot in the fiery pits of hell. Ironically, religion may have little to offer to individuals and families who arguably most need the social support a religious community can provide: divorcing couples, single-parent families, rebellious teenagers, and conflicted homosexuals.

Demanding Devotion in a Secular World

It can be very difficult for families to be devoutly religious in a society perceived to be at odds with a godly lifestyle. In predominantly religious societies, because almost everyone is devout, parents don't have to worry about their children acquiring "undesirable" beliefs from friends, teachers, colleagues, or spouses. The problem only exists in culturally diverse societies where children are likely to be exposed to friends, teachers, and ultimately work colleagues and marriage partners who are significantly less religious than they are or who have very different religious beliefs.

This situation poses a serious problem for highly religious parents and their churches: To ensure that their children acquire and retain orthodox religious beliefs, they need to control the children's social environment and restrict their friendship choices to those with compatible religious beliefs (Kelley & DeGraaf, 1997). You'll recall that this sort of concern led the Scheibners to reject the trappings of mainstream U.S. culture.

A crucial dilemma, of course, concerns the desire that one's children marry within the faith. In a society such as the United States—where individuals have considerable choice over mates, are likely to interact with many persons of different religions, and feel less pressure to "switch" faiths when they marry—interfaith marriages have become more common (Roof, 1999). On a personal level, parents are likely to be concerned that their grandchildren will be raised in a different religious tradition or raised without any religion at all.

Religious leaders are often concerned that interfaith marriage will erode membership in their congregation and result in more secular values throughout society. Marriage between people of different faiths is especially troublesome in those religions whose numbers are already small. For instance, according to recent figures the percentage of Jews in the U.S. population has declined from 4 percent to about 2 percent in the last 50 years (Safire, 1995). Whereas one Jew in ten married a non-Jew in 1945, one in two does so today. A lower birth rate coupled with the propensity to not raise children Jewish can explain, in part, why the Jewish population is dropping so precipitously.

A statement issued in 1973 by Reform Judaism's Central Conference of American Rabbis (the most liberal, and therefore the most tolerant, branch of American Judaism) defined interfaith marriages as "contrary to Jewish tradition" and discouraged rabbis from officiating at them (Niebuhr, 1996). Indeed, most U.S. rabbis today refuse to perform interfaith weddings, even though there is some evidence that interfaith couples who have been married by rabbis are likely to raise their children as Jews.

. . . .

Whereas one Jew in ten married a non-Jew in 1945, one in two does so today.

. . . .

Ammerman's (1987) study of fundamentalist families illustrates further the dilemmas faced by very religious families in a less religious society. For fundamentalist Christians, for instance, the ideal home is one in which the wife is a full-time homemaker. Husbands are assumed to be the unquestioned authority, the family "priest," and wives are expected to submit to their husbands' wishes. A statement of beliefs issued at the 1998 national convention of Southern Baptists included a declaration that a woman should "submit herself graciously to the servant leadership of her husband," whereas a husband should "provide for, protect and lead his family" (quoted in Niebuhr, 1998, p. 1). The wife has the God-given responsibility to respect her husband and serve as his helper. "Submission," according to one Christian women's organization, "is a place of honor" ("The Promise Keepettes," 1997, p. 15).

The economic and social demands of contemporary life often make it impossible for fundamentalist families to live up to these expectations, however. Ammerman found that of the mothers she inter-

viewed with children under 25, only about 15 percent were able to stay out of the labor force entirely while their children were growing up. In fact, most worked outside the home, about half of them in full-time jobs. Unwilling to abandon their religious beliefs entirely, though, fundamentalist women learn to subtly influence family decision making while still deferring to their husbands' authority:

> I regard my husband as the real leader of the family, and the children know I am not trying to usurp that authority out from under him. I bucked this at first, but have made a conscious choice to maintain the Biblical perspective. I have made a concerted effort not to be the iron fist in the silk glove, as many women end up doing. . . . His role is to lead the family well, and I am to support that leadership. (quoted in Vela, 1996, p. 258)

People often try to find ways to reconcile the tension between personal or family realities and conflicting religious doctrines. For instance, many gay and lesbian couples who wish to have their relationships publicly validated—something few religions are willing to do—create and perform their own religious ceremonies. Individuals in mixed-faith families often creatively merge rituals from different faiths (Roof, 1999).

It's not just couples or families that find themselves making such compromises. Some religious organizations make compromises as well. For example, in a study of conservative churches that prescribe very traditional gender roles, a pastor described how he would counsel a family faced with the necessity of the wife working outside the home. After questioning them about whether they really needed the money,

> I would encourage them and offer support. I would help that family find a quality, Christian, inexpensive, preschool. I would help them find employment which might allow them to work around certain hours so that she could make as much money as possible yet maybe still be at home. Maybe find some sort of work where she could stay home and make money. (quoted in Demmitt, 1992, p. 10)

Despite resistance in some quarters, some religious organizations have found ways to accommodate changing families.

Promoting Oppression of the Powerless

The conflicts we've just described pertain to situations in which families find it difficult to live up to the expectations spelled out by their religious ideologies. However, problems can also arise when families are too successful in meeting their religion's expectations. In some situations, living up to religious teachings can come at the expense of an individual's own happiness. One wife in Ammerman's study talked about how she interpreted the Bible to mean that she was stuck in an unhappy marriage:

> I remember one time coming home and screaming at my husband, opening the Bible and saying, "See this? See this? That's why I'm here. Not because I want to be here, but I have to be here. The Bible says I have to be here. God says that I have to be here, and that's why I'm here." (quoted in Ammerman, 1987, p. 136)

When people think of religious ideologies being "oppressive," they typically think of radical regimes in other countries that use religious dogma to reinforce conformity and justify their persecution of dissenters. For example, in 1996 the Taliban, a radical fundamentalist Islamic movement, took control of Afghanistan. Before the takeover, women accounted for 70 percent of Afghanistan's teachers, 50 percent of its civil servants, and 40 percent of its physicians. The Taliban immediately issued religious edicts forbidding women to work outside the home, attend school, or leave their homes unless accompanied by a husband, father, brother, or son. They were not permitted to wear white socks—because white is the color of the Taliban flag—or to wear shoes that make noise as they walk.

These restrictions had a profound effect on women's physical and mental health. About 62 percent of Afghani women experienced a decline in access to health care after the takeover. Most were so frightened of being flogged or beaten in the streets that they were often reluctant to seek what little help was available to them. Shortly after the Taliban took control, 86 percent of Afghan women showed signs of anxiety, and 97 percent demonstrated evidence of major depression (Rasekh, Bauer, Manos, & Iacopino, 1998).

This case is extreme, but the potentially harmful consequences of people adhering to strict religious belief systems can be found in more democratic societies as well. In some religions, there is a widely held conviction that children enter the world with a wayward will and it is up to the parents to break that will, so that the child can better respond to parental guidance and submit to the will of God (Greven, 1991). But many parents have taken this directive to "break the child's will" as a mandate to inflict severe physical punishment. Central to this approach to parenting is the parents' religiously inspired belief that they are inflicting pain and sometimes injury for the child's own good and not out of their own anger or vindictiveness (Capps, 1992).

For instance, 90 state troopers and 50 social workers raided the compound of the Northeast Kingdom Community Church in Island Pond, Vermont, in 1984. They rounded up 112 children—ranging in age from 9 days to 17 years—and took them to a courthouse in nearby Newport where they could be examined for evidence of child abuse. The children were eventually released to the custody of their parents. Church members didn't dispute that they used corporal punishment, usually with thin rods, to discipline the children. But they claimed they did so in accordance with their God-given right to discipline and in a spirit of love:

> Discipline comes from love. Without discipline, children will not have any respect for God or for authority. They have no sense that there are consequences for disobedience. Discipline is not a joyful experience, it hurts, but [children never feel] unwanted or unloved. (quoted in "Trip home to stand," 2000, p. A16)

More recently, a conservative religious leader in Eau Claire, Wisconsin, showed a group of parents how to inflict corporal punishment. Demonstrating on a teenage boy, he stated, "You spank them right here on the gluteus maximus, which God made for that purpose" (quoted in "Conservative leader urges parents to spank children," 2000). The minister urged parents to start spanking children around age 2, claiming that it builds self-esteem because it lets children know they are loved. However, research on corporal punishment has found that such disciplinary tactics are likely to result in overly aggressive and easily frustrated children (cited in Crary, 2000).

In other situations, the harm caused by religious beliefs is less direct. Consider, for example, parents who refuse to seek medical treatment for their sick children because of their religious beliefs. Some states allow parents to refuse certain medical procedures for their children on religious grounds, such as immunizations, eye drops for newborns, screenings for lead poisoning, and physical examinations (CHILD, Inc., 2000). But it's unclear what ought to be done when parents' religious beliefs result in injury or death to a child. Twenty-six states allow religion as a defense in cases of child endangerment, criminal abuse or neglect, or cruelty to children. Delaware, West Virginia, and Arkansas allow religious defenses in cases where parents kill their children.

· ·

It's unclear what ought to be done when parents' religious beliefs result in injury or death to a child.

· ·

Nevertheless, there have been cases where parents have faced criminal charges in such matters. In 1995, an Anderson, Indiana, couple who postponed medical treatment for their 6-year-old son and relied, instead, on prayer was charged with homicide and neglect of a dependent when he died of streptococcus pneumonia meningitis (Labalme, 1995). In 1996, the U.S. Supreme Court let stand a ruling by the Minnesota Court of Appeals that awarded $1.5 million to the father of an 11-year-old boy who died after his mother, stepfather, and two Christian Science practi-

tioners tried to use prayer to heal his diabetes. In its ruling, the Court stated, "Although one is free to believe what one will, religious freedom ends when one's conduct offends the law by, for example, endangering a child's life" (Greenhouse, 1996, p. A12).

Straining Family Resources

Another source of stress that can weaken family ties stems from the religious organization's financial and time demands. For example, among Muslims and certain Christian churches, families are expected to tithe, or donate, a certain amount of their income (10 percent, in most cases) to support their religious establishment. Although it's a charitable thing to do, tithing can create problems for families that are already financially strapped. Americans pay an average of $440 a year to their religious organizations, and those in conservative Protestant groups tend to give even more (Hoge & Yang, 1994). Moreover, members of conservative religious denominations donate considerable time to religious organizations, which can detract from time spent with their families (Hoge & Yang, 1994).

These sorts of expectations can take needed resources away from families. One study found a high rate of divorce among members of very conservative denominations (Nazarene, Pentecostal, and Baptist), despite these religious groups' strong disapproval of divorce. The researchers concluded that "the strong demands these denominations make on the time, energy, and money of their adherents, . . . may negatively affect marriages if the spouses are not also adherents" (Glenn & Supancic, 1984, p. 568). When evaluating the role of religion in family life, it's important to consider how religion can harm families alongside how it can help them.

Something to Think About

In the past, religious and family institutions had a mutually supportive relationship. Religion served to legitimate marriage and child rearing and to support and guide family life. In exchange, families were an extension of the religious community, inculcating religious values, beliefs, and practices (Roof, 1999). Although society has not become completely secular, as some have feared, this close relationship between family and religion has weakened because of a wide variety of challenges facing contemporary families. The benefits to be gained from the close tie between family and religion are therefore not experienced by as many Americans as in the past, especially by those who might benefit from religious affiliation.

1. Should religious organizations compromise their position on various issues (such as premarital sex, divorce, homosexuality) if their message makes some groups or individuals feel unwelcome? How could such compromises benefit families, religious organizations, and society in general? At what costs? Explain.

2. Have you or someone you are close to grown up in an interfaith family? What do you see as the disadvantages? Is children's religious socialization nec-

essarily weakened in such families? What are the advantages?

3. Should one spouse in an interfaith marriage convert to his or her spouse's religion so that everyone within the household shares a common faith? Would you advise newly formed blended families to adopt one religion? Why or why not? Would the benefits that come from sharing a faith outweigh the costs of giving up one's faith? Explain your position.

4. Should parents have complete freedom to homeschool their children if they believe public (and even parochial) schools cannot instill proper religious values? What role should the government play in ensuring that these children receive adequate educational experiences? Should religious organizations help subsidize these children's education? Why or why not?

For More On . . .	See . . .
Keeping marriages intact	"Divorce American Style" in Chapter 11
Spirituality and raising children	"The Social Complexities of Child Rearing" in Chapter 9
Interfaith marriage	"Exogamy and Endogamy" in Chapter 6
Oppressive religious ideology	"Child Abuse" in Chapter 10

Thinking Sociologically About Families

The four chapters of Part II provide an introduction to the sociological perspective, a lens that will be used throughout this book to understand key family-related phenomena. We describe the major theories and methods sociologists use to generate research on family. We also investigate how crucial sociological concepts—gender, race and ethnicity, and social class—influence people's family experiences. Does family look and feel different to men and women? To people of different racial and ethnic groups? To wealthy people and poor people? This section of the book is a crucial introduction to the structural and cultural forces that help determine the form and function of families and people's everyday lives within them.

The Sociological Study of Family Life

The Elusive Family

Family sociologists seek to answer questions about the form and function of families. Because families are such an important part of society, the answers to these questions have real-life relevance for all of us. But family is the most private of all social institutions, and so the vital information needed to fully understand family life often occurs in private, well outside the view of others—including, or maybe especially, researchers.

Families typically present a stable, conflict-free, happy image in public.

But such an image offers a somewhat unrealistic portrait of family life and can obscure a very different reality.

In contrast to the typical, well-ordered, "front-stage" image that we see in family photographs, "backstage" family life can be significantly messier. It's no wonder that people are reluctant to let others observe the private, intimate moments of family life.

What sorts of backstage behavior, to which researchers have very little access, might really help us understand what families are and how they operate?

What research strategies might allow researchers to study what really goes on behind closed doors?

One important aspect of intimate family life that is very difficult to observe firsthand is sexuality. Sexuality has long been depicted in art, but only relatively recently have social scientists attempted to uncover its mysteries.

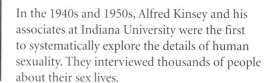

In the 1940s and 1950s, Alfred Kinsey and his associates at Indiana University were the first to systematically explore the details of human sexuality. They interviewed thousands of people about their sex lives.

You can see from this photograph that Kinsey (seated with the bow tie) and his colleagues were white men. How might this fact have shaped their findings and, in turn, the public's understanding of sexuality?

Although other types of research on families are somewhat easier than research on sexuality, researchers still run up against people's reluctance to make their private lives public. Consider the barriers facing government agencies like the Bureau of the Census, whose task is to compile trustworthy statistical information on American families and households. For years, census takers have engaged in the tedious work of contacting all U.S. citizens to gather important demographic data.

Gathering information on "nontraditional" families is especially difficult. Here a census taker talks to homeless men in a Houston shelter. Families without stable homes are frequently undercounted by the Census Bureau, adding to their societal invisibility.

There's been a lot of talk about the inaccuracy of the census and the difficulty census workers have in surveying all citizens. Can you think of a better way to gather information about American families?

Why is such statistical information important?

Social research is all around you. Throughout our lives we are flooded with a sea of statistics that are supposedly the result of scientific research: which detergents make clothes brighter, which soft drinks most people prefer, which chewing gum four out of five dentists recommend. Many of the important decisions people make, from purchasing a car to voting for a political candidate, are supported by some sort of research.

Of all the topics scholars research, none is more popular or has more immediate personal relevance than family. You can hardly pick up a newspaper or turn on the television these days without someone making a claim about how families are changing or about the problems they face in the twenty-first century. Answers to questions about families are not just important to sociologists and other researchers. A variety of professionals deal directly with family issues, including counselors, social workers, psychologists, psychiatrists, lawyers and judges, teachers, doctors and nurses, police officers, and politicians. Anyone who supervises or manages other people must also be attuned to the family lives of employees.

At the same time, the general public wants to understand how families are formed, why people act the way they do within them, why some succeed and others fail, how best to raise children, and so on. In fact, probably one of the reasons you are taking this course in family sociology right now is that you want some answers to questions about families in general that you can apply to your own family.

In this chapter we provide a broad overview of theory and research as it applies to family. We describe how sociologists and other social scientists go about answering questions regarding family experiences and identify some factors that may help you evaluate the trustworthiness of social research. This knowledge is crucial because it provides a grounding not only for understanding what research findings mean and how they're generated but also for assessing whether they're credible as well. Because we are exposed to so many statistical claims regarding family, it is important that we be critical, informed consumers of this information.

Everyday Research

Whether you realize it or not, you spend a significant proportion of your life doing research. Every time you seek out the opinions of others, try to gauge the attitude of a group of friends, or draw conclusions about an event, you are engaging in a form of research. Say, for example, that you thought your score on the next exam would improve if you studied with others. You then formed a study group. After the exam you compared your grade with the grade you received on the previous exam. If you noticed any significant improvement, you'd likely attribute it to the study group. This is the essence of research: You had an idea about some social process, and you went out and tested it to see if you were correct.

Although useful, such casual, everyday "research" can be fraught with problems. People may make inaccurate or selective observations, overgeneralize on the basis of a limited number of observations, or draw conclusions that protect their own interests (Babbie, 1992).

In contrast, the research that social scientists perform helps answer questions through a systematic, careful, and controlled process of collecting information, interpreting that information, and drawing conclusions. To that end, researchers do the following:

- Methodically record observations across a variety of situations
- Design and choose questions in advance, and ask them in a consistent way of a large number of people

- Use sophisticated techniques to ensure that the characteristics of the people in a study are similar to those of the population at large
- Use computers to generate statistics from which confident conclusions can be drawn

Furthermore, published social research is subjected to the scrutiny of colleagues who point out any mistakes and shortcomings. Researchers are obligated to report not only their results but also the methods they used to collect data and the conditions surrounding the study. Such detailed explanation allows **replication** of the study—that is, it allows other researchers to perform a similar study themselves to see if the same results are obtained. The more a particular research result is replicated, the greater its acceptance as fact in the scholarly community. Presumably, flawed research is corrected and ultimately displaced by more accurate and better designed research (Furstenberg, 1999).

Social scientific research, then, is a more sophisticated and structured form of the sort of individual inquiry people use every day. And because published research tends to be couched in scientific and highly sophisticated terms, the general public is likely to assume that the information is accurate and credible. However, research results cannot always be trusted. When picked up and presented in the popular press, social scientific research is often oversimplified and key qualifications are glossed over. Small differences between groups—for instance, that children from divorced families are 20 percent more likely to fail first grade than children from "intact" families—take on more weight when published uncritically in the popular press (Furstenberg, 1999). Unfortunately, the tendency to believe research findings just because they appear in print can sometimes get people into trouble.

In April 2001, the U.S. Census Bureau released a report titled "The 'Nuclear Family' Rebounds," which claimed that the number of children living in a traditional nuclear family with their biological mother and father had increased between 1991 and 1996 (U.S. Bureau of the Census, 2001b). Traditional U.S. families, the report concluded, were making a comeback. Was such an optimistic conclusion warranted? Probably not. Rather, a rise in the number of people of marrying age accounted for the increased number of marriages. True, more people were getting married and having children, but more people were also marrying but remaining childless, living together without getting married, having children without getting married, living alone, and so on.

Indeed, barely a month later the Census Bureau released a profile of U.S. families based on new data from the 2000 census. These figures showed that the proportion of U.S. households consisting of married-couple families with children had, for the first time, dropped below 25 percent. And the number of unmarried couples living together had nearly doubled between 1990 and 2000 (U.S. Bureau of the Census, 2001d).

See Issue 2 for more on whether these trends indicate the decline of U.S. families.

But people must be cautious about concluding that married-couple families are in jeopardy. The apparently dramatic increase in cohabitation obscures the continuing importance of marriage in U.S. society. Over 90 percent of Americans marry at least once by the time they reach their 50s (U.S. Bureau of the Census, 2000b). Even though the numbers of cohabiting couples and single-parent families are growing faster than married-couple families, they still constitute a relatively small percentage of all families (see Exhibit 1.1).

You can see that it's impossible to separate what people know about families from how that knowledge is acquired. So to become informed consumers of social research—and to form accurate conclusions about family life—you always need to ask, How accurate is this information? And how well does information about a specific case generalize to the entire society?

Changing
Makeup of U.S.
Families

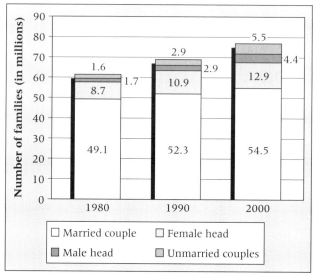

Note: Number for male-headed families is approximate.
Data source for 1980 and 1990: U.S. Bureau of the Census. 2001b. *Statistical Abstract of the United States: 2000,* Tables 57 and 62. Washington, DC: U.S. Government Printing Office.
Data source for 2000: Simmons, T., & O'Neill, G. 2001. *Households and Families: 2000. Census 2000 Brief.* Available at www.census.gov/prod/2001pubs/c2kbr01-8.pdf. Accessed November 30, 2001.

Theory and Research

Unlike a personal quest for answers, which may be motivated by a hunch, whim, or immediate need, most social research is guided by a particular theory. A **theory** is a set of statements or propositions that seek to explain or predict a particular aspect of social life (Chafetz, 1978). Theories ideally concern phenomena as they exist, not morality or ideological preference—that is, they deal with the way things are, not the way they ought to be.

Research and theory depend closely on each other. Research without any underlying theoretical reasoning is simply a string of meaningless bits of information (Mills, 1959); theory without research is abstract and speculative.

Theoretical Perspectives on Family

Sociologists use a variety of theories to explain the structure and dynamics of families. Each theory makes different assumptions about human nature and social behavior (see Exhibit 1.2). Yet they are not necessarily mutually exclusive. Some are broad frameworks that attempt to explain the origin of families and the existence of family as a social institution. Others are more narrowly conceived, focusing on specific family issues such as mate selection, interpersonal communication, power relations, conflict, and so on. Here we look at five of the theoretical perspectives that have commonly been used to examine family life. We should note that although some research is clearly linked to a particular theoretical perspective, researchers typically draw on multiple theories to better understand a particular behavior or experience.

EXHIBIT 1.2

How Sociological Theories View Families

Theoretical Perspective	Key Assumptions About Families
Sociobiology	Individual, couple, and family patterns are determined by biology.
Structural-Functionalism	Families' purpose is to fulfill certain roles in order to keep society as a whole functioning smoothly.
Conflict Perspective	Inequality is an inherent part of families. Some family members benefit more than others from these arrangements.
Feminist Theory	Inequality within families and society is structured along gender lines. Men benefit more from family practices than do women
Social Exchange Theory	Enduring family relationships and interactions are those that offer the greatest rewards and fewest costs.
Symbolic Interactionism	Families are created through day-to-day interactions. Communication is central to the creation and maintenance of family bonds.

Sociobiology   Some theorists focus on the biological imperatives that underlie human family relationships. They assume that some features of families are the natural end products of a long evolutionary process. This perspective, known as **sociobiology** (or to some, *evolutionary psychology*), seeks to understand human behavior by integrating relevant insight from the natural sciences into traditional sociological thinking. This perspective suggests that biology always interacts with culture in creating certain family forms (Walsh & Gordon, 1995).

Several brands of sociobiology exist: Some argue that cultural influence is minimal and that underlying physical states determine *all* human behavior; others acknowledge the strong effect of social experience and the environment. However, the fundamental assertion of the sociobiological perspective, no matter what its emphasis, is that people are endowed by nature with a desire to ensure that their genetic material is passed on to future generations (Lindsey, 1997).

According to this perspective, human families reflect the biological characteristics of the species' mating and reproductive system (van den Berghe, 1979). Family patterns in humans, sociobiologists argue, evolved over millions of years to ensure that mothers and infants remain closely attached and that adults mate and reproduce healthy offspring who will survive to adulthood, when they too will reproduce. A central tenet of this perspective is that the dominant family forms existing today—most notably, the nuclear family—are those that have proved most effective in ensuring species survival (Buss, 1994).

Structural Functionalism   Other sociologists see families as essential for survival not because they ensure genetic fitness but because they serve as an individual's primary source of emotional and practical training in society. Such an image of family derives from a theoretical perspective in sociology called **structural functionalism**.

This perspective emphasizes how a society is structured to maintain its stability. Societies are thought of as massive organisms, with the various social institutions working together to keep society alive, maintain order, and allow individuals to live together relatively harmoniously.

When examined from this framework, family becomes not simply a place in which people live out their intimate lives but an important—even necessary—institution for the very survival of the larger society (Parsons & Bales, 1955). This perspective forces people to look at the family in terms of its contribution to society.

Structural functionalists identify several important social functions that are best performed by the family. One such function is the control and regulation of reproduction. All societies need to have a system by which new members are produced and trained. Obviously, children can be, and with increasing frequency are, born outside of "conventional" families. But most societies do not encourage, and in many cases strongly discourage, reproduction outside the family setting.

Another important function served by families is socialization—the process by which individuals learn the values, attitudes, and behaviors appropriate for them in a given society. Families provide members with a sense of self and identity, as well as a set of beliefs and attitudes. It is within families that people get their first sense of their own worth in the eyes of others and their first taste of what's expected of them as males or females.

Of course, in recent years families have surrendered much of the responsibility for socialization to religious and educational institutions and to the media. Schools, for example, transmit the skills and values people believe are necessary to being a good citizen in society. But balancing the relative influence of schools and families can create conflict. Some families are glad to relinquish all responsibility for education to schools. Others want to retain control. When parents protest against the teaching of certain subjects in school or the reading of certain books, or when they fight for the right to choose the schools their children attend, they are attempting to reclaim the family's right to train their children.

Although the family plays a less prominent role in educating children than it did in the past, it continues to serve the necessary function of providing affection and emotional security. To some, a family's most useful service to society is to be a "haven in a heartless world" (Lasch, 1977), where one can find safety and protection and escape the stresses and strains of public life. Families are supposed to provide intimacy, warmth, and trust, an antidote to the dehumanizing and alienating forces of modern society.

According to structural-functional theory, when families serve these important functions, not only do families work more smoothly, but so does society at large.

The Conflict Perspective   Structural functionalism was the dominant theoretical tradition in sociology for most of the twentieth century. Prior to the 1970s, much about families was simply taken for granted: that they're pretty much the same everywhere, they're generally harmonious, men's and women's roles within them are necessary and inevitable, and the daily realities of family life correspond to norms about the ways families are supposed to work (Skolnick, 1996).

Within the past 3 or 4 decades, however, such assumptions about families have been challenged. Structural functionalism, in particular, has been criticized for emphasizing the usefulness of existing social arrangements without examining why those arrangements are created and maintained and how they might exploit or otherwise disadvantage certain groups or individuals.

In contrast, the **conflict perspective** examines society not in terms of stability and agreement but in terms of conflict and struggle. The focus is not on how all the elements of society contribute to its smooth operation and continued existence but on how social structure promotes divisions and inequalities between groups. Social order, then, arises not from the societal pursuit of harmony but from dominance and coercion. Political, religious, educational, and economic institutions foster and legitimate the power and privilege of some individuals or groups at the expense of others. The key question that the conflict perspective asks is, Who benefits from and who is disadvantaged by particular social arrangements?

The famous philosopher Karl Marx was interested in how larger systems of inequality found in many societies influence family life. He felt that in modern societies, two classes of people emerge: *capitalists*, who own the means of production (land, commercial enterprises, factories, and other forms of wealth) and can purchase the labor of others; and *workers*, who neither own the means of production nor have the ability to purchase the labor of others. Instead, the workers must sell their own labor to survive. In such a structure, capitalists inevitably tend to use their power to create more wealth for themselves, to act in ways that will protect their interests and positions in society, and to exploit the workers to meet those ends.

Conflict sociologists see families both as an element of a larger class system and as a small version of society, in which relationships and expectations benefit some family members more than others. They are particularly likely to focus on the link between families and larger systems of political and economic inequality. For instance, how does racial discrimination in politics, education, and employment affect family life? How does a family's position in the class structure affect its ability to act on its own behalf? How do economic trends such as corporate downsizing, falling wages, and the globalization of economic marketplaces change the power structure in families?

Inequality can also exist *within* a particular family. The well-being of one family member sometimes results from the oppression and exploitation of another. Because families are organized principally around age and gender, the benefits of family life tend to be distributed unequally between parents and children, women and men, boys and girls (Thorne & Yalom, 1982). Family relations can be characterized by a competitive struggle to control scarce social, emotional, and economic resources within the family. Members often have different interests and desire different outcomes as they go about trying to get their way. Conflict can arise over a wide range of issues—from how loud the stereo ought to be, to whether or not the family should relocate to another city. Every parent knows what it's like when his or her desire to have a child go to bed comes into conflict with the child's desire to stay up late. Indeed, it's the rare parent who is able to avoid battling with his or her children over meals, homework, fashion, hygiene, and sibling conflicts. Likewise, spouses commonly compete with each other over how to spend money, where to go on vacations, and how to raise children. Sometimes the competition occurs through bargaining and negotiation; at other times, through force and aggression.

One particularly noteworthy and influential version of conflict theory is **feminist theory**. This approach attempts to explain women's subordination in families by arguing that men's dominance within families is part of a wider system of male domination. An early example of this perspective is provided by the nineteenth-century German philosopher Friedrich Engels (1884/1972). In tracing the origin of human families, Engels argued that in primitive human groups sexuality was casual and unregulated, making it difficult to establish who a child's father was with any certainty. So the first family form was based on the biological link between mother and child. A person's family identity was likely to be traced through the female line. Women, therefore, wielded significant power.

Gradually, though, a pattern of stable sexual relations between heterosexual pairs arose in the interests of establishing more permanent bonds between people. The result, according to Engels, was the subjugation of women, who came to be regarded by men primarily as their sexual property. Hence the monogamous, married-couple family form so common today emerged hand-in-hand with the first form of systematic oppression in human society: that of women by men. Engels felt that women in contemporary society could be emancipated only if the monogamous, male-dominated family was abolished.

Similarly, contemporary feminists argue that the way gender is defined and expressed in families is linked to the way it's defined and expressed in the larger society. For instance, women have been encouraged—or in some cases, required—to perform unpaid household labor and child care duties, whereas men have been free to devote their energy and attention to earning money and power in the economic marketplace. Women's lower wages when they do work are often justified by the assumption that their paid labor is secondary to that of their husbands.

The oppression of women exists not just in specific household arrangements but in the *ideology* of family. Centuries ago, women were considered the sexual property of men, and the marriage contract legally obligated women to abide by the wishes and desires of their husbands. Although such formal contractual obligations no longer characterize marriages, overall male dominance in society and general beliefs about women's "proper place" are still closely linked to gender inequality in families.

The conflict perspective paints a rather pessimistic picture of family life. Its emphasis on conflict and coercion tends to overlook the cooperation, agreement, and stability that exist in many families. Nevertheless, it sensitizes us to the reality that people in families often have conflicting needs, and with limited resources, some will get what they want and others won't.

Social Exchange Theory   Like the conflict perspective, **social exchange theory** uses the principles of economics to explain family experiences. But it pays special attention to the way people make decisions and choices. In particular, it focuses on why we are attracted to some people and not others and why we pursue and remain in some relationships and avoid or leave others.

This theory assumes that humans are motivated by the same forces that drive economic marketplaces: a desire to maximize rewards. Rewards can assume many forms: money, desired goods and services, attention, status, prestige, approval by others, and so on. At the same time, people are also motivated by a desire to minimize their costs—to avoid unpleasant, undesirable, or painful experiences. Humans choose a particular line of action over other lines of action because it produces the best profit (rewards minus costs).

When applied to intimacy, this fundamental premise implies that relationships that are the most "profitable" to both partners are the most satisfying and the most likely to last. Intimate relationships provide obvious rewards—such as love, sexual gratification, warmth, desirable characteristics of the partner, companionship, and so on. But they present certain costs as well—time and effort spent trying to maintain the relationship, undesirable characteristics of a partner, bickering, and so on. Research has shown that the couples who indicate high levels of happiness are providing each other with many rewarding experiences and few costly ones (Birchler, Weiss, & Vincent, 1975; Rusbult, 1983; Vincent, Weiss, & Birchler, 1975).

Unlike purely economic exchanges, whose rewards and costs are objective and defined in terms of money, the rewards and costs in an intimate, family context are likely to be matters of subjective definition. One person may define sensitivity as a rewarding characteristic, whereas another may define it as wimpiness and find it costly. Even so, such preferences are, in many ways, embedded within the larger society's definitions of desirability. As long as people have generally agreed-on standards of a person's worth and as long as certain people have a competitive advantage over others in terms of what they can offer to a relationship, intimate preferences and relationships will share some features of the economic marketplace (Becker, 1981).

Social exchange theory also directs our attention to people's expectations. These expectations are derived from past experiences. People judge the attractiveness of the outcomes they receive in present relationships by comparing them to outcomes received in previous ones. If a present relationship exceeds expectations—that is, it is "better" than any relationship in which someone has been involved before—satisfaction is likely to be high. However, if the present relationship doesn't provide what a person has come to expect, that person probably won't be very happy.

People also compare the attractiveness of a present relationship to the kinds of profits they think are available in an alternative relationship (Thibaut & Kelley, 1959). If an individual perceives that available alternatives would be more rewarding than the present relationship, he or she will be less inclined to remain. But when people feel they have few, or no, or more costly alternatives, they tend to stay in the relationship, even if it is far from satisfying.

Symbolic Interactionism   A final sociological perspective on family is **symbolic interactionism**. This perspective seeks to understand society and social structure by examining the personal day-to-day interactions of people as individuals, pairs, or groups. These forms of interaction take place within a world of symbolic communication. The symbols people use—language, gestures, posture, and so on—are influenced by the larger group or society to which they belong. When you interact with others, you constantly attempt to interpret what they mean and what they're up to. Most human behavior, then, is determined not by the objective facts of a given situation but by the subjective meanings people attach to it.

This perspective presents an image of family as a reality that must be negotiated. *Family* is not a "thing" that is self-evident. You can't really "see" a family. You can only see people and infer from the way they live, treat one another, and resemble one another whether or not they can be considered a family.

In everyday life we use language to refer to many objects that we can't see: feelings, attitudes, notions, and so on. We come to know these "things" through our experiences with them. We learn the shape of and give meaning to these "things" when we speak of them, act toward them, and respond to them (Gubrium & Holstein, 1990). For instance, think about your own family. You can probably describe the characteristics of the people in it and their feelings for and relationships to one another. You can also talk about its structure, its geographic location, its financial wherewithal, and its quirky traditions. In doing so, you give shape and meaning to this "thing" called *family*.

Simple enough, right? But is the family you describe the same one your parents or siblings would describe? Probably not. The definitions depend on everyday experiences such as housework, leisure time, financial and physical well-being, and so on. Two individuals in the same family are unlikely to "see" the same thing. For instance, children have very different family experiences from parents and therefore are likely to define family differently. Consider a child's perception of a "single-parent family." If a divorced parent remarries, does that automatically turn the "single-parent family" into a "married-couple family"? It probably would to the parent, who now has another adult with whom to share parenting responsibilities. But it may not be perceived that way by the child, who may rebel against considering his or her parent's new spouse a parent. Hence the child may still "see" a single-parent family even though two adults are present (Trost, 1988). And how do those people at the edges of a particular family—grandparents, aunts, uncles, cousins, close friends, and so on—see it? Finally, even if everyone in your family could agree on a definition of what it is, that definition may bear little resemblance to the self-definition of the Nguyen family or the Garcia family or the Davis family or, for that matter, the vast majority of families that exist in the world today.

In sum, although all families consist of identifiable statuses, roles, and norms, each individual family adapts these structural features to its own everyday experiences. The reality of family life is not fixed and inevitable. It is created, sustained, and changed through the day-to-day interactions that take place among members.

Variables and Hypotheses

The concepts that are the basis of family theories are usually abstract and not amenable to empirical observation. You can't directly observe concepts such as "marital satisfaction," "gender expectations," or "attachments to parents." So researchers must translate these concepts into measurable entities called *variables*. A **variable** is any characteristic, attitude, behavior, or event that can take on two or more values or attributes. For example, the variable "sex" has two categories: male and female. The variable "attitudes toward divorce" has categories ranging from very favorable to very unfavorable. The variable "social class" ranges from upper to lower.

Social researchers distinguish independent from dependent variables. An **independent variable** is the factor that is presumed to cause changes in or influence another variable. The **dependent variable** is the one assumed to depend on, be caused by, or change as a result of the independent variable. If you believe that a person's gender affects his or her attitude toward abortion (for instance, women will hold more favorable attitudes than men), then "gender" is the independent variable and "attitude toward abortion" the dependent variable.

To test theories, sociologists must translate abstract theoretical propositions into testable hypotheses. A **hypothesis** is a researchable prediction that specifies the relationship between two or more variables. Say that you suspected, because of the tenets of conflict theory and social exchange theory, that household income is related to marital happiness. You might hypothesize that as income increases, marital happiness would also increase. To test this hypothesis, you would figure out a way to measure the independent variable (income) and the dependent variable (marital happiness) and compare them statistically.

The Modes of Research

Once a sociologist has formulated a hypothesis, the next step is to decide which mode of research will be best for gathering the data needed to support or refute the hypothesis. Although the answers to important sociological questions are not always simple or clear, the techniques sociologists use to collect and examine data allow them to draw informed and reliable conclusions about human behavior and social life.

Experiments

An **experiment** is typically a research situation designed to elicit some sort of behavior and is conducted under closely controlled laboratory circumstances. In its ideal form, the experimenter randomly places subjects in two groups and then deliberately manipulates or introduces changes into the environment of one group of subjects (called the "experimental group") and not the other (called the "control group"). The experimenter takes care to ensure that the groups are relatively identical except for the variable that he or she manipulates. Any observed or measured differences between the groups can then be attributed to the effects of the experimental manipulation (Singleton, Straits, & Straits, 1993).

Experiments have a significant advantage over other types of research: The researcher can directly control all the relevant variables. Thus conclusions about one factor causing changes in another can be made more convincingly. The artificial nature of laboratory experiments, however, may make subjects behave differently from the way they would in their natural settings, leading some people to argue that experimentation in sociology—and, in particular, in family research—is practically impossible.

To overcome this difficulty, some sociologists have created experimental situations outside the laboratory. In 1974 two social psychologists, Donald Dutton and Arthur Aron, devised an experiment to determine the degree to which physiological arousal influenced people's feelings of sexual attraction. In the experimental condition, the researchers had an attractive female assistant stand in the middle of a fear-inducing suspension bridge—a 450-foot wobbly footbridge that swung in the wind 250 feet above the raging Capilano River in British Columbia. When she saw a lone male hiker walking along the bridge who appeared to be between the ages of 18 and 40, she would approach him and ask if he would be interested in participating in a study she was doing on "creativity in scenic places." If he agreed, she'd ask him to write some brief stories based on a picture she'd show him. When the man was done writing the stories, she would tell him, "I'm sorry I can't tell you any more about the study until it is over, but it will be over tonight, and if you want you can phone me to learn more about it." She would then give him her name and phone number.

For the control condition, the researchers found another bridge upriver, built of heavy cedar beams and only 10 feet above a shallow rivulet. There, the female assistant followed exactly the same procedure.

Dutton and Aron believed that those men on the rickety footbridge would perceive their state of arousal (which was actually fear) as attraction to the female researcher. Therefore, they would be more likely to call her later that day than those on the safe bridge, who had no physiological basis for making an attribution of attraction.

In the experimental condition on the rickety bridge, nine out of eighteen subjects called the interviewer later that day; in the control condition on the more solid bridge, only two out of sixteen called her. In addition, the stories the subjects in the experimental condition wrote contained significantly more sexual imagery than those written by the control subjects. The researchers concluded that physiological arousal is indeed linked to the level of sexual attraction people feel for others.

Field Research

In **field research**, sociologists typically seek to obtain in-depth information about some issue or question by observing it firsthand. Such research involves spending a significant amount of time with subjects, observing the context of their lives to gain familiarity with their everyday experiences. It relies less on quantitative data than other forms of social research do. Findings are typically presented with long quotes of and stories about real people, as opposed to sets of statistics, tables, charts, and so on. Such research frequently provides rich and detailed information about people's family experiences.

For her book *Families on the Fault Line*, sociologist Lillian Rubin visited the homes of 162 working-class and lower middle-class families who lived in a variety of cities all across the country. Twenty years earlier she had interviewed some of these families as part of a previous study. She had kept in touch with some of them over those 20 years, playing the role of friendly adviser when needed. Whenever possible, she spent time with wives, husbands, and teenage children—eating meals, sitting in living rooms, and so on. Because of the nature of the topics Rubin was studying, it wasn't always easy to get people to cooperate. So she devised a strategy:

> Experience long ago taught me that my best chance for getting cooperation is to approach the woman in the family first. If I could convince her, she almost always became my ally in helping to persuade the other family members. So I phoned the woman, introduced myself, and explained what I was doing and why it was important for me to talk with her. . . . Some of the women were able to secure the promise of cooperation from their husbands and, where they had any, their teenage children, even before I arrived on the scene. In other families, it had to wait until afterward, by which time I had become something of a family event, provoking the curiosity of other family members sufficiently so that they didn't need much convincing to talk to me. (Rubin, 1995, pp. 14–15)

Through her close observations, Rubin was able to go directly to the experiences of ordinary people and show how social, political, and economic changes influence the ways families organize and reorganize themselves.

Field research is a useful method of studying families because it allows the researcher to observe the subtle attitudes and behaviors that can't be seen in paper-and-pencil questionnaires or structured interviews. Rubin's vivid accounts of working-class people's frustrations, anger, fears, hopes, and dreams could not have been obtained through any other research method.

As a general rule, it's always better to observe people interacting than to ask them questions about their interactions, because their answers may be inaccurate or biased to give a good impression of themselves or their families. For instance, observing a parent disciplining a child usually produces more accurate information than asking that parent how she or he has disciplined the child in the past.

But field research does have its drawbacks. For one thing, it usually requires a significant investment of time. Arlie Russell Hochschild's (1997) examination of how people balance their work and family lives involved in-depth observations and interviews of employees at a single corporation over 3 years. Conceivably she could have mailed the employees questionnaires, thereby gathering data—albeit less trustworthy data—in only a fraction of the time.

Furthermore, because fieldwork is so time consuming, researchers can conduct only a limited number of interviews and can observe only a limited number of people. Hochschild may have collected rich information about people's work/family tradeoffs, but she was able to study only one corporation. It's rather risky to generalize from the experiences of a small group of workers in one company to all workers in all sorts of work environments.

The possibility also arises that the researcher will unwittingly change people's behavior simply by being there. As you well know, people act differently when they know they are being watched. However conscientious researchers are in minimizing their influence on subjects, the fact remains that their presence changes things.

Surveys

Sociologists often seek information from a large number of people when they want to draw conclusions about an entire population. In such cases, experiments and field research are impractical or impossible. Hence, they often employ survey research, the most common sociological method. **Surveys** require that the researcher pose a series of questions either orally or on paper.

Survey researchers typically use standardized formats to ask all the subjects the same questions in roughly the same way, and large samples of the target population are used as subjects. The questions should be understood by respondents the way the researcher wants them to be understood and measure what the researcher wants them to measure. In addition, respondents are expected to answer the questions honestly and thoughtfully.

All of us have had experience with surveys of one form or another. Every 10 years we are required to fill out questionnaires for the U.S. Census Bureau, the source of most statistical data on families. At the end of some college courses you have probably filled out a form whereby you can evaluate your instructor and the course.

Surveys are the most common approach to studying marriage and family life. One survey that has provided the basis for much family research is the National Survey on Families and Households. This survey, first conducted in the late 1980s, includes information derived from interviews with over 13,000 respondents. A second wave of the survey, conducted between 1992 and 1994, includes interviews with surviving members of the original sample. The sample comprises a diverse array of households, including single-parent families, families with stepchildren, cohabiting couples, and recently married persons. A great deal of family information was collected from each respondent, including family arrangements in childhood, dating experiences, experiences of leaving home, marital and cohabitation experiences, contact with kin, and economic well-being, as well as education, childbearing, and employment histories. Much of the research discussed in this book is based on analyses of data collected from this survey.

The major advantage of surveys is that they typically require less time and money than field research does. Information can be collected from large numbers of people in a relatively short time. But the disadvantages of surveys are equally obvious. Can a researcher gain an understanding of the rich nuances of family life through a highly structured questionnaire? Certainly not. At best, surveys provide a quick, somewhat shallow glimpse into family life. Consequently, survey research may oversimplify complex issues. Furthermore, through surveys researchers learn about what people say they do, not what people may actually do (Gelles, 1995). Nevertheless, surveys remain useful for research on certain areas of family life that, for ethical or practical reasons, are simply not amenable to direct observation (sexual intercourse, violence, and so on).

Unobtrusive Research

All the research methods discussed so far require the researcher to have some contact with the people being studied: giving them tasks to do in an experiment, watching them, or asking them questions. The problem with these techniques is that the very act of intruding into people's lives may influence the phenomenon being studied. Asking people questions about their voting intentions before an election, for instance, may actually affect their eventual voting behavior. So sociologists sometimes make use of another research technique, unobtrusive research, which requires no contact with people at all. **Unobtrusive research** examines the evidence of social behavior that people create or leave behind. Several types of unobtrusive research exist, including analysis of archived data, content analysis, and historical analysis.

Analysis of Archived Data   One type of unobtrusive research is the analysis of data that were produced for purposes other than scholarly research but can nevertheless be used by researchers to learn about human behavior (Webb, Campbell, Schwartz, & Sechrest, 1966). One of the most popular and convenient sources of data for family research is the U.S. Census, which collects demographic information on all U.S. citizens every 10 years. Government employees collect these data to keep an ongoing record of changes in the population, but sociologists can analyze them to understand marriage and family patterns such as changing marriage, divorce, or premarital childbearing rates. Because the census has been conducted since 1790, researchers can compare current conditions with past conditions to discern trends in family life.

The biggest advantage to using archived data is that few costs are associated with obtaining large amounts of data that would otherwise be prohibitively expensive for one individual or research group to gather.

Content Analysis   Another form of unobtrusive research is content analysis. **Content analysis** is the study of recorded communication—books, speeches, poems, songs, television commercials, and the like. Content analysis can tell researchers about cultural perceptions of family life that would be hard to capture through other means.

For instance, sociologists Sarah Brabant and Linda Mooney (1999) were interested in how families and race were portrayed in Sunday comics and in what messages readers thus receive about families through the media. They studied three cartoon families *(Dennis the Menace, Calvin & Hobbes,* and *Curtis)* by analyzing all the strips from these cartoons appearing in 1994. They found that the comic strip *Curtis,* which depicts an African-American family, showed more family unity and social engagement than the ones that depicted white families. White families were portrayed as more isolated from other families, from the community at large, and from one another.

One limitation of content analysis is that it may tell you more about how one person or group of individuals—poets, songwriters, and so on—feels about an issue than what is really going on. Often the media present an idealized version of family and social life. At the same time, the media can inform us about changing cultural perceptions of the ideal, especially when content is examined over a long period.

See Issue 1 for more on media images of family life.

Historical Analysis   Related to content analysis and analysis of archived data is a third type of unobtrusive research: historical analysis. **Historical analysis** relies on existing historical documents as a source of information. Family is not a static entity. Not only do families change over the life course of individual members, but the social definition of family also changes over time within a society. Charting those changes and reconstructing the lives of past families requires a detectivelike examination of what people in the past left behind.

Historian Lawrence Stone (1979) was interested in how massive shifts in worldviews and value systems between 1500 and 1800 affected British families. Obviously he could not observe or survey people who have been dead for centuries. And existing statistics from the distant past often prove unreliable. So Stone examined every possible type of evidence to pick up hints about how people were incorporating these changes into their everyday lives. He studied personal documents, diaries, autobiographies, memoirs, letters, wills, marriage contracts, and divorce decrees. He sifted through birth, marriage, and death records of towns, villages, and cities. He studied the architectural designs of homes to see how the physical properties of the household affected family interaction. Realizing that accounts of social phenomena can usually be found in the informational and entertainment media of the time, he also examined newspaper columns, novels, plays, poems, and popular art of the day.

The key problem historical analysts encounter is interpreting the records they find. Historical researchers have no way to check the accuracy of diaries, memoirs, autobiographies, and letters, for instance, and therefore must treat these records with a high level of critical scrutiny. Many such documents are often quirky and idiosyncratic. A letter cannot "tell us more than what the author of the document thought—what he thought happened, what he thought ought to happen or would happen, or perhaps only what he wanted others to think he thought, or even only what he himself thought he thought" (quoted in Stone, 1979, p. 25). The best way to overcome these problems, Stone felt, was to examine as many documents as possible, not to rely on a single person's unique interpretation of events.

Furthermore, the reliance on written records necessarily limits any study of the past to a picture presented by the people who were literate and articulate and who had enough leisure time to write detailed accounts of their experiences. This requirement, of course, excludes most people, particularly in the distant past, who could not write a word, let alone keep detailed, thoughtful, and frank diaries of their family life. Women, too, tended to be excluded from the world of literacy long ago. Hence, most written records reflected a distinctly male perspective on events.

Nevertheless, despite the built-in limitations of historical information, historical analyses such as Stone's are able to provide a compelling account of at least some people's experiences with marriage, birth, death, lineage, sexuality, child rearing, and the role of gender in family life.

The Trustworthiness of Family Research

Most family sociologists see research not only as personally valuable but as central to human knowledge and understanding. But you, as a consumer of this information, must always ask yourself how accurate it is. As mentioned earlier, much of what is reported in the popular media is either inaccurate or misleading. To evaluate the results of family research, you must examine for yourself the researcher's units of analysis, samples, indicators, and values and interests.

Units of Analysis

Families are made up of individuals, but they have a structural reality larger than the sum of those individuals. Some family researchers focus on individual family members, some on families as a whole, and some on the institution of family as a part of society's structure. With so much possible variation in who or what is being studied, family researchers must be careful to specify whether the units they wish to study—called **units of analysis**—

are individuals, pairs of individuals, nuclear families, households, extended families, or the institution of family.

Studying individuals in families is not the same as studying families themselves. For instance, if you are interested in whether children from rich families are more likely to attend college than children from poor families, the units of analysis are individual children. If, however, you are interested in whether families with higher incomes contain fewer children than families with lower incomes, the units of analysis are individual families.

Identifying the appropriate units of analysis is not always straightforward. For instance, much research on "families" relies on information acquired from one family member, who reports on the characteristics of the entire family. This strategy is easier and less time consuming than surveying all members of a family, but it assumes that each family member sees the same reality. If you were interested in determining whether rich and poor families differ in the way household tasks are divided, would you be comfortable assuming that the one person from each household you surveyed would have the same perspective as all other members about who does what around the house?

Such an assumption can be dubious. Family members have been known to disagree on even the most fundamental facts. One study of children whose parents had divorced found disagreement about the number of people considered to be in the family. The children were listing absent parents as family members, but the custodial parents were not (Furstenberg & Nord, 1985).

Nor can husbands and wives always provide valid data on their partners' attitudes or perceptions (Deal, 1995). Spouses have been known to disagree on the most obvious facts about their relationship: how they met, how long they've been married, how often they see friends, and so on. In fact, according to one prominent sociologist even happily married husbands and wives disagree on three out of four questions regarding their marriage (Bernard, 1982). Data on socially disapproved or sensitive family issues such as marital violence, marital conflict, and sexuality are especially likely to produce disagreement among partners (Szinovacz & Egley, 1995).

How trustworthy are people's beliefs about the nature of American families if the data fluctuate depending on which member of a family happens to be providing the information? One way around this problem is to acquire information from both members of a couple. Then the researcher can compare partners' answers to the same question and discern systematic differences in their perceptions of the relationship. In one study, the estimated marital violence rate when data were gathered from only one partner was 50 percent to 80 percent lower than the violence rate indicated by couple data, where violence is considered to exist if either partner reports it (Szinovacz & Egley, 1995). Similarly, estimates of the amount of injury to wives caused by marital violence are substantially higher when wives' reports or couple data are used rather than husbands' reports.

Samples

In determining the accuracy of published research, you must also be aware of the people who participated as subjects in the study. Researchers are frequently interested in the attitudes, behaviors, or characteristics of certain groups—college students, women, Americans, and so on. But directly interviewing, surveying, or observing all the people in these categories would be impossible. Hence researchers must select from the larger population a smaller **sample**, or subgroup, of respondents for study.

Ideally, the characteristics of the sample approximate the characteristics of the entire population of interest. A **representative sample** is a small subgroup typical of the population as a whole. For instance, a sample of 100 divorced people should include roughly the same proportion of men and women that characterizes the entire population of divorced adults. Techniques for selecting a representative sample have become highly sophisticated, as illustrated by the accuracy of polls conducted to predict election results—at least when the election is not as close as the 2000 presidential election!

In the physical sciences, sampling is less of an issue. Certain physical or chemical elements are assumed to be identical. A physical scientist need only study a small quantity of nitrogen, because one sample of nitrogen is exactly the same as any other of the same size. Human beings, however, vary widely on every imaginable characteristic. A social scientist could not make a general statement about all American families on the basis of interviewing one family. For that matter, one could not draw conclusions about all families from observing a sample consisting only of white families, working-class families, or families with small children. Samples that are not representative can obviously lead to inaccurate and misleading conclusions.

You may also consider samples unrepresentative if you have reason to believe that the people who chose to participate in the study differ in important ways from the people who chose not to participate. For instance, the people who choose not to participate in a voluntary survey of domestic violence may be more likely than volunteers to have something to hide. Hence, the data derived from a sample of volunteer respondents will, in all probability, underestimate the rate of violence.

Indicators

Another problem sociologists face when doing research on families is that the variables they are interested in studying are usually difficult to observe and measure. What does powerlessness look like? How can you "see" marital dissatisfaction? How would you recognize social class? None of these concepts can be observed directly. So sociologists resign themselves to measuring **indicators** of things that cannot be measured directly. Researchers measure events and behaviors commonly thought to accompany a particular variable, hoping that what they are measuring is a valid indicator of the concept they are interested in.

See Issue 5 for more on measures of religious feeling and on the relationship between religion and family life.

Suppose you believe that people's attitudes toward divorce are influenced by the strength of their religious beliefs, or "religiosity." You might hypothesize that the more religious someone is, the less accepting he or she will be of divorce. To test this hypothesis you must first figure out exactly what you mean by "religiosity." What might be an indicator of the strength of one's religious beliefs? You could determine if the subjects of your study identify themselves as members of some organized religion. Would this measure how religious they are? Probably not, because many people identify themselves as, say, Catholic or Jewish but are not religious at all. Likewise some people consider themselves quite religious but don't identify with any organized religion. So this measure would highlight group differences but would fail to capture the intensity of a person's beliefs or the degree of religious interest.

Perhaps a better indicator would be some observable behavior, such as the frequency of attendance at formal religious services. Arguably, the more one attends a church, synagogue, or mosque, the more religious he or she is. But here too you can run into problems. Regular attendance may reflect things other than the depth of religious commitment, such as family pressure, habit, or the desire to socialize with others. Furthermore, many very religious people are unable to attend organized religious services because they are too frail or disabled.

Frequency of prayer might be a better indicator. People who pray a lot are presumably more religious than people who don't pray at all. But some nonreligious people pray for things all the time. Whichever indicator you use, you are going to affect the type of information you get and thus the conclusions you are able to draw.

Surveys are particularly susceptible to inaccurate indicators. A loaded phrase or an unfamiliar word on a survey question can dramatically affect people's responses in ways unintended by the researcher. If a subject misinterprets what the researcher intended to ask, then the researcher will inevitably misinterpret the subject's response. For instance, people often comprehend differently terms referring to sexual behavior. To some people, a "virgin" is someone who has never had penile–vaginal intercourse. But to others, a "virgin" is someone who has never experienced an orgasm—manually, orally, or otherwise—in the company of someone else. Using a question such as "Are you a virgin?" as an indicator of sexual activity can create an inaccurate estimate if subjects are interpreting the term differently.

Another problem associated with indicators is the **social desirability bias**—the tendency for subjects to report or present characteristics or behaviors they believe are the most socially acceptable or appropriate (Larzelere & Klein, 1987). Even on anonymous surveys, people want to depict themselves in a favorable light. Hence they often accentuate positive attributes and downplay or hide negative ones. In research on marital satisfaction, for instance, couples tend to report more satisfaction and happiness than actually exists. Similarly, in research on marital power, some studies have found a "powerlessness bias"—with each partner claiming the other is more powerful—because they perceive claiming power to be socially undesirable (Brehm, 1992).

You can see that for most sociological variables of interest, indicators seldom perfectly reflect the concepts they are intended to measure. Hence, as you read published research findings you should determine whether the questions people are being asked truly reflect what the researchers intend them to reflect and whether the indicators are likely to elicit socially desirable—and not necessarily truthful—responses.

Values and Interests

In addition to units of analysis, samples, and indicators, the researcher's own values and interests can influence the conclusions drawn from social research and thereby influence sociological information about families. Ideally, research is objective and nonbiased and measures what is and not what should be. The study of social events, however, always takes place in a particular cultural, political, and ideological context (Ballard, 1987; Denzin, 1989).

In fact, because family is such a politically charged topic, research in the area is sometimes designed to support narrowly defined political interests. Many social critics who write about families have strong commitments to certain policy positions, which are revealed in the ways they present empirical evidence (Furstenberg, 1999). You can be reasonably certain that research supported by conservative political organizations, such as the Institute for American Values, will uncover harmful effects of mothers employed outside the home. But it's equally likely that research supported by more liberal organizations, such as the Institute for Women's Policy Research, will find less damaging, even positive effects of mothers' working. It is always tempting to accept the evidence that supports your position and discount the evidence that refutes it, but you must be more open-minded if you want an accurate understanding of families.

Also, remember that sociologists are people too, with their own biases, preconceptions, and expectations. Sociologists' values always determine from which vantage point they will gather information about a particular social phenomenon. In fact, values can influence the questions that researchers find important enough to address in the first place (Reinharz, 1992). For instance, most research on homosexual parenting asks whether lesbian and gay parents subject their children to greater risks or harm than heterosexual parents. Because antigay researchers are looking for evidence of harm, researchers who are sympathetic to homosexual parents defensively seek evidence that the children of homosexual parents are not unduly harmed (Stacey & Biblarz, 2001).

Similarly, the historical tendency for family researchers to be men has affected the questions that they have asked in studying the effects of women's work on their families (Acker, 1978; Thorne & Yalom, 1982). The term *labor force* has traditionally referred to those working for pay and has excluded those doing unpaid work, such as housework and volunteer jobs—forms of employment that are predominantly female. The result of such bias is that findings on labor force participation are more likely to reflect the significant elements of men's lives than of women's lives.

Personal values are not the only thing that can bias social research. Sociologists are also people with their own professional reputations to consider. Hence they are sometimes reluctant to admit that their research interests might be outdated or their conclusions might be incorrect (Furstenberg, 1999). This sort of bias is difficult for the average person to detect, but it's good to keep in mind that a sociologist's opinions, no matter how well supported by his or her data, might be off the mark.

DEMO•GRAPHICS

What Family Statistics Really Mean

One of the most trustworthy sources of data on families is the U.S. Bureau of the Census. As mandated by the U.S. Constitution, the Census Bureau compiles a complete count of the U.S. population every 10 years, called the *decennial census*. The most recent count took place in 2000. For the decennial census, a survey form is sent to every household, as well as to institutions such as prisons, college dormitories, and nursing homes. The Census Bureau also collects annual data from a sample of the population.

All the census data are available at the Census Bureau's Web site (www. census.gov). There you can find an astonishing amount of information about how Americans live, including information on cohabitation, marriage, divorce, childbirth and child care, sexual activities, and so on.

The Census Bureau's basic unit of analysis is households. It gathers information about households and then subdivides them by marital status or living arrangements. According to the Census Bureau, a household consists of a group of one or more persons who live and eat together in a residence with its own access to the outside or to a common hallway. Households consisting of only one person are called "single-person households." A "family household" is defined as a group of two or more persons living together who are related by birth, marriage, or adoption. Nonfamily households include single-person households and house-holds with two or more persons who are not related. Exhibit 1.3a shows that in 2000, 68 per-cent of all households were family households and 32 percent were nonfamily households.

Understanding the differences among such units of analysis as households, families, and married-couple families is crucial for using and interpreting social science data. Findings can look very different depending on which one is used. Take, for example, median annual in-come. (Incidentally, the median is the midpoint in a distribution of values arranged from lowest to highest. It's the point below and above which 50% of the incomes fall.) Using household as the unit of analysis, Exhibit 1.3b shows that the median income in 1998 was $38,885. If the unit of analysis is families, the median income was $47,469, and if you are looking at married couples, it was $54,276. Notice how significantly your choice of unit of analysis impacts the conclusions you draw about the economic well-being of families.

Consider another example of how findings can be affected by the methods researchers use to collect information: the simple wording of a question on a survey. Socially and politi-cally sensitive words such as "pro-life" or "welfare" can bias the way people respond to ques-tions. In 1998 the General Social Survey asked respondents the following question: "Are we spending too much money, too little money, or about the right amount on assistance to the poor?" Nearly two-thirds of the respondents said we spend too little. But look at Exhibit 1.3c to see what happens when these same respondents were asked whether we are spending too much, too little, or about the right amount on *welfare*, which is assistance to the poor. Here, only 17 percent said we spend too little. If public opinion is an important determinant of which policies are enacted, the wording of one question can have an enormous impact on people's lives.

The point here is not that you should have little faith in statistics or that statistics are misleading. Rather, you must be careful to understand who or what was studied and how before you can make meaningful interpretations and comparisons. Often research reported in the media or on the Internet fail to provide details about the unit of analysis or other de-tails of the research, leading to questionable interpretations.

Thinking Critically About the Statistics

1. If you look at Exhibit 1.3a, you can see that the largest category of households is "Mar-ried Couple." Within that category, what different types of families might you find? What does the lack of specificity imply about using households rather than families as the unit of analysis?

2. Have you ever heard the expression "lying with statistics"? Explain how the informa-tion in Exhibit 1.3a could be used to tell two opposite stories about "family values" in the United States today.

3. Exhibit 1.3b shows median annual income based on what is supposed to have been a survey of the entire population of the United States. If it were truly a survey of the en-tire population, you could have a lot of faith in the numbers. But, as census critics have noted, some groups in the U.S. population are likely to be undercounted in any census. Who do you think they are? How do you think the median annual incomes for the three groups shown in Exhibit 1.3b would change if these undercounted groups were included?

4. What do you think the data in Exhibit 1.3c really indicate? What would the U.S. popu-lation really like to do about the poor? How might the results of the surveys change if

EXHIBIT 1.3

How Social Research Affects Public Opinion and Policy

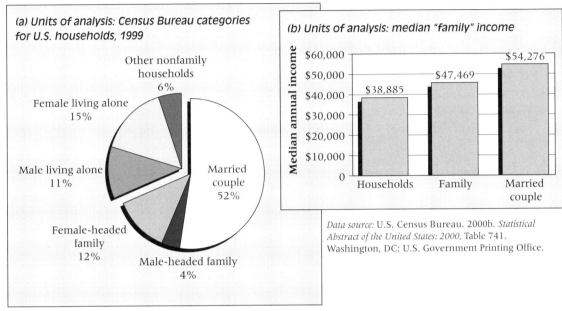

(a) *Units of analysis: Census Bureau categories for U.S. households, 1999*

(b) *Units of analysis: median "family" income*

Data source: U.S. Census Bureau. 2000b. *Statistical Abstract of the United States: 2000,* Table 741. Washington, DC: U.S. Government Printing Office.

Data source: Simmons, T., & O'Neill, G. 2001. *Households and Families: 2000. Census 2000 Brief.* Available at www.census.gov/prod/2001pubs/c2kbr01-8.pdf. Accessed November 30, 2001.

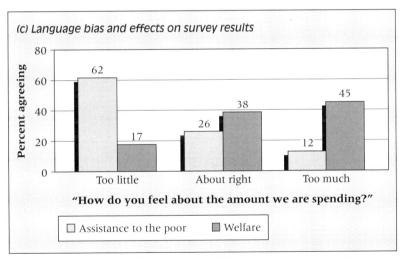

(c) *Language bias and effects on survey results*

"How do you feel about the amount we are spending?"

☐ Assistance to the poor   ■ Welfare

Data source: National Opinion Research Center. 1998. *General Social Survey.* Available at www.icpsr.umich.edu/GSS/. Accessed June 1, 2001.

the entire population of the United States were actually surveyed? In other words, how is the sample likely to be unrepresentative? Keep in mind that the General Social Survey, although administered to a large and carefully selected sample, reflects the individual views of fewer people than the U.S. Census.

Family Privacy and Research Ethics

To produce trustworthy information, researchers must choose an appropriate research method, focus on appropriate units of analysis, select a representative sample, design valid indicators, and avoid incorporating personal biases and interests. They must also take seriously the ethical dilemmas posed by their research. Because most social research represents an intrusion into people's lives, it can disrupt their ordinary activities and often requires them to reveal personal information about themselves. Research on families often deals with sensitive topics and activities. And the most compelling and interesting elements of family life occur beyond the watchful eyes of others. Most sexual acts, for instance, occur in the privacy of the home and aren't amenable to observation. Indeed, unless the researcher uses a hidden camera, the very fact of observing people changes the nature of the phenomenon being studied. Private family life immediately ceases to be private once people are aware that they are being studied.

See Issue 3 for more on the difficulties of family research given the value of family privacy in this society.

Even paper-and-pencil surveys sometimes involve the disclosure of very personal information—such as sexual satisfaction or marital conflict—that can be embarrassing or damaging to the self-esteem of subjects. To a person who has just lost his or her job, answering a simple question such as "What is your annual income?" can be a devastating admission of failure.

Sociologist Christopher Carrington (1999) discovered the sensitivity of social research on families when he studied how lesbian and gay families organize the details of their everyday life. He was particularly interested in how household tasks were divided up within these families. To Carrington's surprise, he discovered that he had actually been the catalyst for at least one long-term relationship breaking up. Here's Carrington's account:

> Several months after these interviews I ran into Richard at the gym. . . . He . . . reported that he and Joe had broken up, and that I was part of the reason. He said he wanted to thank me for helping him to get out of his relationship. I felt perplexed, guilty, mortified. Here is . . . what transpired that day at the gym:
>
> *CC*: I am very sorry; I certainly didn't intend any harm.
>
> *Richard*: Oh, it's okay; it's not really about you, but what you helped me learn about myself.
>
> *CC*: What do you mean?
>
> *Richard*: Well, that interview helped me realize just how much I actually do, and did, for that jerk.
>
> *CC*: Like what are you thinking of?
>
> *Richard*: Well, like all those questions about going out and buying things for the house. You know, I did all of that. . . . The interview made it so clear just how much I had taken for granted. I actually sat down and wrote a list up, thinking of the things that you asked about. . . . I confronted him with it, but he basically thinks those things are my interests, and if I want to do them, that's all about me. Well, I knew I had to get out, and find someone else who appreciates me more. (quoted in Carrington, 1999, pp. 181–182)

Such is the risk we take when we attempt to peer into the private lives of families in order to explain them.

Family researchers, therefore, must take special care to balance the risks posed to participants with the benefits to society of studying something everyone has an interest in: the intimate aspects of family life (Bussell, 1994). Family researchers must try to protect the rights of subjects and minimize the amount of harm or disruption they may experience from being part of a study. Most researchers agree that no one should be forced to participate in research, that those who do participate ought to be fully informed of the possible risks involved, and that every precaution ought to be taken to protect the confidentiality and anonymity of subjects.

Sometimes the desire to secure the most accurate information possible conflicts more directly with ethical considerations. Consider sociologist Laud Humphreys' 1970 study called *The Tearoom Trade*, a study many sociologists found ethically indefensible. Humphreys was interested in studying anonymous and casual homosexual encounters among strangers. He decided to study such interactions in "tearooms"—places, such as public restrooms, where male homosexuals used to go for anonymous sex before the AIDS epidemic significantly curtailed such activity. Because of the secretive and potentially stigmatizing nature of the phenomenon he was interested in, Humphreys couldn't just come right out and ask people about their actions, nor could he openly observe them. So he decided to pose as a lookout, called a "watchqueen," whose job was to warn of intruders as homosexual men engaged in sexual acts in public restrooms. By misrepresenting his identity, Humphreys was able to conduct very detailed field observations of these encounters.

But he also wanted to know about the regular lives of these men. Whenever possible he wrote down the license numbers of the participants' cars and tracked down their names and addresses with the help of a friend in the local police department. About a year later he arranged for these individuals to be part of a simple medical survey being conducted by some of his colleagues. He then disguised himself and visited their homes, supposedly to conduct interviews for the medical survey. He found that most of the men were heterosexual, had families, and were rather respected members of their communities. In short, they led altogether conventional lives.

Although this information shed a great deal of light on the nature of anonymous homosexual acts, some critics argued that Humphreys had violated the ethics of research by deceiving his unsuspecting subjects and violating their privacy rights. Others, however, supported Humphreys, arguing that he could have studied this topic in no other way. In fact, his book won a prestigious award. But more than 30 years later, the ethical controversy surrounding this study persists.

In sum, despite all the potential problems, social research remains an effective and efficient way of providing us with information about families. We just have to be careful and critical consumers of such information, questioning how and from whom it was collected.

Conclusion

We hope you now have a good sense of what family research is, how it relates to theory, how it is done, and what some of its potential pitfalls are. The development of a body of knowledge about families depends on solid research techniques.

Most people learn about the findings of family research not by studying scholarly journals but by reading or hearing others' interpretations of such research. These presentations typically reduce complex statistical findings into brief, easily digested summaries. In the process, much of the information people need to judge the validity of the conclusions (sample, method, indicators, and so on) is left out. Thus you must maintain a healthy skepticism and critically examine the family claims made by social critics, politicians, pundits, talk show hosts, and Web sites. But you must also employ your critical faculties when you do study scholarly journals, because even the most objective scholars are human beings subject to inadvertent blind spots and biases.

Chapter Highlights

- To some degree, everyone is an expert on families. That expertise is based on personal experiences with their own families. However, such information is inevitably biased and idiosyncratic. Systematic social scientific research provides a more sophisticated understanding of family experiences and patterns.
- Sociological research is grounded in a handful of theoretical perspectives: sociobiology, structural functionalism, the conflict perspective, social exchange theory, and symbolic interactionism. Each perspective has something to offer in the effort to understand families and the institution of family; each has shortcomings.
- Sociologists provide useful information about families through a variety of research techniques: experiments, field research, surveys, and unobtrusive research.
- Although systematic research is more trustworthy than informal observation, you still must be a careful consumer of published research information about families. The nature of the people being studied, the way certain phenomena are measured, and the values and interests of the researcher can all skew the results of a study, rendering beliefs about family life inaccurate.

Your Turn

In this chapter we have outlined some of the basic ways sociologists go about understanding families—from the theories that shape their thinking to the methods they use to collect data. One of the key themes has been that you can be an informed consumer of sociological information on families even if you are not a trained researcher. You just need to understand the ways that research can be biased.

Over the span of 2 weeks, collect all the articles you can find in newspapers, weekly news magazines, and news-oriented Web sites that deal with some aspect of families. (You can expand your comparisons by including an assessment of coverage on local and national television news shows.) Try to examine a local source as well as a major national source (*USA Today*, the *New York Times*, the *Washington Post*). Pay particular attention to the information that is presented in these articles as "fact" (census statistics, academic research findings, informal interview results, and so on). How are these "facts" presented? Do the authors provide any information about the way the "facts" were collected or the way subjects were recruited? Does a particular theoretical framework or political ideology seem to guide the article? What is missing from the account that would have allowed a more comprehensive understanding of the "facts" that were presented?

Was a particular event (for instance, a high-profile divorce or custody case) covered in all the sources you looked at? If so, how did their coverage of this event differ? That is, did news magazines or Web sites cover it differently from newspapers or news shows on TV? How did local coverage differ from national coverage? How can you explain the differences you've identified?

What can you conclude about the "trustworthiness" of family information as presented in the popular media? Are some sources more "objective" than others? How do you think this coverage affects the public's "knowledge" of families?

Gender and Families

What Are Girls and Boys Made Of?

We commonly think of the sex categories "male" and "female" as stable, universal, and unchanging. We take for granted that there are two and only two sexes—what sociologists call the "sexual dichotomy." Our entire society is organized around this principle. On closer inspection, however, things are not so straightforward.

In the early 1950s, George Jorgensen was in the U.S. Army.

After his discharge from the Army, George traveled to Copenhagen, Denmark, changed his name to Christine, and made modern medical history by undergoing the first documented sex change operation. Note how Christine's clothing, makeup, hair, and smile convey traditional femininity in the above photo. These visible changes—perhaps more than the surgical sex change—turned George into Christine. We have to rely on such cues to determine sex, because anatomical indicators are generally hidden or invisible.

Do people like Christine Jorgensen threaten or support the sexual dichotomy?

What makes things even more complicated is that sex—a person's biological maleness or femaleness—is different from gender—the behaviors, attributes, and expectations associated with being male or female that we must learn from others. We can see traditional gender images all around us, especially in the cultural events that glorify masculinity and femininity.

 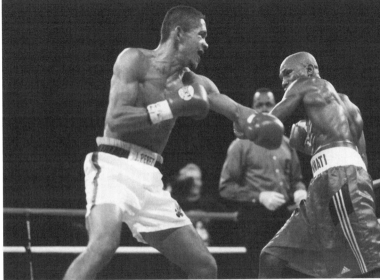

Unlike sex, which is harder (but not impossible) to change, individuals can intentionally manipulate gender. The classic example is the cross-dresser. The beauty queen in the photo is actually a man—20-year-old Chanya Moranon, who was crowned Miss Tiffany's 2000 in Thailand's Miss Transvestite Pageant. "Success" in the pageant depends on looking and acting the part, what sociologists refer to as "doing gender." It's not enough that Chanya dress like a woman, he must also behave in ways that are clearly feminine. The same is true in everyday life for everyone. Labels—"sissy" (for effeminate males) or "tomboy" (for females with masculine ways)—await those who are viewed as acting inappropriately.

From a very young age, children learn how to behave in accordance with gender expectations. Traditional toys not only teach acceptable skills, but they also serve as a sign of gender. We can more easily recognize this individual as a girl—despite somewhat ambiguous hair and clothing—because she is playing with a Barbie doll.

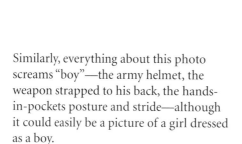

Similarly, everything about this photo screams "boy"—the army helmet, the weapon strapped to his back, the hands-in-pockets posture and stride—although it could easily be a picture of a girl dressed as a boy.

Given the pervasiveness of these early gender lessons, do you think parents can raise their children without emphasizing gender?

Is a "nongendered" childhood desirable?

For individuals who act in ways that violate gender expectations, doing gender is even more urgent and necessary. The women shown here may have huge biceps, rock-hard pectoral muscles, and washboard stomachs, but their feminine bikinis, hairstyles, and smiles serve to eliminate any gender confusion.

Do you think it is more difficult for men to present themselves in feminine ways or for women to present themselves in masculine ways?

Why do you suppose they have more trouble violating gender expectations?

Lisen Stromberg is the mother of a healthy 3-year-old boy. He likes to play soccer and can already hit a baseball out of the backyard. He also likes "girls'" toys and activities. To him, such interests are perfectly normal and unremarkable. Other people, however, have a much different view:

> My son is a cross-dresser. Most mornings he gets up, puts on a hand-me-down dress, wraps an old pillowcase around his head with a ribbon (to create his "long blond hair"), and prances around singing "The hills are alive with the sound of music." . . . At the toy store, he does not want a Batman doll. "I want Batgirl," he cries. When he begs to play with his friend Margo, it is because she has an extensive collection of Barbie dolls and outfits in which he can dress them. . . . His grandmother received the shock of her life when she went to pick him up at preschool one day and he was wearing a blue tutu with beaded gold slippers. . . . "Boys should be playing baseball, not Barbie," my mother-in-law exclaims. . . . Strangers ask, "So when do you think he will grow out of it?" and "How does your husband feel?" (Stromberg, 1999, pp. 42–43)

Daphne Scholinski was a tough kid who got into a fair amount of trouble during her childhood and adolescence. But what got her into the most trouble—3 years under psychiatric observation in three different mental hospitals—was that she refused to act like a girl. A psychiatrist diagnosed her as having "gender identity disorder," and told her that she "wasn't an appropriate female, that [she] didn't act the way a female was supposed to act" (Scholinski, 1997, p. 30).

> I didn't mind being called a delinquent, a truant, a hard kid who smoked and drank and ran around with a knife in her sock. But I didn't want to be called something I wasn't. Gender screwup or whatever wasn't cool. He was calling me a freak. I knew I walked tough and sat with my legs apart and did not defer to men, but I was a girl in the only way I knew how to be one. (p. 30)
>
> The [psychiatric] staff was under orders to scrutinize my femininity: the way I walked, the way I sat with my ankle on my knee, the clothes I wore, the way I kept my hair. Trivial matters, one might say, but trivial matters in which the soul reveals itself. Try changing these things. Try it. Wear an outfit that is utterly foreign—a narrow skirt when what you prefer is a loose shift of a dress. Torn-up black jeans when what you like are pin-striped wool trousers. See how far you can contradict your nature. Feel how your soul rebels. (Scholinski, 1997, p. 29)

In 2000, 6-year-old Aurora Lipscomb was removed from the custody of her parents, Paul and Sherry Lipscomb, by an Ohio children's services agency. The agency cited concern for the child's welfare as the reason the child was taken from her parents. The parents say they love their Aurora and claim they lost custody simply because they had refused to force her to conform to tight gender stereotypes. You see, Aurora was actually born "Zachary" Lipscomb, a biological male. But from the age of 2, the parents raised the child as a female. They noticed early on that Zachary preferred feminine toys, clothes, shoes, and activities. Zachary claimed repeatedly to be a girl and soon announced that her name was Aurora. After years of therapy, which did not "correct" her condition, Aurora, like Daphne Scholinski, was officially diagnosed with gender identity disorder. Nonetheless, the parents decided to enroll her in first grade as a girl. But less than two weeks after school started, the county removed her from her home and placed her in foster care ("Ohio court removes child from parents because of her gender," 2000).

In all three of these cases you can see the social importance of gender. Here are three physically healthy people who contradict widely held gender expectations and therefore exasperate their families, suffer humiliation and ridicule, and end up labeled ill or deprived.

As you will see, everything about people—tastes and desires, intimate relationships, health and well-being, career choices, all behavior—is "gendered," or affected by gender. In turn, the way you are treated by others is shaped by their beliefs about gender (Howard & Hollander, 1997). This chapter focuses on how individuals become gendered and act out gender roles. You'll also see how beliefs about gender shape people's status within families, giving some people more power than others simply on the basis of their gender.

Sex and Gender

Before we examine the role of gender in family life, it is important to distinguish between two important concepts: sex and gender. **Sex** is typically used to refer to a person's biological maleness or femaleness: chromosomes (XX for female, XY for male), sex glands (ovaries and testes), hormones (estrogen and testosterone), internal sex organs (uterus and prostate gland), external genitalia (clitoris and penis), reproductive capacities (pregnancy and impregnation), germ cells produced (ova and sperm), and secondary sex characteristics (shape of hips and breasts, amount of facial hair, and pitch of the voice). **Gender**, in contrast, designates psychological, social, and cultural aspects of maleness and femaleness— that is, masculinity and femininity (Kessler & McKenna, 1978).

Most people view sex as synonymous with gender, assuming that individuals born as biological males will be masculine and those categorized as biological females will be feminine. But as the three case studies at the beginning of this chapter illustrate, things aren't always so straightforward. Although there usually is consistency between sex and gender, one doesn't always determine the other. Thus it is important to think about these concepts as different, though related. Distinguishing between sex and gender allows us to understand with greater clarity the complexity of these concepts and how they interact. It also reminds us that male–female differences in behavior need not spring automatically from biological differences (Lips, 1993).

The Ambiguity of Sex

The relationship between sex and gender is further complicated by the fact that a person's sex is not always as clear-cut as you might think. Most people take for granted that the two sex categories (male and female) are universal (that is, found everywhere), exhaustive (that is, there's no third sex), and mutually exclusive (that is, a person cannot be both simultaneously, or neither). Yet some people are born with features that place them somewhere between male and female, and some are surgically altered to acquire different sex characteristics from those they were born with.

Male, Female, and Other Sexes   The biological "fact" that there are two and only two sexes may seem self-evident, but not every society subscribes to it. For instance, the hijras in India are neither men nor women. They are born as men, but they live as women—dressing, standing, walking, and sitting as women. They undergo an operation in which their genitals are surgically removed, but this transforms them into hijras, not women. There are many figures in Hindu mythology that are neither male nor female; hence traditional Indian culture not only accommodated the hijras but viewed them as meaningful, even powerful beings (Nanda, 1990). As Western ideas about sex and gender seep into Indian culture, however, the hijras have become increasingly marginalized.

In traditional Navajo culture, one could be male, female, or nadle—a third sex assigned to those whose sex-typed anatomic characteristics were unclear at birth (Martin & Voorhies, 1975). Physically normal individuals also had the opportunity to choose to become nadle if they so desired. Nadle were allowed to perform the tasks of both men and women.

Even in this society, the male/female categorization is not always sufficient. Hermaphrodites (or intersexuals), for instance, are individuals in whom sexual differentiation is either incomplete or ambiguous. They may have the chromosomal pattern of a female but have the external genitalia of a male, or they may have both ovaries and testicles. These individuals don't fall neatly into either sex category. Indeed, according to one prominent biologist, Anne Fausto-Sterling, the existence of intersexuals means that instead of two sexes, people have many gradations of sex running from female to male, and along this spectrum lie at least five sexes (Fausto-Sterling, 1993). In addition to males and females, Fausto-Sterling argues there are "true hermaphrodites," people who possess one testis and one ovary; "male pseudohermaphrodites," people who have testes and some aspects of female genitalia but no ovaries; and "female pseudohermaphrodites," people who have ovaries and some aspects of male genitalia but no testes. Indeed, experts estimate that for every 1,000 babies born, 17 are intersexual in some way—falling between unambiguous males and unambiguous females on the sex continuum (Fausto-Sterling, 2000).

The Sex "Reassignment" Controversy   Debate over clinical responses to cases of babies with "ambiguous genitalia" has become more heated recently. In 1973, researchers published an account of an infant boy whose penis had been accidentally cut off by a surgeon who was trying to repair a fused foreskin. Convinced that a boy couldn't adjust to the loss, doctors recommended to the parents that he be reared as a girl even though he had a twin brother. The parents agreed.

The infant's testicles were removed, and a preliminary attempt to construct a vagina was made. The parents treated their genetically male child as a daughter, choosing feminine clothes, toys, and activities. The child appeared to have accepted the new identity and to be content with life as a female. The case was publicized worldwide and entered the scholarly literature as proof that sexual identification has more to do with socialization and exposure to the cultural world of boys and girls than with anatomy or genetics.

In 1997, however, a follow-up study refuted the initial reports of glowing success. The authors reexamined the child's life through adolescence and into adulthood and concluded that the female identity never took. During the elementary school years, the child tore off dresses, rejected dolls, and sought out male friends. Instead of imitating her mother putting on makeup, she mimicked her father shaving. At age 12, she began receiving estrogen treatments so that breasts would grow during puberty, but she disliked the effects and stopped taking treatments. At age 14 she renounced her female identity and chose to live as a man, even undergoing surgery to attempt a reconstruction of the male genitalia. At 25 "he" married a woman and adopted children (cited in Angier, 1997b).

The researchers used this information to underscore the importance of prenatal events such as exposure to hormones in building sexual identity. An editorial accompanying their report stated, "Despite everyone telling him constantly that he was a girl and despite his being treated with female hormones, his brain knew he was a male. It refused to take on what it was being told" (quoted in Angier, 1997b, p. A10). Indeed, according to his twin brother, "There was nothing feminine about [her]. She walked like a guy. She talked about guy things, didn't [care] about cleaning house, getting married, wearing makeup. . . . We both wanted to play with guys, build forts and have snowball fights and play army" (quoted in Colapinto, 1997, pp. 64–65).

This case study is being used to call for changes in the treatment of babies born with ambiguous genitalia. Every month dozens of sexually ambiguous newborns are "assigned" a sex and undergo surgery to confirm the designation (Cowley, 1997). About 90 percent of such infants are designated female, because creating a vagina is considered surgically easier than creating a penis (Angier, 1997a). But the authors of this case study proposed that many of these "constructed females" may not be happy with their enforced identity and may be better off being reared as boys.

What makes these cases even more complex is that success in sex (re)assignment has been defined as living in that sex as a heterosexual. But just as it's possible for persons born with unambiguous sex to vary in sexual preference, so too can intersexuals. Max Beck, for instance, was born intersexual and surgically assigned and raised as a female. In her twenties she married a man, and appeared to have successfully made the transition to being a woman. But within a few years, Beck came out as a lesbian, changed to a man, married his lesbian partner, and became a father (Fausto-Sterling, 2000).

In addition to the social and personal complexities facing intersexuals, many of the surgical techniques used to "correct" the problem of ambiguous genitalia are mutilating and potentially harmful. Critics cite cases of people being robbed of any sexual sensation in the attempt to surgically "normalize" them—that is, give them the physical appearance of either a male or a female. They fear that cases such as the ones described earlier will motivate doctors to simply treat more intersexuals as males and try to construct a penis from a small amount of tissue—not to reduce surgical interventions. The founder of the Intersex Society of North America eloquently summed up her organization's frustration: "They can't conceive of leaving someone alone" (quoted in Angier, 1997b, p. A10).

The medical profession can't leave these individuals alone because to do so would undermine the cultural understanding of sex. Drastic surgical intervention is undertaken not because the infant's life is threatened but because the entire social structure is organized around having two and only two sexes (Lorber, 1989). Biologists usually define cases of hermaphroditism as some variation on the two existing categories, not as a third, fourth, or fifth category unto itself. On the diagnosis, a decision is always made to define the child as either male or female. To suggest that the labels "male" and "female" are not sufficient to categorize everyone is to threaten a basic organizing principle of social life.

The Link Between Sex and Gender

Sex categorization is also culturally important because it marks the beginning of gender construction (Lorber, 1994). As soon as a sex is assigned to an infant, gendered names and dress are assigned as well so that gender becomes apparent. Without knowledge of an individual's gender, interactions can be awkward and confusing. The skit on *Saturday Night Live* in the 1990s portraying "Pat," the character whose gender was ambiguous, poked fun at the extremes to which people will go to properly assign gender when it's unclear. Until gender is assigned, people don't know how to act toward such individuals.

Once gender becomes known, however, others presume to know how to address and treat the individual. And the individual responds to this treatment, eventually coming to experience the world in a distinctly gendered way. According to sociologist Judith Lorber (1994), "Personality characteristics, feelings, motivations, and ambitions flow from these different life experiences so that the members of these different groups become different kinds of people" (p. 15).

New parents can be especially sensitive about the correct identification of their child's sex. Even parents who claim to consider sex and gender irrelevant nevertheless spend a great deal of time ensuring that their child has the culturally appropriate physical appearance of a boy or girl. This sensitivity is not surprising, given the centrality of sex and gender in this culture and people's distaste for ambiguity. Having someone misidentify the sex of their baby can be an embarrassing, even painful experience for some parents, which may explain why parents of a girl baby who has yet to grow hair (a visible sign of gender in this culture) often tape pink ribbons to the bald baby's head. In many Latin American countries, families have baby girls' ears pierced shortly after birth, providing an obvious visual indicator of the child's gender.

The significance of correctly identifying a child's sex and gender goes beyond embarrassment. Because culture is so gendered, if children's gender identities were mistaken "they would, quite literally, have changed places in their social world" (Lorber, 1994, p. 14). One of the most fascinating accounts of how different it might be to live as someone of another gender is provided by James/Jan Morris, a transsexual man-to-woman who experienced life as both genders during adulthood:

> Having . . . experienced life in both roles, there seems to me no aspect of existence, no moment of the day, no contact, no arrangement, no response, which is not different for men and women. The very tone of voice in which I was now addressed, the very posture of the person next in the queue, the very feel in the air when I entered a room or sat at a restaurant table, constantly emphasized my change of status.
>
> And if other's responses shifted, so did my own. The more I was treated as woman, the more woman I became. . . . If I was assumed to be incompetent at reversing cars, or opening bottles, oddly incompetent I found myself becoming. If a case was thought too heavy for me, inexplicably I found it so myself. . . . Men treated me more and more as junior, . . . and so, addressed every day of my life as an inferior, involuntarily, month by month I accepted the condition. (quoted in Lorber, 1994, pp. 29–30)

To most people, who don't have the opportunity to experience personally the difference that gender makes, the gendering process is so pervasive as to be virtually invisible (Lorber, 1994).

Cultural Variations in Gender   As something invented and defined by human beings, gender is, of course, more variable and malleable than sex, which is rooted in biology. What it means to be masculine or feminine has varied over time and from place to place. Although everyone in a particular culture shares certain gender stereotypes and expectations, these perceptions can and do differ by subgroup, depending on race, social class, sexual orientation, age, physical appearance, and so on. For instance, sociologist Noel Cazenave (1984) examined how notions of the "ideal man" vary. Comparing responses from his survey of middle-class black men to results from another survey of predominantly middle-class white men, he found that black men placed greater emphasis than whites on such things as being self-confident, competitive, successful at work, aggressive, warm and gentle, and protective of their family.

The most well-known research illustrating variations in conceptions of masculinity and femininity was conducted by the anthropologist Margaret Mead (1963). Mead studied three cultures in New Guinea in the 1930s. Among the mountain-dwelling Arapesh, men and women displayed similar attitudes and actions. They showed traits people in the United States would commonly associate with femininity: cooperation, passivity, and sensitivity to others. Mead described both men and women as being "maternal." These characteristics were linked to broader cultural beliefs about people's relationship to the environment. The Arapesh didn't have any conception of "ownership" of land, so they never had conflicts over possession of property.

South of the Arapesh were the Mundugumor, a group of cannibals and headhunters. Here, too, males and females were similar. However, both displayed traits that we in the West would associate with masculinity: assertiveness, emotional inexpressiveness, insensitivity to others. Women, according to Mead, were just as violent, just as aggressive, and just as jealous as men. Both were equally virile, without any of the "soft" characteristics we associate with femininity.

Finally, there were the Tchambuli. This group did distinguish between male and female traits. However, their gender expectations were the opposite of ours: Women were dominant, shrewd, assertive, and managerial; men were submissive, emotional, and seen as inherently delicate.

More recently, anthropologists have examined societies where women have significant power and stature. For instance, among the Agta Negritos of northeastern Luzon in the Philippines, women participate in all the subsistence activities men do, including hunting, fishing, and bartering. Consequently they have considerable authority over decision making in the family (Estioko-Griffin & Griffin, 1997). In some regions of Ghana, trade of local food crops in central markets is dominated by women, who are expected to financially support their husbands and children (Clark, 1994).

Studies such as these are important because they show that definitions of masculinity and femininity vary from culture to culture. Women need not be the passive nurturers of children; men need not be the aggressors and breadwinners. Gender expectations are strongly shaped by the social context. For instance, some studies show that when women are rewarded for behaving aggressively, they are just as violent as men (Hyde, 1984). Similarly, some research has found that female athletes often act in stereotypically masculine ways while competing—pushing, shoving, sweating, and using profanity (Watson, 1987). Women can and do act in distinctly nonfeminine ways when the circumstances call for it (and sometimes when they don't).

Gender as a Social Construct   It should be clear by now that sex and gender are separate concepts. When people confuse sex and gender, they all too easily assume that masculine and feminine social roles are inherent, biological phenomena and therefore natural and unchangeable. This assumption overlooks extensive similarities between the sexes and extensive variation within each sex. For most personality and behavioral characteristics, the distribution of men and women generally overlaps. For instance, men as a group do tend to be more aggressive than women. Yet some women are much more aggressive than the average man, and some men are much less aggressive than the average woman. Indeed, social circumstances may have a greater impact on aggressive behavior than any innate, biological traits.

Take as an example one well-established biological sex difference: height. Although men tend to be taller than women, many men are shorter than some women. If biological sex differences such as height explained gender differences, you would expect men to have an advantage in occupations where being tall matters and women to have an advantage in occupations where shortness matters. Of course, there are not many occupations in contemporary society where height is a major factor, with the possible exception of basketball players and horse-racing jockeys. For jockeys, shortness is crucial, which might lead you to conclude that the occupation would be dominated by women. But in fact the opposite is true. From 1875 to 1998, only five women jockeys raced in the prestigious Kentucky Derby ("Derby Connections," 2001"). Women were not even admitted into professional horse racing until 1969. The reason is not biological but rather social: a tendency to assume that sex determines appropriate roles for each gender.

See Issue 2 for a glimpse of changing gender expectations throughout U.S. history.

The assumption that gender differences are natural, as biological sex differences are often assumed to be, also overlooks the fact that gender expectations change. In just the past few decades, for example, it has become more socially acceptable for women to be assertive and ambitious. If such traits were purely biological, they would not have become more prevalent so rapidly. Human genetics evolve on a millennial scale, not within a generation or two. Furthermore, the reliance on biology to explain gender differences overlooks the wide cultural and historical variation in conceptions of masculinity and femininity.

Nevertheless, as long as people continue to believe that gender-linked roles and societal contributions are determined by nature, they will continue to accept sexual inequality in occupational, political, and family life. It's easier to justify women's low wages in the workplace if one assumes women are naturally less ambitious and competitive than men. And it's easier to justify awarding child custody to divorcing mothers, leaving fathers estranged from their children, so long as women are thought to be naturally better at child rearing.

Suggesting that gender is socially, not biologically, based does not dismiss the possibility that biological influences on gender exist. Indeed, the studies on intersexuals that we discussed earlier point to biological influences on behavior. But remember that even sex differences that are, in fact, biological (for instance, hormonal) aren't completely free from societal influence. A society can decide which differences ought to be amplified and which should be ignored.

Learning Gender

Both boys and girls learn at a very young age to adopt gender as an organizing principle for themselves and the social world in which they live (Howard & Hollander, 1997). They begin to distinguish the female role from the male role, learn to see a broad range of activities as exclusively "appropriate" for only one gender or the other, and come to identify themselves accordingly. Most developmental psychologists believe that by age 3 or so most children can accurately answer the question "Are you a boy or a girl?" (Kohlberg, 1966). But to a very young child, being a boy or a girl means no more than being named Jason instead of Jennifer. It is simply another characteristic, like having brown hair or ten fingers. The child at this age has no conception that gender is a category into which every human can be placed (Kessler & McKenna, 1978).

At around age 5 the child begins to see gender as an invariant characteristic of the social world—something that is fixed and permanent. Likewise, children exhibit a high degree of gender typing in their preferences for particular activities (Kohlberg, 1966). Children at this age express statements such as "Men are doctors" and "Women are nurses" as inflexible, objective "truths." Only later are they able to realize that gender roles are more flexible than they once believed.

Gender Differentiation in Childhood

How do children come to understand their gender in a way that is consistent with larger cultural dictates? As you've already seen, the gender differentiation process begins the moment a child is born. A physician, nurse, or midwife immediately starts that infant on a career as a male or female by authoritatively declaring whether it is a boy or girl. It's still common in many hospitals for infant boys to be wrapped in blue blankets and infant girls in pink ones. From that point on, the developmental paths of males and females diverge. The subsequent messages that children receive from families, books, television, and schools not only teach and reinforce gender expectations but also influence the formation of children's self-concepts. This process of gendering is especially powerful because it is supported by religion, law, science, and the society's entire set of values (Lorber, 1994).

Parents, siblings, and other significant people in the child's immediate environment provide these early lessons of gender. Often these individuals serve as models with whom the child can identify and whom the child can ultimately imitate. Other times the lessons are more purposive and direct—as when parents provide their children with explicit instructions on proper gender behavior, such as "Big boys don't cry" or "Act like a young lady."

Evidence suggests that the instructions for boys are particularly rigid and restrictive in this culture and the social costs for their gender-inappropriate behavior are disproportionately severe (Franklin, 1988). The "sissy" has much more difficulty during childhood than the "tomboy." This difference clearly indicates how this society ranks the relative value of men and women.

Typically, parents are their children's first source of information about gender. If you asked parents whether they treated sons any differently from daughters, most would probably say no. Yet considerable evidence shows that what parents do and what they say they do are two different things (Lips, 1993; Lytton & Romney, 1991; Renzetti & Curran, 1989). Gender-typed expectations are so ingrained in American parents that they are often unaware that they are behaving in accordance with them (Goldberg & Lewis, 1969; Will, Self, & Datan, 1976).

In one early study, when thirty first-time parents were asked to describe their newborn infants (less than 24 hours old), they frequently used common gender stereotypes. Those with daughters described them as "tiny," "soft," "fine-featured," and "delicate." Sons were seen as "strong," "alert," "hardy," and "coordinated" (Rubin, Provenzano, & Luria, 1974). A replication of this study 2 decades later found that parents continue to perceive their infants in gender-stereotyped ways, although to a lesser degree than in the 1970s. In addition, mothers are more emotionally responsive to girls and encourage more independence with boys. Fathers spend more time with their sons and engage in more physical play than with their daughters (Karraker, Vogel, & Lake, 1995). Parents also use subtle differences in tone of voice and pet names for their female and male children, such as "Sweetie" for girls and "Tiger" for boys (MacDonald & Parke, 1986; Tauber, 1979).

As children grow older, parents tend to encourage increasingly gender-typed activities. Research consistently shows that children's household tasks differ along gender lines (Antill, Goodnow, Russell, & Cotton, 1996). For instance, boys are more likely to mow the lawn, shovel snow, take out the garbage, and do the yardwork, whereas girls tend to clean the house, wash dishes, cook, and babysit the younger children (White & Brinkerhoff, 1981).

Parents also influence their children's gender through the things they routinely purchase for them, such as clothing. Not only do clothes inform others about the sex of an individual, they also send messages about how that person ought to be treated. Clothes direct behavior along traditional gender lines (Martin, 1998) and encourage or discourage certain gender-typed actions. Even very young girls understand that some behavior is not appropriate when in a dress. Consider the following scene at a children's preschool with a group of 5-year-old girls:

> Four girls are sitting at a table—Cathy, Kim, Danielle, and Jesse. They are cutting play money out of paper. Cathy and Danielle have on overalls, and Kim and Jesse have on dresses. Cathy puts her feet up on the table and crosses her legs at the ankle; she leans back in her chair and continues cutting her money. Danielle imitates her. They look at each other and laugh. They put their shoulders back, posturing, having fun with this new way of sitting. Kim and Jesse continue to cut and laugh with them, but do not put their feet up. (Martin, 1998, p. 498)

You can see that feminine dress and adornments restrict girls' movements, which leads them to take up less space with their bodies. Nor do dresses lend themselves easily to rough and dirty play. Likewise, it is difficult to walk quickly or assertively in high heels and skirts. Clothes for boys and men rarely restrict physical movement in this way.

Toys, too, serve to distinguish between the sexes. The toy industry has been built on a solid foundation of gender stereotypes. War toys, competitive games of strategy, and sports paraphernalia have been long-standing staples of the toy industry's boy market. The words *hero, warrior, battle,* and *speed* characterize boys' toys. Dolls, makeup kits, and toy kitchens continue to be profitable items for girls. The vocabulary of girls' toys consists of terms such as *nurturing, love,* and *magic* (Lawson, 1993). Boys' toys encourage invention, exploration, competition, and aggression. Girls' toys encourage creativity, caregiving, and physical attractiveness (C. L. Miller, 1987). Gender-specific toys foster different traits and skills in children and thereby further segregate the two sexes into different patterns of social development.

Androgynous Socialization

Many people today, concerned with the overemphasis on male–female distinctions and sex stereotyping, are pushing for less restrictive ideas about gender (Lips, 1993). This is not a new development. Even a generation or two ago, very few adults ranked "acting like a girl (or boy)" as a desirable trait for a child to have (see Exhibit 2.1).

To diminish gender distinctions, some people advocate **androgynous socialization**— bringing up children to have both male and female traits and behaviors (Bem, 1974). Advocates for androgynous socialization see no reason, except for a few anatomic and reproductive differences, to differentiate between what males and females can do.

Modern parents are probably more likely than their predecessors to be concerned about gender stereotypes and to attempt to overcome them in the raising of their children. Yet parents' ability to carry out androgynous socialization may be somewhat limited (Sedney, 1987). At 4 and 5 years old, children often engage in strongly gender-stereotypical play, regardless of the attitudes and beliefs expressed by their parents (O'Brien & Huston, 1985). In fact, sociologists have found that when with their peers even children raised in feminist households—where they are taught that men and women are equal and that no activity needs to be sex-linked—act in ways that are fairly gender stereotypical (Risman & Myers, 1997). Such findings have led some researchers to suggest that the effects of androgynous socialization are more likely to show up in adulthood rather than in childhood, after individuals have developed the cognitive maturity and the confidence to incorporate nontraditional gender attitudes and beliefs into their everyday lives (Sedney, 1987).

See Issue 3 for an overview of the conflict between societal interests and parents' right to raise their children as they see fit.

EXHIBIT 2.1

Desirable Traits in Children, 1972–1987

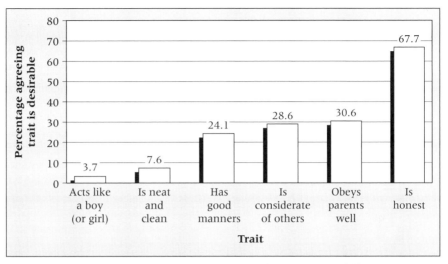

Data source: National Opinion Research Center. 1998. *General Social Survey.* Available at www.icpsr.umich.edu/GSS/. Accessed June 1, 2001.

But some sociologists question whether parents or anyone else has the ability to change such deeply ingrained lessons as gender roles (Lorber, 1994). Gender structures every organization and shapes every interaction in society, often in ways people are not consciously aware of. Individual parents may have little hope of seriously altering their children's understanding of gender. Remember the case of Aurora/Zachary, whose parents lost custody of their child because they failed to properly "gender" him/her? The efforts of some parents to break gender barriers can quickly be undermined by the larger society.

Doing Gender

Sociologists have come to understand gender as an accomplishment rather than an attribute of each individual (West & Zimmerman, 1987). In other words, gender isn't acquired in the sense that once it's learned, it's with that individual for a lifetime. True, young children acquire knowledge about gender through socialization and, in most cases, learn to display behaviors and attributes appropriate for their gender. But what they learn are the gender rules that allow them to be perceived as masculine or feminine. Simply having knowledge of these rules does not make a person feminine or masculine.

To accomplish that, people must "do gender" appropriately and continuously through everyday social interaction. How do people "do gender"? They do it by behaving in ways that are considered appropriate for their gender. For women, it means not acting in masculine ways (for example, not burping in public, sitting in a "ladylike" manner," paying attention to appearance, wearing makeup and jewelry). For men, it usually means not acting in ways that are typically defined as feminine, such as not overtly displaying certain emotions and not nurturing others, especially other adults.

Is it possible not to do gender? Not really. People might not do gender well or do it in culturally inappropriate ways, but if they try not to display or do gender at all, others will do it for them. For instance, sociologist Betsy Lucal (1999) describes what it's like to be a woman, identify as a woman, but be mistaken for a man because she doesn't bear the traditional markers of femininity:

> I am six feet tall and large-boned. I have had short hair for most of my life. . . . I do not wear dresses, skirts, high heels, or makeup. My only jewelry is a class ring, a "men's" watch (my wrists are too large for a "women's" watch), two small earrings (gold hoops, both in my left ear), and (occasionally) a necklace. I wear jeans or shorts, T-shirts, sweaters, polo/golf shirts, button-down collar shirts, and tennis shoes or boots. . . . I prefer baggy clothes, so the fact that I have "womanly" breasts often is not obvious. (pp. 786–787)
>
> Each day, I experience the consequences that our gender system has for my identity and interactions. I am a woman who has been called "Sir" so many times that I no longer even hesitate to assume that it is being directed at me. I am a woman whose use of public restrooms regularly causes reactions ranging from confused stares to confrontations over what a man is doing in the women's room. (p. 781)

According to Lucal, although she can choose not to "do" femininity, she cannot choose not to "do" gender. People she encounters always attribute one or the other gender; it just so happens they often make a misattribution. But for Lucal, as with most of us, gender is a significant part of her identity, and she is deeply embedded in the "gender system." Her failure to "do" femininity doesn't mean she's not a woman or that she doesn't want to be seen as a woman. Lucal writes,

> I am not to the point of personally abandoning gender. . . . I do not want people to see me as genderless as much as I want them to see me as a woman. . . . I would like to expand the category of "woman" to include people like me. . . . I do identity myself as a woman, not as a man or as someone outside of the two-and-only-two categories." (pp. 793–794)

Gender and Sexuality

It's important to realize that by "doing gender" people usually are also "doing heterosexuality." A gay student recently remarked that he "does gay" when he's with homosexual friends (for instance, he feels more free to touch and show affection toward men) but knows he must "do straight" among heterosexuals, in part for his own safety. To him, "doing straight" is the same thing as "doing masculinity." In this culture, being seen as heterosexual usually involves enacting fairly traditional gender roles.

When men or boys display "feminine" behaviors, they risk being labeled "sissy" or "faggot." Tommi Avicolli's (2000) powerful account of growing up as a "sissy" provides insight into how doing heterosexuality and doing gender merge:

> What did being a sissy really mean? . . . It means not being interested in sports, not playing football in the street after school; not discussing teams and scores and playoffs. And it involved not showing fervent interest in girls, not talking about scoring with tits or *Playboy* centerfolds. Not concealing naked women in your history book; or porno books in your locker. (p. 123)

Likewise, when women or girls act in typically masculine ways, they risk being labeled "lesbian." Perhaps their desire to avoid such labeling is one reason why women often feel the need to wear makeup in public (Dellinger & Williams, 1997) or why female athletes go to great lengths to act and appear very feminine when not competing (Watson, 1987). Presenting "appropriate" images of gender can also be of concern to larger organizations that cater to public tastes. In his field study of the Ladies' Professional Golf Association (LPGA), sociologist Todd Crosset (1997) found that conventional definitions of sport and gender, along with financial considerations, have forced the LPGA to actively try to counter what it calls its "image problem": the public's tendency to perceive female golfers as lesbians:

> The tour's promotion of itself is very similar to that of the annual Miss America contest—a simultaneous promotion of wholesomeness and sexuality. . . . It produces swimsuit pictorials . . . and consistently promotes the tour's most attractive players to the media and the general public. . . . The LPGA staff frequently produce articles that discuss the dilemmas faced by the mothers/wives on the tour. (p. 126)

Clearly, the way people do gender also conveys messages about their sexual orientation. If people do gender in ways deemed culturally acceptable, they're likely to be perceived as heterosexual. If they do gender in ways deemed culturally unacceptable, they may be perceived as gay or lesbian. And because being labeled homosexual still tends to be stigmatizing in this culture, most heterosexuals and many homosexuals prefer to conform to traditional gender expectations.

The Rewards of Doing Gender Well

To understand why people care so much about doing gender appropriately requires thinking about gender on both individual and cultural levels. On an individual level, people may do gender to experience the rewards and privileges that come from acting in ways consistent with society's gender expectations. For instance, by acting incompetent at housework—a characteristic typically associated with masculinity—a man may be able to get a female friend or partner to cook and clean for him. Women who wear makeup at work are more likely to be seen as heterosexual, healthy, and competent than women who do not (Dellinger & Williams, 1997). Both men and women who do gender well may find that they are more successful at attracting mates.

The way people do gender may also help them avoid hostile reactions, whether because of their own characteristics, as in Betsy Lucal's case, or because of the social context. For instance, doing gender can be difficult for men in predominantly female occupations, such as nursing, where their masculinity is likely to be questioned. In these cases, men may employ special strategies (such as emphasizing the tough, physical nature of their work) to accentuate their masculinity.

In other cases, an individual may lack the social or personal resources to do gender appropriately. Unemployed men, for example, especially those who perceive breadwinning as integral to their masculinity, face a difficult dilemma—how to seem masculine when circumstances don't allow them to do gender the way they think they should. Many unemployed men may resist doing housework or child care even more vehemently than they would if they were employed, to avoid further threats to their masculinity.

Disabled men also face the challenge of doing gender appropriately (Gerschick & Miller, 1997). Obviously, doing masculinity (which emphasizes physical strength and independence) can be difficult for someone in a wheelchair and dependent on others for even the most basic care. But even disabled men find ways to do gender. One individual, a 72-year-old quadriplegic who required around-the-clock care, remained "in control" and, at least in his mind, masculine, by becoming commanding and domineering:

> People know from . . . [the start] that I have my own thing, and I direct my own thing. And if they can't comply with my desire, they won't be around. . . . I don't see any reason why people with me can't take instructions and get my life on just as I was having it before, only thing I'm not doing it myself. I direct somebody else to do it. So, therefore, I don't miss out on very much. (quoted in Gerschick & Miller, 1997, p. 106)

On the individual level, there is often much to gain from being able to perform culturally prescribed roles well—not the least of which is recognition from others that you are a success at doing the gender you believe yourself to be. On a broader level, doing gender appropriately sustains and legitimizes the larger institution of gender (West & Zimmerman, 1987). Because just about every aspect of social life is gendered, collectively declining to do gender would involve dismantling and reorganizing how people work, relate, eat, parent, show emotions—everything. Further, by doing gender, people acquiesce in the view that gendered social arrangements are natural and normal. Differences between women and men that are created by this process can then be portrayed as fundamental and enduring traits. If, in doing gender, men are also doing dominance and women are doing deference, the resulting social order is perceived to reflect "natural differences." In the end, the "rewards" of doing gender well are that people reinforce and legitimate power arrangements between men and women both inside and outside the family (West & Zimmerman, 1987).

Gender and Power

In understanding families, gender is not just important because it is a key variable on which people's experiences and behaviors differ. It is also important for the privileges and ultimately the power it provides some people and not others. Feminist theorists argue that the problem with current gender arrangements is not just that males and females act or feel differently. The problem is that sex differences are perceived as gender differences, which then get translated into power differences:

> Females are born a little smaller than males. This difference is exaggerated by upbringing, so that women grow into adults who are less physically strong and competent than they could be. They are then excluded from a range of manual occupations and, by extension, from the control of technology. The effect spills over into everyday life: ultimately women have become dependent on men to change the wheel of a car, reglaze a broken window or replace a smashed roof slate. (quoted in Lorber, 1994, p. 49)

This author is talking about how gender differences can lead to female dependency in the workplace and in day-to-day activities. Power differences also exist within marriages and families. Not only are power differences important to understand because they shape men's and women's lives so profoundly, but doing so can also help you understand gender inequality within the larger context of a society or the world.

For our purposes, **power** can be defined as individuals' ability to impose their will on others (Lipman-Blumen, 1984). Power can be exercised by punishing (or threatening to punish) people or by rewarding them. Power is most obvious within families when members either achieve, over time, some sort of changes that they want (because they have the power to put them into effect) or are thwarted (because others are able to use their power to create obstacles) (Komter, 1989).

The key to understanding the distribution of power in families is not necessarily knowing who makes the most decisions but who gets to decide which decisions will be made. In addition, having the power to make trivial decisions is not the same as having power over the more important ones (Hood, 1983). Sociologists distinguish between *orchestration power*, making decisions about what will be done, and *implementation power*, making decisions about how it will get done (Safilios-Rothschild, 1976). If a wife decides the family will take a trip and tells her husband that he is to make all the decisions concerning travel arrangements and hotel accommodations, who really has the decision-making power? Although the amount of power that people have in their intimate relationships depends on a lot of personal and situational factors, gender has a considerable impact on power differences in contemporary couples.

Contemporary Power Relationships in Families

On the surface, you might assume that women hold tremendous power within their families because the private, family domain is so closely associated with women's roles. But studies of power within marriage reveal a different story. Sociological research has consistently shown that power imbalances are the rule rather than the exception in intimate and family relationships and that it is typically men, not women, who possess power. In a 1960 study, researchers noted that husbands tend to have more power over their wives than wives over husbands, particularly when wives are not employed outside the home (Blood & Wolfe, 1960).

Although power in contemporary couples is more equal, or egalitarian, than in the 1960s, subtle (and sometimes overt) power differences are still likely to be at work in contemporary marriages. In a recent study, researchers interviewed sixty-one married couples who had faced important work and family choices, to determine what factors influenced their decisions (Zvonkovic, Greaves, Schmiege, & Hall, 1996). Most of the decisions they had to make revolved around the adjustments the wife should make—namely, whether she should either increase or decrease the number of hours she spent at work. These issues were usually related to constraints (such as having a young child) or opportunities (children reaching an age where they could more easily look after themselves) that traditionally affect women. But when the decisions concerned the husband's job, the couples tended to focus on whether he ought to switch jobs rather than on changes in the amount of time he should spend at work instead of at home.

See Issue 4 for more information on how family obligations are divided by gender.

When the husband's job was the focus of attention, both partners tended to know what the other wanted, and both spouses tended to want the same thing from the decision. But when the decision revolved around the wife's job, there was significant disagreement about the most favorable outcome and a general lack of understanding of the other spouse's desires. For example, in one couple the wife enjoyed her part-time job and believed it had beneficial effects on her and on the marriage. Yet her husband viewed her job as just one in a series of rather unimportant temporary jobs. The researchers attributed this sort of disagreement and uncertainty to ambivalence about the wife's participation in the labor force in the first place.

Interestingly, most couples maintained that the decisions they made were "joint" or "mutual." In reality, however, most of the time the husband's preferences prevailed. Husbands' unspoken power over work and family decisions was reflected in one wife's description of how she and her husband make important decisions: "We usually talk and come to full agreement, or I give in and do what he wants on . . . [a] majority of things. I love him, and minor disagreements are a part of life" (quoted in Zvonkovic et al., 1996, p. 98).

See Issue 5 for insights into how fundamentalist Christian families accommodate and negotiate traditional gender roles.

Power differences within families are more clear-cut in some segments of U.S. society. In many fundamentalist Christian families, for instance, most family decisions are apparently made by the wife. But on closer inspection, you would find that she is simply implementing what her husband has delegated to her. Although she is in charge of the household and looks quite powerful, the husband typically claims final authority in decision making (Ammerman, 1987; Balswick & Balswick, 1995).

Interactions between gender and power are even more complex in rapidly changing societies. In Japan, for instance, women have historically occupied a visibly subservient position in families. At one time women were expected to walk several steps behind their husband so as not to offend his dignity by stepping on his shadow (Kristof, 1996c). Wives were legally prohibited from using different surnames from their husbands. Although the 1980s equal rights movement and a booming economy sent many Japanese women surging into the workplace (Naoi & Schooler, 1990), many were still "office flowers"—submissive part-time workers who were expected to smile sweetly, talk softly, pour tea, and answer telephones—with little decision-making power. Indeed, a cross-national study of seven countries (the United States, Norway, Sweden, Canada, the United Kingdom, Australia, and Japan) found that women in Japan are significantly less likely than women in the other countries to hold supervisory or managerial positions in the workplace (Wright, Baxter, & Birkelund, 1995). The recent economic slump in Japan has forced many women out of the workforce and back into their domestic roles.

Within Japanese families, however—even though women are still expected to clean, cook, and tend to the needs of their husbands—they exercise a surprising degree of authority. Many wives control the household finances, giving their husbands monthly allowances as they see fit. Recent surveys have found that about half of Japanese men are dissatisfied with the amount of their allowances. Many wives refuse to give their husbands cash cards for the family bank account. If he wants to withdraw money from the account, the bank will usually phone the wife to get her approval. Japanese men are even starting to take on some of the housework responsibilities, a development that would have been unthinkable a decade ago. One man summed up the situation this way: "Things go best when the husband is swimming in the palm of his wife's hand" (quoted in Kristof, 1996c, p. A6).

By now, you can probably tell that family power can be quite subtle and difficult to detect. For instance, when a husband anticipates his wife's angry response to his desire for her to do more around the house, he may decide to stifle his concerns to avoid what he thinks will be certain conflict. Thus she has successfully exerted power over him (by preventing him from speaking his mind) without any direct confrontation. Such "invisible" power is important because it can maintain inequality even in those marriages that appear harmonious and conflict free.

If women in fact exercise their power within families covertly, they may have more power than sociologists have been able to observe. It has been suggested that women operate from a position of "negative dominance"—for example, withdrawing love or provoking men's guilt feelings to impose their will. This strategy may be strong enough to balance the overt power of their husbands (Holter, 1970).

Anthropologist Susan Rogers (1975) observed this sort of covert power in her studies of peasant societies. Although men's involvement with public positions of authority make them appear dominant, women actually control tremendous informal power. Here's how one couple demonstrated what Rogers called a "myth of male dominance":

> Mme. François wanted a motorbike for fetching the cows from pasture. She argued at length with her husband, who insisted that they could not afford one for at least a year. Two weeks later, she had a motorbike. When I asked her about it, she might very well have said, "I control the budget and I wanted it, so too bad for him, I went out and bought it." But rather, she winked and said simply, "Pierre changed his mind." (Rogers, 1975, p. 741)

Publicly, women in this community insist that the husbands are in control and show them deference when in public. But privately, Rogers suggests everyone in the community—men and women alike—seems to understand that men's power is in fact a myth.

Does the same phenomenon exist in mainstream U.S. society? Without question, many women who are dependent on men for goods and services have probably learned how to subtly influence their partners in such a way that their needs, or their families' needs, are met. But the male dominance we see in contemporary American marriages doesn't appear to be entirely mythical. One important difference between the women in the peasant societies Rogers studied and women in highly industrialized societies such as the United States is that in preindustrial, peasant societies, men and women are equally dependent on each other socially and economically. But in industrialized societies, gender relations have evolved in such a way that women typically control fewer resources than men and are therefore less powerful. As this gap diminishes, mostly as a result of women's successes in the labor force, women have gained greater power in their relationships.

Resources and Dependency

A key factor in power differences within families, according to social exchange theorists, is **dependence**—the degree to which one person relies on the other for important resources. If your partner has something you want or need (money, love and affection, understanding and support, companionship, information, sex, and so on), you'll be motivated to comply with his or her wishes, obey his or her commands, or put up with other undesirable (that is, costly) behaviors in order to get it. In that respect, humans are motivated by the same forces that drive economic marketplaces: a desire to maximize rewards and minimize costs. That is, people seek out experiences, people, objects, and so on that they find pleasurable and avoid those they find unpleasurable.

Each person brings a variety of resources to intimate relationships (for example, money and other possessions, status, attractiveness, emotional support, sex, and affection). People exchange their resources for a desired benefit from a partner. The more resources individuals believe they contribute to a relationship, relative to their partners, the more they expect in return and the more power they're likely to believe they're entitled to (Safilios-Rothschild, 1976).

But control over a resource creates power differences only if the resource is highly valued and perceived as essential. Moreover, it must be something that can't be obtained elsewhere. So if you don't care about sex or financial security or if you have other prospects for acquiring sex or financial security, you won't depend on your partner to provide these things. Therefore, he or she will not be able to exercise much power over you.

When you depend on others to provide resources that you desperately want but that are unavailable elsewhere, you find yourself in a position of powerlessness. Power and dependence are *inversely* related. That is, the more dependent you are on a relationship to meet your needs, the less power you are likely to have. This is as true for emotional resources as it is for financial ones. For instance, a partner who loves more is more dependent and therefore more likely to be submissive. Such submission can be used as a means of keeping the other partner happy, thereby maintaining the stability of the relationship (Winton, 1995).

Because men and women tend to control different types of resources, dependence and power in families are inherently based on gender (Howard & Hollander, 1997). Men's higher earnings and greater access to prestigious occupations have historically given them more power and privilege inside their families. Women who don't work outside the home or who are burdened with the care of young children have considerably fewer opportunities to earn money and are particularly likely to be dependent on their partners economically.

But such power is rarely absolute. Traditional male breadwinners, who can use their economic wherewithal to exert power over their wives, may nevertheless depend on their wives to provide the physical, psychological, and emotional support that allows them to work outside the home. In short, they can be as emotionally dependent on their wives as their wives are economically dependent on them (Hertz, 1986). In addition, women can often claim significant power in families because of their role as "kinkeeper"—the person who controls those relationships that cross generations or that involve relatives outside the nuclear family (Kranichfeld, 1987). These bonds place women at the very center of family life.

Furthermore, as women enter the workforce in greater numbers they have begun to acquire economic resources that let them participate more forcefully in family decision making (Blumstein & Schwartz, 1983; Rubin, 1994). Keep in mind that working women may still defer to their husbands in many situations, and they still retain primary responsibility over domestic work. Even so, employed women, in general, are more likely than nonemployed women to feel they have the right to have their say at home and contradict their husbands. One wife, who oversees a large laboratory, explains why: "I make decisions at the office from nine to five and I think it would be a little strange if I came home and was treated like a pussycat" (quoted in Blumstein & Schwartz, 1983, p. 141).

Conversely, women who drop out of the paid labor force often experience a perceptible decrease in their ability to make family decisions at home: "We don't get along as well as we used to when I was working because then he used to listen to me more than he does now. He tends to boss me around the way he tends to boss his students" (quoted in Blumstein & Schwartz, 1983, p. 142).

What's crucial here is not the objective fact that one partner has more financial resources than the other, but the meaning that couples attach to these resources (Pyke, 1994). The effect that a resource such as money has on marital power depends on whether couples consider it a gift or a burden. For instance, a woman married to a man who sees her employment as a threat to him rather than as a contribution to the household derives less power from her wage earning. This is particularly true when the husband is chronically unemployed or works in a low-status, menial job that exacerbates his dependency on his wife's wages. A woman's employment in these situations may be such a sore spot for her husband that she is actually expected to compensate for it by perhaps doing more work around the house or by deferring to his authority. Sensitive to her husband's feelings of failure, a woman may feel the need to soothe his threatened ego by consciously downplaying her own employment status (Hochschild & Machung, 1989).

However, a woman not working in the paid workforce, and married to a man who sees tremendous importance in her domestic work, may actually derive more power from that role. She may be grateful to him for enabling her not to work for pay, and he may value her choice to stay home, especially when children are present. If her nonparticipation is perceived as her choice, staying out of the paid workforce may actually reflect her power and the ability to make decisions on her own behalf.

The Role of Cultural Ideology

It's highly unlikely that, if there were a sudden redistribution of income so that women began earning more than men, women would be able to claim the lion's share of power and influence in families. Conceptions of gender, power, and family that are deeply embedded in this society would impede such a shift. Indeed, gender inequality has persisted in American society despite women's movement into the labor force in the past few decades and their increasing representation in male-dominated occupations (Ridgeway, 1997). Thus cultural ideology may overshadow the effect of monetary resources on family power.

In this culture, certain family members gain power from social norms, traditions, or laws. That is, certain people in the family are allowed to exert power over others because of the positions they occupy rather than any special or noteworthy characteristics they as individuals might have. The authority of a parent over a child, for instance, is considered legitimate to the extent that the norms and traditions of the larger society uphold this power relationship or perhaps even require it.

In some segments of American society, as in other patriarchal—or male-dominated—cultures, men control most, if not all, of the important social institutions: politics, economics, religion, the media, education, and so on. By virtue of their higher social status in the economic sphere and their roles as husbands and "patriarchs," they can also claim legitimate power over their wives and children. Imagine a traditional married couple in which the husband works and the wife is a homemaker. She wants to begin taking college courses at night, but her husband protests that he needs her at home. She agrees, believing that he has the right to demand that she stay at home and that it is her duty to comply. He doesn't have to argue with her or convince her that it would be beneficial if she didn't work; nor does he have to threaten her. It is a taken-for-granted assumption, beyond challenge or even imagination, that she should do what her husband says. Moreover, in acceding to her husband's demands the wife reinforces the cultural legitimacy of his power over her.

Although many Americans would deny the traditional claim that men have the plain and simple right to enforce their will within their families, people often justify power differentials in more acceptable—but still ideological—terms. For instance, some women now subordinate their careers to their husbands' on the grounds that doing so maximizes family resources and is the most efficient way to serve the interests of all family members (Pyke, 1996). Such a belief, though wrapped in seemingly rational language, still has the effect of undermining women's long-term economic interests and limiting their claims to family power (Blumberg & Coleman, 1989).

Women's economic well-being may also be offset by cultural ideologies that value women primarily for the noneconomic resources they provide. In Korea, for example, research has found that wives who go to work outside the home actually *lose* power in their marriages (Balswick & Balswick, 1995). Because Korean wives already have responsibility and authority to spend the family's money, they gain little personal power from increasing their own financial resources. Furthermore, when they work outside the home, wives lose the emotional power they had. The nurturing resources—such as showering husbands with care and attention after a day's work—are highly valued in Korean society, more so than any extra income wives may provide to their families.

In most American families, occupying the position of husband no longer guarantees power in the family. No longer able to rely simply on cultural tradition, husbands must prove their worth and therefore their legitimacy by fulfilling the expectations and obligations that go with the position, such as earning a living and supporting the family. Men who fail to meet these expectations—such as those who are chronically unemployed—risk losing their family authority.

Cultural diversity yields vastly different conceptions of women's and men's "places" in U.S. society and in families. Among some groups—such as recent immigrants from Latin America, Africa, and Asia—male dominance and authority are the norm. Husbands in these families can wield significant power within the household. Among other groups of Americans, however—such as Unitarians and Reform Jews—families are more likely to approach gender equality. In these more liberal groups, you may find individual women who are more dominant than their husbands. Even so, there is no group within contemporary society where women systematically hold greater power than men.

DEMO·GRAPHICS

How Beliefs About Gender Affect Marriages

Cultural ideology regarding gender is pervasive in U.S. society, coloring attitudes toward everything from the proper roles of women and men in the business, political, and academic worlds to their roles within families. In a society organized so profoundly around differences between males and females, the different roles that men and women occupy are typically attributed to biological differences, not social ones. A good example of this way of thinking is reflected in attitudes toward parenting. When sex and gender are seen as synonymous, women are simply assumed to be *biologically* better suited than men to care for children. In contrast, when people see sex and gender as separate phenomena, they are more likely to attribute differences in child-rearing ability to social factors, such as social inequality.

Consider the reasons given in Exhibit 2.2a for why women are more likely than men to take care of children. Respondents were asked whether each of the reasons was "very important," "important," "somewhat important," or "not at all important" (more than one reason could be listed as "very important"). The largest percentage of respondents—34 percent—cited women's biological predisposition to care for children as a very important reason why women tend to be the ones who tend to children. Close to 90 percent consider biological predisposition at least somewhat important.

But many people also believe that a person's upbringing is important in determining his or her ability to care for children. About 32 percent felt that a very important reason why women parent more than men is that they "are taught from childhood how to care for children." In fact, about the same percentage of people believe that biology is at least somewhat important as believe that upbringing is at least somewhat important. The fact that these two explanations—socialization and biology—coexist in some people's minds is interesting. Perhaps socialization is simply thought to reinforce biological differences.

EXHIBIT 2.2

U.S. Attitudes Toward Gender and Power

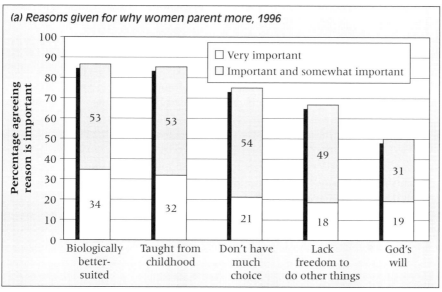

Data source: National Opinion Research Center. 1998. *General Social Survey*. Available at www.icpsr.umich. edu/GSS/. Accessed June 1, 2001.

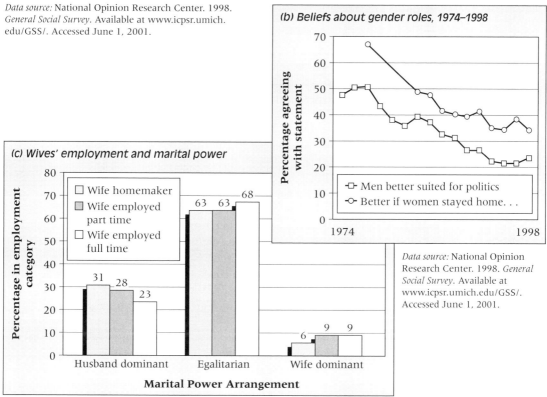

Data source: National Opinion Research Center. 1998. *General Social Survey*. Available at www.icpsr.umich.edu/GSS/. Accessed June 1, 2001.

Source: P. Blumstein & P. Schwartz. 1983. *American Couples*. New York: Morrow, p. 139.

Note also in Exhibit 2.2a how reluctant individuals are to attribute differences in parenting to societal factors such as gender inequality. Only 21 percent of respondents cited "the way society is set up, women don't have much choice" as a very important reason for why women tend to care for children. A smaller percentage, 18 percent, cited "greater freedoms for men" as very important—a slightly lower percentage than those citing "God's will" as a very important reason.

If women are thought to be naturally better able to care for children, it follows that they might be considered better suited than men for other domestic roles as well. Exhibit 2.2b shows that a significant percentage of individuals—35 percent—still, after decades of gains for women in the workplace, strongly agree or agree that "it is much better for everyone involved if the man is the achiever outside the home and the woman takes care of the home and family." It follows too that if women are better suited to the domestic domain, men are better suited to the public domain. In fact, about one in four respondents also agree with the statement "Men are better suited emotionally for politics than are most women." Although such beliefs are being challenged more and more in today's society, as you can see in the declining percentages over the past several decades, such thinking remains a strong part of gender ideology.

So how do such attitudes translate into the sorts of social and marital inequalities discussed in this chapter? For one thing, the gender division of labor contributes to significant income differences between husbands and wives. These differences can further translate into power differences within marriage. As Exhibit 2.2c shows, although most couples claim to have egalitarian decision making, when unequal power exists men are typically seen as more powerful. Even when wives are in the paid labor force, this power differential exists, although it does shrink a bit.

The division of power within relationships can be seen as a logical extension of the gendered division of labor found within many homes. Such patterns die hard in part because people assume they are natural and inevitable.

Thinking Critically About the Statistics

1. Compare Exhibit 2.2a, which is a snapshot of opinions in 1996, and Exhibit 2.2b, which shows trends up to 1998. Despite the fact that women's involvement in the outside world appears considerably more acceptable today than it was a quarter century ago, attitudes toward the parent role in families remain stubbornly gendered. Why do you think individuals today are still less likely to rely on socially based rather than biologically based reasons to explain why women are more responsible for parenting than men (as shown in Exhibit 2.2a)? To what extent might both the invisibility and the pervasiveness of gender in U.S. society be to blame? In particular, why do you think people are more reluctant to acknowledge the possibility that male privilege plays a role in creating and maintaining these patterns? Which groups would you expect are most accepting of social explanations?

2. What social, political, economic, and historical forces might explain the shifting attitudes toward women's role within the home and politics that are shown in Exhibit 2.2b?

3. Exhibit 2.2c indicates that egalitarian power arrangements are most common in American families, even where the wife is a homemaker or employed part time. Which of the other data and ideas presented in this chapter explain why? Given what you have

read, to what extent do you think the attitudes depicted in this exhibit reflect the reality of American families?

4. How might the parenting and decision-making patterns shown in Exhibits 2.2a, 2.2b, and 2.2c reinforce social inequality within the larger society? ■

The Devaluation of Women

One of the most insidious outcomes of these power differences we've discussed is that power translates not only into prestige, status, and independence but also into social worth. The members of any group that systematically lacks power (children, women, minorities) are often devalued on a societal level. You can see signs of women's devaluation in even the most minute social practices, such as language. For example, many more words compare women to animals, such as "bitch" and "fox," than compare men to animals. Women are devalued at the institutional level as well. For instance, the jobs dominated by women are lower paid and less prestigious than those dominated by men.

The devaluation of women and the discrimination that results is often justified by assumptions about their inherent, biologically based skills and limitations. To nineteenth-century Americans, few facts were more incontestable than the notion that women were the products and prisoners of their reproductive systems. Women's place in their families as well as in society was thought to be linked to and controlled by the existence and function of the uterus and ovaries (Scull & Favreau, 1986). Everything about women could be explained by biology: the predominance of the emotional over the rational, the capacity for affection, the love of children and aptitude for child rearing, the preference for domestic work, and so on (Ehrenreich & English, 1979; Scull & Favreau, 1986). Scholars at the time warned that young women who studied too much not only were struggling against nature but would badly damage their reproductive organs and perhaps even go insane in the process (Fausto-Sterling, 1985). The exclusion of women from higher education was thus seen as not only justifiable but necessary for their own health and for the long-term good of society.

Beliefs about the undesirable effects of women's reproductive functioning are not just a thing of the past. Many physicians and psychiatrists today believe that normal biological processes predispose women to certain personality disorders. Consider, for instance, the menstrual cycle. The board of trustees of the American Psychiatric Association continues to debate the merits of including a psychiatric diagnosis called "premenstrual dysphoric disorder" in its official manual of mental disorders.

All societies devalue women to some extent, as anthropologist Michelle Rosaldo (1974) found in her comparison of cultures around the world. In some parts of Papua New Guinea, for example,

> Women grow sweet potatoes and men grow yams, and yams are the prestige food, the food one distributes at feasts. . . . [I]n . . . hunting societies . . . women may help on the hunt but the catch is the men's to distribute, and meat, unlike the nutritious grubs and nuts a woman gathers, is socially valued and shared. (p. 19)

Also, parents in some countries place much higher value on sons than daughters. Figures from the 2001 census in India, for instance, show a growing number of boys compared to girls over the past 2 decades, suggesting that female fetuses are being regularly aborted by parents who undergo sex determination tests prior to the birth of their child. Longer life spans and increasing levels of education among women have not changed the strong

EXHIBIT 2.3

*Illiteracy Rates
in Selected
Countries*

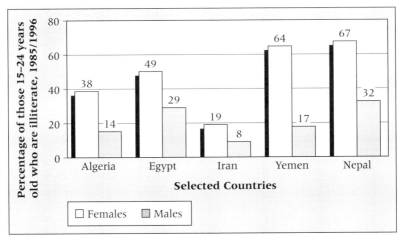

Data source: United Nations Statistics Division. 2000. *The World's Women 2000: Trends and Statistics*. Available at www.un.org/depts/unsd/ww2000/table4a.htm. Accessed September 15, 2001.

cultural preference for sons, who carry the family name, inherit ancestral property, and care for parents in old age (Dugger, 2001). Even when daughters are born, families often invest resources to ensure their sons' future at the expense of their daughters. This practice is reflected in literacy rates in some parts of the world, where it's not unusual for twice as many females to be illiterate as males (see Exhibit 2.3).

Many other examples of female devaluation exist. In many developing countries, laws dictate that a daughter's inheritance automatically goes to her husband on marriage. Furthermore, widows often have no inheritance rights in property owned by their husbands and thus when their husbands die women may lose their homes, the land they've worked on, their household possessions, even their children (Owen, 1996). What value daughters do have in such societies lies in their ability to get married. Among the Masai of Kenya, for example, parents of girls as young as 9 give them to adult men to marry in exchange for money, livestock, food, or any other needed commodity.

In some societies, female devaluation can be fatal. Families short on food commonly see to it that male children are well fed, often at the expense of female children. As a result, girls tend to grow up sicker. Many female babies are so undernourished that they die within the first year (Bryjak & Soroka, 1992).

Certain practices may seem barbaric to most Americans. According to the World Health Organization, between 85 and 114 million girls and women worldwide have been subjected to female genital mutilation (FGM) (cited in Dugger, 1996a). Typically the procedure, which entails the removal of the clitoris and/or the destruction of the labia and vulva, is done under highly unsanitary conditions by a midwife using unclean sharp instruments such as razor blades, scissors, knives, or pieces of glass. Anesthesia is generally not used.

This cultural tradition, often supported by deep historical roots, is a reflection of the extreme powerlessness of women in these societies. Where FGM is common, men demand that their wives be virgins when they marry. Indeed, a girl who has not undergone this procedure may be considered "unclean" or a prostitute by local villagers and therefore unmarriageable. The ritual also serves to perpetuate the idea that the bodies and sexuality of women need to be regulated and controlled.

Ironically, it is often women themselves—usually mothers and grandmothers—who enforce the practice of FGM (Crossette, 1995). But it is unlikely that such pressure is motivated by cruelty. In fact, these older women may have the girls' best interests in mind. If a young woman's marriageability, and therefore her future economic security, requires that she be subjected to FGM, her very survival is at stake:

> In a culture in which men will not marry you unless you have been mutilated and there is no other work you can do and you are . . . considered a prostitute if you are not mutilated, you face a very big problem. Women mutilate their daughters because they really are looking down the road to a time when the daughter will . . . marry and at least have a roof . . . and food. (Walker & Parmar, 1993, p. 277)

Sometimes the violence has no obvious benefit for women. In many Arab countries, for instance, women suspected of being adulterous are sometimes killed by their own relatives to cleanse the family's honor. In fact, women accused of sexual misconduct are often jailed, not to punish them but to protect them from being killed by their families (Jehl, 1999). In Pakistan, women are sometimes killed for marrying against their father's wishes.

One of the most pernicious forms of wife abuse—known locally as "bride burning" or "dowry death"—takes place in India (Heise, 1989; Van Willigen & Channa, 1991). Dowry traditionally consisted of the gifts that a woman received from her parents on marriage. Even though it was officially banned in 1961, dowry is still an essential part of premarital negotiations and now consists of wealth that the bride's family pays the groom. Young brides, who by custom live with their new husbands' parents, are commonly subjected to severe abuse if promised money is not paid. Sometimes dowry harassment ends in suicide or murder. In 1998 about 7,000 wives—an average of 19 a day—were killed by their husbands for not providing adequate dowries ("Bridal dowry in India," 2000). Often the husband and his family try to disguise the murder as an accident by setting the wife on fire and then claiming she died in a kitchen mishap. In the city of Bombay, 19% of all deaths among women 15 to 44 years old are due to "accidental burns" (Heise, 1989).

Although these practices may seem extreme to us, too many American women also experience abuse, mutilation, and murder rooted in gender inequality. For instance, a new trend in cosmetic plastic surgery is "designer laser vaginoplasty"—surgical enhancement of the vulva—for "purely aesthetic" purposes. Plastic surgeons in the United States will also perform "hymen repairs" so that a woman will bleed when she has sexual intercourse, to signify that she's a virgin. Although these surgeries are performed under sterile conditions and by trained professionals, one must wonder how different they really are from FGM. Nor is the devaluation of women through murder an unknown practice here: Many American women who are murdered die at the hands of a husband, boyfriend, or ex-husband bent on exerting control. The intersection of gender and power is perhaps just as volatile in this society as elsewhere.

Conclusion

The sociological study of families relies heavily on the analysis of gender. Most contemporary scholars would argue that it is really not possible to study family without understanding gender. People's gendered selves inform their family experiences.

Every aspect of family life is shaped by gender. Not only do parents respond to their daughters and sons differently, but men and women also parent in different ways. Further, the work men and women do in and outside the home is strongly gendered. Dating behaviors, and experiences with sexuality, aging, divorce, and much more, are also gendered. All these experiences "produce different feelings, consciousness, relationships, skills—ways of being that we call feminine and masculine" (Lorber 1994, p. 14).

By "doing gender" in this way, people are constantly reinforcing the existing social organization of gender, making it difficult for new gender expectations to emerge. Nevertheless, gender relations in this society and, by extension, in American families are slowly but noticeably changing. In one national survey, 79 percent of men and 74 percent of women agreed that the status of women has improved over the last 25 years (Boxer, 1997). Women have increased their participation in the paid labor force and are making greater financial contributions to their families, thus gaining power in their intimate relationships. Likewise, women have become a political and cultural force that can no longer be ignored. The greater societal awareness of sexual exploitation and violence has reduced—although not yet eliminated—this culture's traditional tolerance for sexual harassment, rape, and spouse abuse. To an increasing degree, the public and the media now support women's desire for more sharing and emotional expressiveness from their partners.

Yet as long as people continue to subscribe to the concept of two-and-only-two sexes or genders and to see gender differences as inherent and natural, they are likely to accept the differential treatment of men and women as inevitable. As a result, the power differences in families that are based on gender are likely to persist.

Chapter Highlights

- Whereas "sex" is typically used to refer to a person's biological maleness or femaleness, "gender" designates psychological, social, and cultural aspects of maleness and femaleness.
- Although most people take for granted that there are two, and only two sex categories, cross-cultural and biological evidence suggest that these categories are neither exhaustive nor mutually exclusive.
- Reliance on biology to explain gender differences overlooks the wide cultural and historical variation in conceptions of masculinity and femininity.
- Parents, siblings, and other significant people in a child's immediate environment provide early lessons—both subtle and direct—on how he or she should behave with regard to gender.
- Gender isn't something that is simply acquired through socialization. It is also something people "do"—created and reinforced continuously through everyday social interaction.
- Gender differences are often translated into differences in power and dependence within families.
- Gender inequality takes an enormous economic, psychological, and physical toll on women worldwide.

Your Turn

Gender is said to be pervasive—governing every aspect of life and society—yet invisible. Gender signs are so ubiquitous that people usually only notice the signs when they are missing or ambiguous (Lorber, 1994).

To help you notice gender, deliberately violate a gender norm. Consider the many ways gender is done in everyday society. Pick any aspect of "doing gender," and deliberately act in a way inconsistent with how you identify yourself. It can be as simple as not getting up immediately to clear the table after dinner or leaving the dishes unwashed (if this is part of how you do gender). If you are a woman, consider sitting in a very public place, such as the mall, in a very "unladylike" posture. If you are a man, consider asking someone for help opening a jar or do not automatically get in the driver's seat on a date. Be as daring as you feel comfortable being, but make sure the activity is not illegal or likely to be harmful to you or anyone else.

Pay careful attention to how you feel when preparing to do this activity and when you're actually doing it. Is it fun? Is it scary? How uncomfortable do you feel? Consider the source of these feelings.

Also note others' reactions to you. If possible, arrange to have a fellow classmate watch from a distance to see how others react to you. The additional observer may see things you don't and can also help confirm your impressions.

Finally, explore what your experiences with doing gender "inappropriately" indicated about the pervasiveness of gender in all aspects of social life.

Race, Ethnicity, and Families

Multiracial Families

In the past decade, we've witnessed an increase in the number of biracial or multiracial children. Traditional ideas about what it means to be "black" or "white" or "Latino" or "Asian" no longer apply when the boundaries between racial groups blur.

Although many people think of race as a purely biological trait, most sociologists and anthropologists agree that race is a socially constructed concept that is both subjective and fluid. Multiracial children help to prove their point.

Into what racial category would you place the children depicted in these photos? What pieces of information influence your choice?

Multiracial families can be a bridge between races, helping to overcome the differences associated with race that so often divide and alienate. Grandparents may initially resist their children's interracial marriages, but the arrival of grandchildren can be a powerful tool for bringing people together.

How likely is it that these mixed-race children will be raised to appreciate the ethnic heritage of each side of the family? What concerns might the grandparents have?

In a society that is still bent on seeing race as clear and fixed, where would these children fit?

Do you think children of mixed-race backgrounds ought to identify with one race, or would it be better if they identified themselves as "biracial"?

On the 2000 census, people were allowed to identify themselves as members of more than one race, though they weren't given the opportunity of identifying themselves simply as biracial.

How do you think this policy will influence race relations and our ideas about race in the future?

Gregory Williams is currently the dean of the College of Law at The Ohio State University. He was born in Virginia in the late 1940s, a time when racial segregation was part of the natural order of life in the United States. He led a typical white, middle-class life. He had several black friends when he was young but understood that their "place" was separate from his white world. He went to "whites-only" schools, "whites-only" movie theaters, and "whites-only" swimming pools.

When he was 10 years old, his parents divorced. His father decided to move back to his hometown of Muncie, Indiana, with Gregory and his brother Mike. On the bus ride there, Mr. Williams gave his sons some startling news: Once they reached Indiana, he told them sternly, they could no longer be white. It turned out that their paternal grandmother was black, and this, therefore, made them black too. "Life is going to be different from now on," he told them. "In Virginia you were white boys. In Indiana you're going to be colored boys. I want you to remember that you're the same today that you were yesterday. But people in Indiana will treat you differently" (Williams, 1995, p. 33).

Stunned by the revelation, the boys initially interpreted their new identities in terms of the restrictions that would be imposed on their lives. Gregory's brother shouted, "I don't wanta be colored. We can't go swimmin' or skatin'" (Williams, 1995, p. 33).

Although Gregory initially refused to believe his father's news, his perceptions quickly began to shift:

> I didn't understand Dad. I knew I wasn't colored, and neither was he. My skin was white. All of us are white, I said to myself. But for the first time, I had to admit Dad didn't exactly look white. His deeply tanned skin puzzled me as I sat there trying to classify my own father. Goose bumps covered my arms as I realized that whatever he was, I was. I took a deep breath. I couldn't make any mistakes. I looked closer. His heavy lips and dark brown eyes didn't make him colored, I concluded. His black, wavy hair was different from Negroes' hair, but it was different from most white folks' hair, too. He was darker than most whites, but Mom said he was Italian. That was why my baby brother had such dark skin and curly hair. Mom told us to be proud of our Italian heritage! That's it, I decided. He was Italian. . . . [But when] I glanced across the aisle to where he sat . . . I saw my father as I never had seen him before. . . . Before my eyes he was transformed from a swarthy Italian to his true self—a high-yellow mulatto. My father was a Negro! We were colored! After ten years in Virginia on the white side of the color line, I knew what that meant. (Williams, 1995, pp. 33–34)

Much of Gregory's life from that moment on was a struggle to learn to be black. It was never easy. He was rejected by black and white children alike. Even his aunts, uncles, and cousins resented him because he looked white. In junior high school, Gregory realized that straddling the color line made everyone uncomfortable because it shattered too many racial taboos. Each day, it seemed, brought a new dilemma about his "proper place." Dating was particularly difficult. Because he was considered black, he wasn't supposed to date white girls. But because his skin appeared white, the community couldn't tolerate seeing him with black girls either.

Despite all the obstacles, Gregory managed to excel in academics and sports. He went on to a successful career as a lawyer and a professor. In the process, he came to accept and embrace his multiracial identity. He learned the importance of race in everyday life by living under the simultaneous influence of two different racial labels.

Of course, you don't have to "change" racial identities to know that in this country distinctions among large groups of people are made primarily on the bases of race and ethnicity. We all know the powerful role of race and minority status in American society. And so it would be silly, if not downright misleading, to ignore racial and ethnic variation and talk about *the* American family as if it represented a monolithic, universal form.

And yet focusing on diversity—talking about European-American families and African-American families and Hispanic families and Asian-American families and Native American families and Jewish families and other racial or ethnic types of families as distinctly different—raises other difficult issues. Students of color in the courses we teach are becoming increasingly uncomfortable with compartmentalized treatments of racial/ethnic family types. They worry that the family diversity that exists *within* a particular racial or ethnic group and the similarities that exist *between* groups are being overlooked and slighted. After all, they claim, it's as misleading and erroneous to talk about *the* African-American family, *the* Hispanic family, or *the* Asian-American family as it is to talk about *the* American family. The students also fear that as long as family patterns that differ markedly from the idealized image of the white, middle-class family—whether based on race, ethnicity, religion, class, or something else—are considered "variations," chances are such patterns will be viewed either as curiosities that need to be explained, "dysfunctional" barriers to a minority group's success that must be overcome, or "shortcomings" on which people ought to heap blame for many social ills.

In this chapter we examine the role of race and ethnicity in family structure, paying attention to the commonalities as well as the differences across groups. You'll discover that framing this issue simply as a matter of "racial differences" is woefully inadequate when you consider some of the historical and societal complexities involved.

Racial and Ethnic Identity

Race is an elusive term to define. In common usage, it refers to a category of people labeled and treated as similar because of common inborn biological traits, such as skin color; color and texture of hair; and shape of eyes, nose, or head. Race is usually thought to be a fixed and immutable biological characteristic that can easily be used to separate people into distinct groups.

But the idea that races are pure biological categories with clear boundaries is a myth. Scholars can't even agree on how many human races exist—estimates range from four to more than forty. The practice of identifying distinct races is complicated by the simple fact that since the earliest humans appeared, they have consistently tended to migrate and interbreed. It is estimated that about one in five adults in the United States has one or more close, family members who are of a different race or races (Goldstein, 1999). Some surveys estimate that at least 75 percent of American blacks have some white ancestry (cited in L. Mathews, 1996). There is no gene for race, no gene that is 100 percent of one form in one race and 100 percent of a different form in another race (Brown, 1998). In other words, there is no such creature as a "pure" white—or for that matter, "pure" black—American.

Indeed, the diversity of physical traits within a racial group is often as great as the diversity among groups. People who consider themselves "white" may actually have darker skin and curlier hair than some people who consider themselves "black." And despite obvious differences in physical appearance, Swedes, New Guineans, Japanese, and Navajo are more similar genetically than they are different (Diamond, 1994).

Race is therefore a more meaningful social category than it is a biological one. That is, the characteristics selected to distinguish one group from another have less to do with physical differences than with what that particular culture defines as socially significant. In the United States, for instance, Jews, the Irish, and Italians were once seen as members of separate—and inferior—races. Over time, they became "white" as they entered the mainstream culture and gained economic and political power (Bronner, 1998a). Similarly, as Brazilians climb the class ladder through educational and economic achievement, their racial classification changes, as illustrated by popular Brazilian sayings such as "Money whitens" or "A rich Negro is a white man, and a poor white man is a Negro" (Marger, 1994, p. 441). Gregory Williams didn't "become" black because his skin pigment darkened. He became black because his social circumstances changed.

Race is even more complex because of its connection to *ethnicity*—the learned cultural heritage shared by a category of people with common ancestry. Your history, style, values, vocabulary, tastes, and habits may be more important indicators of your identity than skin color or other anatomic features. Indeed, race and ethnicity need not coincide. For example, Caribbean blacks are quite different ethnically from African blacks and often take great pains to avoid being identified as "African American" (Gladwell, 1996).

Often the variation within an identified racial/ethnic category is significant. For instance, although they all are considered "Hispanic" or "Latino," Mexicans, Dominicans, Puerto Ricans, Cubans, Nicaraguans, Colombians, and other groups have very different histories, dialects, and immigration and citizenship experiences, and they have settled in different regions of the country (Bean & Tienda, 1987; Chilman, 1995). The same can be said for people considered "Asian." Filipinos, Chinese, Laotians, and Japanese differ markedly in cultural expectations and behaviors. Among recent Asian immigrants, some (for example, Chinese, Japanese, Indians, and Koreans) were likely to arrive in this country as educated middle-class professionals with highly valued skills. But others (such as Laotians, Cambodians, Indonesians, and Vietnamese) were likely to arrive uneducated and impoverished. Japanese Americans have an extremely low unemployment rate (about 3.4 percent), whereas the unemployment rate for Hmong immigrants from Laos is over 50 percent (U.S. Bureau of the Census, 1993).

Multiracial Identity

Despite the complexities of defining race, Americans still tend to see it in simple color terms: black, white, red, yellow, brown. As Gregory Williams learned, people typically try to force mixed-race children into specific racial categories.

Since the era of slavery, the United States has adhered to the *one-drop rule* in determining race (F. J. Davis, 1991). The term comes from a common law in the South that a "single drop of black blood" made a person black. For years the U.S. Census Bureau considered a person black if he or she had any known black African ancestry. Anthropologists call this a *hypodescent* rule, meaning that racially mixed people are always assigned the status of the minority group (F. J. Davis, 1991). So a person with seven out of eight great-grandparents who are white and only one who is black could still be considered black.

Many ethnic groups informally establish identity using the hypodescent rule in one form or another. Among Orthodox Jews, for example, a child born to one Jewish and one non-Jewish parent is forbidden to claim Jewish identity (Spickard, 1989). Among older Japanese Americans, a child who is predominantly Japanese with some white blood is considered white by the rest of the community and not fully admitted into the ethnic group. Not surprisingly, a study of 1,500 offspring of Asian-Anglo couples found that the majority of these children (52 percent) identified themselves as Anglo. The rest viewed themselves as Asian (38 percent) or a combination of the two (10 percent) (Saenz, Hwang, Aguirre, & Anderson, 1995).

The dramatic growth in the number of multiracial children has upset traditional views of racial identity. In 1992 the U.S. Census Bureau reported that for the first time in history, the number of biracial babies increased at a faster rate than the number of single-race babies (Marmor, 1996). Today, more and more people of mixed racial heritage are fighting the one-drop rule and refusing to identify themselves as one race or another. They are claiming multiple ethnic identities, a trend that may someday render traditional racial vocabulary obsolete. People have come up with some rather creative ways of expressing their racial or ethnic identity, such as "Korgentinian" (for Korean and Argentinean), "China-Latina," or "Blackanese" (Leland & Beals, 1997). Perhaps the most famous example is from legendary golfer Tiger Woods, who has labeled himself "Cablinasian"—a combination of *Caucasian, black, Indian,* and *Asian* (his father is half black, quarter each American Indian and Chinese; his mother is half Thai, quarter Chinese, and quarter white). In short, the traditional ethnic and racial boundaries that once served as primary societal determinants in everyday life seem to be eroding.

Most people who have multiracial backgrounds have experienced being arbitrarily assigned a racial identity by a school principal or an employer that may differ from the identity of other members of their families or may differ from their identity in other settings. In the late 1990s, these individuals lobbied Congress and the Census Bureau to add a multiracial category to the 2000 census. They argued that such a change would add visibility and legitimacy to a racial identity that has heretofore been ignored. Some even argued that a multiracial category had the potential for softening the racial lines that divide the country (Stephan & Stephan, 1989). When people blend several races and ethnicities within their own bodies, race becomes a meaningless concept, thereby presenting a biological solution to the problem of racial justice (White, 1997).

But not everyone thought such a change was a good idea. Many civil rights organizations objected to including a multiracial category in the census. They worried that it would reduce the number of U.S. citizens claiming to belong to long-recognized minority groups, dilute the culture and political power of those groups, and make it more difficult to enforce civil rights laws (Mathews, 1996). Job discrimination lawsuits, affirmative action policies, and federal programs that assist minority businesses or that protect minority communities from environmental hazards all depend on official racial population data from the census. Furthermore, people who identify themselves as biracial or multiracial are sometimes perceived by members of racial groups as sellouts who avoid discrimination by taking advantage of the confusion their mixed identity creates (Graham, 1995).

In the end, the civil rights organizations won. For the 2000 census, the government decided not to add a multiracial category to official forms. Instead it allowed people, for the first time, to identify themselves on the census form as members of more than one race. The new guidelines specify that those who check "white" and another category will be counted as members of the minority (Holmes, 2000). Preliminary 2000 census data show that 2 percent of the population—or close to 7 million people—identify themselves as belonging to more

EXHIBIT 3.1

Racial and Ethnic Identities in the United States, 2000

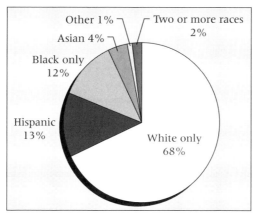

Data source: U.S. Bureau of the Census. 2001d. *Profile of General Demographic Characteristics for the United States: 2000,* Table DP-1. Available at www.census.gov/Press-Release/www/2001/tables/dp_us_2000.pdf. Accessed May 15, 2001.

than one race or ethnic group (see Exhibit 3.1). As you might expect, most of the people choosing this option are young. Blacks under the age of 17 were four times as likely as blacks over 50 to identify themselves as belonging to more than one race (cited in Schmitt, 2001a). The changes in the census form illustrate that when it comes to determining racial identity, politics, not biology, is the determining factor.

Race and Racism

The historical conditions under which any group enters U.S. society are crucial in determining the degree of economic success and achievement it experiences as well as the nature of its family and community life. Those groups that most closely approximate the national ideal in language (English), religion (Protestant), cultural heritage (northern European), and physical appearance (light Caucasian) have historically had an easier time being accepted than groups that were further from these norms. Not surprisingly, those groups whose skin color and traditions were very different from the white majority faced harsher obstacles. Some were simply treated with derision and suspicion; others were persecuted. Slavery was the most dramatic example, but many other immigrant groups have struggled to find a place in American society. Help-wanted ads in late nineteenth-century newspapers routinely carried the message "No Irish need apply." Jews were refused admission to many of the best American universities until the middle of the twentieth century. Limits on Greek and Italian immigration to the United States lasted from 1924 until the 1960s.

Economic status differs significantly by race (see Exhibit 3.2). Social and economic exclusion has forced some racial/ethnic minority groups to adapt their families to deal with hardships imposed by the larger society. Extended families, single parenthood, dual-earner couples, and many other deviations from the mainstream culture's family ideal have been ways of adapting to demanding societal circumstances. Even though these patterns are the products of historical conditions, they are often blamed for a particular group's social and economic difficulties:

See Issue 2 for more discussion of historical variations in family forms.

EXHIBIT 3.2

Median Income by Race or Ethnicity, 1998

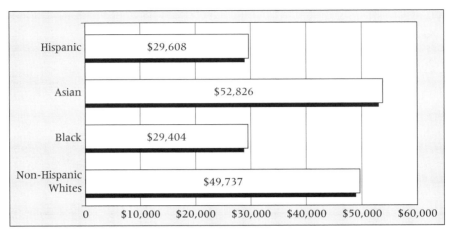

Data source: U.S. Census Bureau. 2000b. *Statistical Abstract of the United States: 2000,* Table 744. Washington, DC: U.S. Government Printing Office.

> Latinos, among whom extended family networks play a crucial role in integrating family and community, [are] criticized for being too "familistic"—their lack of social progress . . . blamed on family values which [keep] them tied to family rather than economic advancement. African-American families [are] criticized as "matriarchal" because of the strong role grandmothers [play] in extended family networks. (Dill, Baca Zinn, & Patton, 1994, p. 16)

This general discussion leaves some interesting questions to ponder: Are the family patterns found in racial and ethnic minority groups really all that different from the mainstream? If so, what social and historical conditions created these differences?

African-American Families

Of all racial minorities in the United States today, African-American families are the most negatively portrayed. The stereotypical image projects marital violence; broken homes; large numbers of children; and a resulting cycle of poverty, illegitimacy, crime, welfare, unemployment, and so on. Black men, especially poor black men, are typically portrayed as being on the outer fringe, either uninterested in or incapable of participating in the lives of their families. How accurate are these images, and how have they developed throughout history?

Slavery, Racism, and Blocked Opportunities

The experiences of African-American families have been unique among ethnic groups in this country because of the direct and indirect effects of slavery. Although accurate and reliable information on slave families has been difficult to obtain, certain aspects of slave life are clear. Because slaves were not allowed to enter into binding legal contracts, there was no legal basis for marriage between slaves. Slave owners determined which slaves could (or even had to) marry and which marriages would be dissolved. Children had economic value, because they were future slaves (Burnham, 1993; Staples, 1992). Slave owners had an interest in keeping slave families intact because married slaves were thought to be more docile and less inclined to rebel or escape. However, when economic troubles forced the sale of slaves to raise capital, most slave owners were not averse to separating the very slave families they had once advocated. The threat of separation "hung like a dark cloud over every slave couple family" (Burnham, 1993, p. 146). Even a "kind" and "sympathetic" master was no assurance of family stability and security.

In this environment, African-American families showed a remarkable capacity to adapt and endure. And families were an important means of survival. It was within families that slaves received sustaining affection, companionship, love, and support. It was here that they learned to cooperate with one another to avoid punishment and retained some degree of self-esteem.

Even when individual families were destroyed, the values of marriage and two-parent households persevered. Sociologist Herbert Gutman (1978) examined marriage licenses, birth records, and census data from 1855 to 1880 and found that two-parent, intact black families prevailed both during slavery and after emancipation. In counties and towns in Virginia, Mississippi, South Carolina, and Alabama, between 70 and 85 percent of black households contained both a mother and a father.

After slavery, blacks had the freedom to legally marry, and they did so in large numbers. Children were of special value to emancipated slaves, who could easily remember having their children sold away during slavery. Indeed, by 1917, 90 percent of all black children were born into existing marriages (Staples, 1992).

During the late nineteenth century, the strong role of women in black families emerged. Because a working woman was seen as a reminder of slavery, many black men preferred that their wives not work. But racism and legal, social, and economic exclusion made it extremely difficult for black men to find employment adequate to support their families. Survival dictated that black women enter the paid labor force. In 1900, 41 percent of black women were in the labor force compared to 16 percent of white women (cited in Staples, 1992).

Despite the difficulties left over from slavery, African Americans were able to create impressive norms of family life over the years. At the same time, though, their family structures were widely disparaged by whites. Negative images received a sort of official legitimacy in 1965, when Daniel Patrick Moynihan, then an assistant U.S. secretary of labor, wrote a report titled *The Negro Family: The Case for National Action*. At the time, the South was still highly segregated, and blacks were at the bottom of all relevant social and economic categories.

Moynihan argued that the root of the problems blacks experienced was not economic but instead was the inherent weakness and deterioration of black families. He described black families as a "tangled pathology," whose key feature was the absence of the father and the unusually large amount of power held by women. Moynihan felt that this "variant" family structure resulted in, among other things, low self-image, low IQ, high rates of school dropouts, delinquency, unemployment, violent crime, drug abuse, and so on—especially among sons.

To add fuel to the fire, the conditions Moynihan originally described with such alarm seemed to get worse over the ensuing 3 decades. Black families, it seems, experienced broad trends and changes more rapidly and with greater intensity than other sectors of society (Tucker & Mitchell-Kernan, 1995). For instance, blacks have a lower marriage rate than whites and wait longer to marry (Cherlin, 1992). Yet despite the increasing tendency for both blacks and whites to delay marriage, blacks begin sexual activity and childbearing earlier. This combination has resulted in a dramatic racial difference in nonmarital births.

It would be impossible to discuss these features of African-American families without examining the broader economic effects of racism, which continue to impede educational advancement and block access to high-paying jobs. African Americans as a group have one of the highest unemployment rates in the country and are heavily marginalized into low-paying jobs. For those who are employed, there's a greater chance of underemployment, inconsistent employment, and lower wages. As a result, 69 percent of African-American children are likely to experience poverty during their childhoods, as compared to 26 percent of white children (Rank & Hirschl, 1999). And half of all African-American children spend at least one year in extreme poverty (that is, their families earn less than 50 percent of the official poverty line).

Long-term exposure to these economic conditions can seriously affect family stability. Sociologists Stewart Tolnay and Kyle Crowder (1999) compared blacks living in northern inner cities with those who recently migrated from the South. They found greater marital stability among those who had migrated. But the longer these families remained in the North, the more their marital behaviors began to resemble those of the northern blacks. The researchers suggest that exposure to "destabilizing conditions" found in the North—such as higher rates of poverty, unemployment, and adult males and families on public assistance—is likely to lead to greater marital instability and a decreased likelihood of children growing up with both parents present.

When men don't work or don't earn sufficient wages, they may become less interested in becoming husbands, because they are constrained in their ability to perform the provider role in marriage (Dickson, 1993; Wilson, 1987). Black single men who are in stable employment are twice as likely to marry as single men who are sporadically employed or unemployed (Testa & Krogh, 1995). In addition, black men's anxiety about being able to provide for their families also increases the likelihood of marital difficulties and divorce, particularly in early marriage (Hatchett, Veroff, & Douvan, 1995). This argument, of course, assumes that male employment is perceived to be a necessary requirement for marriage (Raley, 1996).

Although black men have historically had limited employment opportunities, black women have seen their opportunities increase. More black women than men go to and graduate from college and more work as professionals. In 1997, about 971,000 black women were enrolled in undergraduate and graduate programs at U.S. colleges and universities, compared to 579,000 black men (U.S. Bureau of the Census, 2000a). Between 1977 and 1997, the number of bachelor's degrees awarded to black men increased by 30 percent, whereas the number increased by 77 percent for black women ("Report on black America," 2000). Because they are relatively successful compared with black men, black women have less financial incentive to marry than other U.S. women (Farley & Bianchi, 1991).

Given these trends, policies that take benefits away from poor single mothers who remain unmarried are questionable. The men who compose the eligible marriage market for these women would have difficulty supporting a family (Eggebeen & Lichter, 1991). A more sensible policy might be to encourage movements and programs that are designed to help absent fathers of children on welfare become financially and emotionally involved in the lives of their children (Peterson, 1992). They may be more effective than punitive policies in the long run, because they are attempting to restore the dignity of black men and to make family life an appealing option.

African-American Family Diversity

The stereotype of black family pathology popularized by Moynihan over 3 decades ago persists today. For instance, when asked why blacks are likely to suffer from low income, poor jobs, and inadequate housing, most Americans reject the idea that blacks are intellectually inferior. But they continue to embrace the idea that blacks lack the motivation or willpower to escape poverty (see Exhibit 3.3).

The pervasive image of black family collapse ignores the diversity of African-American family life. The "African-American community" consists of families with widely different histories and experiences. Not all of them have ancestors who entered the country enslaved. Some came to the Americas as freemen; others came as indentured servants who worked off their indebtedness and went on to lead free lives. Today, African-American families come from different classes, different religions, and different geographic areas. Although most have had to deal with racism, discrimination, and oppression, their family structures are quite varied. The despair of poverty, single parenthood, underemployment and unemployment, and lack of opportunity are not uniformly experienced by all African-American families.

In short, the image of black families as "pathological" overlooks the large number of families that don't fit this negative stereotype. One-third of African Americans have incomes, educations, and lifestyles that place them in the middle class. Black incomes are at their highest, and unemployment at its lowest, in 25 years (Cose, 1999). The poverty rate among black families is the lowest it's been since the U.S. Census Bureau began keeping track in 1959 (U.S. Bureau of the Census, 2000b). And poverty rates for black children living in married couple households has fallen over the past 25 years, even as the rate for whites has risen (Loury, 2000).

In two-fifths of all black families with children, two parents are present (U.S. Bureau of the Census, 2000b). In these two-parent families, 52 percent of the fathers work full time, and another 32.7 percent work part time (McAdoo, 1998). It's true that fewer than half of

EXHIBIT 3.3

Explanations for Blacks' Misfortunes

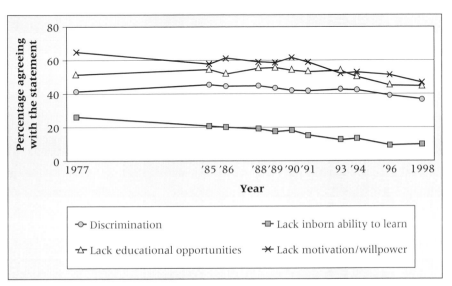

Data source: National Opinion Research Center. 1998. *General Social Survey.* Available at www.icpsr.umich.edu/GSS/. Accessed June 1, 2001.

all African-American adults are married. But contrary to the contention that all black men are averse to marriage, approximately 90 percent of those who are college educated with annual incomes over $25,000 are married and live with their spouses. The black teenage birth rate has fallen 17 percent since 1991, and the proportion of black babies born out of wedlock dropped in 1995 for the first time since 1969 (Holmes, 1996c).

In some ways, African-American families are stronger than other families. Family relationships remain a crucial form of emotional and economic support. For instance, one survey of African Americans found that over 90 percent considered themselves close to their families (Hatchett & Jackson, 1993). Another study (Hill & Sprague, 1999) found that lower middle-class blacks are more likely than whites of the same social class to claim that a long-term goal for their children is for them have a strong and loving family. Extended families tend to be large, often including both blood-related kin and people informally adopted into the family system (McAdoo, 1998). Furthermore, loyalty and responsibility to others in one's family are highly valued. Interestingly, this value is strengthened by the belief that everything a person does reflects not only on his or her family but on other African Americans as well.

See Issue 1 for more on the strengths of "chosen families" among African Americans.

Asian-American Families

When examining the difficulties faced by racial and ethnic minority groups in America, Asian Americans are often considered the "exception" because of their well-publicized educational, occupational, and economic success—especially among highly educated people of Chinese, Indian, and Japanese descent. Japanese Americans, for instance, are sometimes labeled the "model minority" because they tend to show respect for cherished American values such as hard work, achievement, self-control, dependability, good manners, thrift, and diligence (Kitano, 1976). But like all stereotypes, this one doesn't describe all Asian-American families.

Immigration and Racism

Like other ethnic minority groups, Asian Americans have endured a history of prejudice and discrimination that has had a noteworthy impact on the structure of their families. For instance, in the second half of the nineteenth century Chinese immigrants were recruited by industrialists in the western United States to perform the arduous work of extracting wealth from the mines and building the transcontinental railroad. But from the outset they were treated with hostility. The image of the "yellow peril" was fostered by fears that hordes of Chinese would take scarce jobs and eventually overrun the white race.

Initially, working in this country was a means of gaining financial support for one's family back in China. The end goal was to earn enough money to return to China and purchase land there. So most workers assumed they were here temporarily. Indeed, U.S. law in the late nineteenth century prevented Chinese laborers from becoming permanent citizens.

In addition, those who arrived before 1882 were not allowed to bring their wives and were prevented by law from marrying whites (Dill, 1995). Thus for many years the predominant family form among the Chinese in the United States was a *split household,* where financial support was accomplished by one member (the father) who lived far from the rest of the family. Everything else—consumption, recreation, socialization—was carried out by the wife and other relatives in the home village (Dill, 1995). This arrangement required considerable sacrifice—men were separated from their families sometimes for up to 20 years. Many children grew up never knowing their fathers. Wives who remained in China were forced to raise children and care for in-laws on the meager earnings their husbands sporadically sent them. These families became interdependent economic units that spanned two continents (Glenn & Yap, 1994).

Even when they were able to have intact families here, prejudice, violence, and discrimination kept Chinese people poor and segregated. By necessity, Chinese-American communities—which eventually became the "Chinatowns" you can see in many large cities today—were tightly structured and insulated against the threats from white U.S. society. In these close communities people learned to become self-reliant, creating their own businesses, organizing their own social clubs, and so on.

Because of the collectivist nature of Chinese culture, traditional family life required the sacrifice of individual needs and desires in favor of the overall welfare of the family unit (Coltrane & Collins, 2001). In traditional Chinese families, children were taught to be loyal and obedient and to value educational achievement. Although many Chinese wives were more or less equal producers in family businesses, gender roles at home were rigidly defined. Wives were expected to assume major responsibility for the household and child care (Wong, 1998). Fathers tended to have final authority and wielded unquestioned power; others—wives and children—were expected to be obedient (Kitano & Daniels, 1988).

Early Japanese immigrants, who arrived around the turn of the century, were much like the Chinese. In response to prejudice and discrimination, they created separate, insulated communities where children were taught the Japanese language and culture in schools established by their parents. They learned the importance of hard work, obedience to authority, and self-sacrifice. Tight families and a strong work ethic enabled many Japanese families to pool money and resources and achieve relative success.

However, this perceived success motivated lawmakers to enact legislation that limited Japanese people's ability to own or lease land. Fearing a rapid growth in the Japanese population, the National Origins Act of 1924 barred all further Japanese immigration (Takagi, 1994).

Hostility toward Japanese reached its peak in the early 1940s following Japan's attack on Pearl Harbor. Vocal special-interest groups, influential members of Congress, and the military held the Japanese-American community responsible for the surprise attack. The military used suspicion, fear, and racial prejudice to successfully pressure the government to suspend Japanese-American citizens' constitutional rights. The government authorized extensive searches of private residences and businesses. Japanese books, newspapers, and magazines made ordinary families the object of further surveillance. Eventually President Franklin Roosevelt signed an executive order authorizing the relocation and internment of Japanese immigrants and U.S. citizens of Japanese descent in camps surrounded by barbed wire and watchtowers.

Internment had a devastating impact on Japanese families and the Japanese-American community. As part of the registration process, internees were forced to express their loyalty to the United States and renounce their ties to Japan. Many second-generation Japanese (those born here) felt more American than Japanese and thus could express loyalty to the United States more easily than their parents. When they did so, however, Japanese-born parents likely felt their children were betraying their heritage (Broom & Kitsuse, 1956). In addition, the camps undermined the traditional status and authority of "unemployed" parents. Many Japanese Americans interred in the camps were farmers. When the war ended, they found that their farms had been taken over during their internment. These families were forced to resettle in urban areas, making it especially difficult to retain their traditional way of life. Urban living provided many young Japanese-Americans their first opportunity to work and live independently of their parents (Takagi, 1994).

Both Chinese-American and Japanese-American family structures emerged as adaptive strategies for survival in a racially hostile environment. For the most part, because people were forced to turn to their relatives for support, families took on an important economic as well as emotional role in their lives. With such a strong familial foundation, it is not surprising that many Asian-American families have achieved high levels of educational and professional attainment exceeding those of the rest of the population.

Contemporary Asian-American Families

In contemporary Asian-American families—as in other ethnic groups that were originally immigrants—tensions often arise between younger and older generations over the extent to which tradition ought to determine people's lives. As Asian families adapt to the dominant culture, they are more likely to adopt family behaviors characteristic of other American families. For instance, because Asian Americans tend to come from cultures in which relatively few women work outside the home, the contemporary need for two earners in a household has created conflict between young couples and members of older generations.

Moreover, U.S.-born Asian men and women are significantly more likely than foreign-born Asians to marry outside their ethnic group (Lee & Fernandez, 1998). And fewer than one in five Asian-Americans belong to an all-Asian kin group (including aunts, uncles, siblings, spouses, in-laws (Goldstein, 1999). Such trends make it even more difficult to retain traditional culture values.

Nevertheless, Asian Americans are twice as likely as whites to live in extended families and half as likely to live alone. More workers in a family mean more earnings, which may explain why household income is higher among Asian Americans than any other group (U.S. Bureau of the Census, 2000b).

Yet there is considerable variation *within* the Asian-American population. Asian Americans come from some 28 Asian countries or ethnic groups. They have different languages and cultures and different reasons for immigrating to the United States. For the most part, Chinese, Japanese, Korean, Indian, and Filipino immigrants came seeking a better life. They have been here the longest, have a higher proportion of native-born individuals, and are less culturally distinct than more recent arrivals from Southeast Asia (Vietnamese, Cambodians, Laotions, and so on) who typically arrived here as political immigrants or refugees (Parke & Buriel, 2002). Chinese, Japanese, and Korean families are significantly smaller than Vietnamese, Cambodian, and Laotian families and less tied to the traditions of their countries of origin. The more recent arrivals often try to recreate the family structure of their homeland. Immigrant Vietnamese families, for instance, may incorporate friends and neighbors into their extended kin networks, which may not have been part of their concept of family in Vietnam but allows them to maintain some semblance of their traditional, complex extended families despite the disruption of migration (Kibria, 1994a).

See Issue 4 for more on how immigrants try to balance the collectivist family traditions of their native cultures with the demands and expectations of contemporary American society.

Hispanic Families

One of the fastest-growing segments of the U.S. population is Spanish-speaking people who have migrated from Mexico, the Caribbean, Central America, and South America. According to the 2000 census, 12.5 percent of the U.S. population is Hispanic, compared to about 9 percent in 1990 (U.S. Bureau of the Census, 2001c). The Hispanic population grew by over 60 percent in the last decade, making it roughly the same size as the U.S. black population (cited in Schmitt, 2001b). By the year 2030, it's estimated that people of Hispanic origin will compose close to 20 percent of the U.S. population. In California, Hispanics already make up one-third of the population. But as is true of Asian Americans, there is tremendous cultural and familial diversity among groups considered Hispanic. About half the Hispanics in this country consider themselves to be white, 42 percent consider themselves to be "some other race," and 6 percent consider themselves to be two or more races. Exhibit 3.4 shows Hispanic population trends and composition.

Early Immigrant Families

The diversity of the Hispanic population in the United States stems from distinctly different immigration histories. For instance, because Puerto Ricans were granted U.S. citizenship in 1917, their immigration to the United States has been relatively easy and, at times, has been actively encouraged by the government (Sanchez-Ayendez, 1998). Most Puerto Ricans live in the large metropolitan areas of the Northeast.

When Fidel Castro came to power in Cuba in the late 1950s, Cuban immigrants poured into the United States. Because they were fleeing a Communist political regime that was at odds with U.S. political ideals, their initial entry into this country was met with enthusiasm (Suarez, 1998). Many of the early immigrants were middle-class Cubans who had the wherewithal to climb the occupational ladder; some were wealthy executives and business owners who were able to set up lucrative businesses, particularly in Florida. Today, Cuban-American families have the highest median income of any Hispanic group.

The experience of people of Mexican descent is quite different; in a sense, many are not descendants of immigrants at all. In 1848, following war with the United States, Mexico lost more than half its territory, giving up all claims to Texas and ceding much of what is now Arizona, New Mexico, Utah, Nevada, and California (Dill, 1995). Although Mexicans who had been living on the U.S. side of the new border were supposed to be granted all the rights of U.S. citizens, their property was routinely confiscated, and they lost control of mining, ranching, and farming industries. The U.S. takeover resulted in the gradual displacement of Mexicans from their ancestral lands. In the early twentieth century, life continued to be a daily struggle for survival. Frequently, workers had to house their families in primitive shacks with no electricity or plumbing for months on end while they did seasonal labor (Rico & Mano, 1991). Since then, many poor immigrants from the interior of Mexico have crossed the border to seek work, some becoming permanent U.S. residents and some returning seasonally to their home villages. Mexican-Americans make up the largest segment of the Hispanic population.

Roles in traditional Mexican families were strongly defined by gender. Women were valued first and foremost for their household skills. In rural areas they might also be responsible for tending gardens and looking after animals. But high rates of widowhood—caused by the hazardous nature of the work available to men—and temporary abandonment by men in

EXHIBIT 3.4

U.S. Hispanics

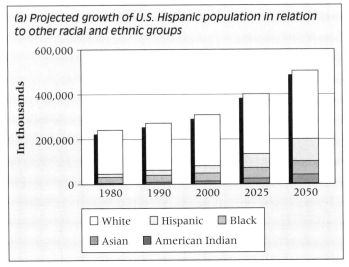

(a) Projected growth of U.S. Hispanic population in relation to other racial and ethnic groups

☐ White   ☐ Hispanic   ☐ Black
■ Asian   ■ American Indian

Data source: U.S. Bureau of the Census. 2000b. *Statistical Abstract of the United States: 2000,* Table 10. Washington, DC: U.S. Government Printing Office.

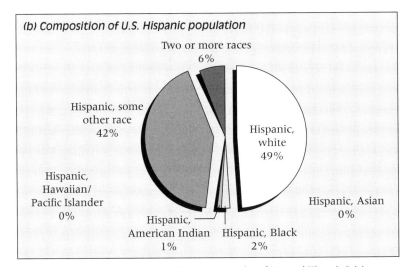

(b) Composition of U.S. Hispanic population

Two or more races
6%

Hispanic, some other race
42%

Hispanic, white
49%

Hispanic, Hawaiian/ Pacific Islander
0%

Hispanic, American Indian
1%

Hispanic, Black
2%

Hispanic, Asian
0%

Data source: E. M. Grieco & R. C. Cassidy. 2001. *Overview of Race and Hispanic Origin: Census 2000 Brief,* Table 10. Available at www.census.gov/prod/2001pubs/c2kbr01-1.pdf. Accessed June 1, 2001.

search of employment created sharp increases in female-headed households during the mid-nineteenth to the early twentieth century (Griswold del Castillo, 1979). Women (and children) began joining the labor force primarily as maids, servants, laundresses, garment workers, cooks, and dishwashers.

Eventually entire families were participating in the labor market, particularly in seasonal, itinerant farm labor. This occupation was a way of increasing earnings and of keeping the family together. Mexican Americans in extended families fared better economically and experienced less downward mobility than people in smaller, nuclear families (Dill,

1995). Extended families could help newly immigrating relatives find housing and employment and could pool their resources to pay for food, housing, transportation, and schooling (Gelles, 1995).

Contemporary Hispanic Families

The consistent decline in white family size over the years has not been mirrored in the Hispanic population (Frisbie & Bean, 1995). Because of the influx of immigrants with large families and religious (Catholic) proscriptions against birth control, Hispanic families tend to be relatively large compared to families of other ethnic groups. In 1999, for instance, 18 percent of Hispanic families had three or more children under 18 in the household, compared to 13 percent for African Americans and 10 percent for whites (U.S. Bureau of the Census, 2000b). By contrast, only 37 percent of Hispanic households had no children under 18 present, compared to 53 percent for whites and 44 percent for African Americans. The average Hispanic woman gives birth to 2.9 children in her lifetime, compared to 2.1 for African Americans, 2.3 for Asian Americans, and 2.0 for whites (U.S. Bureau of the Census, 2000b).

Hispanic families also tend to be more stable than families in other ethnic groups. Although Hispanic families have been affected by rising divorce rates, just like any other group in U.S. society, their rate tends to be lower than or comparable to other groups. In 1999, for instance, 7.6 percent of the Hispanic population was divorced, compared to 11.9 percent of blacks and 9.8 percent of whites (U.S. Bureau of the Census, 2000b). And despite a greater percentage of single-parent families among Hispanics than among whites, a lower percentage of them were created by the breakup of a marriage.

Compared to African American and European-American households, a smaller percentage of Hispanic households has no employed member (U.S. Bureau of Labor Statistics, 2000). Yet Hispanics tend to be more economically disadvantaged than whites, with some variation by subgroup. For instance, approximately 52 percent of children of Puerto Rican descent and 40 percent of those of Mexican descent live in poverty (Roscigno, 2000). Twice as many Puerto Rican families as Mexican families are headed by a single woman (Aponte, 1998). By contrast, only 22 percent of Cuban-American children live in poverty, a rate comparable to that of white children.

A sense of familial responsibility and mutual obligation continues to play a prominent role in Hispanic families (American Association of Retired Persons, 2001; Hines, Garcia-Preto, McGoldrick, Almeida, & Weltman, 1997). Their large kinship networks can best be described as "expanded families" (Horowitz, 1997). Relatives tend to live in the same neighborhood and interact on a regular basis, even though each household comprises a nuclear family. Within expanded families, members are able to exchange important services such as babysitting, meals, personal advice, and emotional support (Becerra, 1992). Feelings of mutual obligation strengthen relationships. Rather than being labeled a freeloader, a person who can survive without money for a long time by going from relative to relative is considered to have a strong, cohesive family (Horowitz, 1997). But in recent years, in light of the rapidly growing elderly Hispanic population, fulfilling familial obligations has become more difficult.

Of all the popular stereotypes surrounding Hispanic families, one of the most prevalent is the concept of *machismo*. Machismo is frequently equated with male dominance, pride in masculinity, honor in being the economic provider, and a sexual double standard. The father

See Issue 4 for a discussion of how race and ethnicity influence attitudes toward family responsibilities.

is considered the head of the household, the major decision maker, and the absolute power holder in the family (Becerra, 1992). Manhood is expressed through independence, strength, control, and domination. Although machismo often has negative connotations, Latino scholars have noted that it also implies many positive traits, such as respect, responsibility, generosity, and loyalty (Mirande, 1988).

For women, motherhood was traditionally seen as the most culturally acceptable identity. The gender stereotypes surrounding Hispanic families imply that women are self-sacrificing and passive caretakers of the entire family. But the ideals of the tradition of machismo are frequently contradicted by the demands of contemporary life, and most scholars agree that the degree of male dominance associated with machismo has been exaggerated. Economic conditions and the types of jobs available to many Hispanic men have often kept them away from their families for long periods. Over time, more and more women have become heads of households and entered the job market. And contemporary Hispanic men appear to share child care, decision making, and household tasks as much as non-Hispanic white men do (Ybarra, 1982). As this Hispanic husband puts it, ideologies can sometimes be compromised by the realities of family life:

> Sharing the house stuff is usually just a necessity. If, as we would hope in the future, she didn't have to work outside the home, then I think I would be comfortable doing less of it. Then she would be the primary house care person and I would be the primary financial resource person. I think roles would change then, and I would be comfortable with her doing more of the dishes and more of the cleaning, and I think she would too. In that sense, I think traditional relationships, if traditional means guy working and the woman staying home, is good. I wouldn't mind getting a taste of it myself! (quoted in Coltrane, 1996b, p. 99)

The Diversity Question

Fortunately, the uniqueness and richness demonstrated by minority families are being more widely acknowledged and appreciated in the United States today. People are more willing than at any time in the past to embrace the racial and ethnic diversity of the U.S. population. Yet this growing cultural tolerance coincides with another social dynamic: the pressure toward **assimilation**, the process by which members of minority groups change their ways to conform to those of the dominant culture. One of the bedrock goals of the U.S. value system has been the ultimate assimilation of racial and ethnic minority groups into mainstream society.

Although there are many views about this issue, 38 percent of Americans tend to believe it's best for racial and ethnic minority groups to assimilate into mainstream society (see Exhibit 3.5). Many immigrants also believe that if they gradually lose their differences and adopt the lifestyle of the majority, they can get high-paying, stable jobs and become accepted members of mainstream society.

However, assimilation has an inherent trap: The only way for a group to conform to the dominant—in U.S. society, European-American—way of life is to abandon many of the family traditions of the culture it left behind (Murray, 1994). Furthermore, assimilation has often been systematically forced on certain groups. Native Americans, for instance, were forced to abandon their traditional family lifestyle by whites who could not accept their distinctive values. When blacks were brought to America as slaves, they were

EXHIBIT 3.5

*Americans'
Attitudes Toward
Assimilation*

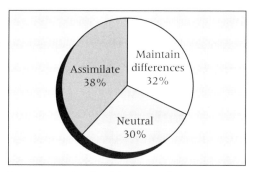

Data source: National Opinion Research Center. 1998.
General Social Survey. Available at www.icpsr.umich.edu/
GSS/. Accessed June 1, 2001.

forced to take new names and forbidden to practice any of the family and social traditions of their native cultures.

Thus some members of minority groups consider assimilation an undesirable goal. Instead, they seek a **multicultural society,** one made up of groups that maintain not only their ethnic identities but also their own languages, arts, music, foods, literature, religions, and family forms. They believe that multiculturalism enriches the society. With the massive influx of foreign-born, non–English-speaking people into this country in recent years, it has indeed sometimes been difficult to think of the United States as one culture and Americans as one people. This issue, of course, remains unresolved, and the entire complex of political and economic events in not only the United States but also the world will continue to shape family life in U.S. society in years to come.

DEMO•GRAPHICS

Racial Variations in Family Patterns

It should come as no surprise that different racial and ethnic groups have created unique family adaptations. Economic and educational realities vary for each of them, shaping the experiences of minority families in profound ways. Consider, for instance, the lower percentage of married couples among African Americans, compared to European Americans and Hispanics. This single variation in family structure has important implications for how individuals, particularly children, experience family life. It means that fewer children are likely to live with both parents. As Exhibit 3.6a shows, about half of black children live in mother-only households, whereas white children are most likely to be living with two parents, as are Hispanic children.

In Exhibit 3.6a, notice the proportion of children living with "no parent." About one in ten black children fall into this category, more than twice the percentage for Hispanics or whites. Interestingly, although these children do not live with one of their biological parents, they are likely to have a "parent figure" in their lives. As you can see in Exhibit 3.6b, of those who do not live with biological parents, 62 percent of black children live with their grandparents, compared to 44 percent of white and 33 percent of Hispanic children. In fact, if you combine the two categories of relatives—grandparents and other relatives—

EXHIBIT 3.6

Race, Ethnicity, and Children's Family Circumstances

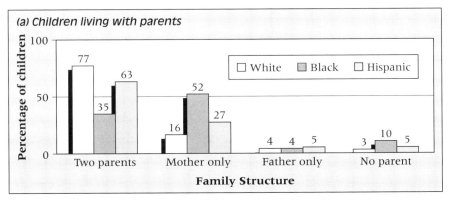

Data source: Childstats.gov. 2000. *America's Children 2000*, Table POP5.A. Available at www.childstats.gov/ac2000/pop5A.htm. Accessed June 1, 2001.

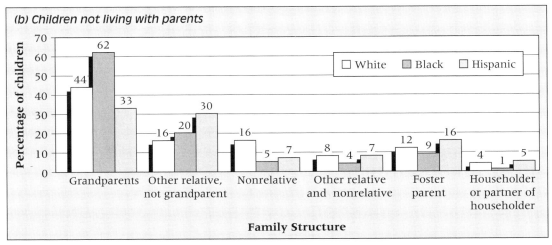

Data source: Adapted from Childstats.gov. 2000. *America's Children 2000*, Table POP5.A. Available at www.childstats.gov/ac2000/pop5A.htm. Accessed June 1, 2001.

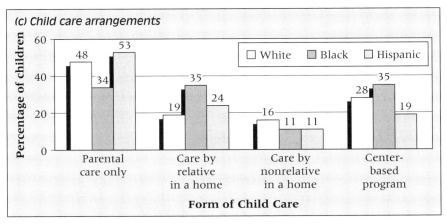

Data source: Adapted from Childstats.gov. 2000. *America's Children 2000*, Table POP5.A. Available at www.childstats.gov/ac2000/pop5A.htm. Accessed June 1, 2001.

about 82 percent of black children who don't live with parents do in fact live with other relatives, compared to 60 percent for whites and 63 percent for Hispanics. These figures suggest a strong reliance on extended family among blacks.

Another indicator of this difference in reliance on extended kin is found in child care arrangements for children who live with their parents. Exhibit 3.6c shows variations in child care arrangements among different racial and ethnic groups for children between infancy and the third grade. (Because children might participate in more than one form of nonparental care, the percentages do not necessarily add up to 100 percent.) About half of both white and Hispanic children are cared for by a parent exclusively, whereas only about a third of black children are cared for only by a parent. A higher percentage of black children are cared for by a relative who is not a parent as compared to white or Hispanic children.

Thinking Critically About the Statistics

1. To what extent to do you think economic differences explain the different racial and ethnic family patterns shown in Exhibit 3.6a? Now compare Exhibit 3.6a to 3.6b. Notice that even though black children are less likely than others to come from two-parent households, when they don't live with their parents they're more likely to live with grandparents and other relatives. Why do you think this is the case? Is the stronger reliance on extended kin among blacks a type of economic survival strategy, or do these differences stem from other cultural and historical circumstances?

2. Exhibit 3.6b also shows that when not living with their parents, two to three times as many white children as black and Hispanic children live with nonrelatives. The source of these data doesn't specify who these nonrelatives are. Who might they be? Why do you suppose white children are less likely than other children to live with extended family members?

3. How are the data shown in Exhibit 3.6c dependent on those presented in Exhibit 3.6b? How might findings concerning child care arrangements by race change if you were looking only at married couples?

4. What can you conclude about the state of U.S. families by looking at Exhibits 3.6a, 3.6b, and 3.6c? Is reliance on extended kin for child care and other needs a positive "family value"? What advantages might accrue to children raised in these situations? What might they be missing? How might the statistics presented in these three tables change if biracial children were included? ■

Conclusion

As you've seen in this chapter, most minority families demonstrate incredible resilience, surviving difficult and sometimes debilitating social circumstances. These families—particularly African-American, Asian-American, and Hispanic-American families—are more often than not a source of strength for their members, providing crucial support and nurturing. From a sociological point of view, the interesting fact is the role that families have played in helping individual members of racial and ethnic minorities to overcome the disadvantages they face in mainstream society.

As U.S. society becomes increasingly multiracial, we are forced to deal with a number of critical issues. Can a society that has been strongly committed to assimilation truly appreciate racial and ethnic diversity? What would such a country look like? Is it possible to address and reduce large-scale economic and educational inequalities that exist by race without threatening the cultural uniqueness expressed by different groups?

Chapter Highlights

- The characteristics that distinguish one racial group from another have less to do with biological differences than with what a society defines as socially significant.
- The dramatic growth in the number of multiracial children is challenging traditional concepts of race.
- The family forms that characterize particular racial or ethnic groups reflect the historical and economic conditions under which that group entered the United States. Minority families must adapt to differing degrees of social exclusion and discrimination.
- Focusing on the unique family characteristics of certain racial or ethnic groups sometimes obscures the diversity that exists *within* those groups.

Your Turn

U.S. society—especially the economic opportunities it provides and the obstacles it sets in place—can look quite different to people from different racial and ethnic groups.

To gain a better understanding of how race and ethnicity influence people's family experiences, interview several adults from each of the following groups:

- White Europeans
- Hispanic nonwhites
- Asian Americans
- African Americans
- A multiracial couple or family

If possible, interview husbands and wives, and also try to maximize diversity within each group. For example, for Hispanic adults, try to locate someone of Mexican descent and someone of Cuban descent.

When you interview your "subjects," first ask them to discuss their cultural heritage(s). When did their families come to the United States? What were the circumstances? Do they have any knowledge of relatives living in the countries of origin? Consider how the circumstances and historical context of their arrival here affect contact with and knowledge of distant relatives who live in other parts of the world.

Ask them about family traditions, such as weekly or daily rituals, holiday celebrations, and so on. Are some of these traditions linked to their racial or ethnic backgrounds? What are the most powerful and important cultural traditions? Ask whether it's difficult to maintain these traditions. Do their family traditions include members of their extended families? What role do these other relatives play in their lives?

Finally, ask about experiences with racial discrimination. What have these experiences taught them about living and surviving in the United States? About the importance of family?

Use your findings to consider whether, when it comes to family, people should emphasize the similarities that exist across racial and ethnic groups or the differences. As society becomes more racially diverse, do you think family patterns among different groups will become more or less distinctive? Do you think U.S. society should aspire to assimilation or multiculturalism? And do you think this society will ever reach a point when racial and ethnic categories are irrelevant in people's lives?

Wealth, Poverty, and Families

Lifestyles of the Rich and the Poor

The United States bills itself as a nation built on the ideal of equality. However, it remains one of the most unequal industrialized societies in the world as the gap between its poorest and wealthiest citizens grows. Such social class inequalities are often felt most strongly in the day-to-day activities of family life. As you look at the photos here, try to put yourself into the circumstances being portrayed. Try to imagine how people in different social classes experience some of the same things. Examine what people wear and what possessions surround them. Think about the advantages and disadvantages that social class creates for families.

The little girl is being tended to by a maid amid lavish, affluent surroundings. The boy—his clothes dirty and his grandfather inattentive—knows only poverty.

In what ways will these two childhoods be different?

How will these differences impact the children's futures?

The differences in the sleeping arrangements in these two photos are striking. But which is better? The closeness of the welfare mother and her newborn baby can foster much greater intimacy than the separate cot and master bed depicted in the other photo.

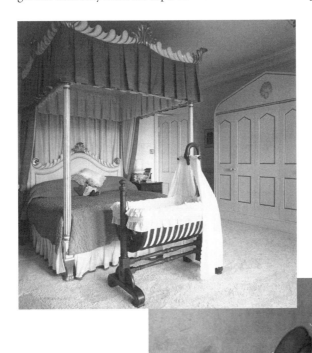

Is it possible that the living arrangements created by poverty can actually strengthen family ties?

Wealth broadens families' social and cultural life. "Eating out" is likely to be commonplace in families that are financially secure. Such experiences help parents socialize children on how to act in public and broaden the children's exposure to other cultures. The cramped kitchen depicted in the other photo affords no such opportunities.

Public transportation not only limits the freedom of families to come and go as they please but also reduces the amount of privacy they enjoy. More affluent families, with their own cars, can conduct private family business as they travel.

Can you think of other situations in which poor people must do in public what more affluent families are able to do in private?

Many of us grew up in middle-class or working-class families. We may not have been wealthy enough to enjoy unlimited freedom and opportunity, but we probably had enough resources to enjoy a level of security and stability far above the circumstances of the impoverished family whose story is told in the following paragraphs.

> One of my sons was diagnosed as having a high lead level in his blood. The Welfare Department placed my son under protective services and told me that I would have to find another place to live or they would put [him] into a foster home. With six children on a welfare budget, it's not easy to find an apartment. And I had to find one within thirty days! To keep the state from taking my son, I was forced to move into the first available housing I could find.
>
> Since I was an emergency case and eligible for a housing subsidy, my name was placed at the top of the list. I had to take the first available unit offered by the Housing Authority. The offer: a brand new town-house-type apartment *fifty miles away* in a white, middle-class suburb!
>
> I knew this move would devastate my family because we would be so far away from our relatives and friends. When you're poor, you have to depend on your family and friends to help you through when you don't have the money to help yourself. At least two or three times every month I take my children to my mother's house to eat. How would we ever be able to get to her house from fifty miles away?
>
> I also knew my neighbors wouldn't welcome me and my children: a black single woman with six children. I imagined the sneers of the merchants as I paid for my groceries with food stamps and the grunts of the doctors as I pulled out my Medicaid card.
>
> I thought about the problems of transportation that were sure to crop up. How would I get my children to school? What if they got sick; how far was the nearest hospital? I envisioned the seven of us walking for miles with grocery bags. . . .
>
> We now live in a totally hostile environment severed from our family and friends. And although we live in a physically beautiful development, life for us is hard. A poor family with no transportation is lost in the suburbs. We are as isolated as if we lived on a remote island in the Pacific. (quoted in Dujon, Gradford, & Stevens, 1995, p. 282)

It doesn't take much of an imagination to see how difficult family life can be for poor families. Poverty brings hardship, even when something good happens—such as placement into a nice apartment.

Of course, the relationship between wealth (or lack of it) and family life is not always so straightforward. Wealthy families are not immune from despair, disappointment, and pain. The lives of children in extremely wealthy families are often tightly monitored and controlled by their parents to avoid any damage to the family's fortune and reputation. Such restrictions can create resentment and rebellion. At the other end of the spectrum, some poor families experience a great deal of trouble and heartbreak, but others are strong, supportive, and emotionally gratifying. Many successful adults who grew up in abject poverty have prospered from the love and guidance of their parents and their relatives.

Nevertheless, wealth and, by extension, socioeconomic standing are an important backdrop to family life. Much of the heated criticism of family we hear these days focuses on poor families. In this chapter, we examine the influence of broad economic forces on family dynamics and structure at both ends of the spectrum and in the middle.

Class Stratification

Contemporary industrialized societies are likely to be stratified on the basis of **social class**—that is, people's economic position in society. Social class distinguishes one group's pattern of behavior from another's and determines access to important resources and life chances. Americans live in a society that is solidly structured along the lines of class distinctions.

Theoretically, class systems are different from other systems of stratification—such as the Indian *caste system,* which bases social position on heredity—in that there are no legal barriers to social mobility. In practice, however, mobility between classes may be quite difficult. As much as people would like to believe otherwise, the opportunities to move from one class up to another are not available to all members of society.

To rank families on the basis of class, contemporary sociologists usually compile information on quantifiable factors such as household income, wealth, occupational status, and educational attainment. But the boundaries between classes still tend to be rather fuzzy. Some have argued that there are no discrete classes with clearly defined boundaries but only a socioeconomic continuum on which individuals are ranked (Blau & Duncan, 1967).

Nevertheless, class designations remain a part of both everyday thinking and social research. Here are some common understandings (from Walton, 1990; Wright, Costello, Hachen, & Sprague, 1982) of who makes up various classes in American society:

- *"Upper" class:* owners of vast amounts of property and other forms of wealth, owners of large corporations, top financiers, and members of prestigious families.
- *"Middle" class:* managers, supervisors, executives, small business owners, and professionals (for example, lawyers, doctors, teachers, engineers).
- *"Working" class:* those who earn modest wages, such as industrial and factory workers, office workers, clerks, and farm and manual laborers.
- *The "poor":* people who work for the minimum wage or are chronically unemployed. These are the people who do society's dirty work and whose lives are the most precarious.

Those in the higher social economic classes control nearly all the nation's wealth. The richest 20 percent of the U.S. population, for instance, control nearly half of the nation's aggregate income (see Exhibit 4.1a). Furthermore, the gap between the richest and the poorest has grown over the past 3 decades, with an increasing proportion of total income accruing to the top 5 percent of earners (see Exhibit 4.1b). The imbalance in the distribution of wealth, or the accumulation of resources such as homes and investments, is even greater. About 99 percent of the wealth in the United States is concentrated in the hands of the wealthiest 20 percent of the population (Wolff, 1995). Since the 1920s, the wealthiest 1 percent of the population has consistently owned about 30 percent of the total wealth in this country (Keister & Moller, 2000).

But class is about more than wealth and occupation; when we talk about social class, we are making broad generalizations about what large groups of people look like and how they live. People's positions in the class system can affect virtually every aspect of their lives, including political preferences, sexual behavior, church membership, diet, health, life expectancy, place of residence, fashion, access to education, dating and marital patterns, child rearing, and treatment by the criminal justice system (Della Fave, 1980; Mantsios, 1995; Reiman, 1998).

EXHIBIT 4.1

*Unequal
Distribution of
Income in the
United States*

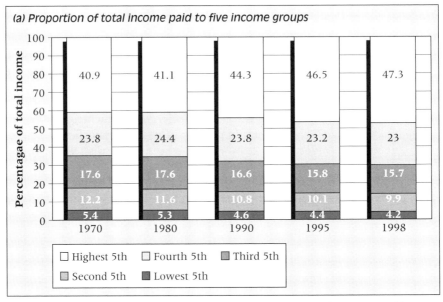

Data source: U.S. Bureau of the Census. 2000b. *Statistical Abstract of the United States: 2000,* Table 745. Washington, DC: U.S. Government Printing Office.

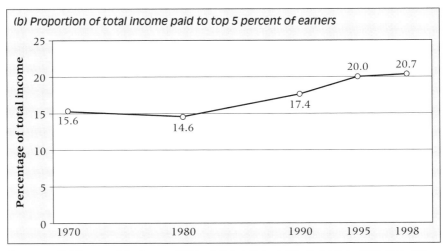

Data source: U.S. Bureau of the Census. 2000b. *Statistical Abstract of the United States: 2000,* Table 745. Washington, DC: U.S. Government Printing Office.

For instance, poor two-parent families are approximately twice as likely to break up as are two-parent families that aren't poor (Rank, 1994). And whereas middle-class preschoolers whose parents work are likely to be cared for by trained day care teachers, the caretakers of lower-class preschoolers are likely to be untrained, unlicensed neighbors or relatives, leading to very different educational experiences and successes later in childhood (King, 1997).

Those at lower levels of the stratification system are more likely to die prematurely as a result of homicide, accidents, or inadequate health care than are people at higher levels

(Kearl, 1989). With each step down the income ladder comes an increased risk of headaches, varicose veins, respiratory infection, hypertension, emotional distress, heart disease, and early death (Shweder, 1997). Lack of adequate health care causes three times more deaths than does AIDS each year (Navarro, 1992).

But keep in mind that families within the same social category—whether one is talking about race, ethnicity, religion, or class—do not represent a monolithic group. There is often as much diversity within a category as between categories. This diversity is especially apparent when social class intersects with race. Mary Pattillo-McCoy (1999) studied the black middle-class residents of an urban neighborhood she called "Groveland." She found that the neighborhoods where many urban, middle-class African Americans live are likely to be in close proximity to poor neighborhoods, whereas white middle-class neighborhoods are typically separated from these areas. In Chicago, for example, 79 percent of blacks are likely to live within a few blocks of a neighborhood where at least a third of the residents are poor; only 36 percent of white, middle-class Chicago dwellers live so close to a poor neighborhood (cited in Pattillo-McCoy, 1999). Thus middle-class black parents who want to protect their children from the negative influences that are often found in poor, inner-city areas face some challenges:

> Groveland parents . . . set limits on where their children can travel. They choose activities—church youth groups, magnet schools or accelerated programs in the local school, and the Boy Scouts and Girl Scouts—to increase the likelihood that their children will learn positive values and associate with youth from similar families. Still, many parents are working long hours to maintain their middle-class incomes. They cannot be with their children at all times. On their way to the grocery store or to school or to music lessons, Groveland's youth pass other young people whose parents are not as strict, who stay outside later, who have joined the local gang, or who earn enough money being a lookout at a drug house to buy new gym shoes. They also meet these peers in school and at the park. . . . For some teenagers, the fast life looks much more exciting than what their parents have to offer them, and they are drawn to it. The simple fact of living in a neighborhood where not all families have sufficient resources to direct their children away from deviance makes it difficult for parents to ensure positive outcomes for their children and their neighborhood. (pp. 211–212)

Pattillo-McCoy found that, in many other respects as well, the structural and social realities for black middle-class Americans are quite different from those of middle-class whites. Still, most families within a particular social class face some common opportunities and barriers.

Upper-Class Families

Members of upper-class families tend to be born into formidable wealth (Langman, 1988), which provides political and economic power as well as insulation from the rest of society. Here's a definition of the upper class, formulated 40 years ago, that still rings true today:

> [A] group of families whose members are descendants of successful individuals of one, two, three or more generations ago . . . the top of the social class hierarchy. They are brought up together and they are friends. They intermarry and have a distinctive style of life. There is a primary group solidarity that sets them apart from the rest of the population. (Baltzell, 1958, p. 60)

An important feature of upper-class families is the rather traditional role that women tend to play (Ostrander, 1984). Many wives, for instance, believe they should put their husbands' interests ahead of their own:

> He's the brain in the family and it's my role to see that he's at his best. I've subjugated everything to that. When he comes home in the evening, this house must be perfectly quiet. . . . He wants me to be pleasant, pretty, and relaxed. I never bring a problem to him, except during forty-five minutes set aside on Sunday mornings for that purpose. (quoted in Ostrander, 1984, p. 39)

Such an attitude seems out-of-date in the twenty-first century. However, as was the case in many nineteenth-century families, these women see such supportive behavior as their essential contribution to their families. They take for granted that their job—their part of the bargain in exchange for a life of luxury—is to "run the house." They rarely do the actual cooking, laundry, and cleaning themselves, but they make decisions about how other people—whose labor they have purchased—perform the housework.

Many upper-class women also tend to have a rather traditional perspective on the mother role. Children's preschool years are typically spent at home in the presence of mothers and nannies, nurses, or other private, in-home caretakers. From kindergarten through college, these upper-class children are usually enrolled in private schools (Domhoff, 1983). There they are set apart from children of other classes or, as one upper-class mother called them, "ordinary people" (quoted in Ostrander, 1984, p. 85). Because inheritance and pedigree in extremely wealthy families are passed down through the children, it is crucial to the family that they be raised to value their social position and understand the responsibilities that come with it. Mothers play a dominant role in enforcing these high standards of behavior and structuring the child's participation in "appropriate" activities and organizations.

The popular belief that upper-class women leave the raising of their children solely to nannies, au pairs, or other hired caretakers may therefore be largely mythical. Many of these women feel it is important to be present in their children's lives, particularly when they are young, even if these other caretakers do take over much of the hands-on, day-to-day care. Upper-class women often arrange their own activities, particularly volunteer work, so they can be home for their children.

What many upper-class parents seem to want most for their children as they get older is a "compatible marriage"—that is, a marriage to someone of equal class standing. To that end, they are often concerned that their children engage in class-exclusive recreational activities and join organizations whose membership is by invitation only. Social clubs are places where "acceptable" people of "the same kind" can meet, ultimately resulting in "acceptable" marriages (Ostrander, 1984). Although marital choices are technically "free," there is a high degree of scrutiny and surveillance of dating and courtship among upper-class youth. Marriage between cousins is often encouraged to ensure proper lineage. Marrying someone of a different social class—or "marrying down"—means not only accepting that person as an equal partner but also blurring class distinctions in the next generation, should the couple have children (Kalmijn, 1991b).

The "New Rich"

Unlike those elite, upper-class families in which vast amounts of wealth are inherited, other affluent families experience a rapid increase of wealth and social mobility through personal achievements. These families are usually headed by high-level executives in large corporations, successful founders of new businesses, and highly compensated lawyers, doctors, scientists, entertainers, and professional athletes. They are the "new rich," people who have made, not inherited, their fortunes. Some executives and professionals were born into poor or working-class families or belong to a disadvantaged racial or ethnic group, but they have been able to climb the social ladder and create a comfortable life for themselves and their families.

Personal effort and achievement are so crucial to the "new rich" that many are opposed to leaving their children huge inheritances. They feel that inherited wealth can corrupt and spoil young people. For example, Microsoft owner Bill Gates—currently one of the richest men in the world—says, "One thing is for sure. I won't leave a lot of money to my heirs because I don't think it would be good for them" (quoted in Linden & Machan, 1997, pp. 152, 154).

Before you start worrying about the deprived lives of the children of such wealthy individuals, remember this: They will never be left destitute. Gates said he will leave his daughter and any of her future siblings $10 million each. This is a tiny piece of a vast estate but a substantial amount of money in its own right. Furthermore, also keep in mind that inheritance involves more than money or property. Parents always "endow" their children with varying amounts of what sociologists call *cultural capital* (reputations, connections, skills, knowledge, and so on) (Becker, 1981). So children of affluent parents inherit a recognized family name and the respect and privilege that goes along with it. Hence, they are likely to have access to opportunities and social advantages that are beyond the grasp of most.

Because they owe their economic position to their occupational achievements, newly rich professionals tend to make their careers the focal point of their lives. Gender plays a key role here. Husbands in particular are likely to work long hours and travel on business frequently. Whereas upper-class wives work to maintain class boundaries in current and future generations, wives in newly rich families tend to be concerned with keeping their husbands in the occupations that put them where they are (Kanter, 1986).

Sudden wealth can create its own brand of family difficulty. For instance, in Silicon Valley—where, at its peak, each day brought 60 new high-tech millionaires and high school parking lots overflowed with SUVs and Mercedes cars—concern has grown over the stressful effects that rapid wealth has on children (Brown, 2000). Children of the newly rich often have little appreciation for the lifestyle their parents provide them. They live in a world where "middle class" is equated with poverty, where families that go to Hawaii only once a year are considered bottom rung, and where having parents who are "only" doctors is humiliating and embarrassing. But unlike upper-class children, whose wealth has spanned generations and whose inheritance and pedigree will likely sustain them in adulthood, these children are intensely anxious about their own ability to achieve the vast amounts of wealth to which they've become accustomed. They see their parents working faster and harder to avoid falling back, and they internalize these pressures. Many believe that if they haven't established their own wealth by the time they're 24, they've somehow failed. Some psychologists and counselors have devoted their practices to treating what has come to be called "sudden wealth syndrome."

Middle-Class Families

Middle-class families are, by definition, those that have "middling incomes." Neither rich nor poor, they are the millions of people who, former President Clinton once said, "work hard and play by the rules" (Zweig, 2000). They are also in the middle of two important constituencies in modern society, the working class and the upper class, and so they share certain interests and concerns of both these groups (Zweig, 2000). For instance, as in most working-class families, both husbands and wives in middle-class families are likely to work in the paid labor force to maintain their standard of living. But like members of the upper class, their relatively secure financial circumstances allow them to purchase services to help manage the demands of work and home, such as child care or housecleaning—luxuries not available to less economically privileged families (Newman, 1999b).

Of course, significant variations in income, status, and lifestyle exist among so-called middle-class families. Those considered "upper middle class" (such as physicians, lawyers, and other well-paid professionals) may have more in common with upper-class or newly rich families than with lower middle-class families. For instance, one study of upper middle-class wives found that their role in the marriage is very much like that of upper-class wives: keeping the household running smoothly, encouraging their husbands emotionally and professionally, moving when their husbands' jobs require it, and so on (Fowlkes, 1987). These women for the most part support their husbands by playing an adjunct role in the family. But women in lower middle-class families are likely to resemble working-class wives, whose own role in the workplace is essential to the family's well-being.

The ambiguous social and economic position of middle-class families shapes family life in significant ways. For instance, wives' employment in middle-class families, especially those of the upper middle class, may not be the absolute necessity that it is in families with fewer economic means. When husbands earn relatively high incomes, their wives' earnings may be viewed as supplemental or even unnecessary (Ferree, 1984). Although a husband may be proud of his wife's accomplishments, he may see himself as the primary breadwinner.

This attitude toward women's work may be shared by children as well. When children view their mothers' employment as a choice rather than an economic necessity, they may resent the time she devotes to work. In Lillian Rubin's study of middle-class and working-class families, she found a level of anger and resentment directed toward parents, especially mothers, among her middle-class respondents that wasn't expressed by individuals in working-class families. She explains,

> In a family where all the material necessities and most of the comforts and luxuries are taken for granted, a child can feel angered and rejected by a father who "works all the time," by a mother whose energy is directed into the kind of volunteerism that engages so many women of the professional middle class, by the one who *chooses* a career. But how can poor children justify or rationalize those feelings when they know that father works two jobs to keep a roof over their heads and food on the table; that mother does dull, demeaning, and exhausting work just to help make ends meet? (Rubin, 1976, p. 27)

Middle-class couples tend to place high value on the ideal of equality in marriages (Cancian & Gordon, 1988; Rubin, 1976). The reality of their everyday lives, however, may be very different. Middle-class marriages are not necessarily more egalitarian than those in other social classes, but the expectation for equality is certainly greater. As a result, when middle-class women confront inequality in their marriages, they may be more angry and mystified by it. Rubin (1976) tells the story of a middle-class couple who faced the difficult decision about whether to have an abortion. The husband, who did not want the abortion, would never have said, "I forbid you to have an abortion!" Such a command would contradict the couple's egalitarian ideology. But what he did say had the same effect:

> It's her choice; she has to raise the kids. I told her I'll go along with whatever she decides. . . . But, you know, if she goes through with it, I'll never agree to have another child. . . . She said I wasn't giving her much of a choice. But it seems to me she ought to know what the consequences of her actions will be when she makes the decision, and those are the consequences. (p. 97)

Not surprisingly, the wife opted to have the child. For this wife, who expects her marriage to be egalitarian, the challenge was to redefine the decision making surrounding this important decision as "mutual" rather than "husband dominant."

The ideology of equality also tends to filter into the parent–child relationship. Shared parenting, or at least greater involvement of men in fathering their children, is a value expressed more among the middle class than other groups (LaRossa, 1992). But here too, the reality is often very different from the ideology. For the most part, in middle-class families—as in families of other classes—women assume primary responsibility for child care.

The importance of understanding middle-class values and lifestyles is clear when one considers that "middle class" is often equated with what is "mainstream" in American society (Pattillo-McCoy, 1999). Middle-class norms often define for this culture what is desirable and, therefore, what others should strive for (Newman, 1999b). By comparison, other family types are often viewed as deviant or problematic. For example, the middle class typically values autonomy, including autonomy among adult siblings and between adult children and their parents (Newman, 1999b). And so the American ideal becomes individual independence, and even lower-class families who find strength in the extended family bonds they rely on for survival begin to wonder whether they shouldn't be living like the middle-class families they see on TV and in the movies.

Of course, not all families can or want to conform to middle-class ideals. To successfully co-parent, fathers cannot work two shifts, as working- and lower-class men may be required to do. It is much harder to realize egalitarian marriages in upper-class marriages if husbands earn significantly more than their wives or if their wives are unemployed. And even for families squarely within the middle class, the realities of contemporary life—including divorce, unemployment, lack of quality child care, and so on—limit their ability to live up to the values associated with the middle class.

See Issue 4 for a discussion of the ways people balance individualism and family obligation.

Working-Class Families

Clearly, the stresses associated with affluence pale in comparison to the stresses felt by families that constantly struggle to make ends meet. The most important characteristic of working-class families is their dependence on hourly wages, which makes them particularly susceptible to downturns in the economy that can result in layoffs, plant closings, and unemployment (Rapp, 1999). These jobs are also less likely than higher-paying, salaried jobs to provide benefits such as medical insurance and retirement plans.

As a consequence of the harsh economic landscape, many working-class young people continue to need their parents' help well after becoming adults. Twenty years ago, working-class women and men were significantly more likely than their middle-class counterparts to marry young, often because of a desire to become independent and leave home. More affluent young people, in contrast, delayed marriage to attend college and enhance their employment prospects.

Working-class people have also tended to have children earlier than members of higher classes, creating further economic pressures. Most working-class women are employed before they marry, and so young couples may expect that two incomes will enable them to maintain a home. But the demands of a baby can make it difficult to pay for day-to-day expenses. Instead of the happy life they imagined, young couples may begin to feel trapped and anxious. Some couples divorce; others are forced to move back in with their parents, which leads to even more stress.

Past research suggested that communication between working-class husbands and wives regarding personal or emotional matters was sometimes difficult. In one comparative study, middle-class and working-class wives were asked what they valued most in their husbands. The middle-class subjects tended to focus on such issues as intimacy, sharing, communication, and the comforts and prestige that their husbands' occupations provided them. Working-class wives were more dismal in their assessments, focusing on the absence of such problems as unemployment, alcoholism, and violence. As one 33-year-old housewife put it, "I guess I can't complain. He's a steady worker; he doesn't drink; he doesn't hit me. That's a lot more than my mother had, and she didn't sit around complaining and feeling sorry for herself, so I sure haven't got the right" (Rubin, 1976, p. 93).

Recent research, however, indicates that such attitudes among working-class couples are weakening. Working-class men and women are significantly more likely to approve of women working outside the home than they were 2 decades ago (Rubin, 1995). According to the General Social Survey, working-class women in the 1970s were likely to feel that the traditional husband/breadwinner, wife/homemaker roles were the best way for a family to be arranged. By the early 1990s, however, working-class women—who were now likely to be employed outside the home themselves—saw their paid employment as a crucial part of a wife's appropriate role (cited in Cherlin, 1999).

See Issue 2 for more on changing family roles and the ideologies that help people make sense out of these changes.

Despite these changing attitudes, working-class families are still vulnerable to fluctuations in the economy. Sociologist Lillian Rubin (1995) held in-depth interviews with working-class families to examine how the economic downturn of the 1980s and early 1990s had influenced their families and their dreams. The title of her book, *Families on the Fault Line,* suggests a precarious life on the edge of disaster. The families she studied aren't considered officially "poor." Nevertheless, the hope that sustained working-class people through bad times two decades ago—the belief that if they just worked hard and played by the rules, they'd eventually grab a piece of the American Dream—no longer existed. It's not so much the possibility of falling into poverty that worries them, it's the fear that there's no possibility of ever moving upward.

To survive psychologically in a world of economic instability and powerlessness, many working-class parents begin to define their jobs as meaningless and irrelevant to their core identity. But instead of focusing on the dreariness or the insignificance of their work, they come to view it as a noble act of sacrifice. A bricklayer put it simply: "My job is to work for my family" (Sennett & Cobb, 1972, p. 135).

Defining a job as sacrifice solves the problem of powerlessness in two ways. First, in return for their sacrifice, working-class parents—especially men—can demand a position of power and respect within their own families. Second, framing degrading work as sacrifice allows them to slip the bonds of the disappointing present and orient their lives toward their children's and grandchildren's future, something that gives them a sense of control and accomplishment they can't get through their jobs.

Ironically, framing work as sacrifice can cause other hidden injuries within the family (Sennett & Cobb, 1972). On the one hand, working-class parents want to spend time with their children and show concern for them. On the other hand, they know that the only way they can provide a "good home" for their family is to work longer hours at an unfulfilling job and be absent from home more frequently. Unfortunately, from the perspective of the child, this absence is precisely what constitutes a "bad home."

In addition, it is more difficult for working-class parents to sacrifice "successfully." Upper-class and middle-class parents make sacrifices so that their children will have a life like theirs. Working-class parents sacrifice so that their children will *not* have a life like theirs. Their lives are not a "model" but a "warning." Hence, the sacrifice does not end the conditions that made the parents prey to feelings of shame and inadequacy in the first place. The danger of this type of sacrifice is that if the children do fulfill the parents' wishes and rise above their quality of life, the parents may eventually become a burden or an embarrassment to them. Thus people who struggle to make ends meet are caught in a vicious trap.

Downwardly Mobile Families

Another group of people whose families are affected by economic insecurities have somewhat different experiences than working-class families. These are the people who have fallen out of the middle class. Even during the relatively prosperous 1990s, many families experienced dramatic turns in their economic well-being. They are the flip-side to the explosive wealth of the "new rich": once successful, financially stable models of the "American Dream," who are "downsized" out of a job or who see their salaries drastically reduced. Some individuals who had invested heavily in the stock market and had experienced increasing wealth during the 1990s and in 2000 lost their fortunes when the stock market plummeted in 2001. The stock market's plunge was followed by massive layoffs, especially in high-tech, high-paying jobs.

A rapid reduction in income has far-reaching consequences. It often means moving to inferior housing and leaving behind familiar routines. It means drastically less money for recreation and leisure and more pressures because of inadequate time and finances. The sudden financial strain also causes social dislocation through the loss of familiar friendships and emotional support networks.

Women are particularly vulnerable to downward mobility. Some plunge when they or their partner lose a job. But for most women, the main cause of downward mobility is divorce. Handicapped by a gender-stratified labor market, divorced women rarely have an income equal to that of their former husbands. They are also hurt by a lack of affordable and high-quality child care and by disproportionate responsibility for child-rearing expenses. What divorced women do earn is thus often not adequate to support a family (Grella, 1990).

Children are hard hit by downward mobility, too. In a study of 429 African-American and white families, sociologists Glen Elder and Jacquelynne Eccles (1995) found that economic pressures can reduce parents' effectiveness in raising their children. Not only does such pressure increase the number of hardships that a family must endure, it can also demoralize parents and significantly reduce their confidence. Children's perceptions of their parents, in turn, may also be affected. The parental authority that sprang from financial control disappears. This father was transformed by losing his job as a successful show business promoter; his 15-year-old daughter describes the loss of the father she once idolized:

> He just seemed to be getting irrational. He would walk around the house talking to himself and stay up all night, smoking cigarettes in the dark. . . . All I perceived is that somebody who used to be a figure of strength was behaving strangely: starting to cry

at odd times . . . hanging around the house unshaven in his underwear when I would bring dates home. . . . In the absence of any understanding of what was going on, my attitude was one of anger and disgust, like "Why don't you get your act together? What's the matter with you?" (Newman, 1999a, p. 96)

Some children of downwardly mobile families never escape the feeling that failure may be lurking around the corner: "The higher they climb, the more urgently they sense they are about to fall" (Newman, 1999a, p. 142). Their experience of social class during childhood has lifelong consequences—as it does for most children.

Poverty and Family Life

The economic woes of working-class or downwardly mobile families are difficult, but nowhere are the stresses of class stratification on family life more apparent than among the poorest of American families. Despair and insecurity are everyday features in families at the bottom of the class structure. Acquiring and keeping basic necessities—food, clothing, and shelter—are daily struggles. Poor families face tremendous difficulty accomplishing the day-to-day tasks that most of us take for granted. Instead, their daily chores, and frustrations, might include

> Having to take one's dirty clothing on the bus to the nearest laundromat with three children in tow; being unable to afford to go to the dentist even though the pain is excruciating; not purchasing a simple meal at a restaurant for fear it will disrupt the budget; never being able to go to a movie; having no credit, which in turn makes getting a future credit rating difficult; lacking a typewriter or personal computer on which to improve secretarial skills for a job interview. The list could go on and on. (Rank, 1994, p. 60)

Large supermarket chains hesitate to open stores in very poor neighborhoods because of security fears. Hence, residents who are without transportation must rely on small neighborhood grocery stores that charge higher prices for food than larger supermarkets do. Poor people may also pay more for winter utility bills because of the lack of insulation in poor-quality homes. Although extremely poor people are eligible for health insurance through Medicaid, nearly half of poor working people in this country have no health insurance, meaning that any sustained illness can turn into a financial catastrophe (Kilborn, 1997b).

Life on the edge of financial survival is precarious. When nothing out of the ordinary happens, people are able to manage. But an unexpected event—a sickness, an injury, the breakdown of a major appliance or automobile—can set off a "domino effect" that imperils everything else. When such events occur, families must make difficult decisions. Imagine being a poor single mother with a sick child. One trip to the doctor might cost an entire week's food budget or a month of rent. Dental work or an eye examination is easily sacrificed when other pressing bills need to be paid. If you depend on a car to get to work and it breaks down, a few hundred dollars to fix it might mean not paying the electric bill that month and having less money for other necessities. When gasoline prices skyrocketed to over $2 a gallon in some places in the summer of 2001, many poor families found that they had to cut down on food purchases so they could afford to drive their cars to work.

One of the most painful choices facing poor households is sometimes called the "heat-or-eat" dilemma: having to choose between paying the heating bill and buying food. A 3-year study in a Boston hospital found that emergency room visits by malnourished children under the age of 6 increased 30 percent after the coldest months of the year. According to one of the researchers, "parents well know that children freeze before they starve, and in winter some families have to divert their already inadequate food budget to buy fuel to keep the children warm. . . . When we say, 'You have to buy more milk for Johnny,' they say, 'But I've got to pay the bills'" ("Study of poor children," 1992, p. A17).

The Feminization and Juvenilization of Poverty

The growing rate of poverty among women and children has prompted both social research and public concern. The term **feminization of poverty** was coined in the late 1970s to refer to the greater likelihood that women, as compared to men, will live in poverty (Bianchi, 1999; Pearce, 1978). Although the poverty rate for women has declined somewhat since the 1970s, it remains about 50 percent higher than the rate for men (Bianchi, 1999).

The women at highest risk of living in poverty are single mothers. As the number of female-headed families has increased, so has the proportion of the poor who live in these families. For example, in 1966, about a quarter of all people living in poor families lived in mother-only families, but by the 1990s more than half did (Bianchi, 1999).

As a result, children are one of the groups at highest risk of living in poverty. Children's poverty rates rose fairly steadily between 1970 and the mid-1990s, reaching a peak of 22 percent in 1993. Since then children's poverty rates have stabilized, and in recent years they have declined a bit. Currently, 17 percent of children live in poverty (U.S. Bureau of the Census, 2000b). Even so, children make up about 40 percent of all people who are officially poor (Bianchi, 1999). In response to these trends, a new term, **juvenilization of poverty** has been coined (Bianchi, 1999; Lichter 1997).

Growing up in poverty has been linked to a variety of problems in children, such as dropping out of school, low academic achievement, teen pregnancy and childbearing, poor mental and physical health, delinquent behavior, and unemployment in adolescence and early adulthood (Caspi, Wright, Moffitt, & Silva, 1998; Harris & Marmer, 1996). In addition, the longer children live in poverty, the worse their cognitive, social, and emotional functioning.

Poverty affects children at every age, but very young children appear to suffer the most devastating effects. Recent research suggests that the preschool period is when economic conditions have the most serious long-term consequences for children (Duncan, Yeung, Brooks-Gunn, & Smith, 1998). For instance, children living in poverty are more likely to be ill prepared for school, which can set off a disastrous chain of events. They may not have learned basic early skills such as naming colors, sorting, counting, recognizing letters, and knowing the names of everyday objects. Hence they start school at a disadvantage compared with children who have mastered these skills (Duncan et al., 1998). Later on, this lack of preparation puts them at risk of lower test scores, grade failure, disengagement from school, and higher dropout rates.

Of course, not all poor children suffer from these conditions. Close, positive supervision and emotional support at home can improve social and emotional development, school performance, and self-worth even among the poorest children (Parcel & Menaghan, 1994).

Poverty and Children's Well-Being

Although poverty rates in the United States have declined some since 1980, children remain at higher risk of living in poverty than most other age groups. Exhibit 4.2a shows the proportion of various age groups who live in poverty. Nearly one in five children up to the age of 17 live below the poverty level (officially defined in 2000 as earnings of less than $17,463 for a family of four). Poverty is most pronounced among minority children: 32.7 percent of black children and 29.9 percent of Hispanic children live in poverty, compared to 12.9 percent of whites.

A closer look at children in poverty reveals significant differences by family type. Exhibit 4.2b shows that families headed by single mothers are far more likely to live in poverty than those headed by single fathers or by two parents. Among all children living in mother-headed households in 1998, nearly half lived in families earning less than $15,000. At the other extreme, over half of the U.S. families with both parents present earned more than $50,000.

Poverty is associated with a wide variety of problems that are detrimental to children. Three of these problems are depicted in Exhibit 4.2c. In addition, 11 percent of all U.S. households with children experience severe problems with housing (such as overcrowding or substandard conditions); among those with very low income, the percentage is 28 percent. Among all children in the United States, approximately 4 percent reported experiencing moderate or severe hunger, but that figure increases to 12 percent for those living below the poverty line. Finally, preschool children from poverty-level families are less likely to be able to recognize letters, count to 20, write their names, or read or pretend to read storybooks. These and other consequences of growing up in poverty increase the risk of lifelong economic hardship.

Thinking Critically About the Statistics

1. Exhibit 4.2a shows differences in poverty rates among various age groups. Why is it that young people (those below age 24) are, by far, the most likely to be poor? You can see that the poverty rate dips when people are between their mid-30s and mid-50s, then rises a bit for people in their 60s. Why do you think this is the case? What do you think this table would look like if it were broken down by sex? By race?

2. As you can see in Exhibit 4.2b, poverty is associated with family structure. What do you think is the nature of this relationship? Do divorce and single parenthood cause poverty? Or does poverty cause divorce and single parenthood? What reasons can you provide to support your opinion? Which household type do you think would have the greatest number of families in the $15,000 to $50,000 range (not depicted in this table)?

3. Exhibit 4.2c shows the effect poverty can have on three areas of a child's life. What do you think are the long-term consequences of these specific variables? What other negative outcomes, not shown in this table, would you expect poor children to experience? This table lumps everyone over the poverty line into one category. What would the table look like if children from middle-income families and children from extremely wealthy families were represented by different bars? Are there factors, other than a family's income, that can impede a child's access to these opportunities? ■

EXHIBIT 4.2

Poverty and Children

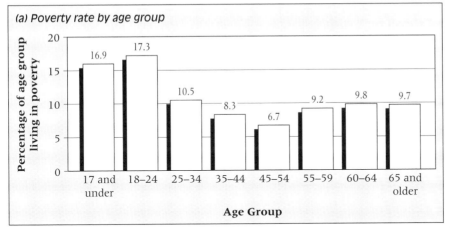

(a) Poverty rate by age group

Percentage of age group living in poverty (vertical axis)

Age Group (horizontal axis): 17 and under 16.9, 18–24 17.3, 25–34 10.5, 35–44 8.3, 45–54 6.7, 55–59 9.2, 60–64 9.8, 65 and older 9.7

Data source: J. Dalaker & B. D. Proctor. 2000. *Poverty in the United States 1999: Current Population Reports,* Table A. Available at www. census.gov/prod/2000pubs/p60-210.pdf. Accessed June 1, 2001.

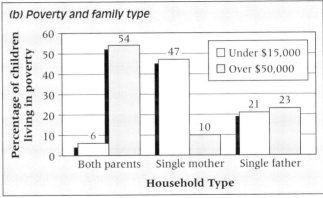

(b) Poverty and family type

Percentage of children living in poverty (vertical axis)

□ Under $15,000
□ Over $50,000

Household Type: Both parents 6 / 54, Single mother 47 / 10, Single father 21 / 23

Data source: Adapted from U.S. Bureau of the Census. 2000b. *Statistical Abstract of the United States: 2000,* Table 70. Washington, DC: U.S. Government Printing Office.

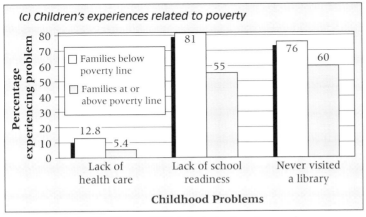

(c) Children's experiences related to poverty

Percentage experiencing problem (vertical axis)

□ Families below poverty line
□ Families at or above poverty line

Childhood Problems: Lack of health care 12.8 / 5.4, Lack of school readiness 81 / 55, Never visited a library 76 / 60

Note: Data for lack of health care, 1997; lack of school readiness and never visited library, 1999.
Data sources: Childstats.gov. 2000. *America's Children 2000,* Table ECON5.B. Available from www.childstats.gov/ac2000/econ5b.htm. Also, U.S. Bureau of the Census. 2000b. *Statistical Abstract of the United States: 2000,* Tables 260 and 326. Washington, DC: U.S. Government Printing Office.

The Debate over Welfare

In 1935 the U.S. federal government developed a social welfare system to help people in need—the aged, the poor, the unemployed, the disabled, and the sick. The system is actually divided into two segments. One segment consists of programs that provide benefits that are "earned" through employment: Social Security, disability insurance, unemployment insurance, worker's compensation, Medicare, and so on. Recipients in these programs are predominantly working and middle class, and, therefore, benefits are neither stigmatizing nor degrading. When it comes time for federal budget cuts, these programs are usually spared.

In contrast, the second segment of the social welfare system consists primarily of aid to the poor. This second segment is most commonly associated with the term *welfare*, which is the object of much hostility these days. When budgets need to be trimmed, these programs are typically the first affected. Entitlement programs for the poor constitute only about 23 percent of all federal entitlement programs but accounted for 93 percent of the entitlement budget cuts enacted by Congress in 1996 ("Harper's index," 1997).

See Issue 2 for more on the idea that American families are in decline and society along with them.

Nearly 70 years after its inception, no one is particularly happy with the nation's welfare system—not the social workers who must administer it, not the politicians who try to fix it, not the poor people themselves who must live under it, and not the working taxpayers who must support it (DiNitto & Dye, 1987). The U.S. public has a deep, underlying fear that welfare for the poor contributes to the breakdown of family by encouraging families to dissolve, women to have more children, extended families to break apart, dependency to be handed down to future generations, single mothers not to marry, and so on (see Exhibit 4.3).

But the conclusion that welfare *causes* such problems is not supported by the evidence. For instance, if it were true that welfare causes or at least perpetuates poverty, you'd expect that increasing welfare payments would lower the incentive to work and lengthen the time it takes to escape poverty. Recent research, however, points out that in the states with more generous payments, women do not spend more time on welfare and they are just as likely as women in lower-paying states to seek employment (Vartanian & McNamara, 2000). Furthermore, higher welfare payments actually hasten the escape from poverty for some single-parent families (Butler, 1996). Even prior to recent reforms, which sharply limit the

EXHIBIT 4.3

Beliefs About People on Welfare

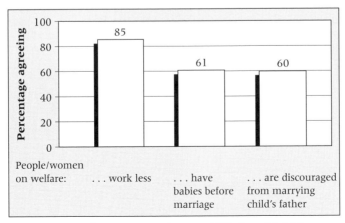

Data source: National Opinion Research Center. 1998. *General Social Survey.* Available from www.icpsr.umich.edu/GSS/. Accessed June 1, 2001.

amount of time people can be on welfare, only 30 percent of recipients stayed on for more than 2 years and only 7 percent stayed on for more than 8 years (Gans, 1995).

What about family breakdown? Welfare spending increased between 1960 and 1970 and decreased between 1972 and 1984, yet there were no accompanying changes in family composition trends during these periods. For instance, the number of households headed by women increased steadily between 1968 and 1983, showing no fluctuation as a result of changes in welfare benefits (Baca Zinn, 1997). Furthermore, differences in welfare benefits from state to state don't produce corresponding differences in family breakdown. In fact, states with higher welfare benefits tend to have lower rates of female-headed households and welfare participation (Darity & Meyers, 1984).

Does drawing welfare benefits encourage single women to have more babies? The common perception is that it does. However, the birth rate of women on welfare is actually considerably lower than that of the general population (Rank, 1994). In fact, the longer a woman remains on welfare, the less likely she is to give birth. The economic, social, and psychological situations in which women on welfare find themselves are not particularly conducive to desiring or having more children. Becoming pregnant and having a child are perceived as making the situation worse, not better, by making it more difficult to ultimately get off welfare—something most welfare recipients want. A study by the National Academy of Sciences found that the overwhelming majority of births to single women were unintended; 70 percent of births to never-married women in general and over 85 percent of births to unmarried teenagers are unintended (cited in Sandefur, 1996). The implication is that most welfare pregnancies are not based on conscious decisions to increase financial benefits.

Family Life on Welfare   The strains and stresses of being on public assistance inevitably influence family relationships. Each benefit—housing subsidies, food stamps, Medicaid, and so on—comes with its own set of rules and regulations that must be followed if participants wish to remain eligible (Dujon et al., 1995). A welfare recipient can be removed from the rolls if she is found to be living with a man without being married to him. If welfare recipients fail to observe child care norms or are believed to use more physical punishment than social workers deem desirable, they can be charged with child neglect or abuse and lose their children to foster care (Gans, 1995).

See Issue 3 for a discussion of the ways that social institutions, particularly those with which the poor come into contact, intrude on family privacy.

To add insult to injury, welfare payments are usually not sufficient to cover ordinary family expenditures. A study of single mothers on welfare in four U.S. cities (Boston, Chicago, Charleston, and San Antonio) found that welfare payments fall short of providing enough money to pay for household expenses by an average of $200 to $400 a month (Edin & Lein, 1997). The average maximum benefit for a family of three is less than $400 a month ("Tough love index," 1996). After covering all other expenses, one 51-year-old divorced mother of two teenage daughters had to provide food, toiletries, and clothing for her family on what amounted to $4 per person per day. She sums up her life:

> This is probably about the lowest point in my life, and I hope I never reach it again. Because this is where you're just up against a wall. You can't make a move. You can't buy anything that you want for your home. You can't go on a vacation. You can't take a weekend off and go and see things because it costs too much. And it's just such a waste of a life. (quoted in Rank, 1994, p. 52)

Contrary to the popular image that welfare parents are neglectful of their children, many of the fifty people that sociologist Mark Rank (1994) studied spoke fondly of the way their children have enriched their lives and the pride they take in their children's accomplishments, their worries about their children's well-being, and their efforts to do what is best for them. They try to teach their children the importance of education as a means of becoming independent so they won't have to rely on public assistance when they become adults. Of course, most of the parents Rank interviewed felt a tremendous amount of frustration over not being able to meet their children's physical, social, and educational needs.

Clearly, trying to lead a "normal life" while on welfare is extremely difficult. Recipients often have to depend on family and friends, boyfriends, or absent fathers to help make ends meet. Some cut back on their own food intake so they can buy shoes for their children; others hire professional shoplifters to get coats so their children can go to school in the winter (DeParle, 1997a). One study of fifty welfare mothers in Chicago found that all of them supplemented their welfare checks fraudulently, with either under-the-table work or money from friends and relatives, and none reported this income to the welfare office as they are required to do (Edin & Jencks, 1992). As one such welfare recipient put it, "We weren't trying to beat the system. We were just trying to make it" (quoted in Penner, 1995, p. 11). The irony of these practices, of course, is that contrary to popular stereotypes, women on welfare are not isolated from the world of work. They're often already working but not earning enough to survive.

So it's not that people on welfare don't want to work. It's that the available jobs often pay too little, demand too much, and offer few opportunities for advancement (Oliker, 1995). What's more, the costs of *going* to work—for transportation, clothes, and above all child care—are so high that the income of a poor single mother who works full time is likely to be the same as or less than the income of a mother on welfare (Edin & Lein, 1997).

Work income is also less stable than welfare income—employers who offer low-wage jobs can seldom guarantee their workers full-time hours. Furthermore, these jobs are often incompatible with parenting. Workers must leave their children in care that may be untrustworthy. Because these jobs rarely offer sick leave or paid vacation days, it is next to impossible to take time off to care for sick children who can't go to school.

Even the most highly motivated job seeker may be thwarted by the biases of employers. For instance, welfare mothers are, by definition, poor and are therefore restricted in their choice of neighborhood in which to live and work. They often lack connections to people or organizations who can help them find a job. Also, long-term welfare recipients have probably been unemployed for a long time or at the very least have a sporadic work history. So employers may feel justified in discriminating against them. Indeed, there is some evidence that employers use information such as neighborhood and welfare dependence in their hiring decisions (Browne, 1997).

Although the road to gainful employment is littered with obstacles, most welfare recipients have worked in the past and want to work in the future. They recognize the stigma that their friends, their community, and the larger society imposes on welfare recipients, and they anticipate a boost in self-esteem and social standing from working.

The Ideals and Realities of Welfare Reform   For decades, the U.S. public has been highly critical of the welfare system. Through the years, state and federal legislators have tried to improve it, but to no avail. Finally, in 1996 President Clinton signed into law an unprecedented welfare-reform bill designed to reduce poor people's reliance on government aid and "end welfare as we know it."

The new welfare system includes a mandatory work requirement, dubbed "workfare," after 2 years of receiving assistance (or enrollment in vocational training or community service); a 5-year lifetime limit on benefits for any family; a transformation of welfare from a federal entitlement to a "block grant" that each state decides how to spend; a massive reduction in food stamps; and other cuts that concentrate on legal immigrants, the disabled, and the elderly poor (Corcoran, Danziger, Kalil, & Seefeldt, 2000). The law also requires states to provide child care and health care for working mothers, but it doesn't specify how long states must offer such support to each recipient (Harris, 1996a). This new system was expected to reduce government spending by $54 billion over 6 years.

In addition to the obvious financial motivation behind this massive effort at welfare reform, another purpose was to promote marriage, parenting within marriage, and "responsible" fatherhood (that is, paternal support) (Curran & Abrams, 2000; Carbone, 2000). To ensure more responsible fatherhood, the new law requires that mothers comply with measures to identify the father of their children before they can qualify for benefits. If mothers do not cooperate with paternal identification efforts, states are required to reduce their benefits. States also now have greater authority to collect paternal support from parents who are delinquent in their child support payments.

One assumption behind this version of welfare reform is that making work mandatory will teach welfare recipients important work values and habits, make poor single mothers models of these values for their children, and cut the nation's welfare rolls. As Columbia law professor Carol Sanger put it, "Welfare reforms are premised on the belief that a working mother as role model is more important for poor children than whatever they may gain from a homebound but publicly supported mother" (quoted in Carbone, 2000, p. 207). The underlying idea is that hard work will lead to the moral and financial rewards of family self-reliance. It is intended to cure poverty and welfare dependence and ensure that new generations of children from single-parent families will be able to enter the U.S. mainstream.

However, the current welfare system can work only if people on welfare have viable employment opportunities and if those opportunities provide a sufficient wage to lift them out of poverty (McCrate & Smith, 1998). Indeed, a major predictor of whether women will leave welfare permanently is whether they can find employment within a year after leaving welfare (Vartanian & McNamara, 2000). However, many studies of state-run welfare-to-work programs show little or no change at all in unemployment rates and only small increases in earnings, which are due primarily to working longer hours, not earning higher wages (Oliker, 1995). In one study, only 16 percent of participants in a welfare-to-work program were able to find a job within the mandated time (Brush, 2000). Most women who leave welfare work in low-paying jobs that offer no benefits (Corcoran et al., 2000). Only one in four are employed full time 5 years after leaving welfare (Cancian & Meyer, 2000). Such people also switch jobs frequently. Only 17 percent were employed by the same company for more than 3 years. Most had new employers every 6 to 9 months (Economic Roundtable, 2000).

When they do work, many former welfare recipients find it difficult to make ends meet. A study conducted by the Economic Roundtable (2000) tracked 100,000 Los Angeles welfare recipients over 8 years. The researchers found that 3 years after leaving the welfare rolls, 70 percent of former welfare recipients still earn below the poverty line. Researchers have found that former welfare recipients who work earn on average $400 less a year than they would have received had they stayed on welfare (cited in DeParle, 1999). And more than half of the women who leave the welfare rolls when they can support themselves with jobs eventually return to welfare because their jobs end or because they aren't earning enough to make ends meet (Harris, 1996b).

Disabled or battered women are at especially high risk of failing under this system. For instance, welfare recipients with low literacy skills tend to be placed in low-paying jobs and denied access to further education that could help them secure better jobs (Rivera, 2000). Battering and its consequences can easily delay or derail efforts to enter the labor market. For example, disfiguring or disabling injuries, or the need to appear in court to obtain a protective order from the abuser, can seriously interfere with a battered woman's ability to attend work or training programs. In one study of 122 women in a job readiness program designed to help welfare recipients make the transition into the workforce, nearly half had experienced violence in their current or most recent relationships (Brush, 2000).

The part of the system aimed at getting men more involved in the financial support of their children on welfare has also not proved very effective. Obviously, in order for fathers to support their children, they must have the financial ability to do so. Yet many of these men have exceedingly low incomes or are unemployed and therefore cannot offer much support (Curran & Abrams, 2000). The job training programs that exist for unemployed men have not significantly increased their employment rates or earnings (cited in Curran & Abrams, 2000).

It's important to note that the reformed welfare system operates under the assumption that all welfare recipients are similar and that all are capable of sustained employment. Yet research has found that there are two types of welfare recipients. One group tends to be older and better educated and to have more work experience. These women tend to be short-term recipients who, on average, remain on welfare less than two years (Carbone, 2000). People in this group tend to be able to get off welfare on their own.

So welfare reforms are really directed at the second group—those who are long-term beneficiaries. Not surprisingly, these women tend not to be very employable. In general, they are not well educated (many haven't graduated from high school), have little or no work experience, and are unmarried (Carbone, 2000). In short, there is likely to be a significant gap between the skills demanded by employers and those offered by these welfare recipients (Corcoran et al., 2000). And although welfare recipients as a whole tend to have fewer children than people not on welfare, this latter group tends to have more. The presence of young children further reduces these women's chances of entering the labor force and thereby increases their need for welfare (Browne, 1997).

What will happen to these women and their children when time limits expire is unclear. Advocates who work on behalf of battered women have expressed concern that new mandates requiring the participation of men who have fathered children on welfare will increase domestic violence (Brush, 2000). And according to one legal expert, the current system "has the potential—particularly when the economy worsens, time limits expire, and less generous states take a meat-ax to what is left of the protections it offers—to make poor children's material circumstances substantially worse" (Carbone, 2000, p. 207). Realities such as these make some observers pessimistic about the long-term consequences of this latest overhaul of the welfare system.

The Long-Term Consequences of Welfare Reform   It's still too early to tell what the long-term effects of welfare reform will be. But there has been some positive news. Between 1996 and 2000, the welfare caseload fell by close to 60 percent, from 12.9 million recipients to fewer than 5.8 million (U.S. Department of Health and Human Services, 2001). Many states are taking the money they're saving and are spending it on transportation, job placement, and programs that let welfare recipients keep more of their benefits even while earning paychecks (DeParle, 1997b). Some states are paying women—often welfare recipients themselves—to set up family day-care centers in their homes. In allowing women to earn a living by caring for the children of others, the states both create jobs for welfare mothers and pave the way for the mothers of the children they care for to go to work (Kilborn, 1997a). If such efforts continue, there's a chance that the welfare reform legislation of 1996 really will end welfare as people once knew it.

But the new welfare program has also created some problems. For instance, there is evidence that the country's poorest families have been driven deeper into poverty. In the first 2 years after reforms went into effect, the poorest 20 percent of U.S. families lost an average of $577 a year (Center on Budget and Policy Priorities, 1999). Typically, these families had left welfare but had not made up lost benefits with wages. In many cases they still face the same problems they faced while on welfare: violent neighborhoods, bare cupboards, absent fathers, depression, and drugs (DeParle, 1999). Moreover, close to 1 million poor parents lost their Medicaid health insurance coverage as a consequence of welfare reform. These parents were forced off welfare and had to take low-paying jobs that didn't offer health benefits. Those who did find jobs that offered insurance were often unable to pay the premiums (cited in Pear, 2000). And it's estimated that about a million additional toddlers and preschoolers are now in day care—which in many cases is of poor quality—as a result of welfare revisions that require their mothers to work (Lewin, 2000).

Welfare reform has had other unforeseen consequences. For instance, although across the country thousands of former welfare recipients are going to work, for the most part they're not entering new jobs created expressly for them, as President Clinton had envisioned when he signed the reform bill into law. Instead, many are taking jobs previously occupied by regular employees. Each state is required to meet annual workfare quotas or risk losing some of its federal money for welfare. So employers are pressured to hire workfare participants. Furthermore, employers can pay workfare participants lower wages than they would pay to regular employees because the government partially subsidizes the welfare recipients. In Baltimore, for example, several school districts hired welfare recipients to clean at $1.50 an hour rather than renew contracts with agencies that charged $6 an hour (Uchitelle, 1997).

Another potential consequence is that welfare reform may actually help reshape the image of motherhood—from one of domesticity to one of working parenthood (Carbone, 2000). The public will eventually realize that inadequate after school care or the lack of flexible family leave policies affects poor families as much as middle-class families. Potentially, putting so many poor mothers to work may pave the way toward a fundamental rethinking of society's responsibility for children.

See Issue 4 for a discussion of gender and family obligation.

In the meantime, how do workfare programs influence the personal lives and parenting strategies of the poor single mothers involved in them? Sociologist Stacey Oliker (1995) observed several state-run workfare programs and interviewed both participants and providers over a 5-year period. Even though program leaders encouraged the women to "go for it" and find the kinds of jobs they would enjoy, all the women interviewed found only low-wage work as cashiers, clerks, kitchen workers, nurses' aides, home health aides, restaurant servers, babysitters, and factory assemblers. Most initially were strongly oriented toward improving the financial well-being of their children and were willing to work long hours and be away from home to do so. Hence they saw the shift from welfare to work as a positive change in their lives. But forced to choose between work and family care, many chose to emphasize caregiving and stopped working.

Interestingly, the women Oliker interviewed spoke of their moral duty to be home with their children in the same way that affluent mothers speak of their role in the upbringing of their children. However, their accounts focused not on the general notion that mothers ought to play a dominant role in enforcing high standards of behavior and maintaining class standing but on the concrete importance of protecting their children's well-being in a threatening environment. In fact, the leaders of the workfare programs that Oliker studied reported that many women dropped out of the program shortly after being victims of or witnesses to burglaries or assaults, when concerns over their children's safety became most urgent.

Poverty and Housing

It is hard to overestimate the importance of safe, decent, affordable housing in the lives of families. It keeps children in school and adults on the job. It allows upwardly mobile families to save money so they can someday buy a house of their own and keeps downwardly mobile families from having to turn to foster care or homeless shelters (DeParle, 1996). The cost of housing breaks the budgets of low-income families or crowds them into unsafe, dilapidated, and sometimes violent ghettos, which are usually some distance from good schools and good jobs.

Unstable housing is particularly hard on children. Poor children whose families do not receive government rent subsidies are more likely to be malnourished and underweight than other children. Some poor families are displaced so often that their children attend half a dozen schools in a single year. The head of foster care in the District of Columbia estimates that as many as half the city's foster children could be reunited with their parents if their families had stable housing (cited in DeParle, 1996).

The federal government defines housing as "affordable" if rent and utilities cost no more than 30 percent of a household's income. By comparison, the average middle-class home owner spends only 23 percent of his or her after-tax income on house payments. According to government statistics, nationwide it takes an average wage of $11.08 an hour—more than twice the federal minimum wage—for a person to afford rental housing. Indeed, nowhere in the United States is the minimum wage enough to afford adequate housing (National Low Income Housing Coalition, 1999). And to add insult to injury, it is estimated that there is a shortage of approximately 5 million housing units for the poor (Arrighi, 1997).

Despite the crucial importance of good housing to family life and its scarcity for the poor, President Clinton signed a housing appropriations bill in 1996 that essentially cut off government rent subsidies. Coincidentally, at the same time, a government report noted that 5 million needy families paid more than half of their pretax income on housing, meaning that other necessities, such as food, were probably being crowded out. In 1997, Congress further burdened the poorest Americans by passing a bill cutting the number of government-subsidized housing units available to very poor families and increasing the number available to "working poor" families—those earning up to 80 percent of the average income in a particular area (Alvarez, 1997; Pader, 1997). Supporters of the bill argued that raising the proportion of tenants with jobs would improve the social environment in most housing projects. If tenants could pay more rent, local housing authorities could afford to better maintain the buildings. Furthermore, the mixing of working and unemployed people would provide needed role models to children in public housing. Others, however, worry that these changes will shut the poorest people out of the only housing they can afford, thereby forcing them to "double up" with relatives or, worse yet, forcing them out onto the streets.

Homeless Families

When people think of homelessness, most conjure up images of single, isolated individuals, cut off from any and all family relationships. In truth, however, the majority of homeless people are married and unmarried couples, single mothers and their children, and intact families (Seltser & Miller, 1993). Families with children, constituting about 43 percent of the entire homeless population, now represent the fastest-growing segment of the homeless (cited in Anderson & Koblinsky, 1995). Ninety percent of homeless families with children are female-headed households, and three-quarters of these families are members of racial and ethnic minority groups (Kondratas, 1991).

In addition to the "official" homeless, countless thousands of other families are one catastrophe away from homelessness—one fire, one broken water pipe, one collapsed roof, one injury, or one job loss. And the families living doubled or tripled up with strained relatives or friends in cramped apartments are always an argument, fight, or ill-conceived comment away from being kicked back out to the streets.

Many families become homeless because of a specific crisis, such as the loss of a job, divorce or desertion, or loss of a house to fire, flood, or some other catastrophe. Others become homeless when a mother takes her children and moves out of an abusive relationship. What they all have in common, though, is that their move into homelessness is less of a fall than a sidestep. These are families already living on the edge of survival. Most homeless families are poor well before they become homeless, often living month to month until they can no longer sustain a residence.

Homeless parents must deal with a double crisis: They must deal with the disruptive and traumatizing effects of losing a home while acknowledging that their capacity to provide protection and support and to respond to their children's needs has been eroded. Studies of homeless parents living in shelters have found that most of them feel that living in the shelter seriously hurts their children. Homeless children, for instance, are often ridiculed at school or suffer the pressure of keeping their home life a secret (Arrighi, 1997).

See Issue 3 for more on the need for a "backstage" area where families can address private matters without being scrutinized by others.

The loss of privacy that comes from parenting in public erodes a parent's confidence, not to mention his or her relationship with the children. In shelters that are noisy, chaotic, and stressful, there is a lot of wasted time, unsupervised activity, and little opportunity to establish a family routine. One observer described the shelter experience as divided into "time that is mealtime and time that is not mealtime" (quoted in Hausman & Hammen, 1993, p. 360). However, in shelters that are small, quiet, and orderly, there can be a lot of nurturing, safety, and support, making effective parenting less difficult.

Whatever the conditions at a shelter, when parenting is visible and public, it becomes open to criticism, particularly in such an emotionally fragile environment. Conflict among mothers is a common characteristic of most homeless shelters (Hausman & Hammen, 1993). Mothers may begin to distance themselves from the unruly behaviors of their children in an attempt to avoid blame from other adults. Under such conditions, parents, and ultimately children, can become irritable and demoralized.

Homeless families tend to lack the emotional resources that might be drawn on in bad times (Bassuk, Rubin, & Lauriat, 1986). Indeed, a lifetime of disappointing, harmful, and traumatic experiences has taught many homeless mothers to be suspicious of everyone—strangers, acquaintances, and relatives—and reluctant to trust anyone, particularly with the care of children (Browne, 1993). Such isolation contributes to the lonely strain of homelessness and interferes with healthy parent-child relationships.

The result of all this is that homeless children suffer higher rates of depression, anxiety, behavioral problems, and academic difficulties than other children. In a comparative study of homeless and housed children, researchers estimate that half of all homeless children demonstrate at least one developmental problem (maladaptive behavior, academic deficiency, emotional problems, and so on), compared to 16 percent of housed children (Rafferty & Rollins, 1989). Not surprisingly, many homeless children either are not enrolled in school or attend sporadically. A few children are able to succeed despite their desperate conditions. But the vast majority of homeless children will suffer well into their adulthood. Once again, you can see the pervasive and long-lasting effects of social class on family life and people's future prospects.

Conclusion

Economic factors—from the amount of money coming in to the day-to-day management of finances and major purchasing decisions—are involved in virtually every aspect of family life. When a family doesn't know how it will pay this month's rent or where its next meal is coming from or whether there will be a warm place to sleep that night, that family will have a difficult time being comfortable, happy, and satisfied. When economic foundations are weak, the emotional bonds that tie a family together can easily crumble.

Over 15 million children in the United States live in poverty (Duncan et al., 1998). As you've seen in this chapter, the most devastating effects of poverty are felt by these youngest members of society. Experiences with poverty early in life are likely to lead to a series of other disadvantages and eventually culminate in long-term economic and social disadvantages. The current modifications to the welfare system are not likely to improve, and may even worsen, the economic circumstances or life chances of these children.

Meanwhile, wealth has become increasingly concentrated at the opposite end of the economic spectrum. As the wealthy get richer, the poorer segments of the population suffer. Even many middle-class Americans are experiencing a decline in their standard of living in the early 2000s.

Numerous strategies to reduce poverty and its effects, such as raising the minimum wage or increasing funding for Head Start programs, have been proposed. However, most have failed to receive widespread popular or political support. In the strongly individualistic and capitalist U.S. culture, it will be difficult to alter attitudes and policies regarding income distribution. But what people may be coming to see is that the indirect costs of poverty (unemployment, nonmarital and early pregnancy, crime, lack of education, and so on) are much greater than are the direct costs of implementing programs to help low-income and poverty-level families.

Chapter Highlights

- American families exist in a society solidly structured along the lines of social class distinctions.
- Social class is about more than wealth and occupation; it determines what families look like and how they live.

- Usually members of upper-class families inherit formidable wealth, which provides substantial political and economic power. "Newly rich" families are more likely to have made, not inherited, their fortunes, leading to a greater emphasis on career mobility.
- Middle-class family norms often define, for the culture, what is desirable.
- The dependence on hourly wages makes working-class families particularly susceptible to downturns in the economy.
- Poor families are often one unexpected event—a sickness, an injury, and automobile breakdown—away from catastrophe.
- Women and children are more likely to be poor than any other segment of the population.
- Although welfare reform has saved the government billions of dollars, it is unclear whether it has improved the lives of most poor American families.

Your Turn

Even people whose income is well above the poverty line can sometimes find it difficult to make ends meet. Imagine a family of four living in your hometown. Suppose that both parents work, that one child is 7 years old and in elementary school, and that the other is 3 and must be cared for during the day.

Make a list of all the goods and services this family needs to function at a minimum subsistence level—that is, at the poverty line. Be as complete as possible. Consider food, clothing, housing, transportation, medical care, child care, entertainment, and so on.

Estimate the minimum monthly cost of each item. If you currently live on your own and must pay these expenses yourself, use those figures as a starting point (but remember that you must estimate for a family of four). If you live in a dorm or at home, ask your parents (or anyone else who pays bills) what their expenses are for such goods and services. Call the local day care center to see what it charges for child care. Go to the local supermarket and compute the family food budget. For those expenses that aren't divided on a monthly basis (for example, the purchase of clothing and household appliances), estimate the yearly cost and divide by 12.

Once you have estimated the total monthly expenses, multiply by 12 to get the subsistence budget for the family of four. If your estimate is higher than the government's official poverty line (around $17,463), what sorts of items could you cut out of the budget for the family to be defined as officially poor and therefore eligible for certain government programs? By looking for ways to cut expenses from your minimal subsistence budget, you will get a good sense of what everyday life in poverty is like.

Describe the quality of life of this hypothetical family that makes too much to be officially poor and too little to sustain a comfortable life. What sorts of things are they forced to do without that a more affluent family might simply take for granted (for example, annual vacations, discretionary income, a second car, eating out once a week)? What would be the impact of poverty on the lives of the children? How will the family's difficulty in meeting its basic subsistence needs translate into access to opportunities (education, jobs, health care,) for the children later in life?

Investigating Families over the Life Course

In Part III of this book we explore how sociologists study specific experiences over the life course. You will see how family relationships are formed, how married couples and other long-term relationships function, how couples balance the demands of family and work, how people become parents and raise children, why intimate violence is so pervasive, what factors affect divorce and remarriage, and how people negotiate the sometimes difficult transitions into adulthood and beyond. The final chapter in this section looks at how the institution of family has changed in the past and what it may look like in the future.

Love, Sexuality, and Attraction

Incurably Romantic

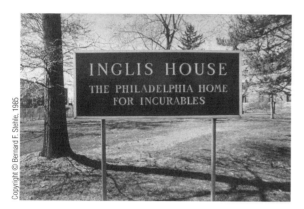

Copyright © Bernard F. Stehle, 1985

The photographs in this essay were taken from a book by Bernard F. Stehle titled *Incurably Romantic* (Philadelphia: Temple University Press, 1985). They are portraits of love and romance between people who reside at Inglis House, formerly known as The Philadelphia Home for Incurables. All of these residents are severely physically disabled. The images are simultaneously disturbing and inspiring—disturbing because they depict people who face significant pain and anguish in their lives, inspiring because they are celebrations of the power of the human spirit.

In the afterword to *Incurably Romantic*, sociologist Joseph Schneider writes:

> We live in a culture that places a high premium on how people look. A conventional-appearing body is prima facie evidence of "normality." It is of course even better to be considered "beautiful" or "handsome." . . . Those considered "unattractive" and physically "abnormal" become, by extension, less personally worthy. . . .
>
> . . . The people we see in [these] photographs are physically, not mentally, disabled. . . . They—indeed, we all—are surrounded by cultural messages that not only is a beautiful body somehow connected to a beautiful person, but . . . that the notions of love, romance, and sexuality are the province of normal and preferably beautiful bodies and people. Couples in love are conventionally described as "radiant," "lovely," "young," "healthy," and expected to be whole. These are appealing, even romantic, notions, and only when we look more closely at the lives of real people do we notice the discrepancy between reality and these cultural images. (pp. 237–238).

As you examine the photos in this essay take note of your own responses to the people depicted. How do these individuals affect your ideas about intimacy? Are you surprised that the couples in this essay are so deeply in love? In what ways are their relationships likely to be similar to those among able-bodied persons? How might they be different? What stake, if any, does society have in setting limits on who can and who can't form long-term, romantic relationships?

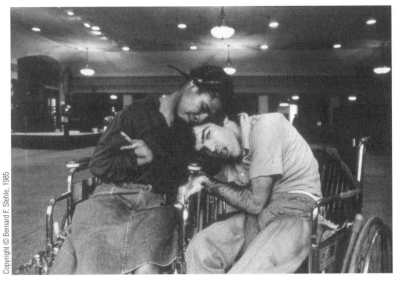

Copyright © Bernard F. Stehle, 1985

Stuart: Diane is the first woman who realized that I had normal feelings of love and of being in love. She makes me happy just holding me and being there. Five years together have taught us a great deal about ourselves. . . . It's a wonderful feeling having someone I can go to for understanding my crazy moods.

Diane: I said it wouldn't work. But his stubbornness made it work—not to give up on me because of our different backgrounds. Now we are working on it together . . . we are talking. (pp. 16–17)

Copyright © Bernard F. Stehle, 1985

One way Diane expresses love for Stuart, who cannot use his hands to feed himself, just as she cannot, is by feeding him using a fork held between her teeth, as she does in this photograph. (pp. xiii, 21)

Copyright © Bernard F. Stehle, 1985

Copyright © Bernard F. Stehle, 1985

Murray: When I married Frances, I swore that I would stay with her till death do us part . . . and I'm keeping my word. . . . I've had a marvelous—a *beautiful*—life with her, even with her handicaps. . . . I can say *one word* and she knows what I'm thinking about . . . because [of] living with me that length of time [fifty years of marriage, the last thirty-five with her multiple sclerosis—the last fifteen of these at Inglis House]. . . . When I come here, I feel *good*; I look for the moment when I have to get in the car to come out here. . . . We're still on our honeymoon, even though she's incapacitated to the point where she's not really a *wife* to me. But as far as a companion? She's all I want. . . .

Frances: . . . When I told my husband how *worried* I was about him once when he wasn't feeling well, he said, "Don't worry"—not to "worry about me"—and all that business—and I said to him: "Don't you *dare* deprive me of that! That's one of my *privileges*." The people for whom I feel sorry are the people that have nobody to worry about. . . . It's a reciprocal thing. (pp. 127–128, 131)

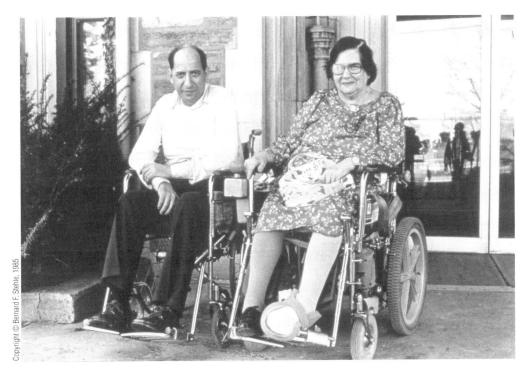

Donald: I have spinal muscular cerebral atrophy; it causes a weakness in the leg muscles. Now I am no longer able to get out of the chair. . . . I try to do for Alice whatever I can despite this—like reach down and adjust her pedals. She gives me shaves with my electric razor.

Alice: I'm a lot older than Donald—twenty-five years. . . . Going with somebody has nothing to do with anything physical, and I feel that the more people learned this it would be a better world. . . . (pp. 104–105)

Do you ever get nostalgic for the good old days, when all people had to do to find a mate was identify someone they found interesting or attractive, awkwardly and nervously approach that person, and ask him or her to go to dinner or to the senior prom? If they hit it off, they'd go on more dates and eventually they'd become a couple. This method wasn't foolproof; more often than not, it was downright painful. And many people just never got the hang of it. But there was something sweet and gratifying about constructing a relationship from scratch.

Against the backdrop of today's technological culture, this old method of dating and courtship is beginning to look hopelessly out of date, time-consuming, and inefficient. Consider the following:

- The top-rated prime-time television show for the week of April 3, 2000, was *Who Wants to Marry a Multimillionaire?*—a show on Fox in which fifty women competed to marry a wealthy man they had never seen. Not to be outdone, executives at NBC-TV decided to air a show called *Chains of Love,* in which a young woman selects four men from a pool of 100 prospects. The four men are then chained to the woman's wrists and ankles for a week while she eliminates them one by one—until she's left with one "Mr. Right." The popular show *Change of Heart* on the WB network arranges for a man or woman who is currently in a relationship to date someone else and then come on the show to discuss the two before deciding either to stay with the first partner or change to the new person.

- In Japan, a product called "LoveGety" is aiding people in their quest to find potential mates. LoveGety is a pendant-shaped radio transmitter (blue for men, pink for women) that is capable of sending out six different electronic invitations: fun, dance, love, movie, chat, or drink. When someone with a pink LoveGety set, for example, on "dance," passes within a few yards of someone wearing a blue one also set for the same activity, a green light flashes and a beeper goes off. The two people can then decide if they want to "hook up" ("Love at first beep," 2000). LoveGety owners can also tell potential partners their whereabouts by advertising on a Web site provided by the manufacturer. Two million units were sold in the first year. The company is already planning more sophisticated versions with display panels showing what a potential lover looks like and other vital statistics.

- Researchers at the M.I.T. Media Lab are working on a computer program that scans a person's e-mail, tallying common and quirky words, and draws conclusions about the person's personality. Another project they're working on is called an "interest tracker." This device is capable of scanning the eye movements of someone browsing the Web to determine what kind of information he or she is drawn to. In both cases, computers then construct a personality profile that dating services can store and cross-reference to assess whether two people might hit it off. When asked whether such technological aids will take the mystery out of courtship, one researcher replied, "Computers will help us understand who we really are as opposed to who we think we are" (Griscom, 2000, p. 93).

- A Web site called "The Romance Institute" has, on its staff, a full-time "romance coach" who provides advice on a variety of relationship-related situations, such as how to introduce yourself to an attractive stranger, how to develop and maintain a long-distance relationship, and how long you should wait before calling someone you've just met.

- Another Web site called eCRUSH.com provides an anonymous, relatively risk-free way of finding out if someone on whom you have a crush likes you back. You simply submit that person's name and e-mail address. Then eCRUSH sends that person a message, saying that someone (you!) likes him or her. If that person lists you as a potential love interest, the Web site matches the two of you. If that person doesn't list you, well, at least you've found out without suffering a public rejection. The site sells itself as a painless way of avoiding the awkwardness and humiliation of unrequited affection. The founders claim to have facilitated over 80,000 matches.

Despite these technological advances in mating techniques, one thing remains the same as always: People actively seek close, intimate relationships with someone special. People expect these relationships to provide a great deal of happiness, recognize that they often serve as a prelude to marriage, and consider them the fundamental building blocks of all family forms. To understand the role of intimate relationships in family life, we need to examine how they develop and what personal and social factors influence them. This chapter looks at the process through which intimate relationships unfold, paying particular attention to dating, courtship, and mate selection. But first we examine the broader cultural contexts of love, romance, and sexuality—the defining characteristics of intimate relationships.

The Cultural Context of Intimacy

Intimacy is the state of being emotionally and affectionately close to another person. It exists in all sorts of relationships, such as those between friends or between parents and children. But in this chapter we focus primarily on romantic and sexual relationships.

This culture's colossal preoccupation with intimacy has given rise to a thriving industry devoted to bringing people together and keeping them together. Singles' bars, singles' apartment complexes, church-based singles groups, and Internet dating services all serve as modern-day matchmakers. International dating services—often in the form of "mail-order catalogs"—have become especially popular, and thousands of U.S. men each year search for potential brides in distant countries such as Russia, Korea, or the Philippines (Egan, 1996).

What's all the fuss about? Why do people devote so much attention to these matters? It no doubt has a great deal to do with the importance of intimate relationships in everyday life. People learn early that these relationships are the standard against which they judge the quality and happiness of their entire lives. Cultural and media images tell people that they can't be truly fulfilled without falling in love, being sexually satisfied, and having a long-term relationship with someone.

Although the need for intimacy continues to occupy a lofty position in the culture, dramatic social changes over the past few decades have made relationships confusing. Young people today become sexually active and involved in intimate relationships earlier than ever before. Heretofore unacceptable forms of intimacy—heterosexual and homosexual cohabitation, for example—are becoming more commonplace and acceptable. At the same time, marriages and other long-term relationships continue to be far from permanent. More people are choosing not to marry or are waiting longer to get married. And the darker side of intimacy—physical abuse, sexual violence, AIDS, and other sexually transmitted diseases—is now impossible to ignore.

The intense need for intimacy, coupled with all these difficulties, has increased the demands people make on their intimate partners. They have come to expect their partners to fulfill all their sexual, emotional, social, intellectual, and economic needs. Under the weight of such a burden, it's not surprising that so many people spend so much time thinking

Issue 2 outlines the debate over whether or not such trends indicate a decline in the institution of family.

about—and will pay good money to find out—how to attract and keep the right person; how to add spice, vigor, and longevity to a sagging relationship; or how to end a relationship that's not working so the search for a more fulfilling one can begin.

Romantic Love

To most of us, love is a magical emotion that defies logical explanation. We don't really know how or why we fall in love. Most of us would have a difficult time describing the point in time when we first knew we were in love. And for the most part we don't want such things explained. Many people feel that too much analysis would defile the wonderful and mysterious essence of the love experience. Nevertheless, a scholarly examination of love provides important insight into common patterns as well as the role that social forces play in its definition and experience.

Webster's Unabridged Dictionary defines love as "attraction or desire for a person who arouses delight or admiration and elicits feelings of tenderness or sympathy." In everyday life, people typically don't use such concepts when they describe love. Indeed, common descriptions of love often include a variety of physical sensations that sometimes seem more like pain and discomfort than an enjoyable emotional experience, as you can see in this characterization: "I have trouble concentrating. . . . I experience heart palpitations and rapid breathing. . . . I experience physical sensations—cold hands, butterflies in my stomach, tingling spine. I have insomnia. I can't think of anyone else but my lover" (quoted in Carr, 1988, p. 53).

Sociologists tend to use a more "sophisticated" definition of **love**:

> Love is a relatively enduring bond where a small number of people are affectionate and emotionally committed to each other, define their collective well-being as a major goal, and feel obliged to provide care and practical assistance for each other. People who love each other also usually share physical contact; they talk to each other frequently and cooperate in some routine tasks of daily life. (Cancian, 1993, p. 205)

What makes one situation between two people who care for each other and revel in each other's company a "friendly relationship" and another a "love relationship"? Of course, at one level the answer lies in the way the people involved define their own relationship. According to the symbolic interactionist perspective, described in Chapter 1, it is not objective reality but one's subjective interpretation of a specific relationship that defines it as either friendship or love. Maybe you know two people who like to do things together, confide in each other constantly, and are very affectionate toward each other in public. They look, for all intents and purposes, as if they're in love. Yet they say they aren't—that they're just very close friends. Or you may know of two people who always seem to be at each other's throats—constantly arguing, fighting, and insulting each other. Yet they maintain that they are very deeply in love and couldn't live without each other. The people involved might themselves experience this sort of definitional ambiguity. You probably know of situations in which the two people have very different definitions of their relationship and expectations for its future.

You can see that love relationships don't necessarily develop smoothly. Instead they "ebb and flow, with false starts and continual negotiations and renegotiations" (Kollock & Blumstein, 1988, p. 481). In the early stages of a relationship, when a clear definition has yet to emerge, a little uncertainty may be tolerable or even enticing. Later on, however, ambiguity can become frustrating. Some may tackle the matter boldly and directly by simply asking, "How do you feel about me?" or "What exactly is going on here?" Others are less direct, looking for signs and clues of the other person's affections, seeking out the opinions of third parties, or dropping subtle hints in an attempt to draw the other person's feelings into the open.

Cultural Variations in Love

One question that has interested social scientists is whether or not romantic love is a universal emotion. Anthropologists William Jankowiak and Edward Fischer (1992) examined cultural folklore and anthropologists' accounts of 166 societies around the world, seeking indicators of the existence of romantic love. They looked for stories of personal longing, use of love songs in romantic involvement, elopement because of mutual affection, and native accounts of passionate love.

On the basis of these indicators, they found that an overwhelming majority of the societies they studied (about 88 percent) recognized romantic love as a component in the formation of intimate relationships. One woman who lived in a hunting and gathering society in the Kalahari Desert of Africa differentiated between companionship and romantic love by contrasting her relationship with her husband and her lover. She used terms such as "rich, warm, and secure" to describe her marriage. But in describing her lover she said, "When two people come together their hearts are on fire and their passion is very great" (quoted in Jankowiak & Fischer, 1992, p. 152). The researchers point out, however, that societies vary a lot in how common such passionate feelings are.

In another study, college students from ten countries were asked this question: "Would you marry someone with all the right qualities if you didn't love them?" (Levine, 1993). The researcher assumed that individuals from cultures that emphasized romantic love would be likely to answer no to such a question. Indeed, 86 percent of the American respondents said they wouldn't consider marrying without love; a similar percentage of Brazilian students also said no. But three-quarters of Pakistani and Indian students said they would have no problem marrying someone they didn't love.

In Pakistan and India, of course, arranged marriages based on family and economic considerations are still commonplace. To people from these countries, the reason Western marriages frequently fail is the inevitable disappointment that sets in after romantic love wears off (Bumiller, 1992). In response to a question about whether she loved her husband, a 20-year-old married Indian woman once replied,

> That's a very difficult question. I don't know. This whole concept of love is very alien to us. We're more practical. I don't see stars, I don't hear little bells. But he's a very nice guy, I get along with him fine and I think I'm going to enjoy spending my life with him. Is that love? (quoted in Bumiller, 1992, p. 123)

You can see in this comment that this woman is fully aware of the ideal of romantic love—equating it with frivolous experiences such as "seeing stars" and "hearing bells." Her perspective is not that romantic love doesn't exist but that it is not and shouldn't be the most important force behind a successful marriage.

Many Americans probably think of arranged marriages as out-of-date and loveless. Yet even though romantic love is not a primary consideration, love often grows in arranged marriages as partners get to know each other. Furthermore, arranged marriages can provide people with significant benefits. For instance, they tend to be very stable. They also strengthen ties with other families, which in turn strengthens the social order of the community (Lee & Stone, 1980).

One could also question just how different arranged marriages really are from marriages formed in cultures that place a high value on romantic love. Arguably, many of the "innovations" in finding mates that we described at the beginning of this chapter (for example, the LoveGety) hint at an arranged system in which chance meetings are minimized. The difference is that technology, not other family members, plays the crucial role in arranging matches. But the reliance on technology to arrange dates also may reflect the frustrations and ineffectiveness of dating in cultures without arranged systems. In cultures where marriages are arranged, couples may experience disappointments and frustrations, but finding a partner and marrying isn't necessarily one of them. The fact that the popular LoveGety was developed in Japan—a society where many marriages in the past were arranged—may suggest that adults there are finding contemporary mate selection too much of a challenge.

Issue 4 explores in greater depth how individualist and collectivist societies vary.

According to some scholars, the presence and importance of romantic love are determined by the broader values and traditions of a given culture. Psychologists Karen Dion and Kenneth Dion (1996) found that romantic love is much more important as a basis for intimate relationships in **individualist societies** than in **collectivist societies**, which emphasize group obligations. When a society celebrates individual freedom, people's intimate choices are likely to be driven by personal feelings and emotions.

In collectivist societies where romantic love is not such a crucial aspect of relationships, people's intimate expectations can seem quite low to Americans. For example, intimate relationships in Japan are sometimes structured on a very different emotional foundation than people in the West would expect. To some Japanese, the strength of their marriages is a matter of patience and low emotional expectations. When asked if he loved his wife of 33 years, one man shared a typical sentiment: "Yeah, so-so, I guess. She's like air or water. You couldn't live without it, but most of the time, you're not conscious of its existence" (quoted in Kristof, 1996d, p. A1).

Ironically, low expectations may help prevent marital breakups. Indeed, the Japanese divorce rate is about half that of the United States. If a couple discovers that they don't love each other or have nothing in common, they really don't have much reason for divorce, because low emotional involvement is par for the course. Only about a third of the Japanese people in one survey would marry the same person if they had it to do over again (cited in Kristof, 1996d).

The Feminization of Love

Culture aside, how people define love relationships and how they express affection are often influenced by their different power positions. Certainly, men and women are more similar than they are different when it comes to intimacy. But the differences that do exist are worth noting. For instance, research suggests that American women generally scrutinize their experiences of love more than men do, leading to more sensitivity and responsiveness to what is going on in their relationships (Holtzworth-Munroe & Jacobson, 1985). Men, in contrast, tend to be less reflective, falling in love more quickly and less intentionally than women. They are more likely to believe in "love at first sight" and less likely to "work" on sustaining or enhancing their love relationships than women (Hochschild, 1983).

Within the context of marriage, research consistently shows that wives disclose more emotional intimacy to their partners than husbands do (Thompson & Walker, 1989). Women also usually experience and express a wider range of emotions in marriage, such as tenderness, fear, and sadness. In short, wives generally seem to be more expressive and affectionate than husbands—a difference that upsets many wives:

> Women tend to complain that their husbands do not care about their emotional lives and do not express their own feelings and thoughts. Women often say that they have to pull things out of their husbands and push them to open up. Men tend to respond either that they are open or that they do not understand what it is their wives want from them. Men often protest that no matter how much they talk it is never enough for their wives. (Thompson & Walker, 1989, p. 846)

In light of these findings, perhaps we should not be surprised that the emotion of love has become *feminized*. The **feminization of love** means that love is culturally defined in terms of emotional expression, verbal disclosure, vulnerability, warmth, and affection—tendencies typically considered "feminine" in Western societies (Cancian, 1993). Expressing tender feelings, being gentle, and being aware of others' feelings—things people would all agree ought to be present in love relationships—are ideal qualities this culture stereotypically associates with women, not men. In contrast, desirable qualities for men usually include being independent, strong, competent, assertive, and unemotional, characteristics that run counter to common ideas about love.

Many studies do indeed show women to be more interested in and more skilled in love than men are (Cancian, 1987). The difference starts early. One study found that during adolescence girls acquire more cultural knowledge about romantic love, including the social norms that guide the expression of those feelings, than do adolescent boys (Simon, Eder, & Evans, 1992).

In heterosexual relationships, feminized conceptions of love can reinforce men's power over women. Many men are emotionally dependent on women, but that dependence remains, for the most part, culturally unrecognized. Meanwhile, women's economic dependence on men is overtly recognized and often exaggerated (Cancian, 1987). Furthermore, the intimate talk about personal troubles that appeals to women requires a willingness to see oneself as weak and in need of support, which further plays into the idea that the man is the stronger, more powerful member of a couple. Being responsive to the needs of others—another feature of women's love—leads to giving up some control and, in a sense, being "on call" to provide care whenever it's required (Cancian, 1993). Hence, the power that women may have—controlling such resources as emotional support, sex, or, in traditional couples, homemaking—remains largely hidden because men's dependence on these abilities is not something that garners much public attention or concern.

According to sociologist Francesca Cancian (1987), love became feminized with the rise of capitalism and the shift from an agrarian to an industrial economy in the nineteenth century. As economic production separated from the home and from personal relationships, women's and men's roles became more polarized. Women became responsible for the "emotional management" of the family relationships. Men took on duties in the larger world of work and became defined by the responsibilities they held there. The masculine ideal in a capitalist economy was to be an independent, self-made man with virtues such as self-control, economic success, courage, and an upright character. Intimacy, emotional expression, and other feminine qualities had no place in the work world and therefore became devalued. Love was what women did in the home; it had nothing to do with what men did at work. In fact, women's "superior" ability to love was seen as enabling them to more effectively comfort and care for their children and husbands.

But men do love effectively, Cancian (1987, 1993) argues—just in a distinctive style that focuses on practical help, shared physical activities, time spent together, and sex. She describes an interview with a 29-year-old man who said that he feels especially close to his wife after they have had sex: "I don't talk to her very often, I guess, but somehow I feel we have really communicated after we have made love" (quoted in Cancian, 1987, p. 77). There is no doubt in this man's mind that he shows his wife how much he loves her every time they have sex. For many women, of course, such an attitude is precisely the problem. To them, the only real communication is verbal communication.

These different ways of expressing love are not equally recognized in contemporary society, however. If sexual behavior were widely regarded in the culture as the primary means of expressing love, the way talking about feelings currently is, then people would be reading all sorts of books and articles about the problem of men wanting love "too much" and women not wanting it enough. But instead, people cast women's yearnings for the form of love they value, as a problem that needs attention.

Even social researchers who study love, friendship, and intimacy often use indicators of love that reflect "feminine" styles. These studies tend to examine such activities as verbal self-disclosure and emotional expressiveness. When less biased measures are used, the differences in men's and women's ability to love are slight. For example, when researchers examine actual contact with loved ones, the differences between men and women essentially disappear (see Exhibit 5.1).

In sum, the fact that women have more close relationships, appear to care more about those relationships, and seem more skilled at expressing feelings doesn't mean that men are

EXHIBIT 5.1

A Gender-Neutral Measure of Love: Spending Time with Loved Ones

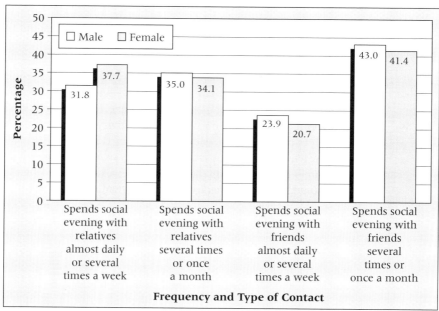

Data source: National Opinion Research Center. 1998. *General Social Survey, 1972–1998.* Available at www.icpsr.umich.edu/GSS/. Accessed June 1, 2001.

distant and unconcerned about love relationships. In national surveys, men and women alike rank family bonds as the most important element of their lives. The feminized perspective on love, however, leads people to conclude that women need love more than men do, even though research on the effect of love relationships on physical and psychological well-being shows that men need it at least as much as women do, if not more (Gove, Style, & Hughes, 1990; Umberson, Chen, House, Hopkins, & Slaten, 1996).

Sexuality

Sexuality is another crucial element of intimate relationships. The United States, as you surely know, is a society preoccupied with sex, overflowing with media images and cultural traditions that emphasize sexuality. A consumer product is rarely marketed without some sexual innuendo or display (Schwartz, 2000). As sociologist Lillian Rubin (1990) describes it,

> In the public arena, sex screams at us at every turn—from our television and movie screens, from the billboards on our roadways, from the pages of our magazines, from the advertisements for goods, whether they seek to sell automobiles, soap, or undergarments. Bookstore shelves bulge with volumes about sex, all of them dedicated to telling us what to do and how to do it. TV talk shows feature solemn discussions of pornography, impotence, premarital sex, marital sex, extramarital sex, group sex, swinging, sadomasochism, and as many other variations of sexual behavior their producers can think of, whether the ordinary or the bizarre. (p. 9)

The "acceptability" of sex as a topic for public discussion reached a new level during the media frenzy surrounding President Clinton's affair with a White House intern in 1998. The publication of the independent counsel's report on the scandal created unprecedented traffic on the Internet as citizens hurried to read the explicit details.

All this attention is a far cry from the United States in the late nineteenth century, when sex was something people spoke about only in hushed, secret tones. So disagreeable was the discussion of sex then that any topic remotely sexual was to be avoided. For instance, people started using the terms "white meat" and "dark meat" to describe poultry so that they could avoid saying the names of body parts such as thighs and breasts (Coontz, 1992).

By contrast, today most Americans openly discuss and express opinions about sexual matters and seem to have a relatively matter-of-fact attitude toward sexuality. According to the General Social Survey (National Opinion Research Center, 1998), 87 percent of Americans favor sex education in public schools, and about 43 percent believe that premarital sex is not wrong at all.

But this apparent comfort with sexual matters in modern society masks an underlying discomfort. Consider the frequent instances of local communities blocking contraceptive ads on television or parents' groups undermining sex education classes in schools (Schwartz, 2000). The irony is that the culture encourages early sexual experimentation while simultaneously forbidding it.

Americans also tend to be reluctant to acknowledge the role of these cultural images on their own sexual attitudes and behaviors (Schur, 1988). Instead, they're inclined to see sexuality as a "natural" phenomenon that they develop into. Admittedly, the expression of affection for another person has obvious biological components. And human genital equipment is pretty much the same worldwide. Consequently, many people simply assume that we are born with sexual drives that emerge at the appropriate stage of development.

But if human sexuality were purely biological, it would fall under strict hormonal control, much like the sexual behavior of other animals. Most animals engage in no sexual behavior at all during most of the year. Mating occurs only when the male and female are fertile and when such activity can lead to pregnancy. This period of time, known as *estrus,* instinctually drives sexual urges. If you've ever had a pet dog "in heat," you know how profoundly its behavior can change during this season.

In humans, as in other mammals, the production of sperm and eggs is controlled by hormones. But human sexuality does not fall under complete hormonal control. We have no limited period of estrus. The average human adult female is able to conceive about once a month, and the average human adult male is more or less constantly fertile. Furthermore, humans regularly have sex at times when conception is not possible and indeed not desired. They can even engage in sexual activity when they don't necessarily want to—and apparently do so fairly often. In one study of American college students, 81 percent reported a recent episode in which they experienced ambivalence about engaging in sex with their date partners, but about half of these individuals did so anyway (O'Sullivan & Gaines, 1998).

Thus sexual activity has symbolic as well as physical significance. Advanced cognitive abilities allow people to become sexually aroused by vivid mental imagery or simply by the sound of a lover's voice. We have sex for fun, as a way of telling others how much we care for them, as a way of living up to others' expectations, as a way to satisfy egos, or for any number of other reasons. In the survey of college students just cited, respondents commonly mentioned not wanting to disappoint, upset, or anger their partners as the reason they eventually engaged in sexual activity.

If sexuality were a universal biological drive, you would also expect to see vast similarities across time and space in the ways people experience and express their sexuality. But sexual diversity is the rule, not the exception. People differ dramatically in what they find attractive and arousing. Some people's sexual appetites are insatiable and indiscriminant; others' are highly particular and selective. For some, sex is a pleasurable physical activity that need not be connected to deep emotions; for others, sex is enjoyable only if it occurs within the context of a long-term love relationship.

Culture and Sexuality

You can see that exclusive reliance on a biological explanation for human sexuality falls short. Individual preferences play a big role. But so does culture. Every society has its own rules and expectations for sexual behavior. Most people in a given society follow the rules; some break them; but none can completely ignore them (Schwartz & Rutter, 1998).

Consider how society's contemporary ideas about sexuality have shifted along with changes in family privacy discussed in Issue 3.

Throughout your life you've been receiving messages telling you which sexual desires and behaviors are "normal" and which are "abnormal" in this culture. These sexual customs and values are passed on by example, through informal and formal teaching, and indirectly through media images. Within that general context, however, different families have their own values and therefore teach widely divergent sexual lessons. A teenager growing up in this permissive culture but in a family in which sex outside of marriage is considered reprehensible may have to suppress feelings of arousal or channel them into "appropriate" pursuits such as competitive sports. Teens raised in a home environment that encourages them to celebrate their sexuality likely have a much different experience. But neither the culture's nor the family's values unequivocally influence sexuality. Siblings raised in the same environment can sometimes express their sexuality quite differently.

Cultural expectations regarding sexuality are most notable for their diversity. In some cultures, sexual contact between people of the same sex is considered a heinous crime punishable by death. In many others, however, it is socially acceptable, at least for certain people at certain times. Among the Sambia of Papua New Guinea, for example, every adolescent male is expected to engage in sexual relationships with other men as part of his initiation into adulthood; as an adult he's expected to enter a heterosexual marriage. In Sweden and the Netherlands, premarital sex is accepted as normal, and both men and women are expected to be sexually experienced when they marry. But in most Islamic societies, virginity at the time of marriage is the norm, especially for women. In some societies, women have no concept of orgasm; in other societies, they become intensely aroused during sex (Schwartz & Rutter, 1998).

Even ideas about sexual dysfunction are culturally determined. Take, for instance, the problem of "abnormal" sexual desire. It is the number one complaint bringing U.S. clients to sex therapists (Rosellini, 1992). On one end of the spectrum of "abnormality" is *hypoactive sexual desire disorder*, which the American Psychiatric Association identifies as a deficiency or absence of desire for sexual activity. The afflicted individual is not motivated to seek sexual stimuli and doesn't feel frustrated when deprived of the opportunity for sexual expression; she or he rarely initiates sexual activity and may only engage in it reluctantly when it is initiated by a partner. This "disorder" is believed to be about twice as common in women as in men.

At the other end of the spectrum are people, sometimes referred to as "sex addicts," who engage in *compulsive sexual behavior*. Their sexual desire is considered too strong. Although no one knows for sure how many people suffer from this problem, experts estimate the prevalence to be roughly 5 percent of the adult population (Rosellini, 1992).

Here are two identifiable sexual disorders that affect millions of people. But what do "too much" and "too little" desire mean? How much sex should a "normal" person want? What is considered normal sexual behavior varies widely from culture to culture. A "normal" amount of sexual activity among Chinese married couples, for example, is generally lower than that among couples in the West, even though approval of pre- and extramarital sex is substantially higher in China (cited in Hatfield & Rapson, 1993). Ideals regarding normal sexual desire change over time as well. In the nineteenth century, low sexual desire was considered a good thing, at least in women; sexuality for purposes other than procreation and outside of marriage was considered evil.

Even within the same culture, one person's idea of normal sexual desire could easily contrast with another's. Researchers of marriage and family have repeatedly found that spouses have different estimates of the frequency and duration of sexual activity (Rubin, 1990). In a scene from the 1977 film *Annie Hall* a split screen shows Alvie Singer (Woody Allen) and Annie (Diane Keaton) as unhappy lovers, each discussing the relationship with their respective therapists. Alvie complains that the couple "hardly ever" has sex anymore—maybe *only* three times a week. On the opposite side of the screen, Annie complains that she feels like they're having sex "constantly"—*as often as* three times per week (Schwartz & Rutter, 1998).

Another common sexual problem that is highly influenced by culture is *premature ejaculation*, defined by the American Psychiatric Association as male orgasm with minimal sexual stimulation before or shortly after penetration and before the person wishes it.

Notice first that this definition suggests heterosexual intercourse. So it is usually considered a problem only within a narrowly defined realm of sexuality. In addition, premature ejaculation can be considered a problem only in a culture that contains some conception of female sexual desire, needs, and pleasure. The idea that a man can achieve an orgasm "too quickly" implies that it occurs before his partner has been satisfied. In cultures where only male sexuality matters or is defined as legitimate, it wouldn't make any difference when the man achieved an orgasm. In fact, in some countries where women's sexuality is of secondary importance, a man who ejaculates quickly is considered healthy, even virile (Schwartz & Rutter, 1998).

So you see that sexuality—from what people want to what people do—is more than just biology. Human beings are constantly involved in complex interactions with others. They all develop their own sexual scripts out of the range of their experiences. These scripts are limited culturally as well—by what they're taught, expect, and believe to be permissible and correct.

Sexual Orientation

Some sociologists have characterized American culture as **heteronormative**—that is, a culture where heterosexuality is accepted as the normal, taken-for-granted mode of sexual expression. Cultural representations of virtually every aspect of intimate or family life—dating, marriage, childbearing, and so on—presume a world in which men are sexually and affectionately attracted to women and women are attracted to men (Macgillivray, 2000). Heterosexuality is socially privileged because these relationships and lifestyles are affirmed in every facet of the culture. Heterosexual privilege includes having positive media images of people with your sexual orientation; not having to lie about who you are, what you do, and where you go; not having to worry about being fired from jobs because of your sexual orientation; receiving validation from your religious community; being able to adopt children; and being able to join the Boy Scouts or serve openly in the military (Macgillivray, 2000).

In such a culture, homosexuality is likely to be considered an aberration. In fact, as Exhibit 5.2 shows, the majority of Americans do consider homosexuality wrong, although the percentage began to decline significantly in 1993.

These changes in attitudes reflect in part the media and scientific attention that has been devoted to discovering homosexuality's causes. Psychiatrists in the 1950s and 1960s wrote extensively about homosexuals as perverts and degenerates who, with the appropriate therapy, could "learn" to be heterosexual. Their underlying assumption was that homosexuality is a choice, a preference, which is not influenced at all by a person's biological inheritance.

Even today, several religious organizations are devoted to "converting" homosexuals. One such organization, called Exodus International, proclaims that "freedom from homosexuality is possible through repentance and faith in Jesus Christ as Savior and Lord. We believe such freedom is increasingly experienced as the former homosexual matures through ongoing submissions to the Lordship of Christ and His Church" (quoted in Ponticelli, 1999, p. 157).

However, a growing body of literature is providing evidence that homosexuality—indeed, sexual orientation in general—is not a choice but is anatomically or genetically determined.

As noted in Issue 1, legal marriage is the most obvious area in which social institutions bestow benefits on heterosexuals that are denied to others (insurance benefits, property and inheritance laws, joint child custody, and so on).

See Issue 5 for more about the stresses that rigid religious attitudes may create in nontraditional families.

EXHIBIT 5.2

*Attitudes
Toward
Homosexuality*

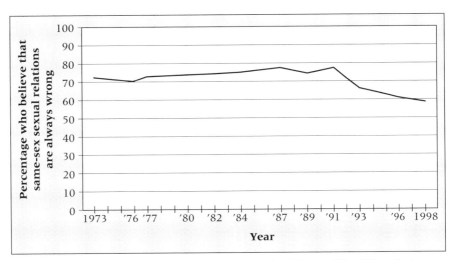

Data source: National Opinion Research Center. 1998. *General Social Survey, 1972–1998.* Available at www.icpsr.umich.edu/GSS/. Accessed June 1, 2001.

Biological Influences   In 1995 two scientists at the National Institutes of Health transplanted a single gene into the bodies of male fruit flies that caused them to display "courtship" behaviors with other male fruit flies (Zhang & Odenwald, 1995). Granted, the notion that a fruit fly could be "homosexual" in the same sense that a human could be is an overstatement, because sexual orientation is a human construction that includes not only physical desires but also psychological imagery and self-identity. Nevertheless, this research added to the mounting body of evidence that sexual orientation is rooted in biology.

In 1991 a California neuroscientist performed autopsies on the brains of men and women of known sexual orientation (LeVay, 1991). He found that a tiny region in the center of the brain was substantially smaller among the gay men he examined than among the heterosexual men. The researcher pleaded for caution in drawing quick conclusions from his findings. He pointed out that his research couldn't determine whether the observed brain differences were the cause or a consequence of sexual orientation or the consequences of AIDS (the gay men he studied had all died of AIDS, and the vast majority of the heterosexual men and women had not). Nevertheless, this study became a catalyst for both scholarly and not-so-scholarly debate on the origins of human sexual orientation (Ordover, 1996).

Another study found that male relatives of known gay men were substantially more likely to also be homosexual (13.5 percent) than were the entire sample studied (2 percent). Indeed, the researcher discovered more gay relatives on the maternal side, fueling the contention that homosexuality is passed from generation to generation through women (Hamer & Coupland, 1994). Some researchers contend that such studies point toward a "gay gene."

As compelling as such findings are, they must be interpreted with caution. One must avoid making too much of any one statistical correlation. The "high" rate (13.5 percent) of homosexuality among relatives of gay men, for example, means that in over 86 percent of the cases these relatives were not gay.

In addition, a single gene is unlikely to be responsible for any complex human trait. Scientists know, for instance, that genes are responsible for the development of lungs, larynx, mouth, and the areas of the brain associated with speech. But such complexity can't be collapsed into a single "talking" gene. Similarly, genes determine the development of penises, vaginas, and brains. But that's a far step from the contention that a single gene determines sexual orientation.

Moreover, these studies really aren't examining the origins of sexual orientation. They're examining the origins of one type of sexual orientation: homosexuality. None of these researchers seems interested in explaining the origins of heterosexuality or bisexuality. For instance, if a certain structure in the brain is small in homosexual men and large in heterosexual men, is it somewhere in between among bisexual men? And no data exist to prove a genetic link or a link based on brain structure with female sexual orientation, whether heterosexual or homosexual.

In short, genetics appears to be one factor among many that can help people understand sexual orientation.

Cultural Influences   Another important factor in determining sexual orientation is culture, which is fundamental to the complex and unpredictable interplay of fantasy, courtship, arousal, and sexual selection that constitute "sexuality" (Horton, 1995). Your genes may enable you to act in certain ways, but because people are all influenced by culture, these actions necessarily take on specific cultural forms.

Consider the terms used today—*heterosexual* and *homosexual*—to refer to the ways in which people can classify their sexual orientation. At the time of Plato, people didn't have a notion of two distinctly different sexual appetites allotted to different individuals. They simply saw various ways of enjoying pleasure (Foucault, 1990).

Concepts such as "the homosexual" and "the heterosexual" originated only toward the end of the nineteenth century when certain behaviors stopped being attributed to particular individuals and came to define certain groups of people (Coontz, 2001). Those who had sexual relations with members of their own sex were now "homosexuals." Those who had sexual relations with people of the opposite sex were a different type, "heterosexual." Medical writers eventually applied these categories to stigmatize same-sex relations as a form of sexual perversion. Men and women could no longer write of their affectionate desire for a loved one of the same gender—as was heretofore commonplace—without causing suspicion (D'Emilio & Freedman, 1988).

This culture's fondness for dichotomous sexual categories was questioned in the 1940s, when Alfred Kinsey published a report arguing that sexual orientation is not an "either/or" proposition. He suggested that it in fact lies along a continuum, with "exclusively heterosexual" at one end of the scale and "exclusively homosexual" at the other. An "exclusive heterosexual," for example, is someone who has never had physical or psychosexual responses to individuals of his or her own sex. In between the two extremes are various gradations of sexuality, suggesting that people could be "bisexual" or "predominantly but not exclusively" heterosexual or homosexual. Note that Kinsey and his colleagues recognized that sexual orientation cannot be measured solely in terms of sexual activity. An individual may be sexually aroused by homosexual fantasies but have had only heterosexual physical encounters. Such a person would fall somewhere in the middle of the continuum.

Kinsey and his colleagues found that only 50 percent of the white males they studied were "exclusively heterosexual" and only 4 percent were "exclusively homosexual" (Kinsey, Pomeroy, & Martin, 1948). The rest fell somewhere between the two endpoints. When they examined only overt, physical sexual contact since adolescence, they found that 37 percent of men had had some homosexual experience that ended in orgasm. Of women, 13 percent had (Kinsey, Pomeroy, Martin, & Gebhard, 1953). These percentages are significantly higher than the percentages of people who identify themselves as homosexual or even bisexual.

As these studies suggest, classifying sexuality into homosexual and heterosexual categories doesn't always fit real experiences. Sexual behavior and lifestyles among men and women vary from day to day and year to year. Whether or not a sexual experience is characterized as homosexual depends on the definition used (A. M. Johnson, 1992). In a fairly recent national survey, many more people reported homosexual desire and behavior than reported homosexuality or bisexuality as their main sexual identity (Michael, Gagnon, Laumann, & Kolata, 1994). About 3 percent of the men surveyed identified themselves as gay, but 9 percent had had sex with a man since puberty. Among women, less than 2 percent identified as lesbian, but about 4 percent had had sex with another woman since puberty.

Biological or Cultural—Does It Matter?   Although the debate over the origins of sexual orientation is far from settled, let's suppose that sexual orientation is, in fact, biologically determined. What would be the social implications of such a fact? Some people argue that understanding sexual orientation as an innate characteristic beyond personal control, like hair or eye color, will make people more open-minded about equality and more protective of the civil rights of gay and lesbian individuals. For instance, the long-standing concern that homosexuals shouldn't work in occupations involving children (Boy Scout leader, elementary school teacher, child care worker, and so on) because of their potentially corrupting influence would disappear, because environmental influence would no longer be considered a factor in the development of a child's sexual orientation.

There is some evidence that the explanations people believe about the causes of sexual orientation do affect their attitudes toward homosexuals. For instance, a decade ago, a *New York Times/CBS News* poll found that 71 percent of people who believe homosexuality is "something people choose to be" said they'd object to having a homosexual as a child's elementary school teacher. But only 39 percent of those who believe homosexuality is "something people cannot change" said they'd object (cited in LeVay, 1996). Incidentally, such negative feelings extended beyond those occupations that offer an opportunity to influence children. People who believe homosexuality is a choice were four times more likely to object to gay airplane pilots than people who believe it isn't a choice.

However, information about the genetic origins of sexual orientation might be used to perpetuate the belief that homosexuality is a "defect" that needs to be fixed, thereby further stigmatizing gays and lesbians. Ideas about biological determinism inevitably carry the threat of encouraging people to try manipulating genes, the brain, hormones, or whatever the purported biological cause, to adapt to prevailing social norms. For instance, some scientists have argued that exposure to certain levels of testosterone at certain times in fetal development is a crucial factor in the development of "sex centers" in the brain. If so, prenatal tests such as amniocentesis could, perhaps, "predict" homosexuality. And if this "condition" can be predicted, "prevention" is but a short step away. So alarming are the possibilities that eleven states currently have laws preventing information derived from genetic testing to be used in a discriminatory fashion (Horton, 1995).

Gender and Sexuality

Although contemporary research indicates that the female sex drive is just as strong as the male sex drive, most people assume that males have greater sexual appetites. For the first 60 years of the twentieth century, sex manuals portrayed female sexuality as either nonexistent, weak, or dormant. A woman was expected to be the passive recipient of orgasms given to her by her husband (Groneman, 2000). Even today people assume that women "want" sex primarily within the context of an intimate relationship or within the security of married life and motherhood (Hollway, 1993).

Men are typically described as preferring more **recreational sex** (sexual pleasure for its own sake) and women as preferring more **relational sex** (sex within the context of ongoing relationships). In truth, both women and men indicate a preference for relational sex (Schwartz & Rutter, 1998). That is, the vast majority of women and men prefer sex with a regular partner or a spouse, as shown in Exhibit 5.3. The difference is that if relational sex is not available, men are more likely to engage in recreational sex than women are.

Certainly some of women's traditional reluctance to engage in noncommitted sex stems from its social costs. Although the **sexual double standard** so prevalent in the first half of the twentieth century—"real" men have lots of sex with lots of women; "good" women have no sex prior to or outside of marriage—seems to have weakened somewhat in recent years, in some ways it is very much alive. Some scholars have suggested that the intense public concern over teen sexuality is really a response to women's—not men's—increased sexual activity: "Teens are demonized as morally wayward—because women have been admitting to engaging in sex at levels that are increasingly similar to men's" (Schwartz & Rutter, 1998, p. 166).

Studies show that women tend to be regarded more negatively than men if they become sexually active at a young age or have sex within casual relationships (Sprecher,

EXHIBIT 5.3

Relationships to One's Sexual Partners

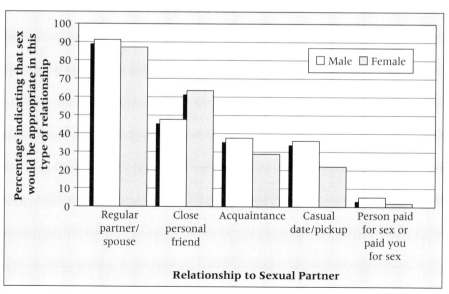

Data source: National Opinion Research Center. 1998. *General Social Survey, 1972–1998.* Available at www.icpsr.umich.edu/GSS/. Accessed June 1, 2001.

McKinney, & Orbuch, 1987). Consider, for example, how this young college student says he would feel toward a woman with whom he had a one-night stand: "[I]f I met a woman in a bar and had sex with her chances are I wouldn't call her because I wouldn't have any respect for her. Because if she did something like that . . . would I want someone like that for the rest of my life? No, of course not" (quoted in Fromme & Emihovich, 1998, p. 174).

Several of the young men interviewed in this study expressed similar ideas, failing to recognize that they were engaging in exactly the same behaviors that they condemned in women (Fromme & Emihovich, 1998). So ingrained is the double standard in this culture that the inconsistencies and contradictions are hardly noticed. After all, with whom are all these men having sex if women are supposedly not having much sex? Amazingly, the double standard has persisted despite women's increased sexual activity.

The double standard also affects attitudes toward contraceptive use. For instance, men who come equipped with condoms on a date are considered safe and responsible, but women who provide men with condoms risk being seen as promiscuous. The lingering cultural reluctance to acknowledge women's control over their own sexuality may be to blame for these perceptions. In fact, college women perceive more negative consequences (for instance, social disapproval from partners) for women who are "contraceptively prepared" than for women who have unprotected sex (Hynie & Lydon, 1995). Such attitudes are certainly one of the more dangerous outcomes of the double standard of sexuality and perhaps explain the relatively low percentage of sexually active unmarried women—even those with multiple partners—who use condoms consistently (see Exhibit 5.4).

Gender differences in sexuality are further illustrated by comparing lesbian couples and gay male couples. In the 1970s and early 1980s, the gay male community advocated a stereotypically male (that is, recreational) approach to sexuality. By the mid-1980s, however, the specter of AIDS brought a noticeable shift toward couplehood. Nevertheless, many gay men still approve of recreational sex and nonmonogamy, even if they are currently in lifetime relationships.

EXHIBIT 5.4

Condom Use Among Sexually Active Unmarried Women

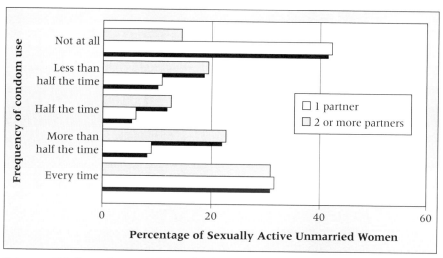

Data source: U.S. Census Bureau. 2000b. *Statistical Abstract of the United States: 2000,* Table 97. Washington, DC: U.S. Government Printing Office.

Research suggests that lesbians, like heterosexual women, tend to prefer sex in the context of ongoing, committed relationships. Despite the growth in recent years of "lesbian sex clubs," which celebrate anonymous sex, relatively few lesbians approve of recreational or nonmonogamous sex. As a group, lesbians tend to have sex less frequently than married, cohabiting heterosexual couples or gay male couples. They also tend to prize nongenital physical contact—cuddling, touching, hugging—more than other couples. Whereas heterosexual women, having to adapt to male sexuality, come to see snuggling and touching as a prelude to intercourse, lesbians are likely to consider these activities as ends in themselves (Blumstein & Schwartz, 1983).

One must be careful, therefore, in assuming that "having sex" means the same thing to people of all sexual orientations. Does the fact that lesbians indicate a lower frequency of sex than heterosexuals or gay men indicate that they "have less sex"? Perhaps not. Consider this: the average duration of a heterosexual sexual encounter is approximately 8 minutes, punctuated by one partner (typically the man) or both partners achieving orgasm. The average duration of a lesbian sexual episode is quite a bit longer—30 to 60 minutes on average—and may not result in either partner achieving an orgasm (Frye, 1992). How many instances of "having sex" are included in an entire evening's worth of cuddling and hugging? To the extent that a standard heterosexual and male definition is used by everyone, the frequency of "having sex" among lesbians will be underestimated. Indeed, if achieving orgasm is defined as the punctuating event that determines whether an encounter is or isn't "having sex," then most lesbian couples (and many heterosexual women) never "have sex."

Adolescent Sexuality

Another example of how culture influences sexual attitudes and behaviors is adolescent sexuality. Much of the concern centers around the timing of sexual activity among today's youth. In 1970, 5 percent of female 15-year-olds were sexually active; by 1995 the figure had increased to 24 percent (U.S. Bureau of the Census, 2000b). Since the 1950s the average age at first intercourse has been decreasing steadily for males and females of all races (Michael et al., 1994). By the time they reach age 20, about 70 percent of girls and 83 percent of boys have had a premarital sexual experience (Abma & Sonenstein, 2001).

Troubling to many is the increasing variety of sexual activities young people are engaging in. Bombarded with warnings about AIDS and other sexually transmitted diseases, young people are turning at early ages to other forms of sexual expression, such as oral sex and mutual masturbation. As one psychologist explains,

> I see girls, seventh and eighth graders, even sixth graders, who tell me they're virgins, and they're going to wait to have intercourse until they meet the man they'll marry. But then they've had oral sex 50 or 60 times. It's like a goodnight kiss to them, how they say goodbye after a date. (quoted in Jarrell, 2000, p. B8)

The increase in sexual activity has been particularly apparent among adolescent girls, who are becoming sexually active at younger ages than ever before and are showing levels of sexual frequency that approach male levels. Among sexually active adolescent girls, 64 percent have had more than one partner, up from 38 percent 2 decades ago (cited in Gibbs, 1993b; U.S. Bureau of the Census, 2000b). The age at which individuals begin having sexual intercourse can have long-term implications for their sexual lives. For example, women who engage in their first sexual intercourse before the age of 16 are much more

EXHIBIT 5.5

Relationship Between Age at First Sexual Intercourse and Number of Lifetime Partners

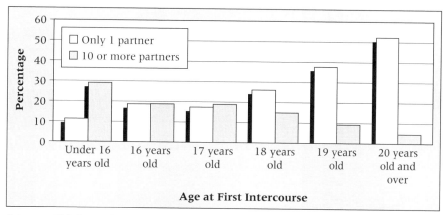

Age at First Intercourse

Data source: U.S. Census Bureau. 2000b. *Statistical Abstract of the United States: 2000*, Table 96. Washington, DC: U.S. Government Printing Office.

likely to have multiple sex partners than are those who become sexually active later in life (see Exhibit 5.5). They are also at greater risk of becoming pregnant and being infected with a sexually transmitted disease (Abma & Sonenstein, 2001).

Although young women are becoming almost as sexually active as young men, their reasons for having sex can be quite different. One national survey found that close to half of all women cited affection for their partner as the reason for having sex the first time. In contrast, more than half the men said they were motivated by curiosity and their "readiness" for sex; only a quarter said they had sexual intercourse for the first time out of affection for their partner. In fact, most men said they were not in love with their first sexual partner, but the vast majority of women said they were (Michael et al., 1994). Furthermore, three times as many women as men report that they did not want to have sex the first time (cited in Schwartz & Rutter, 1998).

Adolescents struggling to establish an identity distinct from their families turn to peer groups for a reference point against which to measure themselves and express their "new self" (Harris, 1998; Rubin, 1990). But like the family, the peer group has its own demands for conformity and its own requirements for acceptance. Sometimes the pressure to become sexually active is direct and specific. But more often the pressure resides in the heightened sexual atmosphere that permeates every facet of adolescent life: fashion, language, music, not to mention daily conversation. In the end, adolescent sexual behavior is influenced not just by the need to belong but also by the need to know:

> A member of the peer group is the first to take the plunge and talk about it. It's news; it's consequential. For those who have not yet had the experience, it's riveting. Someone close has actually done it, can describe it, can say what it feels like. The veil of silence is pierced. But for the uninitiated, the mystery deepens; the pressure to know grows. (Rubin, 1990, p. 66)

Of course, some adolescents resist the pressure. For most, however, even though they may never have any conscious awareness of the pressure, the peer culture in which they reside powerfully influences their sexual decision making (Rubin, 1990).

Young people in our society are also becoming biologically mature earlier and earlier. For instance, the average age of *menarche* (a girl's first menstrual period) has gradually lowered from about 14 years of age a century ago to about 12 and a half today (Darton, 1991; Skolnick, 1991). One study found that 7 percent of European-American girls and 27 percent of African-American girls had begun puberty by the age of 7 (cited in Gilbert, 1997). Yet we haven't responded by socially accepting young people as adults at earlier ages. In fact, the opposite has occurred: Adolescence has been prolonged and adulthood delayed, with a resulting trend toward later marriage. In the past, a child who was physically capable of being sexually active would have already been engaged or married and no longer in her or his parents' home (Schwartz & Rutter, 1998). Today, on average, American girls and boys face over a decade of their lives during which they are sexually mature and single.

Many teenagers, almost by definition, are disqualified from monogamous relationships as "too young" to get serious. The kinds of sexuality they are eligible for—for pleasure rather than reproduction, in relationships that are short term rather than marriage bound—challenge the sexual values of many adults (Luker, 1994). Thus, at the same time that young people are biologically ready to have sex (and bear children), society expects them to wait until they are older.

Teen Pregnancy

Contrary to popular belief, even with high rates of adolescent sexuality, the number of adolescents getting pregnant and having children has decreased since the 1950s (U.S. Bureau of the Census, 2000b). The birth rate among girls between 15 and 17—in all racial groups—is the lowest it's been in 40 years (cited in Lacey, 1999). Indeed, the trend toward lower adolescent birth rates is occurring throughout the industrialized world, in part because of an increased emphasis on education and on goals other than motherhood for young women (Singh & Darroch, 2000). Still, in the United States about 11 percent of white babies, 17 percent of Hispanic babies, and 21 percent of black babies are born to teenage mothers (U.S. Bureau of the Census, 2000b).

What has changed is that young parents today are less likely to be married—or to get married before the baby is born—than their counterparts several decades ago. In 1970 babies born out of wedlock represented about a third of all babies born to teen mothers (Luker, 1994). In the late 1980s and 1990s two-thirds of first births to white teenagers and 97 percent of first births to African-American teenagers were conceived out of wedlock.

However, out-of-wedlock births among adolescents must be placed in the larger context of nonmarital childbearing among all women in this society (see Exhibit 5.6). In 2000, over 1.2 million unmarried U.S. women gave birth, nearly fourteen times the 1940 total of 89,500 (Hollander, 1996; U.S. Bureau of the Census, 2001e). Today one out of every three U.S. births is to an unwed mother (Bianchi & Casper, 2000). Contrary to popular belief, the largest increase in rates of childbearing among single women over the past few years has occurred among older women who are college educated and employed. In 1970 teen mothers were responsible for almost half of all out-of-wedlock births in the United States; today they account for a little less than a third (Luker, 1994).

In light of these trends, why is there still such strident public outcry against adolescent sexuality and childbearing? Conservative and liberal politicians alike speak mournfully of the problems caused by "babies having babies." One national poll showed that 80 percent of Americans thought teen pregnancy was a "serious problem" facing the nation (cited in Luker, 1994). And studies do show that teen parenthood is associated with a variety of harmful conditions, including disrupted education; fewer job opportunities; an increased

EXHIBIT 5.6

Trends in Nonmarital Childbearing

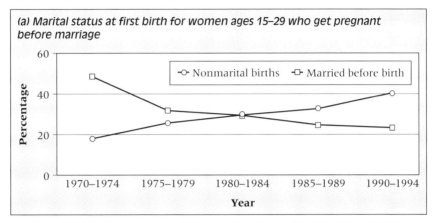

(a) Marital status at first birth for women ages 15–29 who get pregnant before marriage

○ Nonmarital births   □ Married before birth

Data source: U.S. Bureau of the Census. 2000b. *Statistical Abstract of the United States, 2000,* Table 146. Washington, DC: U.S. Government Printing Office.

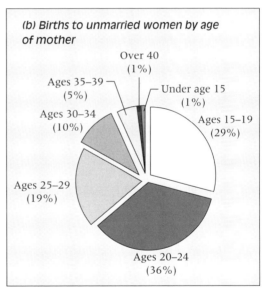

(b) Births to unmarried women by age of mother

Over 40 (1%)
Ages 35–39 (5%)
Under age 15 (1%)
Ages 30–34 (10%)
Ages 15–19 (29%)
Ages 25–29 (19%)
Ages 20–24 (36%)

Data source: U.S. Bureau of the Census. 2000b. *Statistical Abstract of the United States, 2000,* Table 86. Washington, DC: U.S. Government Printing Office.

likelihood of living in poverty; and an increased likelihood of health, psychological, and educational problems for the children of teen parents.

Sociologists have found, however, that such negative outcomes are not simply the result of teenage births (Moore, Manlove, Glei, & Morrison, 1998). Many of the adverse conditions associated with adolescent childbearing—educational failure, low aspirations, fewer employment opportunities, lower self-esteem—in fact contribute to early pregnancy. A teenage woman growing up in disadvantaged circumstances is more likely to become pregnant than teens who do not face such problems (Moore et al., 1998; Wu, 1996; Wu & Martinson, 1993). Because poor and minority youth tend to become sexually active earlier than more "advantaged" young people, they are "at risk" of pregnancy for a longer time. And among youngsters who become pregnant, those who are disadvantaged are less likely to obtain abortions than those who are white, affluent, urban, and of higher socioeconomic status, who get good grades, and who come from two-parent families.

Hence, many, if not most, teenage unwed mothers are already both disadvantaged and discouraged before they get pregnant. No wonder they experience difficulties later in life. As one sociologist put it,

> Teen pregnancy is less about young women and their sex lives than it is about restricted horizons and the boundaries of hope. It is about race and class and how those realities limit opportunities for young people. Most centrally, however, it is typically about being young, female, poor, and non-white and about how having a child seems to be one of the few avenues of satisfaction, fulfillment, and self-esteem. It would be a tragedy to stop worrying about these young women—and their partners—because their behavior is the measure rather than the cause of their blighted hopes. (Luker, 1994, p. 177)

Reducing teen pregnancy would no doubt be a good thing. After all, the United States has a higher teen pregnancy rate than any other industrialized, democratic country in the world, even though its rate of adolescent sexuality is not higher. But by framing the issue of teenage pregnancy as one in which adolescents are too impulsive or too ignorant to postpone sexual activity, use contraceptives, seek abortion, or, failing all that, give their babies up for adoption to "better" parents, Americans can shift responsibility for many serious social problems to adolescents (Luker, 1994). Reducing teen birth rates—either by encouraging or even demanding chastity (the politically conservative approach) or by making abortion, contraception, and sex education more readily available (the politically liberal approach)—is the expedient solution. A greater challenge is to reduce poverty and other social problems, whose deeper causes are more complex and costly to overcome.

DEMO·GRAPHICS

Trends in Teenage Sexuality

One of the most significant and surprising trends related to sexuality over the past decade has been the decline in teenage births. You can see from Exhibit 5.7a that the birth rate—the number of births per 1,000 females in a specified group—for teenage women ages 15–19 dropped considerably between 1991 and 1999. Among the very young (10–14 years) the birth rate in 1999 was the lowest it's ever been. This decrease occurred for all races and was most pronounced for young black women, who experienced a 30 percent decline in birth rates between 1991 and 1999.

Many indirect factors may contribute to the decline in teenage childbearing, such as effective prevention programs and changing cultural attitudes. There are a limited number of possible direct causes as well, such as a decline in sexual activity, more reliable and

EXHIBIT 5.7

Teenage Sexuality

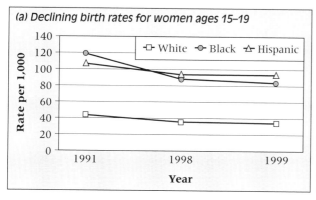

(a) Declining birth rates for women ages 15–19

Data source: S. J. Ventura, J. A. Martin, S. C. Curtin, F. Menacker, & B. E. Hamilton. 2001. Births: Final data for 1999. *National Vital Statistics Reports, 49*(1), Table A. Available at www.cdc.gov/nchs/data/nvsr/nvsr49/nvsr49_01.pdf. Accessed October 4, 2001.

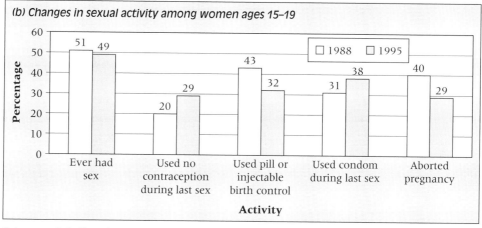

(b) Changes in sexual activity among women ages 15–19

Data sources: J. C. Abma & F. L. Sonenstein. 2001. Sexual activity and contraceptive practices among teenagers in the United States, 1988 and 1995. National Center for Health Statistics. *Vital Health Statistics, 23*(21), Figure 2 and Table 5. Data on abortions from U.S. Bureau of the Census. 2000b. *Statistical Abstract of the United States, 2000*, Table 99. Washington, DC: U.S. Government Printing Office.

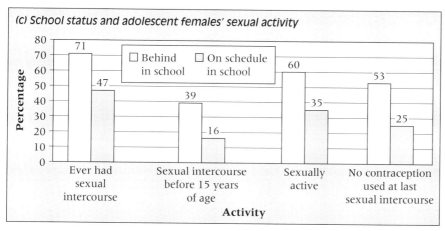

(c) School status and adolescent females' sexual activity

Data source: J. C. Abma & F. L. Sonenstein. 2001. Sexual activity and contraceptive practices among teenagers in the United States, 1988 and 1995. National Center for Health Statistics. *Vital Health Statistics, 23*(21), Figure 14.

effective contraceptive use, and an increase in abortions. Of these, the factors that appear to have directly contributed to the declining birth rates are a slight decline in sexual activity and a slight increase in some forms of contraception (see Exhibit 5.7b). Curiously, the percentage of teenage women who used no contraception at all has increased. Furthermore, the percentage of pregnancies that ended in abortion also declined between 1988 and 1995.

Most likely, people will never know all the complex factors at work that inhibit or encourage adolescent sexuality, but one fruitful approach is to determine who is most likely to become sexually active and therefore at the greatest risk of becoming pregnant. This question has yielded some important research in recent years. Studies suggest that adolescents who become sexually active are likely to be relatively disadvantaged socially. Compare, for example, those female teens who are behind in school (including those who have dropped out) to those who are on schedule (see Exhibit 5.7c). These data are consistent with data from the U.S. Census Bureau (2000b) showing that sexually active adolescents are more likely to have been raised in households without both parents, and to have mothers with relatively low education—factors indicative of lower socioeconomic status. These findings give support to the idea that the unfavorable conditions associated with adolescent pregnancy, such as low occupational status and educational attainment, may be as much a cause as a consequence of teen pregnancy.

Thinking Critically About the Statistics

1. Is the slight decline in the percentage of teenage women who are sexually active (see Exhibit 5.7b) likely to account for the significant decline in birth rates shown in Exhibit 5.7a? What other indirect factors may help explain the decline?

2. Why do you think the percentage of sexually active youth who fail to use contraception during intercourse has risen so much (as shown in Exhibit 5.7b)? As you can see from Exhibit 5.7b, although the percentage of teenage women using condoms increased between 1988 and 1995, the percentage using no contraception at all also increased. How can you explain this apparent contradiction? Given the figures shown here, what role do you think families, schools, religious groups, and media should play in promoting more responsible sexuality among adolescents?

3. Note that the data in all the exhibits shown here pertain to adolescent females. Indeed, most research on adolescent sexuality focuses on females. Why do you think this is so? What are some of the difficulties researchers may face in trying to collect comparable data for adolescent males? What message does the lack of data on males send about men's sexual responsibilities? How might the data presented in these three exhibits change if they reflected male behavioral patterns instead of female patterns?

4. Suppose the U.S. government hired you to develop a program to reduce teenage pregnancy. Considering the data presented in Exhibits 5.7a, 5.7b, and 5.7c, where would you direct your efforts, and why?   ■

Dating and Courtship

Against the cultural backdrop of love and sexuality presented so far, we can now examine the institutional mechanisms through which people meet potential partners. Every society has its own acceptable means of bringing people together, although the process varies markedly from society to society.

In U.S. society, **dating** is the recognized means by which most people move from being single to being coupled. Dating is a somewhat ambiguous phenomenon, blurred by different uses of vocabulary. Terms such as "dating," "going out," "going around," "hanging out," "going steady," and "being involved" often lack clear definition and agreement.

One day one of our sons* (who was 10 at the time) came home from school and happily proclaimed that a girl in his class wanted to "go out" with him. But he was in a quandary. It seems he was already "going out" with someone else. What wasn't clear was where all these fifth graders who were going out with each other actually went. So I asked him.

"Oh, we don't go anywhere," he said, matter-of-factly. Nor did he spend any time at school with the girl or talk to her.

"How do you even know you like each other?" I asked.

"Well . . . if she likes me one of her friends will tell one of my friends who'll tell me. If I like her, one of my friends will tell one of her friends who'll tell her."

"And that's when the two of you are 'going out'?" I asked, hoping to have finally gotten it.

"I dunno," he said, a little surprised that I'd even ask such a question, "I have no idea what she thinks."

Such a conception of "going out" is a far cry from what most adults would consider dating. Although it's difficult to come up with a definition that would apply across situations—first dates, blind dates, double dates, group dates, formal courtship, dating among divorced or widowed people, and so on—all dating seems to involve some degree of companionship, communication, good times, mutual sharing, romantic overtones, and perhaps sexual contact (Laner, 1989). It is these last two features—romance and sex—that typically distinguish "dating" from casual social outings that take place between people who consider themselves "just friends."

The Social Purposes of Dating

Some sociologists (for instance, Waller, 1937) have long argued that one of the key functions of dating in U.S. society—particularly high school dating—is that it serves as a way of gaining social status among one's peers. According to other sociologists, a more important social function of dating—at least in a heterosexual context—is that it lets males and females interact with and learn about one another. It provides an opportunity for exploring romantic intimacy without requiring a rapid escalation toward marriage. It lets individuals learn about the types of people to whom they're attracted. Dating, then, can be seen as a sort of rehearsal for future serious relationships.

Indeed, U.S. dating culture is based on an assumption that dating provides important experiences and valuable lessons that will eventually help people select mates and construct happy marriages. But what exactly is the relationship between dating experiences and future marital success and happiness? Sociologist Martin King Whyte (1990) interviewed 459 women in the greater Detroit area to answer this question. The women, from diverse racial and ethnic backgrounds, ranged in age from 18 to 75. All had been married at least once.

Whyte asked them to recall their premarital dating experiences. Contrary to common perceptions, he found that neither dating variety, length of dating, length of courtship or engagement, or degree of premarital intimacy with a future husband were related to marital success. The amount and type of dating didn't seem to make a difference one way or the

*David Newman's son.

other. Women who married their first loves were just as likely to have long-lasting and satisfying marriages as women who had dated a lot before marrying. Similarly, women who married after only a short acquaintance, and women who knew their husbands-to-be for years, were equally likely to have successful marriages. Marital quality was the same for women who were virgins at marriage and for women who had a variety of sexual partners before marriage.

So apparently dating doesn't really serve as a training ground for marriage. And if you think about it, we really don't have any reason to expect it to. The behaviors that tend to characterize dating—fun, recreation, erotic teasing, and so forth—are not the sorts of activities that necessarily prepare people for the everyday demands of married life.

A Brief History of Dating in America

Even in a 10-year-old's rather hazy conception of dating is a taken-for-granted assumption that the participants involved are solely responsible for deciding whether or not to "go out" with each other. Parents, relatives, or peers may influence these decisions, but they usually don't directly arrange dating relationships.

Americans have never had a tradition of "arranged relationships" or parent-dominated courtship. Eligible males and females, even as early as colonial times, have always taken the initiative to get to know each other, and the decision to marry was always left to them, even if that decision was ultimately subject to parental approval (Whyte, 1992). Later, when large numbers of European immigrants arrived either as single individuals or as nuclear families, ties to extended families—and with them, ties to traditions of arranged relationships—inevitably weakened (Murstein, 1974).

Although Americans have always had a lot of "free choice" in whom they chose to date, dating was (and still is) controlled by social norms. Historical research into U.S. dating practices reveals shifts in social influences and provides a fascinating glimpse into the ways many young people in the past sought intimacy.

Bundling   Before the 1830s, most relationships probably began rather informally. Unmarried individuals had many opportunities to interact in mixed-sex groups (Cate & Lloyd, 1992). These young men and women had typically grown up together in small communities where there were few strangers, so they knew a lot about one another. Even close physical contact was not unheard of, as evidenced by the colonial practice of bundling.

Bundling involved an unmarried woman and an unmarried man, fully clothed, sleeping in the same bed together (Rothman, 1984). Mothers (and daughters) may have favored the practice, perhaps because it was a ritual over which women had significant control. It was up to the young woman to permit or deny access to her bed. In a letter from the late eighteenth century, one man noted that it was "not the fashion to bundle with any chap who might call on a girl, but that it was a special factor, granted only to a favorite lover" (quoted in Rothman, 1984, pp. 47–48).

Although lying in bed together was approved by parents, sexual activity was not. Parents devised a variety of techniques to inhibit sexual contact: "[A] wooden board might be placed in the middle of the bed; the young girl might be encased in a type of long laundry bag up to her armpits; or her garments might be sewn together at strategic points" (Murstein, 1974, p. 317).

Indeed, when you consider that few homes during this time had separate bedrooms for privacy, it would have been difficult to accomplish much sexual activity in the same room

The role of architecture in the emergence of privacy as a valuable family ideal is discussed in Issue 3.

as or in close proximity to the woman's parents and siblings. Difficult, but apparently not impossible. During the latter part of the eighteenth century—a period that has been called the "heyday of bundling"—premarital conception was quite high (for instance, 30 percent in the 1770s) (Cate & Lloyd, 1992; Rothman, 1984).

Bundling disappeared after 1800, in part because women's roles were being significantly redefined. For instance, before 1800 women tended to be viewed as "especially sexual" persons, but in the nineteenth century they came to be seen as "sexually passionless by nature" (Rothman, 1984, p. 48). Gender ideologies that emerged during the nineteenth century emphasized the differences between men and women, and the sexes became segregated in virtually every aspect of their lives (Rothman, 1984). It was during this period that the ideology of "separate spheres," discussed in Chapter 7, emerged. These shifts had profound implications for courtship practices.

Calling and Keeping Company   For one thing, this new gender separation meant that men and women were not able to socialize as freely as they had before. Courtship became more formal, and certain customs and traditions (such as the engagement ring, the formal wedding ceremony, expensive gifts) became common (Rothman, 1984). A new, and highly ritualized, system of dating and courtship known as **calling** emerged during the latter part of the nineteenth century, especially among the middle and upper classes. Young people still could initially meet in a variety of ways—community or church socials, fairs and dances, informally on the street or in school, or through introductions from friends or relatives (Whyte, 1992). But when one or both parties wished to pursue a relationship, the young man was required to visit the young woman at her home, usually during daylight hours. The process entailed many specific guidelines:

> When a girl reached the proper age or had her first "season" (depending on her family's social level), she became eligible to receive male callers. At first her mother or guardian invited young men to call; in subsequent seasons the young lady . . . could bestow an invitation to call on any unmarried man to whom she had been properly introduced. . . . Other young men . . . could be brought to call by friends or relatives of the girl's family, subject to her prior permission. . . . The call itself was a complicated event. A myriad of rules governed everything: the proper amount of time between invitation and visit (two weeks or less); whether or not refreshments should be served . . . ; chaperonage (the first call must be made on mother and daughter . . .); appropriate topics of conversation (the man's interests, but never too personal); how leave should be taken (on no account should the woman accompany [her caller] to the door nor stand talking while he struggles with his coat). (Bailey, 1988, pp. 15–16)

The supervision was so tight—during initial visits the mother remained present in the room at all times; later on she might hover in an adjacent room—that anything resembling recreational enjoyment or romance was next to impossible.

Everyone involved understood that calling was a means by which potential marriage partners could be examined. The practice of calling maintained the social class structure by serving as a test of suitability, breeding, and background (Bailey, 1988). Calling enabled the middle and upper classes to protect themselves from what many at the time considered the "intrusions" of urban life and to screen out the effects of social and geographical mobility that were reaching unprecedented levels at the turn of the twentieth century. It also allowed parents to exert some degree of control over their children's relationships, without going so far as to actually arrange them.

But the courtship process didn't end with calling. If the relationship deepened sufficiently, it might progress to *keeping company*, an early version of going steady (Whyte, 1992). Visits still took place in the young woman's home, but now those visits were limited to one man rather than a host of suitors. They more frequently took place at night rather than in the afternoon, and they sometimes continued after the young woman's parents had retired to bed.

Like couples in previous generations, young people at the end of the 1800s did find time to be alone. Premarital sex and premarital births were not uncommon. According to one study, 13 percent of U.S. women born before 1890 and 26 percent born between 1890 and 1899 engaged in premarital intercourse (Terman, 1938). The premarital pregnancy rate increased from 10 percent in the mid-nineteenth century to 23 percent in the decades between 1880 and 1910 (D'Emilio & Freedman, 1988).

Dating and Rating   The formal tradition of calling began to disappear in the early twentieth century. Economic and educational innovations enabled young people to interact with the opposite sex away from the watchful eyes of parents (Coontz, 1992). The expansion of commercial recreation in the form of movie theaters, dance halls, amusement parks, and so on gave young people new places in which to meet and congregate. Compulsory schooling in public, coeducational institutions provided an arena where young people could see each other daily.

In addition, the growing affluence in the United States and the shift from an agriculture-based economy to an industry-based economy meant that more and more young people had leisure time on their hands. These trends coincided with part-time and after-school employment, which provided young people with spending money that didn't have to be turned over to the family. By the 1920s and 1930s autonomous dating among young people had become a common feature of the interpersonal landscape in the United States (Gordon, 1981).

Technology also played a prominent role in the growth of the dating institution. The innovation that perhaps had the most direct and long-lasting effect was the automobile. Cars were not only a means of transportation away from the home, they also provided a somewhat private space for romantic and sexual activity (Whyte, 1992). The growth of drive-in movie theaters coincided with the growing role cars played in young people's intimate lives. In later years, the borrowed family car was replaced by cars (and then vans) owned by young people themselves.

By the 1930s dating had pretty much moved out of the home and into the public world. In the process, family surveillance was replaced with peer supervision and judgment. Dating now involved activities and places that were virtually off limits to adults, such as private parties and dance halls. In most communities young people identified secluded areas (sometimes referred to as "lovers' lanes") where they could escape the supervision of peers as well as adults.

The gender roles of dating and courtship changed too. For one thing, women came to have less control over the process than they had previously. Dating, unlike calling, required money, which was the man's responsibility. Although men now had a greater financial burden, control over economic resources also gave them greater power in interactions with women (Cate & Lloyd, 1992). Consequently, the initiative shifted from the woman to the man. He asked her out rather than waiting for an invitation to call, as had been the practice at the turn of the century. Finances and transportation were his responsibility. In exchange, she was expected to provide the pleasure of her company and maybe some romance and intimacy. Although women could withhold affection and thereby exercise some control over the event, the absence of parental oversight and absence from the safe confines of their home placed women in a more vulnerable position than they had occupied during the era of calling.

Greater privacy and autonomy promoted romantic and sexual experimentation, too, perpetuating the sexual double standard. Men were expected to be the sexual aggressors, and the "success" or "failure" of their date could often be measured by how much intimacy they were able to achieve. Women who "went too far," however, risked destroying their reputations and their ability to attract other desirable men. Women bore the responsibility of setting limits and therefore had to walk a fine line between being too unfriendly and too friendly (Whyte, 1992).

A key feature of the modern form of dating, which emerged during the 1930s and 1940s and continues today, is a primary concern with enjoyment rather than selection of a marital partner. Starting in the 1930s and 1940s, dating was viewed as a necessary first step toward marriage, but that wasn't its primary purpose. Both young men and young women were encouraged to "play the field," and the frequency of dating was often used as a barometer of popularity.

Sociologist Willard Waller (1937) coined the phrase **rating-dating complex** to describe the process by which young adults during this period established their desirability and popularity through dating. Individuals, he claimed, were "rated" according to their status and prestige. Men having access to cars, money, and belonging to high-status fraternities had high dating status. For women, higher ratings were associated with such things as attractiveness and membership in prestigious sororities. Dating someone of higher status could increase one's own prestige and popularity. Thus dating was sometimes more about maintaining or enhancing social status and having fun than about making a commitment and possibly marrying.

Going Steady   By the 1950s an intermediate phase between dating and marriage developed: *going steady*. It was considerably different from the turn-of-the-century notion of "keeping steady company," which was a preliminary to engagement. Going steady simply entailed a recognizable commitment on the part of both people to date each other exclusively. Few steady couples expected to marry each other, although they often acted as if they were married. Going steady typically involved exchanging some symbolic token of commitment such as a class ring or school sweater and often led to heightened expectations regarding intimacy (Bailey, 1988). Not surprisingly, many adults feared that going steady would inevitably lead to more serious sexuality between young people. Some dating manuals of the 1950s even argued that a young woman was better off dating a series of strangers than having a steady boyfriend (Bailey, 1988). Teenagers, in contrast, simply viewed going steady as a form of "social security"—guaranteeing a date for major school functions and for most weekend nights.

These patterns of dating and going steady from the 1950s persisted well into the 1970s and 1980s (Cate & Lloyd, 1992). On first dates, in particular, traditional gender roles persisted:

> On a first date . . . a man is supposed to control the public domain (make plans and transport the date) as well as the physical and economic resources (car and money).

> Women's control and resources (beauty, sexuality, and charm) are supposed to be in the private sphere. (Rose & Frieze, 1989, p. 266)

However, some important changes did occur. For instance, opportunities for informal mixed-sex interaction became more plentiful in the 1970s and 1980s, and getting together at a friend's apartment with a large group of friends became an acceptable date. The development of a relationship, through a series of recognizable stages, also became less structured, and cohabitation emerged as a more common stage in the courtship process (cited in Cate & Lloyd, 1992). Strict gender roles also began to weaken a bit. It was now more acceptable for women to initiate dates than in previous decades, and they were encouraged to pay their own way to avoid the presumption of sexual activity.

Contemporary Dating

Contemporary culture approves of young people pairing off with various romantic partners without adult supervision (Whyte, 1990). In contrast to earlier generations, teenagers today feel entitled to make their own choices about sex and tolerate all kinds of sexual behaviors, as long as they meet the norms of peers. Dating is defined more in terms of immediate gratification than the goal of choosing a life-long partner.

Parental Influence   Even though they don't "arrange" their children's relationships, parents today still may exert influence over their children's romantic lives. They always indirectly influence their children's dating choices by their financial status and lifestyle, their decision to live in a particular neighborhood, and the general values and beliefs they instill in their children from early childhood.

But in a world of interpersonal relationships that seems to get more dangerous with each passing day, more and more parents are opting for greater direct control over their teenage children's dating patterns and choices. The strategies they employ can be quite varied. At one extreme is complete prohibition—those parents who simply refuse to allow their teenage children to date at all. Here's how one family dispenses with the dating game:

> If a young man wants to date a young woman, he contacts her father to ask permission. During that first meeting or phone call, the father explains that the family believes in courtship, which means that the young man must be spiritually and financially prepared to marry the young woman if they fall in love—otherwise, he shouldn't even bother to start a relationship. (As for our sons, they know they must meet the same requirements before they can begin courting a young woman.) This means, in effect, that there will be no courtship or dating during the high school years, and perhaps not until after college graduation. . . .
>
>   Courtship . . . brings practical benefits. For one thing, bringing Dad into the picture takes the responsibility for saying yes or no to a relationship off a daughter's shoulders. . . . Courtship includes time spent with the entire family. In our home, a young man interested in Heather or our youngest daughter, Catharine, is apt to find himself playing basketball with our . . . sons . . . or helping out in the kitchen after dinner. (Ryun & Ryun, 1997, pp. 28–29)

At the other extreme is the "if you can't beat them, join them" strategy. Some parents allow their teenage children (primarily sons) to sleep with their dates—as long as they stay

See Issue 3 for more on the delicate balance within families between parents' responsibilities and children's privacy rights.

in the parents' home. Frightened by the specter of AIDS, drugs, street crime, and other realities of teenage life today, these parents are deciding that acknowledging their children's sexuality and providing them a "safe" environment is better than pretending the sexuality doesn't exist. However, these parents sometimes find themselves torn between the desire to protect their children from harm and the nagging fear that they are encouraging their children to engage in sex. As one mother of a 17-year-old son put it, "It's not that I think it's wonderful. But I don't want my son and his girlfriend hiding in basements or the back seat of a car, getting mugged. I feel better knowing where my child is, so I decided that his room is his territory, his privacy" (quoted in Lawson, 1991, p. C1).

Most parents probably fall between these two extremes, trying to gradually loosen the reins over their children's sexual behavior while still trying to ensure that their children's actions reflect their own values.

Gender and Dating in Contemporary America   Women today are more likely to initiate dates and share expenses than they ever were in the past. And women have greater cultural "permission" to be sexually assertive than they once had. These changes, coupled with the informality and absence of clear norms that characterize contemporary dating, can cause tremendous anxiety and confusion among young people. Rules are constantly being defined and redefined.

Given what you already know about gender differences in sexuality, you probably aren't surprised that men and women may evaluate dating experiences differently too. For instance, research has found that men tend to perceive sexually suggestive behavior on the part of a dating partner (for example, leaning close when sitting together, repeated touching) as an indicator that things are moving toward more intense sexual activity, whereas women are more likely to be uncomfortable with sexually suggestive behavior. Men also tend to see rejection of their sexual advances as a sign of a "bad date" (Alksnis, Desmarais, & Wood, 1996).

Disagreement over signals of sexual desire is one of the most notable problems in contemporary dating. One study found that 53 percent of female high school students had been in a dating situation in which they believed a boy overestimated the level of sexual intimacy the young women desired; 45 percent of male students had been in situations where they felt girls underestimated the boy's level of desired sexual intimacy (Patton & Mannison, 1995). As you can see, the old double standard may have weakened, but it still plays havoc with people's attempts to get together with the opposite sex.

Social Theories of Intimate Relationships

Social theorists have developed several ways of explaining patterns of attraction and relationship development. Three of them are presented here: the sociobiological model, the stage model, and the social exchange model. Unfortunately, their cold, scientific language contradicts U.S. culture's deeply held and romantic visions of how intimate relationships begin and grow. But theories provide important insights into the possible ways relationships develop. And although many people like to think their love experiences are unique, theories can reveal patterns in the ways couples interact. We can begin to see that intimate experiences, although deeply personal, are also shaped by social forces.

A Sociobiological Model of Attraction

To some scholars—most notably sociobiologists—attraction is less a matter of choice than a matter of fulfilling genetic destiny. They argue that all species must evolve efficient ways to pass on their genetic material through successful reproduction (van den Berghe, 1979).

Different strategies require different levels of **parental investment**—the relative contribution parents make to the fitness of offspring. Some species, such as most fish, have evolved a strategy in which parental investment in offspring is quite low. Female fish produce and lay thousands of eggs at a time. Males produce billions of sperm, which they spread over the eggs that have been laid. In this strategy, males and females don't have to "pair up" to raise their offspring. Thousands of eggs are fertilized during the process, but most are eaten by predators or otherwise die. Only a tiny percentage survive and grow to adulthood. But even that small percentage of survivors allows the species to continue. Other species, such as humans, use a strategy that invests a great deal more effort in each fertilized egg. Both men and women gain an evolutionary advantage—as does the entire species—from producing as many healthy offspring as possible and ensuring that enough of them live long enough to perpetuate the gene pool.

Some sociobiologists hypothesize that to maximize the chances of species survival, men and women have evolved different mate selection strategies, based on biological differences in the reproductive process (Buss, 1994). Compared to some other animals, human females make an enormously high investment in the reproduction process. They produce very few eggs, perhaps between twelve and fifteen a year. A single act of sexual intercourse can close off the woman's other mating opportunities for at least 9 months. While pregnant, she obviously can't become pregnant again. Women also bear exclusive responsibility for lactation—which can last up to 3 or 4 years after the child is born.

Human offspring also take a long time to mature in the mother's womb and are completely helpless at birth. Because of the large size of human babies' heads and the small size of the mother's pelvis (a consequence of walking upright), human babies are born at a much earlier stage of development than other animal babies. A day-old human baby can't get up and gallop away like a newborn colt. Human babies need a great deal of supervision and care to ensure their survival until they are independent enough to survive on their own—which may take 20 years or more! From the perspective of species survival, human babies are a scarce and precious resource. As a result, women in our evolutionary past may have had to be extremely selective in their mating and "stingy" in offering their reproductive resources. Their taste for sex within the context of an ongoing relationship and the greater significance for women than men of each sexual act are thought to be consistent with women's high reproductive investment.

The picture is strikingly different for men. They have just as much interest in species survival as women do, but their investment in the process is not that much higher than that of a male flounder. To put it crudely, sperm are plentiful and cheap relative to eggs. One man can fertilize as many eggs as his stamina and the sexual availability of ovulating women will allow. The most prolific human parent, according to *The Guinness Book of World Records*, was an eighteenth-century emperor of Morocco who reportedly fathered more than 1,000 children. (In contrast, the female record is held by a Chilean woman who claims to have given birth to about 60 children.) A single act of sexual intercourse for a man requires minimal investment. Once he "deposits" his sperm, he is free—in a physiological sense—to do anything he wants, even impregnate other women. If so inclined, he could walk away from a casual coupling without any biologically necessary obligations.

According to some sociobiologists, men's apparent "fondness" for recreational sex and their desire for a variety of partners are consistent with their evolved reproductive strategy. Their sexual interest is more easily aroused than women's because sex has fewer biological costs to them. Some sociobiologists cite the fact that prostitution is a service overwhelmingly sought by males rather than females and is common around the world as evidence of men's biologically based sexual strategies.

Some sociobiologists also argue that because of sex differences in reproductive investment, men and women are genetically programmed to desire different traits in a mate. They claim that women's reproductive need for protection and stability means they have evolved a preference for mates who are capable of acquiring resources and who are willing and able to support their mates and their children and protect them from harm (Hatfield & Rapson, 1993). A study by British and Japanese psychologists found that women's preferences in men change during their menstrual cycle. Most of the time they prefer slightly feminized male facial shapes. But when they are ovulating (and chances of conception are highest) they prefer more rugged, masculine features, which, according to sociobiological thinking, are associated with reproductive success. The researchers also noted that women's general distaste for the way men smell diminishes when their fertility is at its peak (Penton-Voak et al., 1999).

Following this logic, men can afford to be less choosy. Because of their low level of investment in the reproductive process, they have evolved a powerful desire for engaging in sexual encounters with a wide array of partners. In the interests of reproducing offspring with the highest likelihood of survival, they are attracted to women who show signs of reproductive fitness: physical appearance, health, and youth. One study of 1,500 college students in the United States, Russia, and Japan found that in all these cultures men rated physical attractiveness as more important than did women. In all cultures, women rated intelligence; ambition; potential for success; money, status, and position; kindness and understanding; and expressiveness as more important than men did (Hatfield & Sprecher, 1995).

In sum, according to this sociobiological argument, sexual tendencies in humans evolved because a certain kind of sexual partnership and division of labor maximized the probability of survival for individuals, groups, and ultimately the species. However, scientists have no way of proving unequivocally that these tendencies stem exclusively or even primarily from biological imperatives. Historically, norms and laws were designed to protect men's sexual property—namely, women. Even today, sexually promiscuous women are substantially more likely to be called derogatory names (*slut, whore,* and so forth) than are sexually promiscuous men. Given such a cultural context, one would expect men and women to show different sexual proclivities.

Furthermore, if the sociobiological model is correct, you'd expect that men's and women's preferences in partners and mates would remain the same even as social conditions change. A recent study, however, found that people's mate preferences in the United States have changed over time (Buss, Shackelford, Kirkpatrick, & Larsen, 2001). For instance, men today place greater importance on finding a mate with good financial prospects than they did in the past. Other research suggests that, as women's social and economic position improves, their romantic preferences change too. In societies where women are economically independent, they tend to focus more on sex appeal than on practicality (that is, the ability of the other person to be a good provider) in choosing sexual partners (Gangestad, 1993). Thus the role of biology in attraction and mate selection is still a question mark.

A Stage Model of Relationship Formation

Although some sociologists insist that biological factors play an important role in human behavior (for example, Massey, 2000), most argue that mate selection is less a matter of innate biological drives than of social and interpersonal processes. Even the most personal elements, such as whom one initially finds attractive, is affected by social forces.

According to sociologist Ira Reiss (1960), once mutual attraction takes place, emotional attachment develops in a series of stages: rapport, self-disclosure, and mutual dependency and need fulfillment. Before people disclose intimate information about themselves, they must first achieve a certain level of rapport and compatibility with that person.

Attraction and Initiation   Before any relationship can develop, two people must overcome a number of culturally based barriers. For instance, the perception that someone interesting is "out of my league"—meaning too attractive, too rich, too popular, and so on—is strongly influenced by cultural ideals of attractiveness. Gendered patterns of communication can also interfere with relationship formation. If a woman feels uncomfortable approaching someone and initiating a date, she must try to make her interest known indirectly and discreetly. Because her cues are so subtle, the object of her desire might misinterpret her behavior as a lack of interest. Men's reluctance to approach women due to their fear of rejection can likewise be misinterpreted by women as a lack of interest (Vorauer & Ratner, 1996).

Social psychologists have long argued that (mutual) attraction is one of the most critical factors in determining whether a romantic relationship develops (Murstein, 1987). Interestingly, the emergence of virtual relationships (where initial contacts are made over the Internet) may be altering this dynamic in significant ways (Cooper & Sportolari, 1997). Physical attributes—so crucial in real-life interactions—are not evident online, which can lead to the development of relationships that otherwise might never have gotten off the ground. Attraction in cyberspace relies more heavily on other factors, such as common interests. Whether a relationship begun online can override the possible lack of physical attraction when the couple finally meets face-to-face is not clear.

Rapport   When two people first start forming a relationship, their interactions tend to be somewhat superficial. Nevertheless, they are attempting to establish **rapport**—a general sense of compatibility (for example, "My favorite ice cream flavor is Vanilla Swiss Almond, I like to play tennis, and my favorite group is the Dave Matthews Band").

At this stage, interaction may be complicated by deliberate attempts to manipulate information about oneself. Individuals may try to present values, opinions, and biographical information that they think the other person will find appealing. They don't want to say or do things that will upset, anger, or repel the other person. They want to present idealized images of themselves and at the same time accept the idealized image of the other person.

Intimate Self-Disclosure   As people grow more comfortable and trusting of each other, the disclosures become more intimate and revealing—and therefore more risky. This next stage of relationship development is characterized by **intimate self-disclosure,** a willingness to go beyond providing basic background information to reveal some very personal facts, thoughts, and feelings. These disclosures can include problematic events in one's past, the depth of one's feelings toward the other person, fears and vulnerabilities, and so on. They not only convey information, they are symbolic gestures meant to tell the other person, "I feel close enough to you to share this with you. I trust you not to laugh, belittle, devalue, or fear what I am going to tell you." Research has shown that the greater the level of self-disclosure between partners, the greater their satisfaction in the relationship (Altman & Taylor, 1973; Hendrick, 1981).

Self-disclosure is governed by a clear set of social norms and expectations. One important, but often unspoken, expectation is that the intimate self-disclosure should be reciprocated (Derlega, Harris, & Chaikin, 1973). People provide more and more intimate facts about themselves in hopes that their partners will do the same. When people complain about communication problems in their relationships, they are usually referring to an imbalance in the nature and amount of information that partners are sharing.

Such reciprocity is particularly important in the disclosure of the depth of one's affection. Often people go through a great deal of strategic maneuvering before first disclosing to partners how they feel about them. But once they do disclose, they expect similar levels of disclosure from their partners (Cunningham, Strassberg, & Haan, 1986). If partners don't reciprocate, they are forced to acknowledge that their definition of the relationship is not mutual.

So you can see that self-disclosure is a potentially hazardous stage in a relationship. When their partners do not disclose enough, people don't know what the partners are truly feeling. But they don't want to appear pushy by constantly asking for feelings and reassurances, so they sometimes resign themselves to quiet suffering. In the absence of clear information, people frequently let their imaginations run wild. They find themselves attributing feelings that they think their partner has. They scrutinize every sentence, every gesture for some tiny morsel of information—some shred of evidence that will tell them what the other person is feeling.

In contrast, disclosing too much and too quickly can also be problematic (Altman & Taylor, 1973). Those who tell everyone, even complete strangers, every intimate detail of their lives and feelings have not learned about the importance of timing self-disclosure. The recipient of prematurely personal disclosures usually feels quite uncomfortable in the role.

Mutual Dependency and Need Fulfillment   When a relationship endures beyond the point of shared self-disclosures and partners begin to interpret as serious their level of commitment to the relationship, they enter the next stage: **mutual dependency and need fulfillment** (Reiss, 1960). Eventually the everyday lives of the partners become intertwined. People get used to doing things that require the other person—an audience for jokes, a confidante for the expression of fears and wishes, a partner for sexual experiences, and so on (Reiss & Lee, 1988). As a relationship progresses to this point, people begin to rely on the partner to satisfy psychological and physical needs. These needs can be as basic as sexual appetites but may also include the desire for someone with whom to share feelings, someone who can take care of a partner and vice versa, and someone who will reinforce a partner's own sense of worth and identity (Brehm, 1992).

Endings and Beginnings   As you can see, establishing and maintaining an intimate relationship is no easy feat. To get to the last stage of Reiss's model, many couples must endure conflicts, disappointments, and ambivalent feelings. Reiss viewed his stage model of relationships as a wheel, with rapport, self-disclosure, dependency, and need fulfillment as the spokes. As couples pass through each stage or spoke, the relationship deepens, and so too does their rapport, intimacy, dependency, and so on—each one reinforcing the other.

At some point, couples may decide to formalize their commitment through marriage or some other "permanent" living arrangement. But not all relationships endure. In fact, most don't. And as you may already know, ending a relationship with someone you've shared your deepest hopes and fears with, someone you've come to depend on, can be extremely difficult, even traumatic. If the breakup is not mutual, one person is left having to come to terms with feelings of inadequacy and failure.

Interestingly, what initially attracts one individual to another may be precisely what spells its demise. Sociologist Diane Felmlee (2000) calls this dynamic "fatal attraction": It occurs when people are drawn to the very aspects of another person that they later find troublesome. For instance, the person who was initially attracted to someone because he or she was "exciting" may later find this very same quality "scary." Felmlee found that about 44 percent of her sample of college students reported fatal attractions, although not all had ended the relationship.

The Social Exchange Model

The stage model simply identifies the steps in a process of relationship development. The exchange approach tries to explain why we are attracted to some people and not others (Blau, 1964; Emerson, 1962; Homans, 1961; Rubin, 1973; Thibaut & Kelley, 1959). People evaluate their own qualities (for instance, economic standing, physical attractiveness, and so on) and seek partners whose assets match their own.

The exchange approach also explains why we pursue some relationships and avoid others. Intimate relationships provide obvious rewards—such as love, sexual gratification, warmth, desirable characteristics of the partner, companionship, and so on. But they present certain costs as well—time and effort spent trying to maintain the relationship, undesirable characteristics of a partner, conflict, and so on.

Like sociobiologists, economist Gary Becker (1981) argues that men and women look for different things in a relationship. However, he focuses less on unseen genetic urges and more on the cultural capital individuals have at their disposal and the demands of the relationship marketplace. According to Becker, relationships develop when the arrangement is mutually beneficial to those involved. These benefits are maximized when each partner can contribute to the relationship what he or she does best. So, if women are more "efficient" at household labor and child care and men are more "efficient" at earning money, both benefit if the wife specializes in housework and the husband specializes in paid work. In such a traditional environment, women are compelled to search for "good providers" and men are likely to search for "good homemakers."

Since Becker first presented these ideas, the cultural climate has changed dramatically. People's preferences are less likely than perhaps they were in the past to be confined to specific skills or traits. For instance, both men and women are now likely to prefer a mate who is gainfully employed (South, 1991). Nevertheless, the social exchange perspective's assumption that people seek out others whom they perceive as potentially rewarding remains intact.

Expectations   In addition to taking into account costs and benefits, social exchange theory also considers people's preferences and expectations. These go a long way in shedding light on the curious and sometimes inexplicable things people do in their intimate relationships. Surely you've seen people who remain in relationships that to outside observers seem undesirable or unrewarding. Why would they stay if, as social exchange theorists argue, people form and maintain relationships only if they find them profitable?

The person's expectations and perceptions of alternatives may play a role. For example, if a woman receives certain necessary resources (such as financial support) from her obnoxious, wine-swilling partner and feels she can't get those resources elsewhere, she may stay in the relationship out of necessity. If a man has had a history of bad relationships, his expectations may be quite low to begin with; hence, it wouldn't take much to exceed them. So he may be satisfied in a relationship that others would find intolerable.

Availability of Partners   Our evaluations of our relationships are also influenced by larger social or "market" conditions. Marital opportunities vary by age, race, and educational attainment (South & Lloyd, 1992). Even where you live can influence your chances of finding a partner.

You must have some contact with someone before you can fall in love and begin a relationship. So where you live will clearly determine whom you come into contact with on a regular basis and ultimately your pool of prospective marital partners (Lichter, LeClere, & McLaughlin, 1991). People who end up marrying usually—but, of course, not always—meet where they spend most of their time: in their neighborhood, in school, at work, at a friend's house. Many people are involved in "long distance" relationships, but even those require some sort of contact at the outset to take shape at all.

In addition, marriage rates can be affected by the overall supply of men and women of marriageable age and, to be more precise, the number of potential mates with desirable economic and social characteristics (Lichter et al., 1991). Thus the shortage of marriageable, well-educated, and employed black men may account for the lower marriage rate among African Americans than other groups. Such an explanation of mate selection is important because it suggests that improving the socioeconomic status of black men could increase the number of "marriageable" men and thus have a stabilizing effect on black families.

Perhaps you disagree with this contention. Don't people who face a shortage of attractive potential partners simply lower their standards a bit? This question was addressed by sociologist Dan Lichter and his colleagues (Lichter, Anderson, & Hayward, 1995). They found that a favorable marriage market—that is, lots of possibilities—indeed increases the likelihood of marrying someone with a good education and a good job. However, they found that people forgo marriage altogether in an unfavorable market—that is, when no "suitable" mates are available.

Conclusion

Trying to shed intellectual light on something so precious and so personal as love relationships has several inherent dangers. One is that on close inspection the dark side of intimacy will appear. You have seen in this chapter that intimacy often involves conflict and even exploitation. Such facts fly in the face of popular images of intimacy and therefore shake the foundation of what is so culturally and personally valuable: love relationships.

Another danger is that the attempt to intellectually examine intimacy will appear too cold and emotionless. Who wants to equate love with a marketplace where people seek to maximize benefits and minimize costs through negotiation, bargaining, and comparison shopping? These concepts conflict with deeply held, romantic visions of what love relationships are or should be. The fact that people desire, establish, and maintain intimacy with others only because they find it profitable to do so or that nonromantic factors such as race, class, religion, and geography determine, to some degree, who is attractive is a bitter pill most people would prefer not to swallow. The idealized image of love in U.S. culture largely denies control and rationality. People "fall" in love; are "swept off their feet"; are "carried away;" or love "puts a spell on them."

And yet we're all aware, at least at some level, that these nonromantic factors are important, that many of them influence intimate choices. We secretly express doubt over the staying power of a relationship between two people who love each other very much but who have no visible means of support and no future prospects. "Starry-eyed romance" may make for enjoyable novels, but it may not be enough to sustain a relationship through the practical demands of day-to-day family life.

Chapter Highlights

- Although love exists everywhere, people do not experience it in the same way in all cultures. The role that love plays in people's intimate lives is determined by the nature of the culture in which they live.
- In this society, love has become a "feminized" emotion, making it incompatible with such socially valued traits as power, independence, and control. Consequently, men and women tend to express love differently, although they are equally capable of loving.
- Human sexuality is more than just a biological drive. Its expression is subject to strong societal norms. Hence, the way individuals experience it varies from culture to culture and among different groups within the same culture.
- Unlike societies in which relationships are arranged by families, U.S. society recognizes dating as the means by which most people move from being single to being coupled.
- Dating is not a matter of completely free choice, however. Parental influence, cultural conceptions of gender, concerns over social class, and other societal constraints may determine who dates whom. Over the years the nature of dating has been changed by economic, educational, and technological changes in society.
- Attempts to identify the biological underpinnings of intimate relationships remain controversial. More useful at this point are the stage model and the social exchange model. They attempt to explain how people become attracted to each other and why they stay together. Relationships appear to develop in stages, and they are influenced by partners' expectations and availability.

Your Turn

The formal purpose of college is to provide students with a quality education. But colleges also informally provide students with countless lessons about friendship, intimacy, sexuality, and so on. To delve deeper into the role that colleges play in creating or reinforcing gendered expectations regarding intimacy, consider all the ways people meet others and establish intimate relationships on your campus. Distinguish between informal mechanisms (meeting someone in class or at the library) and *institutional* mechanisms that are designed explicitly to bring people together, such as university-sponsored social events, fraternity and sorority parties, and so on. Have some places in the surrounding community (bars, clubs, and so on) gained a reputation for being good spots to "meet people"? What proportion of students use computer or video dating services? Does your campus newspaper or local newspaper have a "personals" section? Are programs in place to help students deal with problems of intimacy (for example, information about sexually transmitted diseases, sexual assault support networks, pregnancy testing, and/or abortion information)? Try to find out how many students use these services in a given month.

Describe how each of the institutional mechanisms you've identified incorporates broader beliefs about gender and intimacy. Do they tend to reinforce or contradict traditional gender expectations? What does each tell about the pervasiveness of gender ideologies in everyday campus life?

Now think about other social factors at work. For instance, did you notice any variations attributable to age, race or ethnicity, social class, or sexual orientation in the amount and type of student use of these mechanisms? Do any of these events or services segregate students? Do they actively seek to integrate students from varied social backgrounds?

More generally, what should be the college's role in creating or enhancing intimate relationships among students? Should it be liable for any harm that these relationships might cause (for example, sexual violence)?

Couplehood and Marriage

What It Means to Be a Couple

In most societies, the wedding ceremony is the most widely recognized symbol of romantic commitment. It publicly announces that two people are now, officially, a couple. Although the specific details of the wedding ceremony vary from culture to culture or from group to group within a culture, all societies have some way of marking this transition.

But beyond this moment, there are actually few visible signs that symbolically mark this level of commitment. So we must ask ourselves, aside from marriage licenses and public ceremonies, what actually distinguishes a "couple" from other types of close relationships, such as siblings, friends, or roommates.

Marriages and other committed relationships are defined not by the events of the wedding day but by private moments of intimacy and the performance of the day-to-day tasks required to sustain a relationship and a household.

Could the couples shown here be brother and sister? Could they be neighbors? Friends?

What indicates to you that they are romantically connected? Or what is missing?

In a more general sense, how exactly do long-term romantic relationships differ from close friendships or casual sexual couplings?

If it's true that marriage is defined by the unremarkable, everyday things that partners do with and for each other, then same-sex couples are able to establish extensive life-long bonds just like those found in long-term heterosexual couples.

Compared to the people depicted on the previous page, is it more or less difficult to define the individuals shown here as couples? What are the clues?

Weddings occupy an ambiguous place in U.S. society. On the one hand, they are perhaps our most treasured ritual. Most of us are taught, from a very young age, that someday, if we're lucky, we'll find that right person and have a grand wedding. In many Western fairy tales, marriage is the ultimate goal. The wedding ceremony has long been recognized as the epitome of romantic commitment, the most desirable—and most recognizable—public declaration of love and devotion that exists in this society.

The esteemed cultural position of weddings is reflected in their portrayal in the media. Television networks commonly draw on the universal appeal of weddings to boost their ratings:

> The 1997–1998 [television] season opened [with weddings] in *Dharma and Greg*, and closed with them on *Friends, The Nanny, Jag, Spin City, Baywatch, Suddenly Susan, Dr. Quinn, Everybody Loves Raymond, NYPD Blue*, and *For Your Love.* . . . The 1998–1999 season [began with the conclusion of the *Friends* wedding that closed the previous season, carrying the wedding theme through a total of four episodes]. *To Have & To Hold* and *Will & Grace* each began their . . . seasons with weddings. Made-for-TV movies *Forever Love, The Marriage Fool, A Marriage of Convenience*, and *I Married a Monster* all [featured] a wedding. (Ingraham, 1999, pp. 5–6)

Prime-time shows such as *Friends, Once and Again,* and *Frasier* all prominently featured weddings in the 2000–2001 season.

A similar trend can be seen in the film industry in recent years with the box office success of movies such as *Father of the Bride* and *Father of the Bride II, Three Weddings and a Funeral, My Best Friend's Wedding, The Wedding Singer, In & Out, Muriel's Wedding, The Other Sister, The Wedding Banquet, The Polish Wedding, Runaway Bride, The Bachelor,* and *The Wedding Planner.* The Internet Movie Database Web site lists 250 movie titles that contain the word *wedding* and over 500 that contain the word *marriage, marry,* or *married.*

But although weddings retain their revered place in the culture, there also exists a somewhat darker side. A film critic, writing about yet another movie that focused on a wedding, put it this way:

> Say what you will about the institution of marriage, but without it the possibilities of romantic comedy would be impoverished. Not only is the fantasy of everlasting love capable of melting the most cynical heart, but weddings, with their ridiculous formal wear, pretentious catered food, free liquor and cheap sentiment, also overflow with potential for comic disaster. (Scott, 2001, p. 1)

In addition, lurking behind the romance of weddings are some common negative images of marriage that have existed for decades: the nagging wife; the beer-drinking, television-addicted, couch potato husband; the domestic grind; the "ball and chain"; the possessiveness, deceit, and suspicion. Even popular jokes depict a sinister side of marriage:

- Marriage is a three-ring circus: engagement *ring*, wedding *ring*, suffe*ring*.
- Marriage is not a word, it's a sentence.
- Marriages are made in heaven, but then again so are thunder and lightning.
- Marriage is a great institution, but I'm not ready to live in an institution.

The ambivalence toward marriage tends to vary along gender lines. Consider, for instance, the ritual of the prewedding bachelor party, which has traditionally symbolized the groom's last precious hours of freedom before settling down to married life. Strippers, exotic dancers, and various sorts of pornography are not uncommon. The wedding is seen more for what it is ending (the carefree life of singlehood) than for what it is beginning. Notice how such a ritual portrays marriage not as fulfilling but as constrictive, more like a prison than a paradise. At one university, which has a rather large population of students in fraternities and sororities, men who become engaged often find themselves stripped naked by their fraternity brothers, duct taped to a chair, taken to the living unit of their love interest, where they are publicly ridiculed, and then thrown unceremoniously into a nearby pond.

In contrast, the female equivalent of the bachelor party—the wedding shower—is usually a gift-giving, happy affair that reinforces the "goodness" of getting married. Despite the occasional gag gift—such as edible underwear—the atmosphere is usually one of eager anticipation. You don't hear many women at wedding showers bemoaning the impending loss of freedom. At the same university where engaged fraternity men suffer considerable abuse, sorority women who become engaged are serenaded by their "sisters" in a candlelight ritual that involves lots of hugging.

In general, because love tends to be feminized in this society (see Chapter 5), weddings and marriages have traditionally taken on heightened importance for women:

> We [women] love marriage. We love to dream about it, prepare for it, enter it, exit it, and do it all over again. What do women talk about within ten minutes of meeting each other? Marriage. Upcoming marriages. Outgoing marriages. The marriages of movie stars. Marriages from hell. Our last marriage. The marriage we will have if we ever marry again. The glory of marriage. The agony of it. (Heyn, 1997, p. xii)

But despite its sometimes negative portrayal, marriage remains highly valued in contemporary society. It's no surprise, then, that only about 10 percent of unmarried men and women say that they don't ever want to marry and that 80 percent expect to get married someday (Sweet & Bumpass, 1992). Furthermore, even people who decide not to marry will likely experience living in a long-term committed relationship at some point in their lives.

In this chapter we take a close look at life in marriages and other long-term intimate relationships. We examine these relationships both as intensely personal experiences of individuals and as a social institution, which can only be fully understood in its cultural context. And we compare marriages to other types of relationships to see how different and how similar they are.

Cultural Influences on Intimate Relationships

The cultural ambivalence toward marriage goes beyond bachelor parties and wedding showers. Surveys of U.S. adults show that fewer than half believe married people are generally happier than single people, even though most unmarried people would like to be married if the right person came along. In 1993, the General Social Survey asked adults about the things they value the most in life. Interestingly, respondents ranked being married below such other values as having faith in God, being self-sufficient and financially secure, and having children. Exhibit 6.1 depicts some of the findings from these surveys.

People's attitudes toward intimate relationships are clearly shaped by social, historical, and cultural forces. In Chapter 5 we discussed this influence with regard to dating. As couples of all sorts—heterosexual or homosexual, unmarried or married—move into

EXHIBIT 6.1

How Americans Feel About Marriage

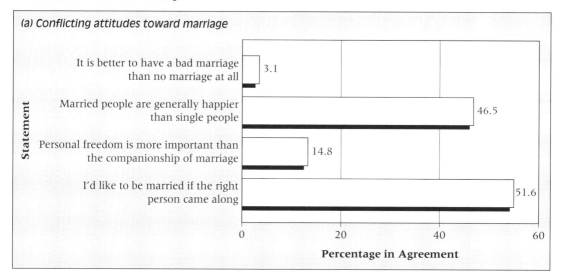

(a) Conflicting attitudes toward marriage

Statement

- It is better to have a bad marriage than no marriage at all — 3.1
- Married people are generally happier than single people — 46.5
- Personal freedom is more important than the companionship of marriage — 14.8
- I'd like to be married if the right person came along — 51.6

0   20   40   60

Percentage in Agreement

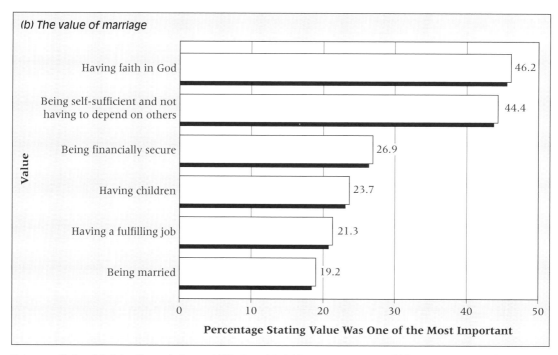

(b) The value of marriage

Value

- Having faith in God — 46.2
- Being self-sufficient and not having to depend on others — 44.4
- Being financially secure — 26.9
- Having children — 23.7
- Having a fulfilling job — 21.3
- Being married — 19.2

0   10   20   30   40   50

Percentage Stating Value Was One of the Most Important

Data source: National Opinion Research Center. 1998. *General Social Survey, 1972–1998.* Available at www.icpsr.umich.edu/GSS/. Accessed April 14, 2001.

more committed, long-term relationships, they continue to be influenced by culturally pre-scribed norms. Comparing cohabitors and married couples, sociologists Julie Brines and Kara Joyner (1999) noted that the idea of cohabitation initially attracts some people because it appears more flexible and experimental than marriage: "In short, it bespeaks few 'rules'" (p. 350). In fact, though, these researchers found that violating the rules in a rela-tionship where no such rules are believed to exist can be more disruptive than any compa-rable violation in marriage. Cohabitors were more likely than married couples to end their relationship when women earned more than their male partners—that is, where a tradi-tional social norm regarding the male breadwinner role had been violated.

You can learn a lot more about attitudes toward marriage and other long-term rela-tionships by examining the following national statistics on marital trends.

DEMO•GRAPHICS

Changing Marriage Patterns in the United States

Shrinking marriage rates, the increasing average age at first marriage, and the growth of nonmarital living arrangements reveal a reluctance on the part of some contemporary Americans to embrace marriage. For instance, take a look at the marriage trends presented in Exhibit 6.2a. As you can see, the percentage of the population that is married has steadily declined in the latter half of the twentieth century. Nevertheless, the percentage is roughly comparable to that in 1900. The percentages of the population that have never married and are divorced have also increased over the past 50 years.

The popular media have made much of the increase in unmarried persons, suggesting that Americans are rejecting the institution of marriage. But the increase in people who have never married is at least partially the result of men and women postponing marriage, not rejecting it altogether. As you can see in Exhibit 6.2b, the median age of first marriage for women and for men has been rising since the 1960s. In 1960, for example, the median age at marriage was 22.8 years for men and 20.3 years for women. In 1998, it was 26.7 for men and 25 years for women. Even though these figures appear to be merely a return to trends of the early twentieth century, the median age at first marriage for men and women reached record highs in the 1990s.

Interestingly, however, median age at first marriage for men has taken a slight down-turn since 1996, whereas the median age for women has continued to climb. These patterns have contributed to a shrinking "gender gap" in median age at marriage over the past cen-tury (see Exhibit 6.2b). Men almost always used to marry women several years younger than themselves. But this age gap declined steadily throughout the twentieth century. In 1900, for example, men, on average, were 4 years older than their wives. In 1998, the gap was only about 1 year.

Perhaps as a function of Americans waiting longer to marry, more people are cohabit-ing than ever before. There were about 1.6 million cohabitors in 1980, but about 5.4 mil-lion in 2000 (U.S. Census Bureau, 2001d). About 7 percent of women aged 15–44 years old are currently cohabiting, and 41 percent have cohabited at some point in their lives. But as you can see from Exhibit 6.2c, of women who have cohabited in their lifetimes, most do so as a prelude to marriage, not as a permanent alternative.

EXHIBIT 6.2

Trends in Marriage in the United States

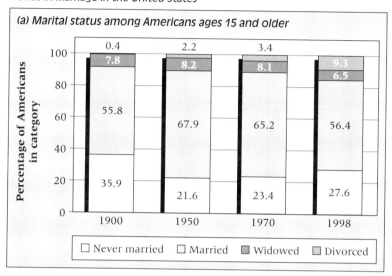

(a) Marital status among Americans ages 15 and older

Data source: U.S. Bureau of the Census. 1999a. 20th-century statistics. *Statistical Abstract of the United States: 1999*, Table 1418. Washington, DC: U.S. Government Printing Office.

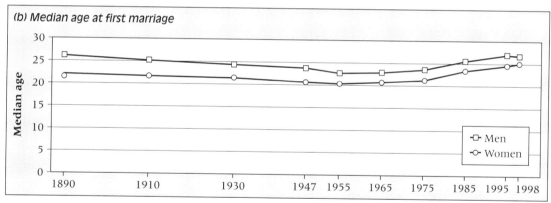

(b) Median age at first marriage

Data source: U.S. Bureau of the Census. 1999b. Internet release, Table MS-2. Available at www.census.gov/population/socdemo/ms-la/tabms-2.txt. Accessed June 1, 2001.

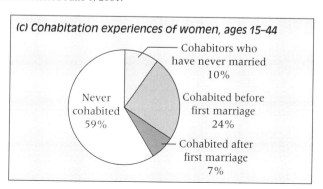

(c) Cohabitation experiences of women, ages 15–44

Cohabitors who have never married 10%

Never cohabited 59%

Cohabited before first marriage 24%

Cohabited after first marriage 7%

Source: U.S. Bureau of the Census. 2000b. *Statistical Abstract of the United States: 2000*, Table 58. Washington, DC: U.S. Government Printing Office.

Thus an increase in cohabitation does not necessarily indicate that people are rejecting marriage. In many cases, cohabitation is part of the courtship or marriage process. In fact, cohabitors are more likely than noncohabitors to eventually marry. In one study of cohabitors, 74 percent said they either had definite plans to marry or thought they would marry the person with whom they were living (Bumpass, Sweet, & Cherlin, 1991).

Thinking Critically About the Statistics

1. In Exhibit 6.2a, including data from 1900 provides a very different picture of marriage trends in the United States than if you only went back as far as 1950. How might you explain the high percentage of never-married people and the relatively low percentage of married people in 1900? Can you think of any cultural or demographic similarities in U.S. society in 1900 and 1998 that could explain why the proportions of never-married and married individuals in these two periods are so comparable?

2. Examine the trends depicted in Exhibit 6.2b. Why might young adults at mid-century have married earlier than young adults today or a century ago? Consider the kinds of social and economic experiences these different groups had during significant points in their lives such as childhood, adolescence, and young adulthood.

3. What could account for the narrowing of the gender gap in median age at first marriage over the last century (see Exhibit 6.2b)? What kinds of changes have occurred in the ways men and women meet that could be related to their ages? If you consider age to be an indicator of social power, with older people typically having more power than younger ones, how might the changing gender gap affect the power relationship between husbands and wives?

4. Exhibit 6.2c shows the cohabitation experiences of women between the ages of 15 and 44. In what ways would you expect men's cohabitation experiences to be similar or different to those of women? How would you explain such differences? What do you think the pie chart would look like if it included people over age 44? (*Hint:* Again, think of the larger social forces that influence people's intimate relationships.) ■

Exogamy and Endogamy

Intimate relationships are governed by many varieties of cultural influences. Long before people settle into a long-term relationship, powerful social norms are at work, influencing whom they are likely to end up with. Two important social rules that limit the field of eligible partners are exogamy and endogamy.

Rules of **exogamy** require that an individual form a relationship outside certain social groups to which he or she belongs. In almost all societies, exogamy rules prohibit people from marrying members of their own nuclear family—siblings, parents, and children. Rules of exogamy usually extend to certain people outside the nuclear family, to include cousins, grandparents, and, in some societies, stepsiblings. In South Korea, people are strongly discouraged from marrying someone with the same surname, not a trivial rule considering that 55 percent of the population is named Kim, Park, Lee, Choi, or Chong (WuDunn, 1996).

One advantage of exogamy rules is that they encourage alliances between groups larger than the primary family. But exogamy rules can also be extremely restrictive and create severe hardships for individuals who violate them. In some parts of India, for example, the prevailing rule of exogamy is that a husband and wife must come from different villages. In 1999, a 23-year-old man and 17-year-old woman from the same village who had fallen in love and eloped were mauled and hacked to death by members of the woman's family. Her mother said, "My daughter ran away and our whole family was humiliated. We killed her to protect our honor" (quoted in Bearak, 1999, p. A4).

Less obvious, but just as powerful, are the rules of **endogamy**, which limit marital choices to people within their social group, however that group is defined. Royal families of the past often encouraged members to marry blood relations to keep the power and wealth of the group intact. Although U.S. society doesn't have such formal endogamy rules, the vast majority of relationships occur between people from the same religion, race or ethnic group, social class, and age. These similar backgrounds increase the likelihood that the two people will share common beliefs, values, and experiences. But more importantly from a sociological point of view, rules of endogamy reflect society's traditional distaste for relationships that cross group boundaries.

Religion   Marrying outside one's religion is more common than it once was. But although the traditional norms that once obligated people to marry within their faith have diminished, most religions still actively discourage interfaith marriages. Their concern is that such marriages may weaken people's religious beliefs and values, lead to the raising of children in a different faith, or take religion out of the family entirely. Religious leaders often worry about the bigger problem of maintaining their ethnic identity within a diverse and complex society (Gordon, 1964).

See Issue 5 for more information on religious proscriptions against interfaith marriages.

Consequently, somewhere between 80 and 90 percent of Americans marry someone of the same religion (Kalmijn, 1991a), although sociologists note that these figures may overestimate religious endogamy because some spouses convert to their partners' religion before or shortly after marrying. Nevertheless, the high rate of religious endogamy reflects the influence of religion on individuals' behaviors and expectations—even (or especially) taking into account that some spouses feel it's important enough that they're willing to convert. For very religious individuals, marrying someone of a different faith or even no faith would be unthinkable—they'd probably not find those individuals attractive in the first place.

As the number of people who belong to a particular religion shrinks, though, endogamy becomes more difficult. For instance, the percentage of Jews in the U.S. population has dropped by nearly half since the mid-twentieth century. Many Jewish leaders fear that the outcome of this trend will erode and perhaps extinguish an entire way of life. They believe the survival of U.S. Jewry depends on maintaining the integrity of traditional Jewish values and institutions. According to some, young people who decide to marry outside the faith "are threatening to transform Judaism into a religion of half-remembered rituals, forgotten ancestors and buried beliefs" (Rosen, 1997, p. 7).

Others, however, are more accepting of interfaith marriage. In the Annual Survey of American Jewish Opinion conducted by the American Jewish Committee, most respondents did not oppose interfaith marriage, and about 16 percent said they felt it was actually positive. Fewer than 25 percent felt that rabbis should refuse to officiate at interfaith marriages (cited in Niebuhr, 2000).

Race and Ethnicity   Even though marriages that cross racial and ethnic lines have become more common—they've tripled over the past 30 years—they still remain rare relative to marriages between people of the same race or ethnic group. In 1970 there were 310,000

EXHIBIT 6.3

Interracial Marriage in the United States

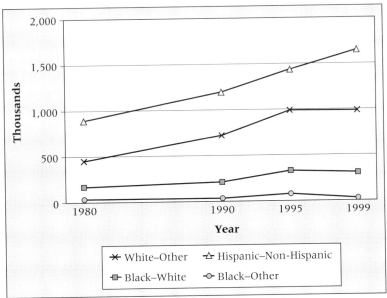

Data source: U.S. Bureau of the Census. 2000b. *Statistical Abstract of the United States: 2000,* Table 54. Washington, DC: U.S. Government Printing Office.

interracial couples in the United States; by 1999 there were 1.3 million. Still, this figure constitutes only 2.3 percent of all U.S. marriages. Exhibit 6.3 shows the trends in interracial marriage since 1980. Twenty-three percent of interracial marriages are black–white unions, but they account for just 0.5 percent of all marriages (U.S. Bureau of the Census, 2000b). Among people who identify themselves as Hispanic, 28 percent are married to someone of non-Hispanic origin.

The strength of racial and ethnic endogamy varies from group to group. Historian Paul Spickard (1989) compared the intermarriage experiences of Japanese Americans, Jews, and African Americans. For Jews and Japanese Americans, intermarriage has become more prevalent with each succeeding generation. Less than 2 percent of eastern European Jews who immigrated to the United States in the early twentieth century married non-Jews; between 5 and 10 percent of their children married outside the faith, and upward of 30 percent of their grandchildren married non-Jews. The same generational pattern holds for Japanese Americans. First-generation immigrants tended to maintain their Japanese identities and were mindful of traditional prohibitions against intermarriage. Following generations tended to be more ambivalent about their minority ethnic heritage and more enthusiastic about "being American."

Today, compared to other racial and ethnic groups, Asian Americans in general have fairly high rates of intermarriage—23 percent versus about 2 percent for the general population (Lee & Yamanaka, 1990). Most scholars have attributed this high rate of intermarriage to the process of assimilation, whereby minority identity gradually dissolves as individuals adjust to the practices of the dominant culture (see Chapter 3 for this and other effects of assimilation).

Black patterns of endogamy are distinctive among U.S. racial minorities (Tucker & Mitchell-Kernan, 1990). African Americans are the least likely of all racial and ethnic groups to marry someone from another race. Furthermore, unlike every other group, African-American men are more likely than women to marry nonblacks.

Note, however, that intermarriage rates for all groups are affected by societal factors and are not uniform from one region to another. For instance, intermarriage rates for African Americans are highest in the West, where attitudes toward interracial relationships and race in general are more permissive and tolerant than in other parts of the country. Intermarriage rates are lowest in the South, where attitudes tend to be the least tolerant (Tucker & Mitchell-Kernan, 1990).

Where ethnic communities are strong and concentrated, rules of endogamy tend to powerfully impede intermarriage. For Jews, intermarriage has traditionally been lower in eastern cities with large Jewish populations and has been higher in the South and West, where the Jewish population tends to be smaller. Intermarriage among Chinese Americans and Korean Americans is significantly higher in Hawaii, which has no large Chinese or Korean communities exerting control over marital choice, than in Los Angeles, where ethnic communities are strong (Kitano, Yeung, Chai, & Hatanaka, 1984).

In short, sociologists have found that the strength of the ethnic community is crucial in determining how much the rules of endogamy will influence mate selection. These communities provide a large supply of ethnically similar marital candidates. Ethnic institutions in these communities (fraternal organizations, churches, synagogues, and so on) often actively discourage intermarriage. Gossip and ostracism from within the community can sometimes be enough to dissuade people from choosing a mate from outside the group. But where these community structures and social networks are weak, personal interests and desires can easily override group constraints.

The issue of racial/ethnic endogamy is an especially emotional one in U.S. society. Fear and condemnation of interracial relationships have been a part of American culture, politics, and law since the first European settlers arrived here close to 400 years ago. The first law against interracial marriage was enacted in Maryland in 1661, prohibiting whites from marrying Native Americans or Africans. Over the next 300 years or so, thirty-eight more states put such laws on the books, expanding their coverage to include Chinese, Japanese, Koreans, Indian, and Filipino Americans. These laws were supported by biological and evolution-based theories of race, which spelled out essential differences (and therefore implied superiority or inferiority) among the races. Laws were enacted to prevent a mixing of the races (referred to as "mongrelization") that would destroy the racial purity (and superiority) of whites. The irony, of course, is that racial mixing had been taking place since the country's very beginning, much of it through white slave owners forcing sexual activity on black slaves.

Violent disapproval of intermarriage persisted well into the twentieth century. The gruesome murder in 1955 of Emmett Till, a black youth thought to be overly friendly with a white woman, brought to light the deep-seated feelings that some people harbored over even the suggestion of interracial intimacy. In 1958, when white Richard Loving and his new wife, black Mildred Jeter, moved to their new home in Virginia, a sheriff arrived to arrest them for violating a state law that prohibited interracial marriages. The Lovings were sentenced to 1 year in jail but then learned that the judge would suspend the sentence if they left the state and promised not to return for 25 years. Nine years later, in 1967, the U.S. Supreme Court ruled on the suit they had filed, concluding that using racial classifications to restrict freedom to marry was unconstitutional.

People in this country are no longer murdered or banished for expressing intimate feelings for people of a different race. In fact, the percentage of Americans who believe there

EXHIBIT 6.4

Declining Hostility Toward Interracial Marriage

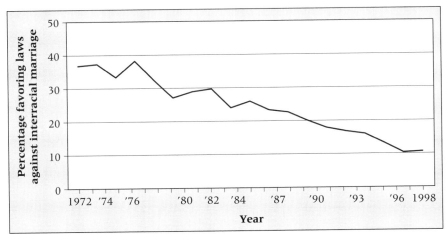

Note: Only nonblack respondents were counted.
Data source: National Opinion Research Center. 1998. *General Social Survey, 1972–1998.* Available at www.icpsr.umich.edu/GSS/. Accessed June 1, 2001.

should be laws against blacks and whites marrying has declined dramatically since the 1970s (see Exhibit 6.4). A recent nationwide survey conducted by the Henry J. Kaiser Family Foundation also shows that Americans are becoming more accepting of interracial relationships, although the level of acceptance varies between different groups. The study found that 77 percent of blacks, 68 percent of Latinos, 67 percent of Asians, but only 53 percent of whites said it makes no difference whether a person marries someone of his or her own race or someone of a different race (Fears & Deane, 2001).

Yet many Americans, especially those in black–white relationships, still lack family support when choosing to marry someone of a different race (Lewis & Yancey, 1997). In 1998, about two in five whites surveyed said they would oppose having a close relative or family member marry a black person (National Opinion Research Center, 1998). About half of the black–white couples in the Kaiser study felt that biracial marriage makes things harder, and 65 percent reported that their parents had a problem with the relationship, at least initially.

The legal system can also be less than accommodating. Two states—South Carolina and Alabama—had laws against interracial marriage on the books until the mid-1990s. Even today, rural judges can sometimes make it difficult for interracial couples to marry (Staples, 1999).

Social Class   If people were to base their ideas about the formation of romantic relationships on what they saw in movies, they might be tempted to conclude that divisions based on social class—that is, people's economic position in society—don't matter or perhaps don't exist at all. Films such as *Titanic, Good Will Hunting, Fools Rush In, Ever After, Inventing the Abbotts, Pretty Woman, White Palace, Love Story,* and *Pretty in Pink* send the message that when it comes to love, we're all really alike. In these stories the power of love is strong enough to blow away differences in education, pedigree, resources, and tastes. When it comes to love, Hollywood's United States is a classless society.

In reality, however, social class is a powerful factor in mate selection. People face strong pressures to choose marital partners of similar social standing (Kalmijn, 1998). Even if two individuals from different races or religions marry, chances are they will have similar socio-economic backgrounds. Certainly some people do marry a person from a different social class, but the class tends to be an adjacent one—for instance, an upper-class woman marrying a middle-class man. Cinderella-like marriages between people of vastly different class rankings are quite rare.

One reason is that individuals from similar social classes are more likely to participate in activities where they come into contact with people who share their values, tastes, goals, expectations, and backgrounds (Kalmijn & Flap, 2001). The U.S. education system plays a particularly important role in bringing people from similar class backgrounds together. Neighborhoods—and thus neighborhood schools—tend to be homogeneous in social class. College often continues class segregation. People from upper-class backgrounds are considerably more likely to attend costly private schools, whereas those from the middle class are most likely to enroll in state universities, and those from the working class are most likely to enroll in community colleges. These structural conditions increase the odds that the people whom college students meet and form intimate relationships with will come from a similar class background. Indeed, the tendency for spouses to have similar educational backgrounds has increased in the United States since the 1920s (Kalmijn, 1991a).

Age   In most societies, husbands are older than their wives, sometimes considerably older. For example, in some countries of sub-Saharan Africa one-half to three-quarters of girls between the ages of 15 and 19 are married, often to men in their 30s. In Nepal, 40 percent of girls are married before they turn 15 and 7 percent before they are 10 (UNICEF, 2001). Parents may feel that marrying off a daughter at a young age can help them economically and keep the girl "safe" from unwanted sexual advances. But such differences in age can have devastating effects. Young brides are usually pulled out of school. And pregnancy-related deaths are the leading cause of death for girls between 15 and 19 worldwide (UNICEF, 2001).

In the United States, marriages tend to be age-endogamous. Husbands and wives are usually fairly close in age (see Exhibit 6.2b). In fact, about 32 percent of U.S. marriages consist of couples who are within one year of each other, whereas fewer than 10 percent of all marriages involve one spouse who is 10 or more years older (U.S. Bureau of the Census, 2000b). When age discrepancies in U.S. marriages do exist, it is almost always men who are older. Only about 12 percent of all marriages consist of wives who are 2 or more years older than their husbands (U.S. Bureau of the Census, 2000b).

Expectations for Couples

Rules of exogamy and endogamy help determine who marries whom. But even after relationships are formed, cultural forces continue to exert influence on couples' lives, affecting what they expect of each other and the relationship.

The Expectation of Interdependence   Sociologists maintain that the key feature of close relationships is **interdependence**, the degree to which partners rely on each other to provide affection, companionship, sex, money, and so on (Berscheid & Peplau, 1983; Scanzoni, Polonko, Teachman, & Thompson, 1989).

Traditionally, because they were less likely than men to work outside the home, wives tended to be economically dependent on their husbands. In return, wives usually managed the household, the children, the couple's social life, and the emotional quality of the marriage. Although both men and women were likely to depend on and benefit from the exchange, some sociologists argue that women's economic dependence, which made it difficult for them to survive outside of marriage on their own, is mainly what stabilized marriages (Nock, 1999; Popenoe, 1999). But, they say, as women have gained greater economic independence and more couples have become dual-earners, economic interdependence is becoming a less common reason for two people to stay married. Some fear that the declining expectation of interdependence reduces interest in marriage and leads to higher divorce rates.

Issue 2 examines the claim that women's growing economic dependence is partially responsible for a decline in the institution of family.

But studies show that economic interdependence is still likely to exist in contemporary relationships, including dual-earner ones. Each partner comes to rely on the other's income to provide the higher standard of living it affords. Furthermore, committed relationships involve more than just economic interdependence. Couples tend to depend on each other for everything from practical assistance to emotional support. Often this sort of interdependence leads to what social scientists call **specialization**—each partner developing some skills and neglecting others, "because each can count on the other to take responsibility for some of the work involved in making a home or living" (Waite & Gallagher, 2000, p. 26).

The Expectation of Equity   Nowadays, most people enter marital or cohabiting relationships with certain expectations about equity (that is, fairness) and the balance of power. According to the social exchange model (see Chapters 1 and 5), in forming relationships, people are motivated to maximize their benefits and minimize their costs.

But judgments of how much "profit" is to be derived from a relationship and of how well it compares to past experiences and perceived alternatives are not made by one partner alone. Being in a relationship means that another person is simultaneously interested in maximizing rewards and minimizing costs. Once established, relationships work best when the exchange is fair, or *equitable*—when both partners are deriving benefits from the relationship that are proportional to what they are investing in it. The presence or absence of such **interpersonal equity** has profound effects on the satisfaction felt by individuals as well as on the stability of the relationship itself (Hatfield, Traupmann, Sprecher, Utne, & Hay, 1985; Utne, Hatfield, Traupmann, & Greenberger, 1984). Indeed, research has consistently shown that the happiest couples are those in which partners are providing each other with many rewarding experiences and few costly ones (Birchler, Weiss, & Vincent, 1975; Rusbult, 1983; Vincent, Weiss, & Birchler, 1975).

An *investment* is anything someone has to offer to the relationship, such as time, money, interest, or personal characteristics, such as good looks or a sense of humor (Brown, 1986). Investments are important because they create feelings of entitlement or deservedness. When a friend says to you, "You deserve better than her" (or him), or "You're entitled to some happiness," an implicit statement of equity is involved: "Given what you have invested or what you have to offer, in all fairness you should be receiving greater benefits."

As you might suspect, not every relationship is perfectly equitable. When things become disproportional, feelings of unfairness result. In general there are two types of inequity: *underbenefited inequity* (that is, you feel you are not getting out of the relationship what you feel you deserve) and *overbenefited inequity* (that is, you feel you are getting too much for what you have to offer). Each kind of inequity can threaten the stability of the relationship.

Social psychologist Elaine Hatfield and her colleagues (Hatfield, Walster, & Traupmann, 1978) interviewed 537 college men and women who were dating someone. She asked them whether they expected to be with their partners in 1 year and in 5 years. Those who felt their relationships were perfectly equitable were much more likely than others to think the relationships would last. Interestingly, the overbenefited subjects were just as doubtful as underbenefited subjects about the future prospects of their relationships. Presumably, the underbenefited individuals felt they would do better in the future, and the overbenefited individuals didn't expect their luck to last. Incidentally, a follow-up study 3 months later indicated that the equitable relationships were, in fact, more likely to still be intact.

Both types of inequity are uncomfortable and motivate individuals to restore either actual or psychological equity (Brehm, 1992). Underbenefited partners may attempt to reduce their investments in the relationship or demand more from their partner. For example, if you feel you're being underbenefited, you may decide not to do as many favors for your partner or you may stop showing affection. If that fails, you may start to demand more benefits or more investments from your partner: "Do you think you could start showing some appreciation for all that I do for you around here!?" Overbenefited partners, in contrast, may try to increase their contributions (such as taking more responsibility for planning social events) or increase the benefits they offer their partner (such as showering the partner with gifts).

The problem with these strategies is that they may backfire. For instance, your reduction of contributions to the relationship may be met by a similar reduction on the part of your partner. Or your partner may take advantage of your attempts to increase his or her benefits. Hence, individuals often resort to attempts to restore equity psychologically—to convince themselves that, although it seems otherwise, equity does in fact exist (Brehm, 1992). If you are the underbenefited partner, you may talk yourself into believing that your partner is a special person who deserves more than you do. Perhaps she or he has had terrible experiences in the past and deserves to be treated well in this relationship. If you are the overbenefited partner, you may convince yourself that, because of some particularly noble quality you possess, you truly deserve the favorable inequity.

Inequity is fairly obvious when the imbalances involve things that are easy to see: financial contributions to the relationship or the performance of certain chores around the house. But an imbalance in feelings—in emotional investment—is more difficult to identify. Most people know about relationships in which one partner seems more in love than the other partner. Such imbalances in emotional attachment can create serious and potentially dangerous power differences in relationships. The person who loves less or does not express unconditional affection has the upper hand in the relationship, because the other person will presumably suffer more if the relationship should end (Blau, 1964). Hence, the individual who loves less can dictate the terms of the relationship and can, if so inclined, exploit the other by making heavy demands. The partner who loves more has greater interest in maintaining the relationship and may be forced to put up with a lot to do so.

Such a situation implies a rather depressing reality about intimate relationships. The less-dependent partner—that is, the one who has more alternatives outside the relationship—has more power in it because that person can more easily abandon the relationship. This phenomenon—referred to as the **principle of least interest**—suggests that control over the relationship rests with the partner who has the least interest in continuing it. If so inclined, this person can dictate the conditions of the relationship, make demands of the other, and even exploit that person's dependence. You've probably seen relationships in which one partner is so much more "in love" than the other that he or she is willing to tolerate a lot of pain and nastiness in hopes that the relationship will continue.

The Expectation of Commitment   To understand the true nature of enduring relationships, expectations surrounding interdependence and equity need to be viewed within a broader context. After all, why do people make investments in their relationships? How can people justify continuing what objectively appears to be an inequitable arrangement? Why would an individual become economically or emotionally dependent on a relationship if the option to be more independent exists elsewhere?

The answer to these questions is that enduring relationships involve a certain degree of commitment to the relationship. **Commitment** can be thought of as personal dedication to the relationship, a desire to maintain and improve the relationship for the benefit on both parties (Stanley & Markman, 1992). In U.S. culture, people expect couples to express commitment and concern for each other, and to come to the other's defense when threatened. What characterizes a committed relationship is genuine concern for the partner's well-being, not just one's own (Stanley & Markman, 1992). Committed partners worry about each other and feel responsible for each other (Waite & Gallagher, 2000). Here's how one wife describes what commitment means to her:

> [W]e are responsible for each other . . . for each other's health, each other's well-being, mental health, financial stability . . . we are each other's keeper . . . we have a responsibility to go to a fair amount of trouble in order to make sure that we stay together and we continue to be responsible for each other. (quoted in Waite & Gallagher, 2000, p. 9)

When you're committed to a relationship or a partner, you are more likely to make sacrifices for the relationship and to invest in it. In a highly committed relationship, partners are willing to tolerate a certain amount of powerlessness or inequity because they believe that things will balance out in the long run. For instance, a husband may be willing to forgo his own educational plans so his wife can pursue an advanced degree because in the long term he expects to benefit from her higher income.

The Expectation of Permanence   Another cultural expectation that characterizes committed intimate relationships is that of permanence. Despite the high rate of divorce in the United States, most couples still marry with the expectation that they will be married forever. Even Glynn Wolfe, who, according to the *Guinness Book of World Records*, is the most married man in the monogamous world and whose shortest marriage lasted about 2 months, claims he expects permanence. When Mr. Wolfe, at age 81, was preparing to marry his twenty-ninth bride (a 15-year-old who was the sister of his current wife), he insisted in an interview that "I marry 'em for keeps" ("Perpetual groom plots 28th wedding," 1990, p. C1). And although cohabiting relationships are often shorter than marriages, many cohabitors still expect their relationships to be permanent.

This conflict between whether to stay married, despite the quality of the relationship, echoes the struggle between individualism and family obligation, discussed in Issue 4.

Expectations of permanence vary widely among different social groups. For instance, conservative religious groups, such as fundamentalist Christians, are opposed to divorce and feel it is better to stay in an unsatisfying marriage than to divorce. Others, however, feel that permanence, simply for the sake of permanence, is not necessarily desirable.

The Expectation of Sexual Access   In the United States, another distinguishing feature of long-term intimate relationships is the expectation of sexual access. Traditionally, marriages have been created by establishing sexual ties; thus the first act of sexual intercourse on the wedding night symbolically ratifies the marriage. If two people who are legally married have never had sexual intercourse, they are said not to have "consummated" the marriage. Such a situation used to be grounds for annulment, because a key term of the marriage contract had not been put into effect.

For generations, most men probably had some sexual experience before marriage, but for women marriage usually meant their initiation into an adult sexual relationship. Even for those people who did have some sexual experience before marriage, there was a big difference between "the guilty, if passionate, tumblings in the back seat of a car, the corner of a park, or the living room couch and the luxury of a bed of their own, unconstrained by concerns about time or parents" (Rubin, 1990, p. 161).

Today, however, marriage usually follows a period of sexual exploration with a variety of partners and is just as likely to be the continuation of an already existing sexual relationship as the beginning of a new one. Nevertheless, spouses and other long-term partners still expect to have relatively unimpeded sexual access. The two people may have different levels of desire or different levels of adventurousness, but they know they will be able to have sex with their partner without the anxiety and auditioning that often characterizes sexual behavior in casual relationships.

Because of sexual access on a daily basis, married couples and long-term cohabitors have sex more frequently than single people (Laumann, Gagnon, Michael, & Michaels, 1994). But frequency declines precipitously after the early years of a relationship, and every year thereafter sex gets a little rarer: "There is an old saying that if a couple puts a penny in a jar for every time they have sex in the first year of marriage and then takes a penny out of the jar for every time they have sex the rest of the marriage, the pair will never empty out the jar" (Schwartz & Rutter, 1998, p. 132). The reason typically cited for this decline is that access breeds boredom. Once the novelty and uncertainty disappear, sex becomes mundane. Both men and women can become bored by predictability (Schwartz & Rutter, 1998). Furthermore, the distractions of daily life—which multiply exponentially if children are around—can also reduce desire and energy.

The Expectation of Sexual Exclusivity   An expectation of sexual access is usually accompanied by an expectation of sexual exclusivity, which is apparent in the kind of sexual possessiveness that frequently characterizes U.S. heterosexual relationships. For instance, in this society marriage is considered a contract for exclusive sexual rights between two spouses (Collins, 1992).

But the expectation of sexual exclusivity has historically applied more to women than to men. In traditional societies a woman's body was the exclusive sexual property of her husband (which explains why more emphasis was placed on the bride being a virgin at marriage than on the husband's being so). A husband's property rights over his wife were threatened if she had intercourse with another man. Under English common law, a man was legally incapable of committing adultery. Indeed, the offense of adultery was not the sexual betrayal of one partner by the other, but the wife's engaging in acts that could taint the husband's bloodlines (Stoddard, 1992).

The vast majority of individuals in the United States—about nine out of ten, in one national survey—believe that extramarital sex is morally wrong (Laumann et al., 1994). But as with the ideal of permanence, such attitudes reflect an expectation, not necessarily the reality. When sociologist Edward Laumann and his colleagues asked married individuals, "Have you ever had sex with someone other than your husband or wife while you were married?" about 25 percent of men and 15 percent of women answered yes. The researchers also found a slight tendency for cohabitors to report affairs more often than did married people, even when the duration of the relationship was the same.

Interestingly, for heterosexual couples, extramarital affairs are defined almost exclusively by sexual infidelity. Emotional infidelity seems of less concern. But among gay couples, fidelity is defined more in terms of emotional commitment and betrayal (Steen & Schwartz, 1995).

Technology is also changing the definition of infidelity. The Internet affords individuals the opportunity to talk to, flirt with, or seduce virtually anyone, no matter how distant. It is possible to connect with another person every way but physically via the Internet, and for some people, still feel completely faithful to one's partner. And there may be a greater tendency to self-disclose and experiment on the Internet than one would in real life because of a sense of anonymity and security. But some therapists insist that these "cyber-affairs" can be as threatening to a relationship as real-life affairs (Greenfield, 1999).

The Expectation of Being a "Couple"   One of the major expectations surrounding couples is that they behave like couples. In U.S. culture, for instance, people typically expect married couples to live together and spend time together, pool financial resources, entertain other couples, and so forth. Imagine a newlywed couple in which the husband wants to continue hanging out with his old single friends. To the wife (and others), such actions might lead to questions about his commitment to the relationship, and even his desire to be married in the first place.

But being a couple involves something far more important than simply acting the part. It involves feeling and thinking like a couple. In other words, it involves the expectation that the two people involved will create a new *identity* as a couple. It means thinking less in terms of "me and mine" and more in terms of "we and ours." For many individuals, one difficult challenge they face when entering long-term relationships is balancing their new "couple" identity with their old "individual" identity. Such a balancing act is especially difficult in marriages, where institutionalized expectations encourage, and sometimes even require, a person to abandon his or her identity as a single person.

As relationships progress, couples create this new couple-identity for themselves and, through interaction with each other, reinforce this identity (Berger & Kellner, 1964). As this identity becomes more salient and central to one's self-concept, it has greater and greater impact on present and future behavior and choices.

Third parties also play an important role in reinforcing the couple's new identity. Whether outsiders approve of the relationship ("You two make a lovely couple") or disapprove of it ("I think you can do better"), on some level they are validating the couple by responding to them as a couple, acknowledging that a "couple" entity even exists (Berger & Kellner, 1964). Such external validation is important to developing in intimate relationship. Sometimes partners don't even consider themselves a couple until they are publicly recognized as such by their friends and peers.

Once others recognize two people as "coupled," they are likely to impose a new and complex set of expectations. The couple may be issued joint invitations to social gatherings, be expected to accompany each other to public events, or be assumed to know each other's whereabouts at all times.

The power that these expectations have over how people act and think reinforces the contention that personal relationships always develop within a social context. As much as people would like to believe otherwise, intimacy—even love—is not just a phenomenon that occurs between the two involved. "Third parties," especially parents, peers, and children—indeed, anyone who has a vested interest in the couple's well-being—can play a significant role in shaping a couple's relationship.

Even the most private aspects of the couple's interactions, such as their sexual activities, can be subjected to third-party influences (Laumann et al., 1994). For instance, childless married couples often feel pressured to have children; children may actively discourage their single parents from dating and becoming sexually intimate with people they deem unacceptable; and everyone seems to have a lot to say about husbands or wives who engage in extramarital relations.

Couples' Lives

If all relationships are similarly governed by a culture's rules and expectations, it would seem that couples, at least those within a given culture, should be pretty similar. But of course, this isn't the case. As you're well aware, no two relationships are ever exactly alike.

It's true that people enter a relationship with a set of religious beliefs, ethnic traditions, and community norms that shape their desires and give them an idea about what to expect. They also bring along information from parents' and friends' relationships and the images of relationships they see in the media. But despite possible similarities, no two people's ideas, experiences, and expectations are identical. Thus each couple faces the task of forging its own unique relationship while at the same time conforming to broader social norms.

Private Culture

Issue 3 discusses the broader role of privacy in shaping family experiences.

Through interaction and over time, couples create a unique pattern of interaction—a set of habits, rules, and shared reality. They develop a sort of **private culture**—their own particular way of dealing with the demands of everyday life, such as how to make everyday decisions, what expressions of sexuality are appropriate, and how to allocate household labor (Blumstein & Kollock, 1988). The private culture includes things as mundane as a weekly dinner schedule or a Sunday morning ritual of breakfast and newspaper reading in bed, or as serious as the distribution of power and the handling of household finances. Some rituals and habits disappear as the composition of the family changes (for instance, with the arrival of children); others persist and are passed on to future generations.

The private culture of marriages and other enduring intimate relationships creates for individuals a sense of order and connection (Berger & Kellner, 1964). Committed, intimate relationships validate the participants and the worlds they live in. This sense of order is key to a sense of well-being. Sociologists have long recognized that people who lack such connections can feel profoundly alienated (Durkheim, 1897/1951). But simply being married or in a committed relationship doesn't make someone impervious to these negative feelings. Undoubtedly, some married persons feel alienated and distant from their spouses.

Communication Styles

Sociologists, especially symbolic interactionists (whose perspective is described in Chapter 1), believe that communication patterns are essential to establishing a shared reality and private culture and ultimately building a successful relationship (Berger & Kellner, 1964). For decades social scientists have tried to explain—by looking at factors such as income, education, age at marriage, and the age difference between husband and wife—why relationships succeed or fail. But many now believe that these factors may be less important than communication between partners. For instance, it's not simply a lack of money that causes problems in a relationship, it's how the couple discusses and negotiates with each other about financial difficulties (Fitzpatrick, 1988). Indeed, couples seeking divorce frequently cite "communication problems" as a reason for the breakup (Kincaid & Caldwell, 1995).

There is no one recipe for communication success. What works for some couples may not work for others, as sociologists John Cuber and Peggy Harroff (1965) found. To uncover the patterns of communication that emerge in enduring marriages, they conducted extensive interviews with over 400 upper middle-class husbands and wives ages 35 to 50. All their respondents had been married at least 10 years, and all claimed they had never considered divorce or separation. In other words, these were not couples in crisis.

Cuber and Harroff found that stable couples are quite diverse. They identified five different types of marriage based on different patterns of communication:

- *Conflict-habituated marriages* are marked by a pervasive and constant air of tension. These are the couples who seem to constantly fight and argue. Simply being in each other's company is enough to trigger an argument. To the outside observer, such conflict would appear to characterize a marriage doomed to failure. But these couples had no intention of ending their relationship. The conflict-habituated way of interacting could last a lifetime.
- *Devitalized marriages* involve couples who were once deeply in love, but who have drifted apart over the years. Communication is minimal and usually devoted to specific tasks or problems. Most of the time they spend together is "duty" time: entertaining guests, spending time with the children, pursuing community activities. They realize their marriage isn't what it used to be, but remain together out of a sense of obligation and loyalty.
- *Passive-congenial marriages* look, for all intents and purposes, like devitalized marriages—except they have been this way from the start. The couple rarely argues, but they also have no expectation of love or passion. The marriage provides stability for the couple so they can direct their energies elsewhere. They define their lack of intense involvement as the way they want their marriage to be.
- *Vital marriages* conform most closely to what the ideal image of marital communication should be. They involve spouses who truly share intimacy in all important aspects of their lives. Their primary satisfaction in life is derived from the time they spend with each other, although the spouses do not lose their separate identities.
- *Total marriages* differ from vital marriages in the degree to which couples share time with each other. They are completely absorbed in each other's lives. Chances are, they even work together. Twenty-four hours a day in each other's company is still not enough. Privacy from each other is a foreign concept.

Although Cuber and Harroff's typology of marriages was based only on upper middle-class couples and therefore may not be applicable to all marriages, it shows us that stable relationships needn't always be the picture of happiness. Different communication styles suit the needs of different couples. As long as both partners in the relationship agree that a particular pattern of communication suits them, things are fine. Trouble can arise, though, when individuals expect different sorts of conversations and responses from their partners. One factor that can cause different expectations is gender.

Gender and Communication

Some of the most popular books on intimate relationships—such as John Gray's *Men Are From Mars, Women Are From Venus,* and Deborah Tannen's *You Just Don't Understand*—focus on the different ways that men and women communicate. To state that men and women are from different planets, even figuratively speaking, is obviously overstating the effect that gender can have on marital communication. Men and women are more alike than different when it comes to communication. But gender undoubtedly influences the way people interact in relationships. For heterosexual couples, gender can pose significant challenges if men and women bring different understandings and communicative experiences to the relationship. But even for same-sex couples, gender can shape communication and lead to problems.

Communication in Heterosexual Relationships   Research on gender differences in communication have consistently shown that women's and men's conversational patterns differ in many ways (Maltz & Borker, 1982; Noller, 1993; Parlee, 1989). For example,

- Women tend to ask more questions.
- Women use more positive minimal responses, such as "mm-hmms."
- Men tend to interrupt more.
- Women are more likely to use modifiers and hedges (such as "sort of," "kind of," and "I guess").
- Women are more likely to use tag questions at the end of declarative sentences (for instance, "It's cold outside, *isn't it?*").
- Men are more likely to change the topic of conversation.
- Men are more likely to want to problem solve; women are more likely to want to listen.
- Men are less open and less likely to engage in intimate self-disclosure.

Such differences can have important implications for the way private cultures develop in long-term relationships:

> Women may feel it is essential to keep conversation going, which they do by encouraging other speakers, filling silences, and asking questions. Men, on the other hand, may view such supportive devices as weak, and prefer to use strong tactics such as making statements and interrupting other speakers. . . . Women seek consensus in making decisions, because their primary objective is to maintain the emotional link between partners. Men seek to make decisions more expeditiously, with the more powerful person deciding the outcome. In responding to others' concerns or problems, men are likely to suggest solutions or possible actions, whereas women are more likely to express sympathy by sharing similar feelings or experiences, thus creating the intimacy that is women's goal in conversation. (Steen & Schwartz, 1995, pp. 310–311)

In everyday conversation, but especially during arguments, these differences can hinder effective communication and, as a result, interfere with the sense of connection in a relationship. For example, if a man interrupts or changes topics frequently in conversation, it may appear to his partner that he isn't paying attention, even if he is (Noller, 1993). During conflict, these gendered patterns of interaction can result in what has been termed the "demand-withdraw pattern," in which the woman's attempts to confront a problem are met by her male partner's withdrawal (Noller, 1993). Obviously, if the key to successful relationships is clear communication, such gender differences can pose a serious barrier.

Communication in Homosexual Relationships   In heterosexual relationships it is the gender difference in conversation patterns that may hinder communication, but in homosexual relationships, similarity can be problematic. For instance, "if both women are committed to reaching complete consensus, discussions may go on interminably, erupting in anger when frustrated partners cannot reach mutual agreement" (Steen & Schwartz, 1995, p. 316).

The opposite problem can arise for gay men who may have acquired more traditional male communication patterns: "It was much different in the beginning of the relationship, because we didn't realize how much we didn't communicate. You tend to overlook familiar things and they don't come out. We were ignorant—or afraid—about how to discuss things" (quoted in Blumstein & Schwartz, 1983, p. 542).

Interestingly, many same-sex couples actually experience communication dynamics very similar to heterosexual couples. That is, one partner is likely to be more open and work harder to keep the "conversation" going, whereas the other is more withdrawn. Consider how this gay man describes a particularly difficult stage in his relationship with a married man:

> I was very emotionally unsteady at the time. . . . What I needed was someone who was very, very verbal, and tactile, and Ted is neither. He is very reserved. His feelings are quieter than most people's. . . . That was a source of conflict, that constantly milking him for verbal approval and reinforcement and stuff like that. . . . (quoted in Blumstein & Schwartz, 1983, pp. 510–511)

What this man is describing is the typical interactional work that women have historically tended to do: working hard at keeping the conversation going (Fishman, 1978).

Power in Intimate Relationships

Clearly, gender is not the only factor shaping communication patterns in long-term relationships. Sociologist Cathryn Johnson (1994) conducted an experiment in which men and women were instructed to play either a managerial role or an employee role in a fictitious office setting. She found that positions of authority were far more important than gender in understanding conversational patterns. Subordinates exhibited more conversational support and were less assertive than those in the manager role, regardless of their gender.

When researchers examine conversational patterns and dynamics in intimate relationships more closely, they find that the person in power—no matter what the gender—tends to dictate the nature and direction of communication. Sociologists Peter Kollock, Phil Blumstein, and Pepper Schwartz (1985) examined taped conversations between intimate partners in heterosexual, gay male, and lesbian couples to see if positions of power influenced people's conversational behavior. They were particularly interested in such conversational norm violations as interrupting, talking over the other person, and monopolizing the conversation. They found that regardless of the sexual composition of the couple—the factor that in past research had been used to explain differences in conversational behavior—people in positions of power interrupted more, overlapped their partners more, and talked for longer periods of uninterrupted time than the partners with less power. In other words, power can create a conversational division of labor. And because men tend to be more powerful in relationships than women, as we noted in Chapter 2, they do tend to dominate conversations. But these differences stem from being more socially powerful, not simply from being male.

Power is important in the context of intimate relationships not simply because it provides conversational privileges to some people and not others. Power can affect all aspects of a couple's intimate life. Being part of a couple requires many decisions and choices. When two people fall in love and want to spend their lives together, they must choose whether to maintain separate residences or live together (whether married or not). If they decide to live together, they must decide where to live, how to decorate the home, and who will be responsible for certain domestic tasks. They must make decisions on how their respective careers will influence family life, whether to have children, how to discipline them, and so on. The way they make all these decisions—from the trivial ones such as what to have for dinner to the important ones such as whether to accept a job transfer to another state—depends on the way relationships of power and authority have been structured.

The expression of power in intimate relationships certainly emerges from the interactions and personalities of the specific individuals involved. But one must also not forget that couples are embedded in a social system that perpetuates unequal rewards and life chances in society. In a society stratified along gender lines, for example, women will continue to have limited opportunities to claim legitimate power in the larger society. These variations in social power can play out in interesting ways within couples' lives.

Power arrangements that were once taken for granted—such as who's going to sacrifice a career to stay at home and raise children—are now more than ever likely to be the product of decisions arrived at by partners through open negotiation. At the very least, people entering into long-term relationships are starting to acknowledge that not every woman wants or expects to have children and take care of the household and not every man wants to be a primary breadwinner. More and more women are in the paid labor force and are therefore less dependent economically on their husbands than they once were. In addition, an increasing number of employed wives are now earning more than their husbands. For instance, a recent study of dual-earner couples found that 20 to 25 percent of wives earn more than their husbands (Winkler, 1998). Most importantly, gender norms are changing. Hence more and more couples today are trying to establish relationships in which power is balanced (Schwartz, 1994).

Yet as discussed in Chapter 2, most relationships in the United States continue to be male dominant in part because resources are unequally distributed by gender and because gendered norms are deeply entrenched in society. Sociologist William Goode (1981) suggests that people in positions of power are usually reluctant to sacrifice their privilege. Because of their historical position in society, men are less likely to see gender inequality as unjust or to see change as necessary. Indeed, most men do not see gender inequality—either in their families or in society at large—as their fault or their problem; it's a "woman's issue." Like most people whose interests are being served by the system, men are largely unaware of the small and large advantages that the social structure and prevailing family ideology provide them (Goode, 1981).

Even couples who identify their relationships as egalitarian and their roles as nongendered sometimes show male-dominant patterns. For instance, one study (Kudson-Martin & Mahoney, 1998) found that among egalitarian couples, wives were more likely than husbands to accommodate their partners' desires and needs, worry about upsetting their partners, do what their partners wanted, and try to fit their lives around their partners' schedules. Such studies are important because they show us that even though women have gained ground economically, traditional gender expectations continue to exert powerful influence over people's family experiences.

Marriages

As you may have noticed, all enduring relationships, whether same sex or heterosexual, married or unmarried, are likely to share these common features: patterns of exogamy and endogamy, expectations regarding couplehood, patterns of communication, and power. Some sociologists have argued that because all close relationships contain similar features, there is nothing particularly unique or special about marriage. They argue that it makes more sense to talk about and study "sexually based primary relationships," regardless of legal status (Scanzoni et al., 1989).

Issue 1 looks more closely at the debate over legalizing gay marriage.

But are marriages really like any other committed intimate relationship? Is there nothing special about marriage? If there isn't, the fight to ensure that same sex couples have the right to marry may be unnecessary, except on symbolic grounds. In this section, we examine the differences between two similar relationships—cohabitation and marriage—and the implications for persons in these unions.

Cohabitation versus Marriage

In terms of everyday relationship issues such as sexual activity, decision making, parenting, and concerns about employment, cohabitors look a lot like married couples (cited in Scanzoni, 2000). But beyond the obvious differences in legal status, cohabiting relationships differ from married ones in several ways. The following are among the most significant and noteworthy findings:

- Cohabitors report significantly lower satisfaction and happiness with their relationships than spouses do (Booth & Johnson, 1988; Nock, 1995).
- Cohabitors report lower levels of commitment to the relationship (Nock, 1995).
- Cohabitors are almost twice as likely as spouses to report that they believed their relationship was in trouble over the past year, even after controlling for age of the partners and duration of the relationship (Bumpass et al., 1991).
- Cohabiting relationships tend to be shorter-lived than marriages. Most either dissolve or end in marriage (reported in Smock, 2000). In addition, people who cohabit before marriage are at greater risk of marital dissolution than people who did not cohabit (DeMaris & Rao, 1992).
- Male cohabitors are much more likely than husbands to say they overbenefit in their relationships, although men in both types of relationships view themselves as benefiting more from the relationship than do women (Kollock, Blumstein, & Schwartz, 1994).
- Cohabitors tolerate less inequality in their relationships and are more likely to dissolve the relationship under these circumstances, especially when inequality takes the form of women earning more than their partners (Brines & Joyner, 1999).
- Cohabitors report having poorer relationships with their parents (Nock, 1995).

Some research suggests that cohabitors actually look more like single people than married ones in terms of such things as childbearing intentions, schooling, homeownership, and employment (reported in Smock, 2000). However, such findings may depend on what type of cohabitors are studied. Cohabitors who plan to marry may look more like married couples; those who don't intend to marry may look more like single persons (Brown & Booth, 1996).

Overall, it does appear that cohabitation differs from marriage on several important counts. But such differences don't necessarily mean that married and cohabiting relationships operate on fundamentally different principles. Rather, the extent to which these organizing principles operate may simply be a function of degree. In other words, many of the principles, such as the expectation of sexual exclusivity or permanence, may apply to both types of relationships, but seem to be more important to spouses than to cohabiting partners. By contrast, the principle of equity appears to play a more important role in cohabiting relationships than in married ones (Brines & Joyner, 1999).

Unique Aspects of Marriage

Then is marriage like cohabitation, only more so? Probably not. Other forces besides the dynamics of the relationship are at work in marriages. A variety of cultural and structural features of marriage can make it more stable and secure than cohabitation or any other type of relationship.

The Marriage Contract   The legendary actress Katherine Hepburn once said, "It's bloody impractical to love, honor, and obey. If it weren't, you wouldn't have to sign a contract" (1997, cited in Ingraham, 1999). In some sense, she's right, of course. The legal contract that binds married couples in marriage adds formality to the union, as well as a set of rights and obligations. It can also make terminating the marriage difficult and complicated.

By contrast, no state has determined all the legal rights and duties of cohabitors. In some sense, the lack of a clearly defined contract might make termination of the relationship easier, but it is also likely to inhibit the investments in the relationship that might bring couples closer together (Brines & Joyner, 1999). Cohabitors could create such investments if they choose to—for example, by pooling incomes and signing written agreements that would make their relationships more comparable to marriages—but few do.

Increasingly, though, marriages have also become less subject to regulations by the state. Some traditional provisions of the marriage contract—for example, that husbands were legal heads of households, responsible for support, and wives were responsible for housework and child rearing—have been eliminated. In addition, many companies now grant unmarried cohabiting employees the same rights and benefits as married employees. In this sense, the legal contract has probably become a less distinguishing aspect of marriage.

Indeed, some scholars have insisted that the idea of a contract is no longer appropriate for describing marital arrangements. Law professor Margaret Brinig (2000) suggests that while husband–wife (and parent–child) relationships are bound by a contract—a legally enforceable agreement—this contract is really only relevant when entering into family arrangements (marriage, adoption) or exiting them (separation, divorce, termination of parental rights). A contract "does not have the right concepts or language to treat love, trust, faithfulness, and sympathy, which more than any other terms describe the essentials of family" (p. 30).

Brinig (2000) proposes that the term *covenant* should replace the more traditional idea of the marriage contract:

Covenants are those agreements enforced not by law so much as by individuals and their social organizations. Though rich in religious provenance . . . "covenant" refers to the solemn vows that create and characterize the family. Enforcement stems from that solemnity and from the values of the family members. Thus, while some covenants draw power from religious values, today we find families whose covenants derive most of their power from the family members' mutual commitment to one another and to the preservation and protection of the family itself." (p. 1)

The covenant between husbands and wives implies unconditional love and permanence. Of course, such a covenant could exist between nonmarried partners too, but people in marriage covenants are also "bound not only to each other but also to some third party, to God or to the community or both" (Brinig, 2000, pp. 6–7). The covenant implies duties and obligations that reflect the needs of the wider community in a way that nonmarital relationships do not. For some individuals, marriage also involves a sacred covenant, one inspired by a divine being; cohabitation and nonmarital sexual relationships most certainly do not have this status.

Issue 5 discusses whether or not religious beliefs and practices strengthen families.

The Wedding Ceremony   One of the most obvious ways that legally married couples differ from others is that they have the option to engage in a public wedding ceremony. Although there are likely to be variations across social classes, religions, and racial or ethnic groups, the wedding ceremony usually includes some common roles, rituals, and images. Whether they're religious or secular, large or small, highly formal or relatively informal, traditional or alternative, a first marriage or a remarriage, most weddings involve:

- A supporting cast of formally clad bridesmaids, groomsmen, flower children, ring bearers, ushers, and musicians
- An authoritative figure—usually a justice of the peace or a clergy person—who pronounces the marriage valid and legal
- An audience of witnesses who are obligated to be supportive and cry when appropriate
- Children dressed in uncomfortable clothes who can't sit still
- The exchange of vows and rings between spouses and a kiss that seals the deal
- Some sort of celebratory reception afterward, typically with dancing, food, and alcohol
- A particular script for the reception that includes the best man's toast, the cutting of the cake (and the common "mashing of the cake into the new spouse's face to the laughs and cheers of onlookers"), the first dance "as husband and wife," the throwing of the bouquet and the flinging of the garter, the vandalizing of the bride and groom's car, and ultimately the couple's getaway

The symbolic importance of the wedding ceremony is undeniable:

[A] public wedding ceremony is a ritual in the sense that it is believed to transform the couple from what they previously were into an entity that is "totally other"—a wholly different and distinctive reality. At the time of their wedding, their kin and friends, along with the state and often the church or synagogue, bestow on the couple a type of approval, honor, and esteem that is unique and obtainable by no other discernible means. What is more, that esteem follows them beyond the wedding, because whenever they happen to make known their marital status, strangers immediately accord them the respect appropriately due that position (Scanzoni, 2000, p. 58).

Wedding ceremonies also reaffirm the heterosexual norm of society (discussed in more detail in Chapter 5). Sociologist Chrys Ingraham (1999) argues that weddings are a prime means by which the heterosexual standard is sustained: "Weddings are one of the major events that signal readiness and prepare heterosexuals for membership in marriage as an organized practice for the institution of heterosexuality" (p. 4).

Of course, couples who are barred from legally marrying (that is, same-sex couples) can also have public wedding ceremonies. And when they do, they tend to have the same reasons heterosexual couples do—so that friends and family members can bear witness to the couples' love and commitment and for spiritual or religious ratification (Haldeman, 1998). But unlike weddings of heterosexual couples, this ceremony is not recognized as legitimate by other social institutions.

The Honeymoon   The honeymoon is another cultural tradition that is uniquely linked to marriage, and more specifically, the wedding ceremony. Although the term *honeymoon* probably originated in the sixteenth century to refer to the couple's emotional state, its meaning today is universally understood as "a specified period of time in which the newlyweds exclude themselves from their social networks, engage in passionate and sexual behaviors, and establish themselves as an autonomous unit" (Bulcroft, Smeins, & Bulcroft, 1999, p. xiii). This particular conception of the honeymoon, as a romantic and secluded getaway, is a relatively new phenomenon, dating back only about 100 years (Bulcroft et al., 1999). Prior to that time, it was not uncommon for the entire wedding party to join the bride and groom in their bedroom after the wedding. Often the newlyweds were the object of pranks such as tying bells to the bed frame or nailing the door shut.

You might expect that increases in cohabitation and rates of premarital sex would render the honeymoon an obsolete social custom. But it continues to be a prominent feature of weddings. So what function does the honeymoon now serve? Perhaps most important, it provides newlyweds with a powerful opportunity to forge a new identity as a couple. This identity-building aspect of the honeymoon marks a significant transition for the couple and contributes to their ability to create a new, shared reality:

> The newlyweds begin their lives together as a process by which they select events to create a shared history and collective vision of their social world. Thus, the purchase of souvenirs or the documentation of the honeymoon through photographs or video provides the beginnings of this shared reality. Nowhere is the social construction of a collective identity more evident than in today's honeymoon homepages. These Web-based homepages provide a world even larger than the couple's immediate friends and family with a view of the marriage. . . . The homepages provide the opportunity to define and frame not only the honeymoon experience but the emerging identity as a couple." (Bulcroft et al., 1999, p. 5)

There simply is no comparable, publicly sanctioned ritual or opportunity afforded cohabitors or other unmarried couples.

The Institutionalized Nature of Marriage   Finally, one cannot ignore the fact that marriage is far more institutionalized than even the most serious cohabiting or dating relationships. Marriage is a patterned way of life that includes a set of commonly known roles, statuses, and expectations: "People know about it; they can describe it; and they have spent a lifetime learning how to react to it. The *idea* of marriage is larger than any individual marriage. The *role* of husband or wife is greater than any individual who takes on that role" (Blumstein & Schwartz, 1983, p. 318).

Despite its alleged state of disrepair and public concern with its disintegration, marriage remains the pinnacle of committed intimacy in the United States. It is the cultural standard against which all other types of intimate relationships are judged. For instance, the campaign to legally recognize permanent homosexual relationships is, in essence, a campaign to elevate those unions to the status of marriage.

Because marriage is an institutionalized form of intimacy, people can anticipate what it will be like long before they actually marry. There is no longer clear agreement on what it means to be a wife or husband, but as sociologist Steven Nock (1995) claims, "there are clearly traditional standards of propriety and decorum associated with one's relationships with married individuals" (p. 56). By contrast, what it means to be a "cohabiting" person is much less clear. Consider the fact that the English language lacks any term to describe one's cohabiting partner. "Significant other," "life partner," "lover," or "intimate roommate" just don't capture the nature of this type of relationship. In contrast, telling someone, "This is my spouse" —or "wife" or "husband" —immediately conveys a world of information about the couple's relationship and evokes a set of expectations on the part of others, whether or not the couple consciously attempts to live up to these expectations. Thus marriage

> is really a very public package of expectations about how two people should behave and about the benefits that help them fulfill these obligations: A wife should spend weekends with the family, not friends; a husband can give his pregnant wife (but not his pregnant sister) his insurance benefits; a man or a woman should put his spouse first before the demands of parents, friends, or other family members; married people should support each other financially as well as emotionally. (Waite & Gallagher, 2000, p. 20)

Another implication of living in a highly institutionalized relationship such as marriage is that it integrates one firmly within the social networks of other married couples. These networks, especially those between parents and adult children, can represent an important source of support for the couple. Cohabiting couples may receive less approval and support (emotional and economic) from family than do married couples, which can adversely impact the relationship (Nock, 1995).

The law provides further support for the institution of marriage. By contrast, cohabitors are in a position of "legal insecurity" (Seff, 1995), which can have long-term economic disadvantages. For instance, you may have relied on your partner for financial support for many years. However, if the relationship breaks up you may have no clear right to support payments (whereas a spouse would automatically be entitled to such support). You may also have no clear right to share in the assets your partner may have accumulated during your relationship (whereas in a marriage such assets would be considered community property). Likewise, if your partner becomes ill and unable to make medical decisions for him or herself, you have no legal right to make decisions for him or her. In these situations, married partners have greater opportunities to protect their financial assets.

The Marriage Benefit

If marriage, more than other types of intimate relationships, fosters a sense of meaning, generates greater social support, and provides greater legal protection, it seems reasonable to expect that marriage would have positive effects on the well-being of individuals. Indeed, research shows that for some people marriage is associated with a wide range of health and economic benefits.

However, it is important to note that individuals with more resources (for example, health and income) are more attractive as mates in the first place and are therefore more likely than those without such resources to marry. Hence it is difficult to determine whether marriage itself leads to these benefits or whether already advantaged individuals are more likely to be married. Although such a "selection bias" is clearly at work, some research has attempted to disentangle such effects and suggests that marriage does in fact offer an added bonus.

Health Benefits   Research has shown that married people experience fewer health problems than the unmarried. For example, sociologist Linda Waite (2000) followed a national sample of men and women over a 20-year period. She noted their marriages, divorces, and remarriages as well as their deaths and the deaths of their spouses. Waite found that married men and women faced lower risks of dying at any point than those who had never married or who experienced divorce.

Marriage apparently benefits physical health by reducing risky and unhealthy behaviors. For instance, married men are less likely to be problem drinkers than unmarried men (cited in Waite, 2000). Marriage also increases material well-being, leading to better medical care, better diet, and safer neighborhoods for married people.

Marriage also seems related to mental health. Research indicates that becoming married is associated with lower levels of depression, especially for those who believe in the desirability and importance of marriage. In contrast, separating and divorcing is associated with greater depression, especially for people who believe most strongly that marriage should be permanent (Simon & Marcussen, 1999).

One explanation for such findings is that good marriages provide people with a sense of being cared for, loved, and valued as a person. Having someone to confide in and to count on for understanding and help can serve as a buffer against emotional distress. But marriage itself may not be what creates psychological benefits; the quality of the relationship may be far more important. For instance, people in unhappy marriages experience greater psychological distress than those who are single or who are happily married (cited in Waite & Gallagher, 2000).

Despite the health benefits of marriage that have been documented, we're not recommending that everyone rush out and find a spouse. Marrying simply for the sake of marrying would undoubtedly result in a certain percentage of bad marriages, which would not confer many benefits on the partners. In fact, the long-range costs of bad marriages, to individuals and to society, especially if children are present, is likely to be tremendous. Moreover, the very characteristics that can make marriage rewarding—for example, privacy and the investment of emotions, resources, and time—are precisely those factors that can lead to violence in marriage (Gove et al., 1990). The key appears to be whether the relationship is supportive and interactions are positive. People in problematic and unsupportive marriages, characterized by neglect, conflict, or abuse, tend to experience greater psychological distress than those in more supportive marriages (Gove et al., 1990; Horwitz, McLaughlin, & White, 1997).

Economic Benefits   When the model Anna Nicole Smith, aged 27, married billionaire J. Howard Marshall II, aged 90, virtually everyone in the country assumed she married him for money. But Smith insisted otherwise: " 'I'm very much in love,' Smith told an interviewer, flashing her asteroid-size 22-carat engagement diamond and her diamond-dusted wedding band. . . . 'I could have married him four years ago if I'd just wanted to get rich' " (quoted in Ingraham, 1999, p. 109).

Of course, imagine how shocked you'd be if Smith, or any bride or groom to be, bluntly stated they were marrying for "money." People getting married today generally downplay the impact of marriage on their standard of living. In 1994, for instance, only 17 percent of adults interviewed for the General Social Survey agreed that the main advantage of marriage is financial security. People are more likely to view the benefits of marriage in terms of overall happiness, emotional security, and an improved sex life than in terms of an improved standard of living (South, 1992). Interestingly, however, economically disadvantaged groups (for example, Hispanic and black women) and older people seem to have a more realistic picture of the role that economics plays in a marriage.

But marriage in many other societies is also recognized openly as an economic arrangement, a contract between families. Marriages are important not because they are personally fulfilling to partners who are in love with each other but because they provide economic links between kin groups. In societies that have an elaborate and highly structured stratification system, such as India and Pakistan, a family's social status is extremely important in determining who is eligible to marry whom. Marriages are usually arranged from within the same caste, although the ideal situation is that the man's family be of slightly higher status than the woman's. Under such circumstances little thought is given to the desires or shared affections of the partners.

Although people raised in the United States tend to emphasize the importance of love rather than money and tend to resist the idea that marriage is economic in nature, marriage clearly has economic benefits. When you look at wealth among older couples—those who have had time to feel the economic effects of marriage—married individuals have significantly higher median incomes and net worth than older widowed, divorced, or never married adults (Seigel, 1993).

The economic benefit of marriage takes shape in a variety of ways (Wilmoth & Koso, 1997):

- The division of labor in marriages allows each spouse to specialize in specific skills and tasks. In time, this specialization can become efficient and productive.
- Married couples benefit because they can share resources, such as housing, food, and utilities, which minimizes the cost of living and provides insurance against unemployment or an unexpected illness.
- Marriage broadens social support systems and increases participation in other social institutions. Connections established in these activities can lead to additional opportunities and benefits.
- Married couples usually have access to benefits such as health or life insurance through a spouse's employment.

Marital status is also related to wages. Married men have higher incomes, educational attainments, and labor force attachments than unmarried men (Nock, 1998a). Some argue that these differences exist because married men are more productive and have spouses who can take over household tasks, freeing their time and energy for work. Marriage may also increase men's incentives to perform well at work so they can successfully meet their family obligations (Waite, 2000).

Another economic advantage relates to the fact that marriages tend to last longer than other types of relationships. In the early years of a relationship, cohabitors may not differ much from married couples in terms of combined earnings. In fact, women's earnings in the early years of a cohabiting relationship are much more likely to approximate their partners' and they are more likely to earn more than their partners do, compared to married women (Brines & Joyner, 1999). However, as couples age, the balance of economic benefits shifts in favor of married couples.

The Marriage "Problem"

Given these sorts of benefits, it's not surprising that many politicians and social scientists feel that stronger support for marriage could solve many of society's woes— including welfare dependency, the federal deficit, antisocial behavior, and public incivility (Flanders, 1996; Ingraham, 1999). Some recommend establishing a clear legal preference for married couples. For instance, sociologist Steven Nock (1999) suggests that states grant special economic benefits to couples who are willing to participate in premarital and marital counseling and who are willing to forgo the option of no-fault divorce.

Politicians have been working recently to increase the economic benefits of marriage. In 2000, Congress approved a bill easing what is often called the "marriage tax penalty." Up to this point a husband and wife who both worked and made similar incomes often would have to pay more in taxes than if they were single. This tax disadvantage wasn't noticeable when it was common for one spouse to work and the other to stay at home. But as more wives have entered the workforce and started earning salaries similar to men's, the number of married people paying more than their share of taxes has jumped. These days, about 21 million married couples pay on average an extra $1,380 in taxes a year, according to figures from the Congressional Budget Office ("Congress approves bill," 2000).

But not everyone believes that the future stability of society depends on strengthening the institution of marriage. Over the past few decades feminist sociologists have shown that marriage can burden women:

> Women are the marital partners responsible for a family's emotional intimacy, for adapting their sexual desires to their husbands', for monitoring the relationship and resolving conflict from a subordinate position, and for being as independent as possible without threatening their husbands' status. (Blaisure & Allen, 2000, p. 161)

They argue that the traditional structure of marriage has overwhelming emotional, psychological, and economic costs for women. Women may be more attracted to marriage than men, but they end up getting less out of it. Women experience more legal, social, and personal changes upon becoming wives than men do when they become husbands. Women still make more concessions and adjustments to their lives upon marriage than men do. For instance, married couples are more likely to relocate because of the husband's career than the wife's. And wives are more likely than husbands to leave the workforce upon the birth of a child. Consider also the common practice of wives giving up their last names when they marry. Even today, deviation from this norm can be met with hostility, as evident in the following letter to Ann Landers:

> Dear Ann: When our son married, he informed us he and his wife were going to use a hyphenated name: "John and Jane Smith-Jones." . . . My husband and I were very upset. Our name should be good enough for her by itself. I refuse to recognize my son's new name and have told him so. This has caused a rift in our relationship. . . . His wife is a control freak. (Landers, 1993)

Furthermore, because women are likely to marry men who are older than they are, have more education, and earn more money, their identity often becomes subordinate to their husbands'. In traditional marriages, wives tend to be known more for their husbands' accomplishments than for their own.

Is there any validity to the feminist arguments? Let's take a closer look at the marital benefits described earlier. For instance, the relationship between marital status and wages is different for women than it is for men and may even vary along racial lines. Childless black women, for example, earn substantially more if they're married than if they're single, but this advantage shrinks with each child they have. Among white married women, only those who are childless enjoy increased wages. Once white women become mothers, marriage actually decreases their earnings, because many mothers choose or are forced to reduce their hours at work (Blaisure & Allen, 2000).

And what about the psychological benefits of marriage? Two decades ago, sociologist Jessie Bernard (1982) made the startling claim that marriage was good for men but made women sick. She based her claim on research showing that men seem to enjoy greater health benefits than wives. Research on this topic continues to reveal that married women experience higher rates of mental and physical illness and distress than married men (Gove et al., 1990). Also, problems in the marriage affect women more than men (Horwitz et al., 1997), especially when only the man is employed (Barnett, Brennan, Raudenbush, & Marshall, 1994).

One explanation for the different effect that marriage has on men's and women's mental health concerns the types of roles women play in marriage and society (Gove, 1980). For instance, women's increased labor force participation has not been matched by men's increased involvement in the home (Hochschild & Machung, 1989). For the most part, women are expected to take primary responsibility for household work once they get married, even if they work full time outside the home (see Chapter 7 for more detail). Such a heavy burden, especially when women enter a marriage expecting that the division of labor will be more balanced, can lead to psychological distress. Indeed, wives experience less depression when their husbands contribute significantly around the house (Glass & Fujimoto, 1994).

Interestingly, economically independent women who remain unmarried may not necessarily forgo the noneconomic benefits of marriage. Research suggests that the health benefits that married women experience are often the result of their greater economic resources (provided by their husbands' income), which affords them safer living conditions, better health insurance plans, and so on (Lillard & Waite, 1995). Men, in contrast, appear to benefit from simply living with a spouse who encourages them to look after their own health needs.

Thus it might appear that marriage does have more benefits for men than for women, especially women who could be economically self-sufficient. Still, the majority of U.S. women and men find marriage to be a source of benefits unavailable anywhere else.

Conclusion

Marriage is a series of contradictions. It is both revered and ridiculed; it is considered by many to be the foundation of society, but it is also relentlessly criticized as weak and ineffectual. It is dynamic and changing in some ways but static and traditional in others; it is an intensely private relationship, but it is shaped by broad social forces such as the law, economics, religion, culture, and so forth. Many single men resist it, and many single women long for it, but men seem to benefit from it the most. It represents the summit of our romantic hopes, but also the pit of our intimate fears.

Clearly there is no fail-safe path to a successful marriage. It would be nice if we could end this chapter with a checklist of actions or beliefs that would guarantee a satisfying relationship. But no such list exists. For all marriage's popularity and commonality, for all the prior expectations people form about it, and for all the influence social and cultural forces have on it, each marriage must be constructed from scratch by the people involved.

At the same time, at this point in history people can't even agree whether marriage is a good or bad thing. Marriage rates are declining in the United States, but it seems as if marriage as an institution matters to Americans more than ever. Surely people who legally marry enjoy numerous benefits. So many, in fact, that politicians of all stripes continue to assume that marriage can be the solution to many of the most pressing individual and social problems. But others do just fine without marriage.

So one is left to ponder the question of whether people's need to feel connected to another person in an ongoing, committed relationship ought to be satisfied only in the context of a legally recognized marriage. Although more and more couples are exploring various types of living arrangements such as cohabitation, most still want some kind of formal recognition of their love for each other. This is not surprising in a society such as this, which values romance so highly and continues to privilege marriage above all other relationships. Perhaps, in addition to "strengthening" marriage, this society should also focus on increasing the socioeconomic and psychological well-being of cohabitors and individuals who do not or cannot enjoy the benefits of marriage.

Chapter Highlights

- Mate selection is strongly influenced by cultural rules of endogamy and exogamy. Although people are not supposed to marry close relatives, they tend to find partners among people of the same religion, social class, and race and ethnicity.
- Although modern relationships are more flexible than ever before, they are still governed by expectations of interdependence, equity, commitment, permanence, sexual access, and sexual exclusivity. Couples still feel pressured to be "coupled" —that is, to act and think like a couple.
- To some degree, each relationship is unique and is characterized by a private culture that arises from a couple's interactions and communication. But social forces always influence these interactions, even the most personal and private ones, such as communication and sex.
- Power, a part of all intimate relationships, is reflected in couples' communication and interactions. Despite women's increased economic role intimate relationships, men continue to have more power.
- Cohabitation and marriage vary in several important ways. The institutionalized nature of marriage appears to bestow both health and economic benefits on many individuals.

Your Turn

For any intimate relationship to survive, couples must communicate frequently and openly about a wide range of issues and concerns. But couple communication involves much more than simply negotiating schedules and expressing one's feelings. Communication in intimate relationships also contains underlying messages about respect, authority, and power.

To explore this "hidden language" in couple communication, ask any two couples you know to tape-record their conversation for 30 minutes. Try to choose two different types of couples (for instance, dating along with married or cohabiting, heterosexual along with homosexual, affluent along with working class, dual earner along with single earner). Ask them to choose a time when they're likely to be engaged in a casual discussion about their day—for example, when they're making or eating dinner together—and to simply leave the recorder running. Assure them that it's fine if they are not talking about anything really important. It's best, in fact, if they are simply conversing about the mundane aspects of their days.

Listen to each tape, and record the following data for each person. You will probably have to listen several times to each conversation to pick up on these details, to which you would usually pay no conscious attention.

- How many questions did each partner ask?
- How many times did each partner not answer a question?
- How many times did each partner interrupt the other?
- How many "modifiers" (for example, "sort of," "I guess") did each partner use?
- How many tag questions (for example, "You had a busy day, *didn't you*?") did each partner use?
- How many times did each partner change the topic of the conversation?

Next, answer the following questions about each couple's interaction:

- Who, if anyone, tended to do more "interaction work" (that is, tried to keep the conversation going)?
- Who, if anyone, tended to ignore the other person more?
- Who, if anyone, tended to be more silent in the conversation?

Compare your results to those of other students in the class. Consider what you know about these couples (for instance, do they both work outside the home? Have they been together a long time?). Look for the following patterns in your data.

- Do men or women tend to do more interaction work, ask more questions, use more modifiers and tag questions?
- Do men or women tend to not answer questions, ignore their partners, use more silence, interrupt and change the topic more?
- Do communication patterns differ when both partners work outside the home versus when one does and the other doesn't?
- Are the patterns observed among heterosexual couples different from those of same-sex couples?
- Are the patterns observed among dating couples different from those of cohabiting or married couples?
- Do you notice any variations among couples of different social classes or racial/ethnic groups?

Discuss how consistent your data are with findings discussed in this chapter. What might account for any differences? Reflect on what you've learned about couple communication through this exercise. Did anything surprise you? How do you think your own communication is influenced by your gender, status, race, and so on?

Work Life and Family Life

When Home Is Work and Work Is Home

For most couples these days, both partners are likely to work in the paid labor force. In fact, people are putting in longer hours on the job than ever before. As a result, the boundary between home life and work life can sometimes become blurry.

The demands of work can especially overload parents and put strains on their relationships with their children. Small children simply aren't capable of suppressing their needs for the sake of their parents' convenience. When needs conflict, frustration and tantrums can ensue.

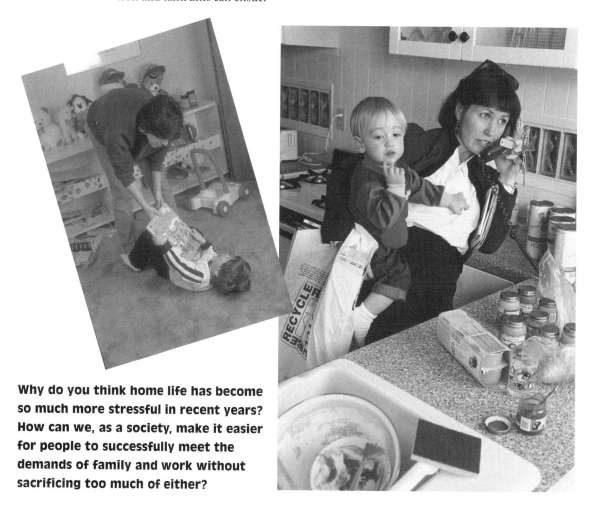

Why do you think home life has become so much more stressful in recent years? How can we, as a society, make it easier for people to successfully meet the demands of family and work without sacrificing too much of either?

Because more and more parents are struggling to juggle their work and family obligations, many employers now offer services to lighten their employees' burden. Some offer on-site child care facilities; others offer flexible schedules that allow parents to work out of their own homes.

Giving workers access to workplace day care facilities and the option of working at home are typically presented as positive, family-friendly workplace innovations because they allow people to spend more time with their families. However, can you see some possible problems in such arrangements?

Ironically, while the home is becoming a more harried place, the workplace is becoming more nurturing and personally satisfying. For many people, working late has become an opportunity not only to catch up with work but also to put off confronting the stresses of home life. Working overtime is especially easy to do when the emotional ties to those at home don't seem as strong or as attractive as the emotional ties to work associates.

Not surprisingly, many people report that their jobs provide them with a sense of personal growth and achievement, offer them opportunities to develop close friendships, and perhaps even give them a feeling of having a "second family" with whom to share their leisure time.

How might the combination of a more stressful home life and a more nurturing workplace influence people's expectations about their family lives?

What impact might these developments have on marriage? On the bearing and rearing of children?

Over 40 years ago a 14-year-old Albanian woman named Sema Brahimi decided to become a man. Sema's father had recently died, leaving a widow, four daughters, and an infant son to survive on their own. In Albania's heavily male-dominated society, such a task would have been hard enough. But in the isolated, mountainous, rural area in which the family lived, it was inconceivable that they could run a household without a man in charge. So Sema, the eldest daughter, decided to take the job (Demick, 1996).

She cut her hair short, put on men's clothes, and went to work in the fields. She changed her name from Sema to Selman (the masculine equivalent). Her mother and siblings began to use male pronouns when they referred to her. Gradually Selman assumed responsibility for tending the family's crops and making the regular 3-hour trips by mule to the nearest city to sell them. Later on, as the head of the household, Selman took responsibility for selecting a wife for her brother and wore a suit and tie to his wedding, taking the role of father of the groom.

Looking back on the decision, Selman, now in her late 50s, has no regrets:

> I've lived my whole life as a man. I've got the habits of a man. . . . If anyone has a problem with it, I've got my gun to deal with them. . . . Until I was 18 to 20, I had proposals of marriage. My brother was old enough to work, and my mother said that I should follow the fate of my sisters and get married. But once something is decided, you can't undo it, and I already thought of myself as a man. . . . I've had to work very hard to earn bread for the family and to be honest and correct in my relations with others. But, no, I have never regretted the decision. I've not had a bad life as a man. (Demick, 1996, p. C8)

Interestingly, nobody else has had a problem with Selman's choice either. Selman has long been accepted by men in the village as a man among equals.

Selman's family has benefited from her decision to live as a man, but arguably, she herself has been better off too. Under local law, women have few legal protections. They can be beaten or chained if they disobey their husbands and have no property or inheritance rights whatsoever. The only path to self-determination is to assume the life of a man. In fact, this practice is actually part of an age-old tradition. The folklore of northern Albania is filled with stories of women who took an oath never to marry so they could fill voids left by a shortage of males. As "men" they often became fierce warriors and village leaders.

All societies have clear conceptions about what men and women are obligated to do or what they're entitled to, particularly when it comes to meeting the financial needs of the family. Gender and economics are tightly intertwined. In her male-dominated society, the only way Selman could support her mother and siblings and acquire some degree of authority in her community was to "become" a man.

In U.S. society today, the traditional barriers to financial stability are no longer as impenetrable as they once were. However, earning capacity and professional credibility have always been linked in some way to gender. In the past, women had few opportunities to enter prestigious occupations, own property, or be financially independent. And U.S. women still lag behind men economically and politically and continue to encounter frustrating cultural barriers and closed doors.

American women don't have to "become" men in the literal sense that Selman did, but they have nonetheless attained economic stability and social power only by drifting away from their traditional family roles and entering historically male realms of occupational life. In the 1996 film *The Associate*, Whoopi Goldberg plays a bright Wall Street stock analyst whose insightful ideas are repeatedly trivialized because she's a woman. So she quits her job in disgust, opens her own firm, and creates a fictitious, invisible male partner to whom she gives credit for all her best ideas. Her business thrives, and "he" soon becomes one of the best-known, most successful advisers on Wall Street. The message of the film is clear and not all that different from that conveyed by the experience of the young Sema Brahimi halfway across the world: It's easier to achieve economic power as a man than as a woman.

In this chapter we examine the ways that the different work experiences of U.S. women and men, both inside and outside the home, influence family life. The intersection of work and family is centrally important in a society, such as that of the United States, where both men and women are expected to make an economic contribution.

Two Worlds: Work and Family

Up until the mid-nineteenth century, the nation's economy was primarily agricultural. People's lives centered around the farm, where husbands and wives were partners not only in making a home but in making a living (Vanek, 1980). The word *housework*—distinct from work done in other places—was not even part of the language. Research suggests that men and women performed different tasks, to be sure. But they worked together:

> In the division of responsibility, women got the bulk of internal domestic chores. Normally, they took care of the house—including the preparation of food, cloth, candles and soap—and supervised farm animals and kitchen garden, while husbands did the plowing, planting, and harvesting. Yet interaction never stopped. Husbands helped at the spinning and weaving when farm work was done. In the southern colonies, wives hoed and female servants worked in the fields. Male apprentices often found themselves doing household chores. Female servants spent as much time in the workshop as in the household. Mothers taught young children their letters, while fathers tended to take over the educational process as offspring grew older. Wives routinely developed competency in their husband's [sic] businesses; they could and did inherit them when death demanded it. (Kessler-Harris, 1982, p. 7)

With the advent of industrialization, though, things began to change. New forms of technology and the promise of new financial opportunities and a good living drew people away from the farms and into cities and factories where they could earn wages for their work. Many of the first factory workers were actually women. Sociologist Linda Haas (1995) suggests that as factory work came to be seen less as a peripheral activity and more as the primary feature of the new economy, men took control of this new source of income, power, and prestige. For the first time in U.S. history, the family economy was based outside the household, and the majority of families depended on wage labor for their financial support. Instead of being self-sufficient, people now operated under the rules and regulations of factory owners, who were likely to believe that family responsibilities were incompatible with productivity (Glass, 2000).

So industrialization relieved men of many of their domestic duties. And women no longer found themselves involved in the day-to-day supervision of the family's business as they had once been. Instead, they were consigned to menial and powerless positions in the workforce and the only domestic responsibilities that remained: caring for and nurturing children and running the household. Because this work was low-paid or unpaid and because visible goods were no longer being produced at home, women's work was devalued in the emerging industrial economy (Hareven, 1992).

Looking at these changes from men's point of view, one can see that industrialization had a profound effect on their lives too. Researchers have estimated that in hunting and gathering societies, men provided only about a fifth of the resources needed for their family's subsistence (Boulding, 1976). In colonial times, as well, women were instrumental in providing for their families. They ran inns and taverns, managed shops and stores, and sometimes even worked in the fields (Bernard, 1981). The common notion of men as "primary breadwinners" or "good providers" emerged around the 1830s with the rise of the market-based industrial economy. Men became almost solely responsible, at least in the eyes of the community, for their family's economic well-being. Men were judged by their family's prosperity. Men's presumed "primary breadwinner" role didn't "officially" end until 1980, when the U.S. Bureau of the Census stopped automatically assuming that the head of the household is male (Bernard, 1981).

The Ideology of Separate Spheres

In the first decades of industrialization, the divergence between men's and women's labor resulted in the ideology of **separate spheres**. It promoted the idea that women's place is in the home (the *private sphere*) and men's is in the work world outside the home (the *public sphere*). This ideal fostered the belief that men and women are naturally predisposed to different pursuits. Women were assumed to be inherently nurturing, demure, and sacrificial—a perfect fit for their restricted domestic roles. Women's "natural" weakness and frailty were assumed to make them ill suited to the dog-eat-dog life of the competitive labor force and to justify their limited job opportunities. The ideal image of men, in contrast, was that of the rugged individual whose virtue came from self-reliance, power, and mastery of his job and family. Men were thought to be naturally strict, aggressive, calculating, rational, and bold—a perfect fit for the demands of the marketplace.

For women in the nineteenth century, this ideology gave rise to what has been labeled the "cult of true womanhood." For a woman to be truly feminine or womanly, she had to devote herself to home and family. Thus, the ideal, glorified role for women focused entirely on the more limited and less socially valued domestic role. In addition to caring for the home, women came to be seen as primarily responsible for child rearing.

The unpaid work that most women did in the home was accorded little social value. This devaluation reflected the difference in power between the public and private spheres (Sidel, 1990). As long as men controlled the public sphere, they could wield greater economic and political power within society and translate that power into authority at home.

Discounting Women's Work in Industrial Society   The reality of U.S. family life has never quite fit the image painted by the ideology of separate spheres. Even in the late nineteenth century, well after the advent of industrialization, men weren't the only ones who left their homes each day to work in factories. Many children worked long hours to help support their families. At the turn of the century, for example, 120,000 children—some as young as 11—worked in Pennsylvania coal mines and factories; and children made up close to one-quarter of all workers in southern textile mills (Coontz, 1992).

Many women, too, entered the industrial labor force. By 1900, one-fifth of U.S. women worked outside the home (Staggenborg, 1998). But the experiences of working women var-

As discussed in Issue 2, these historical facts conflict with cherished and nostalgic images of what family life was like in the past.

ied along class and race lines. For middle- and upper-class white women, few professions other than teaching and nursing were available, and these jobs paid poorly. Most entered and exited the labor force in response to family demands or took up volunteer work to fill up their free time.

In contrast, poor women worked mostly in unskilled jobs in clothing factories, canning plants, or other industries where working conditions were often dangerous and exploitative. Female factory workers often faced an exhausting pace of work and serious health risks, sometimes for 14 hours a day. Some were forced to pay "rental fees" for the machines and equipment they used on the job (Staggenborg, 1998).

Conditions for women of color were especially bad. Black domestic servants, for instance, were often forced to leave their own families and live in their employer's home, where they were expected to work around the clock. But most had little choice. Throughout history, black women have rarely had the luxury of being stay-at-home spouses and parents. In 1880, 73 percent of black single women and 35 percent of black married women reported holding paid jobs. Only 23 percent of white single women and 7 percent of white married women reported being in the paid labor force at that time (cited in Kessler-Harris, 1982).

Immigrant women, especially from southern and eastern Europe, rarely worked outside the home and would therefore seem to support the ideal of separate spheres. However, they often contributed significantly to the family income by taking in boarders, sewing, making paper flowers and cigars, or taking on a variety of other money-earning tasks that could be done in the home. Italian men routinely employed their wives and sisters as helpers, although they weren't officially considered employees.

Thus, women of color and poor white women were excluded from the "cult of true womanhood." Ironically, the privileged, upper-class women who could afford to embrace this ideology were able to do so only because they depended on other women—servants—to do much of the household labor (Boydston, 2001).

Despite these discrepancies, the ideologies of separate spheres and the cult of true womanhood became powerful forces. Their imagery was used to justify restrictions on women's involvement in economic and political activity and men's lack of involvement in family and community. Because domestic work was considered incompatible with wage labor and factory productivity, the majority of women were excluded from full participation in the emerging industrial economy. Those who did work outside the home were paid significantly less than men and were confined to "female" jobs (Cowan, 1987).

The ideology of separate spheres became a powerful force in society by developing appealing imagery to justify its restrictions on women. For instance, belief in separate spheres made Mother's Day the popular national holiday it is today. Most people, when they think of Mother's Day, think of a day for celebrating each mother's devotion to her own family. However, a look at history reveals quite a different story.

The original proposal for a day for mothers occurred in 1858. Mothers' (plural) Day was intended to celebrate women's roles as community organizers and activists. It was meant to honor women who acted on behalf of the entire generation of children, not just their own (Coontz, 1992). Some time later, Mothers' Day became a vehicle for organized social and political action by all mothers.

But the eventual adoption of Mother's (singular) Day by Congress in 1914 represented a reversal of everything that the nineteenth-century mothers' days stood for. Politicians began making speeches linking Mother's Day to domestic life. They repudiated mothers' roles outside the household. Merchants hung testimonials to their own mothers in stores, hoping to entice others to buy things for their mothers. What was once an occasion for supporting activism and controversial causes in the community was reduced to an occasion for political posturing and marketing, all pushing the image of mother as a domestic servant to her family.

The doctrine of separate spheres has been weakened from time to time by larger historical, political, and economic needs. During World War II, for example, the government initiated a massive public relations program designed to lure women out of their homes and into factories where they would take up the productive work of men who had gone off to fight in the war. Government motivational films depicted child care centers as nurturing environments where children would flourish while their mothers worked, and in 1942 the Lanham Act was passed, allowing the federal government to establish and fund child care centers. Between 1940 and 1945 the female labor force increased by over 50 percent. Three-fourths of these new workers were married, and a majority had children (Coontz, 1992).

After the war ended, however, the message was very different. Women were encouraged to return to their "natural" domestic roles. Child care centers were now depicted as horrible, dangerous places. Working mothers were labeled as selfish and irresponsible. Practically overnight, the political atmosphere had changed and with it the perception of women's appropriate place in the family and in the economy. Although many women remained in the labor force, especially those who had moved into high-paying jobs during the war, others quit their jobs or were laid off (Kessler-Harris, 1982). Those who quit, not surprisingly, tended to be young married women, many of whom were, or were soon to be, young mothers.

The years right after the war represented the heyday of the separate spheres ideology. Media messages heavily emphasized women's obligations to take their rightful position on the domestic front. Men began to pursue advanced educational opportunities during this period, but few women entered college. Of those who did, two out of three dropped out before graduating. Most women left because they feared that a college education would hurt their marriage chances (Mintz & Kellogg, 1988) or because they had already married and chose to abandon their educational pursuits to turn their attention to raising a family (Weiss, 2000). The ideology of separate spheres had returned in full force.

Taking Stock of Separate Spheres Today   Since the 1950s, the boundary separating men's and women's spheres has steadily eroded. Prior to 1960, about a third of female high school graduates enrolled in college (compared to over 50 percent of male graduates). By 1998, the percentage of women going to college was 69 percent, higher than the percentage of men (62 percent) (U.S. Bureau of the Census, 2000b). In 1950 a little over 30 percent of adult women were in the paid labor force; today, over 60 percent of all women over age 18 work in the paid labor force (U.S. Bureau of the Census, 2000b). At the same time, men's labor force participation has declined from about 87 percent of all men in 1950 to a little over 70 percent today. About 46 percent of all people in the paid labor force today are women, compared to a little under 32 percent in 1950. Furthermore, 62 percent of married mothers and 68 percent of single mothers with children under 6 are employed (Beeghley, 1996; Reskin & Padavic, 1994; U.S. Bureau of the Census, 2000b).

Yet despite these trends, the separate spheres ideology still exists. For instance, when we examine the percentage of women employed full time, year round, differences in gender expectations become apparent. Only about 35 percent of married women with young children worked full time, year round in 1998 (Cohen & Bianchi, 1999). Thus, women's labor force decisions appear grounded in a slightly evolved separate spheres ideology: It's appropriate for women to work outside the home, but they are still primarily responsible for child rearing.

In addition, many Americans still perceive domestic work as women's sphere and outside employment as men's sphere:

> Few Americans admit that job discrimination against women is acceptable, yet most feel uncomfortable when confronted with a female mechanic or a CEO in a dress. . . . When it comes to marriage and family life, Americans are even more ambivalent about women's roles, wanting them to be generous self-sacrificing mothers even if they are also expected to be dedicated professionals. Although women are encouraged to go to college and pursue their careers as never before, they are still held accountable for what was once called "women's work." If their houses are a mess, or if their children are unkempt, women . . . are still subject to blame. . . . Although eight out of ten Americans believe it is OK for women to work, half still think that men should be the real breadwinners. Americans want fathers to be more involved with their children, but most feel uncomfortable if a man takes time off work "just" to be with his kids. (Coltrane, 1996a, p. 26)

In some corners of U.S. society, calls can still be heard for a return to the traditional division of labor between male breadwinner and female homemaker. But how likely is it that vast numbers of U.S. women will willingly withdraw from paid employment and happily return to the domestic sphere? A growing number of women are now the primary source of financial support in their families. And it isn't just money that motivates them. One national poll found that only about a third of working women said they'd prefer to stay home rather than work even if money were no object; they value the respect, esteem, and friendship networks their jobs provide (cited in Coontz, 1997). Women are just as likely as men to feel successful in their work lives and their family lives, as well as in balancing the two (see Exhibit 7.1).

Issue 2 examines whether or not mothers' employment outside the home has harmful effects on their families.

EXHIBIT 7.1

Success in Family Life and Work Life

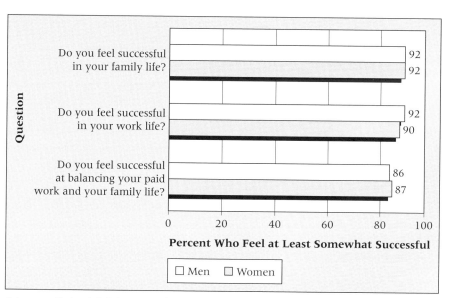

Data source: National Opinion Research Center. 1998. *General Social Survey, 1972–1998.* Available at www.icpsr.umich.edu/GSS/. Accessed June 1, 2001.

DEMO•GRAPHICS

Separate Spheres or Equal Spheres?

The ideology of separate spheres continues to shape family life as it has for over 150 years. But the ways in which this gender ideology is played out in contemporary families is neither simple nor straightforward.

Judging from the labor force participation rates shown in Exhibit 7.2a, one could convincingly argue that the ideology of separate spheres is dead. Over the past 40 years, the labor force participation rates of women have steadily increased, whereas the rates for men have decreased. Currently, as many married women with children between 6 and 17 are in the labor force as married men (77 percent for both). Note that married men with children ages 6–17 still have a higher labor force participation rate (about 92 percent) than similar women (U.S Bureau of the Census, 2000a). Even so, the notion that men are solely responsible for supporting their families financially is a thing of the past.

But responsibility for economic breadwinning is only half the separate spheres story. The other half, of course, concerns responsibility for what happens in the domestic world: housekeeping and child care responsibilities. For the 1994 General Social Survey, researchers asked married couples who was responsible for certain chores around the house. As you can see in Exhibit 7.2b, housekeeping chores are clearly gendered, with women doing most of the housekeeping and caretaking. The one area where men outperform women is in doing small repairs around the house.

An interesting statistic hidden in Exhibit 7.2b is the exceedingly low percentage of families who hire others to help with housekeeping. Many dual-earner families could afford to hire someone to do some of the laundry, shopping, and housekeeping, yet very few families do. This finding reflects another dimension of the separate spheres mentality. Not only is it women's responsibility to care for the home—regardless of her other work activities—but such labor is expected to stay within the family. This expectation reinforces the idea that housework is not really work and therefore does not deserve to be paid.

Perhaps the most important indicator that the separate spheres ideology persists shows up in data on how women and men feel about the unequal division of labor. If women and men perceive their work arrangements to be unfair, it could be argued that the ideology—if not the reality—of separate spheres, is defunct. But as you can see in Exhibit 7.2c, the vast majority of women and men state that the division of labor in their households is fair.

Together, the statistics depicted here reveal a lingering but contradictory separate spheres ideology. Clearly, the revolution in women's labor force participation has not been countered by a revolution in men's domestic contributions. The perception that this division of labor is fair and equitable are powerful reminders that women's primary place is still thought to be in the home.

Thinking Critically About the Statistics

1. Why do you think married women with children have higher labor force participation rates than do married women in general? What factors other than children's age might help explain variations in labor force participation rates for men and women? Consider especially how race and childbearing experiences might affect labor force participation rates.

EXHIBIT 7.2

The Division of Labor in U.S. Families

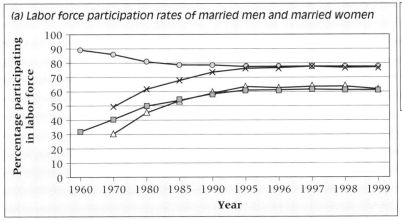

(a) Labor force participation rates of married men and married women

- ○ All married men
- ■ All married women
- △ Married women with children under age 6
- ✻ Married women with children under age 6–17

Data source: U.S. Census Bureau. 2000b. *Statistical Abstract of the United States: 2000,* Tables 651 and 653. Washington, DC: U.S. Government Printing Office.

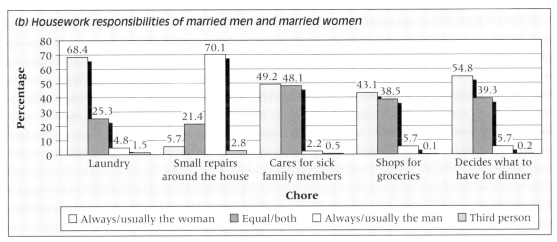

(b) Housework responsibilities of married men and married women

□ Always/usually the woman   ■ Equal/both   □ Always/usually the man   ▦ Third person

Data source: National Opinion Research Center. 1998. *General Social Survey, 1972–1998.* Available at www.icpsr.umich.edu/GSS/. Accessed June 1, 2001.

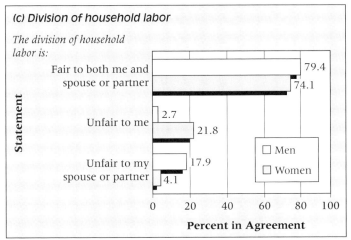

(c) Division of household labor

The division of household labor is:

Fair to both me and spouse or partner — 79.4 / 74.1

Unfair to me — 2.7 / 21.8

Unfair to my spouse or partner — 17.9 / 4.1

□ Men
□ Women

Percent in Agreement

Data source: National Opinion Research Center. 1998. *General Social Survey, 1972–1998.* Available at www.icpsr.umich.edu/GSS/. Accessed June 1, 2001.

2. As you can see in Exhibit 7.2a, the U.S. Bureau of the Census breaks down statistics on the employment status of women by the presence and age of children. But it provides no comparable statistics for men. Why not? What does such a discrepancy indicate about gendered work expectations in this society?

3. Note in Exhibit 7.2b that the household chore with the highest percentage of "equal" or "both" responses is caring for sick family members. Reflect on your own experience when someone in the family is ill. What happens when the primary caretaker—usually the mother—becomes ill? Who cares for this person? Does anyone take over the other chores during this person's convalescence? How might these caretaking practices explain why men gain greater health benefits from marriage than women do, as discussed in Chapter 6?

4. Look at the significant difference in the length of the bars in Exhibit 7.2c. Why do you think so many husbands and wives perceive the division of household labor to be fair? Can you think of some factors that might alter these perceptions?

5. Check the source notes for Exhibits 7.2a, 7.2b, and 7.2c. It is no coincidence that the data on household labor shown here come from the General Social Survey (an ongoing academic project) and the labor force participation data come from the U.S. Census (a government project). The U.S. Bureau of the Census keeps highly detailed accounts of labor force participation but no data on housework. Why not? What message does this statistical focus convey about the importance of paid versus unpaid work?   ■

Gender Ideology in the Workplace

Although women and men are now both in the workplace, traditional gender ideologies still affect their experiences there. As discussed in Chapter 2, gender ideologies are the ways people identify themselves regarding the work, marital, and family roles that are traditionally linked to gender (Greenstein, 1996b). Gender ideology is what distinguishes the man who believes that breadwinning is "men's work" and housework is "women's work" from the man who believes that "being male" means sharing breadwinning responsibility and cooperating with household chores. Employers as well as the public at large still believe women and men are naturally inclined to behave in a certain way in the workplace and to do certain jobs in the paid labor force (Reskin & Hartmann, 1986). Those beliefs translate into unequal rewards for women and men who work outside the home.

Discrimination Built into the System   Think for a moment about what you must do to be considered a good worker by your boss. Obviously you must show competence and a deep, serious commitment to the company. But how do you show you're committed to the job? You'd have to show a willingness to work extra hours, travel to faraway business meetings or professional conferences, attend special training programs, work unpopular shifts, entertain out-of-town clients on weekends, relocate if necessary, and so on. Although this job description is not gendered by definition—women or men could perform these tasks—when work is structured in this way women find it much harder than men to conform to the "ideal worker" mold (Williams, 2000). Because women, especially mothers, still tend to have the lion's share of responsibility at home, they have more difficulty making time for these activities and therefore are less able to demonstrate to their bosses that they are good, committed employees. By hiring, rewarding, and promoting those workers who successfully separate work from family responsibilities, most workplaces operate as if the model of male provider and female homemaker was still the norm (Acker, 1989).

Assumptions about what constitutes an "ideal" worker can run deep. Imagine for a moment that you're a boss who's just been told that your most valuable employee, Chris, is engaged to be married. How will you respond?

If Chris is a man, chances are his impending marriage will be seen as a "stabilizing" influence. His carefree days of bachelorhood will soon give way to the serious responsibilities of family life. Job security will now be extremely important to him, perhaps making him an even more committed and dependable worker. He might even need a raise, because fatherhood is probably looming not far down the road. You'd be unlikely to think that these new family responsibilities will somehow prevent Chris from devoting himself entirely to his job. For instance, if his new wife has a job in another town, it's probably unlikely that Chris will give up his job and relocate so she can pursue her career. On the contrary, family obligations will likely motivate him to work even harder and longer so he can support his family.

Now suppose Chris is a woman. How might your response to the nuptial news change? Chances are that the impending marriage will now be seen as a potential impediment to career mobility. You might begin to question whether she'll be able to remain fully committed to the job. Will she move if her husband finds a good job somewhere else? Perhaps you begin to wonder how long it will be before Chris becomes pregnant and seeks maternity leave or quits altogether. Rather than marriage making her a more dependable worker, you may fear that it may actually make her less dependable, less stable, and less invested in the company.

In the real-life workplace, these gender-based expectations can play a decisive role in hiring and promotion decisions (Reskin & Hartmann, 1986). Even an "ideal worker" might be discriminated against by an employer who assumes that she will be less productive because of her family responsibilities or will become pregnant and quit work.

Not surprisingly, about 90 percent of male executives but only 35 percent of female executives have children by the time they turn 40 (cited in Schwartz, 1989). Furthermore, married men earn 10–40 percent more than single men (Waite & Gallagher, 2000). These differences are not necessarily the result of outright sexism and overt discrimination but a more subtle consequence of a pervasive ideology that underlies beliefs about gender, family, and the workplace.

The Wage Gap   In addition to facing restrictions on the sorts of jobs they are expected to be able to fill, women still also face disadvantages when it comes to wages, promotions, and authority (Reskin & Padavic, 1994). In particular, U.S. women still face a **wage gap**: Their earning power—and thus their ability to financially support their families—lags behind men's. In 1998, the average earnings for all U.S. men working full time, year-round was $35,345. All women working full time, year-round earned an average salary of $25,362 per year (National Committee on Pay Equity, 1999). To put it another way, for every dollar a U.S. white man earns, a woman still earns only about 73 cents. The differences are even more pronounced for African-American women, who earn 63 cents for every dollar a white man earns, and Hispanic women, who earn just 53 cents. In addition, 61 percent of employed women have little or no ability to advance in their jobs, 40 percent of those over 55 have no pension plan, and 34 percent have no health insurance through their jobs ("Working women's woes," 1994).

These figures are clearly an improvement over past wage differences (see Exhibit 7.3). In 1973, for instance, all women earned only 56.6 cents for every dollar a man earned. Advances in work experience and job-related skills have enabled some women—particularly middle- and upper-class women—to improve their income levels relative to men's.

EXHIBIT 7.3

Trends in Earnings for Female and Male Year-Round, Full-Time Workers

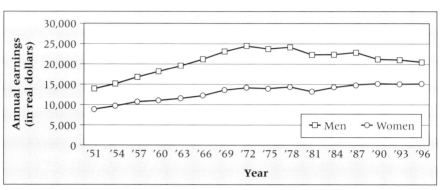

Data source: I. Castro, 1998. *Equal Pay: A Thirty-Five-Year Perspective*, Table 1. U.S. Department of Labor. Available at www.dol.gov/dol/wb/. Accessed June 1, 2001.

However, some sociologists argue that the wage gap has narrowed somewhat, not because women's earning power has improved but because men's has worsened (Bernhardt, Morris, & Handcock, 1995). Also, the discrepancy between men's pay and women's pay has proved remarkably resilient over the years, despite the 1963 Equal Pay Act, which guaranteed equal pay for equal work, and Title VII of the 1964 Civil Rights Act, which banned job discrimination on the basis of sex (as well as race, religion, and national origin).

Mothers are particularly susceptible to wage penalties. One study that charted the work experiences of over 5,000 women over a 10-year period found that mothers see wages reduced by 7 percent per child (Budig & England, 2001). The penalties are larger for married mothers than for unmarried mothers. The researchers concluded that only about one-third of this penalty is attributable to deficiencies in past work experience or lack of seniority. They suggest that the bulk of the penalty results from the effects of motherhood on productivity or employer discrimination. Research consistently shows that mothers earn lower wages than women without children. The "wage penalty" for working mothers doesn't disappear even when different levels of work experience are taken into consideration (Waldfogel, 1997).

Note that the wage gap is not an exclusively U.S. phenomenon. To varying degrees in every country around the world, men earn more than women. In the developing countries of Latin American, Africa, and Asia, a typical unskilled female worker is likely to earn three or four times less than what a skilled male worker would earn (Tiano, 1987). In other countries, however, such as France, Sweden, Australia, and Denmark, the wage gap is narrower than here, with women earning 80 to 90 percent of what men earn (Reskin & Padavic, 1994).

Why does the U.S. wage gap continue to exist? Some economists and policymakers argue that the wage gap is an institutional by-product of men's generally higher levels of work experience, training, and education. The U.S. Bureau of the Census, however, reports that gender differences in education, labor force experience, and seniority—factors that might justify discrepancies in salary—account for less than 15 percent of the wage gap between men and women (cited in National Committee on Pay Equity, 1995). For instance, the average income of full-time female workers in the United States is significantly lower than men's with the same level of education or training. In fact, women with a bachelor's degree can expect to earn only slightly more than men who ended their education with a high school diploma (see Exhibit 7.4). And whereas men with professional degrees earn the

EXHIBIT 7.4

*Education
and Income
for Women
and Men*

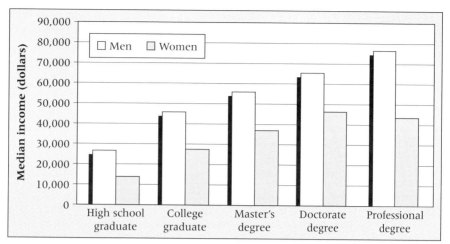

Data source: U.S. Bureau of the Census. 2000b. *Statistical Abstract of the United States, 2000,* Table 750. Washington, DC: U.S. Government Printing Office.

highest median incomes overall, women with professional degrees actually earn less than men with bachelor's degrees (U.S. Bureau of the Census, 2000b). Hence, the continuing gap seems to have little to do with men's and women's different abilities or credentials.

A more likely reason for the wage gap is the types of jobs women typically have. It is true that in the United States, women have made remarkable progress in overcoming traditional obstacles to employment. The increase in female labor force participation has been particularly dramatic in such male-dominated fields as medicine, law, and administration. In 1983, for instance, 15 percent of lawyers in the United States were women; by 1999, the figure had increased to 29 percent. Women now make up the majority of students in law school (cited in Glater, 2001). During that same period, the proportion of female physicians increased from 16 percent to 24.5 percent (U.S. Bureau of the Census, 2000b). In addition, 36 percent of all U.S. businesses are owned by women (U.S. Bureau of the Census, 2000b).

But segregation in the workplace on the basis of gender is still the rule and not the exception. The majority of employed women work in jobs that are extensions of their traditional family roles. According to the U.S. Bureau of the Census (2000b), women constitute 99 percent of all secretaries, 93 percent of all registered nurses, 97 percent of all child care workers, 99 percent of all dental hygienists, and 75 percent of all teachers, excluding those in colleges and universities. Despite their increased presence in traditionally male occupations, women still account for only 17 percent of all dentists, 25 percent of all physicians, 11 percent of all engineers, 29 percent of all lawyers and judges, and 17 percent of all police officers.

"Women's" jobs not only lack social prestige, they are usually on the low end of the pay scale. For the five "most female" jobs in the United States (that is, those more than 96 percent female)—which are secretary, receptionist, preschool teacher, dental assistant, and private house cleaner—the average weekly salary is $336. For the five "most male" jobs (those less than 3 percent female)—which are airplane pilot, aerospace engineer, aircraft mechanic, firefighter, and miner—the average weekly salary is $862 (U.S. Bureau of Labor Statistics, 1999; U.S. Bureau of the Census, 1998a).

But job type does not explain all of the wage gap. For instance, men who work in predominantly female jobs do earn less than men who work in male-dominated occupations, but they earn more than women in these jobs because they are promoted faster. Likewise, women who work in male-dominated occupations earn more than women in female-dominated fields (because these occupations pay better) but they rarely, if ever, outearn their male counterparts in those jobs (Lorber, 1994).

Dual-Earner Families

Despite the wage gap, women remain committed to the idea of participating in the workforce. In 1999, 57 percent of U.S. families with at least one child under the age of 6 had two working parents. That figure was up from 32 percent in 1976. Of those families with children between the ages of 6 and 17, 70 percent consisted of an employed mother and father (U.S. Bureau of the Census, 2000b). The dual-earner family is now the single most common U.S. family type.

One obvious reason for the popularity of the dual-earner family is that the financial strains of modern living—shrinking incomes, increasing cost of housing, and so on—have made it difficult for most couples to survive on one income. Even in the affluent 1990s, median incomes for U.S. families rose quite slowly—from $44,090 in 1990 to $46,737 in 1998 (both figures in 1998 dollars) (U.S. Bureau of the Census, 2000b). Some types of families have been more successful than others, however. Hispanic families, for instance, have experienced virtually no increase in median income over the past three decades. Families with children have seen only a 2.4 percent increase in income, and the incomes of a subset of these families, single mothers, have not changed at all since the mid-1970s. At the same time, childless families have enjoyed a 19.6 percent increase in income (Peterson, 1994).

The image of the traditional family, in which Mom stays home to raise the kids, simply can't work for most people today. By 1990, the percentage of U.S. households that consisted of a married couple dependent on a sole male breadwinner had dropped to less than 14 percent, from a high of almost 60 percent in 1950 (Gerson, 1993). Nevertheless, social institutions, for the most part, still tend to be built around the outdated belief that only one partner (typically the father) in a couple should be working. Such beliefs have created serious burdens for working parents.

Consider the case of a 32-year-old Minnesota woman. She was fired from her job as an accounting clerk at a computer company because she had to stay home from work frequently to care for her sick baby, who had a series of illnesses including pneumonia, influenza, and pinkeye. The company stated that she missed almost half the work time in the previous six months. The state commissioner of jobs and training said she was not eligible for unemployment benefits because she had "voluntarily" put family interests ahead of her employer's interests, which amounted to misconduct (Lewin, 1991). However, her husband was unable to care for the child, and all her nearby relatives worked. In addition, she said, most day care providers do not accept sick children, and bringing somebody into the home to care for the child was far too expensive. Eventually an appeals court overturned the denial of benefits, ruling that her absenteeism was beyond her control and therefore did not amount to misconduct.

Some experts feel that the single most important step this society could take to help dual-earner as well as single-parent families would be to help them deal with child care demands. As recently as 1990, only 52 percent of the nation's largest companies had some form of maternity leave guaranteeing that an employee can use 6 weeks of vacation or sick time and not lose her or his job (Aldous & Dumon, 1990). However, in 1993 President Clinton signed into law the Family and Medical Leave Act (FMLA), which guarantees some workers up to 12 weeks of unpaid sick leave per year for the birth or adoption of a child or to care for a sick child, parent, or spouse.

This law represented a noteworthy shift in the government's recognition of the needs of dual-earner families, but it has some important qualifications that seriously limit its applicability to a significant proportion of the working population:

- The law covers only workers who have been employed continuously for at least 1 year and who work at least 25 hours a week. As a result, temporary, contract, or part-time workers—who are predominantly female—are not eligible.
- The law is of no value to parents who can't afford to take unpaid leave.
- The law exempts companies with fewer than fifty workers; hence, only about 40 percent of the full-time workforce is covered.
- The law allows an employer to deny leave to any employee who is in the highest paid 10 percent of its workforce if allowing that person to take the leave would create "substantial and grievous injury" to the business operations.

Currently, only 58 percent of American workers are covered by FMLA. In 2000, 17 percent of eligible and covered employees actually took leave (U.S. Department of Labor, 2000). According to the Department of Labor, many of the eligible employees who didn't take leave were parents who needed the time off but didn't take it because they couldn't afford to go without a paycheck.

Although this law represents an improvement over past conditions, the United States still lags behind other countries (see Exhibit 7.5). Consider the policies of a few other industrialized nations (Bell-Rowbotham & Lero, 2001):

- In France, mothers are provided 16 weeks off work at 84 percent pay for the first and second child, and 24 weeks for the third and subsequent children. They also receive up to 3 years of unpaid leave with job protection.
- In Norway, parents can take 42 weeks leave at 100 percent pay or 52 weeks at 80 percent. Fathers are entitled to 4 weeks of this leave. Parents can also combine part-time work and partial paternity benefits. For example, one parent could take full leave at 100 percent pay for 42 weeks and the other could combine 80 percent work and 20 percent leave for nearly 2 years.
- In Sweden, parents receive up to 450 days leave per child until the child is 8 years old. Of these, 30 days are reserved for the father and 30 for the mother, but the other days can be split in any way. For the first 60 days, parents receive 85 percent of their wages, and 80 percent thereafter. Furthermore, parents are entitled to take 120 days off work to care for a child under age 12 at 75 percent of their salaries.
- In the United Kingdom, parents receive 18 weeks of maternity leave at 90 percent of their salary and 12 additional weeks at a lower rate. They can also take up to 40 weeks of unpaid family leave.

According to a United Nations survey of 152 countries, the United States is one of only six— along with Australia, New Zealand, Lesotho, Swaziland, and Papua New Guinea—that does not have a national policy requiring paid maternity leave (cited in Olson, 1998).

EXHIBIT 7.5

Government Supports for Families with Children (Benefits Available to All Families, Regardless of Income)

	Health Care*	Maternity and Parental Leave Benefits	Government-Provided Child Care	Family Allowances	Tax Relief for Children
Australia	✓	—	✓	✓	—
Austria	✓	✓	—	✓	—
Belgium	✓	✓	✓	✓	✓
Canada	✓	✓	✓	✓	✓
Denmark	✓	✓	✓	✓	—
Finland	✓	✓	✓	✓	✓
France	✓	✓	✓	✓	✓
Germany	✓	✓	✓	✓	✓
Greece	✓	✓	✓	✓	✓
Ireland	✓	✓	—	✓	—
Italy	✓	✓	✓	—	✓
Japan	✓	✓	✓	✓	✓
Luxembourg	✓	✓	✓	✓	✓
Netherlands	✓	✓	✓	✓	—
Norway	✓	✓	✓	✓	✓
Portugal	✓	✓	✓	✓	✓
Spain	✓	✓	✓	✓	✓
Sweden	✓	✓	✓	✓	—
Switzerland	✓	✓	—	✓	✓
United Kingdom	✓	✓	✓	✓	—
United States	—	—	—	—	✓

*"Health care" in this case refers to varied systems of universal government subsidy and care.
Source: F. M. Cancian & S. J. Oliker. 2000. *Caring and Gender.* Thousand Oaks, CA: Pine Forge Press, p. 116.

The Balance Between Work and Family

Given contemporary realities, many couples and single parents find they must make career tradeoffs to try to balance their work and family lives. A survey of more than 6,000 employees of a major chemical company found that at the managerial and professional level, 47 percent of women and 41 percent of men had told their supervisors they would not be available for relocation; 32 percent of the women and 19 percent of the men told their bosses they wouldn't take a job that required extensive traveling; and 7 percent of women and 11 percent of men turned down a promotion. Among those in manufacturing jobs, 45 percent of women and 39 percent of men had refused to work overtime, and 12 percent of women and 15 percent of men had turned down a promotion (cited in Lewin, 1995b). These data and data from other studies suggest that, although both women and men face difficult choices, women are more likely to make career sacrifices. More generally, the pressures facing working men and women are likely to be different.

The Dilemma for Working Women

Sociologist Kathleen Gerson wrote a book in 1985 titled *Hard Choices: How Women Decide About Work, Career and Motherhood.* The book, a classic in the sociology of work and family, focuses on how women make the difficult choices between work and family commitments. Drawing on the life histories of working- and middle-class women, Gerson paints a vivid picture of the complex and competing forces women face: their aspirations, their commitment to motherhood, their beliefs about children, their perception of their place in their families and in society.

The experiences of Gerson's subjects were quite diverse. Some of these women entered adulthood wanting to become mothers and homemakers; others began adulthood with ambivalence or downright animosity toward motherhood. Some continued on these early paths; others veered off, experiencing a dramatic change in their family plans and desires. But all of them faced tough decisions on how to balance work and family. More than a decade later, the choices for women remain hard.

Such difficulty stems from powerful and sometimes conflicting social pressures, and cultural ambivalence regarding how mothers ought to behave. At one extreme is the image of the traditional mother who stays at home with the kids and devotes all her energy to her family. At the other extreme is the image of the "supermom," effortlessly juggling the demands of home and work. She has a briefcase under one arm, a cell phone in one hand, a baby in the other, and a smile on her face.

The ambivalence comes from the fact that although both images are considered socially acceptable, both are also indicted for their failings. Add to the mix the fact that U.S. culture also seems suspicious of childless career women, and you can see how an adult woman faces a no-win situation (Hays, 1996). If she voluntarily remains childless, some will accuse her of being cold, selfish, and unwomanly. If she is a mother who works hard at her job, some will accuse her of neglecting her children. If she has children, is employed, but puts her kids before her job, some will judge her to be uncommitted. And if she is a full-time homemaker, some will call her an unproductive throwback to the 1950s, content with her subordinate family status.

These images lead many women to *feel* less than adequate. It's difficult for a stay-at-home mother to feel happy and fulfilled when she keeps hearing that she is mindless and bored. It's difficult for a working mother to ably juggle her roles when she hears that she must dedicate *all* her energy in *both* directions to be considered successful.

Under these circumstances, it's not surprising that many employed mothers feel guilty and many stay-at-home mothers feel isolated and invisible to the larger society. Nor is it surprising that both spend a great deal of time making sense of and justifying their position. Employed mothers can come up with lots of compelling reasons why it's good and right to have a career, and traditional mothers can come up with equally compelling reasons why it's good and right to stay home (Hays, 1996).

Issue 4 examines the tension people sometimes feel between satisfying their individual desires and meeting their family obligations.

The Guilt Gap

Because of the lingering notion of separate spheres, men have historically been able to feel they are fulfilling their family obligations by simply being financial providers. A man may have to explain to people why he's chosen a particular career, but he rarely, if ever, has to explain or justify *why he is working*. Most people would interpret his long hours at work as an understandable sacrifice for his family's sake. In contrast, women's employment is sometimes perceived as optional or even potentially damaging to family life. Women have traditionally had to justify why their working outside the home is not an abandonment of their family duties. You'd be hard-pressed to find many journalists and scholars fearfully describing the perilous effects of men's outside employment on the family. But the mountain of

This controversy is examined in Issue 2.

articles and editorials in popular magazines, newspapers, and academic journals focusing on the difficulties women have in juggling the demands of work and family and on the negative effects of employed mothers on their children's well-being perpetuates the idea that their labor force choices are potentially dangerous (Faludi, 1991).

Despite these concerns, research shows that wives' and mothers' employment actually has very little negative impact on their family's well-being (Greenstein, 1995). And most Americans believe that working mothers are just as capable of establishing warm relationships with their children as mothers who don't work outside the home (see Exhibit 7.6). Nevertheless, popular images die hard, and so it's not surprising that few married women with children feel completely self-confident in the choice they make to enter or remain in the paid labor force. They agonize over whether their gains in financial well-being and personal independence are being purchased at the cost of their family relationships (Coontz, 1992).

Men, in contrast, rarely spend as much time worrying about the effect their work will have on their children as mothers do. This gender difference in worrying is referred to by some as the **guilt gap** (Hays, 1996).

The point here is that while many men make sacrifices regarding their careers or their families, in general they don't face the same kind of cultural ambivalence and hard choices that women continue to face. In fact, men's choice, for the most part, is no choice at all. Because men are still expected to attach primary importance to their careers, they seldom feel stress over sacrificing family time for their jobs. The stress some men do feel over balancing their careers and their family commitments can be tempered by the knowledge that they are conforming to cultural expectations if they devote most of their time to work. Indeed, men have historically used job demands to justify limiting their family time. Although women's family obligations and work aspirations have always been tightly intertwined, since the nineteenth century men have typically been able to maintain separate spheres.

EXHIBIT 7.6

U.S. Attitudes Toward Working Mothers

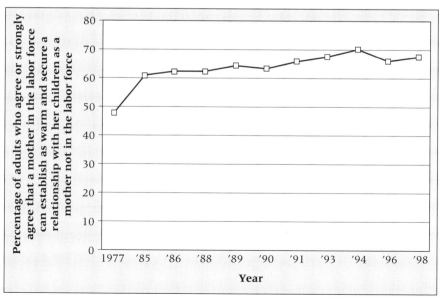

Data source: National Opinion Research Center. 1998. *General Social Survey, 1972–1998.* Available at www.icpsr.umich.edu/GSS/. Accessed June 1, 2001.

In fact, evidence suggests that men benefit from separate spheres. Fathers who are freed of the burden of family obligations—that is, whose wives stay home to take care of the house and children—actually earn more and get higher raises than fathers whose wives work. Such differences hold even after taking into consideration the effects of the number of hours each group of men works, their experience and training, and their field of employment (cited in Lewin, 1994a).

Some argue that these differences exist because men who are the sole breadwinners in their families work longer, produce more, and push harder for raises. In other words, without having to spend time on child care and housework, these men are freed up to pursue their careers with their full attention and energy. Others suggest that the higher salaries of men with nonworking wives simply reflect the fact that highly paid husbands can afford stay-at-home wives. Still others argue that a sort of "daddy penalty" is at work—that employers are prejudiced against men with "nontraditional," working wives (Waite & Gallagher, 2000).

We have no way to determine which of these explanations is correct. But some men with working wives do report feeling that they are being judged more harshly by their employers:

> I do think my boss is very aware that my face time is a little bit less than some of the men who feel like they can work as late as they like because their wives are at home with the kids. I'm as productive as those guys. I work smarter now that I have kids. I take work home. I don't do all the meaningless social stuff that can take up a lot of hours. But I do worry that it's going to slow down my promotions. (quoted in Lewin, 1994a, p. A15)

Another man, whose wife stopped working to be at home with their children, explains his family arrangements differently:

> Knowing a parent is with the kids all day long removes the terrible sense of conflict and guilt if I have to work late. I leave the house at 6:10 in the morning, before the kids are awake and if I don't get home before they go to bed at 8:30 I miss them, and that's hard for me, but I don't feel as worried as I used to that they're not getting enough parent time. . . . Now that my job is our sole source of income, striving to keep it secure and maximize it is more important than ever. (quoted in Lewin, 1994a, p. A15)

"Family Friendly" Workplaces

Many dual-income American families, especially those with young children, continue to struggle with lack of support from employers, government, and businesses. They face difficulty trying to fit in all the tasks that used to be performed by housewives, trying to find dependable day care, having to call in sick themselves to care for a sick child, having to use vacation time as maternity leave, and so on. Some employers demand long work hours or explicitly reward employees who put in long hours, thereby pressuring individuals to work longer and harder to ensure job security or promotions (Clarkberg & Moen, 2001; Golden, 1998).

But each year the number of employers who offer "family friendly" work policies grows. At Hewlett-Packard, for instance, employees are asked to set annual goals, not only for productivity but for personal/family time as well. They are discouraged from checking e-mail and phone messages over the weekend and are applauded if they leave work early to spend time with their children (C. Kaufman, 1999). In some large companies you can now choose to work part time, share a job with another worker, work some of your hours at home, or work on a flexible schedule.

One factor that influences whether an employer does or does not offer flexible work arrangements is institutional constraints (Golden, 1998). Workplaces are often slow to change their structure in response to the preferences and needs of employees. Consider the fact that 73 percent of workplaces do not offer flexible work schedules (Golden, 2001). Even in those that do, workers often must work longer weekly hours than normal to be eligible for flexible work schedules. Flexibility is also less likely to be available to workers who may need it the most: those who are members of racial minorities, women, unmarried, and low-paid (Golden, 2001).

Currently, however, about 27 percent of employees in the United States claim to have the ability to alter their daily starting and ending times of work, but few actually take advantage of these options (Golden, 2001). Given the rhetoric about the importance of spending time with family, you'd expect workers to be rushing to take advantage of these opportunities. A study of 188 companies found that when flexible hours were available, less than 5 percent of employees made use of part-time shifts and less than 3 percent chose to work some hours at home (Hochschild, 1997). And yet the majority of nearly 10,000 husbands and wives surveyed for the National Study of Families and Households study said they were not working the schedule they preferred (Clarkberg & Moen, 2001). Of those who were not working their desired number of hours, two-thirds felt they were working too much. In other words, although many working parents say they want to spend more time with their families and less time at work, relatively few are taking advantage of opportunities that would allow them to do so.

In her study of a Fortune 500 public relations company, sociologist Arlie Russell Hochschild (1997) uncovered a surprising reason behind some individuals' reluctance to work less and spend more time with family. In this company, work had become a sort of refuge. Some of the workers Hochschild interviewed told her that they come to work early and stay late just to get away from the house. At work they can relax, have a cup of coffee, and share jokes and stories with friends without the hectic anxiety that characterizes modern home life. They use terms such as *fun, carefree,* and *emotionally supportive* to describe their work. Not surprisingly, they are perfectly willing to flee a world of unrelenting demands, unresolved quarrels, and unwashed laundry for a world of relative harmony, companionship, and understanding. Work has become their main source of pleasure and personal satisfaction.

A more recent study reveals another dimension to why some individuals prefer work to home life. In some cases, individuals may invest more time and energy at their work—not to escape the chaos of family life, but because there is so little emotional pull from family (Philipson, 2000). Women in this study felt that their emotional needs were met in the workplace, not at home. In some cases, these women had older children or were childless, but even women with young children sometimes felt that growing up with a working mother had made their children so independent that they didn't need much emotional investment from their mother.

Although Hochschild (1997) suggests these patterns reflect a recent tendency to see home as work and work as home, others suggest that there have always been individuals who enjoy work at their families' expense (Maume & Bellas, 2001). Some men and women simply find greater fulfillment at work than at home. In addition, new management techniques have transformed some workplaces into more appreciative, more personal sorts of places. Ironically, the increased presence of women may have fostered a more cooperative and supportive workplace atmosphere.

The unfortunate consequence of working more hours—either by choice or necessity—is that people may "downsize" their ideas about how much care a child or a partner really needs from them (Hochschild, 1997). At the same time, families learn to make do with less time, less attention, and less support at home than they once imagined possible. Sociologists have found that when one or both spouses work long hours (more than 45 hours a week), their quality of life is reduced (Moen & Yu, 2000). But choice appears to be an important factor. There is more work/family conflict, more stress, more overload, and less coping among those people who work more hours than they want to work.

The search for balance between work and family remains a struggle for many U.S. families. Most social and policy research suggests that the solution lies not in individual adjustments and accommodations, but rather in collective ones, such as greater corporate involvement and response to workers' needs.

In the late 1980s, Felice Schwartz (1989) suggested that companies develop alternative work arrangements for working women, such as part-time positions, reduced workloads, temporary positions, flextime, irregular shifts, or jobs that can be performed from home. These innovations—sometimes referred to collectively as the **mommy track**—were intended to provide employed women with less demanding career paths that would enable them to continue meeting their family obligations. In reality, however, the mommy track reinforced a long-term discriminatory practice. Critics argued that there has always been a secondary track for women (Simpson, 1991). More than two-thirds of temporary and part-time workers in this country are women ("Ten facts about women workers," 1997). These jobs tend to be lower paid than full-time jobs and lack the full menu of benefits. They tend to be more insecure than "regular" jobs. Moreover, individuals in these positions are often regarded as less committed to the profession than other workers and therefore are excluded from opportunities that might lead to raises, bonuses, and promotions (Barker, 1993). Thus, rather than being a way to fundamentally restructure the workplace for women's benefit, the mommy track can be seen as a way of further institutionalizing sex segregation in the workplace and feeding the gender wage gap.

The reality is that neither men nor women are going to take advantage of family-friendly policies as long as U.S. attitudes toward work and family remain as they are. As long as workers are evaluated by how many hours they work at the office rather than the quality of their work, the search for balance will remain one of the biggest challenges facing U.S. families (Maume & Bellas, 2001). And as long as employees do not take advantage of new family benefits when offered, the structure of the workplace is likely to remain unchanged (Hertz, 1999).

Work Expectations in Same-Sex Couples

Issue 1 explores the controversy surrounding the legalization of same-sex marriages.

How do the gender-skewed interconnections between work and family apply to those situations in which there are no gender distinctions, as in same-sex couples? In gay and lesbian households domestic and breadwinning responsibilities cannot be automatically based on sex. They must be negotiated.

For same-sex couples, the issue is not who has the right to work or, conversely, the obligation not to work. Instead, the issue is, How can the relationship and the household be kept together given the career demands on *both* partners? The vast majority of same-sex couples emphasize sharing and fairness and believe that both partners in the relationship should work (Blumstein & Schwartz, 1983). Few consider either not working or supporting someone who chooses not to work. But the reasons for their feelings about this issue provide insight into the meaning of work for both men and women, regardless of sexual orientation.

For gay men, work remains a key aspect of self-respect. Unlike many heterosexual men, they don't feel obligated to support their partners financially. Instead, each partner is expected to work because that is what it means to be a man (Blumstein & Schwartz, 1983). Few gay men are interested in being a full-time homemaker. Sociologist Christopher Carrington (1999) describes one gay couple, Rich and Bill, who had a fairly unequal division of labor. Although Bill performs most of the domestic work, his partner goes to great lengths to clarify for the researcher that Bill's not "just a housewife":

> Well, I suspect Bill might be the one to do [more domestic work] . . . but I don't think it's that significant to him, really. *His real love* is his work as an artist, that's where he puts most of his energy. . . . I worry that people will get the wrong idea about Bill. I know that he does a lot of stuff around here, but he really wants to become an artist, and I don't want people to think of him as a housewife or something. He has other interests. (quoted in Carrington, 1999, p. 54)

Asked how he would feel about Bill becoming a full-time homemaker, Rich responds,

> I wouldn't like it at all. I don't see how that could be fair, for one person to contribute everything and the other to give little or nothing to the relationship. Plus, what about one's self-respect? I don't see how one could live with oneself by not doing something for a living. I would not be comfortable at all telling people that Bill is just a housewife. (quoted in Carrington, 1999, p. 54)

For lesbians, work means the ability to avoid being dependent on others and being cast into the stereotypical homemaker role. But lesbians don't expect to be the head of a household in the same way a husband expects to enter the breadwinner role in a heterosexual marriage. Although they understand the importance of earning their own living, rarely do these women think they will have to either support, or be supported by, another person. They are likely to see themselves as "workers," not "providers" or "dependents" (Blumstein & Schwartz, 1983).

Men's Changing Commitments to Work and Family

In contemporary heterosexual households, too, the two partners' work responsibilities are more a matter of negotiation than they were in the days when husbands were expected to be the primary breadwinners. Working wives today make a substantial contribution to their household's income. In 45 percent of dual-earner households, women earn about half or more of the income (cited in Ingrassia & Wingert, 1995). The heretofore unchallenged belief in the superiority of the male "good provider" has been replaced by uncertainty over men's proper place in society. It's no longer obvious what goals men should pursue and how much energy they should devote to pursuing them. At a more philosophic level, it is no longer clear what it means to be a man. Compared to their own fathers, many men today feel less powerful and less confident about making a living (Faludi, 1999). Because women are becoming just as likely as men to bear the responsibility for supporting a family, it has become harder for men to justify advantages based simply on being male.

Along with such uncertainty, men today are facing new choices about how to structure their lives. Sociologist Kathleen Gerson (1993) interviewed 138 men ranging in age from the late 20s to the mid-40s. These men came from diverse social and occupational backgrounds. Less than half of them remained committed to the traditional male breadwinner role and expected women to occupy the traditional female homemaker role. They felt that changes in women's lives had not—or should not—change men's traditional status as dominant breadwinner.

But the remainder of the men Gerson interviewed rejected the traditional male breadwinner role. Of these men, the largest group—about 46 percent (or 24 percent of the total sample)—cited freedom from the breadwinner role as a reason to renounce marriage and parenthood. To these men, marriage always seemed more like a trap than a reward. They felt they had much to lose and little to gain by getting married. Many had negative experiences with other people's children, which convinced them that parenthood was not something they wished to pursue either. Fearing that becoming responsible for a family would rob them of the option to pursue unpredictable careers or nontraditional jobs, these men rejected the whole package of domestic and work commitments that constituted the traditional definition of male success. Freed from the social obligation to financially support a wife and children, these men turned away from family altogether. Those who had already fathered children were quite uninvolved in their lives.

Other men Gerson interviewed—about 39 percent of those who turned away from the breadwinner role (21 percent of the total sample)—simply didn't think or plan for the future at all. But about 15 percent of this nontraditional group saw the decrease in breadwinning responsibilities as an opportunity to embrace a more nurturing parent role and construct a marriage based on equality and fairness. These men believed that a working wife would make a happier, more fulfilled companion than a homemaker. As one man put it, "I just could not see myself being attracted to somebody who was not gonna have their own career, and have the same kind of interest and passion about what they want to do as I had about my career" (quoted in Gerson, 1993, pp. 65–66). They hoped that an employed spouse would lessen their own economic burden and give them the freedom to seek personal fulfillment and not just job security at work. They wouldn't have to worry about earning a big paycheck. These men also showed a deep emotional attachment to their children and devoted much of their time at home to their care. They showed a willingness to parent not seen in their fathers' or grandfathers' generations.

Although still statistically in the minority, such attachments are becoming more socially acceptable. Sociologist Rosanna Hertz (1999) studied a group of family-focused fathers in dual-earner marriages. What made these men interesting was that their commitment to their families tended to be a reversal of earlier patterns. Most of them had spent part of their adulthood focused primarily or exclusively on their careers. So what happened to change their perspectives?

Hertz found that some of the men had made a very conscious decision to put their families above their work commitments, but some came to that decision indirectly. The latter group tended to be working-class men who found themselves without a job or underemployed after they were "downsized" from their jobs. Their wives, by necessity, worked full time or overtime, and these men were forced to assume many of the child care responsibilities. Many of these couples would probably not have chosen to co-parent had their economic circumstances been different, but because they were committed to keeping the family central to their lives, fathers stepped up their involvement and were able to master the parenting role.

The other group of men in Hertz's study were committed to a "new parenting" approach, in which family is organized around children and both parents are full participants. These men tended to hold managerial and professional roles so they were able to negotiate flexible hours or reduced workweeks in order to spend more time with their families. These men were similar to those studied by sociologists Penny Becker and Phyllis Moen (1999), who found that some professional men in their study intentionally limited the number of hours they worked and reduced their expectations for career advancement in order to be more involved with their families. Their decisions were usually prompted by a desire to spend more time with their children and to be more involved than their fathers had been.

A highly public example of such a decision occurred shortly after the 1996 presidential election. Robert Reich, who was secretary of labor in the Clinton administration, wrote a letter to the *New York Times* lamenting the difficulty he faced in balancing his career and his family. Unable to strike the kind of balance he wanted, he made the tough choice to resign from his powerful cabinet position so he could spend more time with his family:

> I have the best job I've ever had and probably ever will. No topping it. Can't get enough of it. I also have the best family I'll ever have, and I can't get enough of them. Finding a better balance? I've been kidding myself into thinking there is one. The metaphor doesn't fit. I had to choose. I told the boss I'll be leaving, and explained why. (Reich, 1996, p. A33)

Reich's story was a poignant one. Unfortunately, the best solution to his problem—and the problem of millions of other workers—lies not in personal decisions made by individuals but in a shift in structural arrangements. Few people have the economic wherewithal that Robert Reich had to leave their jobs and devote more time to their families. A working-class father, for example, isn't about to "resign" from his job to relax and frolic with his children. In fact, recent reforms in welfare laws may actually prevent him from doing so (see Chapter 4). Ironically, Reich, as labor secretary, was the person responsible for federal guidelines concerning workplace policy. He was the very person who could have helped to change the workplace culture to be more conducive to family obligations so that such difficult sacrifices wouldn't have to be made in the first place.

Equality in Dual-Career Marriages

Sociologist Rosanna Hertz (1986) examined a smaller subset of dual-earner couples: middle-classs and upper middle-class working couples in the corporate world. In these couples, not only are both partners employed, but also they are both professionals, committed to their careers. These individuals are, for the most part, economic equals.

Hertz points out that dual-career couples tend not to be politically or socially motivated individuals consciously pursuing an agenda of gender equality. Their desire for equal careers is not driven by any sort of ideology. Instead, they are the by-products of a shifting economy, where the expansion of white-collar employment coupled with the growth of career opportunities for female college graduates combined to make two careers—not just two jobs—in one family a popular option. Their unique position as marital equals is more behavioral than attitudinal. Labor market trends have made them advocates of gender equality, even if they weren't initially supporters of this cause.

How does such equality play itself out in family life? Hertz found important shifts in the roles of these husbands and wives. They understand each other's situation and tend to relate to each other as partners with similar goals, aspirations, and pressures.

The traditional "separate spheres" boundary, between "breadwinner" and "homemaker," dissolves when neither spouse can claim greater power and influence due to working outside the home or earning more money. The marriage can no longer respond entirely to the demands of only one spouse or only one spouse's career. Similar work schedules and employer demands muddy questions about whose work commitments should take precedence.

The blurring of traditional gender boundaries in families leaves plenty of room for differing interpretations of family responsibilities. For instance, some wives who earn a significant income and have an impressive career consider themselves employed homemakers, define their financial contributions to the family as supplementary, or stake a claim to the breadwinner role only reluctantly. Others, however, believe that providing for one's family ought to be as much the responsibility of women as of men and consider themselves "co-breadwinners" (Potuchek, 1997).

Couples trying to make their new reality fit an old, traditional family model often feel frustrated. They constantly struggle not to fall back on the old rules and roles they witnessed as children, when any conflict over work and family was resolved by letting one person's career atrophy.

Hertz found that the dominant mechanism couples used to negotiate these potential conflicts was to view their marriage as a third, shared career that requires commitment, attention, and hard work *from both partners*. Marital equality in this "third career" is not taken for granted; it takes substantial time and energy. As one husband states, "I certainly don't think this is a gloriously equal marriage marching off into the sunset. I think we struggle for equality all the time. And we remind each other when we are not getting it" (quoted in Hertz, 1986, p. 55). In "reminding each other" of inequalities—keeping each other in check so that neither spouse's career becomes favored—partners in dual-career marriages try to strike a livable balance.

Most of the dual-career couples in Hertz's study reported having to be very explicit about fairness in the relationship, adopting a "bookkeeping mentality." They often instituted clear rules about job choices or relocation decisions should one spouse face transfer. For instance, one couple decided that if one spouse received a job offer that required a move to another city, the other spouse always had veto power, retaining the right to reject the city. This agreement operated as a constraint on the pursuit of one career to the possible disadvantage of the other person. Such rules may sound unromantic, but they help to ensure fairness in the marriage.

Despite moments of doubt, ambivalence, or conflict, dual-career couples often create a communication style quite different from traditional marriages. Their work lives, although rarely in the same profession, share a rhythm and a structure. Such a situation is far different from the gulf that can sometimes separate working and nonworking spouses. Dual-career couples have a deep understanding of each other's lives that is at once intimate and empathetic. They both understand, for example, that a last-minute crisis in the office can mean a late night at work, or that one or the other will periodically need to travel out of town on business, or that going out for a drink with colleagues after a particularly rough day can be important. Furthermore, they can both understand inevitable bad moods and therefore can correctly attribute them to job tension and not to their relationship. As one man put it, "She has a sense of what I'm doing because she's out there doing the same damn thing every day" (quoted in Hertz, 1986, p. 77). This heightened understanding of each other's lives offers greater potential for mutual respect.

Hertz's research offers compelling insight into the ways couples strike satisfying balances between work and family. But it's important to note that this balance is still rare among less-affluent dual-earner couples. Furthermore, it is always a struggle. For one thing, these couples still must cope with a culture that assumes male and female roles in the family ought to be divided into separate spheres of influence and responsibility, with one partner (usually the husband) given final authority.

Another caution: Although the marriage of two careers brings a level of autonomy and financial freedom unavailable to most families that rely on a single source of income or on two modest incomes, such arrangements are always contingent on the availability of careers in the labor market, people to help with housework and child care, and the ability of couples to adapt to competing employer demands. In other words, dual-career couples are always dependent on others outside the relationship. Lack of adequate day care or a sudden downsizing at one's place of employment can destroy the delicate balance a couple may have achieved.

Coping Strategies of Dual-Earner Couples

Clearly, couples who want to work and remain committed to their families are subject, to some degree, to the whims of the workplace. For instance, according to the U.S. Bureau of Labor Statistics, the number of people who work outside the typical 9-to-5 shift has doubled since 1991 (cited in Feuer, 2001). As the economy has become more global, more companies require around-the-clock shifts to meet the demands of international customers in different time zones. Therefore, many dual-earner and dual-career couples have had to reconstruct their lifestyles to adapt to these demands.

Shift Work   Approximately 40 percent of full-time employees currently work nonstandard hours (weekends, or not 9 to 5, or both) (Fenwick & Tausig, 2001), and half of dual-earner couples consist of spouses who work different shifts (cited in Greenhouse, 2000). The perception of shift work can vary along class lines. Young, middle-class couples may perceive it as an attractive alternative for the flexibility it offers. For working-class families, however, shift work is likely to be an arrangement over which workers have little control. Parents earning the lowest incomes are more likely to be assigned to work on weekends and on unstable or rotating schedules.

Although shift work is attractive to some couples, it can be a source of tension. It can reduce marital happiness and the amount of interaction that occurs between partners, increase sexual and household problems, and ultimately increase the likelihood of divorce (White & Keith, 1990). Such tension, though, is not inevitable. A recent study found that individuals working on the weekends were the ones who experienced family conflict, lack of balance between work and family, and worker burnout. However, working night shifts and rotating shifts posed few problems for workers or their families (Fenwick & Tausig, 2001). The researchers also found that the amount of control individuals had over scheduling was important in predicting family and health outcomes. When people have choices about their work schedules, shift work does not pose serious problems.

In some cases, parents of young children or single parents have little choice about shift assignments. For these parents, working irregular hours does pose many challenges. Relatively few child care centers operate 24 hours a day or on weekends, but more may begin to do so in the future. Ford Motor Company recently announced it would open thirteen 24-hour child care centers. Although such centers are very costly, management also expects to benefit. As one Ford CEO said, "Not only will it attract and retain the best, but the workers, when they're at work, don't have to worry about their children and where they are" (quoted in Armour, 2000).

But for most parents of young children, such options are few and far between. They must either rely on friends and relatives or work opposite shifts, sacrificing time together so that one of them can be with the children (Hays, 1995).

Commuter Couples   Another nontraditional solution to the problem of balancing work and family is to live apart. It is often difficult to pursue two careers in the same geographic area. The conventional solution, of course, is that one spouse—usually the wife—takes a less desirable job or chooses not to work at all. But more dual-career couples are choosing to meet the incompatible demands of work and family by adopting a commuting lifestyle, living apart for at least three nights a week.

Living apart is not unique to dual-career couples. Some occupations (such as sales, the military, or politics) and some circumstances (such as war, immigration, imprisonment, and seasonal work) have always required some marital separation. However, the husband has historically been the one to leave for some period (Anderson & Spruill, 1993).

Research shows that today's commuter couples tend to be well-educated professionals in their mid-30s. But their commuting characteristics vary widely. The time that separate residences are maintained can range anywhere from a few months to a dozen years or more. The distance between the residences may be short (40 or 50 miles) or span the entire country. Some couples reunite every weekend; others don't see each other for months at a time. Some have children; others don't (Anderson & Spruill, 1993). What they all have in common, though, is that the separation is motivated not by problems in the relationship but by both partners' desire to maximize success in their demanding careers. And it is perceived not as a freely chosen, perfect arrangement but as a necessary, temporary accommodation (Gertsel & Gross, 1987).

Nevertheless, the commuting situation can *create* problems in the relationship. It is a lonely, inconvenient, and expensive lifestyle that takes tremendous effort. Communication, sexual activity, and the economics of maintaining a marriage are issues that must be worked out during infrequent visits.

Yet despite the potential problems, most commuters maintain that the career benefits outweigh the strains of separate living. Spouses report satisfaction with the freedom they have to continue working in their chosen occupations. They can devote long, uninterrupted hours to their jobs without worrying about missing dinners or social events at home. Furthermore, as in long-distance dating relationships, the time spouses in commuter marriages do spend together can be intensely arousing.

Women tend to be more positive about their commuting arrangements than men. Their gains in independence and professional mobility may counteract the costs of reduced emotional closeness. The arrangement can validate the belief that their career is as important as their husband's. Consider the highly positive comments of two commuter wives:

> I was really unprepared for the fierce joy I have felt at being my own woman, being able to concentrate on my own activities, my own thoughts, and my own desires. It's a completely selfish, self-centered existence. It's almost a religious experience when you're fifty years old and have never felt that before.

> Every night I bring work home. If he was here, I'd have to let it go. I would have prepared real meals, made sure the house was neat, had more laundry to do. Oh, you

know, the whole list. But, being alone, it's just easy to do my work. I'm kinda lured into it. (quoted in Gertsel & Gross, 1987, pp. 427–428)

Scaling Back   In some cases, dual-earner couples deliberately reduce their work hours and commitments in order to spend more time with their families and to provide a buffer between family and work. Often such scaling back occurs while couples have young children at home and family demands are most intense. Although women are more likely than men to scale back, husbands too sometimes make very conscious decisions to be more involved in family (Becker & Moen, 1999).

One scaling-back strategy involves placing limits on the number of hours either spouse is willing to work and reducing expectations for career advancements (Becker & Moen, 1999). For instance, some individuals decline a new job offer or a promotion if it is likely to take too much time away from the family.

A second strategy is a return to the traditional one job/one career marriage (Becker & Moen, 1999). In this arrangement, conflict over whose job matters most or who would take time off to raise the children is reduced—priority is given to whichever partner has the career. Not surprisingly, women are more likely to be identified as having the "job" whereas the husbands have the "career." As a result, it is usually women who engage in this type of scaling back (Becker & Moen, 1999). But in these marriages, women may still put demands or limits on their husbands' career choices, effectively exerting veto power over any significant changes in work–family arrangements.

Based on recent studies of couples where one partner has scaled back, these arrangements do seem to offer couples some balance and satisfaction. One study found that women who worked in nonprofessional jobs but whose husbands were professionals suffered little stress and experienced little work–family conflict compared to other women (Moen & Yu, 2000).

Coping Strategies of Single-Parent Families

The coping strategies of dual-earner families simply can't apply to single-parent families. In these households, there is no partner to work a nonstandard shift or commute. And although it may be possible for single parents to scale back, most cannot afford to do so. Rosanna Hertz (1999) found that the single mothers who scaled back were usually professional women. For these women, scaling back required years of planning *before* the child arrived, such as saving money and amassing sick leave to balance out some of the costs of cutting back their hours. Some of these professional women were also able to arrange flexible hours or shorter workweeks. Others switched jobs so they could scale back:

I'm going to have one-third of the number of people reporting to me that I used to and I'm going to walk out of work at 5:15 p.m. . . . And that was a very conscious choice. I didn't want a job that was going to consume me right now because I know that my priority needs to be taking care of Ben. . . . So it's constantly this balance of how much time at work and with my child. . . . How deep am I in the work world with still my arms and my head free to be with Ben and it's a balance that I anticipate continually needing to adjust as the years play out. (quoted in Hertz, 1999, p. 24)

Of course, most single-parent families, especially those headed by women, do not have the financial resources or job status to scale back in this way, nor do they have the status in their jobs to obtain flexible hours (Golden, 2001). In fact, for poor single parents, striking the balance between work and family usually involves working more, not less, hours. The nonprofessional women in Hertz's study, for example, found various part-time jobs—in addition to their full-time jobs—such as cleaning homes, babysitting in their homes, waitressing in the evening, and so on. But such jobs provide few or no benefits, which as Hertz (1999) notes, is crucial: "Making good money without benefits might be doable without a child, but having a child can dramatically change one's financial situation from independence to welfare dependence in a matter of months" (p. 25). When jobs lacked benefits, these women typically were forced to turn to government assistance such as Medicaid.

To complicate matters even further, working multiple jobs requires even more child care. Thus, a major coping strategy for these single employed mothers was building and nurturing an informal but extensive social support system:

Such strategies show how economic circumstances can expand the definition of family, a phenomenon discussed in Issue 1.

> Nearby relatives are frequently tapped for child care; when kin are not available (as happens far more frequently these days), fictive kin like godparents are woven into the family as sources of spiritual and material support. Even more creatively, single mothers often build a "repertory family" . . . by pulling together an ensemble of people who provide some combination of emotional and psychological support, economic contributions, and performance of routine household chores and maintenance. (Hertz, 1999, p. 26)

The Domestic Division of Labor

Work performed for wages, no matter how menial, is always regarded as "work." But work performed within the home is generally invisible, and therefore excluded from typical definitions of "work." Sometimes the invisibility of domestic work is purposeful, as with the following individual:

> I just want to get [the laundry] done, and out of the way, before Andrea gets home . . . I just don't want her to have to deal with it. I really like us to be able to have quality time when she gets here. She has enough pressure to deal with at work, so I try to keep this kind of stuff out of her way. (quoted in Carrington, 1999, pp. 203–204)

But the invisibility of domestic work is more likely to stem from two more important sources: the prevailing notion that housework is really a "labor of love" and not work at all, and the fact that it is unpaid. When you actually detail what has to happen within any given household to make it run smoothly, it is often startling just how much work must actually be done. Consider all that goes into keeping a household going (Carrington, 1999):

- *Feeding work*: planning meals; learning about foods; buying food; preparing the meals; cleaning after meals; and so on
- *Housework*: Cleaning house; caring for clothing and linen; caring for pets and plants; managing household paperwork and financial work; dealing with nonkin (for example, deliveries, service workers); scheduling and monitoring home repairs and maintenance; and so on
- *Kin work*: visiting relatives; writing and sending cards and letters; making phone calls; purchasing gifts (along with all the forethought and decision making that goes into these tasks)

- *Consumption work*: visiting stores; reading about products and services; ordering materials; comparison-shopping; monitoring performance of products and services; record-keeping and organizing manuals and instructions; managing money; and so on

Notice that each one of these tasks involves multiple jobs. For instance, planning meals includes knowing what others will eat, taking into account family members' food preferences and nutritional needs, keeping track of everyone's schedules to know when the family can sit down to eat, and so forth. "Cleaning house" includes vacuuming; scrubbing sinks, toilets, and tubs; sweeping, mopping and waxing floors; cleaning counter tops and stoves, oven, refrigerators, microwaves, and various small appliances; cleaning windows/mirrors; straightening clutter and furniture; dusting; cleaning closets, basements, garages, fireplaces; emptying garbage; recycling; and on and on.

Many sociologists point out that domestic work is invaluable to the entire economic system. However, the people who perform the majority of domestic work—that is to say, women—earn no money for providing these services. Mothers also provide an important service to society by physically and emotionally nurturing the next generation of workers. If a woman were to be paid the minimum going rate for all her labor as mother and housekeeper—child care, transportation, errands, cleaning, laundry, cooking, bill paying, grocery shopping, and so on—her yearly salary would be over $35,000, more than the average salary of male full-time workers ("Mom's market value," 1998). In 1995, women's unpaid work around the world was valued at $11 trillion (compared to the official global output in 1995 of $23 trillion) (Human Development Report, 1995). If women's unpaid work were monetarily valued, they would no doubt constitute the major breadwinners worldwide.

Such work does not afford the prestige it might if it were paid labor because societal and family power are usually a function of who earns the money. It's not that homemakers don't work; it's that they work invisibly outside the mainstream economy, in which work is strictly defined as something one is paid to do (Ciancanelli & Berch, 1987; Voyandoff, 1990).

Furthermore, defining unpaid household labor and child rearing as women's responsibilities upholds male privilege in society. Free from such obligations, men can enjoy more leisure time and take advantage of the opportunity to pursue their own careers and interests. Women burdened with domestic responsibilities have less time and energy to devote to their careers. Hence, the division of labor in the home reinforces the division of labor in the workforce, further solidifying the gender-based power structure of U.S. society described in Chapter 2.

Debate over the devalued perception of domestic work created quite a stir in Canada a few years back. In 1991 a Canadian housewife took issue with a question on her census questionnaire that asked, "How many hours did you work in the last week, *not including volunteer work, housework, [home] maintenance or repairs?*" (Smith, 1996). She had run her household for 19 years, raising three children in the process, and she was furious that her hard work was considered irrelevant. So she refused to fill out the questionnaire, a crime according to Canadian law. Under threat of prosecution, she embarked on a protest campaign, which eventually drew in women from all over the country. She formed a group called the Canadian Alliance for Home Managers, which threatened to boycott the next census if unpaid work remained uncounted. Five years later, Canada became the first country in the world to count on its national census the hours spent performing household labor and child care without pay.

In the pursuit of equal relationships, some men do aim for a better balance between work and family responsibilities. But men in general have found it easier to relinquish some responsibility for the traditional breadwinner role than to take their fair share of responsibility for household labor. Men's involvement in domestic work has not kept pace with women's increasing commitment to paid employment. Some sociologists have referred to this situation as a "stalled revolution" (Hochschild & Machung, 1989).

The reluctance of a sizable proportion of men to share the burden of domestic work contributes to the sluggish movement toward gender equity both inside and outside the home (Arrighi & Maume, 2000). For instance, many wives have opted to quit their jobs rather than continue to argue with their husbands about who should do what around the house. So men's reluctance to take on more of the daily household tasks can be more than just a nuisance. It can indirectly contribute to the disruption of women's tenure in the job market and reduce their earnings (Corcoran & Duncan, 1979).

Even in dual-career couples where wives have prestigious careers, domestic matters are typically assumed to be outside the repertoire of male responsibilities. Consider the swirl of controversy that enveloped the 1993 confirmation hearings of the first two female nominees for U.S. attorney general, Zoe Baird and Kimba Wood. These two women, both highly successful professionals, had employed undocumented immigrants as nannies for their children and thereby avoided paying Social Security taxes. These practices, although technically illegal, are not uncommon among middle-class and upper middle-class working parents. Nevertheless, the news was enough to sink the nominations of both women. Up to that point—and since—no male nominee for any Cabinet post has ever had his household so thoroughly scrutinized, even though such scrutiny would have no doubt found similar transgressions. Questions about nannies would be considered completely irrelevant to his capacity to perform as a member of the presidential Cabinet. Clearly, the assumption regarding these two women was that, despite their professional stature, they were the ones accountable for what went on in their homes. Interestingly, the woman who eventually was confirmed for the post of attorney general, Janet Reno, was single with no children.

Such traditional attitudes toward men's and women's household responsibilities are not unique to the United States. In Mexico, for example, women have entered the workforce and universities in unprecedented numbers in the past decade. The percentage of women in the paid labor force has doubled since 1970. However, their place in the family has changed little. Statistics show that less than half of working men pitch in at all around the house—compared to 94 percent of working women. In 2000, thousands of Mexican housewives went on a day-long strike against housework to protest the imbalance and highlight their contribution to society. For one woman the day of the protest was the first time in *23 years* that she didn't get up at 6 A.M. to fix her husband's meals for the day (Sheridan, 2000).

Women's Work, Men's Help

It's true that men do more around the house than did their counterparts 30 years ago and that they play a more prominent role in the raising of children. And it's also true that women, because they are more likely to be in the paid labor force than in the past, are doing less (Bianchi, Milkie, Sayer, & Robinson, 2000). But despite these changes, domestic work responsibility continues to be predominantly female (Brines, 1994).

The most recent data on couples' housework patterns shows that married women spend on average about 19.4 hours per week doing housework (excluding child care and

EXHIBIT 7.7

Gender Differences in Household Chores

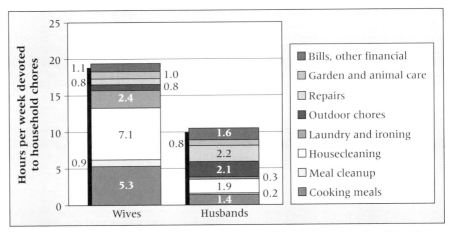

Data source: S. M. Bianchi, M. A. Milkie, L. C. Sayer, & J. P. Robinson. 2000. "Is anyone doing the housework? Trends in the gender division of household labor." *Social Forces, 79,* Table 1.

shopping) compared to 10.4 hours per week for married men. This is a significant change from 1965, when wives did about 34 hours of housework each week and husbands did about 4.7 hours. Thus, the ratio of women's to men's hours doing housework has declined, not because men are doing substantially more but because women are doing a lot less (Bianchi et al., 2000).

Moreover, the housework husbands do tends to be quite different from the work their wives do. As you can see from Exhibit 7.7, women do more of the core housework chores than men. By contrast, men tend to do outdoor chores and home repairs. Men's chores are typically infrequent, irregular, or optional. And notice the difference in time required for these chores compared to the tasks women usually do.

Over a decade ago, sociologists Arlie Hochschild and Anne Machung (1989) pointed out that because of this gender imbalance, the average U.S. wife routinely works two shifts—one at the office and one at home. More recently, Michele Bolton (2000) has suggested that many women actually work a *third* shift—a relentless, psychologically draining period that involves rehashing the events of the day:

> Most of the women I interviewed . . . seemed to use their private, quiet time—in the car, in the shower, before falling asleep at night—as a psychological third shift after finishing the actual first and second shifts that made their days too busy to fully think through their actions and choices. (p. 2)

From a structural functionalist perspective (explained in Chapter 1), traditional gender disparities in household responsibilities may actually reflect an equitable, functional, interdependent division of labor that maximizes benefits for the entire family. But if this were the case, you would expect households in which both partners work full time to distribute domestic labor equally, right? Evidence does indicate that husbands perform more of the mundane household tasks traditionally performed by wives when their wives have a long history of extensive work in the paid labor force (Pittman & Blanchard, 1996). However, in general, the gender discrepancy in household responsibilities does not diminish all that much as a result of women's full-time employment.

Women employed outside the home continue to be primarily responsible for the up-keep of the household (Demo & Acock, 1993). Interestingly, this discrepancy holds even among couples who profess egalitarian, nonsexist values. Husbands who say that all the housework should be shared equally still spend significantly less time doing it than their wives do (Blumstein & Schwartz, 1983). However, compared to other husbands, those with more egalitarian values who are married to women with strong egalitarian values, do perform more housework (Greenstein, 1996b).

Race and ethnicity can play an important role in the domestic division of labor. Asian and Hispanic men tend to do less domestic work than other men (John et al., 1995). This tendency is particularly pronounced in ethnic neighborhoods, where the high proportion of recent immigrants ensures a steady flow of people with traditional, patriarchal values. In contrast, despite stereotypes about black men abandoning their families, they are actually *more* likely than white, Asian, or Hispanic men to be intimately involved in domestic work and child rearing (Rubin, 1995). Black men employed full time may actually spend *more* time doing household labor than unemployed black men, indicating that when men are attached to the provider role they are also committed to their family obligations (Shelton & John, 1993).

Social class appears to have little impact on the gender-based division of domestic labor. One stereotype is that working-class men are less "enlightened" and therefore do proportionately less domestic work than middle-class men. Stereotypically, the macho factory worker whose masculinity is threatened by doing laundry and cleaning the bathroom is contrasted with the "yuppie" father happily cooking meals and pushing a stroller in the park. But research shows that class has little to do with how much housework husbands perform (Wright, Shire, Hwang, Dolan, & Baxter, 1992).

Furthermore, men's economic standing relative to their spouse's doesn't appear to affect how much housework they do, although the reasons behind their involvement may vary. When men earn more than their wives, the fulfillment of traditional gender roles fits well with the exchange of resources: his financial support for her domestic services. But when women earn more, couples sometimes resort to a traditional division of family power in order to reinforce the gender differences that could be undermined by the switching of traditional economic roles. Men who experience challenges to their masculine identity on the job (for example, low pay, lack of autonomy, subordinate status) are especially reluctant to engage in what they consider "feminine" household tasks, because doing so would further threaten their masculinity (Arrighi & Maume, 2000). Men who have suffered through prolonged joblessness are prone to entirely disavow housework, the performance of which would be further evidence of their "failure" at the male provider role (Brines, 1994).

For those couples who do share household tasks, imbalances still exist. For instance, the arrival of children often signals a return to a more traditional division of household labor (Cowan & Cowan, 2000). In fact, employed men may actually *increase* their time at work on becoming parents, whereas women significantly decrease theirs (Shelton, 1992). And men are likely to further decrease their share of housework as the number of children in the household increases (Greenstein, 1996b). In other words, having children often means more work *inside* the house for women and more work *outside* the house for men.

Many women whose husbands make significant contributions to household work and child care report frustration over the fact that they are still "household managers" who are ultimately responsible for planning and initiating household activities. They complain that they must instruct and remind their husbands before the men begin to notice and take care of the tasks necessary to run a home (Coltrane, 1996b). Some women have found that if they want their husbands to do certain household tasks, they must prepare itemized lists every time they leave the house, spelling out exactly what needs to be done (Hays, 1996). Others complain that men seem so blind to what needs to be done that it is often easier just to do the job themselves.

Men's literal and figurative distance from domestic work is also reflected in the ways they define their domestic contributions. Some men distance themselves from the activity by indicating to others that it is not the sort of thing they typically do. Rather than defining the work they do around the house as an ordinary, expected aspect of their family responsibilities, they may define it as "help"—implying that they're assisting the person who's usually responsible for such tasks.

Even men who assume major responsibility for planning and initiating housework and child care tend to define their role as "helper" (Coltrane, 1989). The tendency of many fathers to refer to their child care behavior as "babysitting" verbally aligns them not with the general category of parents for whom taking care of children is a taken-for-granted element of their family role, but with outsiders who periodically care for other people's children. Mothers rarely refer to the time they spend with their own children as "babysitting."

A key social element of "help"—as distinct from "work"—is that it requires expressions of gratitude or at least some acknowledgment on the part of the person "receiving" the assistance (Hochschild & Machung, 1989). Compared to his father or perhaps other men in his community, a husband who does the laundry, dusts the furniture, and washes the dishes may feel he is providing more help than his wife could reasonably expect from a man. Given such a frame of reference, his domestic tasks are something extra—a helpful gift. And his wife should feel grateful. But she has a different frame of reference. If, in addition to her full-time job, she is still responsible for 70 to 80 percent of the domestic work, she may perceive her husband's contribution as little more than what she deserves—not something extra and certainly not a gift.

Hence, he may see her failure to thank him for watching the baby a few hours each afternoon as a lack of appreciation for "all he's done." She, in contrast, thinks he's just done what he should do as a parent and therefore she's not obliged to express any special gratitude. She may even resent him for demanding that she acknowledge his domestic contributions, which, relative to her ordinary responsibilities, are quite small.

Perceptions of Inequity

Imbalances and inequalities exist in most families. However, actual, objective inequality in domestic responsibilities is less important than the *perception* of inequity and unfairness. As you might expect, men in general are less likely than women to perceive the unequal distribution of household labor as unfair (refer to Exhibit 7.2c), although their perceptions of fairness may vary across racial lines. Because, as we've already mentioned, African-American men tend to spend more time on housework than white men, they are less likely to view the household division of labor as unfair to their wives. When comparing their household labor to other men's, African-American men may conclude they're contributing their fair share more than other men (John et al., 1995). What's striking is that relatively few wives (estimates range from one-third to one-fourth) regard the unequal division of labor as unfair either. White, African-American and Hispanic women are equally unlikely to consider housework imbalances as unfair (John et al., 1995).

Research indicates that men and women in general agree that wives should do about twice as much domestic work as husbands do (Lennon & Rosenfield, 1994). In a study of couples of relatively equal economic and professional status, 62 percent of wives said their husbands did a satisfactory amount of domestic work, and 13 percent actually felt their husbands did *too much* (Biernat & Wortman, 1991).

Gender Ideology and Domestic Work   Some people do feel an unbalanced household division of labor is unfair to women (Hochschild & Machung, 1989). But under what circumstances do these perceptions arise? People's perceptions are, in part, contingent on their beliefs and ideologies about gender. In general, husbands with egalitarian gender ideologies tend to see the typically gender-based division of domestic work responsibilities as more unfair to their wives than husbands with traditional ideologies do (DeMaris & Longmore, 1996).

Women's perceptions are somewhat different. Wives with a "traditional" gender ideology are likely to value stability and harmony in their relationships, but "egalitarian" wives may be more concerned with independence and autonomy (Greenstein, 1996a). If a wife truly believes that married women—no matter what their employment status—are *supposed* to do most of the housework, she will probably view inequalities as legitimate and not see them as unjust. In contrast, a wife who enters marriage expecting her husband to share in the household work may perceive even small inequalities as unfair because her expectations are being violated. Such unmet expectations are likely to decrease marital happiness and increase marital discord (Barnett & Baruch, 1987).

One possible source of ideas about gender and domestic responsibilities is culture. Most gender differences are culturally learned, as Chapter 2 explains. The result is different patterns of behavior. In Japan, for example, girls routinely help with housework but boys rarely do.

But gender differences in domestic work aren't just reflections of culturally learned patterns. If women were taught to believe that doing household chores was part of being a woman, gender differences in domestic work responsibilities would be noticeable in all types of household arrangements. But although the amount of domestic work men do is quite similar whether they are married, cohabiting, or single, the amount women do fluctuates considerably (South & Spitze, 1994). Single women do about the same amount of housework as single men. Significant differences between women and men exist only among married and cohabiting couples and are especially pronounced among couples with children.

Differences in contributions to domestic work based on marital status apparently reflect different expectations of how one "does gender" (see Chapter 2). Perhaps women believe that doing the housework is a means of displaying their love of or subordination to men. Single women don't do more housework than single men because they don't feel any pressure to do so (Perkins & DeMeis, 1996).

One comparison of first-married and remarried couples offered some support for this explanation. Women in their second live-in relationship contribute significantly less time to housework than women in first marriages or first cohabiting relationships. Men's housework time was uniformly low across all situations (Sullivan, 1997). The women in second relationships may have started their first relationship under one set of norms and reexamined those norms prior to the second relationship. In another study, a majority of divorced women said they'd left their first marriage because of inequitable treatment

(Schwartz, 1994). So a woman who perceived the domestic division of labor in her first live-in relationship to be unfair might be inclined to seek a more equal division in subsequent relationships.

What determines who will be responsible for housework if gender is no longer a factor? Lesbians and gay men often espouse an ideology of equality but like people in heterosexual households, one partner usually assumes the lion's share of domestic work. Is that because some people are simply better at it or because some enjoy it more (popular explanations for why women in heterosexual relationships do more housework)? On the contrary, most individuals who assume more domestic responsibilities appear to do so not out of choice, interest, or skill but because the nature of their paid work gradually leads them down this path:

> The decision to start the evening meal because one arrives home earlier than others facilitated increased feeding work. For those who work at home, the decision to clean the bathroom or do the laundry during the day led them into increased housework. For those with more flexible work schedules, the time to shop for consumer goods led them into increased responsibility for consumption work. . . . Their domestic careers appear to develop residually, accumulating slowly and unreflectively over the course of their relationships. They then become the experts and begin to feel the responsibility for domesticity. (Carrington, 1999, p. 193)

Because domestic work is a feature of all households, no family type is exempt from questions about how it ought to be divided.

Social Exchange and Household Inequity

Social Exchange and Household Inequity   The social exchange perspective can also shed some light on how men and women perceive domestic arrangements. As Chapter 6 explains, this perspective argues that people can feel deprived without feeling dissatisfied if they conclude that they are getting what they deserve out of their relationships. People with few outside alternatives tend to have lower expectations of a relationship because they stand to lose more from its disruption than people who have more options available to them (Lennon & Rosenfield, 1994).

Thus women who have fewer alternatives to marriage and fewer available economic resources are more likely to view an unequal division of domestic work as fair. If wives have low wages and sense a high risk of divorce in their marriages, they may lower their expectations and feel grateful for whatever household chores their husbands do (Hochschild & Machung, 1989). In contrast, women who are self-sufficient and who perceive available alternatives to their marriage are less dependent on their spouses and are less fearful of divorce. Hence they are more likely to view unequal domestic work as unfair. These women tend to be more distressed and depressed by an unequal division of household labor than women who accept inequality as fair (Lennon & Rosenfield, 1994).

Perceived responsibility for the "breadwinner" role can also be a crucial justification for the unequal distribution of domestic labor (Ferree, 1991). But as you know from the statistics on household labor presented earlier, earning more money excuses men from housework, but not women. In fact, some studies show that, as women's income increases, they actually perform *more* household tasks (Biernat & Wortman, 1991).

In short, what's important is not just the income difference but the meaning attached to that difference. A wife may earn more than her husband, but her earning power won't affect her household responsibilities if she and he don't perceive her as being *responsible* for breadwinning as well (Potuchek, 1997). One study found that only 16 percent of American working wives are "willing breadwinners" who believe that their primary responsibility is to support the family financially (Haas, 1986). But wives who do believe they are the family breadwinners are likely to feel entitled to more assistance around the house.

Manufactured Equity

Inequity in relationships can be uncomfortable for all involved and, as discussed in Chapter 6, people are motivated to reduce it. So in an effort to create the *appearance* of equity in inequitable relationships, some couples engage in a process of "family mythmaking."

Arlie Russell Hochschild's study of gender and domestic work employs detailed case studies to provide insight into the mechanisms couples use to artificially create feelings of equity (Hochschild & Machung, 1989). She describes one couple, Nancy and Evan Holt, who struggled for years over the wife's desire for a more equitable division of labor and the husband's continual opposition to sharing housework. At one point, an exasperated Nancy offered to split the responsibility for cooking dinner so that each would cook 3 days a week and they would go out or cook together on Sundays. Evan's response was that he didn't like "rigid schedules" but he'd try it anyway. The first week he forgot his cooking responsibility 2 out of his 3 scheduled days.

As the pattern continued, Nancy became more frustrated. When the conflict became so great that it began to threaten the marriage, Nancy and Evan created the myth that their marriage would be equitable if Nancy would shift her work hours from full to part time and do all the "inside" housework. Evan would be responsible for "outside" work, such as cleaning the garage and feeding the dog. Nancy convinced herself that taking care of the dog was an onerous task she wanted nothing to do with. In doing so, she elevated this task to a level of importance akin to that of her career—which she was willing, in part, to sacrifice. The solution further "allowed Nancy to continue thinking of herself as the sort of woman whose husband didn't abuse her—a self-conception that mattered a great deal to her. And it avoided the hard truth that, in his stolid, passive way, Evan had refused to share" (p. 44).

Such intricate "solutions" highlight a growing problem facing American families at the dawn of the twenty-first century, a time when changing cultural perceptions of fair relationships are clashing noticeably with families' actual gender-based division of labor. The complexity of trying to "create" equity in inequitable situations results in elaborate mind games. Women and men similarly view men's housework as crucial to fairness (Sanchez, 1994), despite the fact that, by and large, men still don't see domestic work as "their issue" (Coltrane, 1996a).

In sum, men's participation in household tasks has increased only slightly over the years, despite their growing attachment to fatherhood and the dramatic increase in employment outside the home among married women. But as the gender attitudes of men and women gradually become more egalitarian, both sexes may begin to expect men to do more domestic work. Whether these expectations eventually translate into actual behavior may depend on things such as the relative power of the partners, as indicated by differences in education, earnings, and so on. Necessity may also help families more fairly share housework and child care, as irregular work shifts become more common and couples thus find little overlap in their work schedules (Presser, 1994).

Conclusion

What seems quite clear is that, both in fact and as an ideal, the division of labor that as-signed wage-earning responsibilities to men and unpaid domestic work to women is break-ing down. Women are in the paid labor force to stay. Yet at the beginning of the new mil-lennium, women still aren't able to share equally in providing the family income because of persistent inequalities in the labor market and men's persistent lack of interest and full par-ticipation in domestic work.

Nevertheless, men's and women's interests are beginning to converge. Women, in some respects, have become more career oriented but remain committed to family; men, in some respects, have become more family oriented yet still find their primary source of identity in their careers.

Unfortunately, these changes have not been matched by changes in the workplace. Many employers continue to value a workaholic ethic that leaves little time for family life. Couples who equitably share work and domestic responsibilities continue to face a culture that doesn't quite know what to do with them. These couples may shrug off or angrily re-ject others' disapproval, but they still are called on to justify their nontraditional division of labor. Why is he in the grocery store or in the park with his 3-year-old in the middle of the day? Why are they moving to another city to accommodate her career?

At the beginning of the twenty-first century, Americans face the crucial task of inte-grating family and work as smoothly and effectively as possible without sacrificing too much of either. We can resist the social changes that are uniting the once "separate" spheres of work and family—or we can accept these changes and work with them. We can encourage men to sacrifice family life to fit into the rigid structure of the conventional workplace and encourage women to sacrifice careers to meet family needs—or we can learn to value family caretaking and economic productivity in equal degrees. Piecemeal adjustments on the part of individual workers and couples will not be enough. What are needed are adjustments in institutional support systems—for example, the ability to work flexible hours or shorter workweeks, benefits to part-time workers—so men can feel free to act on their emerging interest in family life without fearing a risk to their careers and so women can feel free to pursue their careers without fearing they are placing their families at risk.

Chapter Highlights

- The contemporary belief that work life and family life are separate spheres emerged with industrialization in the nineteenth century. Along with this shift came an expecta-tion that family life was women's domain and work life was men's domain. However, the notion of "separate spheres" has never applied equally to members of different classes and different ethnic groups.
- Work and family are never completely separate. Nevertheless, the ideology of separate spheres was, and continues to be, a powerful force in economics and politics. Conse-quently, women's experiences in the labor force—from the jobs they occupy to the wages they earn—are still tied to broader cultural assumptions about gender.
- Lingering notions of separate spheres shape the way men and women today perceive the balance between their family lives and their work lives.

- Recent decades have witnessed a dramatic increase in dual-earner families. This change has placed unprecedented demands on the workplace to accommodate employees with family obligations and on families to find ways of tending to their needs when time at home is limited.
- The growing presence of women in the paid labor force has not been accompanied by an increase in the responsibility men take for household work. An inequitable division of household labor continues to be a source of strain for many families.

Your Turn

The intersection of gender, family, and work is where you can see most clearly how expectations and beliefs can be translated into action. Locate at least one of each of the following types of couples in which both partners work full time outside the home:

- Cohabiting heterosexual
- Cohabiting homosexual
- Newly married without children (married less than 1 year)
- Married with at least one child living at home
- Married without children (married 10 years or more)
- Stepfamily

Ask each person in each couple (partners must not be in each other's presence when answering these questions) to list all the household chores that need to be done during the course of a week. Ask them to be as specific and exhaustive as possible (for example, "cleaning windows" rather than "cleaning the house"). After the lists are completed, ask each person to indicate which of these tasks he or she is primarily responsible for, which his or her partner is responsible for, and which are shared. Ask the participants also to estimate the total amount of time they spend each week on all these tasks combined. Finally, ask them about how many hours they work outside the home during a typical week.

Compare responses of the following to see if you can find any differences in time each partner spends doing housework and the number of tasks for which each is responsible:

- Partners in the same couple
- Men and women
- Younger and older couples
- Married and cohabiting couples
- Couples with and without children at home
- Married and remarried couples
- Heterosexual and homosexual couples

Do the women still bear the primary responsibility for housework? Are household responsibilities more equitably split by certain types of couples? If partners within the same couple had different ideas about housework responsibilities, to what can you attribute this lack of agreement? Describe the tensions men and women experience when trying to balance work and home responsibilities.

Parenthood and Parenting

Patriarchs, Fathers, and Dads

Although some clearly biological events are involved in becoming a parent, the nature of parenthood is anything but biological. Until relatively recently, the father role was considered less important—and therefore was the focus of less scholarly attention—than the mother role. But the father role has changed dramatically over time, to the point that, in some circles, fathers are now considered as important as mothers in the development and well-being of children.

Fathers of the eighteenth and nineteenth centuries seem to bear little resemblance to contemporary fathers. In the eighteenth-century portrait (above at right), note the position of the mother and the father relative to the children.

In the nineteenth-century portrait (below at right), the father seems to have little interest in the child tugging at his pants.

By the twentieth century, fathers had become somewhat more engaged in their children's lives. In this photo from 1912 (at left), father and child have some physical contact but without much apparent warmth.

By the middle of the twentieth century, fathers were being drawn more into family life. But in the photo below you can see by the father's clothes—which send messages about his "real" place in the world—and his stiff posture that he wasn't perfectly comfortable in the role of the "hands-on" father.

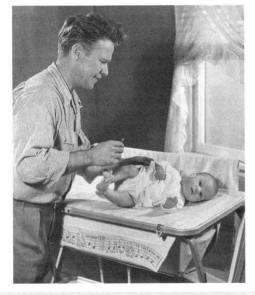

This mid-twentieth-century father (at left) is engaging in the necessary, constant, but not particularly enjoyable task of changing his child's diaper. Note the physical distance between himself and the baby.

In what ways has the father role changed in the past several centuries? Do you think these portraits indicate the true role of fathers in the upbringing of their children? In other words, might fathers have contributed to their children's well-being in less visible ways?

Contemporary images of fathers often portray men as emotionally and physically engaged, attached, and supportive. Although women and men may experience parenthood differently, in many ways today's fathers are expected to act a lot like our traditional picture of "mom." By taking over bottle-feeding, contemporary dads are even able to participate in the care and nurturing of infants that have traditionally been provided by mothers.

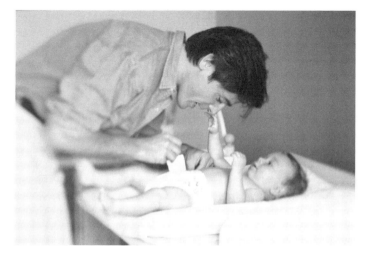

Compare this photo to the photo on the previous page showing the father changing his baby's diaper. Notice that this father is maintaining closer contact and engaging in more playful inter-action with the child.

Fathers choosing to stay home and care for children while their wives work is a fairly recent phenomenon. Increasingly, fathers who have sole or joint physical custody of their children following a divorce assume primary care of children, a role traditionally assigned to mothers.

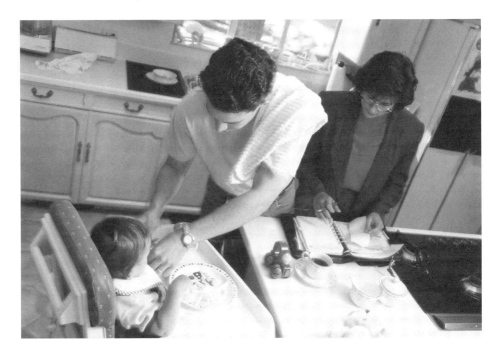

To what extent do images of fatherhood like the ones shown here accurately reflect the everyday lives of most fathers?

Has fatherhood really changed? Or is it just more acceptable today for men to be openly engaged and loving toward children? Or is it simply more acceptable today to *show* men being more openly engaged and loving toward children?

If a Hmong woman in Laos experiences problems becoming pregnant, she resorts to a variety of remedies commonly used by her people. She may consult a shaman, who will ask her to sacrifice a dog, cat, chicken, or sheep. After the animal's throat is cut, the shaman strings a rope bridge from the doorpost to the bed, over which the soul of the couple's future baby, who, it is believed, has been detained by a malevolent spirit, can now freely travel to Earth. A Hmong woman can also take precautions to avoid becoming infertile in the first place. For instance, she will never set foot in a cave because evil spirits who dwell there can make a woman sterile by having intercourse with her.

Once pregnant, the Hmong woman can ensure the health of her baby by paying close attention to what she eats. If she craves ginger but doesn't eat any, the child will be born with an extra finger or toe. If she craves chicken but doesn't eat it, the child will be born with a blemish near its ear. If she craves eggs but doesn't eat them, the child will be born with a lumpy head.

A long or painful labor can be eased by drinking water in which a key has been boiled, in order to unlock the birth canal. If she attributes her labor difficulty to not having treated an elder member of the family with sufficient respect, she can alleviate the problem by washing the offended relative's fingertips and apologizing profusely (Fadiman, 1997).

When a Hmong woman gives birth, she squats on the dirt floor in the center of her one-room house. But the newborn doesn't get dirty, because the mother never lets it actually touch the floor. Instead, she delivers the baby into her own hands, reaching between her legs to ease out the head and then letting the rest of the body slip out onto her forearms (Fadiman, 1997). No birth attendant is present. If she becomes thirsty during labor, her husband can bring her a cup of hot water. But he is forbidden to look at her body. Because the Hmong believe that moaning and screaming can disrupt the birth, she labors in silence, except for an occasional prayer to her ancestors. Chances are that she is so quiet that her other children, sleeping in the same room, will only wake up when they hear the cry of the newborn.

Soon after the birth, the father digs a 2-foot-deep hole in the floor and buries the placenta. If the infant is a girl, the placenta is buried under the parents' bed; if it's a boy, the placenta is buried in a place of greater honor, near a central wooden pillar that holds up the roof of the house. The placenta is always buried with the smooth side, the side that faced the baby in the womb, upward. If it's buried upside down, the baby will vomit after nursing. If the baby develops spots on its face, that means that ants are attacking the placenta, and so boiling water is poured down the hole (Fadiman, 1997).

To most Americans, these practices and rituals seem quite bizarre, even unhealthy—can the parents have the baby's best interests in mind by allowing it to be born into such an unsterile and medically unsupervised environment? But Hmong parents take their parenting responsibilities extremely seriously. To the Hmong, becoming a parent is the most treasured human experience. Although most Hmong families are extremely impoverished, the amount of love, care, and attention Hmong parents heap on their infants is, by Western standards, astounding. A newborn baby is *never* apart from its mother, sleeping in her arms all night and riding on her back all day. Hmong children are almost never beaten, because the Hmong believe an evil spirit who witnesses the mistreatment may take the child, assuming it's not wanted. Research indicates that Hmong mothers are more sensitive, more accepting, and more responsive to their children's signals than are American parents. They hold and touch their babies much more frequently (cited in Fadiman, 1997). So, although their childbirth practices strike the Western observer as somewhat dangerous, the Hmong actually seem to be better parents than are Americans.

In this chapter we discuss some of the important issues associated with parenthood. It's hard to imagine an experience more innate and universal than having children. Reproduction is the essence of life—human and otherwise. Yet as you can see from this description of Hmong childbirth and parenting, parenthood is a phenomenon that, although clearly biological, cannot be separated from cultural norms, values, and definitions. Furthermore, although U.S. society places enormous value on children and the vast majority of U.S. adults want to have children, *becoming* and *being* a parent are seldom problem-free experiences.

Pronatalism

A **pronatalist society** is one in which people believe that married couples should reproduce or should *want* to reproduce. Comparatively speaking, the United States is not as pronatalist as some societies where women's status and social position are determined largely by their reproductive capacities and mothering. But the United States does embrace certain pronatalist beliefs and practices. For instance, most people don't necessarily believe that childless people lead empty lives, but they do tend to believe that watching children grow up is one of life's greatest joys (see Exhibit 8.1). Having children is portrayed as important to self-fulfillment and necessary for the future survival of the society.

All societies, regardless of their economic or political systems, value childbearing, but they do so in different ways and to different degrees. In agricultural societies, couples come to believe that having children is a good thing because children directly contribute to the family's economic potential. In industrial and postindustrial societies, children are valued because of the psychological benefits they provide their parents, serving as an object and source of affection and love, and a way to avoid loneliness (Jones & Brayfield, 1997).

U.S. cultural commitment to parenthood stems from a Judeo-Christian tradition that depicts children as "blessings" and childlessness as a curse or punishment (Miall, 1989). The Bible encourages people to "be fruitful and multiply." These norms—coupled with pro-birth governmental policies, such as income tax deductions for each child—encourage reproduction and reinforce the belief that parenthood is a vital feature of society.

EXHIBIT 8.1

Pronatalist Values of Adults in the United States

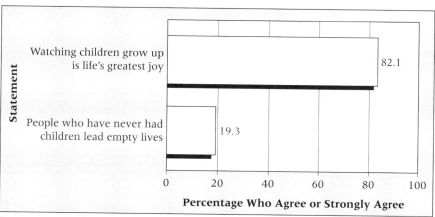

Data source: National Opinion Research Center. 1998. *General Social Survey, 1972–1998.* Available at www.icpsr.umich.edu/GSS/. Accessed June 1, 2001.

The value a society places on having children is often influenced by broader historical factors. For instance, because of the heavy loss of young men during World War I, the French government in the 1920s promised medals of honor to women who produced eight or more children. Nazi Germany in the 1930s and 1940s strongly encouraged Aryan families to procreate, at the same time actively and viciously preventing other ethnic groups from doing so.

In Russia today, many couples are postponing childbearing or are deciding not to have children altogether because of severe economic instability and uncertainty about the future. Russia now has one of the world's lowest birth rates. At the same time, because of skyrocketing rates of poverty, stress, and alcoholism, Russians are dying much younger than people in the rest of the world. As a result, the Russian population has been steadily shrinking since the mid-1990s. Experts fear such a population decline will eventually lead to economic catastrophe. Hence, Russian politicians are promoting a variety of pronatalist policies to reverse the trend, such as a nationwide ban on abortions, financial incentives for couples to have children, and a tax on childlessness (Karush, 2001).

One of the most dramatic examples of governmental childbearing policy took place in Romania 3 decades ago. In 1966, Romanian dictator Nicolae Ceaușescu instituted a plan to increase the country's population from 23 million to 30 million by the year 2000. Ceaușescu declared that "the fetus is the property of the entire society. Anyone who avoids having children is a deserter who abandons the laws of national continuity" (quoted in Breslau, 1990). He outlawed sex education, classifying books on sexuality and reproduction as state secrets (Breslau, 1990). A pregnant woman who had a miscarriage would automatically be suspected of arranging an illegal abortion and could be summoned for questioning. If a child died in a doctor's district, that doctor could lose 10 to 25 percent of his or her salary. The world was given its first glimpse of this policy when Ceaușescu was overthrown in December 1989. The consequences of his "program" were tragic. Not only did thousands, perhaps millions of women suffer through unwanted pregnancies and self-induced illegal abortions, but the country's orphanages overflowed with unwanted and unhealthy children. Under international pressure from the European Union, Romania has improved the condition of its orphanages. But there has been little decline in the number of children who still live in them.

Sometimes a society takes a firm *antinatalist* posture, usually aimed at bringing down birth rates. For instance, China's leadership has been struggling for decades to reduce family size, because its limited resources cannot support a population of close to 1.3 billion people. Since the 1970s the Chinese government has actively *discouraged* couples from having babies, imposing strict waiting periods, yearly provincial birth quotas, local oversight of contraceptive use and women's menstrual cycles, and forced sterilization (Ignatius, 1988; Kristof, 1993b). Couples who have more than one child may be fined as much as a year's salary, lose access to apartments, schools, and free education, or be fired from their jobs. The average number of births per Chinese woman decreased from more than seven in the 1960s to fewer than two in 2000 (Kennedy, 1993; Kristof, 1993a; U.S. Bureau of the Census, 2000b). This antinatalist policy has been so successful that some government officials now advocate phasing it out because they fear it will eventually create a society in which there won't be enough adult children to care for aging parents (Lev, 2000).

At other times, antinatalist policies are focused on specific segments of a population. For instance, to reduce family size among the poor, the Peruvian government promises peasant women cash incentives or gifts of food and clothing if they undergo surgical sterilization (Sims, 1998). In the United States, a Chicago-based organization called CRACK (Children Requiring a Caring Kommunity) offers drug-addicted women $200 in cash if they get sterilized or get long-term birth control. Critics charge that the organizations advertisements target mostly poor, minority neighborhoods (Belluck, 1999).

In American society, most people marry with the expectation that they will have children; and they become parents because parenthood brings social approval and because all relevant social structures deem parenting to be a good thing (Denny, 1994). Having children is not only considered desirable, it is seen as normal and is taken for granted. It's often said that weddings create couples, but it's birth that makes a family (Gillis, 1996). People learn that having children proves their worth and gives them the status of "mature adults."

Issue 1 examines U.S. cultural ideas about what constitutes a family.

Because having children is expected and normal, people with children have a common ground: They can talk about their children to other parents, who will understand them and relate to their experiences. Parents often relate to each other through their children and feel more acceptable to others once they have children. Consequently, people who don't have, can't have, or don't want to have children are often made to feel like outsiders and cultural outcasts.

Adoption and the Primacy of Genetic Parenthood

In this culture, most people consider the biological bond between parents and children to be of paramount importance. One of the most powerful cultural lessons taught is that parenthood gives people genetic identity and immortality (Nelkin & Lindee, 1995). Many of the common questions and comments made to new parents reflect the deep-seated importance of this bond. "He's got your eyes" and "She has her grandmother's mouth" are the sorts of things most new parents hear as friends and relatives try to establish genetic links and physical resemblances. Without thinking, people often ask adoptive mothers of newborns about pregnancy, labor and delivery, breastfeeding, and so on. Physicians seeing an adopted child for the first time may ask about family health history.

In some people's minds, the adoption of a child may provide the experience of being a parent but can never provide the biological connection on which "real" or "natural" families are assumed to be based. Because parenthood tends to be associated with procreation and blood links, adoption is often considered a "debased form of parenting" (Bartholet, 1993). A recent nationwide survey found that although nine out of ten respondents considered adoptive parents both lucky and unselfish, half believed that adopting was "not quite as good as having one's own child" (cited in Lewin, 1997). In a society such as that of the United States, which extols the virtues of having children, adoption is usually a second choice. Most young people don't imagine their life script will consist of growing up, getting married, and adopting a child. They typically expect to grow up, get married, and have kids of their own.

Consequently, some fear that adopted children will always lack a crucial piece of their identity. Indeed, this theme provides the backdrop for the many moving stories we hear about adoptees searching for their biological roots. One researcher found that one in five television characters who are adopted choose to track down birth parents, a percentage that is eighteen times higher than the real-life percentage (cited in "Tune in," 1988). Such stories are framed as holy quests, transformative journeys in search of one's self. These images appeal to the cultural notion that adopted individuals lack an essential element of identity and that one's "real" identity is somehow linked to shared genes.

Some evidence suggests that adopted children are more likely than those raised by their biological parents to experience difficulties, especially during adolescence. Using data from the National Longitudinal Study of Youth, sociologist William Feigelman (1997) compared children raised in adopted homes with those from intact biological families and "attenuated nuclear families" such as foster, divorced, or stepfamilies. Adoptees were similar to children from attenuated families in their tendency to have higher rates of delinquency, youth crime, and alcohol and drug use during adolescence than children from intact biological families. As adults, they were more likely to cohabit prior to marriage and to report lower levels of marital satisfaction. In terms of most other measures such as employment, income, and educational attainment, however, the adult adoptees were just as successful as those adults who were raised in intact homes by biological parents. A review of 66 prior studies comparing the adjustment of adoptees to nonadoptees found higher levels of psychological problems among adoptees (Wierzbicki, 1993). These effects were greater for teenagers than young children, suggesting that adoption may precipitate an "identity crisis" when children reach adolescence (Feigelman, 1997; Wierzbicki, 1993).

But keep in mind that there is tremendous variation in the nearly 1.5 million adoptive families in the United States (Grotevant, Ross, Marchel, & McRoy, 1999). Some children are adopted by their stepparents, others by strangers. Some are infants when adopted, others are adolescents. Some are physically and mentally healthy when adopted, others may have mild or severe disabilities or be at genetic risk of developing problems. Some adopted children have birth parents who are mentally ill or have criminal histories; others do not. Some are placed in families with other adopted children, some enter into homes where they are the only child or perhaps the only adopted child among siblings. Some children have been institutionalized for lengthy periods prior to adoption, some have stayed in a number of foster homes before adoption, and others spend no time in institutionalized care. Some adoptions are interracial, others are intraracial. In short, many factors may explain the problems some adolescent adoptees face, but few studies have controlled for these types of factors or used nonadopted samples as control groups in determining adopted children's adjustment.

Furthermore, most adopted children are raised in nurturing, economically stable homes. After all, adoptive parents must devote a great deal of effort to becoming parents. They *want* to be parents. By contrast, some biological parents conceive by accident and may see parenthood as the least bad of the various bad options available to them (Bartholet, 1993).

Yet the cultural primacy of biological over adoptive parenthood is reinforced by social institutions. For example, in several highly publicized court cases biological parents have been granted custody of children they had earlier put up for adoption. In addition, organizations opposing the sealing of adoption records have grown in recent years. These groups—with names such as Adoption Search and Support Group, Adoptees Liberty Movement, and Concerned United Birthparents—argue that genetics is the primary basis of identity and that adoptees have the same rights as anyone else to know their roots and their heredity.

The move to open adoption records provides mixed cultural messages about the primacy of genetic parenting, however. On the one hand, the practice of "closed" adoptions grew in part from a concern that if an adopted child knew his or her biological parent(s), this genetic connection would be so powerful it would weaken the child's attachment to his or her adoptive parents (Gross & Sussman, 1997). Yet the move to open adoptions also sends the message that the biological parent is an essential part of an adopted child's life, regardless of whether she or he has any emotional, financial, or social connection to the child.

The controversy over open adoptions raises another interesting sociological issue. Such adoptions have the potential to broaden ideas about what constitutes a "family." In some open adoption cases, birth mothers are fully integrated into the family structure. Consider, for instance, how this adoptive mother describes her relationship with her two children's birth mothers:

> She [the birth mother] stays with us for weekends and knows our other birth mother now too. They have talked several times and have actually presented at a meeting together and talked to birth mothers and others interested in open adoption. And we get members from all the families together, just like with in-laws. We try to get together whenever we are in town. At Easter they were at my sister's, and Bob's (second adopted child's) birth grandmother . . . had a big party and she made the cake for it. She had both birth families there. (quoted in Gross, 1997, p. 30)

The extent to which biological ties ought to form the basis for a definition of "family" is discussed in Issue 1.

No one in this situation considers the birth mothers to be the primary parents or in any way a threat to the connections between the adoptive parents and their children. Such families challenge assumptions about the necessity of excluding biological kin from adopted children's lives at the same time that they challenge the primacy of genetic ties.

Infertility

The ideal of pronatalism is clearly illustrated in the societal response to couples who want genetically related children but are unable to have them. In 1995, approximately 15 percent of women in the United States sought services for infertility—and, as Exhibit 8.2 shows, the percentage is higher for older women (U.S. Bureau of the Census, 2000b).

The discovery of infertility can be an acute life crisis (Whiteford & Gonzalez, 1995). It is often unanticipated and unexplained, has no identifiable onset, and lasts for an indeterminate time. It can create overwhelming stress and feelings of guilt and grief. Unlike other stigmatizing disabilities, such as blindness or paraplegia, infertile individuals display no visible stigmatizing features; only the knowledge of their condition distinguishes them from others (Greil, 1991). Because of its invisibility, infertile couples can easily "pass as

EXHIBIT 8.2

Women's Age and Treatments for Infertility

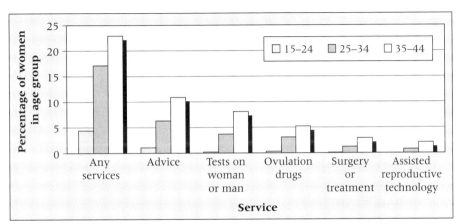

Data source: U.S. Bureau of the Census. 2000b. *Statistical Abstract of the United States: 2000,* Table 101. Washington, DC: U.S. Government Printing Office.

normal" (Goffman, 1959). Nevertheless, people feel the stigma of infertility as deeply as they would feel the stigma of any other "abnormal" condition:

> I feel like I'm isolated in a prison; I have no one who understands how horrible this is. People don't know what to say to you . . . I think I'm alternatively dealt with as either someone who has died or that [I] have a handicap. And I think people approach it like that because they don't understand death; they don't understand handicaps; and they don't understand infertility. (quoted in Whiteford & Gonzalez, 1995, p. 29)

Although infertility can have devastating effects on both men and women, it is especially difficult for women. Women, far more than men, are traditionally socialized to believe that "doing gender" means becoming a mother, as Chapter 2 explains. Sociologist Charlene Miall interviewed or surveyed approximately seventy involuntarily childless women between the ages of 25 and 45. Nearly all the respondents characterized infertility as something negative, and nearly all experienced feelings of anxiety, isolation, and conflict.

Many of these women felt that to admit their infertility publicly was in some way an admission of failure. As one woman put it, publicly acknowledging problems with reproduction was "an admission that you're not a whole person . . . either sexually or anatomically or both. That there's something wrong, and I guess reproduction, the ability to reproduce, strikes at the very essence of one's being" (quoted in Miall, 1989, p. 392).

Another woman was concerned that people's awareness of her infertility would cause them to view her as abnormal: "I do believe it lessens you in some people's eyes, makes you different and possibly even morally suspect, like God is punishing you or something. Somehow infertility lessens your accomplishments for some people" (Miall, 1989, p. 392).

Not surprisingly, these women often engaged in some form of information control. Many of them simply concealed their infertility from everyone except their physicians and counselors. Others used the medical nature of the problem as a way of distancing themselves from blame, saying essentially, "It's beyond my control." Others disclosed the information only to people they knew would not think ill of them. No matter what the strategy, all were motivated by the knowledge that information about their infertility would be judged negatively.

Infertility Treatment   In an attempt to avoid the pain of infertility and become parents, some couples turn to medical interventions. Because of the cultural value placed on children, research on infertility treatment has faced virtually no criticism and has been allowed to expand with little community debate (Rowland, 1990). After all, who would oppose research that could provide infertile couples with the "miracle of a baby"?

Consequently, the field of high-tech infertility treatment is flourishing. In only a decade it grew from 30 clinics to more than 300 (Gabriel, 1996). In recent years, there has been dramatic growth of new reproductive methods such as fertility drugs, artificial insemination, in vitro fertilization, embryo transfer, and surrogate motherhood. Although access is limited primarily to the affluent—some procedures can cost more than $20,000—these techniques have the potential of increasing the reproductive choices and opportunities available to infertile couples (Rothman, 1987; Rowland, 1990).

Despite the availability of these procedures, the choices can mean undergoing years of costly and painful treatment and continuing the stigma and loss of personal identity felt by infertile people. These interventions fail more often than they succeed. Nevertheless, the hope they provide allows infertile couples to define themselves not as "childless" but as "not yet pregnant" (Whiteford & Gonzalez, 1995, p. 27). For some, the pain of being infertile in a pronatalist culture is so great that the high financial and emotional costs of fertility treatments are worth it.

Surrogate motherhood is perhaps the most controversial infertility treatment. It involves the agreement of a woman to conceive artificially on behalf of the contracting parent, to carry the fetus for the full gestational period (9 months), and to relinquish the child at birth (Robinson, 1993). The most common method is artificial insemination of the surrogate with the genetic father's sperm. In such a situation, the surrogate is genetically related to the child, because her egg is being used. In the less common embryo-transfer procedure, however, the child is genetically unrelated to the surrogate, who is simply providing the "gestational environment." In another method, egg donation, the couple receives eggs from a donor that are implanted into a woman. She has no genetic connection to the child. In these cases, sperm from the woman's partner may be used so that the child is genetically related to the father.

Surrogate motherhood pits pronatalist values against individual liberties and against state interest. The U.S. Supreme Court decided years ago that individuals have the right to be free from government intervention in decisions that involve reproduction—rights frequently called "procreative liberty" (Robinson, 1993). And the majority of adults feel surrogacy ought to be available to infertile couples (see Exhibit 8.3). However, the state *can* intervene if certain other societal rights are threatened. For instance, surrogate motherhood may violate several compelling state interests, such as protection against the possible exploitation of poor women as surrogates. Many critics of reproductive technology fear that financial necessity may coerce poor women into becoming surrogates. Compensation sometimes totals $15,000 or more for surrogates and $3,000 or more for egg donors, in addition to payment for all pregnancy-related or medical expenses.

Reproductive technology also calls into question the very nature of the parent role, especially that of the mother. Certainly parental responsibilities and the nature of the parent–child relationship continually change over time. But surrogate motherhood raises the possibility that a child may be born with three mothers: a genetic mother, a gestational mother,

> The tension between family privacy and state interests is examined in Issue 3.

EXHIBIT 8.3

U.S. Attitudes Toward Legalizing Surrogate Parenting

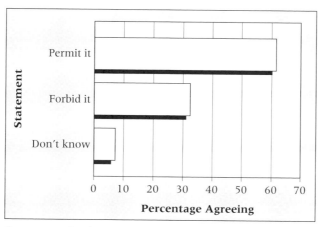

Data source: National Opinion Research Center. 1998. *General Social Survey, 1972–1998.* Available at www.icpsr.umich.edu/GSS/. Accessed June 1, 2001.

and a social mother (Robinson, 1993). Until recently, other than in cases of adoption and stepparenthood, these three roles were occupied by the same person. Surrogate motherhood thus challenges the traditional legal definition of a mother as the woman who gives birth to the child.

Moreover, the technology has advanced more quickly than consideration of ethical and legal issues. Recently in California, a judge ruled that a 2-year-old girl, who had been conceived in a laboratory with donor sperm and egg and who had been carried and delivered by a surrogate, had *no parents* in the eyes of the law. The infertile couple divorced a month before she was born. When her social mother sought child support payments, the social father claimed he was under no legal obligation to support the child, because he had no genetic ties to her. The judge agreed and went even further, ruling that the mother—also with no genetic ties to the child—wasn't "entitled" to be declared a legal mother either (Foote, 1998). Indeed, the only parties with genetic ties to the child were the anonymous donors.

Changing Conceptions of Infertility   The very fact that an entire professional discipline has organized around the task of enhancing people's ability to bear children indicates not only the central place reproduction occupies in this culture but also the fact that it is becoming an increasingly public phenomenon. Not long ago, infertility was an invisible, private tragedy—a topic avoided by the couple in question and spoken about by concerned friends and relatives only in hushed tones. Today, however, considerable attention is focused on the difficulties of those defined as "infertile" (Scritchfield, 1995). The recent medical and public attention devoted to infertility reveals a process of social redefinition. Expectations and definitions of normal patterns of fertility have changed so that couples today are more likely to suspect problems, seek assistance, and expect solutions than previous generations.

Yet infertility does not seem to have become a more prevalent problem in this country. In fact, the rate of infertility has been quite stable over the past 25 years. What has increased is the public's interest in the problem (Scritchfield, 1995). This increase tells us a great deal about the influence of broad social changes on the private experiences of individual people.

Several social factors have contributed to the redefinition of infertility (Scritchfield, 1995). For instance, improved contraception has led many couples to assume that having children is a matter not of deciding if, but of deciding when. The discovery that they are unable to have children is often met with shock and a marked sense of loss of control, motivating them to pursue technological assistance (Greil, 1991). Another social factor contributing to this redefinition of infertility is the trend toward postponed parenthood. Women—particularly employed, college-educated women—are delaying childbearing. The relatively advantaged position of people who postpone childbearing gives them a pretty strong sense of control over all parts of their lives (Scritchfield, 1995). Well-to-do, achievement-oriented couples who have difficulty conceiving may aggressively pursue treatment in an attempt to gain control over their infertility.

In sum, infertility has been transformed from an irreversible private agony that was accepted as fate into a public medical condition for which costly but frequently unfulfilled hopes of rescue exist (Whiteford & Gonzalez, 1995). Stories of happy, beaming parents who have spent upward of $50,000 (perhaps going deeply into debt) for the treatments that helped them have a baby support the powerful cultural idea that the ultimate prize is worth any struggle, any pain, and any cost.

Not even the ticking of the biological clock can stand in the way of our faith that medical technology can "cure" infertility. In 1997, a 63-year-old woman gave birth to a healthy girl. She was being treated in a Los Angeles infertility clinic and had received a donated egg from a much younger woman. This woman wanted to bear a child so badly that to be accepted as a patient by the clinic, she lied about her age (Kolata, 1997b). And so it seems that with eggs donated by younger women and fertilized in laboratories, practically any woman with a uterus has the potential to become pregnant.

Four decades ago infertile couples had limited choices: They could simply resign themselves to the fact that they would forever be childless, or they could adopt. Some would meet their desire to parent by becoming their nieces' and nephews' favorite aunt and uncle. Today, however, it is difficult for couples to choose *not* to have children. The pronatalist expectation is so powerful that those who do not try every conceivable method for overcoming infertility are often considered cultural traitors or objects of pity.

The Stigma of Voluntary Childlessness

Even though having children is still considered the desirable, expected consequence of being married, and the vast majority of married couples have children, more and more people are willfully violating these cultural expectations and *choosing* to remain childless. Exhibit 8.4 shows the percentage of women ages 40–44 who are currently childless. Clearly, marital status is a major determinant of childlessness, especially for white women.

Couples who are childless *in*voluntarily because of infertility may feel stigmatized by others, but they pose no threat to the pronatalist values of society because their *desire* for children remains strong and intact. Voluntarily childless couples, however, directly challenge the commonly held assumption that childbearing is the appropriate course of action in marriage. The voluntarily childless must explain to others not only why they don't have kids but also why they don't *want* them. Even though voluntarily child-free couples report being significantly more satisfied with all aspects of their marriage than couples with children, they still perceive that they are viewed negatively by others (Somers, 1993). Often these couples are maligned for "selfishly" putting their personal needs ahead of the social obligation of parenthood.

EXHIBIT 8.4

Childlessness Among U.S. Women Ages 40–44

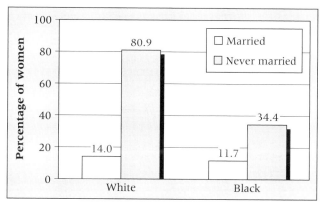

Data source: U.S. Bureau of the Census. 2000b. *Statistical Abstract of the United States: 2000*, Table 95. Washington, DC: U.S. Government Printing Office.

Research suggests, however, that couples' decisions not to have children are more complicated. Sociologist Tim Heaton and his colleagues (Heaton, Jacobson, & Holland, 1999) analyzed changes in parenting desires and behaviors among 1,440 individuals aged 19–39 who participated in the National Survey of Families and Households. When these individuals were initially surveyed in 1988, they were asked about their childbearing desires and plans. They were then interviewed 6 years later to determine whether their plans had changed.

Heaton and his colleagues (1999) found that 43 percent of the respondents were "postponers"—people who originally expressed a desire to have children, but hadn't yet done so by the time of the second survey. An additional 13 percent had originally expressed a desire to have children, but changed their minds by the second survey. Only about 7 percent of those surveyed were "consistently childless"—individuals who never expressed a desire to have children. The remainder of the respondents were people who intended to have children and had in fact had them by the time of the second survey or people who initially didn't want children but then had a child or changed their minds about having one.

You can see from this research how powerful the norms of pronatalism are. Couples who are consistently opposed to having children are actually relatively rare. Most voluntarily childless couples are chronic postponers who remain childless only because they have put off the decision for so long (Veevers, 1980). They start off their marriages assuming they will have children. But through a series of postponements—often for legitimate, credible reasons—they reach a point where having children is either impractical or, because of age, too risky.

Pronatalism and Public Policy

Although the cultural value of parenthood is dominant, not everyone in this society is expected or encouraged to have children. In 1996 the journal *Society* published a symposium on the question of whether parents should be licensed. The underlying rationale used by several authors to argue in favor of licensing was that incompetent parenting is the most important factor associated with costly social problems such as poverty, child abuse, and violent crime (Westman, 1996). The argument is that people should be discouraged—and perhaps even legally prevented—from becoming parents if they do not meet certain basic requirements, such as pledging to protect the well-being of their children or completing some sort of course that provides basic parenting knowledge and skills. Licenses could be revoked if parents showed an inability or unwillingness to care for their children.

Such policy recommendations are unlikely to ever be implemented. However, they illustrate that many people are drawing the conclusion that, although having children is seen as normative and natural, it is also a privilege that under certain circumstances should be restricted or revoked.

Pronatalism and the Poor   Opponents of such proposed policies worry either about too much governmental intrusion into family lives or about yet another form of discrimination against poor people and racial minorities (Jencks & Edin, 1995). But many policies already in place are designed to limit the childbearing of poor people. The debate over whether welfare benefits should be reduced for mothers who have additional children is a case in point (see Chapter 4). Some might argue that preventing mothers on welfare from having additional children reduces negative consequences both for society and for the children themselves. Nevertheless, underlying such a position is the perception that poor mothers—especially unwed poor mothers—are being too fruitful and multiplying too much.

In some situations, parents have been forced to give up their legal right to have children. In 2001, a Wisconsin Supreme Court order barred a man convicted of failure to pay child support from having more children until he is able to show he can support all his offspring. He faces eight years in prison if he violates this order (Lewin, 2001a).

Mothers have sometimes been prevented from having children as well, through court-ordered contraceptive use, as a form of punishment for crimes they've committed. In 1991, for example, after being convicted of several counts of felony child abuse, a 27-year-old mother of four was sentenced to 3 years on Norplant—a contraceptive device that consists of small rods implanted under the skin of a woman's arm. She was given a choice: 1 year in prison and 3 years on probation or 4 months in prison and 3 years on probation using Norplant. Without her lawyer present, she chose the latter option. Although her lawyer later requested that the order be rescinded, the judge stuck to the sentence.

Since then, several similar cases have come to light. Politicians have been eager to exploit Norplant as a means of dealing with "problem mothers." Some legislators have considered mandating Norplant use for *all* poor women convicted of serious drug offenses. Others have proposed it as a solution to what they consider to be the problem of excessive family size of welfare mothers (Young, 1995).

The inconsistency of public attitudes has also become apparent in cases of multiple births. When an Iowa couple had septuplets in 1997, people from all over the country responded with great generosity, sending boxes of diapers, baby care products, and groceries. Locally, the parents were given a fifteen-seat van, free college tuition for the children, even a house. No one suggested they were freeloaders; no one suggested they put a couple of the children up for adoption—advice commonly given to poor pregnant women who already have many children. It's hard to imagine that the admiration and generosity afforded this family would have been forthcoming had the parents been on welfare. Indeed, a working-class black couple who had produced six babies a few months earlier (five survived) received no publicity and no help until the preferential treatment afforded the Iowa family became too obvious to ignore.

Gay and Lesbian Parents   Another segment of the population that is frequently discouraged and sometimes prevented from becoming parents consists of gay and lesbian couples. An estimated 20 percent of gay men and 33 percent of lesbians have previously been in heterosexual marriages; over half of these individuals have at least one biological child (Harry, 1983). Other homosexual men and women have become parents through reproductive technology. And some have become parents through adoption, despite significant societal disapproval.

The oft-heard argument that homosexuality is a threat to the institution of family focuses on the notion that the *capacity* to reproduce (though not necessarily the desire or the success) is a fundamental cornerstone of family and, by extension, society. After all, for a society to survive, there must be a flow of new members to replace those who die. Because gay men and lesbians don't procreate in the traditional biological sense, they are also assumed to be incapable of parenting and establishing kinship ties.

However, such an argument inevitably falls short. Many heterosexual couples are either incapable of reproducing or are committed to not doing so. Yet the state does not

The debate over legalizing gay marriage is discussed in Issue 1.

ask prospective heterosexual spouses if they intend to have children, and the law grants childless married couples the same rights and benefits as married couples with children (F. Johnson, 1996).

The Process of Becoming Parents

The biological facts of parenthood—sexual intercourse, pregnancy, birth, lactation—are, of course, universal. But much more is involved in becoming a parent than biologically creating a child. In every society, the conceiving, bearing, and rearing of children are shaped by cultural and historical beliefs, expectations, and norms.

The Social Construction of Childbirth

As you saw with the description of Hmong mothers at the beginning of this chapter, even something as seemingly natural as giving birth is profoundly influenced by social forces. What are considered normal, healthy childbirth practices in one era, one culture, or even one social class can be seen as dangerous and barbaric in others. What is considered a technological improvement for one age often turns out to be a problem for the next.

Early Attitudes Toward Childbirth   In the seventeenth and eighteenth centuries, pregnancy and childbirth were seen simply as normal events in a woman's life, not as the beginning of an all-encompassing career of parenthood (Gillis, 1996). They were described as an activity—"breeding"—which was no more or less important than a woman's other family activities. The elaborate ritualized attention that many contemporary pregnant women receive—regular doctor's visits, baby showers, medicalized deliveries, and so on—was unknown. Instead, pregnancy was represented as something that happened *to* a woman, an episode in her life in which she was merely the object of natural—and perhaps supernatural—forces.

Because childbirth was not considered a special event, there was little advance preparation for it. In fact, before the nineteenth century, births were hardly anticipated at all. Some people considered it unlucky to interfere with nature or God by preparing for birth too overtly. Most women continued their normal routines right up to the moment of labor. Anything resembling prenatal care was quite rare. Unlike contemporary childbirth, for which labor is sometimes chemically induced, no effort was made to hasten nature (Gillis, 1996).

Up until the nineteenth century, male doctors were almost completely absent from the birthing process. Female midwives and other women in the family or in the community commonly attended women during and after childbirth (Howell-White, 1999). Birth was considered a woman's affair. Only in extremely wealthy families or when the mother's life was in danger was a male doctor consulted (Ulrich, 1990). Indeed, well into the twentieth century, few poor, minority pregnant women had access to doctors and hospitals when they gave birth.

Every effort was made to keep the husbands as far away as possible from the painful, messy, and sometimes lethal process. They typically awaited news of the baby's arrival in the safe company of male friends.

The Medicalization of Childbirth   By the early twentieth century, more and more well-to-do American women chose hospitals as the site of their child's birth. In 1900 only 5 percent of U.S. births took place in hospitals; by 1939 over 50 percent of all births and 75 percent of urban births occurred there. The overwhelming consideration for these expectant mothers was the minimization of pain (Mitford, 1993). Obviously, pain has always been an element of childbirth. But with advances in medical technology, affluent women were beginning to believe that they had a right to avoid pain if at all possible. Initially, women were put to sleep with chloroform or ether throughout labor and delivery. Eventually, localized anesthetics—drugs that alleviated pain but allowed women to remain conscious throughout the delivery—became popular.

The medicalization and hospitalization of childbirth increased women's dependence on the predominantly male medical profession. Little attention was given to the mother's well-being or self-esteem. Typically she was placed in a position with her legs widespread in the air and her genitals totally exposed. Once labor began, doctors commonly resorted to invasive procedures such as the use of forceps and suction. Episiotomies—incisions that increase the size of the vaginal opening to give the baby more room to emerge—became a common part of the birthing process. Today episiotomies are used in 90 percent of all U.S. births, and cesarean sections are performed in almost 25 percent of births (Gillis, 1996). Clearly, medicalization means that the doctor, not the mother, delivers the child.

By the 1950s, however, concern was growing over the possibility that babies might be harmed in some way by the use of drugs and other invasive procedures during delivery. In addition, some women were beginning to complain about the dehumanizing conditions of hospital delivery wards. As one mother of three in the 1950s wrote,

> Women are herded like sheep through the obstetrical assembly line, are drugged and strapped on tables while their babies are forceps-delivered. Obstetricians today are businessmen who run baby factories. Modern painkillers and methods are used for the convenience of the doctor, not to spare the mother. (quoted in Gillis, 1996, p. 173)

Hence, "natural" childbirth, without the aid of anesthetics, became popular in the 1960s and 1970s. It restored women to a more central role in the birth process. Expectant mothers, and their sometimes reluctant husbands, were encouraged to attend childbirth classes to learn special breathing techniques that could ease the delivery without resorting to drugs.

One of the major changes in the process of childbirth that has occurred over the past 30 years is the growing role of fathers. In the past, a father's participation in the event was usually confined to driving his expectant wife to the hospital and pacing the floor in a nearby waiting room until someone came to tell him he had a son or daughter. Today, however, fathers are expected to be present during the delivery—about 90 percent of fathers attend the birth of their child (Griswold, 1993)—although most are passive, sometimes queasy witnesses or cameramen, not active participants. Indeed, their presence in the birthing room is more likely to provide emotional support for the mother than to greet the child as their own. Nevertheless, fathers who choose not to be involved risk being labeled as insensitive and uncaring.

The popularity of "natural" childbirth—less medical intervention, more maternal contact with the newborn right after birth, and so on—has been accompanied in recent years by a nostalgic desire to return to a simpler, less technological childbirth experience. Many hospitals today are turning their cold and sterile "delivery" rooms into homelike, reassuring "birthing" suites. The goal is to re-create, in a safe hospital setting, the benefits of the cozy home birth of the nineteenth century. Most of these rooms are large enough so that the baby and the father can sleep there as well. In addition, more expectant couples are choosing to give birth at home, with the aid of a trained nurse-midwife and with relatives, friends, and other children in attendance.

The Transition to Parenthood

Becoming a parent involves more than giving birth, though. It involves entry into a social role that represents a significant shift in a person's life and identity. Whether the parent is single or married, rich or poor, heterosexual or homosexual, or the birth is planned or unplanned, no transition is more life altering than that from nonparent to parent.

Few role transitions can be as enriching and fulfilling as becoming a parent. For many parents a child is a tangible symbol of the love they share for each other (Neal, Groat, & Wicks, 1989). Children often give parents a sense of meaning and purpose in their lives. Watching children grow and accomplish things can give parents an enormous feeling of pride. Most parents are genuinely thrilled that they have had children and clearly would make the same decision if they were starting over (Cowan & Cowan, 2000). In addition, children expand parents' interaction network by connecting them to other family members—aunts, uncles, grandparents, cousins—as well as the larger community—neighbors, schools, churches, recreational facilities, and so on.

But the transition to parenthood does not come without a fair amount of difficulty:

> It was so scary the first few days, you know. You don't know what you're supposed to do. . . . The awesome amount of responsibility sort of just hits you, and it was just like "oh my God," you know, "we're responsible for this little person now. Nobody is going to help us." (quoted in Fox & Worts, 1999, p. 341)

What makes the transition to parenthood so difficult? Initially, the birth, breastfeeding, and postpartum recovery take a tremendous physical toll on women. Women are expected to be overjoyed after the birth of a child but radical hormonal fluctuations following birth can result in serious postpartum depression for some women. Moreover, the lack of sleep and increased flow of guests and visitors can make the transition into parenthood one of the most physically and emotionally exhausting challenges a person can face.

Social factors also make the transition difficult. For one thing, this transition is irrevocable (Rossi, 1968). Unlike a marriage, which you can dissolve if it is no longer working, or a job, which you can quit if you no longer like it, once you are a parent, you are always a parent. You can have an ex-spouse or an ex-boss or even an ex-friend, but you can't have an ex-child. Parents who try to become ex-parents through abandonment or neglect face prosecution for child endangerment or abuse.

In addition, the transition to parenthood is one that most people are ill prepared to make. "No couple is ever really prepared for the upheavals that accompany the birth of a first child" (Deutsch, 1999, p. 12). Although nowadays most people who are expecting children take classes, what they learn mostly touches on the birthing process, not the day-to-day parenting that follows. Spending time with other people's babies prior to the birth may help somewhat in navigating the terrain of an infant's anatomy. But most of the learning parents experience is "on-the-job" training. Despite 9 months of anticipation, when the baby arrives it arrives abruptly. A person really can't *gradually* become a parent or be a "parent-in-training" until he or she feels more comfortable in the role. The immediate demands of parenthood are especially difficult for single parents, who may not have someone around with whom to share the parent role.

All these things occur within a framework of ambiguity. The goal of parenthood, of course, is to raise competent, well-rounded individuals who will become successful adults. But few guidelines are available to parents on how to reach this goal. Little is known about the long-term outcomes of various child-rearing styles—that is, what works and what doesn't. Hence, parents have no way of knowing whether the things they do with, for, and to their children will ultimately create the sorts of people they want their children to be in 15 or 20 years.

Societal changes over the past several decades have made the transition to parenthood even more difficult (Cowan & Cowan, 2000). Nuclear families have become smaller and are likely to live more isolated lives, often far away from their extended kin. Many young parents today are also trying to create families based on a relatively new egalitarian ideology, in which both partners work and both are expected to share child care responsibilities. These changes require new arrangements to accommodate the increasing demands on parents of young children (Cowan & Cowan, 2000).

Moreover, parenting has become an increasingly private, rather than community obligation. The trend in the culture today is for parents alone to be held accountable for every aspect of the moral and intellectual development of children, often with little institutional support (Glass, 2000):

- They are expected to provide enough income and provide safe housing in neighborhoods with good schools, even if it means working long hours. If they can't afford to live in a good neighborhood, they're expected to volunteer in the child's school and monitor the neighborhood for guns, drugs, pornography, and so on.
- They are expected to exhaustively search for and interview child care providers and continually monitor their quality, because no decent regulatory system has emerged.
- They are expected to read and play music to their children daily to encourage brain development.
- They are expected to constantly supervise children left to play in parks, schoolyards, and neighborhood streets.
- They are expected to provide healthy, well-balanced meals and opportunities for exercise, and protect children from dangers associated with unsafe water, pesticides on food, and exposure to the sun.
- They are expected to monitor children when watching TV or movies to protect them from excessive violence, profanity, and sexually explicit images. Likewise, they are expected to control children's Internet use to avoid exposure to adult Web sites.

Issue 3 examines whether or not such tactics are a violation of children's right to privacy.

- They are expected to teach their children proper moral values and positive behaviors.
- When the children get older, parents are expected to know their friends and friends' parents and watch for signs of precocious sexuality, eating disorders, depression, drug use, or aggression.

Such expectations can be overwhelming to new parents, especially when they see other parents who fail to take such precautions held accountable for the inappropriate or antisocial behavior of their children. For instance, the parents of the two boys who killed 12 people in a Littleton, Colorado, high school in 1999 were sued by parents of some of the victims, who charged that they didn't do enough to prevent the massacre. One of the lawsuits accused the parents of being "negligent in the duties and responsibilities of parental supervision," contending that "by omission and inaction" the parents "facilitated the actions" of their sons (Sink, 1999).

The Stress of Having Children

Given the difficulties associated with the transition to parenthood, it's not surprising that some couples perceive parenthood as a "crisis" that increases stress and decreases marital happiness. Children—as wonderful as they are—represent a substantial drain on time, energy, privacy, and money. The infant's demands for food eventually become the toddler's demands for attention, which inevitably become the teenager's demands for autonomy and the car keys. Parents are pretty much on call 24 hours a day for 18 years—at least. Those quiet, intimate, spontaneous moments of passion that spouses once had quickly become hazy relics of a past life.

Not surprisingly, married couples report that marital quality declines after children are born (Bradbury, Fincham, & Beach, 2000). Over half of the couples with new children surveyed in one study experienced either a severe or moderate decline in the quality of their marriage after the child arrived. For example,

> [New parents] find themselves riding the same roller coaster of elation, despair, and bafflement. . . . [They approached] parenthood full of high hopes and soaring dreams . . . [but] six months or a year after the child's birth they . . . find themselves wondering, "What's happening to us?" (Belsky & Kelly, 1994, p. 4)

Several years ago, researchers asked 1,100 women across the country about their experiences as mothers. About 25 percent of the women said the experience had been mostly positive, and 20 percent said the experience had been mostly negative. The majority (55 percent) had ambivalent feelings about being a parent: Although they acknowledged wonderful aspects of having a child, they also experienced disillusionment over the fact that it wasn't at all what they'd expected (Genevie & Margolies, 1987).

Research on new parents has also found that, although most of them had believed having a child would bring them closer together, the new child in fact represents a significant source of tension (Cowan & Cowan, 2000). Parenthood can sometimes increase feelings of anger, especially for women (Ross & Van Willigen, 1996). Issues of equity become paramount as parents fight over whose turn it is to change the diaper or put the baby to sleep.

Gender and Parenthood

Because of the obvious biological elements associated with bearing children, one could easily conclude that the relationship between parents and their children is an unalterable fact of nature. Parenthood may look quite different in different societies, but underlying these differences is an essential, universal drive.

According to the sociobiological perspective (introduced in Chapter 1), because males and females are physically and genetically different, they logically have different biologically determined roles in raising children. Because women are better equipped anatomically to take care of infant children, the survival of the species depends on their doing so. They are the ones who get pregnant, give birth, and breastfeed. Consequently, they are guided by a different set of parenting expectations from those that guide men.

Sociologist Alice Rossi (1977) argues that biological sex differences affect parental behavior not only during pregnancy but also after birth. Much mothering, she feels, is instinctual. For instance, the cry of an infant is sufficient to stimulate the secretion of the hormone oxytocin in the mother, which triggers nipple erection in preparation for nursing. Rossi also notes that the vast majority of women instinctually cradle their infants in their left arm, regardless of handedness, where the infants can be closer to the soothing sounds of the mother's heartbeat.

But are these observations sufficient to support the claim that mothering is instinctual? The oxytocin secretion is experienced by mothers as a "milk letdown"—that is, the milk rushes to the nipple and sometimes even leaks out. But milk leaks in response not only to hearing the infant cry but also to being sexually or emotionally aroused, running up or down stairs, or simply leaning over (Rothman, 1987). Over time, the let-down response becomes less immediate, eventually taking several minutes of actual sucking to activate. Hence, mothers aren't really responding instinctually to the sound of their infant crying but to the social meaning they attach to it. That is, letdown is a social as well as physiological phenomenon.

Likewise, mothers who hold their infants on the left, over their hearts, may be responding not to instinct but to something they've learned: Infants do calm down when they are held over a human heartbeat. For that matter, babies calm down when they hear *any* heartbeat—even one that is taped. In short, mothers may hold babies this way because it works; it feels right because the baby settles down.

Furthermore, many of the original causes of differences between male and female parenting roles have been done away with by advances in technology. Children's survival no longer depends on a mother's constant care. With day care, infant formula, and so forth, children can survive quite well without a constant maternal presence. Cultural shifts have also made it more acceptable and even desirable for men to take a more active role in parenting. In fact, men who find themselves single parents can successfully raise children from infancy (Risman, 1989).

So the key question is not whether parenting behaviors are biologically programmed but what the social consequences of parenting are. Whether they are instinctual or learned, biological or social, the pregnancy and birth experiences are culturally and personally significant to women. In a culture that places such a high premium on parenthood—and, in particular, motherhood—people have come to believe that women are uniquely, biologically suited to the task. But even in such a culture, not all women want to be mothers. These decisions are influenced by a variety of social factors and experiences and not by some biological predisposition (Gerson, 1985). If having children were solely the result of a biological instinct, there wouldn't be variation in birth rates across cultures, between different social groups within the same culture, and, as shown in Exhibit 8.5, over time.

EXHIBIT 8.5

Birth Rates in the United States

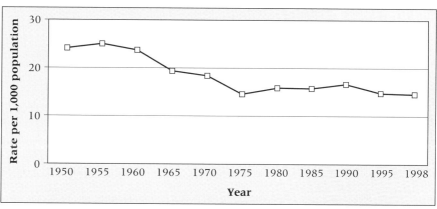

Source: U.S. Bureau of the Census. 2000b. *Statistical Abstract of the United States: 2000,* Table 77. Washington, DC: U.S. Government Printing Office.

In addition, not all women who give birth form nurturant bonds with their infants. Some are indifferent to their children's needs; others are abusive. And although mothers all over the world are similarly equipped to nurse their infants, in many of the world's societies not all are the exclusive caretakers of children after infancy (Epstein, 1988). These temporal, cultural, and group variations give sociologists important insights into the social determinants of parenting.

Nevertheless, the belief in the primacy of the mother–child bond remains strong. Even vocabulary reflects gender-based expectations regarding the different parenting responsibilities of mothers and fathers. Consider the verbs *to mother* and *to father*. In common usage, to *mother* a child is to care for, cherish, or protect that child. *Mothering* is associated with nurturing. In contrast, to *father* a child is to engage in the physical act of procreation, requiring little more than the fertilization of an egg. In common usage, *fathering* a child has nothing to do with a man's parental behavior.

As discussed in Chapter 7, women still bear a disproportionately high degree of responsibility for domestic labor and child care despite significant advances in their workforce participation. Currently, there is no known society where women don't do the majority of child care (Deutsch, 1999). Regardless of children's ages, mothers typically are more invested and involved in the day-to-day lives of their children than are fathers. They also do more of the "emotional" work with children and worry more about their well-being. As a result, women are called on, far more than men, to sacrifice interests and identities outside the family—such as career and education—in order to devote more time to raising the children.

Active, hands-on parenting is required of mothers but is optional for most fathers, whose contribution to parenting—although more visible and more acceptable than ever before—still tends to be defined as "helping" (Thompson & Walker, 1989). As one author put it, "Fathers are volunteer providers; mothers are the staff" (Barry, 1993, p. 70). Even the physical separation of home and work has not created psychological distance for women in the same way it has for men. Mothers never cease being mothers. They are expected to be "mentally at home" in ways fathers rarely are. Men's increased involvement in pregnancy and childbirth has not resulted in equal responsibility for child care *after* the baby is born (Lorber, 1994). Even in households where other forms of housework and breadwinning are shared equally, child care responsibilities still tend to be divided along traditionally unequal gender lines (see Chapter 7).

Images of Motherhood

Women are still socialized to value the rewards of motherhood and to believe that having children is a primary source of self-identity. The following statement reflects this traditional view:

> Motherhood is inevitable; every woman will or should be a mother. A woman's identity is tenuous and trivial without motherhood. A woman enjoys and intuitively knows what to do for her child; she cares for her child without ambivalence or awkwardness. . . . Within the "magic circle" of mother and child, the mother devotes herself to her child's needs and holds her child's fate in her hands. (Thompson & Walker, 1989, p. 860)

These lessons begin early in a girl's life (see Chapter 2). Girls' toys often reinforce the expectation that they will, or should, someday become mothers. For example, My Bundle

Baby, manufactured by Mattel, is a 10-inch infant doll in a padded pouch that can be worn around a child's abdomen. By pressing a button hidden inside the pouch, the child can feel the baby inside "kick" and can hear its heartbeat (Lawson, 1992). The Judy doll, manufactured by the Judith Corporation, looks like any other 11-inch doll except that she is pregnant. She comes with a distended tummy that, when removed, reveals the presence of a cute baby nestled comfortably inside the doll's plastic uterus. The baby can be bloodlessly removed and a flat, nonpregnant tummy inserted in its place. The advertisement reads, "Judy is more than a toy, she's a natural way for your child to learn while playing." Part of what young girls learn through these toys is the cultural value of motherhood.

Having a baby is thought to be essential if a woman is to be whole, because the experiences of pregnancy and motherhood are "the core of women's being" (quoted in Nelkin & Lindee, 1995). As one journalist described it, the unpleasantness of pregnancy is a minor price to pay for the self-validation and social rewards it provides:

> Even though I hated the sweating, the heartburn and the funny underpants I wore when I was pregnant, I liked the feeling that being pregnant was something. SOMETHING! I stuck out and waddled, and society smiled at me and gave me seats on busses . . . I felt queenly and grateful. (Marzollo, 1981, p. 47)

Women who downplay the importance of motherhood have always been the object of concern. In the late nineteenth century, physicians feared that too much thinking would lead to a degeneration of a woman's uterus and ovaries. Young women were often prevented from entering college to ensure their reproductive health. Today, women who pursue intellectual and professional interests and thereby postpone childbearing are similarly led to believe that they might experience reproductive difficulty. Cultural images of ticking "biological clocks" reinforce the idea that working women who have postponed pregnancy are running out of time to reproduce. As one author gravely put it, too many women "have continued to put off childbearing without fully understanding the possible consequences of that choice" (Maranto, 1995, p. 56). This idea is no longer based on some alleged connection between brain use and ovarian development but on modern scientific understanding of the link between infertility and maternal age.

Motherhood and Maternity   To most people, the centrality of maternity (the state of being pregnant and the physical act of giving birth) gives women not only the ability but also the desire to nurture—in other words, maternity fosters motherhood. So it's not surprising that when we hear of mothers abusing or murdering their children we are stunned. When in 2001 a Houston woman named Andrea Yates drowned her five young children, aged 6 months to 7 years, people around the country asked, "How could a *mother* do that to her children?" The fact that she was their biological mother rendered her act even more unfathomable and unforgivable. But the media paid scant attention to Vincent Spik of Findlay Township, Maryland, who in 1998 used a sledgehammer to kill his 5-year-old twins because, he said, they weren't moving fast enough.

Although people today consider the equation of maternity with motherhood universal and timeless, it is, in fact, a relatively recent development. Indeed, until the nineteenth century, anyone who raised a child was addressed as "Mother" regardless of her biological connection to the child. The term was applied to the proprietors of brothels and to innkeepers. In colonial New England all older women—whether they had children or not—were called "mothers" (cited in Gillis, 1996).

The separation of maternity and motherhood in the eighteenth century is particularly evident in what typically took place moments after the birth. Mothers may have had a central role in the physical act of giving birth, but once the child was delivered they became peripheral. Instead of being placed at the mother's breast, the newborn was usually taken to the hearth, symbolically identifying it with the household rather than the mother (Gillis, 1996). It was then swaddled and brought to the father to show to friends and other neighbors. The relative neglect of the mother immediately after the birth was a result of a belief that she wasn't supposed to show too much affection toward the child. Mothers were usually isolated for days, even weeks after the birth. They were rarely present at the church when their children were baptized and played little part in the child's life in the weeks after its birth. The deep love of a mother that is so celebrated today was regarded with suspicion.

Giving birth and giving nurture were often incompatible for demographic reasons (Gillis, 1996). Because birth rates and death rates were so high in Europe and North America up until the mid–nineteenth century, women who gave birth could seldom mother all their children the way people think of mothering today. Only about half of all babies born lived to the age of 21, and mothers were likely to die before all their children had left home. Intensive involvements with each individual child were simply impossible. Consequently, maternity and motherhood were understood to be separable, much as paternity (creating a child) and fatherhood (nurturing a child) are separable today.

But children in these eras didn't lack a maternal presence. Wet nurses—women who would breastfeed other women's children for extended periods—were commonly employed not only by upper-class women, who found breastfeeding distasteful and unfashionable, but also by working-class women, who had neither the time nor the energy to feed their infants. Of the 21,000 babies born in 1780 in Paris, 17,000 were sent to wet nurses (deMause, 1975). But wet nurses commonly took on too many babies in order to make more money. Frequently they ran out of milk, so many babies had to be sent to a series of different nurses, depriving them of a single "mother" figure (McCoy, 1981).

Eventually, the very idea of an infant being breastfed by someone other than its mother became incompatible with cultural definitions of good motherhood. By the late nineteenth and early twentieth centuries, wet nursing had become a thing of the past, associated with primitive, unenlightened times. Mothers either suckled their infants themselves or bottle-fed them.

But intense, continual contact between mothers and their children was rare in the nineteenth century. It was still common for preteen children to be informally adopted by relatives. When kin lived nearby, children often ate meals and slept apart from their biological parents. When families had many children, older ones were frequently sent to live permanently with distant relatives. Girls from poor families were likely to be sent away to work in domestic service. Foundling hospitals and orphanages were common fixtures on the social landscape; parents often placed their children in these institutions because they couldn't afford to raise them. For a mother to give up her children "to the kindness of strangers" was considered neither immoral nor unnatural (Gillis, 1996, p. 155). Not until the 1920s could parents expect most if not all of their children to be their responsibility until the children were married.

Fetal Rights versus Mothers' Rights   One of the great ironies of this culture's conception of motherhood is that although women are believed to be naturally endowed to nurture their children and are expected to place their children's well-being above all else, they are also seen by some as the greatest threat to their children *before* they're born. The contemporary debate that pits **fetal rights** against women's rights has resulted in some of the most contested family issues in contemporary times. Nowhere is this debate more visible, heated and political than in the struggle over abortion. Indeed, for many Americans, abortion is *the* preeminent political issue of our time (Hout, 1999).

Interestingly, abortion was legal in the United States until the mid-nineteenth century. Although some of the reasons behind outlawing it stemmed from concerns about the mother and fetus, others were more political. For instance, as the medical profession became more powerful, physicians sought to gain control from women who performed abortions. Also, the high rate of abortion among white, Protestant, middle- and upper-class women created fears of "overpopulation" by nonwhites, the poor, and immigrants (Mohr, 1978).

In 1973, with the passage of *Roe v. Wade*, abortion was legalized, with some important restrictions. Although pregnant women could obtain an abortion in the first trimester without interference by the state, the U.S. Supreme Court ruled that the state could insist on reasonable standards of medical procedures in the second trimester to ensure the mother's health, and that abortion cannot be performed in the third trimester except in cases where the life or health of the mother is threatened. Since then, there have been numerous legal challenges to a woman's right to obtain an abortion. Although women still have the legal right to terminate a pregnancy, various states have imposed restrictions such as parental notification in the case of teenage women, husband notification, tests of fetal viability, and mandatory waiting periods. Outside the legal arena, protests and violence at abortion clinics and public exposure of abortion seekers and providers are further attempts to restrict women's access to abortion.

But the controversy over fetal rights extends beyond whether women have the right to terminate a pregnancy. In recent years, the behavior of pregnant women who intend to keep their babies has come under heavy scrutiny. Often judges subject pregnant women who commit crimes to harsher sentences than men or nonpregnant women. For instance, several years ago a 29-year-old pregnant Maryland woman was sentenced to 6 months in jail for forging $722 in checks. It was her first offense, which typically would have resulted in probation. The judge acknowledged her differential treatment:

> The extent to which private behavior ought to come under community or governmental control is explored in Issue 3.

> It is true that the defendant has not been treated the same as if she were a man in this case. But then a man who is a convicted rapist is treated differently from a woman. She has also not been treated the same as a nonpregnant woman. But [she] became pregnant and chose to bear the baby who, like most criminal defendants the court sees so frequently, will start life with one other severe strike against it—no father is around. Arguably, [she] should have demonstrated even greater responsibility toward her child. (quoted in Roth, 1993, p. 126)

Concern over the harm mothers pose to their fetuses is particularly strong with regard to using drugs and alcohol. Cigarette packs come with a warning that smoking while pregnant poses health risks to the baby. Restaurants in some states are required to post signs warning pregnant mothers that ingesting alcohol can jeopardize their babies' health. This concern is certainly warranted. An estimated 11 percent of all babies born in this country each year have been exposed to street drugs while in the uterus (cited in Roth, 1993) Four thousand babies each year are born with fetal alcohol syndrome and another 11,000 with fetal alcohol effect (Chasnoff, 1989). But the question remains: What is the state's interest in pregnant women's behavior?

Increasingly, the state's response (other than the printed warnings, which are designed more to relieve companies of liability than to protect the health of babies) has been to prosecute and incarcerate pregnant women who use drugs. Consider the following cases:

- A Kentucky woman who gave birth to three children during her 17-year addiction to drugs was sentenced to 5 years in prison for criminal child abuse (Hoffman, 1990).
- A South Carolina woman was sentenced to 12 years in prison for killing her unborn fetus by smoking crack cocaine. The jury deliberated 15 minutes before convicting her. In an earlier case, the South Carolina Supreme Court had ruled that a viable fetus could be considered a person under the state's criminal code (Firestone, 2001).
- A Wisconsin woman was charged with attempted murder for giving birth to a baby with a blood alcohol level twice the threshold for a legal finding of intoxication. The mother had a history of problem drinking and had been drinking heavily the night of the birth (Terry, 1996).

Since the late 1980s, hundreds of women in thirty states have been arrested or prosecuted for behavior while pregnant that posed danger to their fetuses, the vast majority involving the use of illegal drugs (Terry, 1996). Even more have been deprived of custody of their children or jailed during pregnancy (a practice referred to as "protective incarceration") (Roberts, 1991).

Although the motivation to ensure the health of fetuses is understandable, the societal response is not uniform. Most of the women prosecuted for giving birth to infants who test positive for drugs are poor and black (Roberts, 1991). These women are the least likely to obtain adequate prenatal care. Also, because poor women are generally under greater government supervision—through public hospitals and welfare agencies—their drug use is more likely to be detected and reported than more affluent expectant mothers. Indeed, the government's main source of information about prenatal drug use is hospitals' reporting of infant drug exposure to child welfare authorities. Private physicians, who serve more affluent women, perform fewer drug-screening procedures. One study found that, despite similar rates of substance abuse, pregnant black women are ten times more likely than pregnant white women to be reported to public health authorities (Chasnoff, Landress, & Barrett, 1990). Concern over this imbalance led the U.S. Supreme Court, in 2001, to rule that hospital workers cannot constitutionally test maternity patients for illegal drugs without their consent if the purpose is to alert police to a crime (Greenhouse, 2001).

Far from deterring dangerous drug use, prosecution of drug-addicted mothers often deters pregnant women from using available health and counseling services—out of fear they will be reported to government authorities and charged with a crime. To make matters worse, such mothers can obtain alcohol- or drug-dependency treatment only with extreme difficulty. Because they fear liability, most substance abuse programs will not accept pregnant women. Withdrawal from some drugs can actually do more harm or even kill a fetus (Roth, 1993).

Everyone would agree that babies should receive the best possible start in life. However, focusing solely on pregnant women allows society to ignore other threats to the well-being of children, threats that lie outside the mother's body: poverty, inadequate health care, lack of prenatal care, poor housing, environmental hazards, racism, and so on. Controlling the behavior of mothers allows the government to appear concerned about babies without having to spend any money, change any priorities, or challenge any vested interests (Pollitt, 1991). But even as people become more obsessed with pregnant women's behavior, the health and well-being of American children continues to suffer.

Images of Fatherhood

In the eighteenth century, fathers rather than mothers were considered the primary parents. Fathers were active in all the major nurturing and educational functions we now associate with motherhood (Gillis, 1996). They oversaw wet nurses and carried on the bulk of family correspondence.

The Industrial Revolution of the nineteenth century sent a shock wave through the domestic world that fathers ruled. The male family role became defined primarily as that of the breadwinner. This role, of course, has always varied by social class. The search for work commonly sent poor men away from their families; and aristocratic fathers were typically away in the military or civil service. Men who could do much of their work in the house— artisans, farmers, businessmen—tended to be the ones who took on a more active father role. But it wasn't until the late twentieth century that fathers in all walks of life once more became significant features of their children's daily lives.

Separate Spheres and the Distant Dad   The separation of work and home—the separate spheres ideology explained in Chapter 7—created physical and emotional distance between fathers and children. But throughout the twentieth century, calls for greater father involvement have been heard. Even as early as the 1920s, psychologists warned that lack of fathers' involvement could seriously jeopardize sex role development of children (Weiss, 2000).

During the baby boom period of the 1950s, there was renewed interest in father–child relationships. One father, writing in 1951, claimed, "I couldn't be satisfied to be home and not enjoy our daughter's company part of the time, whether it's listening to her coo, giving her the two A.M. bottle, or, yes, even changing her diapers" (quoted in Weiss, 2000, p. 87). Fathers were believed to play an important, albeit complementary role to mothers, providing children with the stimulation and enthusiasm that exhausted mothers might not be able to give (Weiss, 2000). And concerns about appropriate gender socialization also prevailed. According to two family experts writing during this period: "Father's arms are strong and the child who experiences the security they give him grows up with a warm regard for some of the best qualities of masculinity—tenderness, protection, and strength" (quoted in Weiss, 2000, p. 89).

In part, men's greater involvement in parenting during the baby boom era stemmed from pure necessity. High fertility and the close spacing of children made it common for a family to have three or four children under age 6 in the household at one time. As one family historian put it, "There were simply too many meals, baths, and diapers for one parent to handle alone" (Weiss, 2000, p. 98).

Yet the primary responsibility of these dads—especially those in the middle class—remained breadwinning. Between working 40 or more hours per week and commuting to their suburban homes, many middle- and working-class fathers had little time to spend with their children (Weiss, 2000). Interestingly, these men—as they moved through the life course—sometimes looked back with regret:

> When I was young and started out, I presumed that my work was essentially more important than that of my wife who would shape our children and act as the primary

parent in order to develop them. I have subsequently concluded that, in terms of my satisfactions, that hers is a more lasting and useful and meaningful job than was mine. (quoted in Weiss, 2000, p. 110)

Still, most parents during the baby boom defined fatherhood as supplemental and more peripheral than motherhood, and fathers' primary identity centered around their economic provider roles.

But although men started to show more interest in fatherhood in the latter half of the twentieth century, many expressed doubts about their willingness to become fully involved in their families (Bernard, 1981; Ehrenreich, 1983). The stampede of fathers into delivery rooms to witness the *births* of their children was not accompanied by equally enthusiastic participation in ongoing daily care and rearing (Cowan & Cowan, 2000). One study found that, in two-parent families with employed mothers, fathers still spend about one-third as much time as mothers actually engaged in one-to-one interaction with their child. In addition, they spend about two-thirds as much time as mothers being accessible—that is, ready or available to tend to a child if needed. Finally, mothers carry over 90 percent of the responsibility for their children (making sure they have clothes to wear, get to activities on time, go to the pediatrician, and so on) (Lamb, 1987).

Even fathers who assume primary care of their children while their wives work often look to their wives to anticipate and plan for the child's needs (cited in Russell, 1999). And in families where fathers are primary caretakers of children, that role tends to be seen as a temporary, short-term arrangement. One study found that only one-third of families in which fathers were primary caregivers could be classified this way 4 years later (Radin, 1988). The majority of fathers in this study became less involved as soon as they could.

The imbalance in hands-on parenting found in most families has led some experts to conclude that the *culture* of fatherhood—our beliefs about what fathers should do or what we'd like them to do—has changed more rapidly than the *conduct* of fatherhood—what fathers actually do (LaRossa, 1992).

Moreover, more fathers than ever before are absent from their children's lives because of abandonment and divorce. A growing proportion either deny paternity or shirk parental obligations. In divorced families, contact between children and their noncustodial fathers drops off sharply with the length of time since the parents separated—although it's not altogether clear if the problem is fathers' unwillingness to get involved or mothers' effectiveness at preventing them from doing so (Furstenberg, 1997).

To be fair, fathers who truly want to be involved in their children's lives often feel that their contributions to child rearing are less significant and less necessary than the mothers'. As one new father stated, "[My wife] has the kid on her breast every two hours. And then, for ten minutes, I get to clean up the poop and diaper him and put him back to sleep. What's the point? I might as well be out bringing in some more money" (quoted in Cowan & Cowan, 2000, p. 103). Fathers who feel this way are likely to retreat from active child rearing and make their way back to their work, where they know they can make an essential, measurable contribution to their family's welfare.

In addition, the workplace still discourages men from completely abandoning the breadwinner role. A man who wants to work part time or not at all in order to care for his children is still likely to be looked on with suspicion, disappointment, or amusement by an employer. As one father who took a leave of absence from work when his two children were born put it, "[My boss] was very generous with the time, but he never let me forget it. . . . You don't get a lot of points at the office for wanting to have a healthy family life" (quoted in Gibbs, 1993a, p. 55). Although contemporary fathers are now likely to take substantial pride in their role as nurturer, the breadwinner ideal is still associated with maturity, respectability, and masculinity. And so breadwinning remains the unifying element in the lives of most American fathers (Griswold, 1993).

Despite a significant redefinition of fatherhood over several centuries, fathers are still rarely seen as being at the center of everyday family life in the same way that mothers are (Gillis, 1996). Even today, the U.S. Bureau of the Census can document the 70 million or so mothers age 15 or over in the United States but has little idea how many fathers there are (Gibbs, 1993a).

An Emerging Image of Fatherhood   Nevertheless, images of fatherhood do seem to be evolving. As the percentage of U.S. households that consist of a married couple dependent on a sole male breadwinner has declined (from 60 percent in 1950 to 14 percent in 1990), men have been able to escape somewhat from the excessive burdens of being the primary breadwinner (Gerson, 1993). As a result, contemporary fathers have felt somewhat freer than their predecessors to participate more fully in the upbringing of their children (Furstenberg, 1997). Certainly many men nowadays say they want to take a more active role in raising their children. One poll found that 39 percent of fathers would quit their jobs to spend more time with their children; another found that 74 percent of men would welcome a scaled-down job, off the fast track (cited in Gibbs, 1993a).

And some fathers do appear to be increasingly involved in raising their children. According to U.S. Census figures, fathers are taking care of about one in every five preschool children while mothers work (U.S. Bureau of the Census, 1998c), and the percentage of men who choose not to look for work because of home responsibilities increased from 4.6 percent in 1991 to 8.4 percent in 1996 (cited in Marin, 2000).

Research suggests that, if given the opportunity, fathers can interact with and care for their children just as well as mothers can. For example, although the proportion of children living in father-only families is rather rare—they constitute about 5 percent of all children—such living arrangements have increased dramatically over the last 20 years. These single fathers respond to their nontraditional role with strategies that could be considered stereotypically feminine (cuddling, nurturing, expressing intimacy, and so on). With no wife to depend on, men can be effective "mothers" (Risman, 1989).

What about the father's role in families where mothers are also present? In many cases, because of the mother's employment and the couple's desire or need to avoid the high cost of child care, the father assumes an active role in raising the children. For more and more men today, becoming a father means making a commitment to care for their children emotionally and physically, whether or not they are forced to do so by the mother's employment (Coltrane, 1996a; Furstenberg, 1997). A recent study of parents with preschoolers found that men with liberal gender ideologies, who view fathers as being just as capable and crucial to children's development as mothers, were the ones most likely to be involved in the day-to-day care of their children. But these researchers concluded that ideological beliefs about the father's role may go only so far. Parents' work schedules may be more influential in determining the amount of time men spend as the child's primary caregiver (Bonney, Kelley, & Levant 1999, p. 411). The structure and demands of the workplace often make it difficult for even the most committed fathers to assume very active roles in their children's lives.

Some fathers resolve the dilemma by leaving the labor force to care for their children. In fact, more men are taking time off work to care for their children than ever before. At

AT&T, for example, the ratio of women to men on parental leave dropped from 400 to 1 in the 1980s to 18 to 1 today (cited in "Workplace experts say," 1997). Notice how this father's experience belies the image of the cold, aloof breadwinner-father:

> It was real hard to sit down and hold them when they were sick. I had to keep telling myself that this is important, you need to be here with them doing nothing. Which is the feeling I had—I'm not doing anything—but I was. Eventually those things really paid off with the trust the kids developed in me. (quoted in Coltrane, 1996a, p. 12)

Such participation in children's lives certainly has its benefits. Most child development experts agree that children do better when their fathers take an active, supportive role in their lives. Furthermore, both men and women report greater marital satisfaction when fathers are very involved in caring for their children (cited in Bonney et al., 1999). As one sociologist put it, "When men and women share family work, the entire society benefits" (Coltrane, 1996a, p. 199).

DEMO•GRAPHICS

Fathers' Involvement in Family Life

Most of the research conducted on parenting has focused on mothers, but over the past decade, greater attention has been paid to the role that fathers play in their children's lives. Some of the earliest attention focused on the significant increase in the percentage of father-only families over the past 20 years. Notice in Exhibit 8.6a how the growth rates vary between different racial/ethnic groups.

As you've seen in this chapter, what it means to be a father has also changed in recent decades. Increasingly, U.S. culture has come to expect fathers to be highly involved in their children's lives and even to match mothers' involvement in many aspects of child rearing. As Exhibit 8.6b shows, today there is little difference in what people expect mothers and fathers to provide for their children.

But, of course, expectations do not always match reality. In other words, the culture of fatherhood has probably changed more rapidly than the conduct of fatherhood. One indicator of parental involvement provided by the U.S. Census Bureau is participation in children's school activities. The census breaks down involvement by gender in two-parent families and single-parent families for various school activities. Let's examine parents' involvement in two-parent families first. (For clarity's sake, data for students in grades K–5 only are presented; the gendered patterns of involvement are fairly consistent with patterns found for grades 6–8, but overall involvement is lower at the higher grades.)

As you can see in Exhibit 8.6c, fathers in two-parent households participate more in their young children's school activities when mothers are also present. In other words, both parents are usually present for class events, meetings, and conferences. When only one parent is involved, it's almost always the mother. Also note that the more effort involved in the activity (for instance, volunteering at the school versus attending a meeting), the more likely it is that fathers will be absent.

But what happens when mothers are not present to assume much of the child rearing responsibilities? Do single fathers tend to act more like mothers under these circumstances?

EXHIBIT 8.6

The Changing Role of Fathers

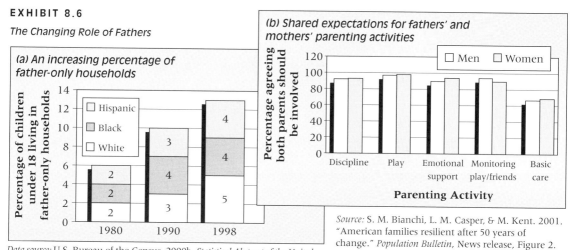

(a) An increasing percentage of father-only households

(b) Shared expectations for fathers' and mothers' parenting activities

Source: S. M. Bianchi, L. M. Casper, & M. Kent. 2001. "American families resilient after 50 years of change." *Population Bulletin*, News release, Figure 2.

Data source: U.S. Bureau of the Census. 2000b. *Statistical Abstract of the United States: 2000*, Table 69. Washington, DC: U.S. Government Printing Office.

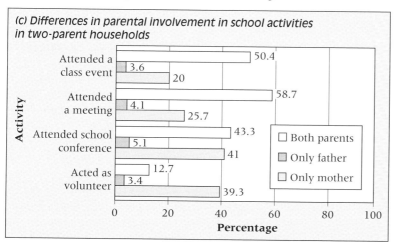

(c) Differences in parental involvement in school activities in two-parent households

Data source: U.S. Bureau of the Census. 2000b. *Statistical Abstract of the United States: 2000*, Table 256. Washington, DC: U.S. Government Printing Office.

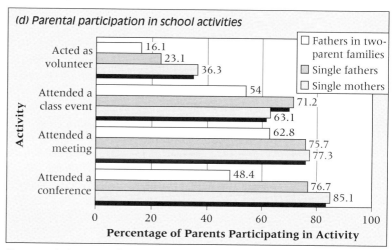

(d) Parental participation in school activities

Data source: U.S. Bureau of the Census. 2000b. *Statistical Abstract of the United States: 2000*, Table 256. Washington, DC: U.S. Government Printing Office.

As you can see in Exhibit 8.6d, single fathers tend to be somewhat less involved in their children's school activities than single mothers, except for attending class events. But they are more involved than fathers in two-parent households.

Thinking Critically About the Statistics

1. Reexamine the data in Exhibit 8.6a. Why do you think there's been an increase in single-father households over the past 20 years? Do you think the increase is simply a function of the high rate of divorce, or does it reflect a more significant trend in how the father role is defined? What other statistics might help you answer this question? How do you account for the racial differences in single fatherhood?
2. How can you explain the discrepancy between the attitudes toward parenting roles shown in Exhibit 8.6b and the actual behavior shown in Exhibits 8.6c and 8.6d? Do you think respondents are more likely to overestimate or underestimate their involvement in their children's lives? Do you think men are more or less likely than women to miscalculate their involvement? Why?
3. Examine the patterns of involvement for "mother only" in two-parent households in Exhibit 8.6c. How do they differ from "father only" involvement? How do you explain the difference? What barriers to involvement exist for mothers? What barriers exist for fathers? Why do you think parents in general are so unlikely to be involved in children's school activities?
4. Compare Exhibits 8.6c and 8.6d. Why do you think fathers in two-parent households are less involved in their children's school activities than single fathers?
5. Considering all four charts in Exhibit 8.6, what do you think the data suggest about parenting responsibilities of men and women?   ■

Conclusion

Parenthood occupies a formidable place in U.S. society. Despite the fact that some people remain childless, becoming a parent is usually considered this culture's pinnacle of family commitment and maturity. Parenthood, as both a social role and a procreative accomplishment, is so deeply ingrained in the culture that its absence in married life still evokes curiosity, pity, or condemnation.

As you've seen throughout this chapter, the cultural ideal of parenthood sometimes doesn't match its ambivalent reality:

- The cultural primacy of biological parenthood persists despite the growing recognition that emotional bonds can be just as strong as genetic ones.
- Parenthood itself continues to be presented as a joyous, valuable, and, of course, normal experience even though it frequently causes unexpected stress, strain, and unhappiness in people's lives and is looked on with ambivalence in the world of work.
- Women are still expected to place motherhood at the top of their list of priorities, even though more and more women consider it a potentially restrictive role and are rejecting the notion that becoming a mother is necessary for their emotional fulfillment.
- The importance of fathers in children's lives is widely acknowledged today even though men's contributions to parenting continue to lag behind women's and they are still drawn by the unambiguous rewards of the traditional breadwinner role.

Perhaps it's not so strange that such discrepancies exist. Certainly the stability of society depends on people seeing parenthood in the most positive light possible. Research on the downside of becoming or being a parent usually remains safely hidden in academic journals, rarely entering the societal discourse on parenthood. A society has much at stake when couples contemplate having children. Indeed, it's hard to imagine a society in which parenthood is not actively promoted and encouraged. Is it any wonder, then, that the dominant cultural messages people receive about parenting emphasize its advantages and downplay its problems?

Chapter Highlights

- Some sociologists characterize the United States as a pronatalist society—one in which married couples are expected to reproduce. Having children is seen as essential to self-fulfillment. Other societies have even stronger pronatalist values, sometimes enacting policies that require people to try to have children.
- The ideal of pronatalism affects the societal response to infertility, which in turn affects infertile couples' feelings of stigma. Because of the value placed on parenthood, medical treatments for infertility have become a booming business.
- Even though having children is still expected of married couples, more and more Americans are choosing to remain childless.
- Even the universal, biological experience of giving birth is profoundly influenced by cultural and historical forces. What is considered normal and healthy in one society or in one era can be considered barbaric in another.
- Although parenthood can be an extremely rewarding experience, the transition from nonparent to parent can be stressful.
- Images of motherhood and fatherhood are often influenced by beliefs about the natural, innate tendencies of mothers and fathers. However, gender differences in parenting behavior are clearly linked to broader cultural expectations.

Your Turn

We've noted in this chapter that the transition to parenthood can simultaneously be a wonderful and a frightening experience. Although most couples look forward to the transition with great anticipation, many experience a sense of dread or general anxiety. Fortunately, prospective parents today have many options available to them to ease the transition: parenting magazines, books, and Web sites; childbirth classes; videos; and so on. These sources of information can relieve some of the tension associated with entering a new world of responsibilities, but they can also inadvertently create an idealized image of parenthood that can lead to unreasonable expectations and worries.

See if you can get permission to sit in on a local childbirth class. Most hospitals offer some sort of program for prospective parents. What sorts of information are these soon-to-be parents provided? What is the balance between the positive and negative information about the transition to parenthood? How are men incorporated into the lessons? Are they treated as "outside observers" or as "equal participants"? It might be useful to talk to some of the fathers to see what their expectations are with regard to their role in the birth and subsequent care of the child.

To get a deeper understanding of the cultural and historical context of the transition to parenthood, see if your library has back issues of a magazine that's devoted to parenting, such as *Parents* magazine. Analyze the contents of a sample of these magazines from the past 3 or 4 decades. Pay particular attention to articles devoted to childbirth, the mother role, and the father role. Such articles serve as a valuable barometer of changing attitudes and expectations regarding mothers and fathers. Do you notice any interesting changes in the type of guidance given to parents? How have society's expectations of parents changed over time? To what do you attribute these changes?

Childhood and Child Rearing

Growing Up in Two Worlds

Children who are members of racial or ethnic minorities grow up in a complex social environment. They live simultaneously in two worlds: their ethnic community and the "mainstream" society. The photos and words in this essay come from a Web site titled "Glass Houses" (www.cmp.ucr.edu/students/glasshouses), created by artist Jacalyn Lopez Garcia: "It is through my art . . . that I am able to explore the complexities of cultural identity and reflections of growing up . . . with a 'Mexican-American' consciousness."

For the most part, as a young person, my life seemed relatively uncomplicated, growing up in middle-class neighborhoods and living in the suburbs of California.

My mother wanted me to live like an "American" with all the rights and privileges and no discrimination. Because I was fair-skinned and light-haired she thought it would be much easier for me. I always wished I had dark skin and dark hair like my mother.

My youth and middle-class status did not protect me from experiencing and witnessing the challenges and hard realities of oppressive environments—especially those of my mother's relatives who lived in Mexico and my Mexican friends who lived in the barrios.

I always wished I had dark skin and dark hair like my mother.

I remember my father was usually exhausted after a hard day's work of manual labor. For six months he played Mr. Mom . . . because a hateful "white" neighbor reported to the authorities that my mother was undocumented. I was only seven years old when my mother was deported; my brother was six. The Christmas tree stayed up until mom returned home in April of the following year.

How does single parenthood, even as a temporary measure, affect the well-being of children?

Despite the risk that her mother's immigration status would be discovered, Jacalyn and her family often drove to Mexico to visit. The experience of crossing from one side of the border to the other highlighted the conflict in her ethnic identity.

As we crossed the Mexican border the border patrol would ask me my citizenship. I would reply, "AMERICAN," because my parents taught me to say that.

"MEXICAN"   "MEXICAN-AMERICAN"   "CHICANA"

But in California, people would ask me, "WHAT ARE YOU?" I guess because they didn't quite know how to ask, "ARE YOU AMERICAN?" I would proudly reply, "MEXICAN."

It wasn't until I became a teenager that I claimed I was "Mexican-American."

It . . . wasn't until I became a re-entry student at UC Riverside (in the '90s) that I developed a "Chicana" consciousness.

What do you think prompted Jacalyn to develop these different identities? How do you imagine the evolution of her identity might have affected her everyday life?

Now Jacalyn has a family of her own. She still faces many of the same issues.

My husband Carlos is the only person in our house who is fluent in Spanish. However, it is not unusual for us to listen to Mexican music while playing English word games.

His mother speaks to me in Spanish and even though I understand her completely, I only speak to her in English. She has an excellent command of the English language and can beat all of us at Scrabble.

While raising my children has helped reinforce my desire to embrace my biculturalism . . . it has also left me questioning "our" assimilation.

Who will preserve the memories of my family's history when I am no longer around?

Will my children re-create the plays we presented with Mexican songs and dances? Will they continue to make tamales at Christmas time and share the story of Las Posadas with others? Who will cook the homemade Mexican meals?

Will they ever learn to speak Spanish?

How do we survive in a world driven by assimilation and maintain our cultural identity?

My oldest son Xavier is a professional actor, and I feel proud that he refuses to accept roles that depict negative stereotypes of Latinos.

Rex can read and write three languages: English, HTML, and Iptscray. He is 12 years old and plays guitar in a punk band.

As I peer into my son's room my heart aches, believing that my children and possibly their children will also experience the pain of "otherness."

I ask myself . . . when they begin to question their own identity, what will they say?

Will it be . . .   Hispanic
Latino
American
Mexican-American
Chicano
or other?

In August 2001, people all across the United States were captivated by the story of a sensational 12-year-old baseball pitcher from the Bronx, New York, named Danny Almonte. Danny was so dominating in the Little League World Series that people were already talking about the brightness of his future in the major leagues. He received congratulatory phone calls from famous major league stars and appeared on national talk shows. He had pitched his way into the hearts of millions.

But then came the bad news: Danny, who with his father had immigrated to the United States from the Dominican Republic 18 months earlier, wasn't 12 at all; he was actually 14 and therefore ineligible to play in Little League. His team had to forfeit all the games they'd won. And it got worse: It turned out that not only had his father falsified his birth certificate, he had purposely failed to enroll him in school so the boy could perfect his pitching skills and improve his future earning power.

The country was outraged, not at the boy—who was sympathetically perceived as a victim in the matter—but at this father. Everybody from ordinary people in the streets and Little League officials to the mayor of New York and the president of the United States expressed anger and vilified the father for his "abusive" parenting. Most of the public response sounded like this:

> [The father] moved his son to the United States, falsified birth documents and kept him out of school just so that he could dominate 12-year-old Little Leaguers on the diamond. Instead of raising his son, he took advantage of him and turned him into a little cheat. He . . . [is] pathetic, the worst stereotype of the Little League parent sprung to life. (Caple, 2001)

Truancy officers and child protection caseworkers investigated the case, suggesting that the father could face charges of criminal neglect.

On the day after Christmas in 1996, the bound and beaten body of 6-year-old JonBenet Ramsey was found in the basement of her Boulder, Colorado, home. The death of a child is always a tragedy. But JonBenet was not just an ordinary 6-year-old. She was a beauty pageant veteran and a star of some repute—the reigning Little Miss Colorado.

Television news shows and supermarket tabloids were saturated with images of this little girl with her false eyelashes, glittering gowns, and high heels, preening for audiences with coy expressions and vaguely sexual poses. One pageant publication had described JonBenet as a "natural . . . who could win the cars and the cash"; a photographer marveled at her maturity, noting that she could "hold a pose forever" (quoted in "The strange world," 1997, p. 44).

Many people immediately implicated JonBenet's parents, not necessarily for murdering the girl—they have never been formally charged in the case—but for selfishly robbing her of an innocent childhood in pursuit of fame, recognition, and fortune:

> In photographs, her characteristic expression is a fixed smile of concentration, earnest and studied. It could be perky, coy or sweet, although the only sure way to tell is by her costume. Strapless ball gown, sailor suit, swimsuit—JonBenet Ramsey . . . worked hard at winning beauty contests, but her mother must have worked even harder. And her father paid for her portfolio of professional photographs, a world beyond the artless family-album snapshots we are accustomed to seeing when a child is killed. But the effect is distancing rather than illuminating: in all the miles of film that were lavished on JonBenet it is hard to find one frame that captures her soul. ("The strange world," 1997, p. 43)

This case exposed a massive beauty pageant culture that few people knew existed—a world that enlists thousands of girls under 12 and their parents and grandparents in about 500 contests a year. They support a billion-dollar industry of contest promoters, costume designers, grooming consultants, and publishers. A hand-sewn gown for a 5-year-old can cost $1,000.

The contestants in these beauty pageants are "child women," whose anxious childhoods are spent trying to attain just the right balance of poise, charm, and good looks. Although parents stress the long-term benefits of participating (greater self-esteem and confidence), the financial stakes are undeniably tempting. Modeling contracts await the best performers. By her sixth birthday, a successful pageant star can win enough money to pay for her college education.

Nevertheless, the sight of JonBenet showing off her body as a competitive activity outraged many people, who liken these pageants to child pornography. Child development experts warn that beauty pageants create hollow children and narcissistic parents and that such activities send the message to these girls that all they need to do to get attention is look pretty. Unlike competitive sports, where skills are clear and success is measurable, girls who excel in beauty pageants are learning simply how to perform for and please other people.

Of course, the beauty pageant culture is not the only place where we can find pushy parents and pushed children. Just spend a few hours at your local youth league baseball or soccer fields, and you will spot moms and dads encouraging hypercompetitiveness in their children as they yell at coaches and jeer at referees. Things have gotten so bad that towns all across the United States are establishing rules and policies designed to control parents. In a Cleveland suburb, the local soccer league forbids parents to yell during their children's matches. In El Paso parents are required to attend a 3-and-a-half-hour class on appropriate fan behavior before their children can play in city-sponsored sports (Wong, 2001).

Although the cases of the Little Leaguer and the JonBenet Ramsey murder are markedly different, they both show how quickly the public condemns child-rearing practices that don't match the general public's sense of what children are and what they're entitled to. Although U.S. culture values family privacy and parents' right to raise their children as they see fit, such ideals are easily sacrificed when conceptions of childhood and beliefs about "appropriate" child rearing are violated.

Fundamental to the powerful image of family is its role as producer and socializer of children. People like to say that the fate of the nation lies in the well-being of its children. So one shouldn't be surprised that when people perceive that parents are "irresponsibly" exposing their children to danger or exploiting them for personal gain, onlookers hurl hostile accusations. However, as this chapter explains, not everybody has, or has had, the same ideas about what childhood is or how children ought to be treated.

The Historical Construction of Childhood

Childhood is such a universal feature of human life that it is easily considered a natural stage of development. After all, doesn't every society, current or past, include some people who can clearly be identified as "children"? Aren't children everywhere younger, smaller, weaker, and generally less experienced than adults? As obvious as the answers to these questions are, sociologists and historians suggest that "childhood," as a special phase of life, has not always been defined the way it is defined today. Western societies at the beginning of the twenty-first century take for granted that children are qualitatively and quantitatively different from adults. It may seem inconceivable that laws, customs, and values regarding children—for instance, the idea that they are dependent and innocent and therefore require and deserve guidance and protection—haven't always been the cornerstone of a "civilized" society. However, current attitudes about the welfare, rights, and requirements of children are, for the most part, relatively new (Ariès, 1962).

Images of childhood don't spring from nature; ideas about childhood and child rearing are tightly connected to a society's culture and organization (Corsaro, 1997). That is, these ideas are socially and historically constructed, emerging from the prevalent attitudes, beliefs, and values of particular societies at particular times (Archer, 1985; Hays, 1996). Thus, notions of parental responsibility, investment, neglect, and abuse vary as cultural and historical definitions of childhood change.

For instance, if people think of children as autonomous, rational beings who can make decisions for themselves, then parents will be inclined to grant them considerable freedom and negotiate with them as they would with fellow adults. If people define children as property or as beings who are born with natural trouble-making tendencies, the appropriate parental course of action is to direct and control them. And if people see children as naturally pure and innocent, parents will be inclined to shelter and protect them as much as possible (Ribbens, 1994).

All these conceptions of childhood have existed throughout history. However, these models are not mutually exclusive. Even within the same society, several different conceptions may exist simultaneously. Indeed, all of them exist, to some degree, in contemporary American society, where conceptions of childhood vary across geographic, racial/ethnic, and class lines.

Children as Miniature Adults

According to some historians, the notion of childhood as a distinct phase of life didn't develop in Western culture until the sixteenth and seventeenth centuries (Ariès, 1962). Before then, childhood wasn't considered a unique and crucial phase of life that required special treatment and protection. Instead, children were viewed as little more than miniature versions of adults. The evidence for this idea comes from examinations of medieval artwork and family portraits, in which children, if shown at all, are depicted as shrunken replicas of adults (Snow, 1997). Their clothes and bodily proportions are the same as those of their elders.

Other historians disagree with the idea that children were not considered any different from adults, pointing out that as early as the thirteenth century some artwork showed children playing with balls and puppets (Gies & Gies, 1989). In the fourteenth century children appeared in artwork in a way that is recognizably "childlike" to modern observers. Parents were sometimes depicted playing with their children and showing affection. These historians also note that in medieval encyclopedias, separate medical sections on children expressed the need for special care to ensure children's proper physical development.

Despite this disagreement, it's clear that children at the time were defined quite differently from the way they are today. Many—though certainly not all—parents, it seems, were rather indifferent to the fate of their children. Between the fourteenth and seventeenth centuries, parents' references to children in diaries, correspondence, and other documents were sparse (Demos, 1986).

Moreover, children were sometimes expected to participate in all aspects of social life right alongside adults (Archer, 1985). According to the diaries of aristocratic children in sixteenth- and seventeenth-century Europe, everything was permitted in their presence: foul language, sexual acts and situations, death, and so on. It was considered perfectly natural for adults to play sexually with children (Ariès, 1962). Children were certainly valued for their role in inheritance and procreation, but they clearly didn't elicit the kind of sentiment to which people today simply assume children are entitled.

In the colonial period in this country, children often worked right alongside adults, doing the same work. Sons were considered miniature versions of their farmer fathers, and girls were modeled after their mothers (Demos, 1986). But although they were subjected to adult expectations, children were in no way considered equal to adults. They were morally and physically inferior and so were given certain tasks considered "children's work." But they were not seen as a group with their own needs and interests.

Such "unsentimental" treatment of children probably had something to do with the demographic realities of the time. Fatal disease during this era was quite prevalent, and infant mortality rates were extremely high. Young children were not expected to live for very long. In seventeenth-century France, for instance, between 20 and 50 percent of all infants died within the first year after birth (McCoy, 1981).

Because childhood death was so common, parents couldn't allow themselves to get too emotionally attached to their children. Many parents of the time referred to a child as "it" until he or she reached an age at which survival was likely. Children were not individuals with their own identities. In some countries, they were considered interchangeable and frequently were given the same name as a sibling who had died before they were born.

The death of a baby, although considered unfortunate, was probably not the long-term, emotional tragedy that it is now. Today, people take for granted that no experience could be more painful or sorrowful than the death of a child. Even parents who experience a miscarriage or a stillbirth are expected to mourn the loss of the fetus as if it were once a living child (Fein, 1998a). In contrast, parents 300 or 400 years ago seldom attended their children's funerals. In some sections of France, when an unbaptized infant died he or she was likely to be buried almost anywhere on the premises, like contemporary families might bury a pet cat or dog (Ariès, 1962). At death, even the children of the rich were sometimes treated as paupers, their bodies sewn into sacks and thrown into big, common graves (cited in Zelizer, 1985).

Children probably weren't seen as deserving of special treatment when they were alive, either. Until the late 1800s, child labor was commonly practiced and accepted (Archer, 1985). Like adults, children were expected to "earn their keep." In poor rural families, children worked on the farm as long and as hard as adults simply to help the family survive. In poor urban families, children often engaged in scavenging and street peddling. Prior to child labor laws, children were sometimes given difficult and hazardous jobs, such as cleaning out the insides of narrow factory chimneys or operating heavy machinery in paper mills.

In addition, family historians maintain that abandoned children were sometimes recruited by unscrupulous adults for use in robbery and prostitution. Some were physically mutilated so they could elicit more sympathy as beggars (Stone, 1979). Historians have little evidence that society completely approved of or tolerated these kinds of practices, but clearly they weren't severely punished either:

> Some [children] had their teeth torn out to serve as artificial teeth for the rich; others were deliberately maimed by beggars to arouse compassion. . . . Even this latter crime was one upon which the law looked with a remarkably tolerant eye. In 1761 a beggar woman, convicted of deliberately "putting out the eyes of children with whom she

went about the country" in order to attract pity and alms, was sentenced to no more than two years' imprisonment. (Stone, 1979, p. 298)

But throughout the nineteenth century concern over the mistreatment of children grew. In 1825 the first House of Refuge in the United States was founded, an institution whose purpose was to provide sanctuary to children who had been abused or neglected. In subsequent years many similar institutions were established.

Even these institutions, however, were not totally sensitive to the welfare of children. On close inspection, social scientists discovered that their purpose was not to protect children but to prevent them from becoming economic burdens and threats to society. It was widely believed at the time that children who had bad childhoods would grow up to be bad adults. The value of removing children from their homes, then, was not to focus on abuse or neglect but to decrease the likelihood that negative parental influence would be transferred to the next generation. The House of Refuge sought to prevent the potential criminal tendencies of poor urban youths from ever surfacing by removing such youth from abusive environments and placing them in institutions. Here they would share a "proper growing up" with other abandoned and neglected youths as well as delinquents who had violated the law (Pfohl, 1977).

Children as Little Monsters

Another conception of childhood that emerged several centuries ago is the idea that children have naturally evil tendencies. In medieval Europe, for instance, infants were often considered inherently corrupt, occasionally referred to as unformed animals or "exasperating parasites" (McCoy, 1981, p. 62). Some parents considered them uncontrollable monsters whose arrival threatened to destroy a heretofore peaceful home. Educators of the time felt it was their duty to continually remind parents of children's natural propensity for evil. In the Christian world, children were believed to be marked by original sin at birth and therefore dangerously prone to evil. If left to their own devices, these creatures would harm not only other people but themselves as well (Hays, 1996). One widespread popular fear, for instance, was that if not restrained by tight swaddling clothes, an infant might "tear off its ears, scratch out its eyes, or break its legs" (Stone, 1979, p. 115). Swaddled babies were often hung on a peg on a wall where they couldn't get into trouble.

In Puritan New England, children were apparently subjected to early obedience training to overcome their sinful nature. Any sign of independent thinking on the part of the child was considered blasphemous and therefore punishable. Only when the child's sinful nature was quashed forever could that child become appropriately obedient to God and family (Hays, 1996).

Some parents probably believed that the responsible way to raise their children was to stamp out the beast in them. The old saying "Spare the rod and spoil the child" reflected this view. Whippings and beatings of children, to "beat the devil out of them," were common (Straus, 1994). Opium was often used to keep them sedated throughout the day (Beekman, 1977). The Puritans sometimes also used psychological terror to overcome their children's sinful nature, locking rambunctious children in dark closets for an entire day or telling them tales of death and hell to purge the sin (McCoy, 1981). In seventeenth-century Europe, children were sometimes forced to inspect the rotting corpses of people who had been executed so they would be reminded of what happens to bad children when they grow up (deMause, 1975).

The relationship between religious beliefs and child rearing is also discussed in Issue 5.

Not all attempts to overcome children's "natural tendencies" toward evil and monstrous behavior were this harsh. For instance, baptism and other religious sacraments were often used to gently expunge the child's sinful nature (Hays, 1996).

Today, of course, most popular images of young children depict them as cute, lovable, and cuddly members of the family. But still, just below the surface, lurks a nagging fear about their monstrous potential. The contemporary image of the "little monster" is likely to refer not so much to children's sinful nature but to the likelihood of them disrupting social life with their animalistic tendencies. People talk of the "terrible twos" as if it were an inevitable stage of development in which the "demonic" impulses that have been lying dormant in the child finally bloom in all their tantrum-throwing, food-flinging fury.

Media portrayals of children often reinforce the idea that they are potentially destructive. An entire genre of horror films—such as *The Exorcist, The Omen, Firestarter, Children of the Corn,* and *The Bad Seed*—and comedies such as *Problem Child* and the *Home Alone* series depict children as precocious and powerful beings who are especially threatening and dangerous to adults (Steinberg & Kincheloe, 1997). Indeed, adults in these films are often depicted as dimwitted buffoons who deserve the havoc these dangerous children offer up. Characters such as Kevin in the *Home Alone* films and television's Bart Simpson never hesitate in devilishly taking advantage of the disorder created by incompetent adults.

Such a conception of childhood is also likely to be associated with negative attitudes toward "permissive" parenting. Parents who allow their children significant freedom from restriction are thought to be "asking for trouble" or "playing with fire." Such responses reflect a belief that if left unrestrained, children's inherent lawlessness might be unleashed. As one mother put it, "[If] you just give in to them all the time . . . as soon as you start doing that they just push you, and push you, and push you, until they're doing the most awful outrageous things, and you're not able to control them at all" (quoted in Ribbens, 1994, p. 150).

Children as Natural Innocents

As early as the late 1700s, ideas about children's inherent evil were beginning to be challenged. In his writings during the eighteenth century, the famous French philosopher Jean-Jacques Rousseau portrayed children as sacred, noble, and innocent. He was appalled by what he felt was parents' tragic insensitivity to the needs of their children and argued that child-rearing practices should follow from the development of the child's inner nature rather than from adult interests. He believed that children shouldn't be beaten into submission but rather should be "treated with love and affection, and protected from the corruption of the larger society" (Hayes, 1996, pp. 25–26).

By the mid-nineteenth century, reformers and child advocates had achieved some success in convincing people that children were neither miniature adults nor naturally evil. Drawing from the work of Rousseau and others, they argued persuasively that children, if anything, are naturally weak and need to be treated with care and compassion; that they should be sheltered from the harsh realities of adult life.

This more sympathetic belief in childhood innocence, though, did have a darker side: It implied that children's inherent innocence makes them susceptible to temptation (Stone, 1979). It wasn't that they were inherently evil, it was that they were easily influenced. Without adequate oversight, they might easily succumb and get into trouble. Thus, it's likely that many parents continued to believe that only through harsh discipline could they properly shape their children. Children were often beaten, not to subdue the devil inside them but to teach them right from wrong and give them the strength to avoid temptation. Such beatings of children in the nineteenth century could sometimes be particularly cruel, although people usually offered religious justifications for them. One theologian suggested a theory that God had formed the human buttocks so that they could be severely beaten without incurring serious bodily injury (Stone, 1979).

Protecting Innocence   A century later, the dominant model of childhood is that children's "natural" innocence is to be cherished. It must be protected for as long as possible because once gone, it is gone forever. People now take for granted that childhood ought to be carefree and full of fun, play, and creativity (Ribbens, 1994). Children are given license to act in ways that are unacceptable for adults. A child can talk to him- or herself in public, play with imaginary friends, throw tantrums, wear mismatched clothes, or simply do nothing and be scarcely noticed by others. Their inherent "silliness" is a counterweight to the rationality and responsibility that awaits them in adulthood. Indeed, people don't expect, nor do they want, children to worry about paying bills, or impressing bosses, or addressing any of the other multitude of concerns that adults fret about.

People still believe parents have an abiding duty to guard their children against the corrupting and tempting influences of society (Ariès, 1962; Lee, 1982). But most parents are likely to consider this duty in terms of protection and shelter rather than harsh, punitive discipline. For instance, in Western cultures, many people simply assume that children should not be exposed to potentially disturbing images of sexuality and death. Discussion of these topics awaits a time (usually adolescence) when, it is generally believed, children have the cognitive ability to appreciate the gravity of such topics.

Indeed, the media often portray society as an overwhelmingly dangerous place filled with constant threats to children's innocence and well-being: child abuse, child pornography, incest, child molestation, harmful rock lyrics, violent web sites, child abductors, and so on (Best, 1993). The concern over childhood innocence has evolved into a powerful belief that all children are potential victims.

Childhood innocence also implies that small children are incapable of making rational decisions for themselves (and, therefore, are not responsible for their acts). Hence parents are sometimes held liable for their children's transgressions. Many states across the country—including California, Michigan, Virginia, Florida, and Ohio—are beginning to aggressively enforce truancy laws by prosecuting parents. In Springfield, Illinois, for example, six mothers were charged with a misdemeanor for allowing their children to cut class; they risked up to a month in jail and a $500 fine (Meredith, 1999). Other states have enacted laws allowing parents to be cited for contributing to their children's unlawful behavior:

- In West Virginia, parents of a child caught defacing a public building can be liable for up to $5,000 in fines.
- In Louisiana, parents can be found guilty of "improper supervision of a minor" and fined up to $1,000 and imprisoned for up to 6 months if their child associates with a convicted felon, drug dealer, or members of a street gang (Applebome, 1996b).
- In Florida, parents of juvenile offenders can now be forced to pay some of the costs of keeping their children in state custody, which can be as much as $50 a day (Hollis, 2000).
- In 1996, after their son repeatedly defied them in public, smoked marijuana, and stole $3,500 from his church, a couple from St. Clair Shores, Michigan, was convicted of violating a city ordinance that requires parents "to exercise reasonable parental control" over children. The parents were fined $100 each and ordered to pay $1,000 in court costs (Applebome, 1996a).

Implicit in such laws is the belief that parents must be forced, under threat of punishment by the state, to take more seriously their obligation to protect the innocence of their children.

In one sense, the value of childhood innocence reflects a societal concern that letting children become adults too soon is harmful. The collective worries people have about the effects of divorce on children, for instance, are worries that innocent children will be forced to deal with the sort of pain, seriousness, and inconvenience that many people believe children shouldn't have to deal with. You often hear people say that children of divorce are forced to grow up too soon.

Undermining Innocence   Yet this conception of childhood as a time of innocence and dependency has been undermined in recent years by children's access to adult knowledge about the world (Meyrowitz, 1984; Steinberg & Kincheloe, 1997). Children today are exposed to events, devices, and ideas that would have been inconceivable a generation ago. The cultural "secrets" of adulthood—death, illness, violence, sexuality—are revealed to them in their homes, in their schools, on television, and over the Internet. As a result, children speak, dress, and act more like adults than they used to.

The idea of childhood as a sheltered, innocent time, free from adult worries, has become a nostalgic relic. We read about 12-year-olds becoming pregnant, 7-year-olds being tried for such crimes as rape and drug smuggling, and 11-year-olds convicted of murder. In Columbus, Ohio, an 8-year-old girl was charged with attempted murder for allegedly pouring poison into her great-grandmother's drink because the two didn't get along. In Pensacola, Florida, a 5-year-old girl faced assault charges for beating a 51-year-old school counselor. A spate of school shooting rampages has made victims and mass murderers of scores of children over the past few years. As you can see from Exhibit 9.1, in 1998 approximately 25 out of every 1,000 teenagers ages 12–17 were victims of serious violent crimes (aggravated assault, rape, robbery, and homicide); the rates are higher for males and for blacks. About 27 out of every 1,000 youth committed serious violent crimes.

The fear of juvenile crime created by such publicized incidents has led to a further erosion of childhood innocence. Since the late 1980s, 44 states have adopted new laws enabling

EXHIBIT 9.1

Crime Victims and Offenders Among Youth Ages 12–17

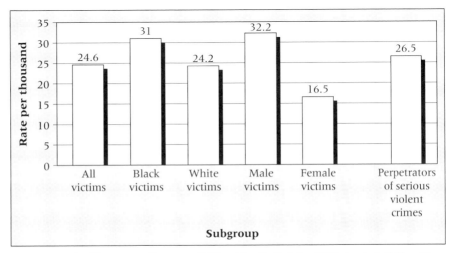

Data source: Federal Interagency Forum on Child and Family Statistics. 2000. *America's Children: Key National Indicators of Well-Being, 2000,* Tables BEH4.A and BEH4.B. Washington, DC: U.S. Government Printing Office.

them to try more children as adults. Each year approximately 6,000 children are sent to adult prisons (Bradsher, 1999).

But the loss of childhood innocence is not just the result of exposure to serious social problems and adult issues. Pressures to perform and succeed—often from parents themselves—rob childhood of its anxiety-free state. Many feel that young people today are overworked and overscheduled. Compared to those just a generation ago, children today spend more time on school, organized sports, and housework and less time in unstructured play and television watching (see Exhibit 9.2).

The increasingly competitive nature of social life is making some parents feel obligated to give their children every conceivable edge to help them succeed. For instance, parents may pay as much as $70 an hour for private coaches to sharpen the athletic skills of their children or send their 4-year-olds to intensive foreign language camps (Johnson, 1999). At increasingly younger ages, children are being asked to "put away their childish things" and get on with the serious task of growing up and measuring up:

> Preschoolers read, fifth graders take S.A.T.'s for admission to summer college programs and high school juniors are told they need three advanced-placement or college-level courses for Ivy League consideration. And they are urged to build a

EXHIBIT 9.2

Changes in Weekly Time Use by Children Ages 3–11

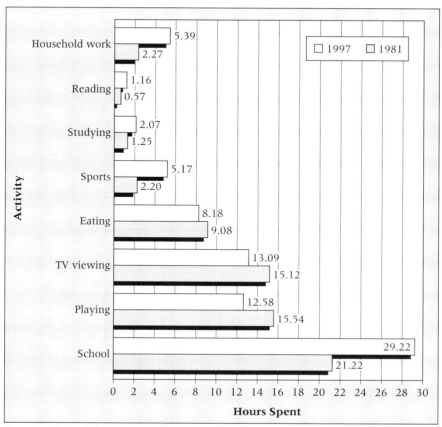

Source: Population Reference Bureau. 2000. "How Do Children Spend Their Time? Children's Activities, School Achievement, and Well-Being." *Today's Issues*, No. 11. Available at http://156.40.88.3/about/cpr/dbs/pubs/ti11.pdf. Accessed June 1, 2001.

curriculum vitae that includes sports, student government, music, volunteer work, summer courses and internships. Children are drowning, up until midnight. (Gross, 1997b, p. 22)

The pressure increases when the achievements of U.S. children are compared to those of children in other countries. One international comparison of schooling found that students in other countries consistently outperform U.S. students in fields such as mathematics and science. The author of the study bleakly proclaimed, "Our best students in mathematics and science are simply not world class" (quoted in Bronner, 1998b, p. A1).

Such findings are cause for alarm among many educational experts and political leaders. They point out that U.S. 13-year-olds spend an average of 178 days a year in school, compared to 198 in Russia, 220 in Japan, 222 in Korea, and 222 in Taiwan (National Center for Education Statistics, 2000). Japanese schools, in particular, are famous for producing high achievers. Approximately 97 percent of Japanese students stay in school until they are 18, and over a third go on to college ("Less rote, more variety," 2000). Some Japanese 3-year-olds may spend hours a day memorizing stories, learning vocabulary, making calendars, and taking achievement tests so that they can pass the grueling entrance exams to get into the best elementary schools, which in turn serve as gateways into the top high schools and universities (WuDunn, 1996).

Not everyone agrees that the United States should emulate other countries' educational models, which can result in high-achieving yet hyperstressed children and parents. In fact, some critics feel that U.S. society already places far too much emphasis on performance and achievement (Mannon, 1997b). And some people are taking steps to reduce the pressure many children now experience. For instance, one community in Minnesota is seeking "family friendly" policies in its recreational programs. A group that calls itself Family Life 1st asks coaches, dance instructors, and youth group leaders to cut back on practices, rehearsals, and meetings and to loosen policies that penalize children for missing events. Their larger goal is to slow down the frenetic way of life that pervades many children's lives (Belluck, 2000a).

Nevertheless, concern over the ability to compete in the global marketplace has led to nationwide calls for various educational reforms: heavier emphasis on math and science, more time spent on foundational skills such as reading and writing, increased computer literacy, and training in political geography and international relations. Some school districts have even done away with recess, a period of the day for relaxation and play. And newly passed education reforms now mandate annual testing in reading and math, which will undoubtedly increase the pressure on schoolchildren. In the end, changes such as these—and the concerns and worries that spawn them—are eroding the belief that childhood ought to be a time of playful innocence.

Children as Property

Another common conception of childhood that has existed to greater and lesser degrees throughout history is that children are a form of "property." In the distant past, children literally belonged to their parents. In ancient Rome, for instance, a father could treat his children any way he saw fit, even put them to death if he wished. As late as the seventeenth century, children were considered possessions with no individual rights. They sometimes ended up as security for their parents' debts, as marriage partners for their father to use in expanding his business alliances and property holdings, even as slaves sold for profit (McCoy, 1981).

The matter of family privacy and parental rights is explored in more detail in Issue 3.

Today in U.S. society people don't think of parents as *owning* their children. Nevertheless, parents do retain certain rights over them and often act vigorously to defend those rights. Parents have the power to keep children in the parents' house, send them to school, or take them places the parents want them to go. Parents can direct children's behavior in many respects, determining how they dress, who they spend time with, what their religion (if any) is, and so on (Collins, 1992).

Related to the notion of property is the idea that children represent economic assets. Not so long ago, children were expected to help support their families financially by working without pay in the family business or on the farm or by going out and getting a job. Even today, children's incomes are legally the property of their parents until the children reach the age of majority.

In this country, the shift from a predominantly agricultural economy to an industrialized one in the nineteenth century revolutionized the "property value" of children. Children were a crucial source of labor in the family economy, and they were a source of financial support in old age (LeVine & White, 1992). Consequently, the birth of a child was hailed as the arrival of a future laborer who would contribute to the financial security of the family (Zelizer, 1985).

By the middle of the twentieth century, however, children were no longer seen primarily as economic necessities. In most families, the main source of income was now the parents, or more accurately the father, working outside the home. As a result, children became economically useless. In fact, people began to see them as downright costly to raise (LeVine & White, 1992). At the same time, though, the culture was beginning to recognize their emotional value. Today's parents are more likely to look to their children for intimacy and less likely to expect anything tangible in return, such as economic support in old age. The contemporary "property" value of children is determined not by their labor potential but by their emotional worth (Zelizer, 1985).

You can see the strength of the emotional value of children when parent–child ties are threatened. In contemporary divorce proceedings, for instance, a key point of conflict is custody of the children. Some noncustodial parents have gone so far as to defy court orders and kidnap their children. The fact that parents are willing to commit a felony to "have" their children and that courts are willing to prosecute such cases with so much vigor shows how important emotional property rights over children can be (Collins, 1992).

As you can see, childhood is not simply a biological stage of development. Rather, it is a social category subject to changing definitions and expectations. Consequently, parental investment in children is less a function of instinct than a function of parents' perceptions of their responsibilities toward their children. Cultural notions of appropriate parenting—or, for that matter, of child exploitation, neglect, and abuse—are fluid and varied.

Children's Power in Families

As conceptions of children have changed, so too has children's position within the family. For instance, despite tremendous variation in how much parents today involve their children in decision making, many families strive to be more democratic than would have ever been permitted when children were viewed as little monsters or as property. In today's single-parent households, it's not at all uncommon for children to assume an almost parental role, making decisions and helping manage the household (Arditti, 1999).

The shift toward recognizing and accepting children's power within families has not necessarily been a smooth one. The trend toward greater power for children conflicts with traditional conceptions of parent–child relationships, which emphasize parental control and authority. In nuclear families, power is still expected to reside mostly with parents—at least until they become enfeebled or incapacitated with age. Most people would argue that parents have the right—indeed, the obligation—to make decisions regarding their young children's health, education, and morality. Among other things, such legitimate authority over their children means that parents are granted the legal right to use physical means—such as physical punishment—as they see fit. Nonrelated adults have no such right. If they spank or slap someone else's child, they are committing a crime.

Even in traditional families, however, parental power is rarely absolute. As much as parents hate to admit it, children can at times exert considerable control over them. The cries of a newborn infant can easily alter parents' sleep, recreational, and eating patterns. A toddler's supermarket temper tantrum can force a parent to visit the ice cream section. An adolescent's volatile emotions can leave even the strongest of parents trembling.

Thus, ideology and practice often conflict. Many parents believe, for instance, that they shouldn't have to resort to rewards, punishments, force, or persuasive arguments to get their children to comply. But, as every parent knows, the legitimacy of their power frequently goes unrecognized or ignored by children. Indeed, most parents bargain, cajole, cut deals, manipulate, even plead with their children from time to time, to get them to behave as they want them to.

Paradoxically, children gain this sort of power from the very source of their powerlessness—their dependency and helplessness. Because children are completely or (later) partially dependent on their parents for survival, parents are required to act in ways that protect their children's interests. Sociologists have called this the "norm of social responsibility"—the expectation that individuals should help others in need (Schopler & Bateson, 1965). In their role as parents people are expected to sacrifice many of their own needs for their children and to willingly share resources. In some cases, parents may feel they should place their children's needs above their own. In addition, parents who wish to promote their children's self-esteem or feel that families should be more democratic may actively solicit their children's input on various family decisions.

Remember, power relations change as families change. As children age, their dependence on their parents diminishes. Ties to peer groups and to nonfamily groups give children a source of power outside the family (Goode, 1964). Teenagers may be employed outside the home or have access to their own or a friend's car, so their reliance on their parents for allowances or transportation declines. It's not unusual to hear parents of teenagers say that they feel they've lost control of their teenagers and that their authority is constantly being challenged. For some critics, such decline in parental authority signals a more serious decline in family values, such as children's respect for their parents. For others, however, it marks a normal transition as children move from childhood to adulthood.

The debate over family decline is explored in Issue 2.

Adolescence

Like childhood, the definition of **adolescence**—that gut-wrenching, noisy, awkward, tumultuous, ill-defined, but recognizable stage of life that hovers between childhood and adulthood—varies in different eras and different cultures. Adolescence is usually thought to be synonymous with puberty. But as you'll see, the two aren't necessarily the same.

The Social Construction of Puberty

Certainly people throughout human history and all over the world experience the physical changes of **puberty**: the maturing of genital organs and development of secondary sex characteristics (for example, breasts and hips in girls; facial hair and deepening of the voice in boys). For both sexes, the onset of puberty often coincides with society's first acknowledgment of the person's sexual capacity.

But the physical changes themselves are not solely responsible for what happens to young people during and after puberty. Much more crucial are the social reactions to these changes and the meanings that are assigned to them. Consider, for instance, the different meanings attached to the dramatic biological events that mark the onset of puberty for males and females. For males, that event is the arrival of the ability to ejaculate. Some adolescent males have their first orgasm while they are asleep, having erotic dreams. *Nocturnal emissions* or *wet dreams* are quite common for young males who have no other sexual outlet. Eventually they realize that they can bring about the pleasurable experience of orgasm through masturbation. Despite the guilt and anxiety that can surround this activity, virtually *all* males are thought to have masturbated to orgasm before their first sexual experience of any kind with another person (LoPresto, Sherman, & Sherman, 1985; Rubin, 1990).

Now think about the social characteristics of masturbation: Its *only* motive is sexual pleasure; it is gratification for its own sake. And it is something over which the individual has complete control. It isn't tied to romance, nor does it depend on the availability and willingness of sexual partners.

For females, the signifying physical event that marks puberty is menstruation. Menstruation is neither sexually stimulating nor controllable. It is associated with the ability to become pregnant, not the ability to experience sexual pleasure. Hence, unlike males, adolescent females are not provided with the same physical incentive to begin active sexual behavior.

Indeed, the social meaning attached to menstruation has always been somewhat ambivalent. At one time, the onset of menstruation was seen as a serious threat to a girl's emotional and physical well-being. In 1900 the president of the American Gynecological Society stated that "many a young [girl's] life is battered and forever crippled on the breakers of puberty" (quoted in Ehrenreich & English, 1979, p. 110). Physicians advised mothers to do whatever they could to delay the beginning of menstruation in their daughters.

Today, although girls generally equate menstruation with growing up and being normal, some still find it an anxiety-producing event. A survey of adolescent girls found that many of them consider menstruation embarrassing, disgusting, and annoying or dislike the idea of its not being controllable. The vast majority felt that it was a subject that should never be discussed with males (Golub, 1992).

As discussed in Chapter 5, adolescent girls do become sexually active in their early teens, and the long-standing sexual double standard is beginning to crumble. But for teenage girls, puberty marks a time when parents and peers perceive them as someone for whom dating and relationships are now appropriate, not necessarily a time when they may pursue sexual pleasure for its own sake (Golub, 1992).

In sum, the cultural focus on ejaculation (for males) and menstruation (for females) as the key biological events associated with puberty serves to reinforce Western attitudes toward male and female sexuality in adolescence and beyond. For young men, puberty is associated with sexual pleasure for its own sake. For young women, however, sexual pleasure is a small part of their experience with puberty.

Not surprisingly, adolescent girls consistently show lower levels of masturbation than boys, and they are less aroused by explicit sexual material. Their entry into sexual activity is usually associated with romance, love, and affection rather than simple physical desire (Rubin, 1990). These differences—male adolescent desire for sex and female adolescent desire for affection—set the stage for the conflicts and awkwardness that characterize adolescent heterosexual relationships.

The meaning and significance of puberty vary across societies too. Some societies take no note of the physical changes of puberty, and the transition from childhood to adulthood takes place without any sort of community recognition. Among the Rungus of Borneo, for instance, the onset of menstruation does not constitute a recognized stage in a girl's development. Indeed, the Rungus have no institutionalized rites of passage for either males or females on reaching puberty. Instead, sometime between ages 12 and 15 girls and boys have their teeth filed and blackened to make themselves more attractive to the opposite sex (Appell, 1988).

Other societies have elaborate initiation rituals publicly declaring that a child is now an adult. The ritual may require that the child undergo a difficult and dangerous task, such as going off alone into the wilderness to hunt an animal, or it may consist of a painful alteration of his or her body. Among the Temne of Sierra Leone, the initiation of a girl into womanhood can last for 1 year. The girls are first taken into the forest for a genital operation and 2 weeks of healing. Then they must move to a special house where they are enclosed for the remainder of the year, hidden from the eyes of men except for brief trips to fetch water. The ritual is so secret that it is considered a serious crime for an initiated girl to discuss the details of what happens to her with a prepubescent, uninitiated girl (Lamp, 1988).

In other cases, the ritual may simply consist of a festive, happy celebration. Among the Asante of Ghana, a girl who reaches puberty sits in public view under an umbrella (a symbol usually reserved for kings and other dignitaries). There she receives gifts and congratulations and observes singing and dancing performed in her honor. When the festivities are over, she is eligible for marriage (Buckley & Gottlieb, 1988).

Sometimes the ritual isn't tied to biological changes at all. In traditional, historical Jewish culture, for instance, a boy became a man when he turned 13, the day of his *bar mitzvah* ceremony. (The female equivalent, *bat mitzvah*, is a recent development that doesn't carry the same developmental meaning as the bar mitzvah.) During the ceremony, he would read from the sacred Torah, something that only adults—and until recently, only men—were allowed to do. He needn't have reached puberty to have a bar mitzvah ceremony. But from that day forward, he would occupy adult status within the community. Today such a ritual is largely symbolic and festive and doesn't carry the same legal significance within the community.

The History of Adolescence

For the most part in the United States, elaborate rituals have not been a part of the arrival of puberty or the entry into adulthood. Prior to the Civil War era, youth was an ill-defined category (Skolnick, 1991). Puberty didn't mark any particularly significant status change or life experience. For the vast majority of young people who lived on farms, life as a worker began early—say, around age 7 or 8. As they grew older, they were given more responsibility, and they would gradually move toward maturity. Where occupations were passed down from parent to child, each generation quietly merged into the next.

Adolescence as people in the United States know it today appears to have evolved in the late nineteenth century, a consequence of social and economic changes that extended childhood dependency into the teen years. As industrialization gradually moved paid labor away from the home, the gap between adult responsibilities and children's activities widened. As young people were removed from the labor market, child labor laws went into effect. The movement to regulate working conditions and set a minimum age at which children were allowed to work outside their own families helped segregate teenagers from the rest of society and extend their dependence on their parents.

Furthermore, to limit young people's free time, compulsory education became necessary. School attendance was now required, and truancy became defined as a punishable act. The age-graded school system created separate worlds for children and youth. High schools separated young people from the rest of society and helped create a youth culture.

These social changes helped make adolescence a legally and psychologically recognizable stage of life. It became known as the period between puberty and the ages specified by the law for ending compulsory education and beginning employment. Soon people began writing about the *adolescent experience*, which included the urge to be independent of the family, the search for personal and sexual identity, and the questioning of adult values.

As adolescence emerged as a recognizable stage of life, family ties between parents and their teenage children intensified. Adolescents began depending more completely and for a longer time on their parents than in the past. At the same time, as family size decreased mothers were encouraged to devote themselves to nurturing their children.

But the growing intensity of family life increased the emotional strains of adolescence. A young person's awakening sexuality—particularly that of young men—was likely to have been more disturbing to everyone in the household than it was when young men lived away from home, a common practice before industrialization. Not surprisingly, fear of adolescent sexuality became intense and widespread. Medical books of the late nineteenth century identified masturbation as one of the most destructive and evil of sins.

By the beginning of the twentieth century, *adolescence* had become a household word and part of the social structure of modern society. It also became an important stage in an individual's biography—a recognized, intermediate period of being neither a child nor an adult. At various times during U.S. history, adolescence has gained tremendous visibility and has powerfully shaped the culture. For instance, a distinct "youth culture" emerged during the 1960s and 1970s, as baby boomers reached adolescence. During this period of economic prosperity, youth gained greater spending power than any previous generation of young people had. Since then, a youth culture—identified by distinctive music, movies, clothing, language, even food—has become a major part of the U.S. consumer market.

But this socially recognized stage of life is notoriously problematic for young people. Everyone has heard the horror stories: uncontrollable, awkward, hormone-drenched adolescents getting into trouble, disrespecting their parents, locking themselves in their bedrooms, and swooping around on emotional roller coasters.

Adolescent girls may have a particularly difficult time. In 1990 the American Association of University Women polled 3,000 boys and girls between ages 9 and 15 on their attitudes toward self, school, family, and friends. They found that for the average American girl, adolescence is marked by a loss of confidence in her abilities, especially in math and science; a scathingly critical attitude toward her body; and a growing sense of personal inadequacy (cited in Orenstein, 1994). Although all children experience confusion and a faltering sense of self during adolescence, girls' self-regard drops further than boys' and, for many, never recovers.

This decrease in esteem is particularly true for white and Latina girls. Between the ages of 9 and 15, the number of girls who are "happy with the way I am" decreases by 38 percent for Latinas and drops 33 percent for whites. But it drops only 7 percent for African-American girls, perhaps because African-American women play a more influential role in their communities and families and less emphasis is placed on weight and body shape (Molloy & Hertzberger, 1998).

In many areas of the country, young people of both sexes are at physical risk as well. In the 1996–1997 school year, for instance, 10 percent of all schools in the United States reported serious violent incidents to police. Among high schools in cities, 48 percent reported such incidents (U.S. Bureau of the Census, 2000b). In 1997, there were more than 1 million violent crimes against students, 201,800 of which were serious. One out of every five U.S. public high schools now has at least one police officer stationed there full time ("Harper's Index," 1998). In 1999, the Centers for Disease Control (2000) reported that about 5 percent of teenagers felt too unsafe to go to school during one or more days during the month preceding the survey. About 8 percent had been threatened or injured with a weapon on school property during the prior year.

Three-quarters of the deaths of young people between the ages of 15 and 24 occur not from disease but from preventable causes (U.S. Bureau of the Census, 2000b), including traffic accidents and violence. And youth ages 12–19 have the highest victimization rates of any age group over 12 years of age (U.S. Bureau of the Census, 2000b). Also, according to the Centers for Disease Control (2000), over the past 8 years there has been an increase in the number of teen-agers who use marijuana, cocaine, and steroids.

Social inequality and widespread changes in family structure also place many adolescents at risk. The U.S. Bureau of the Census (1997e) reports that 50 percent of youth ages 16–17 live with at least one of the following risk factors: poverty, welfare dependency, both parents absent, one-parent families, unwed mothers, and a parent who has not completed high school. As Exhibit 9.3 shows, the more of these social risk factors teenagers are exposed to, the more likely they are to not be in school and not working, or, in the case of

EXHIBIT 9.3

Effect of Social Risk Factors on the Future Success of 16- and 17-Year-Olds

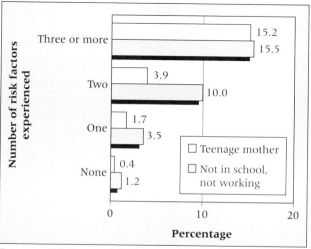

Data source: U.S. Bureau of the Census. 1997e. *America's Children at Risk.* Census Brief, CENBR/97-2. Washington, DC: U.S. Government Printing Office.

teenage women, to become mothers prematurely. Either outcome is a serious handicap for someone just about to take on adult responsibilities.

The risks to adolescents are many, but one shouldn't overstate them. People usually don't hear how the risks have declined. For example, the death rate among males ages 15–24 declined from 172 per 100,000 in 1980, to 118 in 1998 (U.S. Bureau of the Census, 2000b). Similarly, the death rate for young women during this period dropped from 58 to 43 per 100,000. The number of suicides by teenagers ages 15–19 remained essentially the same in 1997 (1,802) as it was in 1980 (1,797)—but at least it didn't increase (U.S. Bureau of the Census, 2000b). Between 1991 and 1999, there was a decline in teenagers who were involved in physical fights at school and who seriously considered suicide (Centers for Disease Control, 2001). Furthermore, between 1993 and 1999, the percentage who had carried a gun during the past month decreased from 8 percent to 5 percent, and those carrying any sort of weapon on school property sometime during the past month decreased from 12 percent to 7 percent (Centers for Disease Control, 2001).

True, there has been an increase in juvenile arrests for violent crimes, weapon law violations, and drug abuse, and there has been an increase in the number of delinquency cases disposed of by juvenile courts between 1980 and 1998 (U.S. Bureau of the Census, 2000b). But these increases may be a function of greater vigilance and law enforcement rather than actual changes in behavior.

Thus the period of adolescence isn't inevitably dismal. For most young people, adolescence is marked by mild rebelliousness and moodiness. Although it is difficult time for everyone involved, most youth don't become deeply alienated from conventional values (Skolnick, 1991). One national poll found that the majority of adolescents trust their government, admire their parents, and believe in God (cited in Goodstein & Connelly, 1998).

In fact, parents may suffer more during adolescence than do the adolescents themselves. Some research has found that when children reach puberty, parents themselves experience tremendous changes in their lifestyle, and their attitudes toward their children change. Marital satisfaction—which typically declines over the course of a marriage—reaches its lowest point when the oldest child reaches adolescence (Rutter, 1995).

The Social Complexities of Child Rearing

Because of their continuous interaction with their young children, parents have a crucial effect on their children's social and emotional development. Later on, peer groups have growing influence. However, parents typically provide children with their earliest emotional attachments, basic communication skills, a sense of right and wrong, and the basic skills to eventually become functioning adults in the social world.

These things are accomplished through the process of child rearing. **Child rearing** encompasses the actions parents take that enable their children to develop a sense of personal identity, learn what people in their particular culture believe, and learn how people are expected to behave. Through support, control, modeling, moral lessons, and direct instruction, parents socialize their children so that they can be transformed from helpless infants into more or less knowledgeable members of society.

Child rearing is a developmental process for all involved. People often assume that a child grows, changes, and interacts with a fixed entity: the adult parent. But parents grow and change too. And children are not just passive recipients of parental influence. They are energetic actors who frequently influence their parents' outlooks, attitudes, and behaviors as much as parents influence the children's. Indeed, a being from another planet might very well conclude that a newborn infant is the most influential and powerful member of the family, judging from its ability to train the parent to respond to an elaborate array of cries and squeals.

Parental influence over child rearing is also limited by the fact that many socializing functions that families provided in the past now commonly occur in other social settings: in school, with peers and friends, in front of the television. These **agents of socialization** typically become more influential as children get older and are exposed to forces that discourage conformity to parents' wishes. Indeed, as children mature and spend more and more of their time in school, they collectively construct a "peer culture"—a set of shared activities, routines, artifacts, and values—that becomes significantly more influential than their parents in guiding their behavior (Corsaro, 1997).

To make matters more complex, child-rearing practices are always shaped by a variety of other factors, including birth order of siblings, child spacing, family structure, overall family size, neighborhood, the unique personalities of parents and children, and so on. Sociologists are especially interested in the influence of broad, societal factors, such as culture, social class, and race and ethnicity, which can exert enormous influence on parents' values and expectations regarding their children's development. Sociologists have also been enlisted to study the influence of parents' sexual orientation on child rearing.

Culture and Child Rearing

You have seen how notions of childhood and conceptions of children can change over time. Parents form attitudes about how to raise their children based on cultural definitions of childhood and appropriate child-rearing strategies. The diversity of cultures in the world naturally supports a wide variety of beliefs and values about child rearing.

In most cultures, child rearing means looking after small children until they reach an age at which they are considered able to participate in some aspects of the adult world (Hays, 1996). At a minimum, child rearing usually consists of protecting the child from physical harm and providing enough food and clothing to ensure survival. When environmental, economic, medical, or cultural conditions make survival uncertain, many cultures develop strategies that provide for the well-being of some family members at the expense of others, such as selective neglect, abandonment, even infanticide.

But whether minimal care is provided for every child or not, all cultures seem to acknowledge that early child rearing means more than just ensuring survival. And all societies develop child-rearing practices designed to produce individuals who can fit well into that particular society. Yet different cultures have developed different ideas about who children are, what they need and deserve, what their development entails, and who should raise them. Exhibit 9.4a shows the variation among cultures on just one expectation for children's development: fostering a sense of independence. You might conclude there is no universal definition of the needs of children. As you can see in Exhibit 9.4a, Americans have mid-range attitudes toward the importance of developing independent children. Exhibit 9.4b shows in more detail what U.S. parents feel are important and unimportant life lessons.

Most Americans also feel that children are innocent and priceless and that their upbringing ought to be primarily the responsibility of individual parents, who should focus

EXHIBIT 9.4

Cultural Attitudes Toward Teaching Children Independence

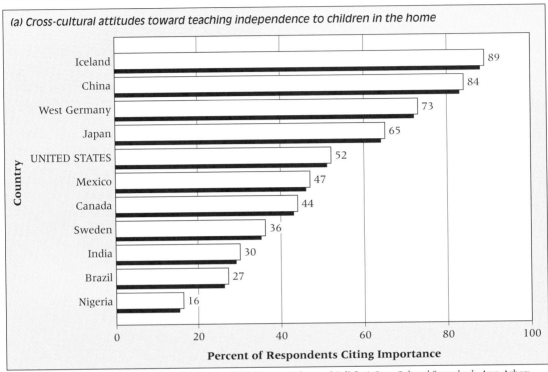

(a) Cross-cultural attitudes toward teaching independence to children in the home

Data source: R. Inglehart, M. Basanez, & A. Moreno. 1998. *Human Values and Beliefs: A Cross-Cultural Sourcebook.* Ann Arbor: University of Michigan.

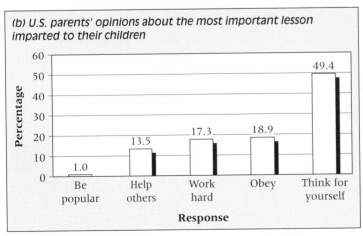

(b) U.S. parents' opinions about the most important lesson imparted to their children

Data source: National Opinion Research Center. 1998. *General Social Survey, 1972–1998.* Available at www.icpsr.umich.edu/GSS/. Accessed June 1, 2001.

on the child's needs (Hays, 1996). Furthermore, people assume that if parents attend to the child's drives and desires with consistency and affection, that child will learn to trust the parents, adopt their values, develop a sturdy self-concept, and turn out to be a well-rounded, normal individual.

In contrast, in the highlands of Guatemala, parents believe their child's personality is determined by the date of birth (Kagan, 1976). The parents are almost entirely uninvolved in the child's life, standing aside so he or she can grow as nature intended. In many societies—Nigeria, Russia, Haiti, the Dominican Republic, and Mexico, to name a few—many parents think the best way to teach children to be respectful and studious is to beat them. In contrast, most American child development experts believe that hitting a child can deaden his or her spirit and lead to violence later in life (Dugger, 1996b).

Culture sometimes combines with social standing to produce unique child-rearing philosophies. Among the somewhat wealthy Rajput caste in northern India, for example, child-rearing practices are directed toward training the child to function within the structure of his or her family, caste, and village (Hitchcock & Minturn, 1963). From infancy, Rajput infants are trained to be emotionally unresponsive. Although they are attended to when they are hungry or fussy and are never left alone, babies are not the center of attention. They spend most of the time lying on their cots, wrapped in blankets to keep off insects. Adult interaction with babies is more likely to be aimed at stopping a response (for example, crying) rather than stimulating one (for example, laughing). Children aren't praised by their parents, who feel such behavior would spoil them and make them disobedient. But they receive little pressure to become self-reliant either, and hence no encouragement for toilet training, walking, or talking. This lack of self-reliance is consistent with the caste culture, which emphasizes group orientation over individual achievement.

In addition, the Rajputs have little feeling that children should be given chores to do simply to teach them "responsibility." This lack of responsibility training is consistent with the Rajputs' caste values. Manual work is considered degrading and spiritually unclean. Most Rajputs are wealthy enough to employ servants to do the menial tasks that would otherwise be done by children.

Despite the dramatic differences from society to society in what people believe to be the "appropriate" way to raise a child, most children in all cultures grow up equally well adapted to their particular society.

Social Class and Child Rearing

Although people in the United States don't have a caste system, the process of raising a child within U.S. society can also be influenced by a family's socioeconomic standing. As discussed in Chapter 4, a family's financial stability has a direct and dramatic effect on the way childhood is experienced. According to the U.S. Department of Agriculture (Lino, 2001), a two-parent family earning between $38,000 and $64,000 a year (what the government considers middle class) spends over $165,000 to feed, clothe, transport, and shelter a child to the age of 17. That represents a 13 percent increase in real terms over what a comparable family spent in 1960 ($146,000 in 2000 dollars). Families that earn over $64,000 will spend over $241,000. Single-parent families that earn above $38,000 a year can expect to spend around $243,000 to raise a child. These costs tend to be higher in the urban areas of the West and Northeast, and lower in rural areas and the Midwest. These figures don't

EXHIBIT 9.5

Social Class and Children's Participation in Enrichment Activities

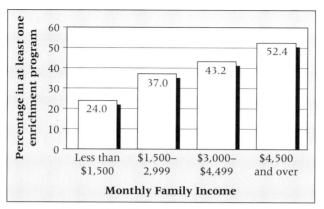

Data source: K. Smith. 2000. Who's Minding the Kids? Child Care Arrangements: Fall 1995, Table 12. *Current Population Reports*, P70-70. Washington, DC: U.S. Bureau of the Census.

include costs incurred before birth, such as prenatal health care and costs related to childbirth, or after the age of 17, such as college tuition or children's weddings.

Children from different social classes are likely to grow up with different experiences. Affluent children obviously grow up in more abundant surroundings than less affluent children and therefore have access to more material comforts and enriching opportunities such as music lessons, sports, clubs, and after-school programs (see Exhibit 9.5). These differences in child-rearing practices serve to reinforce and reproduce the social class structure discussed in Chapter 4.

Money doesn't always buy happiness, of course. For instance, a national survey of children between the ages of 13 and 17 found that teenagers who come from households with an annual income of over $75,000—no matter what their race or gender—were significantly more likely than children from more modest backgrounds to report that their lives were harder than their parents' lives when they were teenagers (Lewin, 1999b). Parents living on the edge of poverty are likely to pass on stories about childhoods filled with struggle and hardship. Compared to them, less affluent teenagers seem to feel their lives aren't so bad. They commonly cited new technologies and new opportunities as making their lives considerably easier than their parents had it. In contrast, many affluent children in the survey heard parents' stories of childhoods that were care free, leisurely, and safe. Furthermore, affluent children face higher parental expectations, more pressure to succeed, and a faster pace of life. They attribute their difficulty to too many activities and too many consumer choices.

Nevertheless, parents from all social classes are aiming to do what's best for their children and want their children to have a sense of accomplishment, self-satisfaction, and self-confidence. But the values and orientations that children learn as they're growing up are influenced by their family's class standing. Imagine how the experiences of the child of a CEO of a large corporation would differ from those of the child of a single parent on welfare. What sorts of values would the upper-class parent instill in his or her child? What would the welfare parent teach his or her child about how to survive in U.S. society?

Sociologist Melvin Kohn (1979) provided evidence to support the contention that children from different classes are socialized by their parents to have different values and outlooks on life. He interviewed 200 working-class and 200 middle-class couples who had at least one child of fifth-grade age. He found that the middle-class parents were more likely to value characteristics that promote self-direction, independence, and curiosity than were the working-class parents. Conversely, working-class parents were more likely to value characteristics that emphasize conformity to external authority. They want their children to be neat and clean and to follow the rules.

These differences may be related to the conditions that working-class and middle-class parents experience in their jobs. Middle-class occupations are likely to involve considerable task complexity, flexibility, discretion, and freedom from supervision. Working-class occupations, in contrast, typically involve standardized tasks, rigid schedules, and closer supervision. These conditions can readily be translated into the conceptions of social life that parents of different classes instill in their children.

Of course, not every parent in any given social class raises children the same way. Nevertheless, Kohn felt these general tendencies were consistent regardless of the sex of the child or the size and composition of the family. Moreover, such differences are directly related to future goals. Working-class parents tended to believe that eventual occupational success and survival depend on their children's ability to conform to and obey authority. Middle-class parents saw future success as stemming from assertiveness and initiative. Hence, middle-class children were much more likely than working-class children to feel that they had control over their own destiny.

Poor parents also have their own values and outlook on life, which exert similar influences on their children's socialization. Perhaps more basically, however, poverty itself is a serious obstacle to successful child rearing (see Chapter 4). The proportion of children under the age of 6 who live in poverty has remained high over the past 2 decades. Poverty poses significant health risks for these children; infant mortality, malnutrition, and homelessness are all higher among poor children than others. Poverty also hinders children's development of a strong sense of self-worth and self-confidence. According to the Children's Defense Fund, the United States, unlike most Western industrialized nations, lacks federal policies that could help poor parents raise their children. Such policies might include free or inexpensive medical care for all workers and their dependents, guaranteed prenatal care for poor pregnant women, federally funded child care facilities, and guaranteed paid maternity/paternity leave programs for all workers (cited in Aulette, 1994). Such help would at least ensure U.S. children a healthy start in life, regardless of social class.

Race, Ethnicity, and Child Rearing

Given the powerful role that race plays in U.S. society (see Chapter 3), it's not surprising that racial and ethnic differences exist in the way parents raise their children. For instance, a review of research on racial variations in child rearing (McLoyd, Cauce, Takeuchi, & Wilson, 2000) found, among other things, that:

- African-American fathers spend more time in primary caregiving such as bathing and feeding than do fathers from other races.
- Hispanic fathers spend more time with children in shared activities than do European-American fathers.
- African-American and Hispanic fathers monitor and supervise their children's activities more closely than do European-American fathers.
- African Americans are more likely than European Americans to use physical punishment to discipline their children.

Even with these differences, though, some aspects of child rearing are similar across all groups of American parents. One study of parenting styles found that European-American, African-American, Hispanic, and Asian-American parents are more similar than different in their parenting attitudes, their parenting behaviors, and their involvement with their children (Julian, McKenry, & McKelvey, 1994).

Thus sociologists must be careful not to overgeneralize. They must also acknowledge significant differences *within* the same racial or ethnic group. Middle-class African-American parents, for instance, are likely to have high educational and occupational expectations for their children. So they try to teach them to have positive attitudes toward hard work, thriftiness, and property ownership (Blackwell, 1985). Many poor African Americans, in contrast, are so disillusioned and alienated that they see little chance of breaking out of their economic circumstances. These parents are likely to be somewhat limited in their ability to provide guidance for their children and may have difficulty controlling their children's behavior (Willie, 1981). Yet not even all low-income African-American families are the same. They too have diverse beliefs about desirable child-rearing values, goals, and practices (Abell, Clawson, Washington, Bost, & Vaughn, 1996).

Child Rearing Among Racial Minorities   The U.S. educational system is designed to socialize children from various racial, ethnic, and religious backgrounds into the dominant culture. Thus the family remains the primary institution for passing along ethnic traditions and for instilling in children a sense of group identity (Klaff, 1995). When parents downplay, ignore, or conceal racial or ethnic traditions, their children typically adopt more "mainstream" views and may lose touch with their heritage.

In 1999, shortly after an unarmed West African immigrant was shot and killed by four white police officers in Bronx, New York, some of our students became embroiled in a heated discussion of the incident. One student, who was white, expressed concern that because of the terrible actions of these individual officers, young children of all races would now grow up mistrusting or even hating the police. As a child she had been taught that the role of the police is to help people and that if she were ever in trouble or lost she could approach an officer for help. She never questioned whether or not the police could be trusted. She then speculated how awful life would become for kids without the sense of safety and certainty she had been socialized to take for granted.

Some of the black students in class immediately pointed out to her that their socialization experiences had been quite different. Parents and others in their neighborhoods had taught them never to trust the police because officers were just as likely to exploit and harass them as to help them. They were taught to seek out neighbors, not the police, if they ever needed help. To them the police were not knights in shining armor but bullies with badges.

In the wake of several incidents where people of color were killed by overzealous police, some parents and civic leaders now teach black and Latino children how to respond when approached by the police. The NAACP, the Allstate Insurance Company, and the National Organization of Black Law Enforcement Executives have published brochures and held community forums on "guidelines for interacting with law enforcement officials." Among other things, children are taught to speak when asked to speak, stop when ordered to stop, never make any sudden movements, and always display their open hands to show they aren't armed (Barry, 2000; Herbert, 1999).

Although the two perspectives of the students discussing their attitudes toward the police are not representative of every white person or every black person in this country, the interchange illustrates the powerful impact that race can have on the lessons parents teach. The values taught to white children are likely to mirror those of the wider society. Chances are that schools and religious institutions will reinforce the messages expressed to them in their families—for example, that "hard work will pay off in the long run."

For racial minorities, however, child rearing occurs within a more complex social environment (Taylor, Chatters, Tucker, & Lewis, 1990). These children must live simultaneously in two different worlds: their ethnic community and "mainstream" society. To simply survive, they must become knowledgeable of the dominant, "white culture" as well as their own. Parents have to teach their children to deal with the realities of racism they will encounter every day (Staples, 1992). Childhood training frequently involves preparation for living in a society that has been and still is set up to ignore or perhaps actively exclude them. Even minority children from affluent homes in integrated neighborhoods need reassurances about the racial issues they will encounter (Comer & Poussaint, 1992). They are more likely than white children from affluent homes to be taught that "hard work" alone might not be enough to get ahead in this society.

Dealing with such prejudices can be complicated in biracial families. Many white parents of biracial children are unprepared for just how central race can be in the lives of their children. Consider the following scenario, described by the white mother of a biracial son (Reddy, 1994):

> Your nine-year-old son likes to play hide-and-seek games around the neighborhood with other children. One afternoon, you look out the kitchen window and see him crouching behind a neighbor's hedge, with his dark jacket pulled up over the back of his head for camouflage. Suddenly realizing that your child is now tall enough to be mistaken for a teenager, you call him into the house, away from the game. He thinks his greatest danger is being found by the child who is "It," but you know that he is at risk of being shot by someone who sees not a child playing, but the urban predator of television-fueled nightmares, ready to spring from the bushes.
>
> You know that you have waited too long to warn him about this danger, and about others that are real and present now that he resembles an adolescent. He has to be told to keep his hands out of his pockets when he is in stores, for instance, lest he be seen as a shoplifter. He also must learn how to talk to the police who will surely stop him when he is out riding his bike some day soon. You ask your son to feed his pets and to make his bed, hoping the chores will give you enough time to figure out how to explain these facts of life to him without destroying his innocent sense of fun. You never faced such dangers as a child, and so you have no model to follow. (p. ix)

It is a constant struggle to raise a biracial or minority child so that she or he doesn't internalize the negative images of racial minorities that pervade U.S. culture.

Transracial Adoption   The importance of race in child rearing is further illustrated in the contentious debate over transracial adoption. Transracial adoptions are relatively uncommon. Eight percent of all adoptions in the United States involve parents and children of different races (National Adoption Information Clearinghouse, 2001). And the vast majority of these adoptions involve white parents adopting minority children. Only 2 percent of adoptions in the United States involve nonwhite parents adopting white children, and a significant proportion of these are parents who adopt children from other countries (National Adoption Information Clearinghouse, 2001).

A key issue in transracial adoptions is whether children adopted by parents of a different race should and can receive the cultural socialization of their ethnic group. In the 1995 film *Losing Isaiah*, a black lawyer representing a black mother who abandoned her infant son argues during a custody trial that the child should be removed from his white adoptive parents and returned to his birth mother, a recovered crack addict. He states simply, "Black babies belong with black mothers." At one point he asks the white adoptive mother, an affluent pediatrician, whether any of the bedtime stories she reads her son have black characters. She replies that the stories contain characters of all colors. The lawyer responds, "So who is this child to identify with? The yellow 'muppet'"?

The answer to this question is not easy. Experts in child psychology and racial identity differ widely on whether children of color—particularly African-American children—are harmed by being adopted by white families (Williams, 1995). The question is whether a child's racial, ethnic, and cultural identity are essential to the development of a positive self-image or whether race is irrelevant and ought to be minimized or ignored in the interests of finding a solid and loving home for a child.

Studies that have followed transracially adopted black children from infancy to beyond adolescence have found that, despite periodic racial taunts at school and in other public situations, these individuals do not have problems identifying themselves as black Americans, are well adjusted for the most part, and show high self-esteem (Simon, Alstein, & Melli, 1994; Vroegh, 1997). A long-term, longitudinal study of white, Asian, and black children adopted by white parents found similarity across the groups in terms of health, academic achievement, behavioral problems, and overall adjustment. In fact, the group experiencing the most difficulty overall was that of white male adoptees, not transracial adoptees (Brooks & Barth, 1999).

But other studies have shown that minority children who have been transracially adopted have a weaker racial identity (Hollingworth, 1997) than those adopted by same race parents. In a study of thirty adolescent black children adopted by white parents, only ten identified themselves as black, six said they were "mixed," and the rest simply said they were "human" or "American" (McRoy & Zurcher, 1983).

To opponents of transracial adoption, these findings signal a tragic loss of cultural and ethnic heritage. Advocates of transracial adoption, however, see a new generation emerging that is not as concerned about race as previous generations have been, a generation that may lead the way in transforming a racially divided society into a more racially integrated one.

Sexual Orientation and Child Rearing

Researchers believe that between 6 and 14 million U.S. children live with gay male or lesbian parents (Patterson, 1992). Given this society's reluctance to acknowledge the legitimacy of gay families, it's not surprising that some people worry about the ability of gay parents to successfully raise children. Some people are concerned that these children will suffer confusion about their own sexual identity and are more likely to become homosexual themselves. Others feel these children will be less psychologically healthy and exhibit more adjustment and behavioral problems than children growing up in heterosexual homes. Finally, some people worry that children raised by homosexuals will experience teasing, ostracism, or traumatization by peers and the public at large (Patterson, 1992).

Are these beliefs about the dangers of growing up in a gay or lesbian household warranted? Can a parent's sexual orientation impose excessive burdens on a child? Over the

Issue 1 examines the controversy over legally recognizing same-sex marriage.

past 20 years, numerous studies have compared children growing up with homosexual parents (usually lesbian mothers) with the children of heterosexual parents. Researchers have consistently found few or no differences between the two groups of children in the development of gender identity, gender role behavior, sexual orientation, self-concept, intelligence, peer relations, personality characteristics, likelihood of being sexually abused, or behavioral problems (Savin-Williams & Esterberg, 2000).

In short, we have no evidence to suggest that the psychosocial development of children growing up with homosexual parents is compromised. In fact, a review of all the research on this issue reveals not a single study that has found children of lesbian or gay male parents to be disadvantaged in any significant respect. "Homosexual" home environments are just as likely to support and enhance children's psychosocial growth as "heterosexual" homes are (Patterson & Chan, 1999; Savin-Williams & Esterberg, 2000).

When researchers find differences between children raised in these different environments, they tend to be the result of the parents' gender or the social conditions under which lesbian and gay families live, not of the parents' sexual orientation in itself (Stacey & Biblarz, 2001). Indeed, homosexual parents are likely to be more sensitive to their children's development than heterosexual parents are. Some studies, for instance, show that lesbian mothers are more child oriented (Miller, Jacobsen, & Bigner, 1981) and self-confident (Greene, Mandel, Hotvedt, Gray, & Smith, 1986) than heterosexual mothers. Furthermore, lesbian mothers' partners are often more involved in parenting than heterosexual fathers are (cited in Patterson & Chan, 1999).

Despite this evidence, many individuals view homosexuality and parenthood as incompatible. Judges sometimes ignore the research evidence when ruling on custody and adoption cases. In a 1996 Florida case, for instance, a lesbian mother lost custody of her 10-year-old daughter to her ex-husband, who was a convicted murderer. More recently, judges in Pennsylvania ruled that gay and lesbian couples could not legally adopt children (Stack, 2000). Florida, which has a similar ban on adoptions by gays and lesbians, actually entrusted one gay couple to raise three children from infancy as foster parents but would not allow this couple to legally adopt the children they were raising ("ACLU sues Florida," 2001).

Given the current legal and social climate surrounding gay and lesbian parenthood, homosexual couples raising children must confront not only the daily challenges of child rearing, but also heightened fears of losing custody because of their sexual orientation.

The Issue of Child Care

Judging from the statistics, the welfare of children living in homes with two working parents or with a single parent who works is actually a greater problem than the welfare of children living with homosexual or poor or minority parents. Some social critics question whether working parents can possibly devote sufficient time to their children's needs. Although some research has found that parents in dual-earner families spend less time with their children than do parents in single-earner, "traditional" families (Nock & Kingston, 1988), other studies show that today's mothers spend as much time with their children as did mothers in 1965 (Salmon, 2000). To spend more time with their children, working moms sleep 5 to 6 hours less per week and have 12 fewer hours of free personal time compared to stay-at-home moms.

Working parents do face the question, however, of how to ensure the welfare of their children while they're working. With the increase in dual-earner families (discussed in Chapter 7), more and more children are being cared for at least some of the time by people other than their parents. For families with preschoolers, the need for child care is especially pressing, and many parents turn to private babysitters, day care centers and preschools, or relatives. And rather than go home to an empty house, millions of school-age children around the country now stay after school, playing, studying, creating art projects, and so on. To meet the demand, there has been a dramatic increase in after-school programs nationwide—federal financing of these programs ballooned from $1 million in 1997 to $454 million in 2000 (Wilgoren, 2000).

Often parents feel great guilt about using outside child care and worry about the effects that such arrangements will have on the child. The research on this question is mixed. For instance, one highly publicized 2001 study of more than 1,100 children in ten U.S. cities found that children who spend most of their time in child care—30 hours a week or more—are significantly more likely than children cared for primarily at home to exhibit traits such as aggression, defiance, and disobedience (cited in Stolberg, 2001). Critics of this study point out that it shows only a link between time spent in child care and undesirable behavior; it doesn't explain why a youngster in child care is more likely to be aggressive or disobedient. Moreover, although it found that 17 percent of children in long-term child care experience behavior problems later on, the remaining 83 percent show no problems at all.

Other research suggests that the simple fact that a child spends time each day with a caretaker other than his or her parents is not sufficient to cause harm. Instead, the child's development is affected by the quality of care both inside and outside the home. A long-term study by the National Institute of Child Health and Human Development found that children who receive good care and a lot of attention at home seem unaffected by day care (cited in "Child care caste system," 1998). And regardless of the quality of the care and the age when the child enters it, the emotional attachments between parent and child do not appear damaged by the experience (Vobejda, 1996). Only those children who spend time in day care and don't get good parenting at home are less securely attached to their parents.

Indeed, high-quality child care offered by sensitive and committed providers can actually enhance a child's development. A study that tracked poor children from infancy to age 21 found that those who received high-quality day care consistently outperformed peers who didn't on cognitive and academic tests. They were also more likely to attend college and hold high-skill jobs when they became adults (cited in Wilgoren, 1999).

What complicates matters for U.S. parents is the lack of a coherent national policy regarding child care. Virtually all western European countries have a policy of universal but voluntary preschool for children from age 2 to when they begin compulsory education (Kamerman & Kahn, 1995). The preschools tend to be heavily subsidized by the governments and so cost little to parents who want their children to attend. These programs are seen as part of the overall education system and are therefore designed to enhance children's development and prepare them for school. They are so highly valued for the cognitive stimulation they are believed to offer that even parents who aren't employed send their children to preschool. In Germany, Denmark, Finland, and Sweden the vast majority of children between the ages of 3 and 5 attend preschool; in France, Belgium, and Italy over 90 percent of children attend (Kamerman & Kahn, 1995).

In contrast, most U.S. child care providers fall under private auspices, both nonprofit and for-profit. Some are licensed, many are not. The hodgepodge of providers includes

EXHIBIT 9.6

*Quality of Child
Care in the
United States*

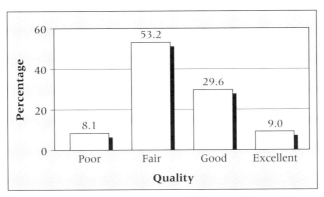

Source: D. L. Vandell & B. Wolfe. 2000. "Child care quality: Does it matter and does it need to be improved?" Table 9. NICHD Study of Early Child Care Research Network. Available at http://aspe.hhs.gov/ hsp/ccquality00/index.htm. Accessed May 1, 2001.

nannies, au pairs, relatives, day care centers, and private homes. Their quality tends to be uneven (see Exhibit 9.6). The average child care worker in this country earns about $6 an hour, which is less than the wage earned by the average parking lot attendant. Moreover, federal changes in welfare laws—which force most women with young children to start work after 2 years of receiving benefits—have increased the demand for jobs that require little education or job training. Consequently, more and more child care centers are hiring untrained welfare recipients to whom they can pay minimum wage (Lewin, 1998b).

Parents are forced to "shop around" for the best—or for many families, least expensive—situation. A full-time nanny may provide the most personal and attentive care but can cost from $250 to $2,000 per week. The average day care center costs considerably less—about $90 per week—but often day care centers have a high child-to-adult ratio, and they are frequently staffed by untrained and underpaid workers. For low-income families, especially poor single-parent families (who have the most critical need), good child care is for the most part, unaffordable.

The one exception is the federally funded Head Start program, whose aim is to integrate child care with high quality early educational experiences for low-income families and families with disabled children. In 2000, 857,664 children were enrolled in Head Start (Head Start Bureau, 2001). The majority of these families earned less than $9,000 annually (Head Start Bureau, 2000). Research indicates that these children make good academic progress, especially in reading and math, once they enter public schools (Ramey et al., 2000). Unfortunately, only a tiny percentage of children who would qualify for Head Start have been able to enroll.

Child care has long received relatively little attention in this country because of people's lingering devotion to the "traditional nuclear family." However, most Americans today have begun to see child care as an inevitable feature of modern family life. Other changes in society—in particular, welfare reforms that require mothers to work—have crippled the argument that all mothers should stay at home with their children. Welfare policies now provide a year of transitional child care assistance for women who leave welfare to work. And some states provide child care assistance to low-income families even if they haven't been on welfare.

Just where child care stands on the political agenda is still unclear. In 1998 President Clinton proposed a major child care initiative, including increased subsidies for low-income families and expanded tax credits for child care expenses. In 2000, Congress increased federal child care funding by $817 million so that states could provide child care to 241,000 additional children (National Women's Law Center, 2001). And in 2001, several members of Congress formed a bipartisan Congressional Child Care Caucus to investigate ways of improving the nation's child care policies. However, early in his administration President Bush proposed a budget that included major cuts in child care programs for low- and middle-income families and eliminated the Early Learning and Opportunities Act, which was enacted in 2000 to enhance the quality of child care.

DEMO·GRAPHICS

Who's Minding the Kids?

Two major social trends—the increase in mothers' paid labor force participation and the increase in single-parent households—have created a tremendous need for child care. Currently, about 75 percent of children under age 5 years are in some form of regular child care.

As you'd expect, the child care rate is higher for mothers who are either employed or in school than it is for mothers not employed or in school. But notice from Exhibit 9.7a that a surprisingly large percentage of nonemployed mothers (43 percent) also have some regular child care arrangement—about the same percentage of employed mothers who use child care when they're not at work. This figure suggests that parents view child care as something more than a necessary evil to be used only when they are at work.

Paradoxically, the increase in nonmaternal child care may mean that children today actually spend more time with other family members than in the past. As you can see from Exhibit 9.7b, other family members represent a crucial piece of the child care puzzle. Relatives—most often the other parent or grandparents—are caretakers for about half of all the children with working mothers today. About 30 percent of preschoolers receive care from grandparents, and 18 percent receive care from the other parent (Smith, 2000). Thus children today probably spend more time with fathers, grandparents, and other relatives, than they did during the last century. Observe too that older children rely heavily on enrichment activities such as after-school lessons, clubs, and sports and that less than a fifth are so-called latchkey children who care for themselves.

One common criticism of child care is that it adversely affects the emotional quality of the parent–child relationship. Yet most parents (including stepparents, adopted parents, and father figures in the household) report that their relationships with their children are extremely or very close (see Exhibit 9.7c). They also claim to engage frequently in very loving behaviors with their child, such as hugging, expressing their love, talking and joking, and so on. Interestingly, the percentage of parents who describe their relationships in these positive ways declines as their children age. With older children, parents are more likely to engage in activities with their children such as household chores, reading, talking about the family, doing homework, building or repairing something, playing computer or board games, and sports. What's unclear from these data is whether the parent or the child is responsible for the reduction in "loving" behaviors that occurs when children get older. Apparently, though, the increasing reliance on child care is not destroying family relationships.

EXHIBIT 9.7

Child Care Arrangements in the United States

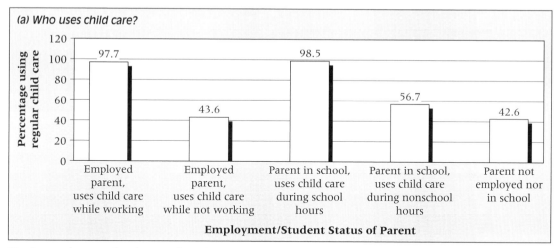

(a) Who uses child care?

Note: *Parent* refers to mothers in married-couple families or the custodial parent in single-parent families.
Data source: K. Smith. 2000. *Who's Minding the Kids? Child Care Arrangements: Fall 1995,* Table 1. *Current Population Reports,* P70-70. Washington, DC: U.S. Bureau of the Census.

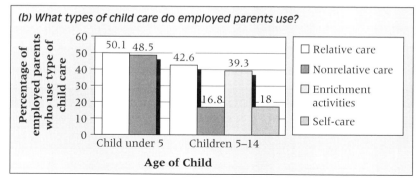

(b) What types of child care do employed parents use?

Note: Because children may participate in more than one type of child care, the percentages within an age group may exceed 100%. Data source: K. Smith. 2000. *Who's Minding the Kids? Child Care Arrangements: Fall 1995,* Tables 2 and 9. *Current Population Reports,* P70-70. Washington, DC: U.S. Bureau of the Census.

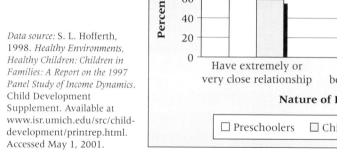

Data source: S. L. Hofferth, 1998. *Healthy Environments, Healthy Children: Children in Families: A Report on the 1997 Panel Study of Income Dynamics.* Child Development Supplement. Available at www.isr.umich.edu/src/child-development/printrep.html. Accessed May 1, 2001.

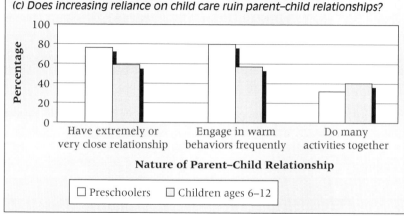

(c) Does increasing reliance on child care ruin parent–child relationships?

Thinking Critically About the Statistics

1. Look at Exhibit 9.7a. Besides those who use child care while they are at work or in school, notice the fairly high rate of usage (slightly above and slightly below 50 percent) among parents who seemingly shouldn't need child care services. Why do you think these parents would put their children in child care when they are available to care for them? What factors, not represented by the data in this exhibit would be important to consider? This exhibit doesn't distinguish between mothers and fathers. How do you think these charts would differ if parent's gender was taken into account? Do you think Exhibit 9.7a could be used as evidence that society has become more approving of child care over the past few decades? Explain.

2. Look at Exhibit 9.7b and compare the percentages for relative care and nonrelative care for the two age groups. How would you explain the change that you see as children age? Why is the decrease in the use of nonrelative care as children age so much larger than the decrease in relative care? The note on the exhibit states that the percentages may add up to more than 100 percent. What do you think are the most likely overlaps for children ages 5 to 14?

3. Recall from this chapter that children's value to parents today is largely emotional. Do the percentages in Exhibit 9.7c seem to reflect this emotional bond, or are they lower than you'd expect? What historical and cultural factors might influence the emotional quality of the parent–child relationship?   ■

Conclusion

As a society, we express great love for children. They occupy a hallowed place in this culture, and it is upon their tiny shoulders that people place their most precious hopes and dreams for the future. On a personal level, most parents today tend to regard their children with deep pleasure. To many parents, there is no greater delight than seeing the first sign of recognition on an infant's face or coming home to children's hugs after a tough day at work. These are the gifts that sustain parents.

But this society's cultural and personal ideals regarding children don't always match the reality of their lives. Many children today face a miserable life filled with poverty, ill health, and violence. Others face a life of parental indifference or worse. Even those children who are fortunate enough to have parents who love them or to be born into a family with the economic means to sustain a comfortable life can sometimes bear the heavy burden of unrealistic expectations and excessive pressures to grow up and measure up.

Such societal ambivalence is made even more complex by the inherent irony of child rearing: Parents never really know what the long-term effects of their parenting will be. As they watch their own children develop, they can't help but wonder if the way they're raising the children is the "right" way. Most parents have gnawing worries that they'll say something or do something to their children that will somehow tarnish them for life.

What makes child rearing all the more unsettling is the knowledge that parents can never completely determine and control the course of their children's lives. Much as some parents would like to believe otherwise, powerful forces over which they have absolutely no control profoundly affect the way they raise their children. Societywide economic conditions, for instance, can place extraordinary financial and emotional strains on parents, which spill over into the relationship they have with their kids. Even more directly, much of parents' influence over their children stops at the front door. Children easily forget lessons about the virtues of nonviolence in the throes of playing a friend's shoot-'em-up video game. To be part of the group out in the schoolyard, they blithely ignore our pleas to judge other children as individuals, not on the basis of their gender or other social attributes.

In short, it's worth remembering that childhood and adolescence are not just universal stages of growth and that child rearing is not simply a preprogrammed skill. They always take place within a particular cultural and historical context. And they are always influenced by prevailing values, social forces, and cultural definitions. These things can either markedly enhance or drastically impede even the most loving and competent parents' ability to raise their children "successfully."

Chapter Highlights

- The experience of being a child is influenced, to a large degree, by broader social definitions of childhood. But childhood is not merely a biological stage of development. It is a social category, subject to changing definitions and expectations. Throughout history, children have been seen as miniature adults who deserve no special treatment, little monsters that need to be tamed, innocent beings who deserve nurturance and love, and parental property with no special rights.
- The power dynamics in families are a lot more complicated than people tend to think. The power and influence contemporary children have conflicts with traditional conceptions of parent–child relationships, which emphasize parental control and authority.
- Like childhood, adolescence is a socially defined stage of life. It marks the transition between childhood and adulthood. Adolescence, as people today know it, emerged in the late nineteenth century as a product of social, economic, and educational changes that extended childhood dependency into the teen years.
- In some societies, the change from child to adult is marked by an elaborate rite of passage. In other societies, as in ours, the change is much less explicit and much more gradual.
- Broad gender ideologies affect the ways males and females experience adolescence, especially regarding sexuality.
- The ways that children are raised depends on cultural definitions of appropriate child rearing, on social class, and on race and ethnicity. Sexual orientation of the parents, which has been a concern of some social critics, appears to have little or no effect on child-rearing practices or effectiveness.
- Institutional child care has become a common feature of U.S. family life. Its quality, though, remains uneven; and despite some recent high-level attention, it remains a low political priority.

Your Turn

Throughout this chapter we've seen the importance of how a society defines childhood and adolescence. One way to glimpse these definitions is by analyzing cultural products such as the media. The media often reveal a society's unspoken, shared understandings and assumptions about who children and adolescents are, and who others want them to be. Because multiple definitions of childhood and adolescence can and do exist simultaneously, people often send contradictory messages, or show a discrepancy between what they say they want and what they actually expect from youth. For instance, although they say young children should be shielded from sexual messages and discouraged from forming romantic attachments, popular media presentations designed for young children are replete with such messages, sometimes subtle, sometimes not.

To see firsthand the unspoken assumptions about childhood and adolescence, select a particular type of media to examine, such as music, cartoons, comic books, books, videos, or computer games. Most public libraries allow users to check out videos, CDs, and games, in addition to books. Here, you'll find media aimed at a various ages. Examine some aimed at young children and some created for adolescents.

First, carefully examine the materials directed at young children for "hidden" messages about race, social class, gender, and sexuality. Pay attention not only to what's happening in the foreground (the spoken message) but also to "background" messages—those not central to the main action. To what extent do media directed at young children introduce readers to issues such as racism, poverty, discrimination, violence, and sexism? When present, how are these messages conveyed? What underlying assumptions about children are implied by the treatment of these messages? Does this medium imply that children are "miniature adults"? "natural innocents"? "little monsters"? "parental property"? If you're looking at books, you may also want to compare recently published books with those from earlier decades to determine whether and how messages have changed.

Next, examine media directed at adolescents. What messages do preteens and teens get about some of the issues just noted? How do they differ from messages in younger children's media? Are you surprised by the explicitness of some of these messages? What do these media seem to imply about adolescents? Do they portray them as adults, children, or something in between?

Do you think manufacturers are simply responding to market demands (that is, do they produce this type of media because that's what people want), or do manufacturers play a role in creating those demands?

Intimate Violence

A Violent Society Begets Violent Homes

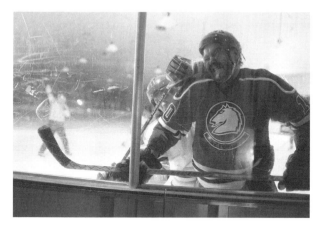

There's no question that we live in a violent society. From gang-related drive-by shootings and schoolyard slayings to earth-shattering acts of terrorism, violence can and does intrude on all aspects of everyday life. Violence even invades the privacy and comfort of American families. Indeed, as much as we'd like to believe otherwise, outside of wars and riots, the home is the most violent location in U.S. society. This sort of violence crosses class, race, and religious lines. It happens in every corner of the country. It happens between spouses, between siblings, and between parents and their children. It happens to the very young, the very old, and every age group in between. We can't begin to understand violence in homes without examining the violence that pervades the larger society and culture.

The glorification of violence in the media and in sports is often credited with promoting violent responses to frustration and perceived injustices.

To what extent do you think that sports events and media depictions of violence encourage actual acts of violence? Do you think acts of bullying are relatively harmless forms of violence? If you were a social researcher, how would you go about answering these questions?

Most people associate spouse abuse with violence toward women. Although women are more likely to be severely victimized in their homes than men, some men also find themselves the victims of violence in their homes.

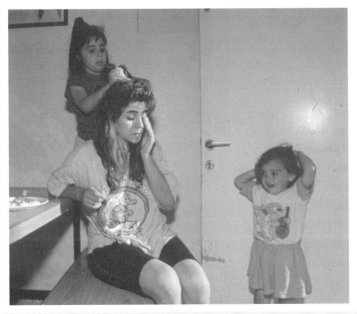

The woman and her children shown here are residents at a domestic violence shelter. How important are shelters in protecting victims? Given that most shelters accept only women and children, where would male victims of domestic violence seek refuge?

Children can be both direct and indirect victims of abusive violence in the home. Given their dependent status and limited resources, they can also be victims of neglect.

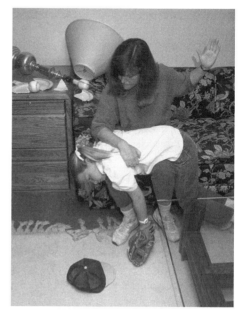

To some, spanking is a dangerous form of violence; to others, it is an acceptable aspect of child rearing.

Do you think spanking is a form of child abuse? If so, how could such behavior be monitored and controlled? If you don't think it is a form of abuse, how should we, as a society, distinguish between acceptable spanking and unacceptable abuse?

The past few years have been awash in highly publicized cases of intimate violence. Hardly a week goes by without some famous actor, musician, or athlete being accused of beating his wife or girlfriend. One professional football player sits in prison, convicted of masterminding the murder of his pregnant girlfriend; another was shot and killed by his wife after one of their many heated arguments. And the name O. J. Simpson still evokes images of spouse abuse, mayhem, and murder.

What is perhaps even more disturbing than these high-profile cases is the sheer volume of incidents that few of us ever hear about—those stories that never make the national news and remain tucked away in the back sections of local newspapers. The following is just a sampling of domestic violence incidents reported in one newspaper, the *New York Times*, during the first 4 months of a single year. All occurred in New York City. None was considered newsworthy enough to appear as front-page headlines:

- *January 1:* A 38-year-old mother of three was charged with reckless endangerment in the death of her 10-month-old daughter, who was found with a fractured skull, fractured leg, and multiple blunt-force traumas.
- *January 5:* A 49-year-old man was charged with assault and attempted murder after he threw rubbing alcohol on his wife and set her on fire.
- *January 6:* A 22-year-old mother was arrested and charged with murder for throwing her newborn girl out of a third-story window into an alley.
- *February 12:* A 35-year-old man who spent 16 months in prison for killing a baby in 1985 was taken into custody on charges that he fractured the skull of his girlfriend's 5-month-old son.
- *February 22:* A pregnant mother and her boyfriend were each charged with seven counts of aggravated assault and endangering the welfare of a child after all seven of her children were found with bruises and welts.
- *March 7:* A 26-year-old man was arrested after a rampage in which he beat his five young children. Two of the children—ages 3 and 4—suffered broken legs.
- *March 27:* A 23-year-old man was charged with kidnapping and murdering his fiancée just days after she had obtained a court order of protection against him.
- *March 31:* A 27-year-old woman was charged with murder after taking her 5-year-old son—his bruised body already lifeless from weeks of starvation and abuse—to a nearby hospital.
- *April 2:* A 33-year-old woman was arrested on charges that she severely burned her 7-year-old daughter by forcing her to sit on a radiator as punishment for fighting with her siblings.
- *April 10:* A 28-year-old woman was charged with attempted murder for trying to strangle her 8-year-old daughter on a busy sidewalk; meanwhile another woman tried to shield them from view.
- *April 11:* A 22-year-old man was charged in the beating death of his girlfriend's 3-year-old son. The boy died from stomach wounds, blunt trauma, and internal bleeding.
- *April 21:* A 33-year-old man was charged with attempted murder for beating his girlfriend's 14-month-old son into unconsciousness.

We can only imagine how many other cases took place during the same period that either didn't result in debilitating injury or death, or simply never came to the attention of the police or the press. Had a different 4-month period in a different year or newspapers from a different major city been examined, there's a good chance that a similar array of tragic stories would be unearthed.

In this chapter we take a close look at the nature, prevalence, causes, and consequences of intimate violence and abuse. With such a broad and emotionally volatile topic, it is impossible to cover every aspect or acknowledge every opinion. For instance, perhaps the most prevalent and taken-for-granted form of violence in families occurs between siblings. But such violence rarely escalates to the point of life-threatening injury. Hence, we focus primarily on four types of violence: dating violence, spouse or partner abuse, child abuse, and elder abuse. Furthermore, although intimate violence usually includes emotional, psychological, and sometimes financial abuse as well, we pay particular attention to its physical dimension. Finally, we use terms such as *intimate violence, domestic violence,* and *family violence* interchangeably to refer to acts of violence and aggression that take place between people related by blood or involved romantically.

The Roots of Intimate Violence in the United States

No one would deny that the United States is a violent society. Rates of violent crime here—although decreasing in recent years—still exceed those of any other industrialized nation. Americans have long been committed to the use of violence to achieve desirable changes and resolve interpersonal problems. It is in the streets, schools, movies, television shows, toy stores, spectator sports, and government. It's even in the everyday language: Americans *assault* problems, *conquer* fears, *beat* others to the punch, *pound* home ideas, and *shoot down* opinions (Ewing, 1992).

Although there's no questioning the violent nature of U.S. society, it is surprising to many that the majority of violent acts occur between people who know each other (see Exhibit 10.1a). Certainly most people are reluctant to label U.S. families as violent. "Violence" and "families" are words that don't seem to naturally go together. One of the most enduring popular images of family is that it is a "safe haven"—the one place in society to which people ought to be able to escape when life becomes overwhelming. Family is not a place where you'd expect to get screamed at, emotionally belittled, punched in the face, raped, or have your life threatened simply because you came home too late, got a *C* on a calculus test, said the wrong thing at the wrong time, or just happened to be there. But that is precisely what awaits a large number of people in this country, especially children and women.

The tragic truth is that, outside of wars and riots, the home is the single most violent location in society (see Exhibit 10.1b). Intimate violence happens in rich homes and poor homes, black homes and white homes, heterosexual and homosexual homes, rural and urban homes.

As recently as 40 years ago, most Americans saw intimate violence as an unfortunate, but nonetheless "normal" part of family life. In the popular 1950s sitcom *The Honeymooners,* Ralph Kramden (played by Jackie Gleason) would routinely threaten to hit his wife so hard he would send her "to the moon." Such scenes never failed to elicit laughs from the audience.

The relationship between family privacy and domestic violence is examined in Issue 3.

At the same time, though, intimate violence wasn't something a family wanted to publicize. It was typically considered a secret that was better kept out of sight. Because it remained so well hidden—particularly among the middle and upper classes—the public didn't believe such behaviors constituted a serious social problem. Instead, most people thought family violence was mainly characteristic of poor and minority families—those segments of the population unable to keep their private lives private.

EXHIBIT 10.1

Violent Crime in the United States

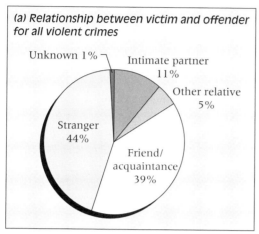

(a) Relationship between victim and offender for all violent crimes

- Unknown 1%
- Intimate partner 11%
- Other relative 5%
- Friend/acquaintance 39%
- Stranger 44%

Data source: U.S. Department of Justice. 2001a. *Criminal Victimization in the United States, 1999,* Table 43A. NCJ 184938. Available at www.ojp.usdoj.gov/bjs/pub/pdf/cvus99.pdf. Accessed January 28, 2001.

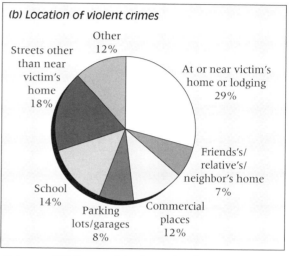

(b) Location of violent crimes

- Other 12%
- At or near victim's home or lodging 29%
- Friends's/relative's/neighbor's home 7%
- Commercial places 12%
- Parking lots/garages 8%
- School 14%
- Streets other than near victim's home 18%

Data source: U.S. Bureau of the Census. 2000b. *Statistical Abstract of the United States: 2000,* Table 342. Washington, DC: U.S. Government Printing Office.

The hidden, private nature of domestic violence prevented the vast majority of victims from seeking help. What's more, they had little choice but to keep their experiences to themselves. They couldn't call for help, because no help was available.

Since the 1970s, however, we have witnessed a marked change in public conceptions of domestic violence. Child abuse, spouse abuse, elder abuse, and other forms of intimate violence have been publicly redefined. Although still cloaked in secrecy, domestic violence no longer has the sort of tacit approval and look-the-other-way tolerance it once enjoyed from police, courts, and the public at large. Every major city now has shelters for battered women and self-help groups for victims and former abusers. Hospitals sponsor special treatment programs concerned with abused and neglected children.

Families themselves are no longer the harsh little dictatorships they once were, where fathers ruled with iron fists. Children now have recognized rights and are not expected to submit to their parents' will with unquestioned obedience. Women are no longer expected to be docile and subservient. They are now likely to enter marriage assuming they will have a high degree of autonomy and sufficient opportunity to assert themselves educationally and professionally (Pleck, 1987).

Public perceptions have also changed. Intimate violence is more likely to be reported and prosecuted than it once was, which has, ironically, produced what appears to be a rising incidence of intimate violence. College students today overwhelmingly oppose the use of violence and coercion in dating situations (Cook, 1995). Few people would dare argue that wife battering is justifiable when wives disobey their husbands or that regular beatings are the best way to raise a child.

And yet, despite the dramatic changes that have taken place in this society, old attitudes and expectations die hard. Several years ago, after his team had barely beaten a much weaker team, star basketball player Charles Barkley said, "This is a game that, if you lose, you go home and beat your wife and kids." That same year, after his college football team lost a heartbreaking game, Penn State head coach Joe Paterno "jokingly" told reporters, "I'm going to go home and beat my wife" (both quoted in Nack & Munson, 1995). To our knowledge, neither of these men did, in fact, go home and beat their wives or children. But such statements do show that those old attitudes toward domestic violence are far from extinct.

Perceptions of family violence are always influenced by broader historical and political conditions. Ideas about what constitutes unacceptable intimate violence and how people should respond to it are linked to the political moods that characterize this historical era. For instance, over the past century the women's rights movement has been most influential in confronting and publicizing family violence and demanding that action be taken against it. Historically, concern with family violence has grown when feminism was strong and has receded when feminism was weak (Gordon, 1988). Similarly, during conservative periods intimate violence tends to be explained in terms of the individual psychologies of batterers and victims. When progressive political attitudes prevail, explanations tend to revolve around broader social conditions, such as economic uncertainty and changing power relationships in families or in society as a whole.

Violence in Dating Relationships

When people think of violence between intimates, they usually think of violence that occurs within nuclear families. But a great deal of intimate violence occurs even before couples marry. A recent survey of approximately 2,000 high school girls between the ages of 14 and 18 found that 20 percent had been hit, slapped, shoved, or forced into sexual activity by a dating partner (Silverman, Raj, Mucci, & Hathaway, 2001). Other research reveals that as many as three-quarters of all U.S. college students may have experienced violence in a current or past dating situation (Carlson, 1996). Dating violence crosses lines of race, ethnicity, age, class, and sexual orientation (Levy, 1991).

You'd expect violent episodes to shatter the romantic images held by dating partners and signal the end of the relationship. However, in many cases the violence seems to enhance rather than destroy the illusions of romance. According to one study, one out of four victims and one out of three offenders interpret dating violence as a sign of love (Henton, Cate, Koval, Lloyd, & Scott, 1983).

When sociologist Jan Stets (1992) examined dating violence, she found several patterns of aggression, each with a different cause. A one-time-only violent outburst is likely to be caused by a disagreement over some sensitive issue (spending habits, sex, future plans, and so on). Such an act is likely to come as a surprise to both partners. But aggression that happens many times may be caused by a more persistent, long-term issue such as basic and repeated value conflicts in the relationship. For instance, a person who tends to neglect the partner's needs, concerns, and wishes and to put his or her desires first may repeatedly act aggressively.

What's important about these different patterns of dating aggression is that they elicit different interpretations. When violence is a single instance, the partners are likely to interpret it as an instantaneous means of expressing feelings. If the aggression is immediately challenged, chances are it won't happen again.

When a person is violent more than once, however, it may not be so much a spontaneous expression of feelings as an instrument to get what he or she wants. Repeated aggression may be deliberate, calculated, and planned (Stets, 1992). If the conduct is not challenged, it can become part of a person's behavioral repertoire and become solidly embedded in the relationship (see Chapter 6 for more on power in intimate relationships).

Sexual Coercion

Young women consistently report that the thing they dislike most about dating situations is unwanted pressure to have sex. The prevalence of **sexual coercion** in dating relationships is well documented (Reinholtz, Muehlenhard, Phelps, & Satterfield, 1995). Studies have found that as many as one in three women engage in unwanted sexual activities because of pressure from dating partners.

Still more women—perhaps more than half the population—engage in unwanted sexual activity for reasons other than pressure from a partner, such as general peer pressure; fear of appearing shy or afraid, unfeminine, or inexperienced; and a desire to be more popular. This sort of pressure comes not from a partner but from one's own expectations about how one should behave sexually (Reinholtz et al., 1995). About a quarter of both men and women cite peer pressure as one of the main reasons they had intercourse for the first time when they didn't want it (Laumann et al., 1994). Sexual coercion, although not as violent in a direct, physical way as rape and sexual assault are, is often the precursor to these crimes.

Rape

Although the official number of rape victims appears to have fallen over the past few years (Butterfield, 1997), forcible rape remains the most frequently committed but least reported violent crime in the United States today (U.S. Department of Justice, 2001).

According to the National Crime Victimization Survey—an annual assessment of crime victimization carried out by the U.S. Bureau of Justice Statistics—more than 333,000 women are raped or sexually assaulted annually, three times the 93,000 incidents of rape that were officially reported to the police in 1998 (U.S. Bureau of the Census, 2000b). Such violence is especially prevalent on college campuses, where about 3% of college women experience a completed or attempted rape during a typical college year. In the vast majority of these cases, the victim knew her attacker (see Exhibit 10.2).

Cultural beliefs about gender, sexuality, and intimacy influence societal and legal responses to rape:

- In 1999 the highest appeals court in Italy overturned a rape conviction because the victim wore jeans. The court ruled that it is impossible to take off tight jeans "without the collaboration of the person wearing them," implying that the woman must have been a consenting participant in a sexual encounter rather than a victim of a violent crime ("Italy," 1999, p. A8).
- In Peru, a man who rapes a woman—whether he knows her or not—can be absolved of all charges if he offers to marry her. As one Peruvian man put it, "Marriage is the right and proper thing to do after a rape. A raped woman is a used item. No one wants her. At least with this law the woman will get a husband" (quoted in Sims, 1997, p. A8).

EXHIBIT 10.2

*Offender's
Relationship to
Victim in College
Rape Cases*

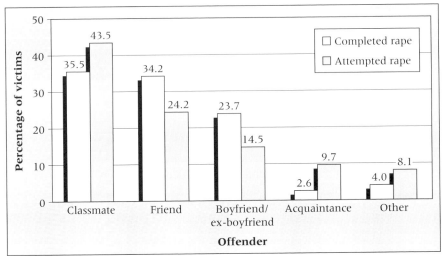

Source: B. S. Fisher, F. T. Cullen, & M. G. Turner. 2000. "The Sexual Victimization of College Women."
Exhibit 8. NCJ 182369. Available at www.ncjrs.org/pdffiles1/nij/182369.pdf. Accessed June 1, 2001.

Likewise, in Taiwan a woman may be encouraged to marry her rapist in order to preserve her honor and chastity (Luo, 2000).

- In Kenya, 300 boys at a boarding school raped 71 girls in a dormitory. Several of the girls were killed in the attacks. The vice principal explained, "The boys never meant any harm against the girls, they just wanted to rape" (quoted in Cooper, 1999, p. 355).

In the United States, people have a somewhat more sympathetic response to rape victims. Even so, rape has one of the lowest conviction rates of any violent crime. According to a report by the Senate Judiciary Committee (1993), 98 percent of rape victims never see their attacker caught, tried, and imprisoned. And of those rapists who are convicted, close to 25 percent never go to prison and another 25 percent receive sentences in local jails, where the average sentence is 11 months.

Unlike any other crime, rape trials typically require the victims to prove their innocence in addition to requiring the state to prove the guilt of the rapist. This state of affairs stems partly from a definition of rape that is based on a traditional model of sexual intercourse (penile–vaginal penetration) rather than the violent context within which the act takes place. In other words, rape, especially in dating situations, is still largely viewed in terms of women's sexuality rather than men's coercion (Sheffield, 1987). The notion that sex is synonymous with penile–vaginal intercourse also means that forced oral sex, nonconsensual fondling, or same-sex coercion may not be considered rape (Reinholtz et al., 1995).

The exclusive focus on the sexual component of the crime requires the court to consider information about the social circumstances around the act and about the relationship between the people involved. Victims must provide some evidence that they were "unwilling" and tried to resist. No other violent crime requires that the victim prove lack of consent. People aren't asked if they agreed to having their car stolen or if they did something to provoke being robbed.

If women cannot prove they resisted or cannot find someone to corroborate their story, consent is often presumed. Even in cases of stranger rape, anything short of vigorous and repeated resistance calls the victim's motives into question. In 1992 in Austin, Texas, a man forcibly entered a woman's apartment. The woman fled and locked herself in the bathroom. He broke down the door, held a knife to her, and demanded sex. Fearing for her life, not only because of the knife but also because of the chances of contracting a sexually transmitted disease, she begged the man to put on a condom. He agreed and went on to assault her for over an hour. The next day he was arrested for burglary with intent to commit sexual assault. In a sworn deposition he admitted that he had held a knife to her and had sex with her. But the grand jury originally refused to indict the man on the rape charge because the victim's act of providing a condom was taken to mean consent. Only after widespread public outrage was the man tried, convicted, and sentenced to 40 years in prison.

Excusing the Rapist   Cultural norms and beliefs about male sexuality (see Chapter 5) also influence people's understanding of sexual coercion and rape in dating relationships. One such belief is that men's sexual urges are uncontrollable. Men are frequently portrayed as overwhelmingly sexual beings who, once aroused, are compelled by forces beyond their control to seek sexual gratification. Thus sexual coercion and violence are rendered inevitable.

In 1993 a group of teenage boys in Lakewood, California, who called themselves the "Spur Posse" made national headlines for their practice of keeping a tally of the many girls with whom they had sex. These boys were predominantly well-known athletes from middle-class families. Nine of the boys—aged 15 to 18—were arrested and charged with various crimes, including forcible rape, rape by intimidation, unlawful intercourse, oral copulation, and child molestation. Within a week all but one were set free. The district attorney's office explained that it does not file charges in sexual assault cases if the perpetrator and the victim are of roughly the same age and social experience (Allen, 1993). You can see in one father's response the belief that these behaviors were an inevitable product of male sexual nature: "Nothing my boy did was anything that any red-blooded American boy wouldn't do at his age" (quoted in "The body counters," 1993, p. 36).

Rape in dating situations is thus viewed less as an act of deviance and more an act of overconformity to cultural expectations; less an act by abnormally brutal individuals and more an act by "normal" men behaving in ways they think are appropriate. As one author wrote, rape is the "all-American crime," involving precisely those characteristics traditionally regarded as desirable in men: strength, power, domination, and control (Griffin, 1989).

Blaming the Victim   Related to this belief in uncontrollable male sexuality is the belief that women are ultimately responsible for men's sexual behavior. That is, women "do something to" men that arouses their sexuality, and men cannot resist. A woman who is raped is therefore held responsible for failing to control the man's behavior (Reinholtz et al., 1995).

Many people also regard women as partly or wholly responsible for being victimized when they purportedly place themselves at risk by acting seductively, wearing provocative clothing, or telling dirty jokes. Research indicates that the cultural belief that women provoke rape is pervasive. One survey of 400 teens (Goodchilds, Zellman, Johnson, & Giarusso, 1988) found that approximately half of the boys and about 30 percent of the girls felt it was acceptable for a man to force sex on a woman when

- She is going to have sex with him and changes her mind.
- She has "led" him on.

- She gets him sexually excited.
- They have dated for a long time.
- She lets him touch her above the waist.

In another study, male and female high school students were given a list of statements and asked to indicate the extent to which they agreed with them (Kershner, 1996). Fifty-two percent agreed that most women fantasize about being raped by a man. Forty-six percent felt that women encourage rape by the way they dress, and 53 percent said they felt that some women provoke men into raping them. Thirty-one percent agreed that many women falsely report rapes. Thirty-five percent felt that the victim should be required to prove her innocence during a rape trial.

The important sociological point of these findings is that many men and even some women don't always define violent sexual assault within dating relationships as wrong, and that they think it is what men are expected to do under certain circumstances. These views have become so entrenched in this culture's view of rape that many women have internalized the message, blaming themselves for not doing enough to prevent their own victimization. Outside of fear, self-blame is the most common reaction to rape; it is more frequent than anger (Janoff-Bulman, 1979).

The crucial consequence of these attitudes is that women must bear most if not all of the responsibility for preventing rape. When asked, What can people do to stop rape? most individuals list things such as, Don't hitchhike. Don't walk alone at night. Don't get drunk at parties where men are present. Don't initiate sex play. Don't engage in foreplay if you have no intention of "going all the way." Don't miscommunicate your intentions. Don't wear provocative clothing. Don't accept invitations from strangers. But note that these suggestions focus exclusively on things that women should avoid in order to prevent rape and say nothing about the things men can do to stop it. Because it is primarily men who rape, ultimately the responsibility for stopping rape is men's.

Certainly, given the violent nature of today's society, women should communicate their sexual intentions clearly and not put themselves in dangerous situations. The implication of such instructions, however, speaks volumes about the nature of rape, expectations in intimate relationships, and the place of women in this society. Confining discussions of rape prevention solely to women's behavior suggests that a woman cannot dress the way she wants, walk where and when she wants, talk to whom she wants, enjoy "partying," or change her mind about having sex.

Without a fundamental restructuring of society, it seems, no significant reduction in sexual violence in dating situations is likely to occur. People would have to transform male–female relationships and childhood socialization, override the cultural beliefs and images that perpetuate certain sexual attitudes, and institute a more equitable sharing of political and economic power. Until that time arrives, the most practical response may be to clarify the fuzzy boundary between seduction and coercion, helping men and women understand the conflicting values and expectations they bring to dating relationships.

Violence Between Spouses and Partners

A form of intimate violence that has received substantially more attention than dating violence is that which takes place between spouses and long-time intimate partners. Research on this type of intimate violence shows it can take several forms (MacMillan & Gartner, 1999):

- *Interpersonal conflict* involves relatively minor acts of random and sporadic violence, such as pushing, grabbing, and slapping
- *Nonsystematic abuse* involves a range of violent acts from threats to kicking and hitting but generally does not involve life-threatening acts
- *Systematic abuse* involves a relatively high risk of all types of violence, including life-threatening violence, such as beating, choking, and attacks with knives or guns.

Although all three forms of violence between intimate partners are serious and deserving of attention, one cannot get a clear picture of the nature of spousal and partner violence if they are all lumped together. For example, reported research can be somewhat misleading if incidents of systematic abuse are lumped together with incidents of interpersonal conflict.

Exact statistics about the prevalence of spousal or partner violence are also difficult to collect, because it is concealed and private, usually occurring in seclusion, beyond the watchful eyes of relatives, neighbors, and strangers. Even with the more stringent rules for police reporting of domestic calls that have been instituted in the past decade or two, most incidents are never reported; others are dismissed as accidents. Furthermore, definitions of abuse and reporting practices vary from state to state.

The statistics on spouse and partner abuse that do exist indicate that it is a widespread problem, although it has declined somewhat in recent years. According to the U.S. Bureau of Justice Statistics (2000), about 1 million violent crimes were committed by spouses, boyfriends or girlfriends in 1998. These figures only include lethal (homicide) and nonlethal (rape, sexual assault, aggravated assault, simple assault) offenses. If one were to count other, relatively minor, acts of interpersonal conflict (pushing, slapping, shoving, throwing things) the figures would, no doubt, be much higher.

There is some debate as to whether men or women are more likely to be victims of intimate violence. In some cities around the country a quarter of arrests for domestic violence are of women (cited in Goldberg, 1999). It's true that men are sometimes beaten by their intimate partners, yet women account for about 85 percent of victims of domestic violence nationwide (U.S. Bureau of Justice Statistics, 2000). Most of the women who are arrested in cases of intimate violence were acting in self-defense. Furthermore, because violence committed by men tends to be more severe and more difficult to escape than violence committed by women, women clearly are the disproportionate victims of the most dangerous and life-threatening forms of violence. In fact, violence in the household represents the single largest cause of injury to women in the United States today. Half of the victims are beaten three or more times a year (Straus, Gelles, & Steinmetz, 1980). In some areas of the country, domestic violence sends as many women to hospital emergency rooms as any other type of injury, illness, or assault.

In 1998, over 1,800 murders were attributed to intimate partners. Three out of four of the victims were women, accounting for about 30 percent of female homicides in this country (U.S. Bureau of Justice Statistics, 2000). Although the number of men murdered by intimates has dropped by 69 percent since 1976, the number of women killed by intimates has remained fairly stable and has only begun to drop of in the past 10 years (see Exhibit 10.3).

Given the shame and stigma associated with such violence, you can probably assume that the figures on assault are *under*estimates of the actual incidence of violence between intimates. Only about half of the cases of nonlethal violence against women are reported to the police (Rennison & Welchans, 2000). Murder estimates, in contrast, are likely to be more accurate. It's safe to say that many people—mostly women but also some men—face significant physical danger in their homes each day.

EXHIBIT 10.3

Murder of Intimates in the United States

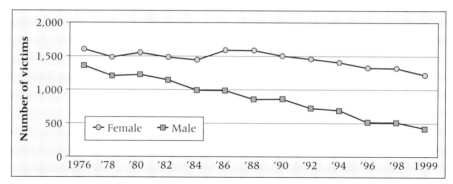

Data source: U.S. Department of Justice. 2001c. "Homicide trends in the U.S.: Intimate homicide." Available at www.ojp.usdoj.gov/bjs/. Accessed May 1, 2001.

DEMO•GRAPHICS

Lovers, Friends, or Strangers

As you've already seen in Chapters 5 and 6, women often place a higher value on marriage and intimate relationships than do men. It is especially tragic and ironic, then, that these relationships actually place women at greater risk of violence than men. In fact, if you were to examine the overall rates of violent crimes in society (homicide, rape, robbery, and assault), you'd see that men are more likely to be victimized than women. However, these men are usually not victimized by women, but by other men. Yet when we look at rates of *intimate* violence, the opposite pattern emerges (see Exhibit 10.4a).

Unquestionably, intimate relationships are more dangerous for women than for men. But are women actually at greater risk of being victimized by an intimate partner than by a nonintimate? Probably not. Examine, for example, the data in Exhibit 10.4b on the relationship between women who were sexually or physically assaulted and the offender. Women are more likely to be sexually or physically assaulted by a stranger than by an intimate partner—but much more likely to be victimized by a friend or acquaintance than any other type of intimate. In contrast, the majority of men who are assaulted are victimized by strangers, usually other men (U.S. Department of Justice, 2001).

If friends and acquaintances are more likely than closer intimates to victimize women, you might also expect less committed relationships to be more violent than more committed ones. But are they? The best data available to answer this question are homicide statistics, which show that between 1976 and 1996, 31,260 women were killed by husbands, ex-husbands, or other intimate partners. Of these, the vast majority were murdered by husbands. The rates are similar for men who were murdered by intimates (see Exhibit 10.4c). You can't necessarily conclude, however, that spouses are more likely to murder each other than divorced spouses or cohabiting partners are. The statistics may simply be a function of risk: There are many more married couples than dating or divorced couples, so the number of murders by spouses would of course be greater.

The question remains: Does marriage itself place women at risk? The available data break down crime rates by gender or marital status but not both. Looking at the victimization rates in Exhibit 10.4d, you see that married people are actually less likely to be victimized overall than are divorced or separated, or never married people. Widowed people—

EXHIBIT 10.4

Violence Against Spouses and Partners

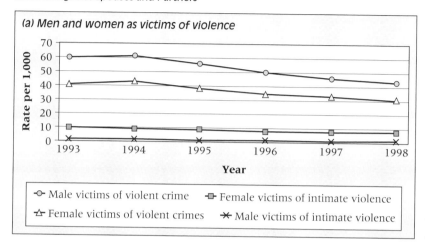

(a) Men and women as victims of violence

— Male victims of violent crime   — Female victims of intimate violence
— Female victims of violent crimes   — Male victims of intimate violence

Data sources: U.S. Department of Justice. 2000. "Violent Crime Levels Declined Between 1998 and 1999, Rates for Men and Women Are Getting Closer." Available at www.ojp.usdoj.gov/ bjs/glance/vsx2.htm. Accessed May 1, 2001. Also C. A. Rennison & S. Welchans. 2000. *Intimate Partner Violence,* Table 2. Available at www.ojp.usdoj.gov/ bjs/pub/pdf/ipv.pdf. Accessed June 1, 2001.

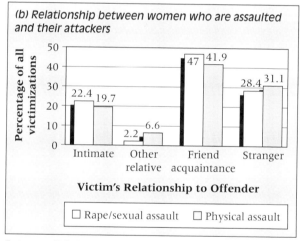

(b) Relationship between women who are assaulted and their attackers

☐ Rape/sexual assault   ☐ Physical assault

Data source: U.S. Department of Justice. 2001a. *Criminal Victimization in United States, 1999.* Table 43A. NCJ 184938. Available at www.ojp. usdoj.gov/bjs/pub/pdf/cvus99.pdf. Accessed January 28, 2001.

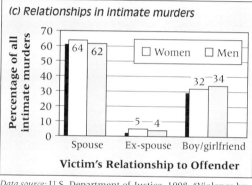

(c) Relationships in intimate murders

☐ Women   ☐ Men

Data source: U.S. Department of Justice. 1998. "Violence by Inimates: Analysis of Data on Crimes by Current or Former Spouses, Boyfriends, and Girlfriends." NCJ-167237. Available at www.ojp.usdoj.gov/bjs/pub/pdf/vi.pdf. Accessed May 1, 2001.

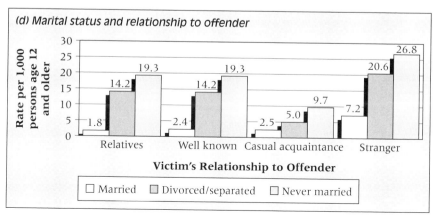

(d) Marital status and relationship to offender

☐ Married   ☐ Divorced/separated   ☐ Never married

Data source: U.S. Department of Justice. 2001a. *Criminal Victimization in United States, 1999.* Table 35. NCJ 184938. Available at www.ojp.usdoj.gov/bjs/pub /pdf/cvus99.pdf. Accessed January 28, 2001.

not shown in Exhibit 10.4d—have the lowest rates of all. So perhaps marriage is not as dangerous to either women or men, as the statistics shown in Exhibit 10.4c indicate.

The study of domestic violence is complicated by many factors, including underreporting and the hodgepodge of available data. Clearly, however, both men and women are at less risk of being victimized by intimates than by people they don't know so well. But equally clearly, women are much more likely to be victimized by their intimate partners than men are. Thus the study of intimate violence is also a study of how gender, power, and intimacy interact in everyday life.

Thinking Critically About the Statistics

1. In any other setting except intimate relationships and families, women have lower rates of victimization than men. As Exhibit 10.4a shows, however, the rates of victimization for men and women are converging. Look at the trend lines. When did the rates for all violent crimes begin to converge? What broader social changes might explain this trend? Are women being victimized more, or are men being victimized less? How do the trends in rates of *intimate* violence for men and women compare?

2. Compare each pair of columns in Exhibit 10.4b. In which category are the differences between sexual and physical assault rates most pronounced? (*Hint:* Calculate the percentage difference between the rates.) How can you explain this discrepancy? Most people have only one spouse but encounter many acquaintances, friends, and strangers. Thus it could be argued that one's chances of encountering violence from a nonspouse is higher simply because of the exposure risk. Given this, are the rates of intimate violence higher than what you'd expect?

3. What does Exhibit 10.4c tell you about men's exposure to the risk of intimate murder as compared with women's? Assuming the data show statistically significant discrepancies, how can you explain the differences in risk for men and women?

4. Exhibit 10.4d shows a complex set of data about marital status and the risk of violence. Study the exhibit carefully for any unusually small or large discrepancies in the grouped columns. For instance, divorced/separated and never-married individuals face the same risk of violence at the hand of relatives as at the hand of other people who are well known to them; yet married individuals face less risk from relatives than from others who are well known to them. How might you explain such differences? How do you suppose the length of a relationship would affect the statistics reported in this exhibit? ■

Spousal Violence Across Cultures

When we examine *all* forms of family violence, it appears that most people around the world have either been the victim of, perpetrator of, or witness to violence within their families (Levinson, 1989). According to one study, wife beating is the most common form of family violence around the world, occurring at least occasionally in about 85 percent of the societies examined (Levinson, 1989). Husband beating is less common—occurring in about 27 percent of societies—and occurs less often than wife beating in those societies where both are present. Husband beating occurs only in those societies where wife beating also occurs.

In cultures that consider men's dominance legitimate, husbands control their wives and use violence to maintain that control when they believe it is necessary. In South Korea, for instance, more than one-third of women report being physically abused by their husbands

(UNICEF, 2000). Although things are changing—especially among young, better-educated couples in large cities—and most people say that beating is wrong, violence continues to be a "normal" part of Korean family life. One man, when asked if he had ever beaten his wife replied, "I was married at 28 and I'm 52 now. How could I have been married all these years and not beaten my wife? For me it's better to release that anger and get it over with. Otherwise, I just get sick inside. . . . Of course, you have to apologize afterward" (quoted in Kristof, 1996a, p. A4).

Some Korean women's attitudes also support men's authority and right to beat their wives:

> Of course my husband beats me. But it was my fault because I scolded him. Maybe there are some cases where it's just the man's fault, but ultimately the woman is to blame, because if she won't argue with her husband, he probably won't beat her. I told [my daughter], "if he hits you, just sit back and take it." (quoted in Kristof, 1996a, p. A4)

In South Africa, it's estimated that nearly 70 percent of marriages involve some type of violence (Dangor, Hoff, & Scott, 1998). In that culture, with its legacy of apartheid, black women in particular have had to bear the brunt of such violence. As you can see in the following quotes, these women are often acutely aware of their vulnerability:

- "Black women are the worst off because they're the wrong color and the wrong sex."
- "[There's] a lack of respect for women—men want to prove their superiority and show us that we are objects of manipulation to suit their needs."
- "Men like being in control, and abusing women gives them power." (quoted in Dangor et al., 1998, p. 134)

In the Central American country of Belize, men have historically exercised almost complete economic and political power over women. In families, they have always exerted their authority and control through physical battering. Husbands frequently beat their wives with anything they can get hold of: guns, knives, crowbars, machetes, electric wire, bottles, mop handles, rocks, boards, rope, and so forth. These violent acts go unacknowledged by the community, go unreported to the police, and are rarely discussed among friends and families (McClaurin, 1996). Despite the fact that local papers periodically run stories of women mutilated, burned, and murdered by their husbands or partners, wife battering doesn't warrant any mention in the country's official crime documents.

Women's dependence is so deep in Belize that they are usually willing to accept abuse and tolerate offensive behavior in exchange for economic security. Over the past decade, however, frustrated Belizean women have formed several organizations aimed at increasing women's status, decreasing their dependence, and ending domestic violence. Their efforts came to fruition in 1993 with passage of the Domestic Violence Act, which lets women acquire legal restraining orders against their husbands and grants police the power to make arrests in domestic disputes.

Explanations of Spousal Violence

Trying to figure out why spousal violence occurs is not a simple task. It's tempting to see such violence in purely individualistic terms: Men who beat their wives are cruel individuals who are incapable of controlling their rage or who gain some sort of pathological pleasure and feeling of power by inflicting pain on their spouses.

Alcohol is often cited as a key culprit in spousal violence. To some researchers, the relationship between alcohol and family violence is undeniable: "Just as high alcohol intake leads to cirrhosis of the liver, brain damage, and heart failure, so does high alcohol intake lead to violence in the family" (Flanzer, 1993, p. 171). However, the contention that alcohol—as well as other drugs such as cocaine and crack—directly and inevitably produces violent and abusive behavior has little scientific support. Evidence from laboratory studies and blood tests of men arrested for wife beating indicates that although alcohol may be an immediate antecedent to some acts of violence, it is far from being a necessary or sufficient cause of domestic violence. Findings from a study of 5,159 couples nationwide revealed that alcohol is involved in only about 25 percent of instances of wife abuse (Kanter & Straus, 1990), which means the vast majority (75 percent) take place when neither person has been drinking. Furthermore, about 80 percent of men who are defined as heavy or binge drinkers *do not* beat their wives at all. Hence, although the stereotype of the violent, drunken husband has a kernel of truth, domestic violence cannot simply be explained as the result of alcohol.

Attributing spousal abuse to mentally defective or drunken husbands might be psychologically comforting to the public at large, but one can only truly understand spousal violence as the complex product of psychological, interpersonal, societal, historical, and cultural forces. Each act of domestic violence brings these forces together. As one sociologist puts it, "Compressed into one assault are our deepest human emotions, our sense of self, our power, and our hopes and fears about love and intimacy, as well as the social construction of marriage and its place within the larger society" (Yllo, 1993, p. 47). In short, spousal violence is best understood by going beyond individual-level explanations to an examination of the sociocultural environment in which it takes place.

The Social Organization of Families   Families have several organizational characteristics that promote intimacy but at the same time increase the probability of conflict and violence. One such characteristic is the greater amount of time people usually spend with family members compared to the time they usually spend at work or with others. From a strictly quantitative perspective, people are at greater risk for violence at home because that's where they spend so much of their time (Gelles & Straus, 1988).

But what goes on during time at home is much more important than the sheer number of hours people spend there. Not only are they with family members a lot, they also interact with others in the family across a wide range of situations. The intimacy of these interactions is intense. Emotions sometimes run deep. It's ironic that those who people can care about most are also the ones who can make them the most angry. The anger people may feel toward a stranger or an acquaintance never approaches the intensity of the anger they feel toward a spouse—or for that matter toward a sibling or a child.

People also know more about family members than they know about other individuals in their lives. They know those others' likes and dislikes, fears and desires. And those others know such things about them, too. If someone in your family insults you, you know immediately what you can say to get even. Married couples usually know the "buttons" they can push to hurt or infuriate each other. Arguments can escalate into violence when one partner focuses on the other's vulnerabilities and insecurities.

Long periods of intense contact with people you know virtually everything about can elevate even trivial matters into conflict situations. In many families, everyday decisions occur in a context of winning and losing. Hence, some of the most serious family conflicts occur over seemingly insignificant issues such as what program to watch on television or what restaurant to go to for dinner.

Finally, family life contains endless sources of stress. For one thing, people expect a lot from their families: emotional and financial support, warmth, comfort, and intimacy. When these expectations aren't fulfilled, stress levels escalate. Moreover, the birth and raising of a child, financial problems, employment transitions (voluntary or involuntary), illness, old age, death, and so on are all events that potentially increase stress. Research indicates that the likelihood of domestic violence increases with the number of stressful events that a family experiences. Indeed, stressful life circumstances are the hallmark of violent families (Gelles & Straus, 1988).

Power and Family Inequality   Focusing exclusively on the role that family structure plays in intimate violence can obscure the role of gender and power. Family life is characterized by significant inequality. The more resources—whether personal, social, emotional, or financial—that a person controls, the more influence he or she has over the relationship.

As conflict theory tells us (see Chapter 1), power, power confrontations, and perceived threats to dominance and authority are underlying issues in almost all acts of domestic violence (Gelles & Straus, 1988). And research has consistently shown that the balance of power within families has a noticeable effect on domestic violence. Sociologists Murray Straus, Richard Gelles, and Suzanne Steinmetz (1980), for instance, found that the level of violence against wives is lowest among couples who follow a pattern of egalitarian decision making. Fewer than 3 percent of these wives had suffered a severe violent attack within the previous year. In contrast, the rate of wife beating among couples in which the wife dominates is 7.1 percent, and where husbands dominate, the rate is 10 percent.

In male-dominated households, husbands sometimes turn to violence to maintain the subordination of their wives. But why is the rate of spouse abuse so high where *wives* tend to have the most say over decisions? Husbands in these families may be lashing out violently when they feel their masculinity is under attack. In other words, husbands may use violence as a final resource to gain control when other resources are insufficient or lacking (Goode, 1971). In an achievement-oriented society, husbands who lack the financial, occupational, and educational resources necessary to establish household dominance may turn to violence or coercion (Yllo & Straus, 1990).

Men have traditionally maintained their edge in family resources through their employment. The effect of men's employment on violence was demonstrated in a study of 12,000 Canadian women over the age of 18 (MacMillan & Gartner, 1999). The researchers found that wives' exposure to spousal violence had little to do with whether or not they were employed. But when their husbands were unemployed, employed wives' risk of violence increased significantly. Not only were these women at greater risk of physical violence, they also were subjected to greater "coercive control," such as when a husband expresses jealousy and doesn't want his wife to talk to other men, tries to limit her contact with family and friends, insists on knowing with whom and where she is at all times, and prevents her from knowing about or having access to the family income.

Power and Structural Inequality   The forces of power operate at the societal level as well as the family level. In most societies, economic and social structures support male domination, which is revealed in the relatively low position women hold in the workplace, schools, politics, and other social institutions (Yllo & Straus, 1990). In many patriarchal societies, men blatantly classify and treat women as possessions. Globally, male dominance has a long history. Roman law, for instance, justified a husband's killing his wife for reasons such as adultery, wine drinking, and other so-called inappropriate behaviors (Steinmetz, Clavan,

& Stein, 1990). The "rule of thumb" in English common law recognized a husband's right to beat his wife with a stick that was no bigger than the circumference of his thumb.

In the United States, too, male dominance is part of a centuries-old legacy of domestic violence. Early American law provided that on marriage a husband acquired rights to his wife's person, the value of her paid and unpaid labor, and most property she brought into the marriage. The wife was obliged to obey and serve her husband. Her legal identity "merged" into his so that she was unable to enter into contracts without his approval. The husband, in turn, was responsible for his wife's conduct. As master of the household, he could subject her to corporal punishment or "chastisement" as long as he didn't inflict permanent injury (Siegel, 1996).

Prior to the Civil War, corporal punishment became the subject of widespread controversy, and campaigns against it began to develop. These movements coincided with early campaigns for women's rights. Over time the U.S. legal system did respond. In 1871 an Alabama court declared that a husband no longer had the privilege of beating his wife:

> The wife is not to be considered as the husband's slave. And the privilege, ancient though it be, to beat her with a stick, to pull her hair, choke her, spit in her face or kick her about the floor, or to inflict upon her like indignities, is not now acknowledged by our law. (quoted in Siegel, 1996, pp. 2121–2122)

But because this "privilege" had such a long tradition in married life, it didn't die easily. The legal system continued to treat wife beating differently from other violent crimes, intervening only intermittently in cases of marital violence. To protect male authority and the privacy of families, courts granted most men formal or informal immunity from prosecution, implying that it was easier for a wife to forgive her husband's impulsive violence than for a husband to suffer the loss of authority entailed in having his behavior scrutinized by public authorities.

> The need for family privacy—and the problems this need creates—is discussed in Issue 3.

At the beginning of the twentieth century, judges, clergy, and social workers routinely urged couples to reconcile and preserve the marriage rather than punishing those who assaulted their partners. Battered wives were discouraged from filing charges against their husbands, urged to accept responsibility for their role in provoking the violence, and encouraged to remain in the relationship and rebuild it rather than separate or divorce (Pleck, 1987; Siegel, 1996). Physical violence in the home was not viewed as criminal conduct; it was viewed as an expression of emotions that, through counseling, needed to be re-channeled into the marriage. Such a "therapeutic" framework regulated marital violence for much of the twentieth century.

Not until the late 1970s did the feminist movement mount a significant challenge to male primacy and authority. Since then, many reforms have been secured, such as shelters for battered women and their children, new arrest procedures, and federal legislation that makes gender-motivated assaults a civil rights violation and prevents people convicted of domestic violence from purchasing handguns.

But the tradition of male dominance persists. For instance, the laws relating to rape in many states in this country, and in most countries around the world, include what is commonly known as "the marital rape exemption." These laws typically define rape as "the forcible penetration of the body of a woman, *not the wife of the perpetrator*," making rape in marriage a legal impossibility (Russell, 1998, p. 71). In eight states, husbands cannot be prosecuted for raping their wives unless they are living apart or legally separated. In twenty-six other states, they can be prosecuted in some circumstances but are totally exempt in others. For example, in some states rape imposed by force but without the wife's suffering additional degrees of violence, such as kidnapping or being threatened with a weapon, is not considered a crime (Russell, 1998). At present, only 15 states have abolished the marital rape exemption entirely (Burgess-Jackson, 1998).

When the American Law Institute—an organization devoted to clarifying and simplifying the law through legislative reform—most recently revised the Model Penal Code provisions on rape, it decided to preserve language that exempted husbands from rape charges in hopes of protecting family privacy:

> The problem with abandoning the [marital] immunity in many . . . situations is that the law of rape, if applied to spouses, would thrust the prospect of criminal sanctions into the ongoing process of adjustment in the marital relationship. . . . Retaining the spousal exclusion avoids this unwarranted intrusion of the penal law into the life of the family. (quoted in Siegel, 1996, p. 2174)

Legal definitions such as these are based on the assumption that rape is a private matter between an individual wife and an individual husband. However, focusing instead on the power structure of society shows that spousal rape—not to mention battering, economic abuse, coercion, intimidation, and emotional abuse—is not simply a "family problem" isolated from the rest of society. It is the manifestation of a broad patriarchal system, with male domination and control built into the very structure of society.

Such sociological explanations make intuitive sense. But, for the most part, they have not been tested empirically. One exception has been a study by sociologists Kersti Yllo and Murray Straus (1990), who examined the relationship between the structural inequality of women and wife beating. They ranked all fifty states in terms of women's status as a group relative to men's, taking into consideration four social institutions: economics, education, politics, and the law.

Yllo and Straus found that the rate of wife beating is highest in those states where economic, educational, political, and legal inequality are greatest. As the overall status of women improved, violence declined—but only to a point. Surprisingly, in those states where the status of women is highest, the rate of wife beating is also quite high.

The researchers suggest that two different processes are at work. When social inequality is high, more coercion is needed to maintain an unbalanced system. Thus force is used to keep wives "in their place" in those states where women have the lowest status. But rapid changes in sex roles and shifts in the balance of power between the sexes, found in states where women's status is high, may contribute to increased marital conflict because of the threat these changes pose to men.

Even though these forces provide a fertile social environment for violence, they don't make it inevitable. After all, most husbands who live in this violent, male-dominated society don't abuse their wives. Nevertheless, if a significant percentage of people do beat their partners because they feel that such behavior is appropriate given their position in society and in their families, then we would be wrong to conclude that abusers are simply psychotic, deranged, "sick" individuals. Rather, they are people who believe that violent domination is their birthright.

Privacy and Spousal Violence   Even though many Americans currently accept the principle of male dominance, most of us are horrified at the thought of a person beating or killing a spouse. At the same time, Americans also dislike the thought of the state intervening in the private affairs of families. But the privacy of family life can be life threatening to certain members. An eminent anthropologist once observed that among the societies she had studied, violence between family members tended not to occur when families lived communally. Only when the walls of separate houses went up did the hitting start (cited in Gelles & Straus, 1988).

In this society, people who are socially isolated from neighbors and relatives are more likely to be violent against family members. For instance, cohabiting couples are more likely to be isolated from their network of kin than either dating couples or married couples. Not surprisingly, research indicates that much more, and more severe, violence takes place among cohabiting couples than among married or dating couples (Stets & Straus, 1990). Conversely, when families are well integrated into their communities and belong to groups and associations, violence becomes less likely (Gelles, 1995).

The relationship between family privacy and spousal violence is clear when we look at where and when such violence is most likely to take place. According to sociologists Richard Gelles and Murray Straus (1988), most domestic violence occurs in the kitchen, living room, or bedroom between 8 P.M. and midnight. As the evening wears on, family members have fewer places outside the home to escape to if problems arise. Similarly, weekends are the most violent time of the week for families because members are usually at home, away from school or work.

A thorough examination of family privacy appears in Issue 3.

The cultural value of family privacy has also helped to reinforce a perception that spousal violence is somehow less bothersome and more tolerable than other types of violence. Even when violence between spouses occurs in public, it is often perceived as a private matter.

Psychologists Lance Shotland and Margaret Straw (1976) performed an experiment that involved staging what appeared to be a heated altercation between a man and a woman as they emerged from an elevator. The researchers set up two scenarios that were identical except for one important detail. In the first, the woman, who is the object of the man's verbal and physical threats, shouts, "Get away from me! I don't even know you!" In the second (with identical actors and identical behaviors), she says, "Get away from me! I don't know why I ever married you!" In the first situation, involving apparent strangers, 65 percent of the bystanders attempted to stop the fight. In the second situation, involving apparent spouses, bystanders intervened only 19 percent of the time. Clearly, the second case was defined by observers as a domestic dispute between spouses, conjuring up a set of norms that stopped them from "getting involved" in the private affairs of a married couple.

The family privacy so valued in the twentieth century has diminished the impact of neighborhoods, extended kin, and other informal networks in protecting people against violence from intimates. Although more and more urban neighborhoods band together to organize crime watch groups to prevent street crime or patrols to watch out for local teens who might get into trouble, such organizations rarely, if ever, address the violence that occurs off the streets, in neighborhood homes (Mannon, 1997a).

The Escape from Abusive Relationships

One question that has captured the attention of many family researchers is, Why do victims stay in abusive relationships? During the 1960s the *masochism thesis*—that is, women derived pleasure from being humiliated and hurt—was the predominant reason offered by psychiatrists (Saul, 1972). Even today, many psychiatrists believe masochism, or *self-defeating personality disorder,* as it is now called, should be a "legitimate" medical explanation for women who stay in abusive relationships. Other contemporary explanations focus on the women's character flaws, such as weak will or abnormal emotional attachment.

A substantial proportion of the public subscribes to various stereotypes about battered women and the nature of domestic violence. In one study of 216 predominantly white registered voters, more than a third of those surveyed believed that a battered woman is at least partially responsible for the beatings she suffers and that if she remains in the relationship she must be either masochistic or emotionally disturbed. Nearly two-thirds believed that battered women can "simply leave" a relationship when it becomes abusive. Interestingly, women were more likely than men to subscribe to these stereotypes (Ewing & Aubrey, 1987).

These explanations and attitudes focus solely on the victim while paying little attention to her social situation. Many battered women end up staying in abusive relationships not because they are masochistic or weak willed but because they come to believe that there are worse things than being beaten. For instance, they may fear that if they are unsuccessful in escaping the relationship, the violence may get worse and if they escape, they may be killed. In addition, they may be concerned for the well-being of children or possible retaliation against their parents or other close relatives.

According to social exchange theory, explained in Chapter 1, one of the most powerful reasons why women stay in abusive relationships is dependence. That is, an individual will be inclined to stay in a relationship—even a bad or abusive one—if she believes she has no other options. As one woman put it, "I had no place to go and no help. . . . I need to take care of my family" (quoted in Baker, 1997, p. 61). Women who are not in the paid labor force and cannot support themselves financially are significantly less likely to leave an abusive marriage than women who are employed and therefore have their own source of income (Strube & Barbour, 1983).

Some women in abusive relationships develop beliefs that help them accept the fact that they are staying in a situation generally condemned by society. Kathleen Ferraro and John Johnson (1983) were participant observers at a shelter for battered women in the Southwest. They gathered information from 120 women, ranging in age from 17 to 68, who came to the shelter over the span of a year. Some women had convinced themselves that they must endure the abuse while helping their "troubled" partners return to their "normal," nonabusive selves. Others claimed that their abusive partners were "sick" and that their actions were beyond their control; in other words, their partners were also victims. Finally, many women blamed themselves, taking the responsibility away from their spouses.

But the perception that battered women simply sit back and take the abuse, thinking they somehow deserve it, is inaccurate. One study of 1,000 battered and formerly battered women nationwide found that they tried a number of active strategies to end the violence directed against them (Bowker, 1993). They tried to talk men out of beating them, extracted promises that the men wouldn't batter them anymore, avoided their abuser physically or avoided certain volatile topics, hid or ran away, and even fought back physically. Many of these individual strategies had limited effectiveness, however, and so most of these battered women eventually turned to people outside the relationship for informal support, advice, and sheltering. From these informal sources, the women generally progressed to organizations in the community, such as police, social service and counseling agencies, women's groups, and battered women's shelters. Some of these women were able, eventually, to end the violence; others weren't. The study points out that most women actively try to end their victimization.

Issue 5 explores the relationship between religion and family violence.

The Lack of Institutional Support   One reason why so many battered women are unable to get out of abusive relationships is that the social organizations and institutions designed to help them have traditionally been ineffective. In 1980 a bill was introduced in Congress that would have provided federally funded local community shelters for battered women and their children. Some religious groups vigorously—and successfully—opposed the bill, arguing that the shelters would become "anti-family indoctrination centers" (Scanzoni, 1983, p. 202). These groups didn't approve of violence, but they believed that such matters were best left to families.

Throughout the years, hospital personnel, police, and courts have been notoriously unsympathetic to the plight of battered women. As recently as 10 years ago, for instance, emergency room workers routinely interviewed battered women about their injuries with their husbands present. Police departments, in particular, have traditionally been reluctant to get too involved in domestic disputes. For instance, in the O. J. Simpson case in 1996, police were called to his home on at least nine occasions because of his physical abuse of his wife, Nicole. Some departments have arrest policies called "stitch rules," which specify how serious an injury a victim must sustain, measured by how many surgical stitches are required, to justify an arrest of the assailant (Gillespie, 1989). One study found that the majority of domestic disputes and family violence incidents reported to the police resulted in no arrest; either the police did nothing or the offender was referred to other agencies (Bell & Bell, 1991). Given this sort of response, people should not be surprised that the majority of battered women never contact the police (Straus & Gelles, 1986).

The courts, too, have historically treated spousal violence less seriously than other crimes, making it even more difficult for women to seek help. In 1978, for instance, an Indiana prosecutor refused to prosecute for murder a man who beat and kicked his ex-wife to death in the presence of a witness and then raped her as she lay dying. Filing a manslaughter charge instead, the prosecutor said, "He didn't mean to kill her. He just meant to give her a good thumping" (quoted in Jones, 1980, p. 308).

Consider also the case of Kenneth Peacock, a long-distance truck driver. One night in 1994 he returned home unexpectedly from a delivery run and found his wife in bed, naked, with another man. He chased the man away at gunpoint. At about 4 A.M., after hours of arguing, he shot his wife in the head with a hunting rifle.

He pleaded guilty to voluntary manslaughter. The judge in the case sentenced him to 18 months in prison—a sentence half as long as the prosecution recommended—stating that he wished he didn't have to send him to prison at all because the feelings of anger the man had were understandable under the circumstances. The judge said, "I seriously wonder how many men married five, four years would have the strength to walk away without inflicting some corporal punishment" (quoted in Lewin, 1994b, p. A18).

For centuries, the law has either explicitly or implicitly recognized a "heat-of-passion" defense in domestic homicide cases. Under such considerations, killings may be treated less harshly if a reasonable person would have been so distraught as to be incapable of exercising proper judgment. In such cases—the most prototypical example being a man finding his wife in bed with someone else—prosecutors allow the defendant to plead guilty to the lesser charge of voluntary manslaughter, knowing that a jury would be unlikely to hand down a murder conviction. In fact, as recently as the early 1970s killing an adulterous wife found in bed with another man was considered justifiable homicide.

Today, however, as a result of the battered women's movement and others who have worked hard to educate the public about domestic violence, the legal system has become somewhat more responsive to the needs of abuse victims. For one thing, many police departments around the country have revised their unspoken "hands-off" policies toward domestic violence cases. In Indianapolis, for example, after the number of domestic violence cases doubled between 1990 and 1991, officers were required to make an arrest even if they didn't directly witness the assault. In addition, officers were required to have 30 hours of in-service domestic violence training each year. In other cities, domestic violence victims cannot drop assault charges once they are filed.

As a result, battered women are now expected to get away and stay away from their abusers. Those who stay with or return to abusive partners violate this new cultural expectation. Yet many battered women find these expectations overly narrow and unrealistic. Consider, for example, recent reforms in the welfare system (see Chapter 4). As many as two-thirds of women who received welfare payments in the form of Aid to Families and Dependent Children (AFDC) had abuse in their backgrounds, suggesting that welfare may have been an escape route for many battered women with children (Gordon, 1997). Today, however, the inadequacy and unpredictability of the revised welfare system may force many of these women to stay in relationships with men who abuse them or their children.

Sometimes the resources in place to assist battered women are simply inadequate. In rural areas with no public transportation, shelters exist but may be inaccessible to women who live miles away and don't own a car. In small towns, confidentiality is virtually impossible. The fact that people tend to know one another can dissuade a woman from calling a local sheriff's office for help, because the person answering may be a friend or relative of her abusive partner.

The problem of inadequate resources is not limited to scarcely populated rural areas, however. For instance, in New York City several years ago the mayor launched a massive campaign against domestic violence. Most buses and subways now display posters encouraging battered women to come forward and seek help from city-supported shelters and other services. Every day sixty-five battered women who feel they're in danger call the Victim Services hotline requesting shelter. But every day about sixty of them are told no spaces are available (Sontag, 1997). Some of these women are so desperate that they agree to be bused hundreds of miles away to a place where shelter is available. This remedy may get them out of harm's way, but it may also wreck their work lives, isolate them from family and friends, endanger welfare checks, and disrupt their children's schooling.

In other cases, standard procedures can work against women trying to escape their abusive situations. In 2000, a social services agency that runs a shelter for battered women in California sued Pacific Bell, alleging that the company printed the shelter's confidential address in the White Pages telephone book. The agency was immediately forced to close the facility and move its residents.

Other times rules and regulations work to the disadvantage of battered women. Here's how one woman who had been viciously brutalized by her husband describes the system failure that led to her decision to leave a shelter and return to him:

> He [her husband] would get my phone number and he would call me and call me and I'd have to pay $50 to get the number changed, and I'd tell the authorities, "Well, he called me and he called me," . . . They'd say, "Well, do you have proof or do you

have it documented?" Well, how do you do that if you don't have a device on your phone that is gonna cost you. That's how he always got me to go back to him because he would just harass me until I would just be like "Fine, go meet him." (quoted in Baker, 1997, p. 59)

In sum, the decision to stay in an abusive relationship may be the result not of irrationality or mental dysfunction but of rational choices women make in response to an array of conditions, including fear of and harassment by the abuser, the complex everyday realities of dependence, and the lack of institutional support (Baker, 1997). When people encourage battered women to leave abusive situations, they mean to be helpful, of course. However, without adequate institutional support often all they accomplish is making these women feel guilty about their already difficult and dangerous decision to stay.

Women Who Kill Their Abusers   There comes a time for some battered women when they realize they can't escape the situation, can't make the violence stop, and can no longer explain it away. So, seeing no way out, they resort to more drastic, violent measures. About 750 battered women kill their abusers each year (cited in Roberts, 1996). Most, as in the following case, are making a "last ditch" effort to get out of a situation that they perceive as life threatening:

> Judy and Thomas Norman had been married for twenty-five years, since she was 14; he had beaten her for twenty years, "frequent assaults that included slapping, punching . . . kicking . . . striking her with various objects . . . throwing glasses, beer bottles . . . putting his cigarettes out on her, throwing hot coffee on her, breaking glass against her face and crushing food on her face. He forced her to make money by prostitution . . . routinely called [her] 'dog,' 'bitch,' and 'whore,' . . . made her eat pet food out of the pet's bowls and bark like a dog . . . deprived her of food and refused to let her get food for the family. He threatened to cut off her breast and, increasingly frequently, to kill her. On a day when he made these threats continually, Judy Norman shot him as he took a nap." (quoted in Gordon, 1997, p. 25)

During Judy's trial in 1989 the court ruled that her attorney was not entitled to present her history of abuse as evidence. And because she shot him while he was asleep, she was unable to make a self-defense plea: There was no *imminent* threat to her life. She was convicted of manslaughter.

This case became a focal point for the frustration many victims, defense attorneys, and women's rights activists feel over the unsympathetic legal response and the high conviction rate of battered women who kill their abusive partners. The day after a judge reluctantly sentenced Kenneth Peacock to 18 months in prison for murdering his wife "in the heat of passion," another judge handed down a 3-year sentence to a woman who pleaded guilty to voluntary manslaughter for killing her husband after 11 years of abuse (Lewin, 1994b). The judge gave her a sentence *three times longer* than the sentence the prosecutors had sought.

Why have women who kill their abusive partners been treated so harshly by the courts? For several reasons, battered women have traditionally had trouble claiming self-defense. One study found that in over 70 percent of trials in which self-defense was raised, the defendant was still found guilty of some form of homicide (Ewing, 1987). First, a finding of self-defense requires that the defendant had reason to believe that death or grievous bodily injury was imminent at the time of the killing (Schuller & Vidmar, 1992). Battered women, however, often develop a keen ability to predict attack from a long history of observing their abuser's actions. Hence, many kill their abusive partners *before* the situation reaches the precise point at which the court could consider it life threatening. Furthermore, because of fear, women are likely to wait until a time when their partner is least dangerous and most vulnerable. One study found that in two-thirds of the cases reviewed, the woman had committed the killing outside of a direct confrontation, when no "imminent" threat seemed apparent to an outside observer. Commonly, the husband was walking away or asleep (Ewing, 1987).

Second, in some states self-defense stipulates that people in harmful situations first have a "duty to retreat." That is, as an alternative to using force, they must first attempt to escape from the situation. Only when no such opportunity exists can they legally use lethal force. With regard to domestic violence cases, the "duty to retreat" has become for many judges, attorneys, and juries a duty to leave a relationship in which violence has been occurring for a long time. During the course of the trial, prosecutors usually ask, "Why didn't the woman leave, if she was really being abused?" (Roberts, 1996). Such a question implies either that she hadn't really been beaten (therefore nullifying the self-defense claim) or, if she were being victimized, that she could have and should have "retreated," thereby putting an end to the violence.

Finally, self-defense requires that the victim respond with "proportional" force. For example, shooting someone you find rummaging through your garbage can is not usually considered self-defense. Historically, in domestic violence cases, courts have ruled that a woman cannot use lethal force against a man who slaps her around or is psychologically abusive. But because of the differences in physical strength between a woman and her male abuser, hitting back with proportional force is not easy for a woman. Hence, the force she is likely to use will probably involve a deadly weapon.

Because of activism by feminists in the battered women's movement, things have changed in recent years. Since the 1980s, courts have increasingly allowed women to introduce a history of abuse as a legal defense against crimes they are accused of committing against their abusers. Courts now understand the **battered woman syndrome** as a state of mind that occurs when a woman's exposure to long-term physical and mental abuse makes her feel psychologically trapped in a relationship. This syndrome affects her judgment in such a way as to make her believe she is in imminent danger and that the use of force is the only way to escape.

The court's acceptance of the battered woman syndrome as a legitimate defense marked a turning point in the judicial treatment of battered women. It helped to shift the focus from the defendant to the person responsible for the victimization and helped overcome bias among the many judges who refused to recognize that self-defense laws apply to battered women. Now a long history of abuse could in itself constitute a reasonable expectation of attack.

Realizing that scores of women were in prison because of convictions that had occurred prior to these legal changes, the governor of Ohio in 1990 granted clemency to 26 women who were incarcerated for killing or assaulting their abusive partners. Since then, governors in twenty other states have freed more than 100 battered women who were in prison for similar crimes (cited in Gross, 1997a).

The use of the battered woman's syndrome defense is not limited to cases in which women strike back at their abusers. It can also be used in cases of abused women who are accused of committing crimes against others, including their own children. In 1995 an

Indiana woman was convicted of criminal neglect and sentenced to 20 years in prison for leaving her 4-year-old daughter in the care of a boyfriend, despite evidence of prior abuse and the fact that he threatened to kill them both. He eventually beat the girl to death. But 2 years later, her conviction was overturned because it was determined that the mother suffered from battered woman's syndrome and feared for her own life so much that she was incapable of protecting her daughter (McNeil, 1997).

Advocates for battered women say that these legal actions, and others like them, mark a positive shift in attitudes toward domestic violence. They are an indication that people are finally realizing that some women are trapped physically and emotionally in abusive situations and are unable to simply walk away.

Critics, however, argue that such legal actions send a very dangerous message to women and to society. According to the president of the Ohio Prosecuting Attorney's Association, "The fact that you're battered does not give you license to kill. Now instead of going to the courts, or getting a divorce, these women will think, 'Maybe I'll kill him.'" Another Ohio prosecutor said, "Our concern is that in the future we're going to get a lot of women claiming to be battered. In our view, it is not a proper defense for murder" (quoted in Wilkerson, 1990, p. 11).

Others argue that the battered woman syndrome is a setback for the women's movement because it depicts battered women as psychologically impaired and helpless rather than as rational individuals responding to perceived danger (Bowker, 1993; Downs, 1996). They point to the most famous case—or infamous, depending on your perspective—involving the use of the battered woman syndrome defense, that of Lorena Bobbitt. In 1993 she was acquitted of charges that she maliciously wounded her husband John when she cut off his penis with a kitchen knife while he slept. The jury decided that Bobbitt was not responsible for her actions, because a history of physical, psychological, and sexual abuse by her husband had rendered her temporarily insane. Instead of focusing public attention on the societywide problem of domestic violence, this case simply became a sensational news story about an individual woman who had "gone crazy" and was unable to control her actions.

Power and Violence in Gay and Lesbian Households

Although domestic violence between heterosexual partners gets most of the attention, a growing number of researchers point out that domestic violence is also becoming more common in gay and lesbian relationships (Lockhart, White, Causby, & Isaac, 1994; Renzetti, 1992). The violence that takes place in long-term homosexual relationships appears to be as prevalent as battering in heterosexual relationships (Coleman, 1996).

The causes of domestic violence are also much the same. For example, although most gay and lesbian couples embrace the ideal of equal power in their relationships, inequality is not uncommon. Power differences may not automatically generate violence, but they are associated with heightened levels of physical and psychological abuse (Elliot, 1996).

Furthermore, stress—which is a major contributor to violence in heterosexual families—is prevalent in same-sex relationships, too. This stress can come from sources heterosexual couples typically don't have to face. For instance, many gay and lesbian couples must deal with neighbors and extended family who disapprove of their relationship. They must struggle to create and sustain intimate ties without the legal protection of marriage, while protecting themselves and perhaps their children from antigay violence and harassment. Employment and housing discrimination can create further financial stress in these households.

For the most part, homosexual domestic violence has remained invisible to the public, making it especially difficult for victims to get help. Battered gay men, for example, cannot get sympathy for being the victims of sexism and male dominance, as battered heterosexual women sometimes get. Indeed, many gay male victims themselves believe battering is something that happens only to women and are extremely uncomfortable identifying themselves as battered (Letellier, 1996). A "real man"—regardless of sexual orientation—is supposed to be able to protect himself in any situation.

Many gay male victims of intimate violence do try to protect themselves when being beaten by striking back at their partners. Such retaliation—whether effective or futile—enables these men to characterize the violence as "mutual combat," an explanation implying that both men are equally capable of and willing to commit violence. Unfortunately, such a characterization suggests that the violence is a "relationship problem" for which they are both equally responsible, not an act of aggression inflicted by one partner on the other.

Battered gay men and lesbians have an especially difficult time escaping the violence and getting help because of the denigration and animosity directed toward homosexuals in the larger society and because of the gay community's failure to acknowledge domestic violence as a serious problem. Consequently, battered homosexual partners are even less likely than battered heterosexual wives to tell anyone about the abuse and seek help, putting themselves at risk for more severe and more frequent violence. Resources available to assist them are almost nonexistent. For instance, half a million gay men or more are battered each year, yet only six agencies or organizations nationwide exist specifically to help them (Letellier, 1996).

Child Abuse

The U.S. Bureau of the Census (2000b) reports that there were 861,000 substantiated cases of child abuse and/or neglect in 1998. But if we take intimate violence to mean *any* act of physical aggression directed by one person toward another—including a parent spanking and slapping a child—perhaps as many as nine out of every ten American children under the age of 3 have been subjected to violence at the hands of their parents or caretakers (Straus & Gelles, 1990). And if we look at the more abusive forms of violence (kicking, biting, punching, beating up, burning, hitting with an object, scalding, and threatening with a knife or a gun), approximately 6.9 million American children are physically abused by their parents or adult caretakers each year (Straus & Gelles, 1990). This figure is about eight times higher than the annual number of substantiated cases officially reported, suggesting that the vast majority of child abuse incidents remain hidden from the police and social service agencies. To make matters worse, a study by the Department of Health and Human Services confirmed that the number of child abuse cases rose dramatically during the 1990s—although it's not clear whether this rise represents an actual increase or better reporting of cases ("Child abuse," 1996).

Child abuse is often fatal. Homicide is one of the five leading causes of death for children between 1 and 18 years of age in this country. About 600 children under age 5 are killed by another person each year, usually by parents (see Exhibit 10.5a).

Another type of child abuse that has received a lot of public attention is sexual abuse. Although sexual abuse represents only about one out of every ten cases of substantiated abuse or neglect, a high percentage of all sexual assault cases reported to law enforcement agencies involve children under age 18 (see Exhibit 10.5b). Definitions of sexual abuse vary

EXHIBIT 10.5

Violence Against Children

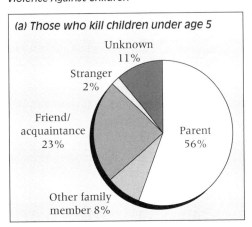

(a) Those who kill children under age 5

Unknown 11%
Stranger 2%
Friend/ acquaintance 23%
Parent 56%
Other family member 8%

Data source: U.S. Department of Justice. 2001b. *Homicide trends in the U.S.: Infanticide.* Available at www.ojp.usdoj.gov/bjs/. Accessed May 1, 2001.

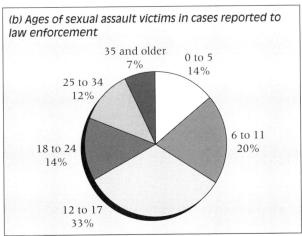

(b) Ages of sexual assault victims in cases reported to law enforcement

35 and older 7%
0 to 5 14%
25 to 34 12%
6 to 11 20%
18 to 24 14%
12 to 17 33%

Data source: H. N. Snyder. 2000. "Sexual assault of young children as reported to law enforcement: Victim, incident, and offender characteristics." Table 1. NCJ 182990. Available at www.ojp.usdoj.gov/bjs/pub/pdf/saycrle.pdf. Accessed June 1, 2001.

widely, but usually include intrusive acts (for example, oral, genital, or anal penetration), genital contact (actual genital contact, without penetration), and other sexual acts, such as genital exposure, or fondling breasts or buttocks (Sedlack & Broadhurst, 1996; Winton & Mara, 2001). One study found that about 12 percent of prepubescent girls are victims of sexual abuse involving genital fondling, or vaginal, oral, or anal penetration by an older person (Browning & Laumann, 1997). In over 92 percent of these cases, the abusers were older males. Girls are about three times more likely to be victims of sexual abuse than boys (Sedlack & Broadhurst, 1996). About 50 percent of the cases involving child sexual abuse involve parents or parent substitutes (Sedlack & Broadhurst, 1996).

Child Abuse Across Cultures

Around the world, most acts of direct violence against children are carried out by their parents or by other caretakers with their parents' approval. Anthropologist David Levinson (1989) studied ninety small-scale and folk societies in all major cultural regions of the world to determine the extent to which violence against children is present in family life worldwide. About 74 percent of the societies he examined allowed some form of physical punishment of children. Such punishment included slapping, spanking, hitting, beating, scalding, burning, pushing, pinching, and switching.

In most societies where physical punishment of children is used, it is used infrequently. But some cultures, such as the Goajiro of Colombia, rely on physical punishment as their major method of child rearing:

There are punishments of various kinds. Some . . . consist of striking the child, and these are the most frequent. They slap them on the mouth when they are insolent when given an order or when they give a sharp answer to the father or mother. They are punched and kicked or are whipped with lassos or riding whips, with twigs from woods or cudgels; but the mother generally beats them with a bunch of nettles when they commit any kind of naughtiness. . . . Another quite common form of punishment is to take the child and put him into a mesh bag of agave fiber, sling it on one of the high branches on [a bough-covered shelter] and rotate it until the child is nauseated and vomits, becoming unconscious. He is then lowered and left on the ground until he recovers. (quoted in Levinson, 1989, p. 28)

Ironically, the children most at risk for maltreatment worldwide are those who are most frail: the sick, malnourished, deformed, and unwanted. In many societies—such as the United States—stepchildren are also particularly vulnerable to physical abuse (Kobrin, 1991).

Children in extended-family households that contain many relatives are less likely to be physically punished than children in single-parent or nuclear family households (Levinson, 1989). When child rearing is shared within a supportive community, chances of maltreatment are diminished. Such networks not only scrutinize the actions of parents and enforce standards of child care, they also provide assistance with child-rearing tasks and responsibilities as well. Among rural Hawaiians, for instance, relatives don't hesitate to yell from one house to the next that a spanking has gone on long enough or is too severe for what the child did (Kobrin, 1991).

It's important to remember that the abusive nature of a particular act of violence or punishment lies not in the act itself but in the way it is defined by a particular culture. What people in the United States consider the "healthy" practice of isolating small children in beds and rooms of their own at night some would consider abusive by members of societies in which parents form close bonds with their children by sleeping with them in the same bed. In Turkey, mothers routinely kiss and praise the genitals of their young children when they're playing or when their diapers are being changed, an act that would be considered sexual abuse in this country (Olson, 1981).

Even a phenomenon so universally disagreeable as a parent causing the death of a child can be understood quite differently in different cultures. In one region of northeastern Brazil, for example, mothers show such extreme neglect for some of their children that the infants eventually die. But when one looks at the situation more closely, this apparently harsh treatment makes cultural sense (Scheper-Hughes, 1989). This area is extremely poor with a very high rate of infant and child mortality. Children are most often raised in single-parent households. Mothers commonly leave babies at home alone when they go to work.

The high expectancy of infant death has led to a pattern of nurturing in which infants are divided into two groups: those who are healthy and have a good chance of surviving and those who are sickly and have little chance of surviving. The latter designation is applied to children who are born weak, small, wasted, and passive. They suffer frequent respiratory infections and other common ailments of infancy. People in this region say that such children are born "wanting to die."

The children who are considered "survivors" are nurtured and cared for quite well. The others, however, are purposely neglected. If they develop acute symptoms such as convulsions or very high fevers, food is withheld and they are simply left alone to die. Some die even before they have shown any life-threatening symptoms. Their death is seen as a way of letting nature take its course.

In this area of Brazil, learning to become a good mother means learning when to let go of a child who shows it "wants" to die. Although this emotional detachment contributes to the already high infant mortality rate, it is not seen as abusive within that culture. Instead, it is considered a practical recognition that not all of one's children can be expected to live. Under desperate economic conditions, such selective neglect is a survival strategy that "weeds out" the weakest infants in order to enhance the life chances of healthier siblings and future children.

Poor economic conditions can also influence the treatment of children in industrialized countries. Up until recently, child abuse and neglect—as people understand them in the West—didn't constitute a serious social problem in Japan. Japanese parents rarely inflicted physical punishment on their children. In 1990, there were only about 1,100 reported cases of child abuse. However, in the past decade—a period marked by deteriorating social and economic conditions—there has been a 17-fold increase in the number of reported child abuse cases ("Child abuse cases," 2001). Some observers now feel that child abuse is no less prevalent in Japan than it is in the United States (Kitamura & Kijima, 1999).

The Emergence of Child Abuse as a Social Problem

In the distant past, Roman law and English common law granted parents limitless power over their children, who had no legal right to protection against their parents. U.S. parents in the eighteenth and nineteenth centuries had the right to impose any punishment deemed necessary for the child's upbringing.

There were several attempts to draw attention to the problem of child battering, but none had the backing of groups powerful enough to convince the public that parents who purposely inflict injury on their children should be punished and perhaps even lose custody of their children. Early efforts to fight child abuse generally resulted in institutionalizing beaten or neglected children rather than punishing violent parents.

Terms such as *child abuse, child battering,* and *child neglect* only appeared on the social scene within the past 3 decades or so (Johnson, 1995). Indeed, the United States had no child abuse laws until the early 1960s (Pfohl, 1977).

In 1962 an article titled "The Battered-Child Syndrome" was published in the *Journal of the American Medical Association.* The article was accompanied by an official editorial asserting the grave nature of this new medical problem. The features of the **battered child syndrome** included traumatic head injuries and fractures of the long bones, inflicted most commonly on children under the age of 3. The media paid a great deal of attention to this article. By 1967 every state in the country had recognized the problem and quickly passed legislation calling for its control and punishment.

The fact that the 1962 article had the backing of the powerful medical profession gave it credibility. However, according to sociologist Stephen Pfohl (1977), medical professionals—who would be the most likely to see and report the devastating effects of parental violence—were actually unaware of the problem until forced to recognize it by a relatively obscure subspecialty: pediatric radiology (the interpretation of children's x-rays).

Pediatric radiologists were not particularly heroic (Pfohl, 1977). But unlike other specialties in medicine, they had more to gain than to lose by publicly recognizing the problem of child abuse. Radiologists were near the bottom of the medical prestige hierarchy. The discovery of the battered child syndrome allowed them to work in the higher-status domain of the more prestigious specialties. Furthermore, pediatric radiologists looked at children's x-rays, not the children themselves. The fact that they didn't see patients face-to-face freed them from the restraints of psychological denial and confidentiality that may have inhibited the diagnostic judgment of other medical professionals.

But medical professionals didn't "discover" the problem of child abuse alone. Newspapers, magazines, and television also helped to proliferate the idea of abuse. By 1976, the issue had grown to encompass a much broader array of conditions that threatened the health and well-being of children (Best, 1993). The more general term, *child abuse and neglect,* replaced the narrower concept of the *battered child.* Maltreated children could be abused emotionally, verbally, psychologically, or nutritionally by their parents. Child abuse was now much more than a medical problem to be treated by physicians.

One of the most important actions taken in the fight to detect and prevent child abuse was the formation of Child Death Review Teams composed of a coroner and representatives from medicine, law enforcement, public health, social services, education, child protective services, and mental health. The first group was formed in Los Angeles County, California, in 1978 to examine the circumstances of every child death. Since then, all 50 states and the District of Columbia have established Child Death Review Teams. These groups review the causes and circumstances of each child's death to find hazards that may place other children at risk from neglect, abuse, and violence. They then make recommendations to counties and states on effective strategies to prevent future fatalities (Injury Prevention Web, 2000).

New state laws have expanded the official domain of child abuse. As of 1994, all but five states have laws that, to varying degrees, require health practitioners to report cases of suspected domestic violence (Hyman, Schillinger, & Lo, 1995). Nurses, teachers, social workers, and law enforcement officers, in addition to physicians, are now obligated to report their suspicions. Child protection workers have been granted extraordinary powers to investigate cases and to separate children from their parents if they deem it necessary.

Needless to say, child abuse in recent years has become a well-established social problem. Between 1976 and 1998, reports of suspected child abuse and neglect increased from a little under 670,000 a year to 1.8 million (Besharov, 1993; U.S. Bureau of the Census, 2000b). Polls today consistently show that Americans rate child abuse as very serious.

The term "child abuse" itself has become such a fundamental part of the culture that it is now applied to a variety of concerns, such as failure to pay child support, unusual religious fervor, smoking in the presence of children, parental kidnapping, exposure to explicit rock lyrics, even circumcision (Best, 1993). And child abusers are no longer just parents and guardians; now other relatives, teachers, medical personnel, even other children are potential offenders.

Explanations of Child Abuse

As discussed in Chapter 8, pronatalist ideals form the foundation of American family life. It is simply assumed, in this culture, that "normal" people will have children or at least want to have children. Why, then, in a social environment that idealizes children, would there be such a high rate of child abuse, maltreatment, and neglect?

Individual Factors   Like popular theories of spousal violence, popular theories of child abuse tend to focus on characteristics of individual abusive parents. Many people, for instance, assume that parents who beat their children are alcohol or drug abusers or have some personality or psychiatric defect that renders them incapable of controlling their rage. Abusive parents are sometimes characterized as psychologically immature and unable to see their children as children. Therefore, the parents may expect more responsibility and self-control from their children than the parents themselves are capable of showing, leading to disappointment, anger, and violence. Most experts agree, however, that such characteristics actually account for only a very small percentage of child abuse cases.

A parent's socioeconomic condition would also seem to have something to do with child abuse. Existing data indicate that cases of child abuse are more likely to be reported among parents who have low income, low educational attainment, and long-term dependence on public assistance.

But one must be cautious about drawing the conclusion that child abuse is confined to lower-class parents. Wealthier parents might very well be better able to hide abuse, because they are more likely to live in private homes and less likely to use public services for health care or transportation, where others can scrutinize their actions. Indeed, some studies have found that medical practitioners are more likely to label an injured child as "abused" if the parents are perceived as working class than if they're perceived as middle class (cited in Gelles & Straus, 1988).

Male unemployment, often associated with other risk factors such as low self-esteem, stress, and depression, is another factor frequently associated with child abuse (Gillham et al., 1997). Unemployed people also spend more time at home, increasing their interactions with children. Certainly the resulting tension and frustration can increase the likelihood of child abuse as well as other forms of domestic violence.

It may come as some surprise that women are actually more likely to neglect, physically abuse, or emotionally abuse their children than men. The only type of abuse where men outnumber women as perpetrators is sexual abuse (cited in Winton & Mara, 2001). Women's increased likelihood of abusing and neglecting children is most likely the result of their family roles. Simply put, women have more opportunity to abuse because they tend to spend more time with children, often isolated from other adults. They also tend to be responsible for the arduous and frustrating aspects of child rearing, including disciplining children.

An individual-level factor that has become one of the most popular explanations of child abuse is the so-called **cycle of violence,** which refers to the tendency for people who are abused as children to grow up to be abusing parents and violent spouses themselves. Research suggests that childhood exposure to abuse or neglect doesn't guarantee that people will become violent as adults, but it does increase the likelihood of both juvenile and adult violence. In a study conducted by the National Institute of Justice, 1,575 individuals were followed from childhood to adulthood (Widom & Maxfield, 2001). Of these, 908 individuals had experienced substantiated cases of childhood abuse or neglect between 1967 and 1971. The remaining 667 individuals had not officially been abused or neglected and served as the control group in the study. This latter group and the group of individuals who had been abused were matched in terms of sex, age, family socioeconomic status and race. Criminal records for both groups were then reviewed over a 25-year period.

The study found that although most individuals in both groups had not been involved in juvenile or adult crimes, being abused or neglected as a child increased the likelihood of juvenile arrest by 59 percent, adult arrest by 28 percent, and arrest for violent crime by 30 percent. Furthermore, individuals who had been abused and neglected as children were younger when first arrested, had committed nearly double the number of offenses, and had been arrested more often than those in the control group. Interestingly, males tended to have higher rates of criminality overall, but the effect of childhood abuse and neglect on women was far stronger. Compared to the control group, those who had been abused and neglected as girls were 73 percent more likely to have been arrested for various offenses.

Another important finding from this study was that individuals who were neglected as children, but not physically abused, were also more likely to develop violent criminal behavior than those in the control group.

Other studies suggest that children don't necessarily have to be directly victimized for there to be future problems. Those who *observe* their parents hitting each other may also have an increased likelihood of becoming violent adults. According to Gelles and Straus (1988), seeing such violence teaches a child three things:

- Those who love you are also those who hit you, and those you love are people you can hit.
- Hitting those you love is "morally right."
- If other means of getting your way, dealing with stress, or expressing yourself don't work, violence is permissible.

Although these personal factors may explain the violent outbursts of some individual parents, they do little to explain why child abuse exists as a societal phenomenon and why it is so difficult to stop. To address these issues, we must turn to broader social and cultural conditions.

Parental Rights and State Intervention   On the night of April 18, 1993, Amanda Wallace and her two sons—3-year-old Joseph and 1-year-old Joshua—were visiting relatives. Ms. Wallace began raving that Joseph was nothing but trouble and threatened to kill him with a knife. The boy's grandmother offered to keep him overnight, but Wallace refused. At about 1:30 A.M. she stuffed a sock in Joseph's mouth and secured it with duct tape. She wrapped an extension cord around Joseph's neck several times. She carried him into the living room where she looped the cord around the metal crank arm over the door and, as he waved goodbye, hanged him (Ingrassia & McCormick, 1994).

Amanda Wallace had been a ward of the state since the age of 8. Between 1976 and 1989, when Joseph was born, she had swallowed broken glass and batteries and had attempted to disembowel herself. When pregnant with Joseph she repeatedly stuck soda bottles into her vagina, claiming the baby wasn't hers. When Joseph was born, a psychiatrist who had examined Amanda warned that she "should never have custody of this or any other baby" (Ingrassia & McCormick, 1994, p. 54).

When Joseph was 11 months old, he was removed from his mother because of suspected child abuse. But an assistant public defender persuaded a juvenile-court judge to return Joseph to Amanda. Over the next 2 years, caseworkers removed Joseph from the home two more times following his mother's suicide attempts. A Department of Children and Family Services report recommended that he be sent back to his mother, citing the fact that she had gotten an apartment and had entered counseling. The last time Joseph was returned to his mother—2 months before his death—the judge ignored Amanda's turbulent history, saying to her, "It sounds like you're doing O.K. Good luck."

Each time the state had determined that, in the interests of protecting the mother's parental rights to control her own affairs, it would be best if the child was returned to her. The sanctity of the family, state officials concluded, was paramount, no matter how undesirable the situation might appear to outside observers.

Most cases of child abuse aren't nearly as horrific as this one. Yet even here, where the evidence *against* placing this child with his mother would seem incontrovertible, the decision was still made to do so—on three separate occasions. According to the American Public

Welfare Association, two-thirds of abused or neglected children who are placed in foster care are eventually reunited with their parents (cited in Ingrassia & McCormick, 1994).

Most modern child abuse laws are designed to uphold the family's integrity—that is, keep the family intact by giving abusive parents multiple opportunities to change their ways and retain custody—not to protect children. As these laws read, parents must be given every reasonable opportunity to resolve their problems before a child is removed permanently from the home. Children are not entitled to be free from all harm, just serious harm. Indeed, in 1989 the U.S. Supreme Court ruled that the state had no constitutional duty to protect abused children against "private violence" at the hands of their parents ("Can't sue," 1989).

However, the long-held premise that keeping families intact is the best policy is weakening. More and more parents are being arrested for child abuse and neglect, and many cities and states are beginning to favor child protection over family preservation (Swarns, 1997). Some child welfare and law enforcement officials across the country have been doing everything possible to delay or avoid returning children to potentially abusive or neglectful families.

But as a result, more children are spending longer periods of time in foster care. Since 1985 the population of foster children has nearly doubled—from 276,000 to 500,000. These children stay in foster homes for 3 years on average (cited in Kilborn, 1997c).

In 1997 President Clinton signed into law a bill that helps states take youngsters away from abusive parents. For instance, it requires states to seek the termination of parental rights for any child under 10 who has been in foster care for 15 of the previous 22 months and to seek termination immediately with evidence of severe abuse, including abandonment, torture or physical or sexual abuse, or of the death of a sibling at the hands of a parent. The new law also requires states to set up a permanent placement plan for a child after 1 year of foster care, rather than 18 months, as previous rules stipulated (Seelye, 1997b).

When people weigh the value of parental rights and the desire to keep families intact against the safety of individual family members, the solutions to the problem of domestic violence become complex. On one side are those situations—such as the murder of Joseph Wallace—in which state intervention is considered *too slow* or insufficient to prevent serious harm to a child in danger. In these cases, if families are allowed to function as they see fit or if people hesitate about violating parental rights and family autonomy, some individual members will suffer.

On the other side are those situations in which state intervention is considered to be *too quick* or overzealous, causing unnecessary harm to the family. As you know, by its very nature, child abuse thrives on privacy. So to encourage ordinary members of the community to report cases of suspected abuse, most states let the accusers remain anonymous. Even if the accusers do identify themselves to social workers, the state is required to keep their identities secret.

Research indicates that perhaps as many as two-thirds of anonymous child abuse reports are designated as "unfounded" (Best, 1993). Some false accusations are intentionally false; others may be based on honest mistakes or exaggerated concerns. Authorities in the field say that most baseless complaints come from warring family members, especially ex-spouses looking for revenge or seeking to gain custody of children.

Some states have tried (so far unsuccessfully) to bar social service officials from beginning a child abuse investigation based on an anonymous report. But many states across the nation have been successful in passing laws that make false reports of child abuse a crime. Such attempts, designed to protect the rights of people falsely accused, will unfortunately have a chilling effect on well-meaning relatives. They may not come forward to report real abuse if the government doesn't shield their identities. Therefore, the cloak of privacy may drop over family violence once again.

Corporal Punishment

No one wants to see children hurt, abused, or killed. At the same time, though, the U.S. public generally approves of nonabusive, disciplinary violence: **corporal punishment** (see Exhibit 10.6).

In the United States, hitting one's children "when necessary" is a cultural norm. "When necessary" is usually taken to mean when the child continually misbehaves after being told to stop or does something potentially dangerous. The most famous and popular baby advice book, Benjamin Spock's *Baby and Child Care,* doesn't advocate corporal punishment. However, it states that corporal punishment should be avoided "whenever possible," implying that sometimes it's *not* possible to avoid hitting children. Indeed, most advice books say that corporal punishment ought to be used under certain circumstances. Few, if any, argue unequivocally against it (Straus, 1994).

The distinction between abusive violence and "corporal punishment" is not always clear, though. The only formal difference between the two is that abuse is usually thought to cause perceptible injury while corporal punishment does not (or should not). No parent has the legal right to "abuse" his or her child, but parents in all fifty states have the right to hit their children, provided no serious injury results. Researchers think that about 90 percent of U.S. parents hit their children to punish them (Straus, 1994).

Tolerant laws regarding corporal punishment can be found elsewhere as well. In 2000, the Ontario Superior Court rejected an appeal by child advocacy groups and reaffirmed Canadian parents' legal right to use force to correct their children's behavior. The groups tried to make the claim that the law violates children's rights by making them the only group of citizens that can be legally assaulted for reasons other than self-defense or protecting others. In England, a man who repeatedly beat his 9-year-old son with a 3-foot cane was freed by claiming his actions were "reasonable chastisement" and therefore perfectly legal.

EXHIBIT 10.6

U.S. Attitudes Toward Spanking Children

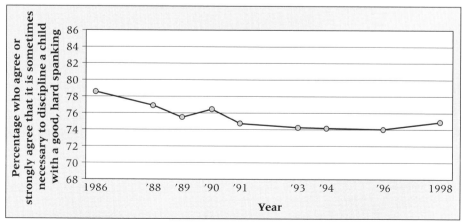

Data source: National Opinion Research Center. 1998. *General Social Survey, 1972–1998.* Available at www.icpsr.umich.edu/GSS/. Accessed June 1, 2001.

As widespread as corporal punishment is, it is an almost invisible part of life. Because most people spank or have been spanked, corporal punishment is so unremarkable and so taken for granted that few people give it much thought (Straus, 1994). In fact, parents opposed to the use of spanking sometimes have to defend their child-rearing philosophy to skeptical friends and neighbors.

Despite its ubiquity, acceptability, and perceived harmlessness, 40 years of research indicate that corporal punishment can have some of the same negative effects on children as child abuse: physical aggression, delinquency, or both. The more violent parents are toward their children—regardless of whether they use "ordinary" corporal punishment or more abusive forms of violence—the more violent these children are toward siblings, friends, and others (Straus, 1994). When these children become adults, they are more likely to show elevated rates of child abuse and spouse abuse than individuals who had never been hit as children. Of course, not all children who are physically punished become abusive adults. Nevertheless, such a finding has important social implications. To the extent that ordinary violence is linked to future child abuse and wife beating, efforts to reduce the incidence of family violence must include attention to the less-extreme sorts of violence that are so typical of American families (Straus, 1990).

In recent years, concerns over the effects of corporal punishment have led several countries (Norway, Sweden, Denmark, Finland, and Austria) to make spanking illegal. These laws are civil, not criminal. They provide no punishment for parents caught spanking their children. Instead, these largely symbolic laws are meant to set national standards, educate and help parents, and make a cultural statement that hitting children is unacceptable.

The Swedish law, for instance, acknowledges that parents need help now and then in dealing with their children, so many kinds of assistance are made available. The law also focuses on teaching children in school and through the media that parents aren't allowed to hit them. As a result, public attitudes have changed. Today, most Swedes favor managing children without corporal punishment.

Although most Americans would prefer to live in a nonviolent society, efforts to impose such antispanking laws here have been rare and futile. The general U.S. cultural tolerance of violence, extreme individualism, fear of unwarranted government intervention in families, and favorable attitudes toward punishment as a child-rearing strategy present formidable obstacles to the passage of such laws. Hitting children is so common in this country that the idea that ending the practice will somehow benefit society is considered ridiculous by most people.

Indeed, the U.S. public is reluctant to get involved in interactions between parents and their children. According to a survey by the National Committee for Prevention of Child Abuse, only 17 percent of its sample said they had "stopped someone they didn't know from hitting a child." But that figure is likely inflated by the vague wording of the question and the desire to report socially desirable actions (cited in Davis, 1991). Moreover, those who do get involved are often made to feel like busybodies who take an undue, even perverse, interest in the personal affairs of strangers.

Elder Abuse

The 1960s and 1970s saw a dramatic increase in the amount of attention paid to child abuse. In the 1980s, spouse abuse gained the cultural spotlight. But as these other social problems were receiving their rightful attention, the problem of elder abuse received relatively little notice. Not until 1987, with the enactment of the Amendments to the Older Americans Act, did the federal government provide definitions of elder abuse, neglect, and exploitation. These definitions serve as guidelines only; individual states determine what actually constitutes elder abuse (National Center on Elder Abuse, 2001).

As more and more adult children find themselves responsible for taking care of their parents, more and more elders are abused by their children. Also, as life expectancies increase, husbands and wives are faced with caring for their aging spouses at the same time they themselves are likely to be experiencing physical and mental decline. The dependency of an older person who was once capable of managing her or his own life places unexpected stress on the caretaker.

Elderly people may be especially vulnerable to several types of abuse (Boudreau, 1993; National Center on Elder Abuse, 2001):

- *Physical abuse*: hitting, slapping, using physical restraints, and withholding personal care, such as food, medicine, and medical attention
- *Sexual abuse*: nonconsensual sexual contact such as unwanted touching, sexual coercion, rape, sodomy
- *Emotional* or *psychological abuse*: using verbal assaults and insults, threats, fear, humiliation, intimidation, treating the individual like an infant, and isolation to control the dependent person
- *Neglect:* failure or refusal to fulfill obligations to the elder, such as not providing food, water, personal hygiene, comfort, and personal safety
- *Abandonment:* deserting the elderly person, often in public places such as hospitals or bus stations
- *Drug abuse*: encouraging elders to take too many drugs so that they are kept sedated and more manageable
- *Financial abuse*: stealing, embezzling, or misusing money and other personal property of the elderly
- *Violation of rights*: forcing a parent into a nursing home or reducing personal freedom and autonomy

A study commissioned by Congress, called the National Elder Abuse Incidence Study, found that approximately 450,000 individuals over age 60 were victims of abuse in 1996 (Administration on Aging, 2001). Of these cases, only 16 percent were reported to Adult Protective Services, the agency responsible for reporting and monitoring elder abuse. About 26 percent of all murder victims over age 65 are killed by a relative or intimate (U.S. Department of Justice, 2000).

The experiences of abused elders can, indeed, be tragic. Listen to how this 79-year-old woman describes the abusive treatment she received from her daughter:

> My daughter locked me in the garage and left me for more than an hour. She always parked the car behind mine in the garage so I could not get my car out except by her permission. . . . Whenever I tried to cook a meal she would appear and turn the gas off and remove the grills so that the only way I could cook would be to hold the pan the right distance over the flame. Also, if she found me using the electric toaster oven, my food was thrown on the floor and the toaster oven was removed and hidden for several days. . . . [My daughter was] always hurting me physically and mentally; kicking me, pushing me, grappling with me, telling me to get out, at one time throwing a drawer down the stairs at me, calling me names, telling me I belonged in a nursing home and why didn't I go to one. (quoted in Steinmetz et al., 1990, p. 472)

Elder abuse seems to be most common in situations where caretakers are overwhelmed by the costs, responsibility, frustration, and stress of caring for the elderly person. Caretakers may resent the extra work, the intrusions on privacy, and the excessive demands on time that result from the elder's presence. As the elderly person gets older and more frail, the care he or she needs can become even more taxing. In the National Elder Abuse Incidence Study, it was the most elderly (those over 80) who were most likely to be abused and neglected (Administration on Aging, 2001).

Issue 4 examines the ways in which people balance their individual desires with their sense of obligation to family members.

To make matters worse, typical family roles can become confused or reversed. Elderly parents may try to retain their traditional authority over family decision making. At the same time, though, the elderly parents occupy a childlike role, depending completely on their adult children to take care of them. Similarly, in the case of elderly spouse abuse, the traditionally dominant spouse may try to maintain his or her authority despite declining capacities. Hostility can increase when the caretakers feel they have been forced into taking responsibility for an elderly family member.

Notice that such an explanation of elder abuse tends to place the blame on the elderly themselves. But focusing on the stress and strain that the elderly cause runs the risk of normalizing the problem, of relieving abusers of much of the blame for their behavior toward a parent who is demanding, difficult, and unpleasant (Pillemer, 1993). People should not relieve abusers of responsibility, but should acknowledge the larger structural factors that make elder abuse more likely to occur. Without condoning the behavior, people must realize that stress and tension have economic and demographic sources that go beyond the individuals involved.

Elderly victims have a particularly difficult time reporting abuse. Victims often refuse to report the abuse for fear of retaliation, lack of alternative shelter, and shame associated with having to admit that a loved one is treating them so poorly. Often the caretaker is providing financial and other resources necessary for survival, which makes it nearly impossible for the elderly victim to leave the situation.

Conclusion

Intimate violence is still defined differently from other forms of criminal violence. Most people still use modifiers such as "intimate," "date," "domestic," or "family" to separate the assaults, rapes, and murders that take place between people who are intimately involved with one another from those that take place between strangers. In so doing, people—perhaps unintentionally—perpetuate the myth that intimate violence is something other than criminal violence and that the relationship between perpetrator and victim is a key factor in determining the severity of a violent act.

Although it would be comforting to believe that intimate violence is rare and is committed only by "sick" lovers, parents, or spouses, you have seen in this chapter that it happens with alarming frequency and is likely to be committed by people you would otherwise consider normal. Dating violence, spouse abuse, child abuse, and elder abuse are found among people of every class, race, and religion. Most people in the world at some point in their lives either experience or witness violence between members of their families. Intimate violence is not an aberration; it is a fundamental characteristic of the way people relate to one another in intimate, family settings.

And so a complete understanding of domestic violence requires an acknowledgment of the social, historical, and cultural environment in which it is embedded. For instance, elder abuse is probably more likely to exist in those societies where the elderly are devalued and perceived as burdensome. Wife abuse is more likely to occur in those societies where men learn that dominating women is appropriate, where gender inequality exists domestically and economically, and where aggression is encouraged by the culture. Child abuse is likely to exist in those societies where physical punishment is tolerated and where parents are granted unquestioned power over their children. As one author puts it, "When the larger culture aggrandizes wife beaters . . . or nods approvingly at child slappers, the family gets a little more dangerous for everyone, and so, inevitably, does the larger world" (Ehrenreich, 1994, p. 62).

Chapter Highlights

- Outside of wars and riots, the home is the most violent place in U.S. society. Family violence crosses lines of class, race, sexual orientation, and geography.
- Although domestic violence is still more likely to occur in private than in public, it no longer has the tacit approval and tolerance it once had from police, courts, and the public at large.
- According to recent research, most dating relationships may be marked by some form of coercion, violence, or sexual assault.
- Spouse abuse is a phenomenon that occurs worldwide. Instead of viewing it as a product of "sick" individuals, sociologists are likely to view it as the product of a culture that tolerates violence in a variety of situations, that traditionally grants men power and authority over women in families, and that values family privacy and autonomy over the well-being of individual members.
- Escape from abusive relationships is often hindered by a lack of institutional support from hospitals, police, and courts. Sometimes the resources in place to help battered women are inadequate to deal with the problem.
- Men's traditional power over women is changing both in individual families and in the larger society, but the power parents exert over their children remains unquestioned. Around the world, most acts of direct violence against children are carried out by parents or by people who have the parents' approval. But the designation of a violent act against a child as abusive lies not in the nature of the act but in the way it's defined by a particular culture.
- As life expectancy increases, more and more elderly people find themselves at risk for various types of mistreatment and abuse at the hands of their children and spouses.

Your Turn

One of the points made in this chapter is that the institutional support necessary to help people in violent home situations is often ineffective. What agencies or organizations in your area deal with domestic violence? Consider shelters for battered women, foster care, individual counseling services, special units within hospitals or police departments, government agencies such as child and adult protective services, support programs for batterers or abusive parents, and so on.

Interview a representative of each agency or program. Can the people you interview provide a statistical breakdown of the people who are aided by their programs—for example, by age, race, social class, or marital status? Can each person you interview identify a "typical" pattern of violence—for example, how the typical incident starts, how long it lasts, how frequent such incidents are in the life of a client?

What do the people you interview see as the primary goals of their programs (prevention, treatment, punishment)? How do they go about achieving these goals? What do they feel are the most serious impediments to their ability to provide services? Are these impediments more likely to stem from individual clients (such as the unwillingness of battered women to press charges against their assailants) or from institutions (such as not enough government or private funding to provide the services necessary to help victims leave abusive situations)?

Considering the information you've collected, what do you think the community's role ought to be in providing services to victims of domestic violence? Should the primary focus be on prevention programs or assistance programs? Would stricter laws and tighter enforcement make the problem better or worse? Explain.

Divorce and Remarriage

Blending Families

In a society characterized by high divorce rates and high remarriage rates, blended families are fairly commonplace. These families, which can consist of any combination of "his," "her," or "their" children, face unique challenges and adjustments. Not only must children forge new ties and relationships with a stepparent, they often must do so with other children who may or may not share common interests and backgrounds. Even their relationships with full siblings can be altered as dynamics shift within the family. The child who was once the oldest sibling in her family may now find herself dealing with an older brother; the "baby" may suddenly become a "middle child."

The blended family depicted in this photographic essay consists of the dad (Jim), his three children from a previous marriage, the mom (Danielle), and her two daughters. Despite similarities in age and background, the children have radically different ideas about the remarriage. A few of them feel that their parent's remarriage has been positive and resulted in a better lifestyle, but others describe the experience as "devastating" and "boldly disruptive."

Under what conditions might children approve or disapprove of a parent's remarriage?

Would it be more difficult to "blend" with a stepparent's children of the same age or of different ages?

When blending children from different households, it's likely that different custody arrangements will be in effect. Complications can arise because the family composition sometimes changes day by day and week by week. Danielle has sole custody of her daughters, so they're home 7 days a week. Jim shares custody of his children with his previous wife, and their schedules vary considerably. For instance, Joshua spends 5 days a week at his dad's house, whereas Nate spends 2 days there.

How would changing family composition complicate common, everyday activities such as meal planning, sleepovers, and family vacations?

In families where custody is shared, children face the challenge of living in and between two separate households. They must always think ahead, remembering to pack whatever they'll need for school later in the week—sports equipment, band uniforms, instruments, homework, and so on.

Because Sara spends half her time at her mother's and half at her father's, on Thursday mornings she boards the schoolbus at her mother's house but must remember to board a different bus, with a different driver, to go home in the afternoon to her dad's.

Planning ahead is a must! One seemingly simple problem for adults but a major one for a young child is ensuring that her library book goes to the right home so that it can be returned to school on the due date, later in the week.

When living in two homes, it's necessary to have duplicates of many things—clothes, contact lens cases, computers, posters, and so on to make it feel like home. This can be a challenge for families with limited financial resources and space. Living arrangements can also vary across households. A child may share a room with a sibling at mom's house but have his or her own room at dad's. In addition, children are likely to have a different set of rules to live by—for example, a child may be allowed to eat in the bedroom at dad's house but not at mom's.

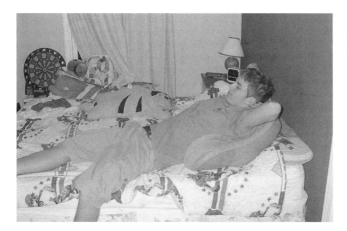

At mom's house, Joshua shares a bedroom with his brother.

At dad's house, he has his own room, television, and video games.

Because women are more likely to be financially disadvantaged than men following divorce, how might children's experiences at mom's house differ from their experiences at dad's? What disadvantages are there to living between two households? What advantages can you see?

One day in second grade my teacher stood at the front of the room after we pledged allegiance to the flag and briefly, nonchalantly announced to the class that Kim Hildebrandt, the girl who sat next to me, would from that point forward be called Kim Louise. That was all she said; she provided no explanation. Then she gave us that day's reading assignment.*

I looked at Kim. She appeared slightly embarrassed, but any 8-year-old kid would look embarrassed if the teacher singled him or her out like that in front of the whole class. So I didn't think much of the teacher's announcement. I just figured her family probably changed their name because "Hildebrandt" was too hard to pronounce.

A few weeks later the teacher made another announcement: Billy Farrell—the dark-haired boy nobody liked because of his fondness for punching people in the arm—would now be called Billy Kuhns. Now I was puzzled. What was going on here? Why were all these kids' families changing their names? I put the question to Billy, who angrily and conde-scendingly replied, "My parents got a *divorce*, stupid!" and walked away. *Divorce*? I didn't know what a divorce was. I'd never heard the word before.

So that night, I asked my mother. She patiently explained to me that sometimes hus-bands and wives stop loving each other. When that happens, some of them decide to stop living together. She said that the kids in my class were changing their names because they were now living with their mothers, who had gone back to using their "maiden" names. I pressed on. "Do we know anyone who's divorced?" I asked.

"Are you kidding?" she replied incredulously. "Of course we do." She reminded me of my cousins, who lived with their mother while their father lived across town with another woman and her two children. (All the time I thought that he lived where he did so he could be closer to his work.) She told me that the nice musician who lived alone across the street was divorced, as was the neighbor a few doors down whose children were only around on weekends and didn't go to my school. She reminded me that my friend, Mike, lived with his mother in a tiny apartment because his parents were divorced and his father lived in Cleveland.

The pathos in her voice as she told me about these people clearly signaled that divorce was not something good and that it should only be spoken of quietly, like cancer or institu-tionalized relatives. She told me not to tease those kids whose parents had divorced, be-cause they were "suffering enough already." The way she talked about the "tragedy" of di-vorce frightened me. I hoped I would never have to hear the word again. But, of course, like everybody else, I *would* hear the word again. Many times.

I don't think I was particularly naive as a child. But the fact that I had no idea what di-vorce was, even though so many people "had" one, showed how hidden and unpopular the topic was 35 years ago. Today, of course, things are quite different. You'd be hard pressed to find an 8-year-old now who doesn't know what the word *divorce* means. Most children have witnessed the end of a marriage, either that of their parents or of someone they are close to. Divorce has become a part of everyday life. It's in our movies, television shows, and novels. The children's sections of book stores stock picture books showing divorcing dinosaurs or Muppet babies worrying about the possibility of their parents divorcing. Hall-mark has an entire line of greeting cards for parents whose young children live elsewhere.

Thirty years ago a divorced politician didn't stand a chance of being elected. Today many of our most influential lawmakers are divorced. In the 1980s Ronald Reagan's divorce

*Reflects the experiences of David Newman.

and remarriage didn't prevent him from being elected president twice. In the 2000 election, people barely mentioned vice presidential candidate Joseph Lieberman's divorce and remarriage. Most people now recognize that in some situations a divorce may be preferable to an unhappy marriage. In short, divorce is as much a part of American family life as, well, marriage.

This chapter examines divorce, single parenting, and remarriage at both the societal and the individual levels. These are profoundly emotional and often disorienting experiences for all involved. Yet with such a high rate of divorce in this society, people must see them not just as personal tragedies but as social processes with cultural and historical causes and consequences.

Divorce in Cultural Context

People's preoccupation in this country with the frequency and consequences of divorce sometimes obscures the fact that divorce exists worldwide. Although it is more common and more acceptable in some places than in others, virtually all societies have provisions—legal, communal, or religious—for dissolving marriages (McKenry & Price, 1995).

Worldwide, divorce rates tend to be correlated with socioeconomic development. The developing countries of Latin America (for example, Ecuador, Nicaragua, and Peru) and Asia (for example, Thailand, Malaysia, Sri Lanka) have substantially lower divorce rates than the developed countries of western Europe and North America (Trent & South, 1989). Practically every industrialized country in the world experienced an increase in its divorce rate between 1950 and 1990 (Goode, 1993).

China provides a good example of the influence of socioeconomic development on divorce patterns. Between 1980 and 1995, the divorce rate in China more than doubled (Yi & Deqing, 2000). This increase has been especially noteworthy among urban residents, women involved in arranged marriages, and women with higher education (Liao & Heaton, 1992). According to some sociologists, several factors related to economic and social change may have contributed to this increase. First, legal restrictions on divorce were relaxed in 1981 with the passage of the New Marriage Law, which made divorce easier to obtain. Second, economic reform permitted more women to control economic resources and gain financial independence. Finally, rapid socioeconomic development and the spread of Western attitudes have loosened traditional Chinese restrictions on divorce (Yi & Deqing, 2000).

In societies where religion plays a dominant role in everyday life, the effects of socioeconomic development on divorce are tempered. In fact, even in some societies that most people would consider modern and developed, powerful religious forces have kept divorce illegal until quite recently. Italians, for instance, have been able to legally divorce for only a little over a decade. In 1995 the Irish government began a campaign against the Catholic Church over the country's constitutional ban on divorce. The government estimated that at least 80,000 people were locked in bad marriages and that they deserved the right to remarry. The Catholic bishops launched a massive advertising counterattack, arguing that even unhappily married people have an obligation to keep their marriages intact to provide a good example for society. But the referendum was passed by a minuscule margin, and in 1997, for the first time, people in Ireland had the right to legally divorce.

In many parts of the world, women have historically had many disincentives to divorce. In traditional Iran, for instance, women who are divorced are entitled to spousal support for only 3 months. To escape a bad marriage, many Iranian women have to forfeit all their possessions to their husbands. Men almost always retain custody of the children and continue to live in the family home. Since Iranian culture discourages women from living by themselves, especially if they are young, they usually end up moving back home so they can be supported by their brothers and father.

In some patriarchal societies women have only recently been granted a say in the divorce process (McKenry & Price, 1995). In Egypt, for instance, men traditionally didn't need a reason to divorce their wives. Women's rights to petition for divorce, in contrast, were severely limited. Divorced women had to wait 3 months before remarrying and were entitled to only 1 year of spousal support (McKenry & Price, 1995). In 2000, however, passage of a new law gave Egyptian women, for the first time, the right to divorce with or without their husbands' consent.

Access to divorce is often seen as a civil rights issue, an important advancement in the personal freedoms and social status of women. In India, for instance, where arranged marriages are commonplace, divorce offers women an escape from the mistakes their families made in selecting a mate for them. In a newspaper article describing the changes in Egyptian divorce laws, the headline read "Egypt's women win equal rights to divorce." The use of the word *win* implies a victory but also suggests that the right to divorce is a valuable thing, something worth winning.

Yet even in those countries that actively and publicly oppose divorce—such as the Muslim countries of the Middle East or the Catholic countries of Europe—large numbers of people have always found ways, such as desertion or separation, to end marriages that don't work. For instance, in 1984—before divorce was permitted in Italy—about 400,000 married couples were living apart (Goode, 1993).

Some people might view the trend toward more divorce worldwide as a welcome end to suffering that people have had to endure under the highly restrictive divorce systems of the past. In China, many people think the increasing divorce rate is a sign of social advancement, a growing indication that people can control their own fates (Faison, 1995). But in most societies, people who divorce are somehow penalized, either through formal controls such as fines, prohibitions against remarriage, excommunication, or forced alimony and child support or through informal means such as censure, gossip, and stigmatization.

Divorce American Style

In the United States, divorce is relatively easy and common. In an average year, close to 1.2 million divorces take place. That works out to a rate of almost 20 divorces per 1,000 married women ages 15 and older (U.S. Bureau of the Census, 2000b). This measure, known as the *divorce rate*, is more meaningful than a simple count of the number of divorces that occur in a given year, because it takes into account only those eligible for divorce and controls for fluctuations in the population. Thus a divorce rate of 20 per 1,000 indicates that approximately 2 percent of married women are likely to divorce each year.

Issue 2 looks at the question of whether a high divorce rate is necessarily a sign that the institution of family is in steep decline.

As Exhibit 11.1 shows, the U.S. divorce rate increased throughout much of the twentieth century, peaking around 1980, then declining slightly thereafter. Although the U.S. divorce rate has more or less stabilized over the past decade or so, it is still more than twice the divorce rate of most other industrialized countries (Clark, 1996).

Probably a little fewer than half of all marriages that begin this year in the United States will end in divorce at some point in the future. Divorce is no longer a rare and stigmatized

EXHIBIT 11.1

Divorce Trends in the United States and Other Countries

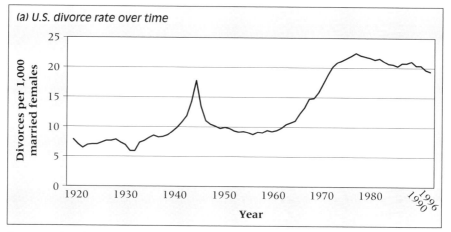

(a) U.S. divorce rate over time

Data sources: Data from 1920–1970 from U.S. Bureau of the Census. 1975. *Historical Statistics of the United States: Colonial Times to 1970.* Series B 216–220. Washington, DC: U.S. Government Printing Office. Data from 1975–1996 from U.S. Bureau of the Census. 2000b. *Statistical Abstract of the United States: 2000,* Table 144. Washington, DC: U.S. Government Printing Office.

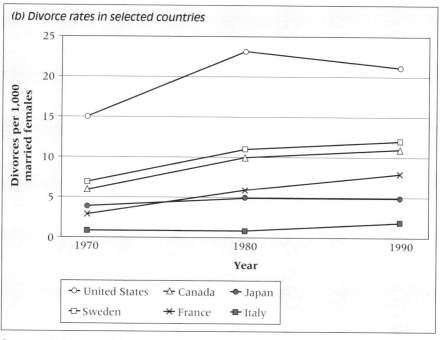

(b) Divorce rates in selected countries

Data source: U.S. Bureau of the Census. 1997d. *Statistical Abstract of the United States,* 117th ed.

Issue 5 examines the stabilizing effect religion can sometimes have on family life.

occurrence; it is an inevitable risk of marriage. One can hardly begin a marriage these days without considering the possibility that it might not last.

The relatively high U.S. divorce rate is often attributed to things such as the decreasing influence of religion in people's lives, the rise of individualism, the liberalization of divorce laws, and women's increasing participation in the paid labor force. These changes have indeed created a cultural shift in the perception of marriage. Marriage has become a *voluntary contract* that can be ended at the discretion of either spouse. In the past, marriage was predominantly an economic agreement, representing the joining of the financial resources of two families. When economic needs—not to mention family expectations and religious norms—held couples together, people "made do" with loveless, unsatisfying marriages because they had to. Now that these constraints are largely absent, people are less willing to make do (Skolnick, 1996). Today people see marriage primarily as an exchange of emotional gratification (Furstenberg & Cherlin, 1991). Hence people are less inclined to stay in marriages that don't provide them with satisfaction and happiness.

Racial and Ethnic Variation

Divorce rates and perceptions of divorce can vary among racial and ethnic groups. For example, studies consistently show that African Americans are more likely than other groups to separate and divorce (see Exhibit 11.2). This difference is sometimes attributed to a weaker emphasis on marriage among African Americans. But on closer inspection, the heightened likelihood of divorce may have less to do with race than with socioeconomic status. Studies that compare whites and African Americans of similar socioeconomic status—that is, similar levels of education, income, occupational prestige, and unemployment—find similar rates of divorce (Cherlin, 1992). Thus lower income, less education, and insecure employment place African-American families at significantly greater risk of marital disruption than other groups.

Conversely, the cultural emphasis on family in most Hispanic groups and the constraining role that the Catholic Church plays in their lives may explain their relatively low rate of divorce. Among Asian Americans, too, who have traditionally stressed the family unit over the individual, divorce still carries a significant stigma. Hence the divorce rate among Asian Americans has consistently been lower than that of the population as a whole. For both Hispanic- and Asian-American groups, though, divorce rates are increasing among younger people, who are generally less influenced than older generations by traditional religious or ethnic values.

E X H I B I T 11.2

Race, Ethnicity, and Divorce

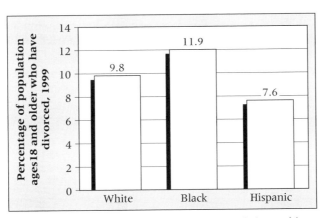

Data source: U.S. Bureau of the Census. 2000b. *Statistical Abstract of the United States: 2000*, Table 53. Washington, DC: U.S. Government Printing Office.

Historical Trends in Divorce

Most people tend to think of divorce as a relatively recent phenomenon, assuming that it was either extremely rare or nonexistent in the distant past. But from a broader historical perspective you can see that divorce has always been a feature of American society. Colonial records throughout the seventeenth and eighteenth centuries reveal a wealth of marital scandals, disruptions, and divorces. Even Puritan settlers condoned and practiced divorce. Indeed, when colonial and state governments attempted to restrict divorce, serious problems immediately became apparent: "Mates mistreated each other, were unfaithful, lived separately, abandoned one another, sought annulments for spurious reasons, obtained divorces in more permissive jurisdictions, and subverted the intent of restrained divorce laws by fabricating grounds that fell within legal limitations" (Riley, 1991, p. 183).

Issue 2 also charts historical developments in U.S. family life.

Such problems led to calls for the re-instatement of more liberal divorce laws (Clark, 1996). Shortly after achieving independence from England, many Americans began to believe that divorce was a citizen's right in a democratic country dedicated to the principles of personal freedom and happiness. Divorce was seen as a civil liberty, not a social ill.

Not surprisingly, divorces began to proliferate. A French citizen touring the United States in the early 1800s noted that marriages were far more easily dissolved in America than in Europe (cited in Riley, 1991). In 1880, two of every 1,000 existing marriages ended in divorce, a rate that was already the highest in the world. By the beginning of the twentieth century, it was apparent that the United States had accepted divorce as a necessity.

After 1900 the divorce rate in this country increased steadily. It reached what many thought were calamitous levels in the 1920s, when 8 of every 1,000 married women divorced each year. In fact, in 1927 the famous psychologist John Watson predicted that the institution of marriage would be obsolete within 50 years. Except for a brief decline during the Depression, the divorce rate continued to rise. Then it increased sharply right after World War II, most likely because many couples had hastily married just before the young men shipped out and realized when they reunited after the war, that they'd made a mistake.

For a brief time during the 1950s, the rate dropped just as sharply as it had risen in the postwar years. But by the early 1960s, divorce began to rise again. The mid-1970s marked the first point in U.S. history when marriages were as likely to end by divorce as by the death of one spouse. By the early 1980s, the American divorce rate had reached a high level that has remained much the same ever since.

A historical analysis of divorce rates does show an increasing incidence overall, but this trend can be somewhat misleading. Comparatively low divorce rates do not necessarily signal a high proportion of happy, satisfying marriages. The rate of "hidden" marital separation a century ago was probably not that much less than the rate of "visible" separation today (Sennett, 1984). For financial or religious reasons, divorce was not an option for many people. A significant number of couples turned to the functional equivalents of divorce—desertion and abandonment—which have been around for centuries. Although the divorce rate may have been lower in the past, families found other ways to break up.

Furthermore, a comparison of divorce rates doesn't take into consideration how often marriages in the past were disrupted by the premature death of one or the other spouse. In fact, when one looks at the total rate of marital dissolution—combining divorce and death—the level is remarkably constant from the mid-nineteenth century to the late twentieth century (Bane, 1976). In short, marital disruption has been around since the inception of the country, even though death made divorce less necessary and economic, legal, and religious barriers made it less available in the past.

Changes in Divorce Laws

Today people involved in unsatisfying marriages can get a divorce more easily than ever. But as recently as 3 decades ago, before they would grant a divorce the courts required evidence of wrongdoing, such as adultery, desertion, or cruelty. A person seeking a divorce had to sue his or her spouse.

The result was a veritable industry of sham divorces. In New York, for instance, where adultery was the only grounds for divorce for most of the twentieth century, people would hire a model and a photographer and stage a phony adulterous situation in a hotel room. If a judge wanted evidence of mental cruelty, a lawyer would advise a client to accuse the spouse of name-calling; if a judge wanted evidence of physical cruelty, the client would be advised to claim to have been slapped by a spouse. Thousands of other troubled couples avoided such schemes by traveling across the border to Mexico to take advantage of its less restrictive divorce laws.

But beginning with California in 1970, every state has adopted a form of **no-fault divorce**. These laws reduce the expense, acrimony, and fraud that typically accompanied divorce proceedings by eliminating the requirement that one partner be found guilty. Instead, marriages could be declared unworkable and simply terminated. In most states, one spouse can now obtain a divorce without the other's agreement and without hiring a lawyer.

No-fault divorce laws also redefined the responsibilities of husbands and wives. The husband is no longer automatically considered the head of the household, and the wife is no longer considered solely responsible for the care of the children. Financial awards—spousal support and child support—are based on each spouse's ability to work. If neither spouse is unable to work, courts usually assume that both are equally capable.

The Unforeseen Effects of No-Fault Divorce   This emphasis on equality in the divorce *process* has been a welcome change, but it has eclipsed any consideration of equality in divorce *outcomes*. Although women tend to show better emotional adjustment than men after divorce, they suffer more than men economically, in all racial groups and at all age levels. Mothers retain custody of their children in the vast majority of divorces, but since the 1970s, many courts have had a tendency to reduce spousal and child support payments for wives on the mistaken assumption that because more women are working, male–female economic equality has been reached. In California, after no-fault divorce laws went into effect in the early 1970s, only 13 percent of mothers with preschool children received spousal support (cited in Tavris, 1992). As a result, no-fault divorce increased the number of divorced women and their children suffering economic hardship (Coltrane & Hickman, 1992). Although Exhibit 11.3 shows some reduction in poverty levels among divorced parents in the 1990s, mothers are still nearly three times as likely to face hardship as fathers.

It's not surprising that separation and divorce have more serious economic consequences for women than for men (Smock, Manning, & Gupta, 1999). For one thing, a divorced woman faces a world in which her earning capacity is significantly less than a man's. Women working full time, year-round earn about 32 percent less than their male counterparts (U.S. Bureau of the Census, 2000b). Divorced women (and their children) experience, on average, a 27 percent *decrease* in their standard of living (Peterson, 1996). Divorce is the single most devastating economic event for American women today.

The picture for men is a little more complicated. Men who relied heavily on a spouse's income during the marriage tend to experience a modest decline in their economic status after divorce. But this decline has a much smaller impact on their standard of living after

EXHIBIT 11.3

Economic Status of Divorced Parents

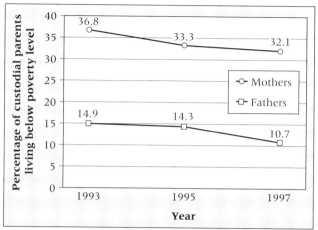

Data source: T. Grall. 2000. Child support for custodial mothers and fathers 1997, Figure 2. *Current Population Reports*, P60-212. Available at www.census.gov/prod/2000pubs/p60-212.pdf. Accessed May 1, 2001.

separation than the decline that most women experience. Men who were the sole or primary breadwinners in their marriages typically gain financially from separation and divorce (McManus & DiPrete, 2001).

Custody of the children imposes further disadvantages on women's economic prospects. As one sociologist put it, after a divorce fathers become *single* and mothers become *single parents* (Weitzman, 1985). Child-rearing responsibility restricts a woman's job opportunities by limiting her work schedule and job location, her availability to work overtime, and her freedom to take advantage of special training, travel, and other opportunities for advancement. So severe are these handicaps that of all children whose family incomes were less than $25,000 in 1998, 57 percent lived in single-mother households; only 6 percent lived in single-father households (U.S. Bureau of the Census, 2000b). It takes, on average, 5 years for divorced women and their children to regain their predivorce standard of living.

Displaced homemakers—divorced women who didn't work outside the home during their marriage—are at even greater disadvantage than other women. Their years off the career path take a toll on their ability to earn a living. Research shows that these women are more likely to be impoverished by divorce than are women who have maintained jobs. Displaced homemakers eventually recover a far lower percentage of the family income they had during the marriage than women who worked prior to the divorce (Arendell, 1987). The situation for divorced women, particularly older divorced women, was so bad in California that the legislature passed the Displaced Homemakers Relief Act, which required judges to consider the future earning potential of each spouse before awarding a settlement.

Both men and women lose a significant part of their identity after a divorce. But divorced women who experience dramatic economic changes often require a fundamental redefinition of self. Their identity as members of a certain social class—and with it the core of their self-esteem—is suddenly shaken by the economic hardship that can result from divorce. Sociologist Christine Grella (1990) interviewed forty previously middle-class divorced women with at least one dependent child at home to explore how they defined their social class after divorce. On average, after divorce, their incomes were cut in half. Yet their assessments of their social class didn't follow neatly from this change in economic circumstances. The contradiction is apparent in the thoughts of a 40-year-old woman who moved to a poorer neighborhood following her divorce:

> I believe I have at least a middle-class and maybe an upper middle-class mentality, my beliefs and convictions, the things I teach my children . . . are definitely a cut above much of what I see in the neighborhood I live in [and] the schools my kids go to. . . . Economically, I'm basically not a whole lot different from anybody in this neighborhood, and this is definitely not a middle-class neighborhood. (quoted in Grella, 1990, p. 46)

Notice that her values and beliefs were more important than economics in her class identity but they were being threatened by the reality of living in a poor neighborhood.

Finally, cultural expectations of mothers contribute to women's disadvantage after divorce. A woman's need to work long hours to earn enough to live on or her desire to educate herself to improve job prospects have typically been seen as detracting from her ability to perform her duties as a mother. For example, in 1994 a Michigan judge ordered a woman to give up custody of her 3-year-old daughter to the girl's father because the child was in day care 35 hours a week while the woman took college classes. The judge decided that the father wouldn't do such a thing and deserved custody ("Day care costs mother," 1994). According to the judge, the mother was not providing the child with a feeling of security and permanence. She was granted visitation on alternate weekends and holidays.

The Movement to Make Divorce More Difficult   Many critics argue that no-fault divorce laws have not only imposed an unfair economic burden on women but have made divorce too easy and too quick. They believe that a majority of divorces occur because the spouses involved simply don't try hard enough to overcome their problems:

> Too many people feel that a bad marriage is like milk—once sour, it can never be made good and it smells up the refrigerator if you leave it there. But every relationship has its high and low points. The thing that distinguishes people in 50-year-old marriages isn't that they're scot-free of problems, but they've confronted those difficulties and persevered when others gave up. (quoted in Clark, 1996, p. 415)

This argument derives from the family decline perspective on family change, described in Issue 2.

The contention is that individuals are simply giving up on marriages that, although not perfect, are "good enough." No-fault divorce has made it too easy for people to dissolve marriages that have not met expectations that were probably too high and unrealistic to begin with.

Some recent research suggests that liberalization of divorce laws did indeed lead to an increase in the divorce rate, especially after 1980. One study found that between 1980 and 1991, while all states had no-fault laws, 32 still allowed one party to raise the question of fault when dividing assets. Those states that took fault into account had lower divorce rates than those that did not (cited in Brinig, 2000). The researchers suggest that no-fault laws reduce the costs of divorce (for example, alimony penalties) and therefore, compared to states where "fault" is taken into consideration, the divorce option seems more appealing. Other research indicates that the shift to no-fault divorce accounts for about 17 percent of the increase in divorce between 1968 and 1988 (Friedberg, 1998; Waite & Gallagher, 2000).

Public opinion appears to favor tightening the laws governing divorce (see Exhibit 11.4). In several states—Iowa, Idaho, Georgia, Michigan, and Pennsylvania, to name a few—legal measures have been debated that would impose mandatory waiting periods for

EXHIBIT 11.4

U.S. Attitudes Toward Divorce

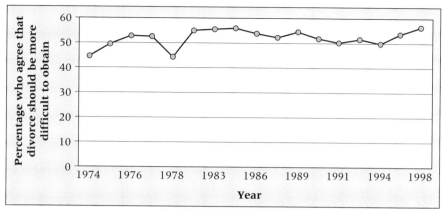

Data source: National Opinion Research Center. 1998. *General Social Survey, 1972–1998.* Available at www.icpsr.umich.edu/GSS/. Accessed June 1, 2001.

couples contemplating divorce or restore the old requirement of proving fault in cases where only one spouse is seeking divorce (D. Johnson, 1996).

Some scholars (for example, Friedman, 1995; Galston, 1995b) suggest that because the effects of divorce are most devastating to children, perhaps a two-tiered system of divorce might work better than the current divorce law. Adults without children would be free to divorce whenever they decided to, much as they're able to now. But once children are present, the adults' legal identity would change from freely contracting individuals to parents. Because society has a vested interest in preventing the breakup of a marriage with children, parents with children under 18 would have to demonstrate that the children would be better off if the marriage broke up. Parental unhappiness and incompatibility would no longer be compelling arguments for divorce.

> The struggle to balance individual needs with family obligation is examined in Issue 4.

In 1997 the Louisiana state legislature passed a measure forcing engaged couples to choose between a standard marriage contract, which permits no-fault divorce, and a "covenant marriage," which could be dissolved only by a mutually agreed-on 2-year separation or proof of fault, chiefly adultery, abandonment, or abuse. The law requires couples who opt for a covenant marriage to receive counseling before the wedding and to seek it again if they experience marital difficulties (Loe, 1997). Arizona followed suit in 1998. But to date only 3 percent of newlyweds in Louisiana and Arizona have chosen the covenant option (Belluck, 2000b).

Instead of making divorce more difficult, other states have tried to strengthen marriage. In Florida, for example, a state law gives couples a $32 discount on their marriage license if they take a marital education course prior to their wedding. Such a course, incidentally, is a high school graduation requirement. The governor of Arkansas has declared a "state of marital emergency" and is exploring tax credits for couples taking a marriage education course.

The governor of Oklahoma provided a clear explanation for the sentiment behind these efforts:

> Tell me the sense of a system where it is easier to get a marriage license than it is to get a hunting or driver's license, easier to get out of a marriage with children than it is to

get out of a Tupperware contract. Ours is an effort to encourage families to appreciate the lifetime commitment of a marriage contract, to recognize that a marriage that can be saved, should be saved. (quoted in Belluck, 2000b, p. A14)

The Case for Retaining No-Fault Divorce   In defense of the current no-fault system, some observers suggest that states' interest in strengthening marriage and making divorce more difficult might be more economic than moral. Divorced families are more likely to need public assistance and to lack health insurance than married families. States spend tens of millions of dollars each year in efforts to collect unpaid child support. There is also the cost to business of lost productivity when employees are going through difficult divorces.

In addition, divorce doesn't always live up to the common cultural images: lonely, neglected children and indifferent, selfish parents willing to break up a happy home (Stewart et al., 1997). Researchers have found that few people divorce easily, for little or no cause (Furstenberg, 1999). In a study of 129 divorced mothers, only 19 percent of them cited "personal dissatisfaction" as the reason they divorced their husbands. The rest cited domestic violence, husband's alcohol or drug abuse, or the husband's involvement with another woman as the cause of the divorce (Kurz, 1995). Other researchers have shown that most women who stay in unsatisfactory marriages do so because they fear that life as a divorced woman will be exceedingly hard (Hochschild & Machung, 1989). In short, the assumption that most divorces consist of people frivolously "walking away" from satisfactory but less-than-perfect marriages simply because they're unhappy appears to be inaccurate.

Furthermore, there is no evidence that repealing no-fault divorce laws will reduce the divorce rate now. In fact, the result of such a repeal may be an increase in contentious, expensive, potentially child-harming divorces. Imagine a woman living with an abusive husband. Without no-fault divorce, she would have to prove fault by spending a tremendous amount of time, money, and resolve to undertake what amounts to a civil prosecution for a violent crime (Whitehead, 1997). This can be a terrifying experience for a battered woman who wants to avoid her husband. She may just choose to endure his abuse at home.

Being forced to find fault during divorce proceedings would also put a greater financial burden on those people who can least afford it. The process may require lawyers, therapists, private investigators, and expert witnesses. Such a costly undertaking would drain the pool of financial resources available to the children of divorce, further contributing to a decline in their standard of living.

Finally, repealing no-fault divorce would intensify the pain that children experience. A divorce can be emotionally draining enough. But forcing children to witness prolonged conflict as their parents go about blaming each other for the marriage's failure so that one can be the "winner" and the other the "loser," can only make matters worse. After such a battle, the chances of ex-spouses engaging in cooperative parenting, which increases the likelihood of a child adjusting well, would be nearly zero.

Some sociologists and social observers argue that instead of making divorce more difficult and more stigmatizing, this society ought to be thinking about ways to improve the quality of life *after* divorce. They argue that the most destructive aspect of divorce, one typically overlooked by reformers, is the poverty that usually ensues when children live with a single mother who earns a low wage. The solution would be to improve the award and enforcement of child support payments and to strengthen the safety net of supportive services, including child care, welfare, and Medicaid.

Uncoupling

Beyond economics, the "spoiling" of a marriage, or of any other long-term, intimate relationship, can create deep emotional wounds akin to those associated with the death of a loved one (McCall, 1982). Those who go through a breakup often experience a wide range of emotions, including anger, bitterness, sadness, self-pity, self-doubt, guilt, and shame. At the same time, as social exchange theory predicts (see Chapter 1), when a relationship ends, so do the interpersonal benefits that came with it. The person loses the partner on whom he or she came to depend for important resources, and loses contact with friends and acquaintances whom he or she came to know through that partner.

The Process of Breaking Up

According to the symbolic interactionist perspective (also discussed in Chapter 1), family experiences are created and given meaning within the context of social interaction. From this viewpoint, divorce can be understood not just as a discrete legal event that occurs when the divorce papers are signed but as a process of definition that occurs over time (Ganong & Coleman, 1994). This "process" part of a divorce is the most significant element in shaping family relationships and individual adjustment.

The divorce process can last for months or even years. More often than not, it begins psychologically well before the two spouses consider separation and continues far beyond the time when the divorce becomes finalized. Here's how one sociologist, Diane Vaughan (1986), describes the slow evolution of divorce:

> I was married for twenty years. As I reflected on the relationship after our separation, the marriage seemed to have been coming slowly apart for the last ten. . . . I could retrospectively pick out turning points—moments when the relationship changed, times when the distance between us increased. . . . Rather than an abrupt ending, ours appeared to have been a gradual transition. Long before we physically separated, we had been separating socially—developing separate friends, experiences, and futures. (pp. xiii–xv)

Using her own experience as a starting point, Vaughan set out to identify the process by which relationships come apart. She collected detailed interviews with 103 divorced or separated men and women. Although each person's experience with uncoupling is unique and the reasons for ending a relationship vary widely, she did find some common patterns, discussed in the following sections. Keep in mind that Vaughan's findings can apply to any long-term intimate relationship, not just heterosexual marriage.

Harboring Secret Unhappiness   According to Vaughan, two partners rarely mutually and simultaneously arrive at the conclusion that they are unhappy and that their relationship needs to end. In most cases, uncoupling begins as a quiet, one-sided process. That is, one partner (whom she refers to as the "initiator") secretly mulls over his or her unhappiness.

This initial solitary reflection can unintentionally create an informational breach between two spouses. Being excluded, the other partner is not given the opportunity to understand the developing situation and either adapt to it or change it.

Making the Initial Disclosure   Eventually, the initiator begins to articulate his or her unhappiness. But these early disclosures are usually framed as complaints, attempts to correct the partner's perceived shortcomings in the hope that he or she will become a more suitable partner. The complaints may focus on specific annoying traits (hair, weight, conversational style, sexual technique, and so on).

These early verbal expressions of dissatisfaction tend to come across as attempts to improve the relationship rather than as a sign of the initiator's desire to end it. But behind the description of annoyances lies the real problem, which usually remains hidden. The other partner's awareness of the initiator's discomfort goes no deeper than these relatively minor complaints, which are all the initiator discloses.

Pursuing Outside Involvements   Sometimes changes in the relationship do occur as a result of these complaints. But they aren't likely to erase the initiator's unhappiness. To avoid the unhappiness at home, the initiator may begin to devote more time and energy to things other than the relationship: children, work, friendships, recreational activities and hobbies, extramarital friendships, or even sexual affairs. By devoting time to these pursuits, the initiator creates a social world from which the partner is excluded. Because the partner's access to these experiences is limited, the breach between the two becomes wider.

In the process of taking up other activities, the initiator often identifies new sources of satisfaction and pleasure outside the relationship. The probability of a relationship ending increases when the initiator begins to see it as less satisfying and less attractive than alternatives and when the costs of ending the relationship (for instance, community, religious, or family disapproval) are low (Cox et al., 1997).

Few studies have attempted to measure the impact of partners' viable alternatives on their marriage. However, sociologists Scott South and Kim Lloyd (1995) examined the relationship between divorce rates and the supply of potential alternative partners in the local community. To estimate the number of potential partners in a particular geographic area, they counted people who were unmarried, not institutionalized, of the same race and ethnicity as their subjects, and in the same age range. In addition to considering the quantity of available potential mates, they also assessed their quality. Current or potential employment is believed to be particularly important to people, so the researchers computed the percentage of suitable men and women in each area who were employed or enrolled full time in school.

They found that the risk of divorce is highest where wives or husbands encounter an abundance of available alternatives. They concluded that many people remain open to alternative relationships even while married and that the more attractive and available these alternatives are, the greater the chance that the spouses will leave their present marriage.

Vaughan points out that up to this point in the uncoupling process, the initiator's creation of a life apart from the partner is not malicious. Rather, it occurs as the initiator attempts to ease his or her painful and disagreeable life situation. But the consequences are still serious. Even though the initiator has made no actual move toward ending the marriage, by creating this independent life and identity, the initiator has taken the first tentative step out of the relationship.

Accentuating the Negative   Disillusioned by the inability to resolve unhappiness at home, the dissatisfied initiator begins to accentuate all the negative aspects of the relationship and to minimize the positive—precisely the opposite of what someone tends to do when initially falling in love. The initiator may begin to redefine the entire history of the relationship. What once were a partner's endearing little rituals become annoying habits in retrospect. The good times get reinterpreted as bad; the bad times are seen as more typical and indicative of the deep problems in the relationship.

As discontent intensifies, it becomes more visible to the partner. The initiator's complaints start to reflect an attitude that the relationship is not only troubled but perhaps unsavable. The initiator may start telling others outside the relationship that all is not well or show his or her displeasure in public settings. Because norms of privacy dictate that couples keep their problems to themselves and present a harmonious public image, such displays mark a public redefinition of the partner and of the relationship.

By focusing on the negative aspects of the partner and of the relationship, the initiator creates in his or her mind something that can and should be left behind. By defining the relationship as "bad," the initiator can justify his or her desire to end it.

Deciding to Separate   For a while, the initiator lives in two worlds simultaneously. Not quite gone from the marriage, he or she still must participate from time to time in the old coupled world. The initiator tends to be uncomfortable in the old role he or she is attempting to shed and therefore simply "goes through the motions" of married life. The initiator may avoid any activity that would bind him or her to the partner for an extended period, such as having a baby, redecorating a room, buying season tickets, or taking out a loan. He or she may also express discomfort with being linked to the partner in public situations, where others still treat them as a couple. Especially troublesome are family gatherings or couple-confirming celebrations such as weddings or anniversary parties.

Eventually the partner begins to notice the changes in the initiator's commitment to the relationship. The partner may realize that the initiator doesn't offer a kiss anymore when leaving or returning home, or that the initiator is undergoing a change in appearance (losing weight, growing a beard, buying new clothes, and so on). The partner may feel excluded but is still not likely to react to the initiator's behavior as a threat to the relationship. However, psychologically and emotionally, the initiator has already left.

How is it possible, you might be wondering, for one partner to slip so far away without the other person noticing? Often partners claim they were unaware that the relationship was deteriorating. Vaughan doesn't think this blindness is due to naivete, ignorance, or a "what you don't know won't hurt you" philosophy of avoidance. Instead, she attributes these contradictions to the way many married couples communicate:

> Unable to witness our partners' every activity or verify every nuance of meaning, we evolve a communication system based on trust. We gradually cease our attentive probing, relying instead on familiar cues and signals to stand as testament to the strength of the bond. . . . As intimate relationships begin to deteriorate, this shorthand method . . . tends to obscure change and can prevent the sending and receiving of new information. (Vaughan, 1986, p. 88)

The result is a sort of collaborative cover-up in which direct confrontation is avoided and facts are suppressed. Since the culture lacks useful guidelines for acknowledging problems and ending a relationship, routines continue and life goes on as usual. As Vaughan puts it, one "tells without telling; the other knows without knowing."

Eventually the "cover-up" breaks down, and the moment of separation arrives. Sometimes the initiator directly confronts the partner with his or her wish to end the relationship.

Other times the initiator uses indirect methods, such as displaying so much discontent and misery that the partner is forced to confront the initiator. Although the initiator may want to be tactful, sensitive, and considerate, more often than not the opposite occurs:

> The truth is, we don't know how to tell our partners we no longer want to be with them. There is no good way, no kind way, no easy way to do it without hurting the other person. Often, we are in such pain ourselves as we consider taking our leave that we act out of frustration rather than rationality, hurting others despite our wish to be humane. (Vaughan, 1986, p. 296)

The actual decision to separate may be the result of discussion and planning, or it may occur spontaneously. It may be mutually agreed on, but chances are it won't be. Disentangling a shared life into two separate ones is never easy. Normal living patterns are disrupted. Economic status, friendship networks, personal habits, sex life, relationships with children—all must be reorganized.

The Pain of Going Public

The process of separation is particularly difficult when it comes time for the couple to tell others close to them that their marriage is ending. Friends, relatives, co-workers, and other interested parties typically want to know whom to blame, whom to help, and whose side to take (Gertsel, 1987). But the explanations offered by each partner will almost certainly be different, because of their distinctive perspectives (McCall, 1982).

Even though they may have noticed serious problems in the marriage, noninitiators are likely to oppose the divorce when their partners first bring it up. Hence they are often able to use a moralistic tone when describing the breakup, talking about sacrifice, the sanctity of the marriage vows, and their efforts to make it work. When dealing with others, noninitiators may seek sympathy, perhaps even wanting to play the victim. At the same time, though, they don't want to advertise the fact that their "value" has plummeted in the former partner's eyes.

In contrast, initiators are likely to face a "tough audience" (Vaughan, 1986). They may feel compelled to provide accounts that forestall any possibility that others will blame them for the breakup. Hence they must frame the partner and the relationship in a way that justifies the termination. They may also begin to highlight the importance of individual needs over commitment or describe the divorce in terms of their emotional and practical needs going unfulfilled:

> I wanted to take care of me. And I knew as long as I stayed in the relationship that I would always take care of somebody else because that's just the way I was. It's probably stupid, but I felt that I couldn't grow and I couldn't be independent as long as I was in that position. (quoted in Hopper, 1993, p. 807)

Further complicating the process of going public is the social stigma associated with the termination of an intimate relationship. Like most things in this achievement-oriented society, relationships—especially marriages—tend to be viewed in success/failure terms. Although studies consistently show a clear decline in disapproval of divorce as a general category, disapproval of divorced *individuals* continues (Gertsel, 1987). Divorced families are still characterized as "broken," "weak," "fragile," "split," or "fragmented." Divorced individuals may come to feel rejected by married friends and experience diminishing self-esteem.

Friends and family close to the couple can increase feelings of stigma by passing judgment and taking sides. As one divorced author describes it, "It's exhausting to be in the company of married people, with children or no. It forces me into a state of emergency alert, in which I have to rescue myself from interrogation and possible disgrace" (Rose, 1996, p. 82).

Private, intimate relationships are never solely one's own possession. In a sense, they also belong to other people—friends and family—who have a vested interest in their continuation. When people marry, they "marry" an entire network of others who often incorporate the relationship into their own sphere of activity. For instance, when family members plan future events, such as group vacations and holiday celebrations, they typically assume that the couple can be counted on to participate as a couple. Hence, a divorce requires the ending of associations with others who also have a strong investment in the relationship.

Divorce and Children

Although divorce is certainly difficult for the adults going through it, most adjust after a couple of years. However, about half of the divorces that occur each year involve couples with minor children (Amato, 2000), who have a more difficult time with divorce. Divorce sets a series of changes in motion with the potential to seriously disrupt children's lives.

A substantial body of research shows that regardless of race or education of parents, children raised in single-parent homes tend to fare worse at every stage of life than children from intact, two-parent families. An extensive review of studies published during the 1990s found that children from divorced families suffer in terms of academic success, psychological adjustment, self-concept, social competence, and long-term health (Amato, 2000). In adulthood, they are at greater risk of low socioeconomic attainment and increased marital difficulties and divorce.

Some scholars have suggested there may be a "divorce inheritance." People who experience parental divorce appear to face a greater likelihood of divorce when they become adults, perhaps because they fail to learn from their divorced parents the conflict resolution skills that can be used in their own relationships (Diekmann & Engelhardt, 1999). Others have found that individuals who came from families where parents stayed together but fought a lot (and arguably lacked good conflict resolution skills) *thought* of divorce more often than those whose parents didn't fight much. But the children of battling parents were less likely than the children of divorced parents to actually divorce (Amato, 2001).

Children's Adjustment to Divorce

Because of the possibility that children's lives will be permanently affected by divorce, researchers have devoted a great deal of energy to investigating the factors that determine how well children will adjust. If we could just figure out the answers, perhaps we could create programs or policies that would help minimize the damage. Maybe we should prevent parents from splitting up; maybe we should help custodial parents do a better job; maybe we shouldn't do anything at all. Unfortunately, the answers to these sensitive questions remain elusive.

The research indicates that how well children adjust to their parents' divorce depends on a lot of things, such as the children's gender, age at the time of separation, duration of life in a single-parent household after the divorce, and so on. Furthermore, the way the children were raised, the economic resources available to them, their sense of emotional security, their enduring relationships with parents or other caring adults, and the amount of supervision they continue to receive can also influence their postdivorce adjustment. No one set of circumstances dooms children to a life of hardship or, for that matter, guarantees that they will come through the divorce experience trouble free.

In an attempt to bring some order to this confusion, sociologist Paul Amato (1993, 2000) has identified five perspectives from which pundits and policymakers seem to view the postdivorce adjustment of children:

- The *parental loss perspective* assumes that a family with both parents living in the same household as the child is *always* a better environment for the child's development than a single-parent household. According to this perspective, both mothers and fathers are crucial sources of guidance, support, information, practical assistance, and supervision. The presence of two adults jointly conducting daily life helps children learn how to cooperate, negotiate, and compromise. Moreover, most children anticipate that they will grow up in homes with a mother and a father. They tend to see themselves as members of a family defined by who lives together (Seltzer, 1994). Most children of divorce are also assumed to suffer from the lack of contact with the noncustodial parent and from the reduction in contact with the custodial parent, whose need to work to support the household decreases the amount of time and energy devoted to the child. According to this perspective, anxiety, depression, and disruptive behavior are to be expected during children's short-term adjustment to divorce.

- The *parental adjustment perspective* focuses on the importance of the psychological adjustment of the custodial parent. This perspective assumes that divorced parents who are supportive of their children and exert moderate control over them tend to enhance the development and well-being of their children. Divorce, however, is a highly stressful process that can decrease a parent's ability to parent and may ultimately jeopardize the well-being of children (Amato, 2000). Some research has found that during the first year after a divorce, custodial mothers were more anxious, depressed, and angry than were married mothers (cited in Amato, 1993). Although the differences in stress between divorced and married women tend to diminish over time, they still remain significant 2 or 3 years after the divorce (Lorenz, Simons, Conger, Elder, Johnson, & Chao, 1997).

- The *parental conflict perspective* suggests that children whose parents ultimately divorce are usually exposed to parents' conflict before separation, during it, and often afterward. Children may react to their parents' conflict with fear, anger, and distress, or they may be drawn into the conflict and forced to take sides. In some cases, children blame themselves for their parents' fighting. Parental conflict may also have indirect effects on children. Parents who are preoccupied with their own problems may be inattentive to their children's needs. During the divorce they may be unable to comfort their children because of their own pain and anger (Seltzer, 1994). From this perspective, conflict and not parental separation is assumed to have the most damaging effects on children. Conversely, children whose divorced parents get along well will do far better than children whose parents remain married but fight like cats and dogs.

- The *economic hardship perspective* assumes that the monetary problems brought about by divorce are most responsible for the problems children face. Money may not buy happiness, but children cannot adjust very easily if they don't have enough to eat or a safe place to live following the divorce. Even if they're not poor, children whose parents separate and who live with their mothers experience, on average, about a 21 percent reduction in family income when their father moves out and sets up a second household (Seltzer, 1994). The economic hardships of divorce can affect children's health and nutrition and their access to books, toys, computers, and other things that can enhance school success. Limited financial resources may force single mothers and their children to live in poorer neighborhoods. Economic deprivation is also associated with frequent residential moves and tense emotional environments.

- The *divorce-stress-adjustment perspective* combines elements of these perspectives, especially the parental adjustment and the parental conflict perspectives, into a single model that highlights the role stress plays. According to this perspective, it is the stress associated with uncoupling and divorce that increases the risk of emotional, behavioral and health problems for children (and adults). As parents begin to uncouple, perhaps years before the legal divorce occurs, intensified marital conflict can lead to children's behavioral problems. When the marriage is ending and during the postdivorce period, children experience more stress because of such factors as less effective parenting from their custodial parent, decreased involvement with their noncustodial parent, moves to new homes, changes of schools, additional parental marriages, decline in economic well-being or ongoing parental conflict. Thus, it is the stress related to divorce, not the divorce itself, that impacts children's well-being. Personal resilience and social support can mitigate the negative effects of divorce.

Amato found that the perspective with the strongest and most convincing support is the parental conflict model, although evidence exists to support each of them. He concludes that most of the behavioral problems that children of divorce exhibit are caused not by the divorce itself but by exposure to conflict between ex-spouses. If one looks at those kids whose married parents are unhappy or are frequently embroiled in conflict, one finds just as many problems as in children of divorce (Furstenberg & Cherlin, 1991).

Furthermore, divorce may only exacerbate some children's existing behavioral and emotional problems (Cherlin, Chase-Landale, & McRae, 1998). One study of children's lives repeatedly surveyed a panel of several thousand U.S. and British children over 4 to 5 years (Cherlin, Furstenberg, Chase-Landale, Kiernan, Robins, Morrison, & Teitler, 1991). The researchers did find that the children whose parents separated or divorced showed more behavior problems at home and behaved worse in school than children whose parents remained married. However, when they looked back at the results from the beginning of their surveys, the researchers found that the children, particularly boys, whose parents were married at the beginning of the study but would later divorce were already showing behavioral problems *well before* the actual divorce occurred. In short, much of the effect of divorce on children can be predicted by conditions that exist before the parents actually separate. Of course, it is possible that divorce was indirectly responsible for these behavioral problems if children were picking up on the stress of parents' "uncoupling," which could have begun years earlier than the actual physical separation (Amato, 2000).

However, even after taking into account possible "predisruption effects," children who had experienced a parental divorce tended to suffer greater mental health problems as adults. Andrew Cherlin and his associates found that, although the differences between these two groups were not great at age 11, the gap widened over time. By age 33, those who had experienced a parental divorce tended to suffer more from problems such as depression and anxiety than did those whose parents had not divorced. The researchers suggest that "the long-term effect [of divorce] may emerge only in adolescence or young adulthood" (Cherlin et al.,

1998, p. 247). They hypothesize that parental divorce may trigger early childbearing, limited education, and other choices that could affect children's well-being in adulthood.

Most of the research on children and divorce focuses entirely on the negative effects of parental divorce. But some studies suggest that divorce can have positive effects. For instance, children, especially daughters, often develop very close relationships with their custodial mothers after the divorce (Arditti, 1999). Postdivorce relationships in which mothers rely on children for emotional support and advice, can contribute to greater equality and closeness:

> My relationship with my mother was just mediocre (before the divorce). After the divorce, things have changed in the sense that there's much more equality between the two of us. Before, it was always me crying on my mom's shoulder, and now it's me crying on my mom's shoulder and my mom cries on my shoulder. (quoted in Arditti, 1999, p. 114)

Other studies have found that children can benefit from the divorce, especially when the marriage was characterized by a great deal of conflict (Booth & Amato, 2001). Furthermore, when children maintain a good relationship with both their parents after a divorce, the negative effects of the breakup can be minimized.

Custody Decisions

Custody decisions—determining where children will live on a day-to-day basis after the divorce (**physical custody**) and who will make the major religious, medical, and educational decisions in their lives (**legal custody**) are frequently the most painful and contentious issues in divorces in our society. But this isn't the case worldwide: The decision of who controls the child after a divorce is irrelevant in *patrilineal societies*, where children always belong to the husband and the husband's family, and in *matrilineal societies*, where they belong to the wife and her kin. However, in *bilateral descent systems*, such as in the United States, both sides of the family have an equal claim on the child. His or her well-being depends on the relationship between both parents.

Providing emotional and economic security for children is a significant challenge in nuclear family systems. From the child's point of view, part of his or her extended family disappears when the marriage ends (Friedman, 1995). Certainly kin and even close non-kin remain deeply attached to children and make significant contributions to their well-being after the divorce. But nothing beyond affection *compels* these contributions. It's ultimately the divorced parents who must guarantee the well-being of their children.

So the most difficult problem in divorced families in the United States is determining which parent ought to have primary responsibility for the child and ensuring that both parents continue to contribute to the child's well-being after the divorce. Unfortunately, most children have relatively little contact with their noncustodial parents. Moreover, the majority of noncustodial parents don't or can't pay the full amount of court-ordered child support. Even the parent who retains custody often reduces his or her contribution to the child after a divorce. Remarriage, for instance, involves time spent dating and courting, investing emotional energy in another adult who has no abiding incentive to contribute to the child, and perhaps even having additional children with the new partner. All these things direct attention, time, and resources away from the child of the first marriage (Friedman, 1995).

Sole Custody   When custody is granted solely to one or the other parent, it is typically granted to the parent who was the primary caretaker before the divorce. The logic of granting **sole custody** to the primary caretaker rests on two principles: (1) It provides continuity for children. The person who provided the most care during the marriage should do so after the marriage. (2) It fairly rewards the parent who has devoted the most time and energy to the child during the marriage.

Today, even though changes in divorce laws over the years have supposedly eliminated sex-based preferences in custody decisions, mothers end up with sole custody in 80 to 90 percent of divorce cases (Fox & Kelly, 1995; Maccoby & Mnookin, 1992). It's important to note that the majority of these cases are agreed to by both parents without any court intervention. In other words, the vast majority of fathers *don't seek* custody of their children.

The fact that fathers tend not to request custody of their children reflects a cultural presumption (discussed in Chapter 8) that, under normal circumstances, mothers are more crucial to their children's development than fathers (Friedman, 1995). Questions about child custody are usually posed as if the mother already has custody and therefore must be determined competent to keep it. In other words, at the time of divorce the court essentially decides whether children *will remain* in their mother's care and control or be taken from her, wholly or partially. In effect, custody "is hers to lose."

Lesbian mothers present the one exception to this maternal custody assumption. Although some states have laws stipulating that sexual orientation should not be an issue in custody disputes, in other states parents who identify themselves as homosexual are automatically presumed to be unfit parents. In 1993 a 25-year-old Richmond, Virginia, woman lost custody of her son—to whom she gave birth while in a heterosexual marriage—when a judge ruled that homosexuality (the woman now lived with her lesbian partner) made her an unfit parent. The woman's mother (the child's grandmother) had sued for custody and won. In 1995 the Virginia Supreme Court upheld the judge's ruling, stating that "active lesbianism practiced in the home" could stigmatize the child and "inevitably afflict the child's relationships with its peers and with the community" ("Lesbian's appeal," 1995, p. 6). The court said that although lesbianism in and of itself didn't disqualify the mother, homosexual conduct is a felony under Virginia law and thus is an important factor in determining custody. The mother was given visitation rights, but the child is not allowed to go to her apartment and is not allowed to have any contact with the mother's partner.

The "Preference" for Maternal Custody   Maternal custody is such a dominant arrangement today that it seems inconceivable that mothers have not always been the preferred parent in divorce cases. Yet up until the early twentieth century, the law actually presumed *paternal custody*. Children were clearly defined as the property of their fathers. In fact, women were often considered legal dependents themselves and therefore couldn't even be awarded custody of children in the event of a husband's death.

But during a span of 40 years—roughly between 1880 and 1920—the presumption that divorced fathers should be granted custody of their children changed throughout the United States. The change was dramatic, as illustrated in the different language of these two custody decisions, the first from 1842 and the second from 1916:

> We are informed by the first elementary books we read, that the authority of the father is superior to that of the mother. . . . It is according to the revealed law, the law of nature, and it prevails even with the wandering savage, who has received none of the lights of civilization.

Mother love is a dominant trait in even the weakest of women, and as a general thing surpasses the paternal affection for the common offspring, and, moreover, a child needs a mother's care even more than a father's. For these reasons courts are loathe to deprive the mother of the custody of her children, and will not do so unless it be shown clearly that she is so far an unfit and improper person to be intrusted [sic] with custody as to endanger the welfare of the children. (both quoted in Friedman, 1995, p. 18)

Changing attitudes toward the proper role of mothers and fathers are also discussed in Chapter 8.

Sociologist Debra Friedman (1995) provides a provocative account of why such a dramatic change in child rearing philosophy occurred when it did. Up until the mid-1800s, when divorce was relatively infrequent, deciding whether a mother or a father should get custody of a child was rarely an issue. The vast majority of marriages ended when one or the other spouse died. If a mother died, the father obviously retained custody. Only if a father died without appointing a guardian for his children would the courts step in to determine where the child should live.

As divorce became more common, however, courts found themselves having to make child custody decisions between two living parents. At the time, it was assumed that fathers were responsible for raising and educating children. Fathers were simply called on to continue honoring those obligations in the event of a divorce; hence the presumption of paternal custody. Notice that these custody decisions were made not in the child's "best interest" but in terms of the father's legal obligation and *entitlement* to custody of his minor children.

Rising divorce rates at the turn of the century put pressure on these laws. New state laws enacted in the early twentieth century established the court's power to use its discretion in child custody matters. Depending on the state, the laws suggested that judges consider the age and sex of the child, the safety, well-being, happiness, comfort, and spiritual health of the child, or the character of the parents. Decisions were based on considerations of child welfare, not parents' rights or obligations. But what exactly constituted children's well-being? Did the benefits of mothers' nurturing outweigh the benefits of fathers' material resources?

At this point, fathers and mothers had equal claims to custody. However, as the sphere of influence for women (especially middle-class women) became restricted to the home, and men's sphere of influence became the workplace (see Chapter 7), fathers began to have less contact with their children and mothers began to play a more active and exclusive role in raising them. At the same time, children were seen less as economic assets that men wanted to control and more as individuals who required significant care, emotional attention, and training to become useful and valuable adults (Friedman, 1995; Zelizer, 1985). Because most fathers were busy elsewhere, the task fell to mothers. So important was this task that motherhood was redefined from a "part-time job" to a "noble calling" (Ehrenreich & English, 1979).

This new conception of motherhood and female domesticity led to a sense that some attention ought to be paid to mothers' claims to custody. If they were assumed to be the superior parent within marriage, they should also be considered the superior parent when the marriage ended. The irony, of course, is that women, even relatively privileged women, were finding they had no way of supporting themselves financially after a divorce, let alone supporting a child or several children.

The old laws favoring fathers made some sense: Fathers of that era were, after all, better able to provide financially for their children than mothers were. Without a paternal prefer- ence in custody decisions, however, fathers were no longer obligated to provide for their children. Thus a dilemma arose: If mothers were to be granted custody, how could fathers be compelled to pay for the care of their estranged children?

By 1930, all but four states had policies designed to address the economic plight of *wid- ows* and their children. It would seem a short step to extend these financial benefits to *di- vorced mothers* and their children. However, widowhood was considered to be a state outside the control of women, whereas divorce was often associated with moral failure. Legislators were reluctant to tell taxpayers to subsidize what many considered an immoral act.

So most states focused on enforcing noncustodial fathers' obligation to provide finan- cial support for their children and the mothers of their children after a divorce. When fa- thers were granted custody, they were obligated to provide only for their children; their ex- spouses were left to fend for themselves. Thus states had a clear economic rationale for presuming maternal custody. It prevented what could otherwise become a severe public burden: providing welfare to both divorced mothers and their children.

In sum, the change from paternal to maternal preference in custody cases did not occur because fathers had suddenly become unable or unwilling to fulfill their parental obliga- tions or because mothers had suddenly become more deserving. Instead, maternal custody represented an effective solution to several societal problems:

- Maternal custody increased the probability that private individuals (that is, noncusto- dial fathers) and not society would pay to support two dependents rather than one.
- Maternal custody put off any efforts by women to claim they had a right to equal pay and employment opportunities. As long as divorced mothers had their estranged husbands to support them, they would have a weak argument for expanding their ac- cess to jobs.
- Maternal custody was favored by both conservatives and liberal feminists (Friedman, 1995): Conservatives favored it because it reduced the welfare obligations of the state; feminists, because it lowered the cost of divorce for women by compelling ex-husbands to subsidize them.

Joint Custody   Over the past few decades, the preference for sole maternal custody has been challenged. Popular child-rearing ideologies now emphasize the importance of *both* parents in a child's life. More fathers than ever are actively seeking shared time with their children and joint decision making on issues such as religious upbringing, education, and health matters. At the same time, more mothers than ever are in the paid labor force and find themselves balancing the practical demands of work and home. Consequently, **joint custody** considerations are becoming more common (Hochman, 1997).

Joint custody policies vary from state to state. In certain states the judge can consider joint custody only when both parents request it; in others, judges can award it when only one parent has asked for it. In most states—twenty-nine as of 1999—judges are required to consider joint custody as the *preferred* custody arrangement. In a few states, joint custody is mandated unless one or the other parent proves that this type of custody would be detri- mental to the child (Flynn, 1991).

Joint custody takes two forms: legal and physical. Joint *legal* custody recognizes the rights of both parents to make major decisions affecting the child's life. Although a variety of living arrangements are possible under joint legal custody, such children usually live with their mothers. Under joint *physical* custody, not only do parents share decision making, but they also share in the physical care of the child. Although the division of responsibilities need not be exactly equal, the child lives alternately for major periods of time with each parent.

Joint custody appears to be the equitable solution to the problem of a child's contact with one parent being curtailed after a divorce. Even when the actual physical custody of the child isn't shared, joint legal custody ensures that each parent maintains some interest in the child and some control over decisions that affect the child's well-being. With joint custody, neither parent needs to be considered a "winner" or a "loser." No one parent's rights are superior to the other's. The intent is to approximate an intact family as much as possible.

Proponents of joint custody believe that shared parenting negates the detrimental effects of the absence of one parent (usually the father). The child's deep sense of loss will be significantly lessened.

This position suggests, however, that parents whose antagonism and incompatibility were severe enough to end their marriage will suddenly be able to work together, in harmony, to decide the best path to raising their children. According to one study, only one out of four divorced couples who were granted joint custody were able to cooperate fully in raising the child (Maccoby & Mnookin, 1992). More commonly, parents continue to fight with each other or develop a pattern of "parallel parenting," wherein the child is shared but the parents don't cooperate at all (Furstenberg & Nord, 1985).

Thus, opponents of joint custody argue that it undermines the continuity and stability that are essential to the child's adjustment. Shuffling back and forth between two parents and two households with different authority figures and different values can be confusing and unsettling.

In addition, the demands of joint custody may restrict the mobility of a parent. He or she may have to forgo a career advancement if it means moving to another city or involves changes that would otherwise interfere with the shared-parenting arrangement.

Research on the effects of joint custody is mixed. Mothers in joint custody arrangements tend to report better relationships with their former spouses, better interactions with them involving child-rearing decisions, and greater levels of emotional support for parenting than mothers with sole custody (Arditti & Madden-Derdich, 1997). Mothers with sole custody tend to show greater parenting stress than joint custody mothers, even though they don't report feeling more burdened and are actually more satisfied with their custody arrangements. Their children might be a major source of stress, but they're also a source of happiness and satisfaction. Sole custody allows women to exercise greater control over child rearing and is also more consistent with society's traditional view of mother as primary caregiver. Perhaps because of those social norms, joint custody mothers may believe that their status somehow reflects negatively on their capabilities as a mother.

Some children in joint custody arrangements seem to appreciate the contact with both parents and the "change of pace" it allows. Others, however, report feeling "torn apart" by the arrangement, especially as they get older. In short, no evidence suggests that joint custody is always best for children, but neither has anyone found evidence that it is more harmful than traditional sole custody.

Joint custody does tend to cause more problems for families when the state mandates the arrangement than when both parents agree it would be best for the child. Because of these problems, some states (for instance, California) have removed the legal preference for joint custody. It seems, then, that children and parents would be better served through policies that make joint custody an available option to those who want it rather than a legal presumption (Flynn, 1991).

The "Same-Sex" Preference   As preference for maternal custody declines and joint custody arrangements become more popular, it has become tempting to search for some type of objective criterion on which to base custody decisions. The same-sex preference is one such standard that has become popular in recent years (Powell & Downey, 1997). In these cases, judges attempt to match children with the same-sex parent. In some cases, siblings have been separated so that sons can live with their fathers and daughters with their mothers.

The typical reasoning behind such decisions is that children, especially adolescents, need a same-sex model to help them become well-adjusted adults. An Illinois judge, for instance, justified his decision to award custody to the same-sex parent as follows: "The court finds . . . , other things being equal, pre-adolescent children and adolescent young people derive substantial benefit from the close personal relationships with the same sex parents to whom they look for a model" (quoted in Powell & Downey, 1997, p. 523).

However, such an advantage may be overstated. Sociologists Brian Powell and Douglas Downey (1997) tested the "same-sex preference" hypothesis using data from the 1990 National Education Longitudinal Study. They examined 386 teenage girls and boys who lived in single-father households and 2,047 who lived in single-mother households. After reviewing more than 70 variables related to children's well-being—including self-concept, relationships, school outcomes, parental involvement, and deviance—they found virtually no evidence of a same-sex benefit. Only three behaviors were significantly different for girls living with fathers compared to those living with mothers—and one (teenage birth) was in the *opposite* direction predicted by the same-sex preference hypothesis. That is, living with the same-sex parent increased teenage girls' risk of giving birth. For boys, only the likelihood of dropping out of school increased when boys lived with mothers.

The Father Role After Divorce

Despite the growing interest in joint custody, maternal physical custody continues to be the most common arrangement. Usually the father is required to pay child support and receives some visitation rights in return—typically the opportunity to take the child out of the mother's home for a few days each week or month. However, this arrangement seldom works well. Divorced mothers sometimes complain that they do not receive the child support payments mandated by the divorce courts. Noncustodial fathers often complain that their visitation rights are inadequate to begin with or are abused by the mother. Society as a whole, which is redefining the father's role in family life, frets that children of divorce growing up without a father's support and influence will suffer long-term harm. People therefore struggle to develop policies that will keep fathers involved—at least financially. But should society insist on fathers' obligations without also protecting some of their rights? Many divorced fathers don't think so.

Child Support Policies   As you've seen, women and children tend to be economically disadvantaged by divorce. One key reason is the inadequacy of court-ordered child support payments. Even more problematic is the failure on the part of many noncustodial parents to pay court-ordered child support. In almost two-thirds of divorces, fathers are required to pay child support (Grall, 2000). Of these, 40 percent pay the full amount, 30 percent pay a partial amount, and 30 percent pay nothing (U.S. Bureau of the Census, 2000b). More than half of divorced mothers with custody of children therefore don't receive the financial assistance they need. And this figure doesn't account for never-married single mothers who receive no financial assistance from the child's father. Award rates are especially low for African-American and Hispanic women, who are likely to suffer from a higher poverty rate to begin with (Grall, 2000). Although custodial mothers suffer economically more than custodial fathers, it is important to note that noncustodial mothers are actually more delinquent in paying child support than are noncustodial fathers.

One key problem seems to be the ineffectiveness or lack of enforcement procedures in child support cases. The kinds of policies that were developed to "take care of" children in single-parent families focused originally on children of widows. In 1960 single-parent families consisted of almost as many widowed parents as divorced parents. But since then the proportion of children living with a widowed parent has dropped considerably, whereas the proportion of children of divorced or never-married parents has increased (see Exhibit 11.5). The courts for the most part, have been ill equipped to deal with these situations.

Up until the 1970s, most states left much discretion to judges and families in setting child support standards, and they had virtually no strategies in place to enforce payment.

EXHIBIT 11.5

*Parent's
Marital Status
in Single-Parent
Households*

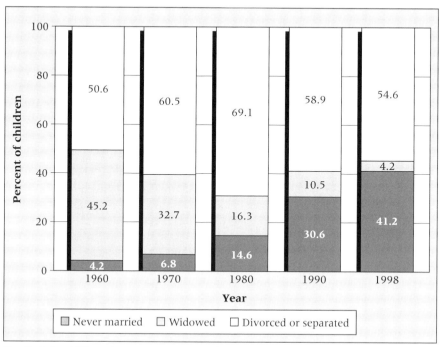

Note: Excludes children whose parents are married with spouse absent, unless parents are separated.
Data sources: U.S. Bureau of the Census. 1998d. Unpublished tables: Marital status and living arrangements: March 1998 (Update), Table A. P20-514. Available at http://www.census.gov/ prod/99pubs/p20-514u.pdf. Accessed June 1, 2001. A. Saluter. 1996. "Marital status and living arrangements: March 1994." U.S. Bureau of the Census, *Current Population Report,* Series P20-484. Washington, DC.

In 1975 Congress created the federal Office of Child-Support Enforcement and required states to establish similar offices to assist in collecting support. However, these agencies had little enforcement power. So in 1984 Congress enacted the Child-Support Enforcement Amendment, which not only required states to set standards for support awards but also mandated such enforcement techniques as withholding money from fathers' paychecks after a history of nonpayment (Klawitter, 1994). This policy targeted unmarried parents as well as divorced parents. However, because determining the identity of the biological father in the case of nonmarital births is often difficult and frequently unsuccessful, these cases became a low priority.

Despite these governmental efforts, a report from the Department of Health and Human Services shows that delinquent parents still shirk court orders in four of every five cases (Clymer, 1997). Thus, some legislators have proposed more dramatic solutions.

In 1996 the Department of Health and Human Services (DHHS) established a national databank of parents who avoid paying court-imposed child support. Officials can now reach across state lines to seize "deadbeat" parents' property (homes, cars, and so forth), garnish wages, and secure money directly from a checking account even if located in another state. In 1997 the federal government began operating a computer directory showing every person newly hired by every employer in the country so that investigators can track down noncustodial parents who move from state to state while owing money to their children. More than 30 percent of the 19 million child support cases in this country are thought to involve parents who don't live in the same state as their children (Pear, 1997).

The DHHS also requires poor mothers to provide the names of their children's fathers and other identifying information before they can receive welfare benefits. Those who refuse do not receive payments, although the policy provides an exception for women who can't identify the father or who are afraid of physical abuse. The goal of the policy, according to then-President Clinton, is not to punish mothers but to enforce fathers' responsibility to contribute to their children: "We're not going to just let you walk away from your children and stick the taxpayers with the tab. We have to make responsibility a way of life, not an option" (quoted in "President tells mothers," 1996, p. 27).

This approach may have a lot of appeal, but simply forcing noncustodial parents to pay more child support may not be a perfect solution to the economic problems associated with divorce. Low-income custodial mothers tend to be associated with low-income noncustodial fathers, who may struggle to provide even for themselves. Indeed, the amount of child support awarded to low-income women is lower than that for other women and remains low relative to the costs of raising children (Klawitter, 1994). Stricter support policies may eventually narrow the differences in award rates for custodial mothers at various income levels, but they are unlikely to significantly alter the poverty rates of low-income women.

DEMO•GRAPHICS

Deadbeat Moms?

There has been much discussion in recent years of "deadbeat dads"—noncustodial fathers who fail to pay child support. In purely numeric terms, noncustodial parents who are delinquent in child support are predominantly male. After all, in 1997 about 85 percent of custodial parents—nearly 12 million—were mothers. Thus the extensive organizational and governmental efforts to collect child support from delinquent fathers are warranted on one level. But women are actually less likely to fulfill their child support agreements than men.

As you can see in Exhibit 11.6a, of those parents awarded child support, fewer custodial fathers (31.6 percent) than mothers (41.9 percent) received the full payment of awards they were due. Note too that there's been a steady increase in the percentage of custodial mothers receiving full payments, but the percentage of custodial fathers who receive full payment has remained about the same.

It's also interesting that a larger number of custodial mothers are awarded child support than custodial fathers. In 1997, about 60 percent of custodial mothers were awarded child support, compared to 38 percent of custodial fathers. This marked a *decline* for custodial fathers since 1993 (see Exhibit 11.6b). In addition, in 1997 the average annual child support amount awarded to custodial mothers was more than that for custodial fathers ($4,172 versus $3,965) (Grall, 2000).

How can these gender differences in child support be explained? In some cases, women resist a reversal of the traditional arrangement, in which the father pays the mother. A woman paying child support to her ex-husband may feel she is being punished for being a bad mother, which for many in this society is a grave insult indeed. The answer to the question of "deadbeat moms," however, most likely lies in understanding who has the greater need for child support payments and the greater ability to finance a household. Custodial fathers' income tends to be, on average, nearly twice that of custodial mothers, regardless of whether or not child support was awarded or paid (see Exhibit 11.6c). Because women's earning power throughout society is significantly less than men's, many women may simply be less able to afford to pay child support than men. Hence, fathers' failure to pay child support probably has a much more devastating effect on children's lives than does mothers' failure to pay, because custodial fathers have relatively high incomes.

Mothers' delinquency in paying court-ordered child support is a problem. However, gender differences in child support payments often reflect women's economic realities following divorce, not simply a stubborn refusal to go along with a court order that defies tradition. And whether "deadbeat" parents are fathers or mothers, people do well to remember that the resulting economic difficulties will, of course, ultimately be felt by the children.

Thinking Critically About the Statistics

1. Judging from the data in Exhibit 11.6a, do you think the campaign to collect child support from fathers has been successful? Given the higher percentage of noncustodial mothers who fail to pay child support, is the campaign to collect support from fathers warranted?

2. Over the past decade or so, fathers have taken a more active role in raising their children. There are more single fathers than ever before. Yet Exhibit 11.6b shows a shrinking proportion of custodial fathers who are awarded child support. How might you explain this trend? Note also that a significant proportion of custodial parents are not awarded any child support at all. What are some of the personal and societal reasons why child support might not be legally granted?

3. If you were to reconstruct Exhibit 11.6c so that all the numbers for custodial mothers were grouped together and all the numbers for custodial fathers were grouped together, what could you conclude about household income and the likelihood of receiving child

EXHIBIT 11.6

Gender, Child Custody, and Support Payments

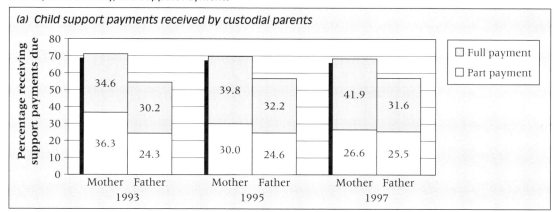

(a) Child support payments received by custodial parents

Data source: T. Grall. 2000. Child support for custodial mothers and fathers 1997, Figure 5. *Current Population Reports*, P60-212. Available at www.census.gov/prod/2000pubs/p60-212.pdf. Accessed May 1, 2001.

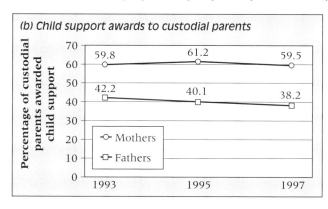

(b) Child support awards to custodial parents

Data source: T. Grall, 2000. Child support for custodial mothers and fathers 1997, Table A. *Current Population Reports*, P60-212. Available at www.census.gov/prod/2000pubs/p60-212.pdf. Accessed May 1, 2001.

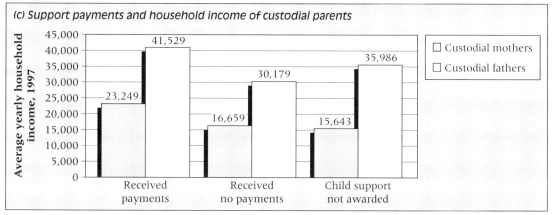

(c) Support payments and household income of custodial parents

Data source: T. Grall. 2000. Child support for custodial mothers and fathers 1997, Table B. *Current Population Reports*, P60-212. Available at www.census.gov/prod/2000pubs/p60-212.pdf. Accessed May 1, 2001.

support for women and men? In other words, how does custodial mothers' income seem to relate to child support payments? How does custodial fathers' income relate to child support payments? How can you explain these patterns? ■

Absent Fathers Financial support isn't the only thing missing from the lives of many children whose parents are divorced. In general, noncustodial fathers tend to play only a minor role in their children's everyday lives. One national study found that half the children whose parents were divorced hadn't seen their fathers in the previous year, and only one out of six had regular, weekly contact with a noncustodial father. Children were most likely to see their fathers immediately after the separation. But after several years, contact dropped off sharply (Furstenberg & Nord, 1985). Another study found that 75 percent of noncustodial fathers never attend their child's school events, 85 percent never help them with homework, and 65 percent never take their children on vacations (Teachman, 1991).

Furthermore, fewer than one-third of divorced parents discuss their children with each other during a 12-month period, and just over 20 percent talk with each other weekly. Even among the estranged parents who do talk about their children, the level of fathers' participation in decision making is limited. Only about 17 percent have significant influence over health care matters, education, religion, and so forth (cited in Arendell, 1995).

What factors influence the frequency and nature of the contact that noncustodial fathers have with their children? One set of factors concerns events that occur *after* the divorce. For example, when fathers remarry, their contact tends to decrease because the new marriage is likely to impose new time constraints and added responsibilities. Divorced fathers are frequently more involved in the lives of their stepchildren than in the lives of their biological children (Stephens, 1996). The remarriage of custodial mothers may also diminish fathers' postdivorce contact because they may feel they've been replaced and view themselves as no longer needed by the children.

Another set of factors that may affect fathers' postdivorce contact with their children are socioeconomic factors. Better-educated fathers are more likely to be exposed to information emphasizing the importance of both parents in children's lives and therefore are likely to maintain significant, regular contact with their children after a divorce. Income may also be positively related to contact, because fathers cannot engage in costly activities (eating in restaurants, going to movies, going shopping, and so on) with their children during visitations if they don't have enough income. Noncustodial fathers must also have the financial resources to provide sufficient space (that is, an extra bedroom) and a duplicate set of child care equipment and toys for frequent contact to occur (Stephens, 1996).

But fathers' absence from their children's lives may also be a purposeful strategy designed to minimize discord with ex-spouses and, to some degree, the children themselves. Sociologist Terry Arendell (1992) interviewed seventy-five divorced men who had at least one minor child and had been divorced or separated for at least 18 months. She found that many fathers stay away from their children to avoid further conflicts and tensions with their ex-wives. Confrontations are especially likely to occur if the end of the marriage was antagonistic. Even though visitation arrangements are legally determined, they are often ambiguous and offer ample opportunity for dissatisfaction and conflict. Most fathers in Arendell's study insisted that their former wives had hindered their access to their children: Scheduled visits were denied, telephone conversations interrupted, messages not conveyed, mail intercepted and not given to the child, and so on. Nearly half the men Arendell interviewed had experienced going to pick up their child for a visit and finding no one at home.

To avoid all these conflicts, some men began to let more time elapse between contacts and visits. In fact, over half of the fathers who were fully absent from their children's lives became nonvisiting parents after a series of confrontations with their former wives.

Absence also served as a means of emotion management for Arendell's subjects. Fathers often felt the need to distance themselves from reminders of happier times and to limit their involvement in situations likely to evoke angry and hostile interactions and perhaps even outbursts of physical violence. Absence also served as a way to avoid unresolved feelings of loss and pain. One father indicated that his sporadic contacts with his son, as opposed to the routine daily contacts they had when the marriage was intact, produced feelings of such unbearable sorrow that he preferred not to see his son at all:

> Every time I pulled up to the driveway to let him off, it was like part of me was dying all over again. I could barely keep myself together long enough to give him a hug goodbye. . . . He would open the door, step out of the car, and I would feel as if I would never see him again. He would walk up the sidewalk and a sense of grief would utterly overcome me. It would take me several days to pull myself together enough to even function at work. I'd have to keep his bedroom door closed; I couldn't bear to see his empty room. I had to break it off totally just to survive; the visits themselves were terrible because I had this constant unease, knowing what was coming. (quoted in Arendell, 1992, p. 577)

Because seeing their children was usually defined as a "visit," and not as a routine part of everyday life, many noncustodial fathers in Arendell's study found their time with their children awkward and uncomfortable. Some sought primarily to entertain their children, with little attempt to establish a routine. Others were extremely anxious and uncertain about how to deal with their children without a mother present. These men probably had little experience dealing with their children during the marriage and were therefore confronted with a kind of on-the-job training with few guidelines. They were not familiar with how to negotiate parent–child interactions. As one father put it,

> I found that I really couldn't control my boys except by getting angry. They just argued and fought when they were around. Every visit was incredibly tense; we were like coiled rattlesnakes just waiting to strike. I'd end up losing my temper which just made it worse because they treated me like I had no right to punish them. (quoted in Arendell, 1992, p. 577)

For their part, the children could also indirectly make contact with their fathers uncomfortable. Some younger children actively resisted leaving their homes or their mothers, often crying and physically fighting against being taken by their fathers. Some fathers felt unappreciated or were blatantly rejected by their older children. Many of these children directed resentment over the change in their standard of living caused by the divorce toward their fathers. Others behaved "too formally" or "too well," as if they were "guests" during the visits. Fathers interpreted such behavior as the child's way of denying the parent–child relationship. Because many of the fathers were unwilling or uncertain about how to talk to their children about these problems, the tensions and feelings of rejection increased over time, making absence an even more viable response.

Most of the men in Arendell's study felt that their former wives could help make the visits less strained and less awkward by intervening with the children. Arendell points out that this expectation is an extension of the traditional marital division of labor, in which women are expected to be the emotional caretakers in the family. Men perceived former wives who refused to intervene as misusing their power to deliberately undermine post-divorce relationships with the children.

But contrary to popular images of absent fathers happy to be free from child-rearing responsibilities, the majority of absent fathers in Arendell's study were emotionally upset by the quality of their relationships with their children. They felt extremely isolated and were unable or unwilling to express their feelings about their children to others. Even men who had remarried felt reluctant to reveal the scope of their feelings to their present wives. Many noncustodial fathers had come to believe that *they* were the unrecognized emotional victims of divorce.

The sociological theories introduced in Chapter 1 give us several ways to understand these fathers' reactions. From a symbolic interactionist perspective, what it means to be a parent is radically altered after divorce. If a "parent" is defined as someone who interacts daily or nearly daily with children, who always looks after the children's well-being and provides continual emotional and financial resources, then one could argue that in a cultural sense, noncustodial parents cease to be parents. If fathers define themselves as "nonparents," they are likely to reduce their involvement in child rearing.

Social exchange theory would suggest that as relationships with their children become less rewarding, fathers are more likely to withdraw from the relationship. It would also follow from this perspective that if fathers remarry and form more rewarding relationships with their new families, their investment in their other children will necessarily decline. One theorist, Gary Becker (1981), further proposes that children are costly to parents because they reduce their remarriage prospects. Thus, not only are the rewards derived from the parent–child relationship likely to decline after divorce, but the relationship becomes more costly as well.

But conflict or feminist theorists would probably argue that the lack of paternal involvement is simply a logical extension of men's lack of investment in the private sphere. These patterns reinforce women's powerlessness in society at large by limiting custodial mothers' involvement in the labor force and their chances of remarriage.

The Fathers' Rights Movement   Many divorced men have begun to fight against what they perceive to be a gender-biased system that discriminates against them during divorce. Lost in the divorce proceedings, they argue, are their rights to fatherhood, discretionary control of their earnings, the exercise of family authority, and the ability to control and handle their own futures (Arendell, 1995). These men report feeling a significant lack of control over the divorce settlement process, leading to greater feelings of dissatisfaction and inequity than women experience (Sheets & Braver, 1996).

What's come to be known as the **fathers' rights movement** borrows the language of the women's movement, arguing that sole maternal custody is sexist and discriminatory, a denial of fathers' equal rights (Williams & Williams, 1995). The names of fathers' rights groups—such as Human Equality Action Resource Team (HEART), Fathers for Justice, and In Search of Justice, to name a few—convey the belief that fathers are being treated unfairly by the legal system. Noncustodial father characters in movies such as *Kramer vs. Kramer* and *Mrs. Doubtfire* have become symbols of the downtrodden, victimized divorced father whose love for his children is squashed at every turn by a gender-biased system unsympathetic to his situation.

The fathers' rights movement identifies several issues as sources of discrimination. One obvious issue is the maternal preference in custody. What fathers' rights groups don't acknowledge is that when fathers formally petition for sole or joint custody, they have a good chance of receiving it. In most cases *both* parents agree that the mothers ought to have sole custody. When pressed, the majority of fathers admit that they don't want sole custody but want liberal, unrestricted access to their children. Few want to have responsibility for their children's everyday care but essentially want to continue the traditional parenting role they held prior to the divorce. In fact, one father went so far as to say that taking on 1 percent of the child care responsibilities would constitute "shared parenting" (Bertoia & Drakich, 1993).

Another issue that concerns the fathers' rights movement is mothers' power to control their children's activities after divorce. Even in cases of joint legal custody, mothers usually decide what schools children attend, what events they participate in, and what doctors, friends, and relatives they see. The loss of control fathers feel is reinforced by their limited access to their children. The change may be very distressing, particularly for men who were either used to exerting power in the family setting or deeply involved in their children's lives before the divorce.

Finally, the fathers' rights movement claims that mothers have often been awarded unjust child support payments. Fathers who pay support resent that they have no way of monitoring how the money is spent. For lower-class fathers in particular, the payments may be a real financial burden, severely affecting a lifestyle that was never particularly comfortable even when they were married. Fathers paying support feel especially victimized when their physical access to their children is limited.

The fathers' rights movement has been somewhat successful in addressing the complaints of noncustodial fathers. As you've seen, in most states, joint custody is becoming the preferred option in divorce settlements. And although single-parent families headed by men are still relatively uncommon, the proportion of such families doubled between 1980 and 1998 (U.S. Census Bureau, 2000b). In some states, judges are forbidding custodial mothers to move out of the state if relocation would make it harder for fathers to see their children. Mothers who fail to produce children for scheduled visits may now face criminal charges or lose custody outright to the father. In other states, fathers who are willing to spend extra time caring for their children—which may include setting up separate bedrooms in their homes, paying for meals, buying them clothes, and taking them to the movies—may be able to reduce their child support payments (Hoffman, 1995). In 1995 the New Jersey Commission to Study the Law of Divorce recommended laws to ensure that parents without custody see their children more often and have a greater say in how they are raised. For instance, it recommended that noncustodial parents have access to children's medical and school records and that a parent who prevents the other from seeing the children be fined.

Women's groups counter that such sanctions are not evenhanded. No similar effort is being made against fathers who don't show up for scheduled visits, and no state restricts a noncustodial father from moving away from his children. Furthermore, they argue that increasing noncustodial fathers' access to children has the potential for creating more strife between ex-spouses. In fact, some cynically note that the fathers' rights movement is less interested in keeping divorced fathers involved in their children's lives than in reducing their support payments.

The bitterness of the debate between men's and women's groups mirrors the bitterness of the debate between many divorcing couples. Once again you see the high level of emotion attending any discussion of children in this pronatalist society (see Chapter 8). Chances are that both sides share some blame and deserve some consideration. What is perhaps needed at a societal level, as has been more common recently at the individual level, is less focus on the rights of fathers and mothers and more focus on the needs of children.

Remarriage and Stepfamilies

The contentious issues surrounding divorce and custody can become even more difficult when former spouses remarry and start new families. Close to half of all marriages today involve at least one partner who was previously married, compared to about one in three in 1970 (U.S. Bureau of the Census, 2000b). Overall, 75 percent of divorced individuals in this country are likely to remarry eventually (cited in Coleman, Ganong, & Fine, 2000). These statistics suggest that although people are quite willing these days to escape a bad marriage, they have not necessarily given up on the concept of marriage. Remarriages that occur in mid-life (that is, after age 40) appear to be more stable than first marriages (Wu & Penning, 1997), but overall the divorce rate for second marriages is higher than the divorce rate for first marriages. Thirty-seven percent of remarriages collapse within the first 10 years, compared to 30 percent of first marriages (Sweet & Bumpass, 1987).

Until the 1960s, the divorce rate and the remarriage rate in the United States rose and fell in tandem. In the 1960s, 75 percent of divorced women and about 80 percent of divorced men remarried. Today, only about 67 percent of divorced women and 75 percent of divorced men remarry (Cherlin & Furstenberg, 1994). But this decline in remarriage is deceptive. At the same time that remarriage rates have decreased, the number of cohabiting couples has increased. Many previously married individuals are not abandoning their desire to live with someone. Instead, many have substituted cohabitation for remarriage.

The Complexities of Stepfamilies

Approximately one in five families today is a stepfamily, and one in four children will spend some time in a such a family (Furstenberg & Cherlin, 1991). Furthermore, 15 percent of all children in divorced families may see the parent they live with remarry and redivorce before they reach 18 (cited in Chira, 1995). This figure is likely to be an underestimate, because it doesn't include couples who live together instead of remarrying. It also doesn't include the nearly one-third of U.S. children who are born to unmarried mothers, many of whom will see their families form, split, re-form, and split again and again.

Remarriage has been described as an "incomplete institution" (Cherlin, 1978), meaning that it lacks the guiding norms, values, and role expectations that first marriages typically have. People have no set of common expectations for relationships between former and current spouses, between stepparents and stepchildren, between step- and half-siblings, and with extended kin following remarriage (Ahrons & Rodgers, 1987). Laws and customs have been slow to catch up to the growing frequency of remarriage. For instance, do stepchildren have legal claims to their stepparents' property? Do incest rules apply to step-siblings?

Issue 1 examines the conflict between the way the government officially defines family and the way individuals informally determine who they consider to be members of their families.

Remarriage creates ties that cross traditional household boundaries. The kinship relationships it produces can be complex and confusing, because they involve original parents (biological or adoptive), stepparents, biological siblings, step-siblings, half-siblings, multiple grandparents, and a seemingly infinite number of aunts, uncles, and cousins. Family alliances can become improvised and unpredictable when remarriage, redivorce, and cohabitation are blended into the mix. If you asked the individuals in a stepfamily who they considered to be in their family, you'd likely get a different response from every one of them. One-third of children in stepfamilies don't mention their stepparent as part of their family; 10 percent don't mention a biological parent (Furstenberg & Cherlin, 1991).

Step-Siblings

Much of the tension in stepfamilies comes from the relationship between step-siblings, who may be asked to share bedrooms or other possessions. If one part of the stepfamily is moving into the home of the other, such sharing may be perceived as an intrusion. Furthermore, children may have a difficult time overcoming the tendency to divide the family into "us" and "them." They often see their connection to their biological parent as giving them a larger claim to that parent's affection and resources. Such situations can create feelings of rejection and envy (Beer, 1988).

Remarriage can also alter children's place in the family hierarchy. A teenager may have gotten used to the responsibilities and privileges of being the "oldest child," only to see that role disappear with the entry of an older step-sibling. Likewise, the "baby of the family" may suddenly have younger step-siblings to contend with. Such changes can create additional tension in stepfamilies.

Despite these formidable problems, most step-siblings adjust well and form close relationships. The bonds that develop between step-siblings occur most quickly when the children are similar in age, sex, and life experience. In addition, most step-siblings do keep in touch with one another when they become adults, although not as closely or as frequently as blood siblings do (White & Riedmann, 1992).

Relationships Between Stepparents and Stepchildren

In American society, the mere existence of a blood tie doesn't necessarily make two people think of themselves as family (Cherlin & Furstenberg, 1994). People typically consider kinship to be achieved by establishing a relationship with a person and making repeated connections. So to be considered a relative, you must do the work of creating and maintaining kinship. Among parents and children, this work usually happens automatically. But among stepparents and stepchildren, it can be problematic.

For one thing, a stepparent who enters a family after a divorce doesn't *replace* a stepchild's nonresident parent, as is the case when remarriage follows the death of a parent. Instead, the stepparent—not to mention all the members of the stepparent's family—is added to the child's stock of potential kin. If both biological parents are involved in the child's life, the stepparent's role remains unclear. Step-relatives are more like in-laws than like kin. In fact, in France the same term—*beau-parent*—means both stepparent and "parent-in-law."

The guidelines and norms are much less clear for stepparents than they are for parents. And stepparents themselves tend to be more uncertain about their roles than are other members of the stepfamily (Fine, Coleman, & Ganong, 1998). One obvious illustration of this lack of clarity has to do with how children refer to their stepparents. *Step-dad* sounds too awkward and indeed is quite rare. Some children use the term *dad,* but many others use the first name, which suggests a relationship somewhere between parent and stranger. Not using the term *dad* or *mom* for a stepparent implies that children aren't granting stepparents the rights and obligations typically associated with parenthood.

After a divorce, single parents and their children establish, usually with some difficulty, new rules, routines, and schedules. They create a system with shared histories, intensive relationships, and agreed-on roles. When a stepparent enters the former single-parent family, the entire system may be thrown out of balance. He or she may be seen as an outsider, or worse, as an intruder. Rules and habits have to change, and for a time, confusion, resentment, and hostility may be the norm. Although conflict is common in all types of families, issues such as favoritism, divided loyalties, the right to discipline, and financial responsibility are particularly likely to arise in stepfamilies. Indeed, studies have found that remarried couples disagree more than couples in first marriages, and that most of their disagreements center around issues related to the stepchildren (Holbart, 1991).

The friction and disruption found in stepfamilies decrease the odds of building durable, intimate bonds. Sadly, some evidence suggests that stepfathers' relationships with stepchildren tend to deteriorate over time (cited in Coleman et al., 2000). Many studies show that the well-being of children in stepfamilies isn't all that much better than that of children in single-parent households (Cherlin & Furstenberg, 1994). In fact, some people who counsel children of multiple divorce say that the trauma of forming a new stepfamily, with a stranger intruding on their time with their parent, can be harder on children than a prior or subsequent breakup (Chira, 1995).

Remarriage can, however, improve the financial well-being of children whose parents had divorced. One national study found that 8 percent of children in mother-stepfather households live below the poverty line compared to 49 percent of children in single-mother households (cited in Cherlin & Furstenberg, 1994). In addition, a stepparent adds a second adult to the household who can interact with the child, serve as a role model for the child, and take some of the burden off the custodial parent.

Many stepparents manage to build strong, durable, and loving relationships with their partner's children. The majority of stepparents and children in a recent national survey described their households as "relaxed" and "close." And most children in stepfamilies are doing quite well psychologically (cited in Coontz, 1997). In fact, the biggest source of problems for kids in stepfamilies may actually be parental conflict left over from the first marriage (Rutter, 1997).

The "success" of remarriages and stepfamilies, then, depends in large part on the nature of the divorce itself. Adults and children who welcomed a divorce or defined it as basically a "good thing" are more likely to anticipate remarriage with eagerness and to see it as a chance for a new start than those who defined the divorce as a "bad thing" or something that should have been avoided.

But, ironically, what works well for divorced spouses may not always work so well for stepfamilies. Ex-spouses who continue to have mutual respect for one another as people and parents, who remain close friends, and who continue to be a significant presence in their children's lives provide a healthy postdivorce environment for their children. But such a situation can be difficult for a stepparent, who may feel threatened by the continuing intimacy maintained by the divorced couple. The open boundaries maintained by the harmonious divorced couple after the breakup (for instance, having and using their key to the ex-spouse's house) can feel to the new spouse like an invasion of privacy. Likewise, the children may resent changes in routines initiated by the stepparent.

Thus, the most conducive postdivorce environment for a stepfamily may be a total lack of contact between former spouses. With no ex-spouses present, stepparents can more easily adopt stepchildren. Defining parental roles is less of a problem because the noncustodial biological parent is out of the picture, and the stepparent can serve as a replacement or substitute parent. Thus the newly formed family can more closely approximate a nuclear family. But what works well for the stepfamily may not necessarily be in the children's best interest, where having a good relationship with both biological father and stepfather seems to be associated with more positive outcomes (White & Gilbreth, 2001).

It seems that stepfamilies can never function quite like first-marriage nuclear families. Family relationships and, as a result, the emotional life of the family are both more complicated (Rutter, 1997). The extensive kin connections established in first marriages cannot be overlooked or ignored. Hence, stepfamilies must remain more flexible and open than nuclear families (Ganong & Coleman, 1994).

As you can see, the high levels of conflict within some stepfamilies are not simply an outgrowth of the spouses' psychological inability to sustain intimate relationships, as some analysts have claimed. The fact that remarriages are not fully institutionalized makes them susceptible to difficulty. The lack of clear role definitions, the absence of established societal norms, and the increased complexity of the family structure all increase the likelihood of tension and turmoil. Perhaps in the future this culture will develop standard ways of defining and coping with remarriage.

Conclusion

Throughout history, some couples have always sought escape from bad marriages. But as long as the community was able to cite the flaws of the individuals involved as the source of the marital problems—one or the other partner was abusive; one or the other partner was unfaithful; one or the other was incapable of sustaining emotional commitment; or, in later years, these two people were simply incompatible—the sanctity of marriage remained intact.

But even though divorce is a tragic personal experience, it is not solely a personal matter. If the only causes of divorce were private unhappiness and mistreatment, *rates* of divorce wouldn't differ over time, between groups, or across cultures. Divorce rates, then, are the product of long-term social and economic changes, not a breakdown of personal values.

Legal restrictions or moral warnings are not likely to alter historical trends that have been building for so long. As long as people live in a society that grants individuals the freedom to choose whom to marry, people will from time to time make bad choices. Perhaps, then, the solution to the "divorce problem" lies not so much in increasing legal and economic sanctions against it, "restigmatizing" it, or restricting access to it, but in helping people develop more realistic expectations and learn better methods for dealing with conflict before and during their marriages.

Or, even more radically, maybe the answer lies in not perceiving divorce as a problem in the first place. Society would have to acknowledge that, although a long-lasting marriage is something all couples should strive for, a certain proportion of marriages will always end in divorce. Instead of punishing divorced people and making their lives, and their children's lives, more difficult, people might consider helping parents make the transition from marriage to singlehood, and children make the transition from two live-in parents to one—and then, if remarriage occurs, giving stepfamilies room to establish working relationships.

Chapter Highlights

- Although divorce is more common and acceptable in some societies than in others, virtually all societies have provisions for dissolving marriages. Nevertheless, no society places a positive value on divorce.
- In the United States, the prevalence of divorce varies among racial, ethnic, and religious groups.
- Changes in divorce laws over the past 2 decades have made it easier for people in unsatisfying marriages to end them. However, no-fault divorce laws have had disastrous effects on some women and children, who are likely to suffer financially as a result of divorce. Thus, some states have attempted to make divorces more difficult to obtain.

- The individual experience of divorce is a process that can extend for months, even years, beginning well before the actual separation and continuing far beyond the time when the divorce becomes final.
- Most societal concern over high divorce rates focuses on the impact on children. However, the bulk of research suggests that the problems children experience after a divorce are caused not by the breakup but by the conflict between the parents. In fact, children who grow up in intact but conflict-ridden families may suffer more than children whose parents divorce but maintain a friendly relationship.
- Although mothers still retain custody of children in the vast majority of divorce cases, joint custody and paternal custody are becoming more common. However, child support policies remain inadequate to meet the economic needs of children in single-parent families.
- The large number of remarriages and stepfamilies challenges traditional notions of what a family is. These families create complex roles, alliances, and loyalties, which can make adjustment difficult, especially for children.

Your Turn

You've seen in this chapter that divorce and remarriage are becoming a common part of everyday family life in this society. Nevertheless, stepfamilies face many unique dilemmas and challenges.

Interview a variety of people who live in stepfamilies. Try to speak to both stepmothers and stepfathers, stepsons and stepdaughters—although they need not be from the same family. See if you can also talk to people from various social class, racial, and religious backgrounds. Try to talk to children who still live at home as well as to grown children who live on their own.

First, get some background information. When did the divorce occur? How long ago did remarriage take place? How long was the respondent in a single-parent arrangement? Are there any step-siblings or half-siblings? If so, what are their sexes and ages? How did the respondent's living arrangements change on remarriage? Did he or she move into someone else's home, or did both sides of the family move into a "neutral" home?

What happened when the respondent first met the new members of the family? Did the situation confirm or contradict expectations? In the new family, what term do the children use to refer to their stepparent? Are they comfortable calling this person Dad or Mom?

Try to get a sense of how certain issues are handled in the stepfamily, such as parental discipline, everyday financial support, leisure time, and so on. What about issues of favoritism between biological and step-relations? Does the respondent feel any confusion, resentment, hostility?

After you complete your interviews, analyze whether parents or children seem to have more problems adjusting to stepfamilies. Considering just the children, compare responses for the following:

- Those whose stepparent is of the same sex and those whose stepparent is of the opposite sex
- Those who were young and those who were older when remarriage took place

What can you conclude from your interviews about the nature of stepfamilies and their place in the larger society?

Family Transitions in Adulthood

Cycles of Change

When we talk about families, diversity is the rule, not the exception. But one thing that characterizes all families, no matter what they look like, is that they are never static. As we grow and mature, we face a constant stream of changes and adjustments. Some are occasions we happily anticipate; others are somber moments approached with uncertainty or dread.

Weddings, pregnancy, and childbirth are transitions commonly associated with early family life. Although not all families begin with such events, they symbolize new identities and roles.

Do you think that these couples are thinking about the challenges and difficulties that await them in the future? How do you suppose the newlyweds' and the expectant couple's perceptions of marriage and family differ from those of the mother whose child is shaking the bride's hand? In other words, how do the expectations of family life differ from its realities?

Child rearing brings its own changes and challenges. Parents are usually so thrilled when their child takes his or her first step that they don't realize it's immediately followed by the exhausting task of keeping up with an active, mobile toddler.

The teen years bring about even more urgent challenges, as willful children begin to gain (and demand) more independence. Finally they leave home to pursue college or work or to establish their own families. Parents and siblings face the task of continually adjusting to changes in composition of the household and its daily rhythms.

How are parents and younger siblings affected when older children leave home? In what ways does the family change? How do the parents' lives change when all the children are gone?

Grandparenthood marks a major transition of later life. Grandparents have always been an important source of knowledge, linking grandchildren with their racial or ethnic heritage and providing them with important information about their own family history. Today, many grandparents are also healthy and financially secure.

In contrast to early stages of family life, the transitions associated with later stages are more likely to revolve around issues of loss and endings. . .

. . . although some elderly people, like these 80-year-old newlyweds, are still able to find opportunities for new beginnings

How have the health and financial well-being of aging grandparents affected your parents? How is your parents' experience now likely to differ from yours as they complete their lives?

My relationship with my father was fairly typical.* We argued sometimes and annoyed each other sometimes, but clearly we always loved each other deeply. Like most fathers in the 1960s and 1970s, he took his breadwinner role seriously and spent a lot of time at work. He'd leave early in the morning, often before I had awakened, and he'd return, usually exhausted, close to dinner time.

Like most children, I created some psychological distance from my father as I became a know-it-all teenager and came to depend less and less on his help and advice. As time passed, I went off to college, got married, and started my own family. My father and I were living separate lives. We'd talk once a week on the phone and see each other two or three times a year. I knew he was proud that I was studying for a Ph.D., and I knew he loved being a grandfather, even if he didn't see his grandson very often. I didn't need him that much, but I just figured he'd be around if I ever did.

Shortly before Thanksgiving in 1987—my last year of graduate school—I received a call from my sister telling me that my father was gravely ill and in the intensive care unit of his local hospital. As far back as I can remember, my father had had health problems of one sort or another. But this time was different. Two days after Thanksgiving my sister called again, saying that I had better get there right away. I caught the next flight and sped directly to the hospital from the airport.

As I approached his room, I saw my sister, brother, and sister-in-law in the hallway, waiting to tell me that my father was hooked up to several machines and was floating in and out of consciousness. They warned me that he looked very different from the way he looked the last time I had seen him.

As I walked into the room, my mother met me with a tearful embrace. I tentatively looked toward the person lying in the bed. For a split second I thought everyone had made a big mistake. That man wasn't my father, I thought. My father was a big, robust man; the fellow in the bed was skinny and frail. His skin was a faint yellow, not the tanned brown my father sported. My father's face was happy and chubby; this man's face had the hollow eyes and sunken cheeks of a skull. But of course it wasn't a mistake. It was my father.

He opened his eyes and looked at me and slightly smiled. He mumbled something, but I couldn't make out what it was. We all stayed there for about 45 minutes making small talk while my father lay there motionless and unaware. "How was your flight?" "How's school going?" "How's the baby?" "How's your job?" As we left I told my father I'd see him first thing in the morning. He didn't respond.

At about 1:30 the following morning the phone rang. It was the hospital. The nurse said my father had "taken a turn for the worse." We all got in the car and rushed to the hospital. A nurse met us in the hallway. Her simple, direct words to us sound as clear in my head today as they did over a decade ago: "I'm sorry, he's gone."

My father was dead. The man who had supported me and loved me unconditionally—even when I didn't deserve it—was dead. Like a character out of some sappy made-for-television movie, I thought of all the things I should have told him but didn't. I had had countless opportunities to tell this man how much he meant to me, but I never did. I had spent far too much time criticizing him and focusing on his flaws and embarrassing habits.

But aside from the guilt, I also came to a frightening realization: My life, from that day forward, would never again be the same. I had experienced a turning point and was now a different person. My family had been transformed. My mother was a widow. What was her life going to be like now? My baby son would never know his grandfather. I missed my fa-

---

*Reflects the experiences of David Newman.

ther, the person. But even though I was a grown man, I also missed *having* a father. The transformation had occurred to my family in an instant, but we would feel its effects forever.

Family life is never static. It is punctuated by transforming events. Some are joyous—a graduation, a wedding, the birth of a child. Others, like the death of a parent, rank as the most painful experiences a person can endure. Some are unexpected; others are anticipated for years. Some take place suddenly; others are gradual changes with ill-defined beginnings and endings.

As people grow, they move from a high degree of dependence on others to greater independence. Their values change. Their tastes change. If you have younger brothers or sisters, you know that right around the time you became a teenager you discovered that your interests no longer matched theirs. The games you once played together now seemed embarrassingly childish.

Nothing is more certain about family life than the fact that it is constantly changing. This chapter looks at some of the important family changes and life transformations that most of us have experienced or will at some point experience. We are constantly defining and redefining our families as such changes occur. In this chapter, we focus on the transitions that occur in adulthood, middle age, old age, and death. You'll see that although most of these transformations are somehow related to biological changes associated with aging, they are all influenced by powerful historical, cultural, and demographic forces.

Family Transitions and the Life Course

Over a typical life span, an individual is likely to undergo many transitions: from baby to toddler, from child to adolescent, from adolescent to adult, from single to coupled, from nonparent to parent, from middle age to old age, from employed to retired, from healthy to frail, and so on. People grow up, change physically, leave home, sometimes return home, form relationships, end relationships, have children, raise children, watch children leave, watch family members die, and eventually die themselves. Although each of these transitions is experienced as an intensely personal event, for the most part major transitions are not unique to individuals. Rather, life transitions are socially defined, and to some extent, predictable. Certainly not all individuals go through the same transitions, and there are multiple pathways to adulthood (Shanahan, 2000), but most people in a given culture at a particular time proceed through life in similar ways. For sociologists, this process is referred to as the **life course**—the sequence of socially defined, age-related events and roles that occur over a person's life (Elder, 1998).

Social scientists interested in the life course emphasize that although many of life's transitions, and even the aging process itself, involve clear and definable biological processes, the meaning of these events is always socially constructed (Elder, 1998). For instance, as you saw in Chapter 9, puberty is associated with obvious biological changes, but the way it is experienced by individuals varies with culture, gender, religion, race, and so on.

In all societies, age-graded institutions guide and constrain individual behavior. In the United States, for instance, laws require children to enroll in school (or be home-schooled) by a certain age, usually by age 6. In old age, Social Security and Medicare benefits determine what many elderly people do and don't do with their time and how aggressively they treat their health problems.

Less formally, behavior is governed by **age norms**, or social expectations about how individuals should act based on age. If this culture didn't have age-related norms about sexuality, for instance, you probably wouldn't hear people refer to a sexually active adolescent as "12, going on 20" or a 50-year-old man dating a 20-year-old woman as a "dirty old man." Family members are also important in this regard, often providing explicit messages about appropriate age-related behavior. Parents may inform their children that they are "too young to date," or children of divorced or widowed parents may inform them that they are "too old to date." Such statements are meaningful only within a life course perspective maintaining that culture, not just biology, defines the appropriate timing of certain events and individual acts.

The Influence of Birth Cohorts

Life course experiences are also influenced by broader historical forces and population trends. One such factor that affects the way people experience family transformations is their **birth cohort**—the set of people who were born during the same period and who therefore face similar societal circumstances. Each cohort has distinctive properties—such as its initial size, ethnic composition, age-specific birth rates, and average life expectancies—and distinctive historical experiences that set it apart from other cohorts.

You've no doubt asked yourself questions such as, What career will I pursue? Where will I live? Will I be able to afford a house? Will I have children? The answers to these questions are obviously influenced by your personal desires, traits, values, ambitions, and abilities, not to mention your social class, gender, sexual orientation, race, religion, and ethnicity. But the shape of your birth cohort and its position and size relative to other cohorts will also determine your responses to these questions. For instance, the sheer number of people graduating from college in a given year will affect the availability of high-paying jobs, which may in turn affect the timing of marriage, the number and timing of children, the timing of retirement, health in old age, and any number of other family-related matters.

Birth cohorts influence the everyday lives of individuals in two fundamental ways (Riley, 1971):

- People born at roughly the same time tend to experience life course events or social rites of passage—such as puberty, marriage, childbearing, graduation, entrance into the workforce, and death—at roughly the same time. Sociologists call these experiences **cohort effects**.
- Historical events (wars, epidemics, economic depressions, and so on) and major social trends, called **period effects**, influence all members of a society at a given point in time. Many historians, for instance, believe that a period of drought and famine caused the abandonment of the great cities of the Mayan civilization nearly a thousand years ago. Those who lived prior to this period enjoyed comfortable lives, reveled in the high culture of the Mayans, and had tremendous prospects for the future. But for their children, born just a generation later, starvation, death, and social dislocation were basic facts of life (Clausen, 1986).

Cohort and period effects combine and interact to profoundly influence the lives of individuals. The same major historical event or world circumstance can affect members of different birth cohorts differently because it occurs at a different stages in the life of each group.

To better understand the combined influence of cohort effects and period effects, consider the research of social historian Tamara Hareven (1994). Hareven studied two cohorts of adult children of immigrants in the industrial community of Manchester, New Hampshire. She found significant differences in the attitudes and practices of these two cohorts. Members of the earlier cohort (born between 1910 and 1919), toughened by the Depression they experienced as teenagers and young adults, were primarily concerned with keeping the entire family afloat economically. They pooled resources, doubled up on housing when possible, scrimped and saved, and supported their aging parents and needy relatives. They held on to traditional beliefs about relying on kin rather than public agencies in time of need.

In contrast, members of the later cohort (born between 1920 and 1929) were very small children during the Depression. They took advantage of the economic recovery brought about by World War II and upon becoming adults were eager to develop middle-class lifestyles. They devoted themselves to improving their own lives and their children's future. They were more likely to live separately from their kin. They were more prepared to accept government help and were more willing to place their elderly parents in nursing homes if necessary.

The earlier cohort was clearly more committed to collectivist family values. Many had actually gone through the experience of caring for elderly parents in their homes or had sacrificed their own marriage to care for a parent. But they had felt significant ambivalence, doubt, and bitterness. The nagging fear that the care they gave their elderly parents had robbed them of the opportunity to start their own families increased the threat that old age would be troublesome for them. Members of the more recent cohort, in contrast, who followed the more individualistic path, were often racked by guilt over the way in which they relinquished responsibility for supporting their aging parents to others.

The very different outlooks of these two cohorts reflect both period and cohort effects. The Great Depression was a major event in this country's history; any American alive during that period was directly affected by it in one way or another. But the fact that it was experienced differently by different age groups also suggests a cohort effect. As one would expect, the older generation, who had more financial responsibility for supporting their families, experienced the Depression differently from those who lacked this responsibility at the time.

Different cohorts develop and mature in what amounts to fundamentally different societal environments. The very nature of society—the size of the population, its age distribution, and its racial or ethnic proportions—varies from cohort to cohort. People start their lives in one historical period, which has its own distinct pattern of behavior for people of different ages and its own set of social norms, and end their lives in another. As you grow older, you develop and change in a society that itself is developing and changing.

The social, cultural, and environmental changes to which a cohort is exposed as it moves through the life course can even affect the way people experience the biological process of aging. People are living longer than ever before, thanks to advancements in nutrition, education, sanitation, and other areas. As a result, cohorts experience the physical consequences of aging in different ways (Riley, Foner, & Waring, 1988). Better health and a longer life span have led to an increase in babies born to middle-aged people. Combined with changing social norms, values, and cultural beliefs, such changes will inevitably delay the point at which people decide they are "too old" to have children.

Certain cohorts are so distinctive that they get pinned with a label. One example is the baby boom generation, consisting of people born between 1946 and 1964. The cohort that came after the baby boomers, called **Generation X,** consists of roughly 48 million people who are now in their late 20s and 30s. The birth rate during the 1970s, when many of these individuals were born, was about half as high as it was during the post–World War II years of the baby boomers.

People in the Generation X cohort are less likely to get married than baby boomers and more likely to delay marriage if they do. Furthermore, the high divorce rate over the past several decades has had a direct and lasting impact on this cohort. Roughly 40 percent of them are children of divorce. Even more of them were so-called latchkey children, the first generation of children to experience the effects of two working parents. For many of them, childhood was marked by dependence on secondary relationships—teachers, friends, day care teachers, and so on.

The most recent cohort to receive the public's attention is known as the **Millennium Generation.** This cohort consists of roughly 70 million individuals born between 1979 and 1994. This cohort rivals the baby boom in size but is different in almost every other way. For one thing, they are more ethnically diverse—one in three is not white, and many are children of mixed marriages. They are also more likely than preceding cohorts to grow up in a nontraditional family (one in four lives in a single-parent household; three in four have working mothers).

Growing up in the affluent 1990s, many in this generation have positive feelings about their futures. Two-thirds of teenage respondents in a recent national survey indicated that they were very optimistic about their chances of having a good job, and many are confident that problems such as sexual harassment and economic discrimination against women are on their way out. But their optimism isn't just about personal interest. Asked to identify the most important concept that will guide their working lives, the most common response was "to help others who need help" (cited in Mogelonsky, 1998).

Furthermore, although they are quick to point out hypocrisy and superficiality (witness the success of the "Image Is Nothing" tag line in Sprite commercials) they may also be more socially conservative than prior generations. For instance, according to the 1972 General Social Survey, only 10 percent of 18- to 24-year-olds said premarital sex was "always wrong." By 1998 that figure for the current 18- to 24-year-olds had more than doubled. Similarly, the proportion who were sexually active decreased between 1996 and 1998 from 83.9 percent to 76.6 percent (cited in Stapinski, 1999). Indeed, rates of pregnancy, abortion, and births for girls between 15 and 17 have all declined since 1990 (Howe & Strauss, 2000). Such trends may very well be reflected later in marriage, divorce, and childbearing statistics for this cohort.

The Transitions of Adulthood

Members of all cohorts must personally experience passage through different stages of the life course. In Chapter 6 we discussed the transition from singlehood to couplehood; in Chapter 8, the transition to parenthood; and in Chapter 9, the transition from childhood to adolescence. But many other transitions await people, including the transition from adolescence to adulthood, from day-to-day parent to "empty nest" parent, from parent to grandparent, from worker to retired person, from middle-aged person to elderly person, and from life—no matter how robust or feeble—to the finality of death. Here we will focus on just a few transitions that are particularly influential in family life.

Entering Adulthood

The presence of a socially recognized but vaguely defined stage of life such as adolescence makes it difficult to pinpoint the exact moment when a person becomes an adult. Depending on how you define "adulthood," a person can be considered an adult anywhere between age 13 and 25. You could consider adulthood to begin when a person is old enough to procreate, drive a car, vote, be drafted for military service, legally drink or purchase alcohol, get married, have an abortion without parental consent, or support him- or herself financially.

Sometimes the age at which a person is thought to be an adult in one situation contradicts the "age of majority" in another situation. In 1990, for example, 50,000 teenagers got married before they turned 18, thereby obtaining the legal right to have sex before they were allowed to watch sexual activity in an X-rated movie (Mogelonsky, 1996). U.S. Americans can purchase cars before they are legally allowed to drive them, and they can do both of these things long before they're eligible to rent cars.

Identifying when adulthood begins became particularly problematic in 1971, when the Twenty-Sixth Amendment to the U.S. Constitution was adopted. This amendment reduced the age at which citizens could vote from 21 to 18. The amendment was passed at a time when 18-year-olds were being drafted in record numbers to fight in the Vietnam War. Many people supported the amendment because they thought it was hypocritical that young people be old enough to fight and die but not old enough to vote for the people who made the decisions to send them to war in the first place.

Definitions of adulthood are often based on cultural ideas about appropriate living arrangements. Since World War II, people in the United States have had a strong cultural expectation that adulthood means college attendance or training away from home and an entry-level position in a career that will lead to sufficient income for independence. People in this society have expected children to live away from home in dorms or apartments during this period and to establish their own households after they complete it. Young adults are expected to marry and have children, all within the context of a union assumed to be permanent. We may think it's appropriate for young married couples to live with one set of parents for a while, but we don't expect children to remain dependent on their parents their entire lives.

These sorts of expectations vary from culture to culture. For instance, a World Values Survey found that Americans have a middling position on the desirability of married people leaving their parents' home and establishing their own households (see Exhibit 12.1). Some cultures, such as that of France, are far more certain that married children need to strike out on their own; some, most notably the collectivist cultures of Asia, believe married children can be happy in their parents' households.

Today, many young adults in this country are having a tough time with U.S. cultural expectations for the transition to adulthood. More and more people are choosing to remain single, delaying marriage, or, if married, deciding not to have children. Buying a home is beyond the means of most young adults, and periodic downswings in the economy can make getting a good job exceedingly difficult, even for college graduates. In short, the traditional indicators of adulthood have become more difficult to attain.

Thus, a new pattern of entry into adulthood has developed among young people, which includes interrupted, delayed, or postponed college attendance; erratic job patterns with no assurance of an income high enough for self-sufficiency; and postponement of marriage and childbearing. Many young people who do attend college live at home and

EXHIBIT 12.1

Cultural Attitudes Toward Living Apart from In-Laws

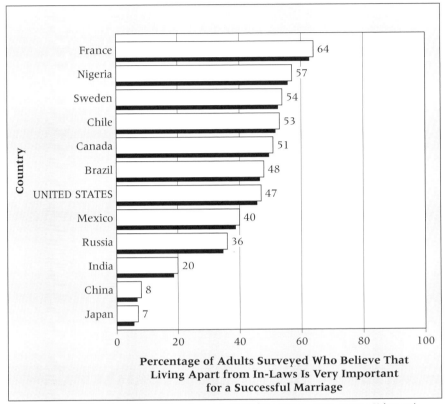

Percentage of Adults Surveyed Who Believe That Living Apart from In-Laws Is Very Important for a Successful Marriage

Data source: Ronald Inglehart, Miguel Basañez, and Alejandro Moreno. 1998. *Human Values and Beliefs: A Cross-Cultural Sourcebook.* Ann Arbor: University of Michigan.

commute daily. According to one study, 25 percent of full-time, first-year college students live at home while they attend school (cited in Mogelonsky, 1996).

Consequently, recent cohorts of young adults have been slower to leave the nest than older cohorts and are more likely to return home after they have tried to leave (Goldscheider & Goldscheider, 1994). About 19 percent of men and 9 percent of women ages 25–29 live with their parents (U.S. Bureau of the Census, 1998d). Among 40- to 44-year-olds, about 6 percent of men and 2 percent of women live with their parents. These figures include children who have never left and those who have left and returned, perhaps more than once. As you can see in Exhibit 12.2, there are significant differences across racial groups, which may reflect underlying cultural and economic differences.

For some, living at home to look after parents is considered selfless and highly responsible. But the prevailing image in an individualist culture is that adults who live with their parents are either slackers who lack the drive to become independent or immature "Peter Pans" who don't want to grow up. According to sociologists Allan Schnaiberg and Sheldon Goldenberg (1989), however, neither is the case. They believe that lack of economic opportunity is the major reason why today's young adults are more likely to remain at home. Between 1976 and 1996, the average per capita income (measured in 1996 dollars) of people between the ages of 25 and 34 dropped from $23,123 to $20,305 (U.S. Bureau of the Census, 1998a). In addition, increases in rents have outpaced entry-level salaries.

EXHIBIT 12.2

*Young Adults
Living with
Parents*

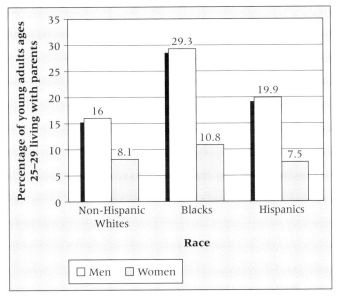

Data source: U.S. Bureau of the Census. 1998d. "Unpublished
Tables—Marital Status and Living Arrangements: March 1998
(update)," Table 2. P20-514. Available at http://www.census.gov/
prod/99pubs/p20-514u.pdf. Accessed June 1, 2001.

Money makes it easier to set up a new household, and a sudden reversal of economic
fortunes can easily force a return to the parents' home. Furthermore, the money spent on
short-term living expenses—rent, food, utilities, and so on—might take away from money
spent for schooling or a "nest egg" for marriage. Thus many young adults conclude that to
have a more secure financial future they should postpone residential independence.

Another factor associated with the delay in leaving home is the rise in the age at which
young people first marry. Between 1970 and 1995, the median age at first marriage rose
from 23.2 to 26.9 for men and from 20.8 to 24.5 for women (U.S. Bureau of the Census,
1999a). The marriage delay gives young adults more time to live with their parents. But it
also increases the number of young adults who live alone or who cohabitate. Thus people
in their 20s are less likely to be married than they were in the recent past, leading to an increase in all sorts of other living arrangements, including living with their parents.

Most adults would probably rather not have to live with their parents. Because people
still tend to take independent living as a primary indicator of being adult in this culture,
adults who live with their parents—even if they're working and saving money for a family
or going to school to enhance their future earning abilities—feel that others see them as
not-quite-adults (Schnaiberg & Goldenberg, 1989). For better or worse, they are deviating
from the cultural expectation that they will separate residentially from their parents during
young adulthood.

Most parents—73 percent in one study (Mitchell & Gee, 1996)—are actually quite satisfied with their adult children living at home. But others do feel a certain level of anxiety.
Parents are particularly likely to be affected negatively by this living situation when their
adult children return home on multiple occasions. Unfortunately, the factors that make
multiple returns necessary, such as downturns in the economy, are largely beyond the control of the individuals involved.

Emptying the Nest

The vast majority of young adults eventually do leave their parents' home, for good. Because more Americans than ever live to be middle aged and beyond, more and more couples experience an extended time together after the children have grown and left home. However, the increase in the proportion of young adults who remain or return home means that this postparental period—referred to as the *empty nest*—has become less predictable and maybe even shorter than parents anticipate (Cote & Allahar, 1994).

A century or so ago, a child leaving home marked the loss of a valued contributor to the household income for most families. On farms, children were an important source of labor. In cities, their earnings helped keep the home together. When all their children had moved out, couples had to face the problem of replacing children's economic contributions. Rural couples often had to hire farm laborers, and urban couples often took in boarders and lodgers to compensate for the child's absence. Hence the postparental period in the last century meant less privacy and more uncertainty (Treas & Bengtson, 1982).

Perhaps because of this history, there is has a pervasive belief that middle-aged parents—particularly stay-at-home mothers—suffer severe emotional crises when all their children grow up and leave home. The idea is that so much energy has been spent raising children that when they are longer there, parents face the "frightening" question of what to do with the rest of their lives. They become depressed and aimless, responding to their children's departure as if they were grieving and mourning. This experience has been dubbed the **empty nest syndrome**. Some psychiatrists believe this syndrome is a clinically diagnosable condition, and medical journals have run full-page advertisements for antidepressants that can be prescribed as treatment (Harkins, 1978).

Such a contention makes intuitive sense. The roles people occupy provide meaning and behavioral guidance in their lives. Historically, as you read in Chapter 8, women have devoted a significant portion of their lives to raising children—in large part because they have found obstacles to developing professional identities outside the home. Consequently, you might expect women to suffer when their children leave, because a key element of the all-important mother role has gone.

But such an explanation operates on some dubious assumptions. First, it assumes that being a parent is the individual's *only* pertinent social role; that when the children are gone, parents—especially mothers—are essentially stripped of their identity. But as you know, everyone takes on multiple roles. Mothers today are likely to have other pursuits, including work, and therefore don't depend totally on mothering activities to determine their self-worth.

Second, this explanation also assumes that when children leave home, parenting abruptly stops. But your parents don't stop being your parents once you leave home. They may not provide you with daily meals or chauffeur you from place to place anymore, but they certainly retain their identity as your parents. In fact, some "empty nest" parents are surprised to learn how much their nonresident children still need them. Listen to how one mother describes her relationship with her son in college:

> My son Josh called me collect from junior college during his first year away from home. "Mom . . . I need your opinion on how [my paper] sounds. I want an *A* in speech." I could have answered, "C'mon Josh . . . you're 19 . . . you're independent . . . I don't need to worry about your schoolwork anymore, especially on my long-distance phone bill." Instead . . . I gave the needed advice, the strokes of support—to a young

man, my son, striving toward adulthood. When I had my babies in the 60s I didn't realize that I would still be parenting in the late 80s. I thought my mother role would end when my children reached 16; they would get their drivers' licenses and speed away toward total independence. I was wrong. . . . I have discovered that parenting is a 25-year commitment. I never suspected that it would last quite this long. (Dardick, 1993, pp. 62–63)

For some, the "empty nest" represents a solution to the dilemma of how to balance individual interests with family obligations, a topic covered in detail in Issue 4.

Contrary to popular belief, research on the "empty nest syndrome" suggests that, for most parents, the departure of grown-up children from home is actually a happy event. When the nest empties, the parents find freedom, relief from responsibilities, and time for themselves. A national study of 402 parents over a period of 4 years found that the "empty nest" is associated with significant *improvements* in marital happiness and life satisfaction (White & Edwards, 1990). The day-to-day pressures of taking care of children end, and couples can look forward to more intimacy with each other. They can also pursue interests that they have set aside in favor of their children's needs.

Still, parents don't want to be completely isolated from their adult children. Parents tend to experience greater improvement in life satisfaction when children maintain frequent contact after they move out. In other words, continuation of the parental role—albeit at a distance—appears to be important to well-being in middle age.

Sociologist Lillian Rubin (1992) interviewed 160 middle-aged women from varied backgrounds whose children had left home to go to college, get married, or start a career. She too found that the stereotype of the painful empty nest is largely a myth. Almost all the women she spoke with responded to the departure of their children with a decided sense of relief. Consider these comments from women whose adult children had recently moved out:

> I can't tell you what a relief it was to find myself with an empty nest. Oh sure, when the last child went away to school, for the first day or so there was a kind of a throb, but believe me, it was only a day or two.
>
> When the youngest one was ready to move out of the house, I was right there helping him pack. We love having the children live in the area, and we love seeing them and the grandchildren, but I don't need for any of them to live in this house ever again. *I've had as much as I ever need or want of being tied down with children* [emphasis in original]. (quoted in Rubin, 1992, p. 263)

Interestingly, many of the women Rubin interviewed seemed guilty about feeling happy that their children were out of the house, even though the majority felt this way. Such guilt illustrates the pervasiveness of gender-based expectations in parenting and the lingering belief that women are supposed to be sad when their children leave:

> To tell you the truth, most of the time it's a big relief to be free of them, finally. I suppose that's awful to say. But you know that, most of the women I know feel the same way. It's just that they're uncomfortable saying it because there's all this talk about how sad mothers are supposed to be when the kids leave home. (quoted in Rubin, 1992, p. 266)

The women feared that such expressions of relief might be interpreted as a lack of commitment to parenting or a lack of love for their children.

Rubin did notice some important class differences in the way mothers respond to their children leaving home. Most middle-class parents know exactly when their children will fly from the nest: the day they leave home for college. Thus middle-class parents have plenty of time to prepare. These mothers frequently reported that the child's senior year in high school served as a time when much of the emotional separation could be done.

In working-class families, however, college attendance is not so easily taken for granted. Children might even be expected to live at home until they marry. Even working-class children who attend college are more likely to attend more affordable campuses close to home, which allows them to continue to live with their parents. The unpredictability of the "departure date" makes preparation for the empty nest more difficult. Nevertheless, the difficulty is usually brief and in no way approaches anything that could rightfully be called "depression."

In sum, parents tend to see the departure of their children not with sadness but with a feeling of accomplishment that they've done their "job" well. For those who do suffer disappointment, the relief can be mixed with painful feelings of failure. Yet none of the women Rubin interviewed yearned for another chance. For better or worse, they were glad the job was done and were ready to move on to the next stage of life.

Becoming a Grandparent

For most parents who make it through the empty nest period, grandparenthood awaits. Historically, the image of the grandparent has been one of a gray-haired, elderly person. However, most people become grandparents while in midlife, when they are married, when they are fully employed, and, with increasing frequency, when their own parents are still alive. For most of the past century, the age at which Americans become grandparents has been in their 40s or 50s. But even today, with delayed marriage and childbearing, grandparenting is not a role most people begin in old age. Contemporary grandparents are more likely than was the case 40 years ago to be healthy, be relatively well off financially, and have a living spouse (Aldous, 1995).

Falling birth rates have had an impact on grandparenting too. In the late 1800s, for instance, American women gave birth to more than four children, on average (Cherlin & Furstenberg, 1987). Many parents found themselves raising young children after older children had left home, married, and started their own families. So parenting and grandparenting often overlapped. It's certainly likely that the responsibilities of raising children who were still at home took precedence over the responsibilities of tending to grandchildren. Hence, most grandparents in the past tended to be somewhat uninvolved in their grandchildren's lives.

In contrast, the birth rate today is lower, and people are getting married and starting families later. Hence parents are more likely to be finished raising their own children before any grandchildren are born. So now when a person becomes a grandparent, fewer parental obligations are likely to be competing for his or her time and energy. In addition, 40-hour workweeks and an increase in available leisure time mean that grandparents today have more time to spend with grandchildren than they did a century ago. Grandparenting has thus become a separate identity and a separate stage of family life.

Some grandparents are centrally involved in their grandchildren's lives. In 1998, 4 million children—about 5.6 percent of all children under 18—were living in homes maintained by their grandparents (U.S. Bureau of the Census, 2000b). Another 1.5 million live with their grandparents in their parents' home (Bryson & Casper, 1999).

Even if they don't live close by, advances in travel and communications make it easier than ever for grandparents to see and talk to their grandchildren. A survey of 823 grandparents nationwide found that over 80 percent of grandparents see their grandchildren or talk to them on the telephone at least once a month (American Association of Retired Persons, 1999). When they see them, the activities include eating meals, watching television, spending the night, going shopping, and so on. Half of the respondents said they frequently play the role of friend or companion to their grandchildren.

Some social changes, however, have made contemporary grandparenthood more difficult. One such change is the high rate of divorce. Often grandparents don't find out that their grown children are getting a divorce until it happens. And they are rarely, if ever, consulted about custody and visitation arrangements for the grandchildren. Because mothers generally receive physical custody of the children after a divorce, maternal grandparents are more likely to be able to continue their relationship with the grandchildren than paternal grandparents, who can experience a sudden loss of contact and have no clear legal rights to visitation. In 2000, the U.S. Supreme Court ruled that grandparents do not have a legal right to see their grandchildren without the parents' consent.

> This case is another example of the debate over who can be legally considered a member of one's family, discussed in Issue 1.

Cultural Expectations of Grandparents   In general, the degree to which grandparents are incorporated into the lives of their children and grandchildren is far stronger in other cultures than in ours. Listen to how one American couple describes the relationships among grandparents, parents, and children in recent Russian immigrant families:

> We have quite a few Russian friends. Now these friends, invariably the mothers are living with the sons, the daughters, with grandchildren—they're all together. . . . The grandchildren have great reverence for the grandparents; they live together. When they go on vacation they take the grandparents with them! I'm just shocked! When they go out eating, they take the grandparents with them! . . . And this is such a new experience because we don't go eating with our children. They go their way, we go our way. . . . The [Russian] grandparents are very much involved with the families of their children. . . . We know a woman who was a famous surgeon in Russia, she's here in America, and she has that same feeling that she has to take care of her grandchild if the mother goes away. She's always obligated to that little girl. Now you wouldn't find the same thing in America. (quoted in Cherlin & Furstenberg, 1997, pp. 361–362)

Although they speak fondly of these family relationships, few older people in this country desire such an arrangement. Like most Americans, they want intimate, satisfying, stable family ties, but at the same time they want to retain their independence from kin. They want affection and respect from their children and grandchildren but don't want to be obligated to them and don't want to be a burden to them (Cherlin & Furstenberg, 1997). As in the case of these Russian immigrants, the price paid for strong family ties is a significant loss of autonomy—a price most American grandparents are unwilling to pay. Consider this comment from an American grandparent who believes that he and his wife have worked hard to raise their children and now deserve to have their own pleasures:

> When we were raising children, we figured when the children got married and moved to their own locales, we'd be free to do as we please. All our lives, we've worked for the kids, to make sure they had an education and everything else. Then we find out when we're grandparents they say, "Uh, Mom, Pop, how about babysitting? We're going away for a couple of days." . . . Once in a while is fine, but we wouldn't want to be tied down to that like three or four times a year. (quoted in Cherlin & Furstenberg, 1997, p. 363)

Ethnic Differences in Grandparenting   Grandparenting styles can vary among different ethnic groups within this country, too. In African-American families, for instance, grandmothers frequently play crucial, involved roles in child rearing and parental support (Hunter, 1997). In fact, African-American children are much more likely than other children to have been "raised" by their grandmothers. Over 12 percent of African-American children live with their grandparents, and close to 40 percent of those have neither of their parents living with them in the household (cited in Morgan & Kunkel, 1998). Most of the literature on the role of African-American grandparents points to crisis situations, such as poverty and single parenthood, as the reason for their involvement. But these grandparents also tend to be younger than those from other racial and ethnic groups, which might also explain part of their greater involvement with grandchildren.

This type of involved grandmothering can also be seen as a time-tested family strategy with roots in black cultural traditions and the economic and social realities of black life (see Chapter 3). Research shows that African-American grandmothers frequently show a style of grandparenting described as "authoritative" or "influential," involving high levels of support and parentlike behaviors (Hunter, 1997). Black children tend to see grandmothers not simply as a fill-in authority figure but as an important teacher of lessons about life, morality, the importance of education, and religious faith (Strom, Collinsworth, Strom, & Griswold, 1992–1993).

To be sure, reliance on grandmothers in raising African-American children is more likely among young single mothers with inadequate financial resources who depend on kin networks for support and survival. But, in addition, mothers perceive that they can count on grandmothers for parenting support (Hunter, 1997). The extent to which young parents are willing to depend on grandmothers reflects not only a response to urgent problems but also a way of thinking about and organizing family relationships.

However, one must be careful not to overgeneralize. Not all families within a particular racial or ethnic group are alike. For instance, one study found that 31 percent of black single mothers with children under the age of 5 received no assistance of any kind from the grandparents—compared to only 23 percent of their white counterparts (Eggebeen & Hogan, 1990). Nevertheless, in general African-American grandparents—especially grandmothers—play a more important, involved role than white grandparents.

Many Native-American grandparents may also have the responsibility for raising grandchildren who have been left without a father, mother, or both. Indeed, depending on grandmothers as primary caretakers of grandchildren is a long-established Native-American child-rearing strategy. However, Native-American grandparents play family roles that are somewhat different from those found among other groups.

Historically, grandparenting roles in Native-American families have been shaped by practical division-of-labor issues and the need to free up younger women so they can participate more fully in the economics of the tribal community; the high value placed on the nurturing of small children so the tribe can continue as a social entity; and the belief that old age represents the culmination of cultural experience. Elders are believed to be the best equipped to transmit culture across generations, thus helping to ensure the cultural integrity of the tribe (Weibel-Orlando, 1997).

Consequently, many Native-American grandparents actively solicit their children to allow the grandchildren to live with them. The express purpose is to expose the grandchildren to the American Indian way of life (Weibel-Orlando, 1997). Grandparents may be annoyed by the disdain that their own urbanized and assimilated children show for this way of life and may feel that the grandchildren are the only hope for the future of the tribe. As one Sioux grandmother puts it,

> The second- or third-generation Indian children out in [Los Angeles], most of them never get to see anything like . . . a sun dance or a memorial feast or giveaway or just stuff that Indians do back home. I wanted my own children to be involved in them and know what it's all about. So that's the reason that I always try to keep my grand-children whenever I can. . . . I'm building memories for them. (quoted in Weibel-Orlando, 1997, pp. 385–386)

Having grandchildren in their home and under their absolute custody for extended periods is one way Native-American grandparents can fulfill their culture's expectations of prop-erly traditional elders. Their grandparenting is not just for the benefit of the grandchildren themselves, but for all future generations.

Old Age

Unless someone dies prematurely, all people at some point enter old age. But just what is meant by "old" is unclear. Different people "become elderly" at different ages. Some people experience serious deficits in cognitive and physical functioning in their 50s; others remain active and energetic well into their 90s.

As Chapter 4 mentions, the degree to which people accumulate social and economic re-sources in their youth and middle age can shape their lives in old age (Stoller & Gibson, 1994). People of color as well as working-class and poor individuals, having lower incomes and less wealth in their peak earning years, may face greater financial and health problems in old age than will middle-class whites. The deficiencies in the health care system and the environment that plague the poor and socially isolated eventually take a toll. A friend re-cently returned from a trip to Hungary, where economic and environmental devastation have made adults look 20 or 30 years older than they are. Hungarians consistently esti-mated his age to be in the mid-20s (he's actually in his mid-40s). One person said to him, "You Americans wear your affluence on your faces."

Culture and the Elderly

Becoming elderly is not determined simply by the number of years a person has lived but by the trajectory of his or her life accomplishments, family relationships, and social cir-cumstances. Larger cultural definitions of and attitudes toward the elderly can also shape the experience of aging. In some cultures, the elderly are highly respected; in others they are either ignored or treated with contempt.

More fundamentally, individualist and collectivist cultures differ widely in beliefs about responsibility to the elderly. In most East Asian countries, for example, the government takes limited responsibility for elder care, relying instead on families to perform this role (Liu, 2000). Indeed, written government policies and tax provisions encourage living near or with one's elderly parents (Liu, 2000). In these cultures, caregiving is expected to be con-tinual and mutual throughout the life span, not something that occurs only when an indi-vidual is too frail to care for him- or herself (Liu & Kendig, 2000). In these cultures, simply "getting old" elicits powerful expectations that younger family members (usually daughters and daughters-in-law) will provide elder care.

The obligations children feel to care for their elderly parents is also discussed in Issue 4.

In contrast, the United States follows a western European model, which supports a greater governmental role in providing elder care. Here, ideas about elder care are deeply rooted in individualist values (Liu, 2000). Individualist cultures tend to value independence above interdependence, so simply being elderly does not evoke caregiving responsibilities. Instead, elder care becomes an issue when the elderly person is incapable of caring for him- or herself. And when this time comes, individualist cultures tend to favor governmental assistance rather than family obligation in caring for the elderly (Liu & Kendig, 2000).

The Elderly in Japan and Korea   The Japanese have traditionally maintained a relatively high level of respect for elders (called **filial piety**), integrating them into work and family (Palmore, 1975). The most common word for the aged in Japanese is *otoshiyori,* which means "honorable elders."

Although the days when elderly people were assumed to be superior simply because they were old are gone, rules of etiquette still give elders priority in most social settings, such as public seating arrangements and serving order at meals. Japan even has a national holiday called Respect for Elders Day. People use the age of 61 as an occasion for celebration, much like the American tradition of celebrating the age of 21. Japan's 1963 National Law for the Welfare of the Elders states, "The elders shall be loved and respected as those who have for many years contributed toward the development of society, and a wholesome and peaceful life shall be guaranteed to them" (quoted in Kart, 1990, p. 203).

Close to 50 percent of Japanese men over 65 are in the paid labor force, compared to less than 20 percent in the United States (Mackellar & Horlacher, 2000; U.S. Bureau of the Census, 2000b). Although most Japanese industries have a mandatory retirement age, which was raised to age 65 in 1986, many large corporations provide some kind of employment for older male workers even after they retire. The employer may extend the old job, create a new one not subject to compulsory retirement, or offer a part-time or lower-paying job (Kart, 1990). Voluntary organizations called Silver Human Resource Centers assist older workers in finding part-time or temporary work, such as supervising parking lots or cleaning parks (Martin, 1989). Those who are not employed remain useful with housekeeping, child care, shopping, gardening, and other household tasks (Palmore, 1975).

Why do the Japanese attach such high social value to their aged citizens? Japanese society is "vertically" structured, meaning that most relationships are hierarchical rather than egalitarian. Age is the most important dimension for determining who is above and who is below. In addition, religious principles of filial piety dating back to Confucius suggest that respect for one's parents is one of the most important virtues an individual can possess. Family patriarchs or matriarchs were once seen as virtual gods in the house. In the past, schoolchildren were rigorously taught moral stories of filial piety, such as the tale of the couple who decided, after running out of food, to kill their child so they would have more to feed their parents. They were rewarded when they dug the child's grave and found a treasure (Kristof, 1997).

So revered are the elderly in some rural areas of Japan that even when they die they remain a respected, everyday presence in the household (Kristof, 1996b). Dead elders are regularly consulted by family members on important matters. People may give them a rundown on the local news; present them daily with tea, rice, and water; and even include a place for them at family meals.

But the venerated position of the elderly in Japan is changing. In recent years—especially in modern, urban areas—attitudes toward the elderly have become more negative, particularly among the young. The belief that children are obligated to care for their aging parents has weakened (Ogawa & Retherford, 1993). Between 1972 and 1999, the number of three-generation Japanese families living under one roof declined from 55.8 percent to 29.7 percent. During that same time, the number of elderly living alone more than doubled (Strom, 2001). In 1950, 59 percent of Japanese in a national survey said they would depend on a child in old age, but in 1990 only 18 percent said they would (cited in Koyano, 2000). In 1963, 80 percent of Japanese respondents said that caring for elderly parents was either a "good custom" or a "natural duty." By 1990, the figure had dropped to 50 percent (Kristof, 1997).

Some scholars suggest that changing attitudes toward the elderly, coupled with the changing age structure of the population, have created a crisis in elder care in Japan (Liu, 2000). The population of Japan is aging faster than any on earth. It is projected that by 2010, close to one-quarter of the Japanese population will be over 65 (Mackellar & Horlacher, 2000), and by 2050 the percentage will be nearly one-third (National Institute of Population and Social Security Research, 2001).

Before 1945 it was exclusively the family that ensured care for the elderly. In those days, institutional care was considered a disgrace and a sign of unsuccessful family life (Hashimoto & Takahashi, 1995). It violated the duty-oriented idea that family members should take care of each other. But shrinking family size, increased female labor force participation, the aging of the Japanese population, and a bad economy have made family care of the elderly more problematic. In response, the Japanese government has recently initiated several programs to help families manage elder care. For example, in 1999, *Kaigo Kyugyouhou*, or the Long Term Care Leave Law, was passed, requiring companies to grant temporary leave for workers to care for frail family members (Ishii-Kuntz, 1999).

Similarly, in Korea, forms of respect for the aged have slowly been changing in recent years as the female labor market expands, multigenerational households decrease, and younger generations emphasize a more individualistic lifestyle (Sung, 1993). But respect for the aged has strong roots in Korean culture, and values based on filial piety have not yet been completely undermined. Over 80 percent of elderly Korean parents still live with their children.

To promote children's respect for their elders, the Korean government in 1973 established the annual Filial Piety Prize, which is awarded during Respect for the Elderly Week. Between 150 and 380 people nationwide—overwhelmingly women—are awarded the prize each year for the respect and responsibility they show their elderly parents. Respect is demonstrated by treating the parent with courtesy and deference; showing exceptional, earnest, and sincere consideration for the parent; and showing extraordinary honor and esteem for the parent. Responsibility is shown by delaying marriage and education or withdrawing from social activities to be fully devoted to parental care, giving care to a parent-in-law after the death of one's spouse or to a mother after the death of a father, and supporting a large family in addition to an aged parent. The prizewinners are individuals who have endured physical, financial, and social sacrifices for their parents. They have disregarded their own comfort and given up the good life, have paid for their parents' medicine or for other forms of care, and may even have quit their jobs to care for their parent.

The high level of sacrifice necessary to be worthy of the Filial Piety Prize is indicated by the fact that the majority of winners are low-income people. More affluent sons and daughters may show just as much respect and take on just as much responsibility, but their acts are not so publicly praiseworthy. They have the financial means to provide care without much personal sacrifice.

The Elderly in Immigrant Families   Cultural values regarding the elderly can cause problems when families migrate from one society to another. Latin-American immigrants to the United States, for instance, bring with them traditional values emphasizing respect for elders (Stanford, Peddecord, & Lockery, 1990). Women are the assumed caregivers of older relatives. Such traditions become difficult to sustain, however, when immigrants face the financial uncertainties and cultural contradictions of living in a new country.

The difficulties that elderly people in Southeast Asian refugee families face are particularly acute. The experience of aging in America is far different from what they had expected for the later phases of their lives in their native countries (Yee, 1992). They must cope with rapidly acculturating children and grandchildren while taking on different roles, under a different set of expectations, in a foreign culture.

For one thing, many Southeast Asian refugee elders find that they aren't considered elderly by U.S. standards. For example, in the traditional Hmong culture one becomes elderly on becoming a grandparent, which could happen at age 35. With grandparent status, these elder Hmong can retire and expect their children to take financial responsibility for the family. But you probably wouldn't find many Americans retiring at the age of 35 so that their children can take care of them for the rest of their lives.

In addition, as is true of the Japanese and Korean societies discussed earlier, filial piety is a strong value in Southeast Asian families. Elders are considered crucial sources of wisdom. But because refugee elders lack knowledge of U.S. culture, their credibility in advising young people on important decisions is diminished considerably. As younger people become more Americanized, they are more likely to reject the teachings of the traditional culture.

In fact, young people tend to be the family members most proficient in the English language, and therefore they act as important mediators between their families and American institutions. Older refugees find themselves increasingly dependent on their children and grandchildren, rather than the reverse. Hence, elders lose many of their leadership roles in the eyes of the family and the larger community (Yee, 1992). Such role reversal can be a source of considerable conflict and shame in refugee families.

Refugee elders also find their socioeconomic status diminished. They may still provide child care assistance and perform household duties, but they can no longer offer financial support, land, or other material goods, as they would have in their homeland. The refugee process strips away these resources and, simultaneously, elders' control of inheritance in the family.

Culture and Old Age in the United States   In this culture people tend to see old age for the losses that accompany it, not the gains it provides. For many, the elderly represent precisely what people spend most of their lives trying to deny: their own mortality. Common stereotypes about the elderly—that they're sick, slow-witted, senile, mean, depressed, and dangerous behind the wheel of a car—reinforce the public perception that they are socially worthless (Neugarten, 1980). Television commercials that advertise products for the elderly portray them as arthritic, constipated, incontinent, wrinkled, and toothless.

Like other forms of prejudice, these perceptions are usually translated into action—that is, overt discrimination. Although the Age Discrimination in Employment Act of 1967 prohibits hiring, firing, or determining wages or other privileges and conditions of employment on the basis of age, age discrimination in employment practices still exists today. Mandatory retirement policies in some businesses operate on the assumption that all people experience a decrease in mental and physical capabilities when they reach a certain age. As long as the elderly are perceived to be rigid, unhealthy, unhappy, and unemployable, discriminatory treatment will seem justified.

Although the elderly tend to be a devalued segment of the U.S. population, they are more likely than any other age group to benefit from existing social policies. Many federal programs are designed to assist the elderly in areas such as retirement, health care, housing, transportation, and other social services. The elderly have been the principal beneficiaries of the federal government's involvement in ensuring health care for high-risk populations (Medicare and Medicaid) and income assistance (Social Security). Thus, the proportion of elderly people who fall below the poverty line has *decreased* over the past 2 decades, even though the proportion of poor young people has *increased* (U.S. Bureau of the Census, 2000b). In fact, over the life course, economic hardship is likely to decline significantly with older age (Mirowsky & Ross, 1999).

The "Graying" of America and Its Effect on Families

Ironically, although Americans tend to devalue old age, they are collectively becoming an older society (see Exhibit 12.3). Two hundred years ago, the median age for Americans was 16; in 1980 it was 30; according to the 2000 census, today it is about 35.3 (U.S. Bureau of the Census, 2001a). Analysts estimate that about 56 million people will be over age 65 by 2020, as the massive baby boom cohort reaches old age, compared to 35 million in 2000 (Federal Interagency Forum on Aging-Related Statistics, 2000).

Two developments in the past several decades have changed the age structure of the United States in dramatic ways. The first has been a decrease in the number of children being born. In 1960 there were approximately 24 births per 1,000 people in the population.

EXHIBIT 12.3

The Growing Elderly Population in the United States

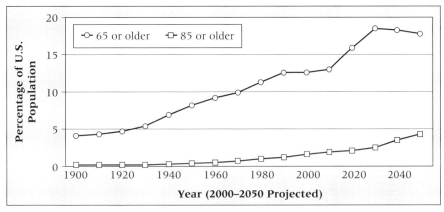

Data source: Federal Interagency Forum on Aging-Related Statistics. 2000. "Older Americans 2000: Key Indicators of Well-Being." Table 1b. Available at www.agingstats.gov/chartbook2000/tables-population.html/. Accessed September 1, 2001.

By 2000 the rate had dropped to 14.2 per 1,000 (U.S. Bureau of the Census, 2000b). In 1960, the typical U.S. family had 3.5 children; today that figure is about 2.0. Between 1980 and 1998, the proportion of the population under 15 decreased from 23 percent to 21 percent (U.S. Bureau of the Census, 2000b), and it will continue to drop for decades to come. The fertility rate is expected to edge up for a while when the baby boomers' children (the Millennium Generation) begin to have their own children. But by then, the percentage of old people will have already shot up.

The second factor changing the age structure has been an increase in the number of people surviving to old age. Several centuries ago, death was an ever-present possibility from the day a person was born. Mortality rates were several times higher than they are today. A white baby girl born today has a greater chance of living to the age of 60 than a white baby girl born in 1870 had of reaching her first birthday (Skolnick, 1991). Young people commonly died of tuberculosis, pneumonia, or one of a host of other infectious diseases.

In the past, old age was a stage of life available only to those segments of the population that had access to adequate health care and nutrition. But technological advances in medicine and nutrition have extended the lives of countless Americans who would have routinely died several decades ago. Old age is now available to a broader cross section of the population, rather than a select few (Treas & Bengtson, 1982). Overall life expectancy at birth has risen from 67.1 for males and 74.0 for females in 1970 to 74.2 for males and 79.9 for females in 1997 (U.S. Bureau of the Census, 2000b). By 2030, the United States will have more old people than children. The number of people over 85 will grow fastest of all, doubling to 6.5 million by 2020 and soaring to 17.7 million by 2050 (Angier, 1995). More than 1 million people will be over the age of 100 by then, as well (cited in Rimer, 1998a).

Why should people be concerned about this "graying" of the U.S. population? At a societal level, the answer is that an aging population will inevitably create increased demands for pensions, health care, and other social services catering to the needs of the elderly. For instance, 1 percent of people between the ages of 65 and 74 require nursing home care. But that figure increases to 22 percent for those over 85 and almost 50 percent for those over 95 (cited in Rimer, 1998a). Moreover, aging populations change the assumptions people make about the economy, such as the size and composition of the labor force, productivity, and patterns of saving, spending, and consuming (Morgan & Kunkel, 1998).

The continuing growth of the elderly population will undoubtedly have an enormous impact on U.S. families as well. Increased life expectancy lengthens the duration of marriage and parent–child relationships, encourages stronger emotional bonds between parents and children, makes grandparenthood likely during the life course, and increases the number of grandparents or even great-grandparents a child will actually know (Skolnick, 1991).

Consider marriage. When life expectancy was lower, the average marriage ended as a result of the death of one of the spouses after only 25 or so years of marriage. At the turn of the twentieth century the median age at marriage was 21.2 for women and 24.6 for men. Life expectancy was about 51 years for women and 48 for men, 35 and 32.5 for African-American men and women (Morgan & Kunkel, 1998). More than half of all marriages were ended by the death of one spouse before the last child had left home (Kart, 1990). So you can see that many people were widowed well before their children were grown.

Today, the average couple may live 30 years or more after the last child has left home. So married couples have more time to compile extensive common experiences and share broad historical changes. But they also have more time to get on each other's nerves

(Preston, 1976). Between 1980 and 1999, the percentage of divorced people over the age of 65 increased from 3.5 percent to 6.7 percent (U.S. Bureau of the Census, 2000b). Now, in a sense, more and more people are "outliving" their marriages.

Increased longevity also extends the amount of time parents spend with their children. In the near future a significant number of parents and children could spend 60 or more years together, of which only 18 or so would be in the traditional parent–child relationship (Riley, 1983). Certainly growing longevity increases the number of important experiences that parents and children can share.

The extended parent–child relationship affords greater opportunity for exchanging resources and ensuring family continuity (Bengtson, 2001). Adult children can (and often do) turn to their parents for support and help in times of need. But the lengthening of parent–child relationships also increases the financial and emotional burdens on the children when they reach adulthood. The likelihood that one's parents will live well into their 80s means that, for many people, their role as someone's child and the accompanying responsibilities will long overlap their roles as someone's spouse and parent and those responsibilities. With these extended responsibilities comes an increased risk of conflict between parents and children.

Increased longevity also means that today's children commonly grow into adulthood without experiencing the loss of a grandparent. In the distant past it was quite rare for a child to know, let alone grow up with, his or her grandparents. But it's projected that by the time children born in the year 2000 reach age 18, 68 percent will still have four living grandparents; and by age 30, 76 percent will have at least one living grandparent (Uhlenberg, 1996). A 20-year-old today is more likely to have a living grandmother than a 20-year-old in 1900 was to still have a living mother. These changes have the potential to both complicate and enrich grandchildren's lives.

DEMO•GRAPHICS

Life Transitions in Old Age

Life is full of transitions. And old age is filled with some of the most significant life changes of all: declining health, death, widowhood, and major changes in long-term living arrangements.

One of the most significant family transitions typically experienced during old age is widowhood. But as life expectancies continue to increase, marriages survive longer. In fact, the majority of American men and women ages 65–74 are still married (see Exhibit 12.4a). After age 75, however, this pattern shifts. Among the very old (age 85 and older), for instance, 1 in 2 men are married compared to about 1 in 10 women.

Marital status, especially widowhood, has a direct effect on the living arrangements of the elderly. In 1998, 73 percent of men aged 65 or older lived with their spouses, compared to 41 percent of older women (see Exhibit 12.4b). Older women were much more likely than older men to live alone or with another relative. But in Exhibit 12.4b you can see significant racial differences in these living arrangements. For instance, white and black women are much more likely to live alone than are Hispanic or Asian-American women. And whites are the least likely to live with other relatives.

EXHIBIT 12.4

Living Arrangements in Old Age

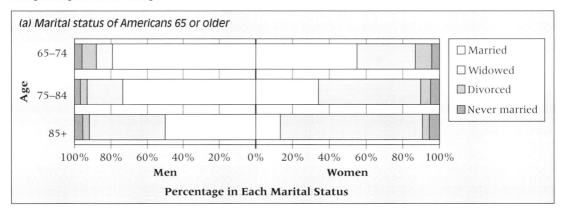

(a) Marital status of Americans 65 or older

Data source: Federal Interagency Forum on Aging-Related Statistics. 2000. "Older Americans 2000: Key Indicators of Well-Being," Table 3. Available at www.agingstats.gov/chartbook2000/population.html/. Accessed September 1, 2001.

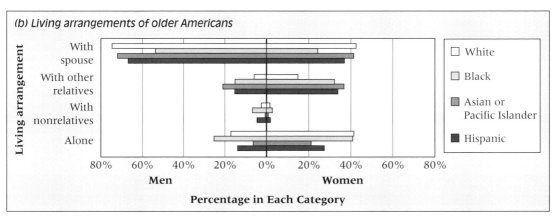

(b) Living arrangements of older Americans

Data source: Federal Interagency Forum on Aging-Related Statistics. 2000. "Older Americans 2000: Key Indicators of Well-Being," Table 5a. Available at www.agingstats.gov/chartbook2000/tables-population.html/. Accessed September 1, 2001.

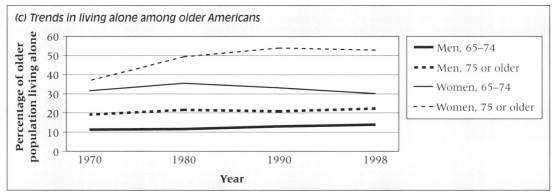

(c) Trends in living alone among older Americans

Data source: Federal Interagency Forum on Aging-Related Statistics. 2000. "Older Americans 2000: Key Indicators of Well-Being," Table 5b. Available at www.agingstats.gov/chartbook2000/tables-population.html/. Accessed September 1, 2001.

One segment of the older population that deserves special attention is the group that lives alone. Research shows that older people who live alone are more likely than other elderly people to live in poverty (Dalaker, 1999). They are also less likely to have caretakers readily available to them. About 19 percent of white older women and about half of older black and Hispanic women who live alone are impoverished (Dalaker, 1999; Federal Interagency Forum on Aging-Related Statistics, 2000). As you can see in Exhibit 12.4c, the percentage of very old women who live alone has increased since 1970. The "old old" in society—precisely those who are likely to need greater assistance and care—are more likely to live alone than are the "young old."

Thinking Critically About the Statistics

1. In Exhibit 12.4a, which age group shows the greatest discrepancy in marital status between women and men? What factors might explain the size of this difference? Do you think this gap is likely to shrink in future decades? Why or why not?

2. Study Exhibit 12.4b carefully. Overall, which racial/ethnic group is least likely to live with a spouse in old age? What are the possible explanations? (*Hint:* Refer to Exhibit 12.4a.) Is this group's tendency to not live with a spouse in old age influenced by some other aspect of their living arrangements? How might feelings of family obligation and reliance on extended kin come into play in helping create the differences represented in this exhibit? Considering the information in Exhibit 12.4b, which sex and racial/ethnic group would you focus on if you were creating a new program to help the elderly?

3. Exhibit 12.4c compares trends in living alone for various age and sex groups. Only one of these groups shows a decline in the likelihood of living alone over the past three decades. What is that group? What are the possible reasons for the decline? Do you consider this trend a positive or a negative development overall? ■

Generational Obligations

In contemporary U.S. society, relationships between adult children and their parents are characterized by two seemingly contradictory sets of norms: obligation and independence (Aldous, 1995). On the one hand, norms concerning obligation specify that adult children and parents should assist and care for each other over the course of their lives. On the other hand, norms of independence specify that adult children must at some point assume responsibility for their own well-being and that nuclear families should maintain themselves, independent of wider kin networks (Lye, 1996). Relations between adult children and their elderly parents sit precariously between these two ideals.

The conflict between obligation and independence is described in Issue 4.

The History of Generational Obligation   The feelings of obligation that cross generations are molded not only by the unique experiences of individuals within a particular family but also by specific historical circumstances. The adaptation of individuals and their families to the social and economic conditions they face in the later years of life is determined by the pathways they took to old age. Wars, migration, depressions, and the decline of local economies can affect patterns of support and expectations for receiving and providing assistance in old age (Hareven, 1994).

Contrary to popular images, early American households were typically nuclear in their structure. Older generations lived in households separate from their married children—

but nearby, often on the same land. Opportunities for contact and cooperation were numerous. Even though adult children were expected to care for aging parents, no laws required them to do so. Even in the colonial period, elderly people couldn't count on the support of their family, though they did get more respect and higher status than they get today (Hareven, 1994). In fact, aging parents had to enter into legal contracts with their inheriting sons in order to secure support in old age. The existence of such contracts indicates that many elderly parents had a great deal of anxiety about what would happen to them when they became too frail to support themselves.

Similarly, in the nineteenth and early twentieth centuries, elderly parents usually didn't live with their adult children and weren't guaranteed their support in old age. In fact, only about 12 percent to 18 percent of all urban households in the later nineteenth and early twentieth centuries contained any relatives other than members of the nuclear family. Today's preferred mode of generational interaction—dubbed "intimacy from a distance"—has persisted since the earliest days of the country, among rural and urban families (Hareven, 1994).

Nevertheless, American families have always been willing to expand their households to include other kin in times of need. When elderly parents and especially widowed mothers were unable to maintain themselves in a separate household, they often lived with their adult children. These arrangements were typically for a limited time, and usually the children moved into the parents' home to care for them rather than vice versa.

Help Across Generations   People often assume that when help is extended from one adult generation to another, it is children who are helping their aging parents. But studies show that assistance usually flows from older generations to younger ones (Bengtson, 2001). For instance, it is much more likely that parents will give financial gifts to their adult children than the reverse.

The higher living standards of today's elderly, discussed earlier in this chapter, may reduce adult children's feelings that they need to help their parents. Furthermore, many people in today's unpredictable economy don't feel they can afford to sacrifice substantial wages and benefits, pass up promotions, or take extended time off their jobs to care for their elderly parents (cited in Rimer, 1999). In addition, high rates of divorce and remarriage, and the complicated family structures that result, make it harder to sort out who is responsible for taking care of parents.

In recent decades, norms of obligation have weakened somewhat while norms of independence have strengthened (Lye, 1996). In fact, on close inspection, researchers have found that there's actually not much help flowing in either direction. A nationwide study of over 13,000 American adults found that half of them didn't routinely give financial help to or receive it from their aging parents (Hogan, Eggebeen, & Clogg, 1993).

This lack of intergenerational support may reflect uncertainty about family obligations. Close to three-quarters of all Americans continue to believe adult children *should* provide financial assistance to their parents (cited in Lye, 1996), and close to half agree that adult children should let their parents live with them when they can no longer care for themselves (see Exhibit 12.5). People are a little less certain, though, about parents' obligations to their adult children. For instance, less than half agree that parents ought to provide financial assistance to their adult children, and slightly more than a third agree that parents should let their adult children live with them (cited in Lye, 1996).

Beneath these statistics is a disapproval of the kind of intergenerational support that creates too much dependence between family members. That concern is stronger among

EXHIBIT 12.5

*American Adults'
Attitudes
Toward Sharing
Their Home
with Aging
Parents*

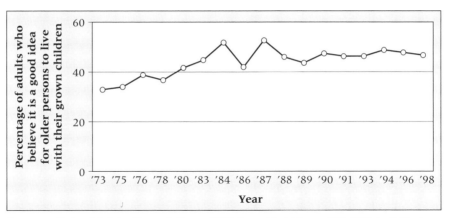

Data source: National Opinion Research Center. 1998. *General Social Survey, 1972–1998.* Available at www.icpsr.umich.edu/GSS/. Accessed June 1, 2001.

the elderly than among their adult children (Lye, 1996). Some elderly people worry about lifestyle differences if two generations live together, struggles over authority and the household division of labor, and the chaos caused by grandchildren as potential areas of conflict. With adequate resources, most older Americans would probably prefer to live independently of their adult children. Many elderly people may perceive living with their children as a last resort before having to live in a nursing or retirement home.

Nevertheless, research indicates that relationships between elderly parents and adult children today can be quite close, characterized by frequent visits, telephone calls, and letters. According to the American Association of Retired Persons (2001), nearly 80 percent of people between the ages of 45 and 55 provide some sort of caregiving services to their parents from time to time, such as shopping, doing housework, talking to doctors, and handling bills and other paperwork. A recent national survey found that over half of adult children live within a 1-hour drive of their parents. Close to 70 percent have weekly contact with their mothers, and 20 percent have daily contact (cited in Lye, 1996).

The closeness of relationships between adult children and elderly parents varies along ethnic lines (American Association of Retired Persons, 2001; Raley, 1995). For instance, by long tradition in the African-American community, adults are expected to care for their parents and grandparents. This tradition arose to address the harsh economic realities of life: limited access to medical care, public support, and good jobs, the sorts of things that would guarantee a secure old age. According to one study, older blacks are twice as likely as whites to receive care and assistance from family members when their health deteriorates (cited in Rimer, 1998b). However, the toll that such caregiving expectations can exact on a family—in terms of stress, lost wages, postponed or missed employment and educational opportunities, and so on—is often quite high. Some experts fear that in coming generations, as African-American families become increasingly mobile, fewer people will be able to take on the traditional caregiving role.

As for Hispanic Americans, within the next 60 years they are expected to grow from 4 percent to 12 percent of the elderly population (Miranda, 1992). Hispanic families are typically close-knit. Around 80 percent of Mexican-American elderly, for instance, have frequent contact with their children, because they either live with them or live within a few minutes of their home. Compared with Anglo Americans, on average, Mexican Americans show significantly higher levels of devotion to their families, more collectivist attitudes, and a greater tendency to help their elderly parents (Freeberg & Stein, 1996). They feel significantly more obligated to avoid conflict and provide assistance. Nevertheless, despite frequent contact, fewer than 20 percent of the elderly respondents in one survey reported receiving direct assistance with meals, shopping, transportation, light housework, or everyday activities such as bathing, dressing, and eating (Dietz, 1995).

Increasingly, adult children of all racial and ethnic groups are having to cope with the burden of caring for elderly parents in addition to the usual demands of work and family. More than 6 million elderly Americans now need help with such everyday basics as getting out of bed, eating, dressing, bathing, and using the bathroom (Beck, 1990). Given the high cost of nursing homes, many elderly parents do end up moving in with their children.

Gender and Elder Care   Both men and women claim to accept responsibility for aged parents, but women are more likely to be called on to act on those responsibilities. Even in eras and among ethnic groups in which individuals were deeply dependent on relations with extended kin, the day-to-day involvement with and responsibility for caring for elderly parents fell primarily to adult daughters (Hareven, 1994). In fact, before World War II norms dictated that a younger daughter would delay or forgo marriage in order to care for her parents until their death (Morgan & Kunkel, 1998).

Although such expectations have diminished over the years, people still expect adult female children to provide needed help to older parents. Sons do tend to perform managerial and maintenance tasks and provide financial support for their parents; but daughters predominantly perform the daily hands-on caregiving. Outside of a spouse, adult female children are the most common caretakers of the frail elderly (American Association of Retired Persons, 2001). According to the National Partnership for Women and Families, two-thirds of women between the ages of 40 and 59 will likely be responsible for the care of an elderly parent in the next 10 years (cited in Toner, 1999). With increases in life expectancy, these caretaking responsibilities can last a decade or more.

Meeting these obligations often comes at the expense of other family roles. Many women who provide care to elderly parents are forced to spend less time with their husbands and children, leading to resentment and frustration and ultimately threatening the structure of family life. Women's occupational roles and financial well-being may also suffer. In an era when most families depend on two incomes for survival, some women have had to switch to part-time work, pass up promotions, or quit their jobs altogether. A study by the American Association of Retired Persons estimated that 14 percent of all part-time adult female workers left their full-time jobs because of caregiving responsibilities. Of those not employed but who once had jobs, 27 percent had taken early retirement or simply quit (cited in Lewin, 1989).

With these conflicting responsibilities come feelings of guilt, inadequacy, and anger, which are similar to the guilt feelings about children's care described in Chapter 7. One woman, who quit her job to care for her mother, who had developed Alzheimer's disease, echoed the thoughts of many:

> I felt like I was going under. I couldn't do my job because I was pretty much in pieces. I was furious at my brother who didn't help at all. My 15-year-old daughter is mad at me because I am so engaged with my mother. My son has stopped visiting me. And the friends who had been wonderful and supportive through the birth of my babies and

my divorce just faded away now that I need them the most. I am alternately so sad about my mother's decline that I can't stop crying and so enraged that my life is being messed up that I want to dump her. I used to think I was good at crises, but this just goes on and on, and I'm falling apart. (quoted in Lewin, 1989, p. 13)

Although the adverse effects of caring for elderly parents on women's well-being are well documented, the experience apparently isn't always so bad. A national study of married persons found that changes in family responsibilities had little effect on female caregivers' well-being, even among those women who worked full time (Loomis & Booth, 1995). The authors offered several possible explanations for why family caregiving responsibilities don't necessarily cause stress:

- *The caregiver knows the individual needing care quite well.* Hence, what that person requires is seldom a mystery or a surprise.
- *The people who take on the added responsibilities may be the ones most capable of doing so.* The people with the stronger marriages were more likely to assume multigenerational caregiving responsibilities than people in weak or unstable marriages. So those who take on additional responsibilities may be the ones who are best equipped to balance family, work, and personal needs.
- *The individuals who take on these responsibilities may value caring for others.* Meeting family obligations may be a source of fulfillment that offsets any negative effects. Many women come to view the care of their elderly parents as a sort of "payback" for the care they received growing up.

The changing economic status of women is likely to have a significant impact on the availability of family caregivers in the future. The mass entrance of women into the workforce, changing attitudes concerning "gender appropriate" roles, and the growing necessity for two incomes in a family have already reduced the number of women who are able to care for elderly parents. Perhaps in the near future sons and daughters will find a way to share the responsibility.

Death and Families

The most devastating transition that a family can experience is the death of one of its members. Like aging, death is a biological event. But also like aging, the experience of death is shaped by culture. In preindustrial societies, sick people were taken care of at home and they died at home. Because life was relatively short, most people could expect to see the death of a sibling or parent during their childhood.

In some cultures today, death continues to be a part of everyday life. In Mexico, for instance, November 1 and 2 are known as *los dias de los muertos*, or "days of the dead." Representations of death pervade every aspect of life during these 2 days. Children eat sugar skulls and candy coffins and play with skeleton puppets. They eat picnic lunches in graveyards and gamble and play board games on the tombstones there. In some areas of Mexico, special bread—called *pan de los muertos* or "bread of the dead"—is baked and eaten only on these days. Families decorate their homes with symbols of funerals (tombs, coffins, and pallbearers) and the afterlife (ghosts, angels, and devils). They build altars and prepare food that they offer to the spirits of dead relatives (Green, 1995).

The inclusion of children in all these rituals reinforces the cultural belief that there is no need to hide death. It is an event with which children are intimately familiar because, like birth, it takes place at home with the family.

In American society, industrialization and the advent of modern medicine have made dying a distant event managed by outsiders. As a result, many Americans have never personally seen someone die—although, ironically, most have witnessed tens of thousands of fictionalized deaths on television and in film by the time they reach adulthood. Dying has become a remote occurrence disconnected from everyday life. Most Americans die alone, in institutional medical settings, surrounded by doctors, nurses, and attendants.

Not surprisingly, then, dying is a strange and fearful process to most Americans, something to be hidden or perhaps even denied. An elaborate vocabulary of euphemisms has developed to refer to death without using the word itself. People aren't dead, they're "gone" or "no longer with us." They don't die, they "pass away "or "expire." Pets aren't killed, they're "put to sleep."

Widowhood

Barring a divorce, practically all marriages end with the death of one or the other spouse. But gender differences in life expectancy mean that widows far outnumber widowers in this country.

Despite its ubiquity, the death of a spouse can be one of the most severe social and personal crises experienced. Widowhood is associated with impaired social and psychological functioning as well as with an increased risk of sickness and death for the surviving spouse. Depression is a particularly common response to widowhood, especially during the first year or two after the death (Umberson, Wortman, & Kessler, 1992). Of course, a number of factors influence people's response to the death of a spouse, such as how close the couple's relationship was before the death and whether the death was the anticipated result of a long-term illness or the unanticipated result of an accident, an acute medical episode, or suicide.

People's response to widowhood is, to some degree, influenced by perceptions of gender within the larger culture. In traditional India, for instance, adult Hindu women had no identity outside of being a wife. Hence, many widows used to commit suicide by ceremoniously throwing themselves on the funeral pyres of their dead husbands. Those who didn't kill themselves were outcasts in the community. Widows are still considered bad luck in India and are often referred to by the pronoun *it*. In Japan, the word for widow, *mibojin*, means "a person who has not yet died."

In U.S. society, the status of widow or widower is likely to be pitied rather than stigmatized. Interestingly, even though men occupy a more advantaged position in the larger society, evidence suggests that they experience widowhood as a more emotionally distressing event than do women (Umberson et al., 1992). Because men are less likely than women to have close, confiding relationships with others outside the marriage, widowhood is more likely to leave men socially and emotionally isolated. This lack of emotional support and social contact may leave them more vulnerable to depression. Furthermore, because men are less likely to handle the bulk of day-to-day household tasks, the surviving husband may be ill equipped to deal with necessities such as cooking, cleaning, laundry, and so on.

Women are by no means unaffected by the death of a spouse. But the source of difficulty is different from that for men. For one thing, women in traditional marriages can experience severe psychological problems because widowhood takes away a key element in their self-identity: being a wife. In addition, because women earn, on average, substantially less than men, widowhood can lead to greater financial strain for women than it does for men. According to one study, the average standard of living of widows drops 18 percent after a husband's death (Bound, Duncan, Laren, & Oleinick, 1991). African-American and Latina women are especially prone to poverty after the death of a spouse.

The Death of a Parent

Because of medical and nutritional advances that have increased life expectancy, only 1 in 10 children today has lost a parent by age 25. Thus, when young children do suffer the death of a parent, they are likely to experience it as a horrible blow. In addition to the emotional tragedy, the loss of a parent can financially devastate the family. As a result, the children may face a series of other significant losses: moving from their home, changing schools and neighborhoods, and so on.

Sociologist Lynn Davidman (2000) interviewed 60 men and women whose mothers had died when they were between 10 and 12 years old. She found that there are few guidelines for coping individually or as a family with such a loss, and no vocabulary to speak about it. As a result, Davidman suggests, silence and a sense of taboo commonly surround early maternal death, making it difficult for children to integrate the experience into their lives. One woman, who was 12 when her mother died, remembers,

> My father said we had to move to get out of that house, because it reminded him of my mother. . . . We went to the house, and it was like she's not there. She never was in that kitchen. She never put something away in this cupboard. She never had those plants. So she just was gone. She was never mentioned. It sort of became like she had never existed. It was our way of dealing with it, I guess. I think to contemplate such a loss would be painful on an ongoing basis, so we just never talked about or thought about it. (quoted on p. 65)

Experiencing a parent's death as a child is "a major disruptive event that creates reverberations that linger throughout the lives of the children they leave behind" (Davidman, 2000, pp. 232–233). For instance, the majority of women and men Davidman interviewed indicated problems with intimacy that they attributed to their mothers having died.

Of course, parental death is more common in adulthood. By age 54, half of all Americans have lost both parents (Umberson & Chen, 1994). Nevertheless, it can adversely affect the physical and psychological well-being of adult children. To them, the death of a parent signifies the loss of a significant part of their living historical record. To lose a parent is to lose one of the few people who have known you your whole life. Furthermore, as you've already seen, parental influence continues to be important throughout adulthood, even in the absence of physical proximity. Finally, because the duration of the parent–child relationship is longer than ever before, the symbolic importance of parent–child relationships may also be greater now than in the past.

Not every adult has a strong relationship with his or her parents. Individuals who feel closer to their parents have a more difficult time adjusting to their death than adult children for whom relationships with parents are an insignificant part of their lives (Umberson & Chen, 1994).

The Death of a Child

Most people assume they will outlive their parents and will therefore have to deal with their parents' death. The death of a child, however, is something few parents assume will happen to them.

In the past, the loss of a child was an expected part of family life. High infant mortality rates meant that parents were likely to experience the death of one, some, or even all of their children. In 1900 half of all U.S. parents experienced the death of a child under the age of 15, compared to well below 5 percent today (Uhlenberg, 1980).

Today, the death of a child is always untimely and unnatural. Often it is sudden and unexpected: the result of an accident, an injury, or a medical emergency. Less frequently it is caused by a progressive disease, which lets parents begin the grieving process before their child actually dies (Raphael, 1995).

Parents have different reactions to the loss of a child, depending in part on when the child dies. Miscarriages, abortions, stillbirths, and deaths in infancy can all be crushing blows to parents, who may mourn the lost opportunity to establish a history and a relationship with the child. The death of a child in childhood or adolescence takes on added significance. This child is known and related to as a real person. Parents who lose a young child or adolescent often plague themselves with thoughts of what could have been done differently. They may become angry and locked into an "if only" state of mind. In some cases parents exhibit little overt grief, just restless, agitated distress. Sadness and depression can persist, unabated, for many years.

Parents who lose their adult children experience intense grief as well. What makes the grieving process especially complex in these situations is the fact that the adult child had probably established his or her own separate life. Hence the grieving process is likely to include a variety of others—a surviving spouse, children, in-laws, and so on—each with his or her own perspective on the loss and own sense of entitlement to sympathy.

The AIDS epidemic has had a particularly transformative effect on the way parents deal with the illness and death of their grown children. Families may unite in support of an infected member, but often conflict erupts, especially if the family focuses on how the disease was transmitted. Families must face social stigma and isolation, fear of contagion and infection, as well as guilt, anger, and grief (Dane, 1991; Macklin, 1988). Most people with AIDS have at least one family member who has ceased having contact with them after learning of the illness.

The difficulties may be particularly acute for gay people with AIDS. Even families who in the past appeared to accept their lifestyle may reject them once the diagnosis is known. The diagnosis of AIDS forces parents to recognize that their children aren't simply gay in some abstract way but have been engaged in activities the parents may find distasteful. Relationships can become strained, formal, and awkward (Dane, 1991).

Families can heighten the sense of stigma by adopting extreme, medically unwarranted anticontagion precautions. A family in one study brought their own sheets when visiting their ill son's home; others refused to allow their infected children to touch any food, share their bathrooms, or come closer than an arm's-length away (Weitz, 1990).

For parents who reject their sick children, death brings many conflicting emotions. They may still experience tremendous grief and sadness over the loss of a beloved child, even though that child pursued a life they either felt uncomfortable with or actively and openly renounced.

The death of a child not only affects parents and other family members as individuals, it affects the structure of the family as well. After the death of a child a process of reorganization must occur within the family. One common dilemma surviving members face is how to now define their families (Brabant, Forsyth, & McFarlain, 1994). People have terms in this society to describe some of the many changes that families experience. "Empty nest," for instance, implies that the children are grown and gone. "Blended family" refers to families resulting from second marriages. But people have no term to describe the family that has lost a child. Some families grieve the loss and no longer include the deceased child as part of the family; others continue to count their deceased children as part of it.

Conclusion

All people reach a point in life when they disengage from the protection of parents and become self-reliant adults. Most people reach a point in life when others address them "Sir" or "Ma'am," stop asking them for identification when they buy liquor, and see them as too old and out of touch to know what life is all about. Many raise children and someday watch them leave the nest to begin their own families. Many someday find themselves responsible for the care of their own parents, and barring some unforeseen illness or accident, they all experience the death of their parents. They all experience the physical changes of aging and with luck all someday know what it's like to be defined as elderly. And all people die.

Most of these changes and transitions are inevitable. They come whether people want them to or not. Nevertheless, a multibillion-dollar industry exists to help people try to ward off aging. They can buy products to dye hair when it becomes too gray or smooth skin when it becomes too wrinkled. Surgery can help people firm up what has begun to sag. People can spend a lot of money trying to avoid old age, but in the end they will always, always fail.

Despite the inevitability of these transformations, their social meaning is far from inevitable. You've seen in this chapter that every life-changing event people experience is shaped and influenced by larger cultural, historical, and institutional forces. We can't understand what it's like to enter adulthood without knowing something about the economic and demographic forces that can impede or enhance such a transition. We can't understand the aging experience without understanding the value of the aged in that particular society. We can't understand the role of death in families without understanding how death is perceived by the dominant culture.

Furthermore, recent social changes mean that the timing of some transformative events will be different for younger cohorts from what they were for their parents or grandparents. People are leaving home later, marrying later, having children later, launching their children later, and living longer than earlier cohorts. These changes will, no doubt, have an enormous impact on people's personal family experiences, on cultural definitions of family, and on political, economic, and other social institutions in society.

Chapter Highlights

- Family transitions are socially defined, influenced by institutional, cultural and historical forces. Transitions occur over the life course, a term used to describe the socially defined, age-related events and roles that take place over the course of an individual's life.

- The way people experience family transformations in adulthood is influenced by their birth cohort. People born roughly at the same time experience personal life course events (graduation, marriage, childbearing, entry into the paid labor force, retirement, death, and so on) at roughly the same point in history, and they experience major historical events at around the same age.

- In American culture people have a pervasive belief that middle-aged parents—particularly stay-at-home mothers—suffer severe emotional crises when all their children grow up and leave home. However, for most parents, the departure of grown children from home actually provides them with freedom, relief from responsibilities, and time for themselves.

- People usually think of grandparents as elderly and retired. But most become grandparents while in mid-life, when they are married, when they are fully employed, and, with increasing frequency, when their own parents are still alive.

- Different cultures and different racial and ethnic groups within this culture vary in the degree to which grandparents are incorporated into the daily lives of families.

- Cultural definitions of and attitudes toward old age can shape the experience of becoming elderly. In some cultures, the elderly are highly respected; in others they are either ignored or treated with contempt.

- Decreasing birth rates and increasing life expectancy mean that the U.S. population is getting progressively older. An aging population changes the assumptions people make about families. It prolongs marriage, prolongs relationships between parents and children, and increases caretaking demands on adult children.

- In U.S. society today, death is something that has become disconnected and remote. Most Americans die alone, in institutional medical settings, surrounded by doctors, nurses, and attendants.

Your Turn

Getting older is not simply a matter of adding an extra year to your age. It is intricately tied to the unique culture and historical era in which you live. Hence the personal experience of aging can differ dramatically in different cultures and even among different ethnic groups within the same culture. Nowhere is this diversity more apparent than when people examine differences in the roles older people play in their own families.

To get a sense of these differences, see if you can interview grandparents from several different groups (white, African American, Asian American, Latino, Native American, recent immigrants, and so on). Try also to interview grandparents from different social classes and different religious groups.

Ask all grandparents a similar set of questions: How old were they when they became grandparents? How often do they see their grandchildren? Do they consider their relationship "close"? Are they satisfied with the amount and quality of time they spend with them? If not, what are the reasons for their dissatisfaction? Do they have any responsibility for raising their grandchildren other than occasional visits? How did their relationship with their children change when they became grandparents? Is being a grandparent any different from what they expected? What sort of support (financial, emotional, practical, and so on) do they receive from their children? What kind of support, if any, do they *provide* to their children?

Pool your findings with those of classmates, and from all the responses see if you can detect any systematic differences across groups. For instance, are grandparents in some ethnic groups more involved in the lives of their grandchildren than others? What do these differences tell about the broader value of older people in the various groups represented? Are some grandparents more or less likely than others to feel like valued members of the family? Were grandmothers and grandfathers any different in this regard? How do the experiences of recent immigrants compare to those of grandparents who have lived in this country all their lives?

Families in a Changing Society

Family Change

Throughout this book we've documented some of the important changes that families have experienced over time. It would seem, looking back, that family is in a constant state of flux. Marriage and divorce rates rise and fall; family size expands and contracts; beliefs about what it means to be a good parent/spouse/ lover/child/sibling shift with the prevailing political/cultural/economic winds. But in many other ways families have remained remarkably consistent over time.

In 1968 a group called the National Women's Liberation Movement demonstrated against the Miss America pageant, claiming that it set false goals for women.

As you look at the photos in this essay, decide for yourself how much families have changed. Is there something enduring about the form and function of families or are they constantly shifting and transforming to the point where they're unrecognizable from one generation to the next? How has your family changed since you were a child? How does your current family compare to the family experiences of past generations?

The women's movement has empowered many women to adopt a more assertive stance in their sexual lives, even to the point of demanding and providing contraception for their partners.

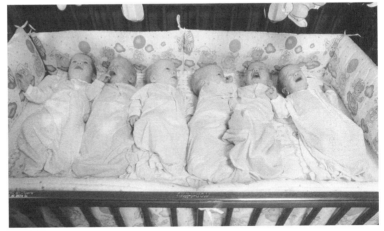

Extraordinary advances in reproductive technology such as in vitro fertilization and embryo transplants have made it possible for infertile couples to conceive and in the process have helped to redefine parenthood.

New reproductive technologies can influence families in sometimes unexpected ways. Multiple births such as these sextuplets can be the unanticipated result of medical treatments for infertility.

Advances in medical technology also allow people to live longer. There are now more four- and five-generation families than ever before. But increased life expectancy increases demands on children to provide emotional and economic support to their elderly parents.

Changes are apparent not only in what happens within family relationships but also in how those relationships begin and end. Divorce is quicker and more accessible than ever before, but does that mean "family" has become any less important in people's lives?

More women are choosing to have and raise their children outside of legal marriage.

The increasing rates of divorce and single parenthood are usually regarded by critics as changes that have had a harmful impact on families. Do you agree? Can you think of any ways that these trends have had a positive effect on the institution of family?

But as much as families have changed, they still engage in activities they enjoy doing together—whether it's listening to a gramophone in the early twentieth century . . .

. . . or watching television at mid-century.

How do you think technology has reshaped family ties and "togetherness"?

Contemporary families have roughly the same composition and function as families of the past, but technological advances like the Internet allow families to share intimate information about themselves with the world.

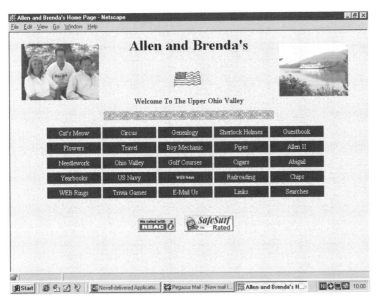

What do the content and design of family home pages tell us about the nature and importance of family in people's lives? How can you explain the willingness of these families to expose such private aspects of their lives to the vast, public domain of cyberspace?

Margaret Atwood's best-selling 1985 novel, *The Handmaid's Tale*, takes place in the not-too-distant future society of "Gilead." A brutal fundamentalist regime has closed all universities. "Enemies" of the state—homosexuals, religious "heretics," people who speak freely, doctors who've performed abortions, and others—are routinely executed, their bodies displayed on walls in town squares for all to see. People's lives are completely controlled by the Guardians, Gilead's regular police force, and a secret organization of faceless spies called the Eyes who use sophisticated surveillance techniques to monitor citizens' activities.

Women have been systematically deprived of any power or autonomy. Many have been fired from their jobs and forbidden access to their credit cards or bank accounts. Following an environmental disaster that has left most women sterile, those few who still have "viable ovaries" and are capable of reproducing are rounded up and assigned to government and military officials for breeding purposes. These women—known as Handmaids—have become faceless reproducers, wearing long red cloaks, red gloves, and white winged hats that hide their bodies and faces. Poor women who cannot bear children have become either Marthas (domestic servants) or "unwomen," who are shipped to some far-off place called the Colonies. Sterile women lucky enough to be married to powerful men—known as Commander's Wives—retain their position as upper-class housewives.

Handmaids occupy a curiously paradoxical role in Gilead. Because there are so few fertile women, the future of the entire society lies in their ability to reproduce. Others are supposed to show them respect because of the vital nature of their service. But their ostensible high status is purely symbolic. They have no authority in the household or in society. They are forbidden to marry. They are treated exclusively as reproductive "machines" with no human feelings or identity. For instance, the story's narrator is a Handmaid named Offred, or "of Fred," meaning she belongs to a Commander named Fred.

Not only are Handmaids not allowed to use their given names, but their everyday lives are completely controlled by their Commanders and Commanders' wives. They may leave the home of the Commander and his wife once a day to walk to food markets, whose signs are now pictures instead of words because women are no longer allowed to read. The sexual intercourse they are required to endure with their Commanders once a month is devoid of any emotion or pleasure. It is a state-controlled procreative necessity. The Commander's wife is present during the act, which is euphemistically referred to as The Ceremony:

> What's going on in this room . . . is not exciting. It has nothing to do with passion or love or romance or any of those other notions we used to titillate ourselves with. It has nothing to do with sexual desire. . . . Arousal and orgasm are no longer thought necessary; they would be a symptom of frivolity . . . : superfluous distractions for the light-minded. Outdated. It seems odd that women once spent such time and energy reading about such things, thinking about them, worrying about them, writing about them. They are so obviously recreational. This is not recreation, even for the Commander. This is serious business. The Commander, too, is doing his duty. (Atwood, 1985, p. 122)

After a child is born, it is immediately given over to the Commander's wife, who is praised by others as if she had given birth to the child. After a few months of breastfeeding, the Handmaid is transferred to another household to become impregnated by a different Commander, thereby maximizing genetic variety as much as possible. Handmaids have no parental rights, no legally or socially recognized relationship to the child they've borne.

They are not considered part of any family. Nor are they considered sexual beings. They are merely reproductive vessels.

Atwood's portrayal of family and parenthood in a society wracked by social change is chilling. Gilead is a society in which intimacy and emotional commitment, the cornerstones of contemporary families, no longer exist. Unlike some other fictional portrayals of future family life—which simply place traditional family structures in a high-tech futuristic setting of carplanes, fully automated appliances, interplanetary civilizations, and robot servants—Atwood's family of the future is dark and alarming. Indeed, the institution of family as we know it has been destroyed.

The book is not meant to be a realistic prediction of the future. Instead, it is speculative fiction, meant as a cautionary tale of what would be the most extreme outcome if some current trends—particularly those regarding societal attitudes about women's place in families and in society—were to continue.

We have used *The Handmaid's Tale* to introduce this final chapter not because we have a dismal, pessimistic view of future families but to show you that the future is never completely separate from the past or the present. It is a continuation and an extension of the events and trends that precede it. Shortly after Atwood's book was published, she told an interviewer, "It's not science fiction. There are no spaceships, no Martians, nothing like that. There is nothing in *The Handmaid's Tale*, with the exception of maybe one scene, that has not happened at some point in history . . . I didn't invent a lot" (quoted in Davidson, 1986, p. 24).

Of course, trying to document and anticipate the events and trends that will impact people's family experiences 10, 50, or 100 years from now is quite difficult. Although the future is always, to some degree, an extension of the past, simply knowing what happened in the past and what is currently happening are never sufficient to project into the future with complete certainty. People have no way of knowing which as-yet-unknown events or forces will shape their social worlds and mark their family lives. A sudden downturn in the economy, a lethal epidemic, a brutal terrorist attack, or a dramatic shift in the political leadership, for instance, could wreak unanticipated havoc on people's family lives.

Underlying any discussion of future families—especially as they relate to the past—is the notion of change. It's important to note that change can occur at different levels. At the individual level, families are always gaining and losing members through births, deaths, marriages, divorces, or migration. The types of transitions discussed in Chapter 12 remind us that change is a universal feature of family life.

But families can also be reshaped in response to change that occurs at the societal or institutional level. In this chapter, we examine some of these broader patterns of family change and explore the sources of these changes. We document current trends, make some tentative projections about what families may look like in the twenty-first century, and discuss society's role in influencing these changes through public policy.

Social Change

Part of the difficulty in talking about families in the future is that the present is so fleeting. Change is the preeminent characteristic of modern human societies, whether it occurs in personal relationships, cultural norms and values, or social institutions. No doubt, the world in which you are living at this precise moment is, in many ways, different from the one experienced when we wrote this book. On several occasions we had to revise or update examples or statistics at the last minute because some things have changed so quickly.

Over the last half of the twentieth century, divorce rates dropped, skyrocketed, then stabilized. People began waiting longer to get married and then, once they did marry, having fewer children. Cultural concerns over gender equality have altered the way men and women relate to each other inside and outside the home. Social and sexual rules that once seemed permanent have disintegrated: Unmarried couples now live together openly, unmarried women routinely have and keep their babies, and remaining single and remaining childless have become acceptable lifestyle options (Teachman, Tedrow, & Crowder, 2000).

> Whether or not these trends signify a breakdown of family institution is a debate addressed in Issue 2.

Fifty years ago, few people doubted the "supremacy" of the female homemaker–male breadwinner family. Functionalist sociologists wrote about how this family type was ideally suited to meet the needs of individuals and social institutions (Gerson, 2000). Today, less than 15 percent of U.S. families fit this pattern. Most families today are either dual-earner, single-parent, "blended," or "empty-nest." Mothers are less likely to be the primary caretakers of their children than they were 30 years ago, forcing them to depend on secondary relationships—paid caregivers, friends, teachers—to fulfill that traditional role. In short, today's American family bears little resemblance to the cultural ideal that existed just a generation ago.

People beginning their families today face tough decisions about issues that past generations simply took for granted:

> In place of compulsory marriage are questions about whether and when to get married or stay married. In place of separate spheres are conflicts between the paid work of supporting family members and the unpaid work of caring for them. In place of full-time mothering and distant but steady fatherhood are tensions between the need to care for others and the need for autonomy and personal achievement. (Gerson, 2000, p. 183)

These new family dilemmas and contradictions are unsettling, but they are simply a correlate of other types of social change.

Sources of Social Change

Although individual families may undergo rapid, sudden changes in their structure and dynamics, changes in the institution of family tend to occur gradually over time in response to changes that occur in other areas of society. Indeed, one can only understand family change in the context of broad social changes in other institutions. Demographic shifts in the population, technological innovation, and cultural, institutional, and economic trends often force families to alter the way they do things. For instance, feminism is often identified as the major reason for family change over the past several decades. But the feminist movement has been able to transform women's lives only because new economic options were available. Most women—and men, for that matter—are now able to live on their own financially and thus are not compelled by economic need to get married or stay married (Gerson, 2000).

Population Pressures   Exhibit 13.1 shows how the population in the United States shifted over the course of the twentieth century from what demographers term a "pyramid" (proportionally higher numbers of young people make up the base and categories shrink with

EXHIBIT 13.1

The Shifting Shape of the U.S. Population

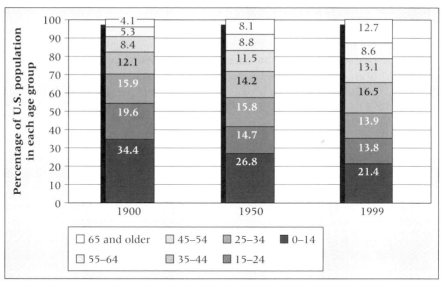

Data sources: U.S. Bureau of the Census. 1999a. *Statistical Abstract of the United States: 1999*, Table 1413. Washington, DC: U.S. Government Printing Office. Also: U.S. Bureau of the Census. 2000b. *Statistical Abstract of the United States: 2000*, Table 12. Washington, DC: U.S. Government Printing Office.

age) to a "beanpole" (age groups are more evenly distributed). This shifting size and shape of a population can create change in society. For instance, the passing of the massive baby boom generation through the life course has been described metaphorically as "a pig in a python." If you've ever seen one of those *National Geographic* films of snakes digesting small animals, you know how apt the metaphor is. As this generation ages, it stretches the parameters of the relevant social institutions at each successive stage of their lives. Baby boomers packed hospital nurseries as infants, school classrooms as children, and college campuses, employment lines, and the housing markets as young adults (Light, 1988). The drastic increase in divorce during the 1970s can be attributed in part to an increase in marriages of short duration initiated by people in the baby boom generation (Teachman et al., 2000).

As the baby boomers reach old age, those institutions concerned with later life—pension plans, Social Security, medical and social care—will be seriously stressed, leading one gerontologist to call the baby boomers a "generation at risk" (Butler, 1989). Over the next 30 years, the size of the aged population is projected to double so that by the year 2030, about one in five people in the United States may be 65 or older (Federal Interagency Forum on Aging-Related Statistics, 2000). At that time there will be over 50 million retirees, about twice the number there are today. Some have even predicted a huge surge in business for the funeral industry by then as this generation reaches the end of its collective life cycle (Schodolski, 1993).

Because of its size, the baby boom cohort's mark on families has been especially influential. That generation was the first to redefine families to include a variety of living arrangements like cohabitation, domestic partnerships, and never-married women with dependent children (Wattenberg, 1986). It was also the first to expect paid work to be a central feature of women's lives. And it was the first to grow up with effective birth control, making delayed childbearing and voluntary childlessness possible.

The consequences of such changes for the well-being of the institution of family is addressed in Issue 2.

Since the appearance of the baby boomers, however, other generations have also made their mark on society and family life. As Chapter 12 explains, the children of baby boomers—often referred to as the Millennium Generation—represent a sizeable generation in their own right. Throughout the 1990s, school districts around the country had to deal with overcrowded classrooms as these children entered the educational system. Political pressure from their parents has led to the building of new schools, increased scrutiny of television programs for children, and heightened concern over the effect of advertising on children.

Technological Innovation   Sometimes change is spurred by scientific discoveries and technological inventions. The discovery of fire and electricity changed the nature of human lives and cultures for all time. The invention of the internal combustion engine, television, telecommunications, and the microchip were instrumental in determining the course of history in the twentieth century. Scientific developments such as improved knowledge of disease processes, medical care, nutrition, and water quality have all helped to reduce illness and therefore increase life expectancy.

As we discuss in Chapter 7, by separating economic production from home life, industrialization in the nineteenth century had a powerful effect on family dynamics and gender roles. Along with these trends came other important changes: Both men and women began acquiring more formal education as access to schools increased and new labor force skills became necessary. Industrialization created greater access to wealth and thereby increased the size of the middle class. Members of the middle class also gained more leisure time, which could be devoted to pursuits such as volunteer work. Birth rates declined, in part because the large number of children who were useful and necessary in a farm-based economy became an economic burden in an industrial one (Staggenborg, 1998; Zelizer, 1985).

A family's religious beliefs, examined in Issue 5, can influence parents' decisions regarding these controversial procedures.

Technological innovations can also increase the moral choices families must make. The growing availability of birth control and reproductive technologies, for instance, has given women greater choice over if and when they will have children. Once they decide to have children, sophisticated techniques in genetic engineering may eventually allow parents to choose the characteristics of their offspring. Some choices won't be easy. Many parents will face decisions about whether or not to abort a child who has a characteristic that is perceived to be undesirable. Indeed, recent advances in cloning technology have raised the possibility that adults may someday be able to create genetic replicas of themselves.

Technology has also raised moral issues regarding the end of life. With the help of respirators and other advanced life support equipment, a person can now be kept alive long after the brain has ceased functioning. Perhaps sometime in the future, death from disease will always be a matter of choice. Scientists also recently discovered a gene mutation in fruit flies that doubles their life span. The same long life gene exists in humans, leading some researchers to predict that future drug therapies could allow humans to double their life spans—to about 150 years (Recer, 2000a). Imagine how such developments would alter our ideas about old age and the life course. For instance, scientists found that female fruit flies with this mutation could reproduce throughout their lives, laying nearly double the normal number of eggs. In humans, such an effect could result in a much more extended childbearing period, or perhaps some women would delay childbearing until age 100 or older. Maybe you'll be sitting down to dinner in the year 2100 with your great-great-great grandchildren!

Society can sometimes be slow to adjust to the changes brought about by scientific and technological innovation. Artificial insemination, in vitro fertilization, surrogate mother-

EXHIBIT 13.2

Households with Selected Electronic Media, United States

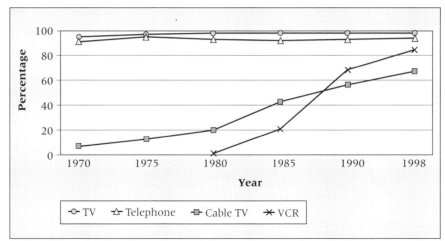

Note: 1998 data point for telephone service is based on data for 1997.
Data source: U.S. Bureau of the Census. 1999a. *Statistical Abstract of the United States: 1999,* Table 1440. Washington, DC: U.S. Government Printing Office.

hood, and other medical advances in the area of infertility have increased the number of infertile couples who can now have children. Yet these technological developments were changing the face of parenthood well before society began to recognize and address the ethical, moral, and legal issues they raised. For instance, because surrogacy and egg donation technology may involve three different "mothers"—the genetic mother, the gestational mother, and the social mother—legal parenthood is unclear. In divorce cases, legal battles rage over which partner is entitled to custody of frozen embryos conceived in a laboratory.

In blurring these boundaries, such devices also weaken the boundaries of family privacy, a topic discussed in Issue 3.

Electronic and telecommunications advances also have undeniable consequences for family life. In the early to mid-twentieth century, telephones and televisions reduced the time family members once spent interacting with each other and with their neighbors. More recently, VCRs, satellite dish TVs, and personal computers have had a similar effect (see Exhibit 13.2). Today, cell phones, pagers, palm-sized computers, and wireless e-mail have created a work day that never ends (Hafner, 2000). These gadgets blur the boundaries between work time and family time to a degree unknown just a few years ago.

Some argue that these changes are good for families. Since the Industrial Revolution, working has meant being physically away from home. Now people can do much of their work while in the presence of their loved ones. Some futurists even point out that homes may once again become workplaces and schools, healing the split between men and women and the split between parents and children that began over 100 years ago (Skolnick, 1996).

Others, however, are not so optimistic. The urge to electronically "stay in touch" with the workplace is robbing some families of uninterrupted time together. Family vacations—at one time a near-sacred ritual of withdrawal from the demands of everyday life—are no longer respites from work responsibilities, especially for families of professional and managerial workers. Many rural resort towns now have cybercafés where hikers and tourists can check their e-mail for important messages. Simply being hundreds of miles away from the office is no longer enough to keep work at bay (Harmon, 1997). With today's technology, there's no excuse for being away from work.

In sum, many of the most difficult family issues people face today derive from technologies that provide benefits few are willing to forgo: longer, healthier lives; the ability to choose when and how many children to have; quicker access to information; and so on. Technological advances have forced people to face conditions that previous generations did not know. And people are unlikely to reverse these changes, rendering moot the nostalgic belief that family difficulties could be solved by returning to a simpler, less technologically sophisticated time.

Cultural Diffusion   Another source of social change that affects families is **cultural diffusion**: the process by which beliefs, customs, and other elements of culture spread from one group or society to another. Most of the taken-for-granted aspects of your everyday life originally came from somewhere else. For instance, pajamas, clocks, toilets, glass, coins, newspapers, soap, even the alphabet and language were once imported from other cultures (Linton, 1937). Japanese innovations in microelectronics have dramatically altered the patterns of communication, housework, transportation, and personal entertainment in American society.

At the same time, American culture, as expressed in fashion, art, music, and food, is being incorporated into the lives of many young people all across the world. The changing value of the elderly in Japan and other collectivist societies (discussed at some length in Chapter 12), for instance, is, in part, traceable to the influx of Western ideals and values into these cultures. The white wedding dress, first popularized in nineteenth-century England (Ingraham, 1999) and now common in the United States, has recently gained popularity in China and Taiwan.

The diffusion process is not always friendly. When one society's territory is taken over by another society, people may be required to adapt to new customs and beliefs. When Europeans conquered the New World, Native-American peoples were forced to abandon their traditional ways of family life and become more "civilized." Hundreds of thousands of Indians died in the process, not only from warfare but also from new diseases inadvertently brought over by their conquerors. Until a few decades ago, Native American children were still being removed from their homes and sent to "Indian schools," to be raised in the mainstream culture and separated from the influence of their parents, extended families, and cultural traditions.

As discussed in Issue 3, legal, educational, and governmental institutions have significantly reshaped the boundaries of parental authority over the past century.

Institutional Diffusion   Changes that occur in one social institution usually create changes in other institutions, a phenomenon known as **institutional diffusion**. For example, changes in the medical and health professions have influenced childbearing decisions, both in terms of controlling fertility and overcoming infertility. Parents' authority over their children has been diminished as a result of children spending more time in schools today. Some agents of the state (for example, social workers) have the ability to remove children from their homes against parents' wishes if they suspect child abuse or neglect.

At the same time, the effects of changes in the institution of family extend to other institutions, such as law, politics, and schools. One cannot be a teacher these days without understanding the psychological effects of divorce and remarriage that many students experience. Some school districts bend residency rules to accommodate children in joint custody situations, hold separate teacher conferences for divorced parents, and make duplicate copies of students' papers, assignments, and report cards to send to both parents (Keller, 1997). In addition, as more and more families find themselves unable to cope with the social problems their children face, schools are being called on to provide students with services that were once the sole province of families. They teach moral values, consumer skills, and technological "literacy," provide adequate nutrition, and administer programs to help students avoid drug and alcohol abuse, teen pregnancy, and sexually transmitted diseases.

Other institutions have been slower to adapt to family changes. For instance, despite some efforts to accommodate family obligations, the workplace, for the most part, is still built on the assumption that job commitment takes precedence over family time. Furthermore, women still face wage gaps, segregated labor markets, glass ceilings, and other workplace disadvantages (Gerson, 2000).

Economic Change   Changing economic conditions have always exerted powerful influences on family life. A slow-growing or stagnant economy, for instance, encourages people to maintain close networks with other relatives and may discourage young people from moving out of their parents' home. Historian Tamara Hareven (2000) also suggests that during periods of extreme economic distress—such as depressions, unemployment, or strikes—patterns of decision making within families are likely to shift. As a result, wives may assume more economic responsibility and gain some marital power:

> Although men were considered to be the main breadwinners and were, therefore, expected to make the major economic decisions for the family, women were much closer to the routine management of household resources. . . . Since the responsibility of feeding and clothing family members was primarily theirs, women were more sensitive to shortages in food and supplies and pursued independent strategies to fulfill these basic tasks. . . . In the Amoskeag Mills, wives went in to work while their husbands . . . were striking. . . . Similarly, during the Great Depression it was the women who surreptitiously went to welfare agencies to receive food staples for the family, while their husbands pretended that the family continued to be self-sufficient. (Hareven, 2000, pp. 96–97)

In contrast, a booming economy leads to higher rates of employment, which can encourage children to leave home and become independent earlier and families to move to better neighborhoods or a new part of the country. The prosperous postwar economy of the late 1940s and 1950s had a tremendous impact on American families. Even young couples could afford to buy homes and start families, which encouraged earlier marriage and childbearing than in the previous generation.

In general, though, outside of the small percentage of families who are independently wealthy, families today generally need two permanent, well-paying jobs to ensure that they remain financially secure. If good jobs become more scarce and are replaced by low-paying and sporadic employment, even two earners may not be enough to safeguard a family from poverty. Furthermore, women and minorities are disproportionately affected by economic downturns producing low wages and underemployment. Most families remain at the mercy of economic change, along with a variety of other trends in the larger society.

Social Movements

Social change is not just something that *happens* to society or families, however. Sometimes change is brought about purposefully by individuals or groups of individuals. These changes are not a by-product of population pressures, technological innovation, cultural and institutional diffusion, or economic change. Rather, they are the result of a concerted effort on the part of people who feel that things aren't the way they ought to be.

When groups of people with common goals and bonds of solidarity make a sustained attempt to bring about change through collective action, targeted at the government or other opponents, they are part of a **social movement** (Staggenborg, 1998). People who participate in social movements take part in a variety of actions—such as violent protest, peaceful demonstrations, lobbying, circulation of petitions, donations, or simple identification with a movement through wearing its symbols or espousing the cause. But underlying all social movements is change: the desire to enact it, stop it, or reverse it.

Family life may seem far removed from these concerted efforts to change society, but in fact some of the most persistent and far-reaching social movements in the last century have had a profound impact on families. The labor movement, the movement to create safe working environments, the women's movement, the environmental movement, the civil rights movement, the abortion rights and antiabortion movements, the gay and lesbian rights movement, and the religious right movement have all directly or indirectly affected people's ability to create, sustain, and direct their family lives.

Ideology   To be effective, a social movement must have an **ideology,** a coherent system of beliefs, values, and ideas that justifies its existence (Turner & Killian, 1987; Zurcher & Snow, 1981). People are almost never neutral about family matters, which lie at the heart of religious, political, and philosophical belief systems. Issues such as welfare, homosexual rights, abortion, sex education, corporal punishment, and divorce often divide people into clear ideological camps.

With regard to social movements that involve the institution of family, sociologists can talk about two broad ideologies. A **traditionalist family ideology** rests on the assumption that "the American family" is in serious decline. To traditionalists, the primary cause of family problems is the disappearance of "family values" and the prevalence of moral decay among people who are either selfish (such as women who would rather work than stay at home to raise their children) or behaviorally corrupt (such as people who have premarital or extramarital sex). In addition, traditionalists believe the foundation of family is duty and obligation. People have a duty to be chaste before legal marriage and monogamous afterward, to have children only within a legal marriage, to live for children and not do anything that might impact negatively on them, and to maintain a permanent marriage "for the children's sake" (Scanzoni, 1991). These are the arrangements and expectations that traditionalists consider "normal" and highly desirable. Hence they would support movements seeking to reverse the trend toward quick and easy divorce and mothers' participation in the paid labor force; to prevent homosexuals from legally marrying; and to restrict easy access to welfare, abortion, and sex education in schools.

A good example of a traditionalist movement is the antiabortion, or "pro-life," movement. Its ideology rests on several assumptions about the nature of childhood and motherhood: Each conception is an act of God, and so abortion violates God's will; life begins at conception; the fetus is an individual who has a constitutional right to life; and every human life should be valued (Luker, 1984; Michener, DeLamater, & Schwartz, 1986). The antiabortion movement subscribes to the belief that everyone can "make room for one more," reinforcing the view that abortion is immoral, evil, and self-indulgent (Luker, 1984).

Although abortion remains legal in this country and the majority of adults support the availability of abortion, at least under certain circumstances (see Exhibit 13.3), the anti-

Supporters of the family decline perspective, discussed in Issue 2, are likely to subscribe to a traditionalist family ideology.

EXHIBIT 13.3

Support for the Availability of Abortion

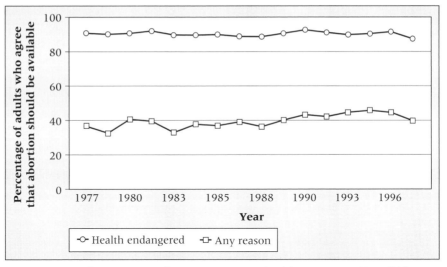

Data source: National Opinion Research Center. 1998. *General Social Survey, 1972–1998.* Available at www.icpsr.umich.edu/GSS/. Accessed June 1, 2001.

abortion movement has achieved some success. Since 1996, for instance, nearly every state has enacted some sort of restriction on abortion. In addition, fewer and fewer medical schools now teach their students how to perform abortions. By 1995, only 12 percent of obstetrics and gynecology programs taught abortion. Today, there are only about 2,000 doctors nationwide who perform abortions and most are in their 50s and 60s. Over 85 percent of Americans lack easy access to abortion (cited in Edwards, 2001).

Although it is difficult to obtain accurate information on such sensitive issues, it appears that the antiabortion movement has had little effect on the actual number of pregnancies that result in induced abortions. For instance, in 1980, 26 percent of all pregnancies in the United States were intentionally aborted. By 1990, 23 percent were aborted and by 1996, the figure was 22 percent (U.S. Bureau of the Census, 2000b). Faced with such a frustrating lack of progress, the antiabortion movement continues to address the underlying theme of family decline to promote its specific goals.

In contrast, the foundation theme of a **progressive family ideology** is that families are not declining but instead are caught up in the continual process of evolution and transition that has been occurring for centuries. Although progressives agree with traditionalists that the family is a vital social institution, they also believe it is a social construction—a product of the attitudes and behaviors of the people touched by it—not a universal form that exists for all times and all societies. In other words, all societies may have something they call "family," but its structure, form, and nature vary widely. The stresses and strains that people experience in their families do not result from forsaking a traditionalist vision but instead emerge from the curious paradox of adhering to traditional norms while behaving in distinctly nontraditional ways. For progressives, the view that a shift away from traditional values has caused the breakdown of families is wrong:

> The [traditionalists] have it backward when they argue that the collapse of traditional family values is at the heart of our social decay. The losses in real earnings and in breadwinner jobs, the persistence of low-wage work for women and the corporate

greed that has accompanied global economic restructuring have wreaked far more havoc on [families] than have the combined effects of feminism, sexual revolution, gay liberation . . . and every other value flip of the past half-century. (Stacey, 1994, pp. 120–121)

Rather than issuing inflexible rules, progressives seek to discover what works and what doesn't work for families across a variety of circumstances (Scanzoni, 1991).

Progressive family ideology pays a lot of attention to the place of women in society: It makes little sense to speak of the well-being of families until adults can be economically secure without regard to gender, until men become more involved in household tasks and child rearing, and until the nation commits to high-quality support for young children (Scanzoni, 1991). For instance, progressives argue that because both women's employment and day care are here to stay, social movements must aim to reduce their costs and maximize their benefits for *both* adults and children. If women's economic well-being improves, kids will ultimately be better off. If children participate in high-quality day care programs, their parents (women and men alike) will be better off.

Ironically, partisan politics and the needs of special interests often blur the boundaries between traditionalist and progressive ideologies. The Family and Medical Leave Act of 1993 granted full-time workers leaves of absence for childbirth, adoption, and family emergencies. Although such a bill would seem to fit a traditionalist ideology, which emphasizes the interests of children, many traditionalist lawmakers were initially opposed to the bill because they felt the policy would impose undue hardships on businesses. These legislators were successful in diluting the original bill, reducing the amount of time workers could take off and eliminating many workers from coverage. As a result, this law has had little effect on the lives of the working families it was intended to help (Marks, 1997).

Clearly, dividing ideologies into broad "traditionalist" and "progressive" categories is an oversimplification. One cannot assume that everyone fits neatly into one category or the other. Indeed, the same person may be rather "traditional" on some issues but "progressive" on others. Yet remember that fundamental ideological and practical conflicts do separate these two positions and can therefore influence the sorts of changes that society experiences.

Movements and Countermovements   Social movements are usually responses to social problems. For instance, the main focus of the women's movement at the turn of the nineteenth century was sexual inequality and oppression in the legal and political arena. It aimed to secure women's right to divorce, to retain custody of children after a divorce, to retain property, to work and keep their wages, and to vote.

The women's movement that gained strength in the mid-twentieth century has had a somewhat different focus, prompted by a different social environment. Beginning in the 1960s, women—particularly white, middle-class, well-educated women—were becoming increasingly aware of the gap between their capabilities and the limiting domestic roles they were consigned to. Women began to realize that the best way to improve their lives was to increase their economic and social opportunities. Through organizations such as the National Organization for Women and the National Abortion and Reproductive Rights Action League, women gained the political clout to have their voices heard.

Some women of color and working-class women have found today's women's movement irrelevant to their immediate needs and concerns. And the major goal of full equality for women has not yet been met. Nevertheless, the movement has been quite successful in securing important economic, political, legal, and familial changes. The vast majority of

EXHIBIT 13.4

Support for the Women's Movement

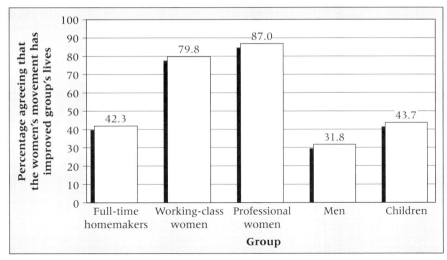

Data source: National Opinion Research Center. 1998. *General Social Survey, 1972–1998.* Available at www.icpsr.umich.edu/GSS/. Accessed June 1, 2001.

women today believe that the women's movement has improved their lives (Wallis, 1989), and more generally, many adults tend to agree that it's benefited women's lives. There's less agreement, however, as to whether it's improved the lives of full-time homemakers, men, or children (see Exhibit 13.4).

There will always be some people who feel threatened by any social movement, which is after all seeking to change the existing social arrangements. Chances are, someone will always be opposed to such changes. Hence movements for social reform often trigger organized **countermovements**, which aim to prevent or reverse the changes sought or accomplished by an earlier movement. Countermovements are most likely to emerge when the reform movements against which they are reacting become large and effective in pursuing their goals and therefore come to be seen as threats to personal and social interests (Chafetz & Dworkin, 1987; Mottl, 1980).

The emergence of the New Religious Right in the 1980s and 1990s, for instance, was provoked by a growing perception that the women's movement of the 1960s and 1970s had created enormous social upheaval, breaking down traditional roles and values and challenging the institution of family (Klatch, 1991). The New Religious Right's position—for family and motherhood, and against equal rights for women—was clearly designed to turn back the feminist agenda. The leaders of the New Religious Right went so far as to articulate the notion that gender equality was responsible for women's unhappiness and the weakening of American families (Faludi, 1991). The rising divorce rate and the increased number of working mothers were seen as eroding the moral bases of family life (Klatch, 1991). As one New Religious Right minister said, "We're not here to get into politics. We're here to turn the clock back to 1954 in this country" (quoted in Faludi, 1991, p. 230).

The overall impact of religion on family life is explored in Issue 5.

Through organizations such as the Moral Majority, the Heritage Foundation, the Eagle Forum, the Christian Coalition, the Family Research Council, Promise Keepers, and many smaller religious groups around the United States, the New Religious Right has sought to restore the faith, morality, and decency they feel American families have lost in recent years. By 1995 the Christian Coalition had 1,100 chapters all across the country and over a million members.

Over the past 2 decades, the New Religious Right has successfully shifted the political and social mood of the country. It first gained legitimacy in 1980, when Ronald Reagan and several Senate candidates supported by the New Religious Right won election; it re-affirmed its influence in 1994 with the Republican takeover of Congress, and again in 2000 with the election of George W. Bush. The movement has learned to make effective use of the media—through thousands of Christian radio stations, cable television networks, and Internet sites—to mobilize its supporters and attack its enemies. Many of its most notable triumphs have been at the state and local levels, where it has succeeded in determining school curricula, in placing limits on divorce, and in passing anti–abortion and anti–gay rights legislation. It will probably continue to have substantial influence until a new countermovement arises to challenge its successes.

Recent and Future Family Trends

Knowing something about the nature of social change and the dynamics and structure of social movements allows us to explain how the institution of family has changed and is changing. It also allows us to extrapolate from current trends to get a glimpse of what family life might look like in the new millennium. But trying to discern the future can be a futile endeavor, according to sociologist Kathleen Gerson (2000): "The looking glass remains opaque not simply because our analytic tools are imprecise. The human capacity for growth and creativity, for responding in unintended ways to new contingencies, renders prediction a risky business" (p. 180).

In fact, when discussing future trends and outcomes, sociologists usually talk about *projections* rather than *predictions*, acknowledging that it's not possible to predict the future with any certainty. At best, sociologists can analyze current trends and factors, and determine what family life will look like if these trends were to continue. In the following sections, we consider some of the most important family trends in recent decades and consider where each might be headed.

DEMO•GRAPHICS

Resilient American Families

American families have undergone significant changes over the past century, giving rise to contentious debates and widespread social movements—and families will continue to change. Those adhering to a traditionalist family ideology fear that the trends signal the breakdown of the family. Those adhering to the progressive family ideology argue that family change is adaptive and necessary, and perhaps even desirable. But both sides agree that families have undergone significant alterations over the past century.

Observing changes over a long period can offer important perspective on the family decline debate. Let's start with one of the most notable changes—marital status—which is depicted in Exhibit 13.5a (For readability, we've included data for women only; the trends for men are essentially identical to those for women). First, you can see that despite an increase over the century in the percentage of divorced women (and men), the divorced

EXHIBIT 13.5

Changes in American Families in the Twentieth Century

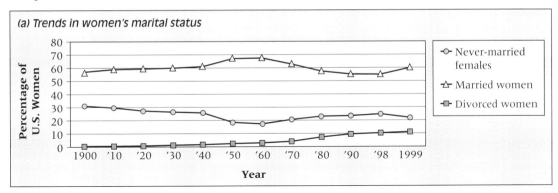

(a) Trends in women's marital status

Data sources: U.S. Bureau of the Census. 1999a. *Statistical Abstract of the United States: 1999*, Table 1418. Washington, DC: U.S. Government Printing Office. Also: U.S. Bureau of the Census. 2000b. *Statistical Abstract of the United States: 2000*, Table 53. Washington, DC: U.S. Government Printing Office.

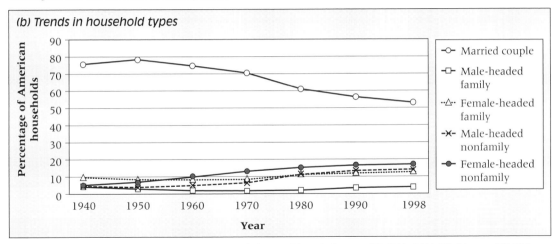

(b) Trends in household types

Data source: U.S. Bureau of the Census. 1999a. *Statistical Abstract of the United States: 1999*, Table 1419. Washington, DC: U.S. Government Printing Office.

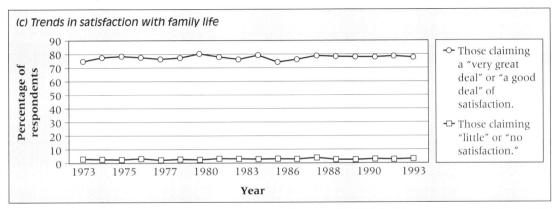

(c) Trends in satisfaction with family life

Data source: National Opinion Research Center. 1998. *General Social Survey, 1972–1998*. Available at www.icpsr.umich.edu/GSS/. Accessed June 1, 2001.

population is, and has always been, a distinct minority. Further, despite a marked increase in the percentage of married women at mid-century, roughly the same percentage of the population was married in 1900 as in 1998. And there were actually more never-married women at the beginning of the century than at the end.

To be sure, changes in individual lifestyle choices and demographic shifts such as those reflected in Exhibit 13.5a leave a mark on families. Families at the end of the twentieth century were clearly structured differently from those at mid-century (household data before 1940 are not available). In particular, the percentage of households consisting of married couples has declined steadily during the second half of the twentieth century, as seen in Exhibit 13.5b. Interestingly, there has been less change in other household types, although a few trends are worth noting. For instance, the percentage of families headed by unmarried men in 1940 was actually higher than it's been in any subsequent decade. Also note that the second most common household type in 1940 was female-headed family households. Today, the second most common type is nonfamily households headed by women—namely, women living alone or with roommates or unmarried partners.

Clearly, over the course of the twentieth century, American families have diversified beyond the traditional nuclear family of mother, father, and children; other kinds of families have emerged to take its place. Yet despite all the changes, Americans continue to derive high levels of satisfaction from their families, a fact that has not changed for nearly 30 years. As you can see in Exhibit 13.5c, about three-quarters of the Americans surveyed for the General Social Survey have consistently reported that they receive either a "very great deal" or a "great deal" of satisfaction from family life. Fewer than 5 percent claim to receive only a little or no satisfaction.

Most people also feel very successful in their family life. For instance, data collected by the General Social Survey for 1996 revealed that 54 percent of Americans felt very successful or completely successful in their family life, 38 percent felt somewhat successful, and only 8 percent felt not very successful or not at all successful. Thus, despite widespread social change, the institution of family is likely to remain a permanent feature of society. It continues to provide individuals with a sense of well-being in a complicated world.

Thinking Critically About the Statistics

1. Suppose you were examining the data on marital status that appear in Exhibit 13.5a only since mid-century. What different conclusions could you draw about family change and possible decline? Why is it important to analyze long-term historical data when available? How might the trends in Exhibits 13.5b and 13.5c on household types and levels of family satisfaction look different if you were able to observe the data over longer periods?

2. Why do you suppose the Census Bureau only began collecting household data (depicted in Exhibit 13.5b) around 1940? What effect might the Great Depression have had on the government's need to document different types of households?

3. Why have levels of satisfaction varied so little over 30 years, despite massive social change? Do you think the high rate of satisfaction seen in Exhibit 13.5c might be caused by people simply giving the socially acceptable answer? Or do you think people really are happy with their families, regardless of what those families look like?

4. What do you think the trends documented here will look like in 10 years? 50 years? 100 years?

Sexual Freedom

Despite energetic attempts to convince young people of the virtues of sexual abstinence, sexuality for most people has become more a matter of personal choice not bound to marriage and childbearing. The old double standard at the time of marriage—female virginity and male sexual experience—is fading fast. Some, perhaps many, young people in the future will decide to "wait" until they marry to begin an active sexual life, but such a decision will undoubtedly be theirs to make.

Advances in medical technology may also have an effect on future sexuality. No disease has had as powerful an impact on people's lives over the last 2 decades as AIDS. By 2000, over 750,000 AIDS cases had been reported in the United States and over 430,000 Americans had died of the disease (Centers for Disease Control, 2001).

However, within the last decade many new drugs have been introduced, creating some guarded optimism that eventually infection with the HIV virus that causes AIDS will no longer mean inevitable death (A. Sullivan, 1996). After rapidly increasing throughout the 1980s, the annual rate of death leveled off between 1994 and 1995 and has steadily decreased ever since (Centers for Disease Control, 2001).

The incidence of new AIDS cases has also slowed dramatically in recent years. At the height of the epidemic in the mid-1980s, the number of new cases from year to year increased as much as 85 percent (Altman, 1997). But between 1993 and 1998 the number of newly reported cases *dropped* by over 50 percent (U.S. Bureau of the Census, 2000b). A survey of gay men in New York City found that one in seven were infected, compared to one in three in 1985 (cited in Altman, 1999).

Although it is premature to declare the epidemic over, the optimistic projection that AIDS can be treated will no doubt have an impact on American sexuality in the near future. But a return to completely uninhibited and unprotected sexuality is not likely, especially because many other sexually transmitted diseases are still "out there."

Will the stigma of homosexuality fade if the disease originally so closely identified with gay sex becomes less ominous? It's hard to say. However, with a smaller and smaller percentage of gay men becoming infected with HIV, the isolation of those who already are infected may actually increase, and those with full-blown AIDS could feel more intensely alone than ever before (A. Sullivan, 1996).

People must also realize that medical breakthroughs in treating AIDS are very limited in scope. Although each day seems to bring an announcement of some new treatment or possible progress toward a cure, no cure has yet been found. In fact, researchers at the 1998 World AIDS Conference indicated that the newest drugs are somewhat less effective than previously thought, dashing hopes that discovery of a cure was imminent.

Furthermore, the vast majority of HIV-positive people around the world have not had access to the very expensive drug treatments available in wealthier countries. Thus worldwide AIDS cases and AIDS deaths have increased dramatically. It's estimated that over 36 million people around the world are currently living with HIV/AIDS and over 21 million have died over the past two decades. Sub-Saharan Africa has been hit especially hard. In 2000, this region accounted for 72 percent of new HIV infections, 70 percent of people living with HIV/AIDS, and 80 percent of AIDS deaths, even though it is home to only about 10 percent of the world's population (Olson, 2000). Only recently have governments, nonprofit organizations, and drug manufacturers started addressing the problem of making the drugs more affordable for the world's most impoverished people. In 2001, the General Assembly of the United Nations convened a special session to address the problem of HIV/

EXHIBIT 13.6

*AIDS Cases in the
United States*

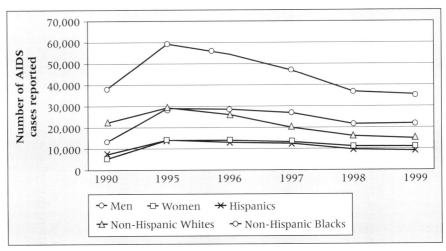

Data source: U.S. Bureau of the Census. 2000b. *Statistical Abstract of the United States: 2000,* Table 217.
Washington, DC: U.S. Government Printing Office.

AIDS and to secure a global commitment to enhancing national, regional, and international efforts to combat it.

Even in this country, the prognosis is much better for some people than for others. The prevalence of AIDS varies by race and gender (see Exhibit 13.6), as does the availability of effective treatment. Before 1986, African Americans accounted for 25 percent and Hispanics 13 percent of all American AIDS cases. Of new cases reported in 1999, 47 percent were African American and 19 percent were Hispanic. Women are experiencing a similar trend. Prior to 1986, women constituted 7 percent of American AIDS cases; today, over 23 percent of new cases are women (Stolberg, 1998a; U.S. Bureau of the Census, 2000b). The decrease in AIDS deaths has been most dramatic for men (54 percent decrease in annual AIDS deaths since 1992) and for whites (66 percent decrease). During that same period, female deaths decreased by only 11 percent, black deaths by 24 percent, and Hispanic deaths by 47 percent (U.S. Bureau of the Census, 1999a). AIDS is now the third leading cause of death for American women between the ages of 25 and 44 and *the* leading cause of death among African-American women in this age group (Stolberg, 1997).

In short, people must be tremendously cautious when interpreting encouraging statistics regarding the AIDS epidemic. Although there is some reason for optimism, it's probably too early to be thinking about a massive societal shift toward carefree sexual behavior.

Life Expectancy

Medical advances in other areas—such as the treatment of heart disease and cancer—will likely contribute to a continued decline in mortality rates and an increase in life expectancy (see Exhibit 13.7). Low death rates coupled with low birth rates will result in an increasing proportion of the population being over 75—the "graying" of America described in Chapter 12. In fact, population experts project that people over 85 will become the fastest-growing age group by the middle of the twenty-first century (Seelye, 1997a). Once only the most durable and healthiest people lived to this age. However, improved medical technology has

EXHIBIT 13.7

Life Expectancy for U.S. Newborns

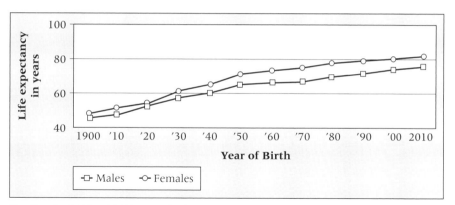

Note: Data for 2000 and 2010 are projections.
Data sources: U.S. Bureau of the Census. 2000b. *Statistical Abstract of the United States: 2000,* Table 116. Washington, DC: U.S. Government Printing Office. Also: U.S. Bureau of the Census. 1999a. *Statistical Abstract of the United States: 1999,* Table 1421. Washington, DC: U.S. Government Printing Office.

increased the longevity of even frail people (Pampel, 1998). Hence society is doubly likely to face increasing demands to care for its elderly population.

The aging of the American population will have serious implications for the way people live their lives within families. The financial responsibility for the care of elderly family members, as well as demands for emotional and social support, will likely still fall on families. And certain issues heretofore unknown to most families will become more common (Riley, 1983). What, for instance, will be the role of great-grandparents in family life? How will they be incorporated into the family structure? Will they be regarded as an obstacle to younger generations' independence, as a "social problem" for family members and for the community, or as valued members of a vastly extended family? What about five-generation families in which a grandparent can also be a grandchild? Such structures will surely require adjustments in patterns of family life and will be a focal point of public policy in the years to come.

Marriage, Divorce, and Remarriage

In the distant past, spouses didn't require much of each other to make a marriage work. Marriages were primarily economic arrangements. If two partners found they could tolerate each other's company and were mildly compatible, that was enough. Today people expect a lot more from their marriages; they want deep intimacy, sexual compatibility, and self-fulfillment. The heightened expectations that accompany marriage have made it all the more difficult for people to keep less-than-perfect marriages together. Furthermore, in the face of increased economic opportunities for women outside the home, their financial incentives to get and remain married have decreased. Hence although the divorce rate has stabilized and even dipped a little recently, all indications are that it will remain high into the foreseeable future.

Cohabitation and voluntary singlehood have also become more commonplace and acceptable. And people are waiting longer to get married. For instance, in 1998 only one-third of white women and 15 percent of black women ages 20–24 had married—a 32 percent drop from 1975 (Teachman et al., 2000).

So what will become of marriage in the future? It still has some distinctive advantages for individuals and for society, which are enumerated in Chapter 6. But some have gone so far as to suggest that people should rethink the long-standing tradition of organizing society around married couples. For instance, feminist scholar Martha Fineman (1995) has proposed that marriage, as a legal category, ought to be abolished. For many, such a suggestion seems ludicrous and frightening. The values surrounding marriage are so ingrained that most people find seriously imagining society without it virtually impossible. But the institution of marriage has undergone so many significant changes and challenges in recent decades that Fineman and other critics suggest a radical rethinking of marriage may be in order.

Fineman proposes that people be allowed to engage in ceremonial marriage, but such an event would have no legal (that is, no court-enforceable) consequences. The decision to define the relationship as a "marriage" would be left to the individuals involved, who may or may not seek religious ratification.

Fineman imagines a future in which the interactions of married people would be governed by the same rules that regulate all other interactions in society—namely, those of property, contract, and criminal law. Equality between adults would be asserted and assumed. No special legal or economic privileges would be granted to husbands over wives or to married couples over unmarried couples. Voluntary, adult sexual interactions would be of no interest to the state, because it would no longer have a preferred model of family intimacy to protect.

Under this legal system, the treatment of children would no longer be based on the marital status of their parents. Children would be protected by the same laws that apply to all citizens. So parents would no longer have the right to hit their children. The category of "illegitimate" children would also disappear and with it the stigma attached to being born "out of wedlock."

In this proposed legal scheme, a new definition of family would focus on the relationship between dependents and the people who care for them, regardless of their blood or marital ties. The caregiving family would become a privileged and protected entity, entitled to special, preferred treatment. Tax breaks would be awarded, regardless of marital status, to stable lower- and middle-income households financially responsible for children, the elderly, or the handicapped. The motivation behind these changes would be not to eliminate marriage entirely but to encourage and sustain stable caregiving households (F. Johnson, 1996).

Such suggestions bring into sharp relief why defining "family," the topic covered in Issue 1, is so important.

This reformed system is similar to another arrangement studied by sociologist John Scanzoni (2000). Scanzoni suggests that the old system of families built primarily on marriage is outdated and generally fails to meet the needs of its members. In its place he proposes a "co-housing" arrangement. Participants—who may or may not be legally married, or heterosexual, or parents—construct neighborhoods where individuals can live in private households but still be intimately connected to other households. Neighbors would share responsibility for children and provide practical and emotional support to each other.

These radical suggestions are unlikely to be implemented any time soon, given the hallowed place in the American psyche that marriage still occupies. So it's likely that the vast majority of the adult population will continue to marry. Marriage, for all its problems and pitfalls, is here to stay.

This fact, coupled with consistently high rates of divorce, means that a growing proportion of the population in the twenty-first century will marry more than once. Families and stepfamilies will continue to become more complex. Consequently, the culture will no doubt need to develop standard, institutionalized ways of defining and supporting step-family relationships.

Gender Equity

American men and women are slowly moving toward a blending of gender and family roles and away from traditional notions of wives and husbands, mothers and fathers. Each year Americans show more accepting attitudes toward women's independence and influence at home and at work (see Exhibit 13.8). Attitudes about men are changing, too. Surveys of high school students over the years show that a growing proportion believe that husbands should take on more household and child care responsibilities. The vast majority believe wives should expect their husbands to participate fully. Most adolescent boys expect that when they get married their wives will work outside the home, and more and more indicate that they intend to take time off from work after the couple has a baby (Coltrane, 1996b).

There also seems to be a growing recognition in this society that the best way to ensure that families with or without children will remain stable is to increase economic opportunities for women as well as men. As couples in which both partners work become the norm, employers will have more and more trouble ignoring the importance of their employees' need to balance their work and family lives. We may see the slow disappearance of the 9-to-5, Monday-through-Friday workweek, an acknowledgment of how employees' needs change through the life course, and a more flexible and less gender-specific definition of what it means to be a good worker.

As working families become more common, fewer people will publicly condemn working mothers as negligent parents. Most people today already say that they believe, at least in

EXHIBIT 13.8

Attitudes Toward Women Working

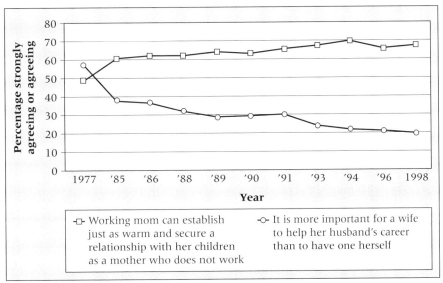

Data source: National Opinion Research Center. 1998. *General Social Survey, 1972–1998.* Available at www.icpsr.umich.edu/GSS/. Accessed June 1, 2001.

principle, in the ideal of equal opportunities for men and women. And if current trends continue, more people will endorse such a belief in the future.

With regard to household work, sociologist Scott Coltrane (1996a) argues that changes in the gender-based division of labor will propel us toward equality between men and women at home. When men take on more of the mundane domestic tasks, the balance of power in the household begins to shift. When fathers take on more child care responsibilities, they begin to develop the sort of nurturing sensitivities traditionally associated with mothers. When parents share responsibilities, children thrive intellectually and emotionally and grow up holding less-rigid gender stereotypes.

As discussed in Chapter 8, some fathers are already becoming more involved in child care and are more likely to want an active role in raising their children. People can expect that men in the future will place even more value on spending time with their children. Of course, not everyone's attitudes will conform to this ideal. Nevertheless, Coltrane (1996b) expects that household tasks will become less tied to gender in the future.

These changes in the home and the workplace have the potential to transform the meaning of gender in future generations and reduce gender-based inequality and discrimination in the present generation. But the road toward gender equity will not be completely free of potholes. Most jobs are still based on the assumption that an employee can and should work long hours without worrying about child care and other household needs. Most employed women continue to work in traditionally "female" occupations and still earn substantially lower wages than men. And the vast majority of women are still responsible for the majority of housework and child care.

Furthermore, work is still structured around a male model of 20 years of schooling, followed by 40 years of employment and then retirement (Skolnick, 1996). This model doesn't work for many women, who must combine work and domestic responsibilities. They often have to step out of the paid labor force to raise a family and return to it later when the children are grown.

Some sociologists feel that despite changing attitudes and the growth of well-intentioned "family-friendly" workplace policies, family status rather than gender may become the most potent discriminating characteristic among workers in the future. As we mentioned in Chapter 7, mothers earn lower wages than women who are not mothers. These sociologists argue that the social and economic gap between "career-oriented" workers (single people and couples who forgo having children in pursuit of career advancement) and "child-oriented" workers (single people and couples who forgo careers in the interests of having and raising children) will inevitably widen. They fear that employers interested in productivity will favor career-oriented workers over men and women who want to spend more time maintaining their intimate relationships (Hunt & Hunt, 1990). If future employers still assume that the most committed employees are those unfettered by family demands, both women and men who openly express a desire to spend more time with their families will continue to risk being passed over for promotions and interesting assignments.

The Science of Childbearing

Advances in reproductive technology such as those we described in Chapter 8 will continue to expand the boundaries of biological parenthood. One issue that will become especially controversial in the years to come is who should be eligible for infertility treatments. For instance, more and more gay male couples are choosing to become parents with the help of

Again, see Issue 1 for more discussion on the controversy over family definitions.

female surrogates and egg donors. These couples are not infertile in the standard medical sense, but they are using these procedures to satisfy their desire to have children with whom they share some biological connection. Such trends will further alter the cultural definition of family.

Advances in reproductive technology will also combine with increased longevity to shatter what were once thought to be impenetrable age boundaries of biological parenthood. In 1997 a 63-year-old Los Angeles woman gave birth to a normal baby girl created from her husband's sperm and an anonymous donor's egg. She became the oldest woman on record to give birth. Although the number of women over 50 who have given birth is small—worldwide fewer than 100 have been reported (Kalb, 1997)—the possibility that someone could become a mother at a time when most women are thinking about becoming grandmothers raises difficult questions about parent–child relationships and, indeed, about the assumptions underlying family. What, for instance, would prevent a couple from waiting until they retire to have children? If they are in good health, they can expect to live over 20 years in retirement. Moreover, with no job to take their time and energy, they wouldn't have to worry about balancing the demands of work and family as so many younger parents have to.

Critics, however, argue that older parents place excessive strains on themselves and their children. They may be unable to keep up with the demands of teenagers; and children may worry that their parents will die at any moment. Note, however, that becoming a parent at age 60 or 70 has always been a biological option for men, especially well-to-do men. The actor Tony Randall and his wife had their first baby in 1996. She was 26; he was going on 77. So-called *start-over dads* have always been fairly commonplace, and their parenthood has never raised the sorts of ethical questions raised by postmenopausal women bearing children.

Another technology with significant ramifications for childbearing is genetic engineering. The understanding of genetic disease will no doubt become more exact in the twenty-first century. Will parents then be able to precisely engineer offspring who are completely free of genetic anomaly? Probably not. But the understanding of the genetics of human disease and defect will transform medical practice as you now know it. Imagine what a prenatal doctor's visit might look like a hundred years from now:

> The patient, let's call her Baby K, has her first checkup when she is an 8-week-old fetus. A technician removes a few fetal cells. Several days later, interviews with the doctor and a genetic counselor provide a detailed picture: a 250-page printout sums up information about the DNA at 50,000 regions of the fetal chromosomes—all those regions whose functions in human development are at last understood. (Kitcher, 1996, p. 124)

With all this information, genetic counselors in the future will be able to provide the expecting parents with reasonably accurate information about Baby K's susceptibility to the major diseases that develop later in life, the strength of her immune system, and perhaps even her future behavioral tendencies:

> The probability that Baby K will develop a particular personality trait might vary quite widely. But, thanks in part to advances made in neurochemistry . . . Mr. and Mrs. K can learn a few things about their daughter . . . : there is no reason to think she will have less than average intelligence; she is not very likely to be hyperactive or suffer from an attention deficit, and she displays no abnormal propensity for depression. (pp. 124–125)

What will parents do with such knowledge in the future? Although it seems technologically as well as ethically and morally unlikely that parents will be able to order a baby engineered to their specifications, they will be able to decide what kinds of children they will carry to term, provided they are prepared to abort fetuses with characteristics they don't like or don't want. The likelihood of genetic prejudice and discrimination is high. Will some parents choose to terminate a pregnancy when the fetal genes indicate a possibility of homosexuality or bisexuality, a risk for heart attack in middle age, a propensity toward obesity or shortness, or a disease that can only be treated at great expense?

The prospect is not all that futuristic. Even today, infertile couples can "adopt" frozen embryos custom made by doctors from donor sperm and eggs to approximate the couple's physical appearance and ethnic background (Kolata, 1997a). At a handful of laboratories, doctors are using a procedure called "preimplantation genetic diagnosis" to detect certain genetic diseases in embryos before implanting them in the womb. This procedure is in its infancy—geneticists can only analyze one gene at a time, and there are only several dozen tests available for detecting genetic disease—but researchers believe that within the next decade there will be hundreds of new tests for genetic problems, including adult-onset illnesses (Jones, 2000).

A few years ago, an American couple was advised that their fetus had a rare extra chromosome that was potentially linked to tall stature, severe acne, and aggressive behavior. The couple responded by aborting the fetus (Shenk, 1997). Thousands, perhaps millions, of women in other parts of the world are already aborting female fetuses or killing infant girls because they believe their daughters, growing up in cultures heavily biased toward men, will not lead happy and healthy lives. Unless prospective parents can rely on tolerance and respect for those who are different, unless they can be assured that their community will do what it can to aid people with disabilities, then the pressure to view reproduction as a process in which the "right" products have the societal stamp of approval and the "wrong" ones should be discarded will be difficult to resist.

In this future vision of childbearing is also the continuing impact of social class. As long as people assign social and economic status to those who succeed by society's prevailing standards, many middle-class and upper-class parents will feel compelled to have only children who satisfy genetic requirements for success. At the other end will be working-class and poor families who cannot afford genetic testing or in vitro therapy. They are more likely to bear children whose genetic shortcomings doom them to unemployment or, at best, to precarious and low-paying employment. They are more likely to bear children with disabilities whose challenging lives are inadequately supported and whose limited insurance coverage or minimal education denies them access to new preventive medicine. Hence some genetic disabilities virtually eliminated in the middle and upper classes will persist in the lower classes. Given today's social attitudes and the persistent gap between the rich and poor, it is not far-fetched to project that socioeconomic inequality could help to create a true genetic underclass in the future.

Ethnic Diversity

The ethnic composition of the U.S. population has been steadily changing over the past several decades and will continue to do so well into the twenty-first century. Eighteen percent of all Americans who are at least 5 years old speak a language other than English at home, up from 4 percent in 1990 (U.S. Bureau of the Census, 2001e). Already, according to

EXHIBIT 13.9

Projected Racial and Ethnic Composition of the U.S. Population

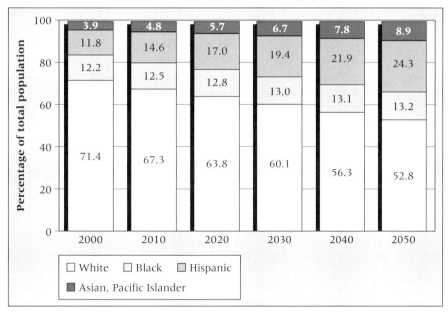

Note: Projections for American Indian/Eskimo, not shown here, are approximately 1 percent for each year.

Data source: U.S. Bureau of the Census. 2000b. *Statistical Abstract of the United States: 2000,* Table 16. Washington, DC: U.S. Government Printing Office.

the 2000 Census, non-Hispanic whites make up less than 50 percent of the population in California. Similar trends are projected in other states, such as New York, Florida, and Texas. In fact, the racial and ethnic composition of the United States has changed more quickly and dramatically in the past decade than at any previous time in the twentieth century. Experts estimate that by the year 2050 the proportion of white Americans will decrease by 9 percent, while Hispanics will see their share of the population increase by 119 percent and Asians by 118 percent (cited in Begun, 2000)—trends depicted in Exhibit 13.9.

What will happen when whites become a statistical minority nationwide? How will these trends affect family life? Certainly the notion that something called "American culture" or "the American family" exists will be noticeably less tenable in the future. Making broad general statements about American families will become increasingly more difficult, because no single family type is likely to dominate the way Euro-American families have for most of the history of this country.

Most people want a society in which racial division and animosity are no longer such potent elements in everyday life. However, for those groups who have historically been ignored, or worse, treated with outright hostility, the unique ethnic elements of family life (see Chapter 3) are a rich and important source of pride and identity. But in the end, the move toward a less white, less European-American society may matter little. Important economic, political, and cultural forces will continue to affect all families, no matter what their ethnic backgrounds.

Whether American families in the future become more similar to one another or more diverse depends on whether the formation of families across racial, religious, or social class lines becomes more common than it is today. As rates of intermarriage and the number of multiethnic children continue to increase, traditional ethnic and racial boundaries will be-gin to blur. In fact, if this trend continues, ethnic differences in family structure may some-day become less noticeable than class differences.

However, it seems unlikely that people will bring an absolute end to racial and ethnic distinctions. Even in a country such Brazil, where racial mixing is common and accepted, status and privilege are still connected to lighter skin color. In the mixed-color future of the United States, there will still be some people who are whiter than others (Cose, 2000). Race may always matter.

The Influence of Globalization

As global influences on everyday life grow stronger, the dynamics of family lives will inevi-tably be affected. Consider, for instance, how the competitive pressures of the international capitalist marketplace have forced many employers to make greater use of so-called dispos-able workers—those who work part time or on temporary contract. These jobs offer no benefits and no security and thus create instability in family life (Kilborn, 1993; Uchitelle, 1993). More and more companies cut costs by relocating their manufacturing facilities to other countries, where they can pay lower wages. Thousands of U.S.-owned manufacturing plants, including plants run by Ford, General Motors, RCA, and Zenith, are now located in northern Mexico alone (Baca Zinn & Eitzen, 1996). These companies obviously benefit fi-nancially, but the displaced American workers and their families do not.

At a deeper level, people are also being forced to understand family problems in a glo-bal context. For many poor American families, each and every day is filled with suffering and despair. In a global context, however, even the poorest of Americans live relatively privileged lives compared to the millions of extremely impoverished people worldwide. The houses, food, clothing, health care, and transportation that poor Americans have ac-cess to may be inadequate to sustain respectable lives here, but they are well beyond the dreams of a majority of families around the world. In short, even poor people in a wealthy country have certain privileges.

We're not suggesting that poor American families don't suffer or that they should feel content with what they have. Instead, we're arguing that global economic inequality will af-fect all of us in the future. It's precisely the fact that even poor American families are in bet-ter shape than poor families in most other countries that brings large numbers of immi-grants—legal and otherwise—into this country each year. They come to escape abject poverty as well as other massive problems, like overcrowding, political unrest, and repres-sive discrimination. All people are touched, in both positive and negative ways, when waves of immigrants leave their countries to seek a better life here for themselves and their fami-lies. Hence, the long-term future of American family life will be linked to the solution of social problems worldwide.

Definitions of Family

In recent years the American definition of family has expanded beyond the traditional defi-nition. Although nuclear families will continue to be important, the term *family* will most likely be used with increasing looseness in the future. In part, the liberal use of the word is a testament to its profound cultural and personal importance. To metaphorically refer to a sports team or a work group as a "family" is to symbolically reinforce the power that family holds over our lives. Yet aside from such usage of the term, the trend toward including various nontraditional relationships under the legal rubric of *family* will be at the forefront of emotional debates for years to come.

For instance, each year more and more major corporations are granting financial benefits to unmarried domestic partners. Huge multinational corporations don't make such policies frivolously, and few of them are making a political statement about the acceptability of certain lifestyles. Instead, these companies have apparently concluded that such policies make good financial sense because they increase workers' motivation and, hence, their productivity and loyalty. To the extent that using an inclusive definition of *family* continues to make good business sense, the list of economically and socially "legitimate" types of families will continue to expand.

Family Policy

With all the heated political rhetoric heard these days about the changing state of "the American family," you'd expect that the U.S. government would have a clear set of family-related objectives and specific measures to achieve them. But unlike most Western industrialized countries, Americans have no formal family policy to guide them into the future (Zimmerman, 1992).

One reason for the lack of a coherent family policy in the United States is the powerful cultural belief in individualism and privacy (Moen & Schorr, 1987). Thus, policies have traditionally been directed toward individuals rather than families. To some people, the very notion of a government plan regarding families is disturbing because it implies state intrusion into family life. Anything that seems to violate families' right to think, judge, and act for themselves is tantamount to sacrilege.

Also inhibiting the development of a family policy in the United States is the diverse nature of families themselves. Regional, state, racial, religious, ethnic, and generational variation in values have precluded agreement on what families are, not to mention what the government should be doing for them.

Certainly, at one level, all government policies—on taxes, education, welfare, health care, and so on—affect families, even if they're not designed specifically to do so. However, the U.S. government and state governments have no systematic and developed plan regarding families. Instead, we have a mishmash of state laws and regulations that lack coherence.

European Family Policies

In contrast to the United States, most European countries have an extensive policy structure for families, which includes national health insurance or services, cash benefits for families based on the number and age of children, guaranteed minimum child support payments, and sometimes housing subsidies for low- and middle-income families (Kamerman & Kahn, 1995). Although specific services and philosophies vary from country to country, the common goal is to support families, particularly families with children, at home and in the community:

> The French want not only to protect the economic well-being of children in vulnerable families but also to ensure that women continue to have children even while entering the labor force in ever-increasing numbers. The Germans and Austrians want

to acknowledge and affirm the value of children and of "family work." The Finns . . . see their policies as supporting the values of parental choice and family work. . . . The Italians stress maternal protection and support for child well-being. The Swedes, and to a lesser degree the Danes, have sought to promote gender equity, child well-being, responsiveness to labor market demands, and support for a strong work ethic. (Kamerman & Kahn, 1995, p. 25)

The policy differences between Europe and the United States are noteworthy because European children tend to be better off, by most statistical measures, than U.S. children. Infant mortality rates are lower in Europe than in the United States, fewer babies are born underweight, childhood immunization rates are higher, and therefore the rates of certain childhood diseases are lower. In most but not all European countries, school learning is more successful, and schools have fewer problems with disruptive students than do schools in the United States. Later on, fewer European adolescents have babies or abortions than do adolescents in the United States (Kamerman & Kahn, 1995).

In the United States, much of the government support for families with children is limited to programs that serve children with behavioral problems, poor children, or children from deprived groups. Such programs provide safety net income or remedial services. However, U.S. policies don't offer basic preventive and development services that can enhance the socialization of children and avert problems as they become adult members of society.

Despite the lack of a formal family policy, the U.S. government and state governments are perpetually considering family-related legislation on such issues as abortion, parental responsibility, family leave, domestic partnerships, welfare, support for the elderly, and tax benefits for families (Schneider, 1996). However, the lack of coherence among all these different initiatives leaves some crucial areas unaddressed and creates confusion in other areas about society's real values and goals.

Points of Debate for Future Policymaking

Decisions made piecemeal over the next few years—within legislatures, government agencies, and the courts—will likely determine the nation's course in regard to families well into the twenty-first century. In large part, the long-term fate of American families will depend on how people define certain social trends. If trends such as the increase in dual-earner and single-parent families are labeled as harmful to family life, then policies will probably develop that oppose family diversity and discourage "nontraditional" households. If, in contrast, such developments are viewed as inevitable—and perhaps even beneficial—then social policies will likely develop to support the needs of new and diverse family forms (Gerson, 1998).

At the forefront of the political debate over these issues will be fundamental questions about government's role in family life, such as the following:

- *Should Americans emphasize "traditional" family values?* One direction the U.S. government might take is to promote and support traditional views on family issues such as marriage, sexual activity outside marriage, maternal child care at home, and so on. Public policies, including taxes, would give preference to married couples with children and discourage or place restrictions on divorce, illegitimacy, and single and gay parenting. Schools would teach children that sex outside of marriage is wrong; the government would not subsidize abortion, and states would repeal no-fault divorce laws.

However, at a time when the country is becoming more diverse, a return to the "traditional family" at the expense of "nontraditional" families seems unlikely.

- *Should Americans promote parental responsibility?* This policy approach would make family planning and sex education a national priority, discouraging people who aren't prepared financially or emotionally from becoming parents unexpectedly. It would strictly enforce existing laws that hold parents responsible for raising children and accountable for their children's legal transgressions. Failure to pay child support, for instance, would be considered a form of child neglect. Divorce and custody arrangements would make the financial well-being of children—not of parents—the highest priority. But this perspective would further complicate the decision to bear and raise children at a time when many people are already struggling to meet the demands of children and work.

- *Should Americans expand the government's responsibility for helping families raise children?* This society has programs designed to help the elderly (Social Security, Medicare), so why not make similar provisions for children? Following models that exist in other industrialized countries, the U.S. government could take steps to lift all children out of poverty. The government would subsidize child care, preschool, health care, and paid parental leave when babies are born. It would also require employers to pay women the same wages that men earn in similar jobs. It would encourage employment practices, such as a shorter workweek, that would help to undercut the career advantage of people who don't place a priority on family life. However, such a policy would require a more pronounced government role in people's lives at a time when a majority of Americans favor limiting government and reducing public spending.

Regardless of which direction government policy ultimately takes, people will need to debate many specific legal issues (Minow & Shanley, 1996):

- *The place of biology in reproduction, custody, and access.* What, if any, claims should those people with biological ties to a child have regarding the child's conception, gestation, birth, and custody? Should grandparents have legally protected access to their grandchildren in the event of a divorce?

- *Sexual orientation.* What relations between adult homosexual partners should the state permit or promote? Should homosexual parents be restricted in their ability to raise children?

- *The preference or privilege accorded to legal families compared to families formed informally.* Should those in legally executed marriages and adoptions receive benefits denied those in informal, legally unrecognized arrangements?

- *The role of the economic marketplace in forming family relationships.* Should people be able to contract for the conception or generation of a child? For a child available for adoption? For sexual services? For a spouse?

- *The role of government money in providing support for families.* Should the government subsidize child care, care of ill or disabled family members, or nursing homes for all enfeebled Americans? Should the government subsidize greater choice in children's education, in the form of charter schools or school voucher systems?

- *The relationship between the workplace and family life.* Should workplaces be structured to favor or support one family type over others? Should workloads in the paid labor force be made more flexible to accommodate the demands of caring for children or elderly relatives or of performing other family duties?

- *The relative power of family members in family-related decision making.* What is the legal or philosophical basis for granting greater power to one member of an adult partnership over the other, as in decisions over abortion and child custody? Should children have as much say as parents in custody decisions? In medical treatment decisions, how should the views of all involved—patients, spouses, cohabiting partners, and other relatives—be collected and given force?
- *Racial, ethnic, and religious identities.* Should the state rely on race or ethnicity or religious identity as a basis for deciding disputes over child custody or regulating foster care, adoption, marriage, divorce, and medical treatment?
- *Dependency, disability, and illness.* Who is responsible for the daily care and financial support of such dependents as children, elderly people, and people with severe disabilities or illnesses? What degree of family relationship establishes such responsibilities?

Each of these issues has arisen because of new technologies, changing social practices, and conflict over norms and ethics. Their resolution will not be easy, because family life is the result of a complex interplay among individuals, institutions, cultural values, and conscious political choices.

A Final Word

We hope that reading this book has motivated you to take a closer, more sociologically informed look at your own family experiences. In families, we have a topic about which everyone has some expertise. It is tempting, therefore, to assume that we can know everything that needs to be known about families by simply looking at our own lives. But, of course, such a subjective view can never be sufficient. Assuming that something that happens in one's own family happens in all families is a little like saying, "Because my older brother likes M&M's, everyone's older brother likes M&M's."

At the same time, though, you have seen in this book that many, if not most, families have certain patterns and features in common. We hope that occasionally you've read something here and felt that we must have been writing about *your* family. It's the patterns and commonalities that are intriguing to sociologists, because they suggest a much larger reality than the private experience of individual families.

Furthermore, families, private and unique though they be, are always tightly intertwined with larger political, historical, economic, cultural, and environmental forces. People can never understand their own families without understanding the social structure within which their families are situated.

Will families exist in the future? Yes. But always keep certain important points in mind:

- It has never been and never will be possible to think of "the family" or "the American family." Family diversity has always characterized family life and will continue to do so in the next century.
- The experiences that individuals have within their own families will always be filtered by their race or ethnicity, social class, gender, sexual orientation, religion, and other social characteristics.
- None of the shifts in family life can be understood in isolation. Each change takes place within a particular cultural and historical context. Furthermore, each aspect of family

life touches on others. People can't begin to understand parent–child relationships, for instance, without understanding something about marriage, gender, demography, culture, domestic and global economics, work, even biology.

As we wrap up this book, we have feelings of both failure and success. On the one hand, we've probably provided few, if any, ironclad answers to the crucial questions that drive discussions and debates over families in American society. People can't agree on what a family is or what the relative importance of biology and culture are in forming family experiences. No one knows for sure what the perfect balance of family privacy and public accountability should be or whether individual rights or family responsibilities should be granted more importance in society. People still argue vehemently over whether American families are declining or merely adapting to changing social circumstances and whether or not divorce or having two working parents hurts children.

But the lack of consensus on these issues is not based on ignorance or stupidity. It's the nature of the beast. None of these important questions has clear, simple answers. Sociological research can provide invaluable information on general tendencies and truths as they apply to the majority of the population, but it can never and will never be able to predict the family experiences of every single person. Sure, some kids are hurt by the divorce of their parents, but others aren't. Some kids with homosexual parents thrive; others don't. Yes, the cultural value of family privacy creates serious and dangerous problems, but it also prevents other problems from occurring. Black families and white families, rich families and poor families are indeed different; but they're also similar in a lot of ways.

So maybe the lack of clear, unequivocal answers isn't a failure after all. Maybe what we've done is succeed in showing you that *no* family issue or experience has an easy explanation. Although sociological theory and research are invaluable tools in understanding the nature of these phenomena, no two people experience their families in exactly the same way; and no two families deal with economic, political, religious, cultural, and educational institutions in the same way. There's an important lesson here: Be wary and skeptical of commentators, critics, politicians, and fellow citizens bearing simple answers to complex family questions. Instead, appreciate families—your family, friends' families, and families in general—for what they truly are: familiar yet confusing, boring yet thrilling, simple yet complex, painful yet wonderful, exasperating yet pleasurable, frightening yet comforting.

Conclusion

The question you probably really want answered after reading this chapter on family change and future family patterns is, What can I expect in my own family life in the next decade or so? Family relationships occupy such a crucial position in people's lives that we all have a powerful desire to know what's in store for us.

But after spending most of this chapter offering speculative thoughts about what families may look like in the future, we can be 100 percent certain of only two things:

- Families will be the same as they've always been.
- Families will never be the same again.

We're only being mildly facetious in making these apparently contradictory predictions. In some not-yet-known ways, as families move further into the twenty-first century, they will be nearly unrecognizable to contemporary observers. No doubt people will encounter some new, frightening things that they haven't yet had to deal with. In other ways, though, families will be much the same as today. People will still worry about the same things they've always worried about and criticize families on the same grounds on which they've always done so.

Consider this account of a family event that, although it took place recently, is likely to become a common, unremarkable occurrence in the future:

> At the recent wedding of my stepson, my husband sat companionably between his former wife (the mother of the groom) and me. The groom, in his toast, warmly acknowledged the bride's ex-husband (the father of son), who was there with his long-time partner, who sat next to the lesbian couple with their new baby. The new husband of my husband's ex-wife introduced us to the daughters of his two previous marriages, one of whom described the difficulties of living with your ex-husband in the apartment right above you. All in all, a typical post-modern family—one typical of Republicans as well as Democrats, conservatives as well as liberals, rich as well as poor. (Tavris, 1996, p. 27)

The scene is humorously bizarre and confusing. Complicated step-relationships and "nontraditional" living arrangements abound. But notice also that age-old things such as long-term, committed relationships and child rearing remain important aspects of family life. In short, even though the structure of people's family relationships may look quite different from the way they do today, people will always need intimacy and commitment and a desire to nurture offspring and therefore will always need to construct some sort of family—whatever it may look like.

Barring some cataclysmic fascist revolution like that depicted in *The Handmaid's Tale*, people in the future will continue to face choices about the things people currently contemplate: whom to date, whether to marry, whether to have children, whether to remain married. The growing racial, ethnic, cultural, and sexual diversity of the population will create substantial variation in the ways people make these choices in the future. But the fundamental needs of human intimacy will always remain.

Chapter Highlights

- When massive social changes occur in a society, their effects are often strongly felt in families. Sometimes these changes occur as the result of major demographic shifts, technological innovations, diffusion between cultures and institutions, or economic change; at other times they are brought about purposefully by individuals or groups of individuals who feel that some aspect of society isn't functioning as it should.
- Although future families will face some issues very different from those faced today, they will also, in many ways, struggle with the same questions and dilemmas families have always struggled with.
- Unlike other industrialized countries, the United States lacks a national family policy. Ironically, some of the most cherished U.S. "family values" (for instance, family privacy and autonomy) prevent the establishment of a coherent state policy.
- At the forefront of political debate over future family trends will be the government's role in family life.

Your Turn

One of the key themes of this chapter has been that change is a permanent characteristic of the institution of family. Such change is sometimes the by-product of changes that occur in other areas of society. At other times, the change comes from the purposeful actions of groups of individuals.

Most communities contain people who are active in one or another major movement for social change that has at its core concern over family roles and responsibilities: the women's movement, the welfare reform movement, and so on. Find a few people who are involved in one such movement. Ask them to describe their experiences. What was their motive for joining the movement? What sorts of activities do they participate in? What goals do they want to achieve? How does the movement reflect their image of what a family ought to be? Do they feel the movement has been effective in accomplishing its goals? If not, why not? What else needs to be done? What do they feel they've personally accomplished?

Attend a gathering in which a movement addressing family needs is involved. It might be an organizational meeting, a town council meeting, a protest march, or a demonstration. What happened at the gathering? What seemed to be the overall atmosphere? Was it festive? solemn? angry? businesslike? Was any opposition present?

What do such movements tell us about the nature of families and their relationship to broader elements of social change?

Abell, E., Clawson, M., Washington, W. N., Bost, K. K., & Vaughn, B. E. 1996. "Parenting values, attitudes, behaviors and goals of African American mothers from a low-income population in relation to social and societal contexts." *Journal of Family Issues, 17,* 593–613.

Abma, J. C., & Sonenstein, F. L. 2001. Sexual activity and contraceptive practices among teenagers in the United States: 1988 and 1995. National Center for Health Statistics. *Vital Health Statistics, 23*(21).

Acker, J. 1978. "Issues in the sociological study of women's work." In A. H. Stromberg & S. Harkees (Eds.), *Women working.* Palo Alto, CA: Mayfield.

———. 1989. *Doing comparable work: Gender, class, and pay equity.* Philadelphia: Temple University Press.

"ACLU sues Florida over ban on gay and lesbian adoptions." 2001. *CNN.com. Online.* Available at www.cnn.com/US/ 9905/26/gay.adoptions/. Accessed May 5, 2001.

Acock, A. C., & Demo, D. H. 1994. *Family diversity and well-being.* Thousand Oaks, CA: Sage.

Adelson, J. 1996. "Splitting up." *Commentary,* September, pp. 63–66.

Administration on Aging. 2001. "The National Elder Abuse Incidence Study: Executive Summary." Available at www.aoa.gov. Accessed May 5, 2001.

Ahlburg, D. A., & De Vita, C. J. 1992. "New realities of the American family." *Population Bulletin, 47,* 2–42.

Ahrons, C. R., & Rodgers, R. H. 1987. *Divorced families: A multidisciplinary developmental view.* New York: Norton.

Albert, S. M. 1990. "Caregiving as a cultural system: Conceptions of filial obligation and parental dependency in urban America." *American Anthropologist, 92,* 319–331.

Aldous, J. 1983. "Problematic elements in the relationships between churches and families." In W. V. D'Antonio & J. Aldous (Eds.), *Families and religions:*

Conflict and change in modern society. Beverly Hills, CA: Sage.

———. 1995. "New views of grandparents in intergenerational context." *Journal of Family Issues, 16,* 104–122.

Aldous, J., & Dumon, W. 1990. "Family policy in the 1980's: Controversy and consensus." *Journal of Marriage and the Family, 52,* 1136–1151.

Alksnis, C., Desmarais, S., & Wood, E. 1996. "Gender differences in scripts for different types of dates." *Sex Roles, 34,* 321–336.

Allen, A. L. 1988. *Uneasy access: Privacy for women in a free society.* Totowa, NJ: Rowman & Littlefield.

Allen, J. 1993. "Boys: Hanging with the Spur Posse." *Rolling Stone,* July 8–22.

Allen, K. R., & Demo, D. H. 1995. "The families of lesbians and gay men: A new frontier in family research." *Journal of Marriage and the Family, 57,* 111–127.

Altman, I., & Taylor, D. A. 1973. *Social penetration: The development of interpersonal relationships.* New York: Holt, Rinehart & Winston.

Altman, L. K. 1997. "AIDS deaths drop 19% in U.S., continuing a heartening trend." *New York Times,* July 15.

———. 1999. "Study says gay men reducing levels of risky sexual behavior." *New York Times,* June 28.

Alvarez, L. 1997. "House passes bill to replace system of public housing." *New York Times,* May 5.

Amato, P. R. 1987. "Family processes in one-parent, step-parent, and intact families: The child's point of view." *Journal of Marriage and the Family, 48,* 327–337.

———. 1993. "Children's adjustment to divorce: Theories, hypotheses and empirical support." *Journal of Marriage and the Family, 55,* 22–54.

———. 2000. "The consequences of divorce for adults and children." *Journal of Marriage and the Family, 62,* 1269–1288.

———. 2001. "What children learn from divorce." *Population Today.* January.

Available at www.prb.org/pt/2001/ Jan2001/children_divorce.html. Accessed July 16, 2001.

American Association of Retired Persons. 1999. "The AARP grandparenting survey: The sharing and caring between mature grandparents and their grandchildren." November. Available at www.research.aarp.org/ general/granpsurv.html. Accessed August 8, 2000.

———. 2001. "In the middle: A report on multicultural boomers coping with family and aging issues." Available at www.aarp.org/inthemiddle/pdf/ inthemiddle.pdf. Accessed July 11, 2001.

Ammerman, N. T. 1987. *Bible believers: Fundamentalists in the modern world.* New Brunswick, NJ: Rutgers University Press.

Anderson, E. A., & Koblinsky, S. A. 1995. "Homeless policy: The need to speak to families." *Family Relations, 44,* 13–18.

Anderson, E. A., & Spruill, J. W. 1993. "The dual-career commuter family: A lifestyle on the move." *Marriage and Family Review, 19,* 131–147.

Anderson, L. 1988. "Property rights of same-sex couples: Toward a new definition of family." *Journal of Family Law, 26,* 357–372.

Angier, N. 1995. "If you're really ancient, you may be better off." *New York Times,* March 27.

———. 1997a. "New debate over surgery on genitals." *New York Times,* May 13.

———. 1997b. "Sexual identity not pliable after all, report says." *New York Times,* March 14.

Antill, J. K., Goodnow, J. J., Russell, G., & Cotton, S. 1996. "The influence of parents and family context on children's involvement in household tasks." *Sex Roles, 34,* 215–236.

Aponte, R. 1998. "Hispanic families in poverty: Diversity, context, and interpretation." In S. J. Ferguson (Ed.), *Shifting the center: Understanding contemporary families.* Mountain View, CA: Mayfield.

Appell, L. W. R. 1988. "Menstruation among the Rungus of Borneo: An unmarked category." In T. Buckley & A. Gottlieb (Eds.), *Blood magic: The anthropology of menstruation.* Berkeley: University of California Press.

Applbaum, K. D. 1995. "Marriage with the proper stranger: Arranged marriage in metropolitan Japan." *Ethnology, 34,* 37–51.

Applebome, P. 1996a. "A carrot and stick for parenthood." *New York Times,* June 16.

———. 1996b. "Holding parents legally responsible for the misbehavior of their children." *New York Times,* April 10.

Archer, D. 1985. "Social deviance." In G. Lindzey & E. Aronson (Eds.), *Handbook of social psychology* (3rd ed., Vol. 2). New York: Random House.

Arditti, J. A. 1999. "Rethinking relationships between divorced mothers and their children: Capitalizing on family strengths." *Family Relations, 48,* 109–119.

Arditti, J. A., & Madden-Derdich, D. 1997. "Joint and sole custody mothers: Implications for research and practice." *Families in Society, 78,* 36–45.

Arendell, T. 1987. "Women and the economics of divorce in the contemporary United States." *Signs, 13,* 121–135.

———. 1992. "After divorce: Investigations into father absence." *Gender and Society, 6,* 562–586.

———. 1995. *Fathers and divorce.* Thousand Oaks, CA: Sage.

Ariès, P. 1962. *Centuries of childhood.* New York: Vintage.

Armour, S. 2000. "Ford plans ambitious child-care program." *USA Today,* November 22. Online edition.

Arras, J. D. 1991. "Beyond Cruzan: Individual rights, family autocracy and the persistent vegetative state." *Journal of the American Geriatrics Society, 39,* 1018–1024.

Arrighi, B. A. 1997. *America's shame: Women and children in shelter and the degradation of family roles.* Westport, CT: Praeger.

Arrighi, B. A., & Maume, D. J. 2000. "Workplace subordination and men's avoidance of housework." *Journal of Family Issues, 21,* 464–488.

Atwood, M. 1985. *The handmaid's tale.* New York: Fawcett.

Aulette, J. R. 1994. *Changing families.* Belmont, CA: Wadsworth.

Avicolli, T. 2000. "He defies you still: The memoirs of a sissy." In E. Disch (Ed.), *Reconstructing gender.* Mountain View, CA: Mayfield.

Ayres, B. D. 1996. "Marriage advised in some youth pregnancies." *New York Times,* September 9.

Babbie, E. 1992. *The practice of social research.* Belmont, CA: Wadsworth.

Baca Zinn, M. 1997. "Family, race and poverty." In A. S. Skolnick & J. H. Skolnick (Eds.), *Family in transition* (9th ed.). New York: Longman.

Baca Zinn, M., & Eitzen, D. S. 1996. *Diversity in families.* New York: HarperCollins.

Bailey, B. L. 1988. *From front porch to back seat.* Baltimore: Johns Hopkins University Press.

Baker, P. L. 1997. "And I went back: Battered women's negotiation of choice." *Journal of Contemporary Ethnography, 26,* 55–74.

Ballard, C. 1987. "A humanist sociology approach to teaching social research." *Teaching Sociology, 15,* 7–14.

Balswick, J. O., & Balswick, J. K. 1995. "Gender relations and marital power." In B. B. Ingoldsby & S. Smith (Eds.), *Families in multicultural perspective.* New York: Guilford.

Baltzell, E. D. 1958. *Philadelphia gentleman: The making of a national upper class.* Glencoe, IL: Free Press.

Bane, M. J. 1976. *Here to stay.* New York: Basic Books.

Barich, R. R., & Bielby, D. D. 1996. "Rethinking marriage: Change and stability in expectations, 1967–1994." *Journal of Family Issues, 17,* 136–169.

Barker, K. 1993. "Changing assumptions and contingent solutions: The costs and benefits of women working full- and part-time." *Sex Roles, 28,* 47–71.

Barnett, R. C., & Baruch, G. K. 1987 "Determinants of father's participation in family work." *Journal of Marriage and the Family, 49,* 29–40.

Barnett, R. C., Brennan, R. T., Raudenbush, S. W., & Marshall, N. L. 1994. "Gender and the relationship between marital-role quality and psychological distress." *Psychology of Women Quarterly, 18,* 105–127.

Barone, C., Ickoviis, J. R., Ayers, T. S., Katz, S. M., Voyce, C. K., & Weissberg, R. P. 1996. "High-risk sexual behavior among young urban students." *Family Planning Perspectives, 28,* 69–74.

Barry, D. 2000. "What to do if you're stopped by the police." *New York Times,* February 27.

Barry, J. B. 1993. "Daddytrack." *Utne Reader,* May–June, pp. 70–73.

Bartholet, E. 1993. *Family bonds.* Boston: Houghton Mifflin.

Bassuk, E. L., Rubin, L., & Lauriat, A. S. 1986. "Characteristics of sheltered homeless families." *American Journal of Public Health, 76,* 1079–1101.

Beal, C. R. 1994. *Boys and girls: The development of gender roles.* New York: McGraw-Hill.

Bean, F. D., & Tienda, M. 1987. *The Hispanic population in the United States.* New York: Russell Sage.

Bearak, B. 1999. "A tale of 2 lovers, and a taboo recklessly flouted." *New York Times,* April 9.

Becerra, R. N. 1992. "Mexican American families." In J. M. Henslin (Ed.), *Marriage and family in a changing society.* New York: Free Press.

Beck, M. 1990. "Be nice to your kids." *Newsweek,* March 12.

Becker, G. S. 1981. *A treatise on the family.* Cambridge, MA: Harvard University Press.

Becker, P. E., & Moen, P. 1999. "Scaling back: Dual-earner couples' work–family strategies." *Journal of Marriage and the Family, 61,* 995–1007.

Beeghley, L. 1996. *What does your wife do? Gender and the transformation of family life.* Boulder, CO: Westview.

Beekman, D. 1977. *The mechanical baby: A popular history of the theory and practice of child raising.* Westport, CT: Lawrence Hill.

Beer, W. R. 1988. *Relative strangers: Studies of stepfamily processes.* Totowa, NJ: Rowan & Littlefield.

Begun, B. 2000. "USA: The way we'll live then." *Newsweek,* January 1.

Bell, D. J., & Bell, S. L. 1991. "The victim–offender relationship as a determinant factor in police dispositions of family violence incidents: A replication study." *Policing and Society, 1,* 225–234.

Bellah, R. N. 1995. "The quest for self." In A. Etzioni (Ed.), *Rights and the common good.* New York: St. Martin's Press.

Bellah, R. N., Madsen, R., Sullivan, W. M., Swidler, A., & Tipton, S. M. 1985. *Habits of the heart.* New York: Harper & Row.

Bell-Rowbotham, B., & Lero, D. 2001. "Responses to extension of parental leaves." Centre for Families, Work and Well-Being. Available at www.uoguelph.ca/cfww/response.htm. Accessed July 10, 2001.

Belluck, P. 1999. "Cash-for-sterilization plan draws addicts and critics." *New York Times,* July 24.

———. 2000a. "Parents try to reclaim their children's time." *New York Times,* June 13.

———. 2000b. "States declare war on divorce rates, before any 'I do's.'" *New York Times,* April 25.

Belsky, J. 1990. "Infant day care, child development, and family policy." *Society,* July–August, 10–12.

Belsky, J., & Kelly, J. 1994. *The transition to parenthood: How a first child changes a marriage; Why some couples grow closer and others apart.* New York: Delacorte.

Bem, S. L. 1974. "The measurement of psychological androgyny." *Journal of Consulting and Clinical Psychology, 42,* 155–162.

Bengtson, V. L. 2001. "Beyond the nuclear family: The increasing importance of multigenerational bonds." *Journal of Marriage and the Family, 63,* 1–17.

Benokraitis, N. V. 2000. "How family wars affect us: Four models of family change and their consequences." In N. V. Benokraitis (Ed.), *Feuds about families.* Upper Saddle River, NJ: Prentice Hall.

Berardo, F. M. 1998. "Family privacy: Issues and concepts." *Journal of Family Issues, 19,* 4–19.

Berger, L. 2000. "What children do when home and alone." *New York Times,* April 11.

Berger, P. L., & Kellner, H. 1964. "Marriage and the construction of reality: An exercise in the microsociology of knowledge." *Diogenes, 46,* 1–23.

Berkin, C. 1996. *First generations: Women in colonial America.* New York: Hill & Wang.

Bernard, J. 1981. "The good provider role: Its rise and fall." *American Psychologist, 36,* 1–12.

———. 1982. *The future of marriage.* New York: Bantam.

Bernhardt, A., Morris, M., & Handcock, M. S. 1995. "Women's gains or men's losses? A closer look at the shrinking gender gap in earnings." *American Journal of Sociology, 101,* 302–328.

Berscheid, E., & Peplau, L. A. 1983. "The emerging science of relationships." In H. H. Kelley, E. Berscheid, A. Christensen, J. H. Harvey, T. L. Huston, G. Levinger, E. McClintock, & D. R. Peterson (Eds.), *Close relationships: Perspectives on the meaning of intimacy.* New York: Freeman.

Bertoia, C., & Drakich, J. 1993. "The father's rights movement." *Journal of Family Issues, 14,* 592–615.

Besharov, D. J. 1993. "Overreporting and underreporting are twin problems." In R. J. Gelles & D. R. Loeske (Eds.), *Current controversies on family violence.* Newbury Park, CA: Sage.

Best, J. 1993. *Threatened children.* Chicago: University of Chicago Press.

Beutler, I. F., Burr, W. R., Bahr, K. S., & Herrin, D. A. 1989. "The family realm: Theoretical contributions for understanding its uniqueness." *Journal of Marriage and the Family, 51,* 805–815.

Bianchi, S. M. 1999. "Feminization and juvenilization of poverty: Trends, relative risks, causes, and consequences." *Annual Review of Sociology, 25,* 307–333.

Bianchi, S. M., & Casper, L. M. 2000. "American families." *Population Bulletin, 55,* 1–44.

Bianchi, S. M., Casper, L. M., & Kent, M. 2001. "American families resilient after 50 years of change." *Population Bulletin,* Newsrelease.

Bianchi, S. M., Milkie, M. A., Sayer, L. C., & Robinson, J. P. 2000. "Is anyone doing the housework? Trends in the gender division of household labor." *Social Forces, 79,* 191–228.

Bianchi, S. M., & Spain, D. 1986. *American women in transition.* New York: Russell Sage.

Biernat, M., & Wortman, C. B. 1991. "Sharing of home responsibilities between professionally employed women and their husbands." *Journal of Personality and Social Psychology, 60,* 844–860.

Birchler, G. R., Weiss, R. L., & Vincent, J. P. 1975. "Multimethod analysis of social reinforcement exchange between maritally distressed and non-distressed spouse and stranger dyads." *Journal of Personality and Social Psychology, 31,* 349–360.

Blackwell, J. E. 1985. *The black community: Diversity and unity.* New York: Harper & Row.

Blaisure, K. R., & Allen, K. R. 2000. "Feminism and marital equality." In N. V. Benokraitis (Ed.), *Feuds about families.* Upper Saddle River, NJ: Prentice Hall.

Blakeslee, S. 1991. "The male link to birth defects figures." *American Health,* April.

Blau, P. M. 1964. *Exchange and power is social life.* New York: Wiley.

Blau, P. M., & Duncan, O. D. 1967. *The American occupational structure.* New York: Wiley.

Blood, R. O., & Wolfe, D. M. 1960. *Husbands and wives.* New York: Free Press.

Blumberg, R. L., & Coleman, M. T. 1989. "A theoretical look at the gender balance of power in the American couple." *Journal of Family Issues, 10,* 225–250.

Blumstein, P., & Kollock, P. 1988. "Personal relationships." *Annual Review of Sociology, 14,* 467–490.

Blumstein, P., & Schwartz, P. 1983. *American couples.* New York: Morrow.

"The body counters." 1993. *People Weekly,* April 12, pp. 34–37.

Bollenbacher, V., & Burtt, S. 1997. "Discipline, assault, and justice: Violent parents and the law." *Law & Policy, 19,* 344–361.

Bolton, M. K. 2000. *The third shift: Managing hard choices in our careers, homes, and lives as women.* San Francisco: Jossey-Bass.

Bonney, J. F., Kelley, M. L., & Levant, R. F. 1999. "A model of fathers' behavioral involvement in child care in dual-earner families." *Journal of Family Psychology, 13,* 401–415.

Booth, A., & Amato, P. R. 2001. "Parental predivorce relations and offspring postdivorce well-being." *Journal of Marriage and the Family, 63,* 197–212.

Booth, A., & Johnson, D. 1988. "Premarital cohabitation and marital success." *Journal of Family Issues, 9,* 255–272.

Boudreau, F. A. 1993. "Elder abuse." In R. L. Hampton & T. P. Gullotta (Eds.), *Family violence: Prevention and treatment.* Newbury Park, CA: Sage.

Boulding, E. 1976. "Familial constraint on women's work roles." *Signs, 1,* 95–118.

Bound, J., Duncan, G., Laren, D., & Oleinick, L. 1991. "Poverty dynamics in widowhood." *Journal of Gerontology, 46,* 115–124.

Bowker, L. H. 1993. "A battered woman's problems are social, not psychological." In R. J. Gelles & D. R. Loeske (Eds.), *Current controversies on family violence.* Newbury Park, CA: Sage.

Boxer, S. 1997. "One casualty of the women's movement: Feminism." *New York Times,* December 14.

Boydston, J. 2001. "Cult of true womanhood." Available at www.pbs.org/stantonanthony/resources/culthood.html. Accessed July 10, 2001.

Brabant, S., Forsyth, C. J., & McFarlain, G. 1994. "Defining the family after the death of a child." *Death Studies, 18,* 197–206.

Brabant, S., & Mooney, L. A. 1999. "The social construction of family life in the Sunday comics: Race as a consideration." *Journal of Comparative Family Studies, 30,* 113–133.

Bradbury, T. N., Fincham, F. D., & Beach, S. R. H. 2000. "Research on the nature and determinants of marital satisfaction: A decade in review." *Journal of Marriage and the Family, 62,* 964–981.

Bradsher, K. 1996. "Rich control more of U.S. wealth, study says, as debt grows for poor." *New York Times,* June 22.

———. 1999. "Fear of crime trumps fear of lost youth." *New York Times,* November 21.

Brehm, S. 1992. *Intimate relationships.* New York: McGraw-Hill.

Breslau, K. 1990. "Overplanned parenthood." *Newsweek,* January 22.

"Bridal dowry in India." 2000. *Morning Edition,* National Public Radio, June 19. Available at www.npr.org/programs/morning. Accessed January 1, 2001.

Brien, M. J., Lillard, L. A., & Waite, L. J. 1999. "Interrelated family-building behaviors: Cohabitation, marriage, and nonmarital conception." *Demography, 36,* 535–551.

Brines, J. 1994. "Economic dependency, gender and the division of labor at home." *American Journal of Sociology, 100,* 652–688.

Brines, J., & Joyner, K. 1999. "The ties that bind: Principles of cohesion in cohabitation and marriage." *American Sociological Review, 64,* 333–355.

Brinig, M. F. 2000. *From contract to covenant: Beyond the law and economics of the family.* Cambridge, MA: Harvard University Press.

Bronner, E. 1998a. "Inventing the notion of race." *New York Times,* January 10.

———. 1998b. "U.S. 12th graders rank poorly in math and science, study says." *New York Times,* February 25.

Brooks, D., & Barth, R. P. 1999. "Adult transracial and inracial adoptees: Effects of race, gender, adoptive family structure, and placement history on adjustment outcomes." *American Journal of Orthopsychiatry, 69,* 87–99.

Broom, L., & Kitsuse, J. I. 1956. *The managed casualty.* Berkeley: University of California Press.

Brown, P. 1998. "Biology and the social construction of the 'race' concept." In J. Ferrante & P. Brown (Eds.), *The social construction of race and ethnicity in the United States.* New York: Longman.

Brown, P. L. 2000. "'Sudden wealth syndrome' brings new stress." *New York Times,* March 10.

Brown, R. 1986. *Social psychology.* New York: Free Press.

Brown, S. L., & Booth, A. 1996. "Cohabitation versus marriage: A comparison of relationship quality." *Journal of Marriage and the Family 58,* 668–678.

Browne, A. 1993. "Family violence and homelessness: The relevance of trauma histories in the lives of homeless women." *American Journal of Orthopsychiatry, 63,* 370–384.

Browne, I. 1997. "Explaining the black–white gap in labor force participation among women heading households." *American Sociological Review, 62,* 236–252.

Browning, C. R., & Laumann, E. O. 1997. "Sexual contact between children and adults: A life course perspective." *American Sociological Review, 62,* 540–560.

Brush, L. D. 2000. "Battering, traumatic stress, and welfare-to-work transition." *Violence Against Women, 6,* 1039–1065.

Bryjak, G. J., & Soroka, M. P. 1992. *Sociology: Cultural diversity in a changing world.* Boston: Allyn & Bacon.

Bryson, K., & Casper, L. M. 1999. "Coresident grandparents and grandchildren." *Current Population Reports,* P23–198. U.S. Bureau of the Census. Washington, DC: U.S. Government Printing Office.

Buckley, T., & Gottlieb, A. 1988. "A critical appraisal of theories of menstrual symbolism." In T. Buckley & A. Gottlieb (Eds.), *Blood magic: The anthropology of menstruation.* Berkeley: University of California Press.

Budig, M. J., & England, P. 2001. "The wage penalty for motherhood." *American Sociological Review, 66,* 204–225.

Bulcroft, K., Smeins, L., & Bulcroft, R. 1999. *Romancing the honeymoon: Consummating marriage in modern society.* Thousand Oaks, CA: Sage.

Bumiller, E. 1992. "First comes marriage—then maybe love." In J. M. Henslin (Ed.), *Marriage and family in a changing society.* New York: Free Press.

Bumpass, L., Sweet, J. A., & Cherlin, A. 1991. "The role of cohabitation in declining rates of marriage." *Journal of Marriage and the Family, 53,* 913–927.

Burgess-Jackson, K. 1998. "Wife rape." *Public Affairs Quarterly, 12,* 1–22.

Burnham, M. 1993. "An impossible marriage: Slave law and family law." In M. Minow (Ed.), *Family matters: Readings on family lives and the law.* New York: New Press.

Burtt, S. 1994. "Reproductive responsibilities: Rethinking the fetal rights debate." *Policy Sciences, 27,* 179–196.

Buss, D. M. 1994. *The evolution of desire: Strategies of human mating.* New York: Basic Books.

Buss, D. M., Shackelford, T. K., Kirkpatrick, L. A., & Larsen, R. J. 2001.

"A half century of mate preferences: The cultural evolution of values." *Journal of Marriage and the Family, 63,* 491–514.

Bussell, D. A. 1994. "Ethical issues in observational family research." *Family Process, 33,* 361–376.

Butler, A. 1996. "The effect of welfare benefit levels on poverty among single-parent families." *Social Problems, 43,* 94–115.

Butler, R. 1989. "A generation at risk: When the baby boomers reach Golden Pond." In W. Feigelman (Ed.), *Sociology full circle.* New York: Holt, Rinehart & Winston.

Butterfield, F. 1997. "1995 data show sharp drop in reported rapes." *New York Times,* February 3.

Call, V. R. A., & Heaton, T. B. 1997. "Religious influence on marital stability." *Journal for the Scientific Study of Religion, 36,* 382–392.

"Canada overturns definition of 'spouse' as heterosexual." 1999. *New York Times,* May 21.

Cancian, F. 1986. "The femininity of love." *Signs, 11,* 692–709.

———. 1987. *Love in America.* Cambridge, MA: Cambridge University Press.

———. 1993. "Gender politics: Love and power in the private and public spheres." In B. J. Fox (Ed.), *Family patterns: Gender relations.* Toronto: Oxford University Press.

Cancian, F., & Gordon, S. C. 1988. "Changing emotion norms in marriage: Love and anger in U.S. women's magazines since 1900." *Gender and Society, 2,* 308–342.

Cancian, F., & Oliker, S. J. 2000. *Caring and gender.* Thousand Oaks, CA: Pine Forge Press.

Cancian, M., & Meyer, D. R. 2000. "Work after welfare: Women's work effort, occupation, and economic well-being." *Social Work Research, 24,* 69–86.

"Can't sue negligent officials in abuse cases, court rules." 1989. *Los Angeles Times,* February 22.

Cantor, M. G. 1991. "The American family on television: From Molly Goldberg to Bill Cosby." *Journal of Comparative Family Studies, 22,* 205–216.

Caple, J. 2001. "Nobody wins when the winners cheated." Available at http://espn.go.com/mlb/columns/caple_jim/1246591.html. Accessed September 27, 2001.

Capps, D. 1992. "Religion and child abuse: Perfect together." *Journal for the Scientific Study of Religion, 31,* 1–14.

Carbone, J. 2000. *From partners to parents: The second revolution in family law.* New York: Columbia University Press.

Carlson, B. E. 1996. "Dating violence: Student beliefs about consequences." *Journal of Interpersonal Violence, 11,* 3–18.

Carr, B. J. 1988. *Crisis in intimacy.* Pacific Grove, CA: Brooks/Cole.

Carrington, C. 1999. *No place like home: Relationships and family life among lesbians and gay men.* Chicago: University of Chicago Press.

Caspi, A., Wright, B. R. E., Moffitt, T. E., & Silva, P. A. 1998. "Early failure in the labor market: Childhood and adolescent predictors of unemployment in the transition to adulthood." *American Sociology Review, 63,* 424–451.

Castro, I. 1998. *Equal pay: A thirty-five-year perspective,* Table 1. U.S. Department of Labor. Available at www.dol.gov/dol/wb/. Accessed May 5, 2000.

Cate, R. M., & Lloyd, S. A. 1992. *Courtship.* Newbury Park, CA: Sage.

Cazenave, N. A. 1984. "Race, socioeconomic status, and age: the social context of American masculinity." *Sex Roles, 11,* 639–656.

Cazenave, N. A., & Straus, M. A. 1990. "Race, class, network embeddedness, and family violence: A search for potent support systems." In M. A. Straus & R. J. Gelles (Eds.), *Physical violence in American families.* New Brunswick, NJ: Transaction.

Center on Budget and Policy Priorities. 1999. "Average incomes of very poor families fell during early years of welfare reform, study finds." Available at www.cbpp.org/8-22-99wel.htm. Accessed June 23, 2000.

Centers for Disease Control. 2000. "Youth risk behavior trends." Available at www.cdc.gov/nccdphp/dash/yrbs/trend.htm. Accessed June 11, 2000.

———. 2001. "Basic statistics—Cumulative AIDS cases." Available at www.cdc.gov/hiv/stats/cumulati.htm. Accessed May 27, 2001.

Chafetz, J. S. 1978. *A primer on the construction and testing of theories in sociology.* Itasca, IL: Peacock.

Chafetz, J. S., & Dworkin, A. G. 1987. "In the face of threat: Organized anti-feminism in comparative perspective." *Gender and Society, 1,* 33–60.

Chasnoff, I. J. 1989. "Cocaine, pregnancy and the neonate." *Women and Health, 15,* 23–25.

Chasnoff, I. J., Landress, H. J., & Barrett, M. E. 1990. "The prevalence of illicit drug or alcohol use during pregnancy and discrepancies in mandatory reporting in Pinellas County, Florida." *New England Journal of Medicine, 332,* 1202–1206.

Chatters, L. M., Taylor, R. J., & Jayakody, R. 1994. "Fictive kinship relations in black extended families." *Journal of Comparative Family Studies, 25,* 297–313.

Cherlin, A. J. 1978. "Remarriage as an incomplete institution." *American Journal of Sociology, 84,* 634–650.

———. 1990. "The strange career of the 'Harvard–Yale study.'" *Public Opinion Quarterly, 54,* 117–124.

———. 1992. *Marriage, divorce, remarriage.* Cambridge, MA: Harvard University Press.

———. 1999. *Public and private families.* Boston: McGraw-Hill.

Cherlin, A. J., Chase-Landale, P. L., & McRae, C. 1998. "Effects of parental divorce on mental health throughout the life course." *American Sociological Review, 63,* 239–249.

Cherlin, A. J., & Furstenberg, F. F. 1987. *The new American grandparent: A place in the family, a life apart.* New York: Basic Books.

———. 1994. "Stepfamilies in the United States: A reconsideration." *Annual Review of Sociology, 20,* 359–381.

———. 1997. "The future of grand-parenthood." In M. Hutter (Ed.), *The family experience.* Boston: Allyn & Bacon.

Cherlin, A. J., Furstenberg, F. F., Chase-Landale, P. L., Kiernan, K. E., Robins, P. K., Morrison, D. R., & Teitler, J. O. 1991. "Longitudinal studies of effects of divorce on children in Great Britain and the United States." *Science, 252,* 1386–1389.

CHILD, Inc. 2000. "Religious exemptions from health care for children." Available at www.childrenshealthcare.org/legal.htm. Accessed October 10, 2000.

"Child abuse a growing problem, report says." 1996. *CNN On-line,* September 18. Available at www.CNN.com. Accessed September 15, 2000.

"Child abuse cases surge in Japan." 2001. *Associated Press Online,* June 21.

"Child care caste system." 1998. *New York Times Magazine,* April 5.

Chilman, C. S. 1995. "Hispanic families in the United States: Research perspectives." In M. R. Rank & E. L. Kain (Eds.), *Diversity and change in families: Patterns, prospects and policies.* Englewood Cliffs, NJ: Prentice Hall.

Childstats.gov. 2000. *America's Children 2000,* Table POP5.A. Available at www.childstats.gov/ac2000/pop5A.htm. Accessed October 3, 2001.

Chira, S. 1993. "Census data show rise in child care by fathers." *New York Times,* September 22.

———. 1995. "Struggling to find stability when divorce is a pattern." *New York Times,* March 19.

Chodorow, N. 1986. "Family structure and feminine personality." In L. Richardson & V. Taylor (Eds.), *Feminist frontiers II: Rethinking sex, gender and society.* New York: Random House.

Christensen, B. J. 1990. *Utopia against the family.* San Francisco: Ignatius Press.

Ciancanelli, P., & Berch, B. 1987. "Gender and the GNP." In B. B. Hess & M. M. Ferree (Eds.), *Analyzing gender: A handbook of social science research.* Newbury Park, CA: Sage.

Clark, C. S. 1996. "Marriage and divorce." *CQ Researcher,* May 10.

Clark, G. 1994. *Onions are my husband: Survival and accumulation by West African market women.* Chicago: University of Chicago Press.

Clarkberg, M. 1999. "The price of partnering: The role of economic well-being in young adults' first union experiences." *Social Forces, 77,* 945–968.

Clarkberg, M., & Moen, P. 2001. "Understanding the time-squeeze: Married couples' preferred and actual work-hour strategies." *American Behavioral Scientist, 44,* 1115–1136.

Clausen, J. A. 19986. *The life course: A sociological perspective.* Englewood Cliffs, NJ: Prentice Hall.

Clymer, A. 1997. "Child-support collection net usually fails." *New York Times,* July 17.

Cohen, P. N., & Bianchi, S. M. 1999. "Marriage, children, and women's employment: What do we know?" *Monthly Labor Review, 122,* 22–31.

Colapinto, J. 1997. "The true story of John/Joan." *Rolling Stone,* December 11.

Coleman, M., Ganong, L., & Fine, M. 2000. "Reinvestigating remarriage: Another decade of progress." *Journal of Marriage and the Family, 62,* 1288–1308.

Coleman, V. E. 1996. "Lesbian battering: The relationship between personality and the perpetration of violence." In L. K. Hamberger & C. Renzetti (Eds.), *Domestic partner abuse.* New York: Springer.

Collins, R. 1992. *Sociological insight: An introduction to non-obvious sociology.* New York: Oxford University Press.

Coltrane, S. 1989. "Household labor and the routine production of gender." *Social Problems, 36,* 473–490.

———. 1996a. *Family man: Fatherhood, housework, and gender equity.* New York: Oxford University Press.

———. 1996b. *Gender and families.* Thousand Oaks, CA: Pine Forge Press.

Coltrane, S., & Collins, R. 2001. *Sociology of marriage and the family: Gender, love & property.* Belmont, CA: Wadsworth.

Coltrane, S., & Hickman, N. 1992. "The rhetoric of rights and needs: Moral discourse in the reform of child custody and child support laws." *Social Problems, 39,* 400–420.

Comer, J. P., & Poussaint, A. F. 1992. *Raising black children.* New York: Plume.

"Congress approves bill easing marriage tax penalty." 2000. *St. Louis Post-Dispatch,* July 23.

"Conservative leader urges parents to spank children." 2000. *Lafayette Journal and Courier,* September 25.

Cook, S. L. 1995. "Acceptance and expectation of sexual aggression in college students." *Psychology of Women Quarterly, 19,* 181–194.

Coontz, S. 1992. *The way we never were.* New York: Basic Books.

———. 1996. "Where are the good old days?" *Modern Maturity,* May–June.

———. 1997. *The way we really are.* New York: Basic Books.

———. 2001. "Historical perspectives on family diversity." In S. J. Ferguson (Ed.), *Shifting the center: Understanding contemporary families.* Mountain View, CA: Mayfield.

Cooper, A., & Sportolari, L. 1997. "Romance in cyberspace: Understanding online attraction." *Journal of Sex Education and Therapy, 22,* 7–14.

Cooper, M. H. 1999. "Women and human rights." *CQ Researcher,* April 30.

Corcoran, M., Danziger, S. K., Kalil, A., & Seefeldt, K. S. 2000. "How welfare reform is affecting women's work." *Annual Review of Sociology, 26,* 241–269.

Corcoran, M., & Duncan, G. 1979. "Work history, labor force attachment, and earnings differences between the races and sexes." *Journal of Human Resources, 14,* 3–20.

Corsaro, W. A. 1997. *The sociology of childhood.* Thousand Oaks, CA: Pine Forge Press.

Cose, E. 1999. "The good news about Black America." *Newsweek,* June 7.

———. 2000. "Our new look: The colors of race." *Newsweek,* January 1.

Cote, J. E., & Allahar, A. L. 1994. *Generation on hold: Coming of age in the late twentieth century.* Toronto: Stoddard.

Cowan, C. P., & Cowan, P. A. 2000. *When partners become parents.* Mahwah, NJ: Erlbaum.

Cowan, R. S. 1987. "Women's work, housework and history: The historical roots of inequality in work-force participation." In N. Gertsel & H. E. Gross (Eds.), *Families and work.* Philadelphia: Temple University Press.

Cowley, G. 1997. "Gender limbo." *Newsweek,* May 19.

Cox, C. L., Wexler, M. O., Rusbult, C. E., & Gaines, S. O. 1997. "Prescriptive support and commitment processes in close relationships." *Social Psychology Quarterly, 60,* 79–90.

Crary, D. 2000. "Survey: Many parents misunderstand discipline, spoiling." *Lafayette Journal and Courier,* October 5.

Crosset, T. 1997. "Outsiders in the clubhouse." In D. Newman (Ed.),

Sociology: Exploring the architecture of everyday life—Readings (2nd ed.). Thousand Oaks, CA: Pine Forge Press.

Crossette, B. 1995. "Female genital mutilation by immigrants is becoming cause for concern in U.S." *New York Times,* December 10.

Cuber, J. F., & Harroff, P. 1965. *The significant Americans: A study of sexual behavior among the affluent.* New York: Appleton-Century-Crofts.

Cunningham, J. A., Strassberg, D. S., & Haan, B. 1986. "Effects of intimacy and sex-role congruency on self-disclosure." *Journal of Social and Clinical Psychology, 4,* 393–401.

Curran, L., & Abrams, L. S. 2000. "Making men into dads: Fatherhood, the state, and welfare reform." *Gender & Society, 14,* 662–678.

Currie, D. H. 1997. "Decoding femininity: Advertisements and their teenage readers." *Gender and Society, 11,* 453–477.

Dalaker, J. 1999. Poverty in the United States: 1998. *Current Population Reports* P60–207. U.S. Bureau of the Census. Washington, DC: U.S. Government Printing Office.

Dalaker, J., & Proctor, B. D. 2000. Poverty in the United States: 1999. *Current Population Reports,* Table A. U.S. Bureau of the Census. Available at www.census.gov/prod/2000pubs/p60–210.pdf. Accessed June 1, 2001.

Daley, S. 2000. "French couples take plunge that falls short of marriage." *New York Times,* April 18.

Dalley, G. 1988. *Ideologies of caring.* London: Macmillan.

Dane, B. O. 1991. "Anticipatory mourning of middle-aged parents of adult children with AIDS." *Families in Society, 72,* 108–115.

Dangor, Z., Hoff, L. A., & Scott, R. 1998. "Woman abuse in South Africa: An exploratory study." *Violence Against Women, 4,* 125–152.

D'Antonio, W. V. 1983. "Family life, religion and societal values and structures." In W. V. D'Antonio & J. Aldous (Eds.), *Families and religion: Conflict and change in modern society.* Newbury Park, CA: Sage.

Dardick, G. 1993. "The long haul." *Utne Reader,* May–June.

Darity, W. A., & Meyers, S. L. 1984. "Does welfare dependency cause female hardship? The case of the black family." *Journal of Marriage and the Family, 46,* 765–779.

Darton, N. 1991. "The end of innocence." *Newsweek* (special summer issue).

Davidman, L. 2000. *Motherloss.* Berkeley: University of California Press.

Davidson, C. N. 1986. "A feminist '1984.'" *Ms. Magazine,* February.

Davidson, J. D., Williams, A. S., Lamanna, R. A., Stenftenagel, J., Weigert, K. M., Whalen, W. J., & Wittberg, P. 1997. *The search for common ground: What unites and divides Catholic Americans.* Huntington, IN: Our Sunday Visitor Publishing Division.

Davis, F. J. 1991. *Who is black?* University Park: Pennsylvania State University Press.

Davis, P. W. 1991. "Stranger intervention into child punishment in public places." *Social Problems, 38,* 227–246.

"Day care costs mother custody of daughter, 3." 1994. *New York Times,* July 27.

Deal, J. E. 1995. "Utilizing data from multiple family members: A within-family approach." *Journal of Marriage and the Family, 57,* 1109–1121.

Della Fave, L. R. 1980. "The meek shall not inherit the earth: Self-evaluation and the legitimacy of stratification." *American Sociological Review, 45,* 955–971.

Dellinger, K., & Williams, C. L. 1997. "Makeup at work: Negotiating appearance rules in the workplace." *Gender & Society, 11,* 151–177.

DeMaris, A., & Longmore, M. A. 1996. "Ideology, power and equity: Testing competing explanations for the perception of fairness in household labor." *Social Forces, 74,* 1043–1071.

DeMaris, A., & Rao, V. 1992. "Pre-marital cohabitation and subsequent marital stability in the United States: A reassessment." *Journal of Marriage and the Family, 55,* 399–407.

deMause, L. 1975. "Our forebears made childhood a nightmare." *Psychology Today, 8,* 85–88.

Demick, B. 1996. "Albanian 'virgins.'" *Indianapolis Star,* August 25.

D'Emilio, J., & Freedman, E. B. 1988. *Intimate matters: A history of sexuality in America.* New York: Harper & Row.

Demmitt, K. P. 1992. "Loosening the ties that bind: The accommodation of dual-earner families in a conservative Protestant church." *Review of Religious Research, 34,* 3–19.

Demo, D. H., & Acock, A. C. 1993. "Family diversity and the division of domestic labor: How much have things really changed?" *Family Relations, 42,* 323–333.

Demos, J. 1986. *Past, present and personal: The family and life course in American history.* New York: Oxford University Press.

Denny, E. 1994. "Liberation or oppression? Radical feminism and in vitro fertilization." *Sociology of Health and Illness, 16,* 62–80.

Denzin, N. 1989. *The research act: A theoretical introduction to sociological methods.* Englewood Cliffs, NJ: Prentice Hall.

DeParle, J. 1996. "Slamming the door." *New York Times Magazine,* October 20.

———. 1997a. "Learning poverty first hand." *New York Times Magazine,* April 27.

———. 1997b. "U.S. welfare system dies as state programs emerge." *New York Times,* June 30.

———. 1999. "Bold effort leaves much unchanged for the poor." *New York Times,* December 30.

DePaulo, B. M., & Kashy, D. A. 1998. "Everyday lies in close and casual relationships." *Journal of Personality and Social Psychology, 74,* 63–79.

"Derby Connections." 2001. Available at www.churchilldown.com/kderby/history/connections/jockeys. Accessed May 1, 2001.

Derlega, V. J., Harris, M. S., & Chaikin, A. L. 1973. "Self-disclosure reciprocity, liking and the deviant." *Journal of Experimental Social Psychology, 9,* 277–284.

Deutsch, F. M. 1999. *Halving it all: How equally shared parenting works.* Cambridge, MA: Harvard University Press.

Diamond, D. 1996. "Keeping tabs on teens." *USA Weekend,* August 30–September 1.

Diamond, J. 1994. "Race without color." *Discover,* November, pp. 82–89.

Dickson, L. 1993. "The future of marriage and family in black America." *Journal of Black Studies, 23,* 472–491.

Diekmann, A., & Engelhardt, H. 1999. "The social inheritance [sic] of divorce: Effects of parent's family type in postwar Germany." *American Sociological Review, 64,* 783–793.

Dietz, T. L. 1995. "Patterns of intergenerational assistance within the Mexican American family: Is the family taking care of the older generation's needs?" *Journal of Family Issues, 16,* 344–356.

Dill, B. T. 1995. "Our mothers' grief: Racial ethnic women and the maintenance of families." In M. L. Anderson & P. H. Collins (Eds.), *Race, class, and gender: An anthology.* Belmont, CA: Wadsworth.

Dill, B. T., Baca Zinn, M., & Patton, S. 1994. "Feminism, race and the politics of family values." Report from the *Institute for Philosophy and Public Policy, 13,* 13–18.

DiNitto, D. M., & Dye, T. R. 1987. *Some welfare politics and public policy.* Englewood Cliffs, NJ: Prentice Hall.

Dion, K. K., & Dion, K. L. 1996. "Cultural perspectives on romantic love." *Personal Relationships, 3,* 5–17.

Domhoff, G. W. 1983. *Who rules America now?* Englewood Cliffs, NJ: Prentice Hall.

Douglas, W., & Olsen, B. M. 1996. "Subversion of the American family? An examination of children and parents in television families." *Communication Research, 23,* 73–99.

Downs, D. A. 1996. *More than victims: Battered women, the syndrome society, and the law.* Chicago: University of Chicago Press.

Dugger, C. W. 1996a. "African ritual pain: Genital cutting." *New York Times,* October 5.

———. 1996b. "Immigrant cultures raising issues of child punishment." *New York Times,* February 29.

———. 2001. "Abortion in India is tipping scales sharply against girls." *New York Times,* April 22.

Dujon, D., Gradford, J., & Stevens, D. 1995. "Reports from the front: Welfare mothers up in arms." In M. L. Anderson & P. H. Collins (Eds.), *Race, class, and gender: An anthology.* Belmont, CA: Wadsworth.

Duncan, G. J., Yeung, W. J., Brooks-Gunn, J., & Smith, J. R. 1998. "How much does childhood poverty affect the life chances of children?" *American Sociological Review, 63,* 406–423.

Durkheim, E. 1951. *Suicide.* New York: Free Press. (Original work published 1897)

———. 1965. *The elementary forms of the religious life.* Trans. by J. W. Swain. New York: Free Press. (Original work published 1915)

Dutton, D. G., & Aron, A. P. 1974. "Some evidence for heightened sexual attraction under conditions of high anxiety." *Journal of Personality and Social Psychology, 30,* 510–517.

Dyssegaard, E. K. 1997. "The Danes call it fresh air." *New York Times,* May 17.

Eckel, S. 1999. "Single mothers." *American Demographics,* May.

Economic Roundtable. 2000. "The cage of poverty." Available at www.economicrt.org/ publications.html#recent. Accessed July 28, 2001.

Edin, K., & Jencks, C. 1992. "Reforming welfare." In C. Jencks (Ed.), *Rethinking social policy: Race, poverty and the underclass.* Cambridge, MA: Harvard University Press.

Edin, K., and L. Lein. 1997. "Work, welfare, and single mothers' economic strategies." *American Sociological Review, 62,* 253–266.

Edwards, T. M. 2001. "How med students put abortion back in the classroom." *Time,* May 7.

Egan, T. 1996. "Mail-order marriage, immigrant dreams and death." *New York Times,* May 26.

Eggebeen, D. J., & Hogan, D. P. 1990. "Giving between generations in American families." *Human Nature, 1,* 211–232.

Eggebeen, D. J., & Lichter, D. T. 1991. "Race, family structure, and changing poverty among African American children." *American Sociological Review, 56,* 801–817.

Ehrenreich, B. 1983. *The hearts of men: American dreams and the flight from commitment.* New York: Anchor.

———. 1994. "Oh, those family values." *Time,* July 8.

Ehrenreich, B., & English, D. 1979. *For her own good: 150 years of experts' advice to women.* Garden City, NY: Anchor.

Elder, Jr., G. H. 1998. "The life course and human development." In W. Damon & R. M. Lerner (Eds.), *Handbook of child psychology: Theoretical models of human development* (1st ed., Vol. 1). New York: Wiley.

Elder, Jr., G. H., & Eccles, J. S. 1995. "Inner-city parents under economic pressure: Perspectives on the strategies of parenting." *Journal of Marriage and the Family, 57,* 771–784.

Elkind, D. 1994. *Ties that stress: The new family imbalance.* Cambridge, MA: Harvard University Press.

Elliot, P. 1996. "Shattering illusions: Same-sex domestic violence." *Journal of Gay and Lesbian Social Services, 4,* 1–8.

Emerson, R. 1962. "Power-dependence relations." *American Sociological Review, 27,* 31–41.

"Employers offer gays more benefits." 2000. *New York Times,* September 25.

Engels, F. 1884/1972. *The origin of the family, private property and the state.* New York: International Publishers.

Epstein, C. F. 1988. *Deceptive distinctions: Sex, gender and the social order.* New Haven, CT: Yale University Press.

Estioko-Griffin, A., & Griffin, P. B. 1997. "Woman the hunter: The Agta." In C. B. Brettell & C. F. Sargent (Eds.), *Gender in cross-cultural perspective.* Upper Saddle River, NJ: Prentice Hall.

Ettelbrick, P. L. 1992. "Since when is marriage a path to liberation?" In S. Sherman (Ed.), *Lesbian and gay marriage.* Philadelphia: Temple University Press.

Etzioni, A. 1993. "How to make marriage matter." *Time,* September 6.

———. 1994. *The spirit of community: The reinvention of American society.* New York: Touchstone.

Ewing, C. P. 1987. *Battered women who kill: Psychological self-defense as legal justification.* Lexington, MA: Heath.

Ewing, C. P., & Aubrey, M. 1987. "Battered women and public opinion: Some realities about myths." *Journal of Family Violence, 2,* 257–264.

Ewing, W. 1992. "The civic advocacy of violence." In M. S. Kimmel & M. A. Messner (Eds.), *Men's lives.* New York: Macmillan.

Fadiman, A. 1997. *The spirit catches you and you fall down.* New York: Farrar, Straus & Giroux.

Faison, S. 1995. "In China, rapid social changes bring a surge in the divorce rate." *New York Times,* August 22.

"Faith healers sentenced in daughter's death." 1997. *New York Times,* June 11.

Faludi, S. 1991. *Backlash: The undeclared war against American women.* New York: Crown.

———. 1999. *Stiffed: The betrayal of the American man.* New York: Morrow.

"Family wins right to end their son's ordeal." 1994. *New York Times,* October 18.

Fan, P. 1996. "Indian brothers marry same women for economic gain." *CNN Online,* September 16. Available at www.CNN.com. Accessed April 5, 2000.

Farber, B. 1987. "The future of the American family: A dialectical account." *Journal of Family Issues, 8,* 431–433.

Farley, R., & Bianchi, S. 1991. "The growing racial differences in marriage and family patterns." In R. Staples (Ed.), *The black family: Essays and studies.* Belmont, CA: Wadsworth.

Fausto-Sterling, A. 1985. *Myths of gender.* New York: Basic Books.

———. 1993. "How many sexes are there?" *New York Times,* March 12.

———. 2000. "The five sexes, revisited." *The Sciences,* July–August, pp. 1–7.

Fears, D., & Deane, C. 2001. "Biracial couples report tolerance." *Washington Post,* July 5.

Federal Interagency Forum on Aging-Related Statistics. 2000. "Older Americans 2000: Key indicators of well-being." Available at www.agingstats.gov/chartbook2000/tables-population.html/. Accessed September 1, 2001.

Federal Interagency Forum on Child and Family Statistics. 2000. *America's children: Key national indicators of well-being, 2000,* Tables BEH4.A and BEH4.B. Washington, DC: U.S. Government Printing Office.

Feigelman, W. 1997. "Adopted adults: Comparisons with persons raised in conventional families." *Marriage and Family Review, 25,* 199–223.

Fein, E. B. 1998a. "For lost pregnancies, new rites of mourning." *New York Times,* January 25.

———. 1998b. "Secrecy and stigma no longer clouding adoptions." *New York Times,* October 25.

Felmlee, D. H. 2000. "From appealing to appalling: Disenchantment with a romantic partner." *Sociological Perspectives.* Forthcoming.

Fenwick, R., & Tausig, M. 2001. "Scheduling stress: Family and health outcomes of shift work and schedule control." *American Behavioral Scientist, 44,* 1179–1198.

Ferraro, K. J., & Johnson, J. M. 1983. "How women experience battering: The process of victimization." *Social Problems, 30,* 325–339.

Ferree, M. M. 1984. "The view from below: Women's employment and gender equality in working-class families." In Beth B. Hess & Marvin B. Sussman (Eds.), *Women and the family: Two decades of change.* New York: Haworth.

———. 1991. "Gender, conflict and change: Family roles in biographical perspective." In W. Heinz (Ed.), *Theoretical advances in life course research.* Weinheim, Germany: Deutscher Studien Verlag.

Feshbach, S., & Feshbach, N. D. 1978. "Child advocacy and family privacy." *Journal of Social Issues, 34,* 168–178.

Feuer, A. 2001. "America 24/7: No matter the time, someone's always working." *New York Times,* April 4.

Fiene, J. I. 1995. "Battered women: Keeping the secret." *Affilia, 10,* 179–193.

Fine, M. A., Coleman, M., & Ganong, L. 1998. "Consistency in perceptions of the stepparent role among stepparents, parents, and stepchildren." *Journal of Social and Personal Relationships, 15,* 810–828.

Fineman, M. A. 1995. *The neutered mother, the sexual family, and other twentieth century tragedies.* New York: Routledge.

Fingerson, L. 1999. "Active viewing: Girls' interpretations of family television programs." *Journal of Contemporary Ethnography, 28,* 389–418.

Finke, R., & Stark, R. 1992. *The churching of America, 1776–1990: Winners and losers in our religious economy.* New Brunswick, NJ: Rutgers University Press.

Firestone, D. 2001. "Woman is convicted of killing her fetus by smoking cocaine." *New York Times,* May 18.

Fisher, B. S., Cullen, F. T., & Turner, M. G. 2000. "The Sexual Victimization of College Women." Exhibit 8. NCJ 182369. Available at www.ncjrs.org/pdffiles1/nij/182369.pdf. Accessed May 2, 2001.

Fisher, I. 1999. "Sometimes a girl's best friend is not her father." *New York Times,* March 2.

Fishman, P. M. 1978. "Interaction: The work women do." *Social Problems, 25,* 397–406.

Fitzpatrick, M. A. 1988. *Between husbands and wives: Communication in marriage.* Newbury Park, CA: Sage.

Flanders, S. 1996. "The benefits of marriage." *The Public Interest, 124,* 80–86.

Flanzer, J. P. 1993. "Alcohol and other drugs are key causal agents of violence." In R. J. Gelles & D. R. Loeske (Eds.), *Current controversies on family violence.* Newbury Park, CA: Sage.

Flynn, C. P. 1991. "Rethinking joint custody policy: Option or prescription." In E. A. Anderson & R. C. Hula (Eds.), *The reconstruction of family policy.* Westport, CT: Greenwood.

Foote, D. 1998. "And baby makes one." *Newsweek,* February 2.

Foucault, M. 1990. *The history of sexuality.* New York: Vintage.

Fowlkes, M. 1987. "The myth of merit and male professional careers: The role of wives." In N. Gerstel & H. Gross (Eds.), *Families and work.* Philadelphia: Temple University Press.

Fox, B., & Worts, D. 1999. "Revisiting the critique of medicalized childbirth: A contribution to the sociology of birth." *Gender & Society, 13,* 326–346.

Fox, G. L. 1999. "Families in the media: Reflections on the public scrutiny of private behavior." *Journal of Marriage and the Family, 61,* 821–830.

Fox, G. L., & Kelly, R. F. 1995. "Determinants of child custody arrangements at divorce." *Journal of Marriage and the Family, 57,* 693–708.

Franklin, C. W. 1988. *Men and society.* Chicago: Nelson-Hall.

Fraser, J. 1987. "The community, the private, and the individual." *The Sociological Review, 35,* 795–818.

Freeberg, A. L., & Stein, C. H. 1996. "Felt obligation towards parents in Mexican-American and Anglo-American young adults." *Journal of Social and Personal Relationships, 13,* 457–471.

Friedman, D. 1995. *Towards a structure of indifference: The social origins of maternal custody.* New York: Aldine de Gruyter.

Frisbie, W. P., & Bean, F. D. 1995. "The Latino family in comparative perspective: Trends and current conditions." In C. K. Jacobson (Ed.), *American families: Issues in race and ethnicity.* New York: Garland.

Fromme, R. E., & Emihovich, C. 1998. "Boys will be boys: Young males' perceptions of women, sexuality, and prevention." *Education and Urban Society, 30,* 172–188.

Frye, M. 1992. *Willful virgin: Essays on feminism.* Freedom, CA: Crossing Press.

Furstenberg, F. F. 1997. "Good dads—bad dads: Two faces of fatherhood." In A. S. Skolnick & J. H. Skolnick (Eds.), *Family in transition* (9th ed.). New York: Longman.

———. 1999. "Children and family change: Discourse between social scientists and the media." *Contemporary Society, 28,* 10–17.

Furstenberg, F. F., & Cherlin, A. J. 1991. *Divided families.* Cambridge, MA: Harvard University Press.

Furstenberg, F. F., Morgan, S. P., & Allison, P. D. 1987. "Paternal participation and children's well-being after marital dissolution." *American Sociological Review, 52,* 695–701.

Furstenberg, F., & Nord, C. 1985. "Parenting apart: Patterns of childrearing after marital disruption." *Journal of Marriage and the Family, 47,* 893–904.

Gabriel, T. 1996. "High-tech pregnancies test hope's limit." *New York Times,* January 7.

Galambos, N. L., & Maggs, J. L. 1991. "Children in self-care: Figures, facts and fictions." In J. V. Lerner & N. L. Galambos (Eds.), *Employed mothers and their children.* New York: Garland.

Galinsky, E. 1999. *Ask the children: What America's children really think about working parents.* New York: Morrow.

Galston, W. A. 1995a. "A liberal-democratic case for the two-parent family." In A. Etzioni (Ed.), *Rights and the common good.* New York: St. Martin's Press.

———. 1995b. "Needed: A not-so-fast divorce law." *New York Times,* December 27.

Gangestad, S. W. 1993. "Sexual selection and physical attractiveness: Implications of mating dynamics." *Human Nature, 4,* 205–236.

Ganong, L. H., & Coleman, M. 1994. *Remarried family relationships.* Thousand Oaks, CA: Sage.

Gans, H. J. 1995. *The war against the poor.* New York: Basic Books.

Gelles, R. J. 1987. *Family violence.* Thousand Oaks, CA: Sage.

———. 1995. *Contemporary families: A sociological view.* Thousand Oaks, CA: Sage.

Gelles, R. J., & Straus, M. A. 1988. *Intimate violence.* New York: Touchstone.

Gellott, L. 1985. "Staking claim to the family." *Commonweal, 20,* 488–492.

Genevie, L., & Margolies, E. 1987. *The motherhood report: How women feel about being mothers.* New York: Macmillan.

Gerschick, T., & Miller, A. S. 1997. "Coming to terms: Masculinity and disability." In M. Baca Zinn, P. Hondagneu-Sotelo, & M. A. Messner (Eds.), *Through the prism of difference.* Boston: Allyn & Bacon.

Gerson, K. 1985. *Hard choices: How women decide about work, career and motherhood.* Berkeley: University of California Press.

———. 1993. *No man's land: Men's changing commitments to family and work.* New York: Basic Books.

———. 1998. "Dismantling the 'gendered family': Breadwinning, gender, and the family values debate." *Contemporary Sociology, 27,* 228–230.

———. 2000. "Resolving family dilemmas and conflicts: Beyond utopia." *Contemporary Society, 29,* 180–187.

Gertsel, N. 1987. "Divorce and stigma." *Social Problems, 34,* 172–186.

Gertsel, N., & Gross, H. 1984. *Commuter marriage: A study of work and family.* New York: Guilford Press.

———. 1987. "Commuter marriage: A microcosm of career and family conflict." In N. Gertsel & H. Gross (Eds.), *Families and work.* Philadelphia: Temple University Press.

Gibbs, N. R. 1993a. "Bringing up father." *Time,* June 28.

———. 1993b. "How should we teach our children about SEX?" *Time,* May 24.

Gies, F., & Gies, J. 1989. *Marriage and the family in the middle ages.* New York: Harper & Row.

Gilbert, S. 1997. "Early puberty onset seems prevalent." *New York Times,* April 9.

Gill, R. T. 1991. "Family breakdown as family policy." *Public Interest, 110,* 84–91.

Gillespie, C. K. 1989. *Justifiable homicide.* Columbus: Ohio State University Press.

Gillham, B., Tanner, G., Cheyne, B., Freeman, I., Rooney, M., & Lambie, A. 1997. "Unemployment rates, single parent density, and indices of child poverty: their relationship to different categories of child abuse and neglect." *Child Abuse and Neglect, 22,* 79–90.

Gillis, J. R. 1996. *A world of their own making: Myth, ritual and the quest for family values.* New York: Basic Books.

Gladwell, M. 1996. "Black like them." *The New Yorker,* April 29 & May 6.

Glass, J. 2000. "Envisioning the integration of family and work: Toward a kinder, gentler workplace." *Contemporary Society, 29,* 129–143.

Glass, J., & Fujimoto, T. 1994. "Housework, paid work, and depression among husbands and wives." *Journal of Health and Social Behavior, 35,* 179–191.

Glater, J. D. 2001. "Women are close to being majority of law students." *New York Times,* March 26.

Gleick, J. 1996. "Big brother is us." *New York Times Magazine,* September 29.

Glenn, E. N., & Yap, S. G. H. 1994. "Chinese American families." In R. L. Taylor (Ed.), *Minority families in the United States.* Englewood Cliffs, NJ: Prentice Hall.

Glenn, N. 1982. "Interreligious marriage in the United States: Patterns and recent trends." *Journal of Marriage and the Family, 44,* 555–566.

———. 2000. "Who's who in the family wars: A characterization of the major ideological factions." In N. V. Benokraitis (Ed.), *Feuds about families.* Upper Saddle River, NJ: Prentice Hall.

Glenn, N. D., & Supancic, M. 1984. "The social and demographic correlates of divorce and separation in the United States: An update and reconsideration." *Journal of Marriage and the Family, 46,* 563–575.

Goffman, E. 1959. *Presentation of self in everyday life.* Garden City, NY: Doubleday.

Goldberg, C. 1999. "Spouse abuse crackdown, surprisingly, nets many women." *New York Times,* November 23.

———. 2000. "Massachusetts is set apart in ratio of older mothers." *New York Times,* June 21.

Goldberg, S., & Lewis, M. 1969. "Play behavior in the year-old infant: Early sex differences." *Child Development, 40,* 21–31.

Golden, L. 1998. "Working time and the impact of policy institutions: Reforming the overtime hours law and regulation." *Review of Social Economy, 56,* 522–541.

———. 2001. "Flexible work schedules: Which workers get them?" *American Behavioral Scientist, 44,* 1157–1178.

Goldscheider, F. K., & Goldscheider, C. 1994. "Leaving and returning home in twentieth-century America." *Population Bulletin, 48,* 1–35.

Goldscheider, F. K., & Waite, L. J. 1991. *New families, no families?* Berkeley: University of California Press.

Goldstein, J. 1999. "Kinship networks that cross racial lines: The exception or the rule?" *Demography, 36,* 399–407.

Golub, S. 1992. *Periods: From menarche to menopause.* Newbury Park, CA: Sage.

Goodchilds, J., Zellman, G., Johnson, P., & Giarusso, R. 1988. "Adolescents and the perceptions of sexual interaction outcomes." In A. W. Burgess (Ed.), *Sexual assault.* New York: Garland.

Goode, W. J. 1963. *World revolution and family patterns.* New York: Free Press.

———. 1964. *The family.* Englewood Cliffs, NJ: Prentice Hall.

———. 1971. "Force and violence in the family." *Journal of Marriage and the Family, 33,* 624–636.

———. 1981. "Why men resist." In B. Thorne & M. Yalom (Eds.), *Rethinking the family: Some feminist questions.* New York: Longman.

———. 1993. *World changes in divorce patterns.* New Haven, CT: Yale University Press.

Goodstein, L., & Connelly, M. 1998. "Teen-age poll finds support for tradition." *New York Times,* April 30.

Gordon, L. 1988. *Heroes of their own lives.* New York: Viking.

———. 1994. *Pitied but not entitled: Single mothers and the history of welfare: 1800–1935.* New York: Free Press.

———. 1997. "Killing in self-defense." *The Nation,* March 24, pp. 25–28.

Gordon, M. 1964. *Assimilation in American life.* New York: Oxford University Press.

Gordon, M. 1981. "Was Waller ever right? The rating and dating complex reconsidered." *Journal of Marriage and the Family, 43,* 67–76.

Gottfried, A. E. 1991. "Maternal employment in the family setting: Developmental and environmental issues." In J. V. Lerner & N. L. Galambos (Eds.), *Employed mothers and their children.* New York: Garland.

Gove, W. R. 1980. "Mental illness and psychiatric treatment among women." *Psychology of Women Quarterly, 4,* 345–362.

Gove, W. R., Hughes, M., & Style, C. B. 1983. "Does marriage have positive effects on the psychological well-being of the individual?" *Journal of Health and Social Behavior, 24,* 122–131.

Gove, W. R., Style, C. B., & Hughes, M. 1990. "The effect of marriage on the well-being of adults: A theoretical analysis." *Journal of Family Issues, 11,* 4–35.

Graefe, D. R., & Lichter, D. T. 1999. "Life course transitions of American children: Parental cohabitation, marriage, and single motherhood." *Demography, 36,* 205–217.

Graham, L. O. 1995. *Member of the club.* New York: HarperCollins.

Grall, T. 2000. "Child support for custodial mothers and fathers 1997." *Current Population Reports,* P60-212. Available at www.census.gov/prod/2000pubs/p60-212.pdf. Accessed May 1, 2001.

Greeley, A. M., & Hout, M. 1999. "Americans' increasing belief in life after death: Religious competition and acculturation." *American Sociological Review, 64,* 813–835.

Green, J. S. 1995. "The Days of the Dead in Oaxaca, Mexico: An historical inquiry." In J. B. Williamson & E. S. Schneidman (Eds.), *Death: Current perspectives.* Mountain View, CA: Mayfield.

Greene, R., Mandel, J. B., Hotvedt, M. E., Gray, J., & Smith, L. 1986. "Lesbian mothers and their children: A comparison with solo parent heterosexual mothers and their children." *Archives of Sexual Behavior, 15,* 167–183.

Greenfield, D. N. 1999. *Virtual addiction: Help for netheads, cyberfreaks, and those who love them.* Oakland, CA: New Harbinger Publications.

Greenhouse, L. 1996. "Christian Scientists rebuffed in ruling by Supreme Court." *New York Times,* January 23.

———. 2001. "Drug tests curbed during pregnancy." *New York Times,* March 22.

Greenhouse, S. 2000. "Poll of working women finds them stressed." *New York Times,* March 10.

Greenstein, T. N. 1995. "Are the 'most advantaged' children truly disadvantaged by early maternal employment?" *Journal of Family Issues, 16,* 149–169.

———. 1996a. "Gender ideology and perceptions of the fairness of the division of labor: Effects on marital quality." *Social Forces, 24,* 1029–1042.

———. 1996b. "Husbands' participation in domestic labor: Interactive effects of wives' and husbands' gender ideologies." *Journal of Marriage and the Family, 58,* 585–595.

Greil, A. L. 1991. *Not yet pregnant: Infertile couples in contemporary America.* New Brunswick, NJ: Rutgers University Press.

Grella, C. E. 1990. "Irreconcilable differences: Women defining class after divorce and downward mobility." *Gender and Society, 4,* 41–55.

Greven, P. 1991. *Spare the child: The religious roots of punishment and the psychological impact of physical abuse.* New York: Knopf.

Grieco, E. M., & R. C. Cassidy. 2001. Overview of race and Hispanic origin: Census 2000 Brief, Table 10. Available at www.census.gov/prod/2001pubs/c2kbr01-1.pdf. Accessed October 3, 2001.

Griffin, S. 1989. "Rape: The all-American crime." In L. Richardson & V. Taylor (Eds.), *Feminist frontiers II.* New York: Random House.

Gringlas, M., & Weinraub, M. 1995. "The more things change . . . single parenting revisited." *Journal of Family Issues, 16,* 194–211.

Griscom, A. 2000. "The blind date: Who is your destiny?" *New York Times Magazine,* June 11.

Griswold, R. L. 1993. *Fatherhood in America: A history.* New York: Basic Books.

Griswold del Castillo, R. 1979. *The Los Angeles barrio: 1850–1890.* Los Angeles: University of California Press.

Groneman, C. 2000. *Nymphomania: A history.* New York: Norton.

Gross, H. E., & Sussman, M. B. 1997. "Introduction." *Marriage and Family Review, 25,* 1–6.

Gross, J. 1997a. "A new life opens, after prison and battering." *New York Times,* February 18.

———. 1997b. "Wall Street's frenetic? Try the eighth grade." *New York Times,* October 5.

Grotevant, H. D., Ross, N. M., Marchel, M. A., & McRoy, R. G. 1999. "Adaptive behavior in adopted children: Predictors from early risk, collaboration in relationships within the adoptive kinship network, and openness arrangements." *Journal of Adolescent Research, 14,* 231–247.

Gubrium, J. F., & Holstein, J. A. 1987. "The private image: Experimental location and methods in family studies." *Journal of Marriage and the Family, 49,* 773–786.

———. 1990. *What is family?* Mountain View, CA: Mayfield.

Gutman, H. G. 1978. "Persistent myths about the Afro-American family." In M. Gordon (Ed.), *The American family in social-historical perspective.* New York: St. Martin's Press.

Haas, L. L. 1986. "Wives' orientation toward bread winning: Sweden and the United States." *Journal of Family Issues, 7,* 358–381.

———. 1995. "Household division of labor in industrial societies." In B. B. Ingoldsby & S. Smith (Eds.), *Families in multicultural perspective.* New York: Guilford.

Haffner, K. 2000. "For the well-connected, all the world's an office." *New York Times,* March 30.

Haldeman, D. C. 1998. "Ceremonies and religion in same-sex marriages." In R. P. Cabaj & D. W. Purcell (Eds.), *On the road to same-sex marriage.* San Francisco: Jossey-Bass.

Hall, M. 1994. "Sentence in infidelity slaying angers activists." *USA Today,* October 19.

Hamer, D., & Coupland, P. 1994. *The science of desire.* New York: Simon & Schuster.

Hareven, T. K. 1978. *Transitions: The family and the life course in historical perspective.* New York: Academic Press.

———. 1992. "American families in transition: Historical perspectives on change." In A. S. Skolnick & J. H. Skolnick (Eds.), *Family in transition* (7th ed.). New York: HarperCollins.

———. 1994. "Aging and generational relations: A historical and life course perspective." *Annual Review of Sociology, 20,* 437–461.

———. 2000. *Families, history and social change: Life-course and cross-cultural perspectives.* Boulder, CO: Westview.

Harkins, E. 1978. "Effects of empty nest transition on self-report of psychological and physical well-being." *Journal of Marriage and the Family, 40,* 549–556.

Harmon, A. 1997. "High-technology: Bliss or bust on vacation?" *New York Times,* July 13.

"Harper's index." 1997. *Harper's Magazine,* February, 13.

———. 1998. *Harper's Magazine,* September.

Harris, J. R. 1998. *The nurture assumption.* New York: Free Press.

Harris, K. M. 1996a. "Life after welfare: Women, work, and repeat dependency." *American Sociological Review, 61,* 407–426.

———. 1996b. "The reforms will hurt, not help, poor women and children." *Chronicle of Higher Education,* October 4.

Harris, K. M., & Marmer, J. K. 1996. "Poverty, parental involvement, and adolescent well-being." *Journal of Family Issues, 17,* 614–640.

Harry, J. 1983. "Gay male and lesbian relationships." In E. D. Macklin & R. H. Rubin (Eds.), *Contemporary families and alternative lifestyles: Handbook on theory and research.* Newbury Park, CA: Sage.

Hartman, A. 1994. "Ideological themes in family policy." *Families in Society, 76,* 182–192.

Hashimoto, R., & Takahashi, M. 1995. "Between family obligation and social care: The significance of institutional care for the elderly in Japan." *Journal of Sociology and Social Welfare, 22,* 47–62.

Hatchett, S., & Jackson, J. 1993. "African American extended kin systems." In H. McAdoo (Ed.), *Family ethnicity: Strength in diversity.* Newbury Park, CA: Sage.

Hatchett, S., Veroff, J., & Douvan, E. 1995. "Marital instability among black and white couples in early marriage." In M. B. Tucker & C. Mitchell-Kernen (Eds.), *The decline in marriage among African Americans.* New York: Russell Sage.

Hatfield, E., & Rapson, R. L. 1993. "Historical and cross-cultural perspectives on passionate love and sexual desire." *Annual Review of Sex Research, 4,* 67–97.

Hatfield, E., & Sprecher, S. 1995. "Men's and women's preferences in marital partners in the United States, Russia, and Japan." *Journal of Crosscultural Psychology, 26,* 728–750.

Hatfield, E., Traupmann, J., Sprecher, S., Utne, M., & Hay, J. 1985. "Equity and intimate relations: Recent research." In W. Ickes (Ed.), *Compatible and incompatible relationships.* New York: Springer.

Hatfield, E., Walster, G. W., & Traupmann, J. 1978. "Equity and premarital sex." *Journal of Personality and Social Psychology, 37,* 82–92.

Hausman, B., & Hammen, C. 1993. "Parenting in homeless families: The double crisis." *American Journal of Orthopsychiatry, 63,* 358–369.

Hays, C. L. 1995. "Increasing shift work challenges child care." *New York Times,* June 8.

Hays, S. 1996. *The cultural contradictions of motherhood.* New Haven, CT: Yale University Press.

Head Start Bureau. 2000. "2000 Head Start Fact Sheet." Available at www2.acf.dhhs.gov/programs/hsb/research/00_hsfs.htm. Accessed July 14, 2001.

———. 2001. "2001 Head Start Fact Sheet." Available at www2.acf.dhhs.gov/programs/hsb/about/fact2001.htm. Accessed July 14, 2001.

Heaton, T. B., Jacobson, C. K., & Fu, X. N. 1992. "Religiosity of married couples and childlessness." *Review of Religious Research, 33,* 244–255.

Heaton, T., Jacobson, C. K., & Holland, K. 1999. "Peristence and change in decisions to remain childless." *Journal of Marriage and the Family, 61,* 531–539.

Heise, L. 1989. "The global war against women." *Washington Post Magazine,* April 9.

Hendrick, S. S. 1981. "Self-disclosure and marital satisfaction." *Journal of Personality and Social Psychology, 40,* 1150–1159.

Henton, J., Cate, R., Koval, J. E., Lloyd, S. A., & Scott, C. F. 1983. "Romance and violence in dating relationships." *Journal of Family Issues, 4,* 467–482.

Herbert, B. "A brewing storm." *New York Times,* February 11.

Hertz, R. 1986. *More equal than others: Women and men in dual-career marriages.* Berkeley: University of California Press.

———. 1999. "Working to place family at the center of life: Dual-earner and single-parent strategies." *Annals of the American Academy of Political and Social Science, 562,* 16–31.

Hess, R. D., & Handel, G. 1985. "The family as a psychosocial organization." In G. Handel (Ed.), *The psychosocial interior of the family.* New York: Aldine.

Heyn, D. 1997. *Marriage shock: The transformation of women into wives.* New York: Delta.

Hill, S. A., & Sprague, J. 1999. "Parenting in black and white families: The interaction of gender with race and class." *Gender & Society, 13,* 480–502.

Hines, P. M., Garcia-Preto, N., McGoldrick, M., Almeida, R., & Weltman, S. 1997. "Intergenerational relationships across cultures." In A. S. Skolnick & J. H. Skolnick (Eds.), *Family in transition* (9th ed.). New York: Longman.

Hitchcock, J. T., & Minturn, L. 1963. "The Rajputs of Khalapur." In B. Whiting (Ed.), *Six cultures: Studying child rearing.* New York: Wiley.

Hochman, N. K. S. 1997. "Fathers play larger roles in custody." *New York Times,* April 20.

Hochschild, A. R. 1983. "Attending to codifying and managing feelings: Sex differences in love." In L. Richardson & V. Taylor (Eds.), *Feminist frontiers.* Reading, MA: Addison-Wesley.

———. 1997. *The time bind: When work becomes home and home becomes work.* New York: Metropolitan Books.

Hochschild, A. R., & Machung, A. 1989. *The second shift: Working parents and the revolution at home.* New York: Viking.

Hofferth, S. 1983. *Updating children's life course.* Bethesda, MD: Center for Population Research, National Institute for Child Health and Human Development.

Hofferth, S. L. 1998. *Healthy environments, healthy children: Children in families: A report on the 1997 Panel Study of Income Dynamics.* Child Development Supplement. Available at www.isr.umich.edu/src/child-development/printrep.html. Accessed October 3, 2001.

Hoffman, J. 1990. "Pregnant, addicted—and guilty?" *New York Times Magazine,* August 19.

———. 1995. "Divorced fathers make gains in battles to increase rights." *New York Times,* April 26.

Hofstede, G. 1984. *Culture's consequences: International differences in work-related values.* Beverly Hills, CA: Sage.

Hogan, D. P., Eggebeen, D. J., & Clogg, C. C. 1993. "The structure of intergenerational exchanges in American families." *American Journal of Sociology, 98,* 1428–1458.

Hoge, D. R., & Yang, F. 1994. "Determinants of religious giving in American denominations: Data from two nationwide surveys." *Review of Religious Research, 36,* 123–148.

Holbart, C. 1991. "Conflict in remarriages." *Journal of Divorce and Remarriage, 15,* 69–86.

Hollander, D. 1996. "Nonmarital childbearing in the United States: A government report." *Family Planning Perspectives, 28,* 29–32.

Hollingsworth, L. D. 1997. "Effect of transracial/transethnic adoption on children's racial and ethnic identity and self esteem: A meta-analytic review." *Marriage and Family Review, 25,* 99–130.

Hollis, M. 2000. "Parents of delinquents to start paying." *Indianapolis Star,* June 24.

Hollway, W. 1993. "Heterosexual sex: Power and desire for the other." In B. J. Fox (Ed.), *Family patterns, gender relations.* Toronto: Oxford University Press.

Holmes, S. A. 1995. "Bitter racial dispute rages over adoption." *New York Times,* April 13.

———. 1996a. "Is this what women want?" *New York Times,* December 15.

———. 1996b. "Quality of life is up for many blacks." *New York Times,* November 18.

———. 1996c. "U.S. reports drop in rate of births to unwed women." *New York Times,* October 5.

———. 2000. "New policy on census says those listed as white and minority will be counted as minority." *New York Times,* March 11.

Holter, H. 1970. *Sex roles and social structure.* Oslo: Universitetsforlaget.

Holtzworth-Munroe, A., & Jacobson, N. S. 1985. "Causal attributions of married couples: When do they search for causes? What do they conclude when they do?" *Journal of Personality and Social Psychology, 48,* 1398–1412.

Homans, G. 1961. *Social behavior: Its elementary forms.* New York: Harcourt Brace Jovanovich.

"Home sweet home." 1995. *The Economist,* September, pp. 25–33.

Hood, J. 1983. *Becoming a two-job family.* New York: Praeger.

Hopper, J. 1993. "The rhetoric of motives in divorce." *Journal of Marriage and the Family, 55,* 801–813.

Horowitz, R. 1997. "The expanded family and family honor." In M. Hutter (Ed.), *The family experience: A reader in cultural diversity.* Boston: Allyn & Bacon.

Horton, R. 1995. "Is homosexuality inherited?" *New York Review of Books,* July 13, pp. 36–41.

Horwitz, A. V. 1994. "Predictors of adult sibling social support for the seriously mentally ill: An exploratory study." *Journal of Family Issues, 15,* 272–289.

Horwitz, A. V., McLaughlin, J., & White, H. R. 1997. "How the negative and positive aspects of partner relationships affect the mental health of young married people." *Journal of Health and Social Behavior, 39,* 124–136.

Houseknecht, S., & Sastry, J. 1996. "Family decline and child well-being: A comparative assessment." *Journal of Marriage and the Family, 58,* 726–739.

Hout, M. 1999. "Abortion politics in the United States, 1972–1994; From single issue to ideology." *Gender Issues,17,* 3–34.

Howard, J. 2000. "The World Congress of Families." *Vital Speeches of the Day, 66,* 301–304.

Howard, J. A., & Hollander, J. 1997. *Gendered situations, gendered selves.* Newbury Park, CA: Sage.

Howe, N., & Strauss, W. 2000. *Millennials rising: The next great generation.* New York: Vintage Books.

Howell-White, S. 1999. *Birth alternatives: How women select childbirth care.* Westport, CT: Greenwood Press.

Huber, E., & Stephens, J. D. 2000. "Partisan governance, women's employment, and the social democratic service state." *American Sociological Review, 65,* 323–342.

Human Development Report 1995. "The revolution of gender equality." United Nations Development Programme. Available at www.undp.org/dhro/e95over.htm. Accessed January 2001.

Humphreys, L. 1970. *The tearoom trade.* Chicago: Aldine.

Hunt, J. G., & Hunt, L. L. 1990. "The dualities of careers and families: New integrations or new polarizations?" In

C. Carlson (Ed.), *Perspectives on the family: History, class and feminism.* Belmont, CA: Wadsworth.

Hunter, A. G. 1997. "Counting on grandmothers: Black mothers' and fathers' reliance on grandmothers for parenting support." *Journal of Family Issues, 18,* 251–269.

Hunter, J. 1991. *Culture wars: The struggle to define America.* New York: Basic Books.

Hyde, J. S. 1984. "How large are gender differences in aggression? A developmental meta-analysis." *Developmental Psychology, 20,* 722–736.

Hyman, A., Schillinger, D., & Lo, B. 1995. "Laws mandating reporting of domestic violence." *Journal of the American Medical Association, 273,* 1781–1787.

Hynie, M., & Lydon, J. E. 1995. "Women's perceptions of female contraceptive behavior: Experimental evidence of the sexual double standard." *Psychology of Women Quarterly, 19,* 563–581.

Ignatius, A. 1988. "China's birthrate is out of control again as one-child policy fails in rural areas." *Wall Street Journal,* July 14.

"Indiana woman says 'Big Brother' made her unwelcome at home." *Lafayette Journal and Courier,* August 23.

Inglehart, R., Basanez, M., & Moreno, A. 1998. *Human values and beliefs: A cross-cultural sourcebook.* Ann Arbor: University of Michigan.

Ingraham, C. 1999. *White weddings: Romancing heterosexuality in popular culture.* New York: Routledge.

Ingrassia, M. 1994. "Virgin cool." *Newsweek,* October 17.

Ingrassia, M., & McCormick, J. 1994. "Why leave children with bad parents?" *Newsweek,* April 25.

Ingrassia, M., & Wingert, P. 1995. "The new providers." *Newsweek,* May 22.

Injury Prevention Web. 2000. "Injury prevention policy: Child death review and injury prevention." Available at www.safetypolicy.org/pm/death.htm. Accessed July 15, 2001.

"The institution of marriage is weakening." 1999. *Society, 36,* 2–3.

Ishii-Kuntz, M. 1989. "Collectivism or individualism? Changing patterns of Japanese attitudes." *Sociology and Social Research, 73,* 174–179.

———. 1999. "Japan and its planning toward family caregiving." In V. M. Lechner & M. B. Neal (Eds.), *Work and Caring for the Elderly: International Perspectives.* Philadelphia: Brunner/Mazel.

"Italy: Rape ruling protested." 1999. *New York Times,* February 12.

Jacobs, A. 1999. "Gay couples are divided by '96 immigration laws." *New York Times,* March 23.

Jankowiak, W. R., & Fischer, E. F. 1992. "A cross-cultural perspective on romantic love." *Ethnology, 31,* 149–155.

Janoff-Bulman, R. 1979. "Characterological versus behavioral self-blame: Inquiries into depression and rape." *Journal of Personality and Social Psychology, 37,* 1798–1809.

Jarrell, A. 2000. "The face of teenage sex grows younger." *New York Times,* April 3.

Jehl, D. 1999. "Arab honor's price: A woman's blood." *New York Times,* June 20.

Jencks, C., & Edin, K. 1995. "Do poor women have a right to bear children?" *American Prospect,* Winter.

John, D., Shelton, B. A., & Luschen, K. 1995. "Race, ethnicity, gender and perceptions of fairness." *Journal of Family Issues, 16,* 357–379.

Johnson, A. M. 1992. "Sexual lifestyles and HIV risks." *Nature,* December 3, pp. 400–412.

Johnson, C. 1994. "Gender, legitimate authority, and leader-subordinate conversations." *American Sociological Review, 59,* 122–135.

Johnson, D. 1992. "Survey shows number of rapes far higher than official figures." *New York Times,* April 24.

———. 1996. "No-fault divorce is under attack." *New York Times,* April 27.

———. 1999. "Seeking Little League skills at $70 an hour." *New York Times,* June 24.

Johnson, F. 1996. "Wedded to an illusion." *Harper's Magazine,* November.

Johnson, J. M. 1995. "Horror stories and the construction of child abuse." In J. Best (Ed.), *Images of issues.* New York: Aldine de Gruyter.

Jones, A. 1980. *Women who kill.* New York: Fawcett Columbine.

Jones, M. 2000. "The genetic report card that will tell you if your embryo will get prostate cancer." *New York Times Magazine,* June 11.

Jones, R. K., & Brayfield, A. 1997. "Life's greatest joy? European attitudes toward the centrality of children." *Social Forces, 75,* 1239–1270.

Julian, T. W., McKenry, P. C., & McKelvey, M. W. 1994. "Cultural variations in parenting: Perceptions of Caucasian, African-American, Hispanic, and Asian-American parents." *Family Relations, 43,* 30–37.

Kagan, J. 1976. *Raising children in modern America: Problems and prospective solutions.* Boston: Little, Brown.

Kain, E. 1990. *The myth of family decline.* Lexington, MA: Lexington Books.

Kalb, C. 1997. "How old is too old?" *Newsweek,* May 5.

Kalmijn, M. 1991a. "Shifting boundaries: Trends in religious and educational homogamy." *American Sociological Review, 56,* 786–800.

———. 1991b. "Status homogamy in the United States." *American Journal of Sociology, 97,* 496–523.

———. 1998. "Intermarriage and homogamy: Causes, patterns, trends." *Annual Review of Sociology, 24,* 395–421.

Kalmijn, M., & Flap, H. 2001. "Assortive meeting and mating: Unintended consequences of organized settings for partner choices." *Social Forces, 79,* 1289–1312.

Kamerman, S. B., & Kahn, A. J. 1995. *Starting right: How America neglects its youngest children and what we can do about it.* New York: Oxford University Press.

Kanter, G. K., & Straus, M. A. 1990. "The 'drunken bum' theory of wife beating." In M. A. Straus & R. J. Gelles (Eds.), *Physical violence in American families.* New Brunswick, NJ: Transaction.

Kanter, R. M. 1986 . "Wives." In J. Cole (Ed.), *All-American women: Lines that divide, ties that bind.* New York: Free Press.

Karraker, K. H., Vogel, D. A., & Lake, M. A. 1995. "Parents' gender-stereotyped perceptions of newborns: The eye of the beholder revisited." *Sex Roles, 33,* 687–701.

Kart, C. S. 1990. *The realities of aging.* Boston: Allyn & Bacon.

Karush, S. 2001. "Russia's population drain could open a floodgate of consequences." *Los Angeles Times,* May 6.

Kaufman, C. 1999. "Some companies derail the 'burnout track.' " *New York Times,* May 4.

Kaufman, G. 1999. "The portrayal of men's family roles in television commercials." *Sex Roles, 41,* 439–458.

Kearl, M. C. 1980. "Time, identity and the spiritual needs of the elderly." *Sociological Analysis, 41,* 172–180.

———. 1989. *Endings: A sociology of death and dying.* New York: Oxford University Press.

Keister, L. A., & Moller, S. 2000. "Wealth inequality in the United States." *Annual Review of Sociology, 26,* 63–81.

Keller, B. 1997. "Divorce increasingly puts schools in the middle of family conflicts." *Education Week,* April 9.

Kelley, J., & DeGraaf, N. D. 1997. "National context, parental socialization, and religious belief: Results from 15 nations." *American Sociological Review, 62,* 639–659.

Kelly, M. P. F. 2000. "Delicate transactions: Gender, home, and employment among Hispanic women." In M. Baca Zinn, P. Hondagneu-Sotelo, & M. A. Messner (Eds.), *Gender through the prism of difference* (2nd ed.). Boston: Allyn & Bacon.

Kennedy, P. 1993. *Preparing for the 21st century.* New York: Random House.

Kershner, R. 1996. "Adolescent attitudes about rape." *Adolescence, 31,* 29–33.

Kessler, S. J., & McKenna, W. 1978. *Gender: An ethnomethodological approach.* Chicago: University of Chicago Press.

Kessler-Harris, A. 1982. *Out to work: A history of wage-earning women in the United States.* New York: Oxford University Press.

Kibria, N. 1994a. "Household structure and family ideologies: The dynamics of immigrant economic adaptation among Vietnamese refugees." *Social Problems, 41,* 81–96.

———. 1994b. "Vietnamese families in the United States." In R. L. Taylor (Ed.), *Minority families in the United States.* Englewood Cliffs, NJ: Prentice Hall.

Kilborn, P. T. 1993, "New jobs lack the old security in time of 'disposable workers.'"*New York Times,* March 15.

———. 1997a. "Child-care solutions in a new world of welfare." *New York Times,* June 1.

———. 1997b. "Illness is turning into financial catastrophe for more of the uninsured." *New York Times,* August 1.

———. 1997c. "Priority on safety is keeping more children in foster care." *New York Times,* April 29.

Kincaid, S. B., & Caldwell, R. A. 1995. "Marital separation: Causes, coping, and consequences." *Journal of Divorce and Remarriage, 22,* 109–128.

King, E. W. 1997. "Social class in the lives of young children: Cross cultural perspectives." *Education and Society, 15,* 3–12.

Kinsey, A. C., Pomeroy, W. B., & Martin, C. E. 1948. *Sexual behavior in the human male.* Philadelphia: Saunders.

Kinsey, A. C., Pomeroy, W. B., Martin, C. E., & Gebhard, P. H. 1953. *Sexual behavior in the human female.* Philadelphia: Saunders.

Kitamura, T., & Kijima, N. 1999. "Frequencies of child abuse in Japan: Hidden by prevalent crime." *International Journal of Offender Therapy and Comparative Criminology, 43,* 21–33.

Kitano, H. L. 1976. *Japanese Americans: The evolution of a subculture.* Englewood Cliffs, NJ: Prentice Hall.

Kitano, H. L., & Daniels, R. 1988. *Asian Americans: Emerging minorities.* Englewood Cliffs, NJ: Prentice Hall.

Kitano, H. L., Yeung, W., Chai, L., & Hatanaka, H. 1984. "Asian American interracial marriage." *Journal of Marriage and the Family, 46,* 179–190.

Kitcher, P. 1996. "Junior comes out perfect." *New York Times Magazine,* September 29.

Klaff, V. Z. 1995. "The changing Jewish family: Issues of continuity." In C. K. Jacobson (Ed.), *American families: Issues in race and ethnicity.* New York: Garland Press.

Klatch, R. 1991. "Complexities of conservatism: How conservatives understand the world." In A. Wolfe (Ed.), *America at century's end.* Berkeley: University of California Press.

Klawitter, M. M. 1994. "Who gains, who loses from changing U.S. child support policies?" *Policy Sciences, 27,* 197–219.

Klein, D. M., & White, J. M. 1996. *Family theories.* Thousand Oaks, CA: Sage.

Kobrin, J. E. 1991. "Cross-cultural perspectives and research directions for the twenty-first century." *Child Abuse and Neglect, 15,* 67–77.

Kohlberg, L. A. 1966. "A cognitive-developmental analysis of children's sex-role concepts and attitudes." In E. Maccoby (Ed.), *The development of sex differences.* Stanford, CA: Stanford University Press.

Kohn, M. 1979. "The effects of social class on parental values and practices." In D. Reiss & H. A. Hoffman (Eds.), *The American family: Dying or developing.* New York: Plenum.

Kolata, G. 1997a. "Clinics enter a new world of embryo 'adoption.'" *New York Times,* November 23.

———. 1997b. "A record and big questions as woman gives birth at sixty-three." *New York Times,* April 24.

Kollock, P., & Blumstein, P. 1988. "Personal relationships." *Annual Review of Sociology, 14,* 467–490.

Kollock, P., Blumstein, P., & Schwartz, P. 1985. "Sex and power in interaction: Conversational privileges and duties." *American Sociological Review, 50,* 34–46.

———. 1994. "The judgment of equity in intimate relationships." *Social Psychology Quarterly, 57,* 340–351.

Komarovsky, M. 1962. *Blue-collar marriage.* New Haven, CT: Vintage.

Komter, A. 1989. "Hidden power in marriage." *Gender & Society, 3,* 187–216.

Kondratas, S. A. 1991. "Ending homelessness: Policy challenges." *American Psychologist, 46,* 1226–1231.

Koyano, W. 2000. "Filial piety, co-residence, and intergenerational solidarity in Japan." In W. T. Liu & H. Kendig (Eds.), *Who should care for the elderly? An East–West value divide.* Singapore: Singapore University Press.

Kranichfeld, M. L. 1987. "Rethinking family power." *Journal of Family Issues, 8,* 42–56.

Kristof, N. D. 1993a. "China's crackdown on births: A stunning and harsh success." *New York Times,* April 25.

———. 1993b. "Peasants of China discover new way to weed out girls." *New York Times,* July 21.

———. 1996a. "Do Korean men still beat their wives? Definitely." *New York Times,* December 5.

———. 1996b. "For rural Japanese, death doesn't break family ties." *New York Times,* September 29.

———. 1996c. "Japan is a woman's world, once the front door is shut." *New York Times,* June 19.

———. 1996d. "Who needs love! In Japan, many couples don't." *New York Times,* February 11.

———. 1997. "Once prized, Japan's elderly feel dishonored and fearful." *New York Times,* August 4.

Kudson-Martin, C., & Mahoney, A. R. 1998. "Language processes in the construction of equality in marriages." *Family Relations 47,* 81–91.

Kulis, S. S. 1991. *Why honor thy father and mother? Class, mobility, and family ties in later life.* New York: Garland.

Kurz, D. 1995. *For richer, for poorer: Mothers confront divorce.* New York: Routledge.

Labalme, J. 1995. "Parents opposed removal of life support." *Indianapolis Star,* December 1.

Lacey, M. 1999. "Teen-age birth rate in U.S. falls again." *New York Times,* October 27.

Lamb, M. E. 1987. "Introduction: The emergent American father." In M. E. Lamb (Ed.), *The father's role: Cross-cultural perspectives.* Hillsdale, NJ: Erlbaum.

Lamp, F. 1988. "Heavenly bodies: Menses, moon, and rituals of license among the Temne of Sierra Leone." In T. Buckley & A. Gottlieb (Eds.), *Blood magic: The anthropology of menstruation.* Berkeley: University of California Press.

Landers, A. 1993. "What's in a name? A lot of discord." *Lafayette Journal and Courier,* December 31.

Landis-Kleine, C., Foley, L. A., Nall, L., Padgett, P., & Walters-Palmer, L. 1995. "Attitudes toward marriage and divorce held by young adults." *Journal of Divorce and Remarriage, 23,* 63–73.

Laner, M. R. 1989. *Dating: Delights, discontents and dilemmas.* Salem, WI: Sheffield.

Langman, L. 1988. "Social stratification" In M. B. Sussman & S. K. Steinmetz (Eds.), *Handbook of marriage and the family.* New York: Plenum.

LaRossa, R. 1992. "Fatherhood and social change." In M. S. Kimmel & M. A. Messner (Eds.), *Men's lives.* New York: Macmillan.

Larson, L. E., & Goltz, J. W. 1989. "Religious participation and marital commitment." *Review of Religious Research, 30,* 387–400.

Larzelere, R. E., & Klein, D. M. 1987. "Methodology." In M. B. Sussman & S. K. Steinmetz (Eds.), *Handbook of marriage and the family.* New York: Plenum.

Lasch, C. 1977. *Haven in a heartless world: The family besieged.* New York: Norton.

Laslett, B. 1973. "The family as a public and private institution." *Journal of Marriage and the Family, 35,* 480–492.

Laumann, E. O., Gagnon, J. H., Michael, R. T., & Michaels, S. 1994. *The social organization of sexuality.* Chicago: University of Chicago Press.

Lawson, C. 1991. "A bedtime story that's different." *New York Times,* April 4.

———. 1992. "Who believes in make-believe? Not these new toys." *New York Times,* February 6.

———. 1993. "Stereotypes unravel, but not too quickly, in new toys for 1993." *New York Times,* February 11.

Lee, G. R., & Stone, L. H. 1980. "Mate-selection systems and criteria: Variation according to family structure." *Journal of Marriage and the Family, 42,* 319–326.

Lee, J. A. 1982. "Three paradigms of child-hood." *Canadian Review of Sociology and Anthropology, 19,* 591–608.

Lee, S. M., & Fernandez, M. 1998. "Trends in Asian American racial/ethnic intermarriage." *Sociological Perspectives, 41,* 323–342.

Lee, S. M., & Yamanaka, K. 1990. "Patterns of Asian American intermarriage and marital assimilation." *Journal of Comparative Family Studies, 21,* 287–305.

Leland, J., & Beals, G. 1997. "In living colors." *Newsweek,* May 5.

Leland, J., & Rhodes, S. 1996. "Tightening the knot." *Newsweek,* February 19.

"Length of workweek doesn't tell whole story." 2001. *Toronto Star,* June 12.

Lennon, M. C., & Rosenfield, S. 1994. "Relative fairness and the division of housework: The importance of options." *American Journal of Sociology, 100,* 506–531.

"Lesbian's appeal for custody of son rejected." 1995. *New York Times,* April 22.

"Less rote, more variety." 2000. *The Economist,* December 16.

Lester, W. 2000. "Poll: Gay marriage not popular, but couples' rights are." *Lafayette Journal and Courier,* June 1, p. A3.

Letellier, P. 1996. "Gay and bisexual male domestic violence victimization." In L. K. Hamberger & C. Renzetti (Eds.), *Domestic partner abuse.* New York: Springer.

Lev, M. A. 2000. "China ready to abandon 1-child rule." *Indianapolis Star,* May 7.

LeVay, S. 1991. "A difference in hypothalamic structure between heterosexual and homosexual men." *Science,* August 30, pp. 1034–1037.

———. 1996. *Queer science.* Cambridge, MA: MIT Press.

LeVine, R. A., & White, M. 1992. "The social transformation of childhood." In A. S. Skolnick & J. H. Skolnick (Eds.), *Family in transition* (7th ed.). New York: HarperCollins.

Levine, R. V. 1993. "Is love a luxury?" *American Demographies,* February, 27–29.

Levinson, D. 1989. *Family violence in cross-cultural perspective.* Newbury Park, CA: Sage.

Levy, B. 1991. *Dating violence: Young women in danger.* Seattle, WA: Seal Press.

Lewin, E. 1996. "'Why in the world would you want to do that? Claiming community in lesbian commitment ceremonies." In E. Lewin (Ed.), *Inventing lesbian cultures in America,* Boston: Beacon Press.

Lewin, T. 1989. "Aging parents: Women's burden grows." *New York Times,* November 14.

———. 1990. "Suit over death benefits asks, what is a family?" *New York Times,* September 21.

———. 1991. "Jobless pay for mother." *New York Times,* March 13.

———. 1994a. "Men whose wives work earn less, studies show." *New York Times,* October 12.

———. 1994b. "Outrage over 18 months for man who killed his wife in 'heat of passion.'" *New York Times,* October 21.

———. 1995a. "The decay of families is global, study says." *New York Times,* May 31.

———. 1995b. "Workers of both sexes make trade-offs for family, study shows." *New York Times,* October 29.

———. 1997. "U.S. is divided on adoption, survey of attitudes asserts." *New York Times,* November 9.

———. 1998a. "Birth rates for teen-agers declined sharply in the 90's." *New York Times,* May 1.

———. 1998b. "From welfare roll to child care worker." *New York Times,* April 29.

———. 1998c. "New families redraw racial boundaries." *New York Times,* October 27.

———. 1998d. "Schools are moving to police students' off-campus lives." *New York Times,* February 6.

———. 1998e. "Study finds that youngest U.S. children are poorest." *New York Times,* March 15.

———. 1999a. "Defining who can see the children." *New York Times,* October 3.

———. 1999b. "It's a hard life (or not)." *New York Times,* November 7.

———. 2000. "Study finds welfare changes lead a million into child care." *New York Times,* February 4.

———. 2001a. "Breast-feeding: How old is too old?" *New York Times,* February 18.

———. 2001b. "Father owing child support loses a right to procreate." *New York Times,* July 12.

Lewis, R., & Yancey, G. 1997. "Racial and nonracial factors that influence spouse choice in black/white marriages." *Journal of Black Studies, 28,* 60–78.

Liao, C., & Heaton, T. B. 1992. "Divorce trends and differentials in China." *Journal of Comparative Family Studies, 23,* 413–429.

Lichter, D. T. 1997. "Poverty and inequality among children." *Annual Review of Sociology, 23,* 121–145.

Lichter, D. T., Anderson, R. N., & Hayward, M. D. 1995. "Marriage markets and marital choice." *Journal of Family Issues, 16,* 412–431.

Lichter, D. T., LeClere, F. B., & McLaughlin, D. K. 1991. "Local marriage markets and the marital behavior of black and white women." *American Journal of Sociology, 96,* 843–867.

Light, P. 1988. *Baby boomers.* New York: Norton.

Lillard, L. A., & Waite, L. J. 1995. "'Til death do us part: Marital disruption

and mortality." *American Journal of Sociology, 100,* 1131–1156.

Linden, D. W., & Machan, D. 1997. "The disinheritors." *Forbes Magazine,* May 19.

Lindsey, K. 1981. *Friends as family.* Boston: Beacon Press.

Lindsey, L. L. 1997. *Gender roles: A sociological perspective.* Upper Saddle River, NJ: Prentice Hall.

Lino, M. 2001. "Expenditures on children by families, 2000 annual report." U.S. Department of Agriculture, Center for Nutrition Policy and Promotion. Miscellaneous Publication No. 1528–2000. Available at www.usda.gov/cnpp/. Accessed July 14, 2001.

Linton, R. 1937. "One hundred percent American." *The American Mercury, 40,* 427–429.

Lipman-Blumen, J. 1984. *Gender roles and power.* Englewood Cliffs, NJ: Prentice Hall.

Lips, H. M. 1993. *Sex and gender: An introduction.* Mountain View, CA: Mayfield.

Liu, W. T. 2000. "Values and caregiving burden: The significance of filial piety in elder care." In W. T. Liu & H. Kendig (Eds.), *Who should care for the elderly? An East–West value divide.* Singapore: Singapore University Press.

Liu, W. T., & H. Kendig. 2000. "Critical issues of caregiving: East–West dialogue." In W. T. Liu and H. Kendig (Eds.), *Who should care for the elderly? An East–West value divide.* Singapore: Singapore University Press.

Lockhart, L. L., White, B. W., Causby, V., & Isaac, A. 1994. "Letting out the secret: Violence in lesbian relationships." *Journal of Interpersonal Violence, 9,* 469–492.

Loe, V. 1997. "New nuptial license gets cool reception." *Indianapolis Star,* September 21.

Loomis, L. S., & Booth, A. 1995. "Multigenerational caregiving and well-being: The myth of the beleaguered sandwich generation." *Journal of Family Issues, 16,* 131–148.

LoPresto, C., Sherman, M., & Sherman, N. 1985. "The effects of a masturbation sermon on high school males' attitudes, false beliefs, guilt, and behavior." *Journal of Sex Research, 21,* 142–156.

Lorber, J. 1989. "Dismantling Noah's Ark." In B. J. Risman & P. Schwartz (Eds.), *Gender in intimate relationships: A microstructural approach.* Belmont, CA: Wadsworth.

———. 1994. *Paradoxes of gender.* New Haven, CT: Yale University Press.

Lorenz, F. O., Simons, R. L., Conger, R. D., Elder, G. H., Johnson, C., & Chao, W. 1997. "Married and recently divorced mothers' stressful events and distress: Tracing change across time." *Journal of Marriage and the Family, 59,* 219–232.

Loury, G. C. 2000. "Twenty-five years of black America: Two steps forward and one step back?" *Journal of Sociology and Social Welfare, 27,* 19–52.

"Love at first beep." 2000. *Utne Reader,* May–June.

Lucal, B. 1999. "What it means to be gendered me: Life on the boundaries of a dichotomous gender system." *Gender & Society, 13,* 781–797.

Luker, K. 1984. *Abortion and the politics of motherhood.* Berkeley: University of California Press.

———. 1994. "Dubious conceptions: The controversy over teen pregnancy." In A. S. Skolnick & J. H. Skolnick (Eds.), *Family in transition* (8th ed.). New York: HarperCollins.

Luo, T. 2000. "'Marrying my rapist?!' The cultural trauma among Chinese rape survivors." *Gender & Society, 14,* 581–597.

Lye, D. N. 1996. "Adult child–parent relationships." *Annual Review of Sociology, 22,* 79–102.

Lynch, M. 1982. "Forgotten fathers." In E. Jackson & S. Persky (Eds.), *Flaunting it! A decade of gay journalism from the body politic.* Vancouver: New Star Books.

Lytton, H., & Romney, D. M. 1991. "Parents' differential socialization of boys and girls: A meta-analysis." *Psychology Bulletin, 109,* 267–296.

Maccoby, E., & Mnookin, R. H. 1992. *Dividing the child: Social and legal dilemmas of custody.* Cambridge, MA: Harvard University Press.

MacDonald, K., & Parke, R. D. 1986. "Parent–child physical play: The effects of sex and age on children and parents." *Sex Roles, 15,* 367–378.

Macgillivray, I. K. 2000. "Educational equity for gay, lesbian, bisexual, transgendered, and queer/questioning students: The demands of democracy and social justice for America's schools." *Education and Urban Society, 32,* 303–323.

Mackellar, L., & Horlacher, D. 2000. "Population aging in Japan: A brief survey." *Innovation: The European Journal of Social Sciences, 13,* 413–430.

Macklin, E. 1988. "AIDS: Implications for families." *Family Relations, 37,* 141–149.

MacMillan, R., & Gartner, R. 1999. "When she brings home the bacon: Labor-force participation and the risk of spousal violence against women." *Journal of Marriage and the Family, 61,* 947–959.

Maltz, D. N., & Borker, R. A. 1982. "A cultural approach to male–female miscommunication." In J. J. Gumperz (Ed.), *Language and social identity.* Cambridge, U.K.: Cambridge University Press.

Mannon, J. M. 1997a. "Domestic and intimate violence: An application of routine activity theory." *Aggression and Violent Behavior, 2,* 9–24.

———. 1997b. *Measuring up: The performance ethic in American culture.* Boulder, CO: Westview.

Mantsios, G. 1995. "Class in America: Myths and realities." In P. S. Rothenberg (Ed.), *Race, class, and gender in the United States.* New York: St. Martin's Press.

Maranto, G. 1995. "Delayed childbearing." *The Atlantic Monthly,* June, pp. 55–66.

Marciano, T. D. 1988. "Families wider than kin or marriage?" *Family Science Review, 1,* 115–124.

Marger, M. N. 1994. *Race and ethnic relations: American and global perspectives.* Belmont, CA: Wadsworth.

Margolick, D. 1990. "Death and faith, law and Christian Science." *New York Times,* August 6.

Marin, R. 2000. "At-home fathers step out to find they are not alone." *New York Times,* January 2.

Markowitz, L. 2000. "A different kind of queer marriage." *Utne Reader,* September–October.

Marks, M. R. 1997. "Party politics and family policy: The case of the Family and Medical Leave Act." *Journal of Family Issues, 18,* 55–70.

Marmor, J. 1996. "Blurring the lines." *Columns,* December.

Martin, K. 1998. "Becoming a gendered body: Practices of preschools." *American Sociological Review, 63,* 494–511.

Martin, L. 1989. "The graying of Japan." *Population Bulletin, 44,* 1–43.

Martin, M. K., & Voorhies, B. 1975. *Female of the species.* New York: Columbia University Press.

Marzollo, J. 1981. "Confessions of a (sort of) grown-up." *Parents,* July 3.

Masnick, G., & Bane, M. J. 1980. *The nation's families: 1960–1990.* Boston: Auburn House.

Massey, D. S. 2000. "What I don't know about my field but wish I did." *Annual Review of Sociology, 26,* 699–701.

Mathews, L. 1996. "More than identity rides on new racial category." *New York Times,* July 6.

Maume, D. J., & Bellas, M. L. 2001. "The overworked American or the time bind?" *American Behavioral Scientist, 44,* 1137–1156.

McAdoo, H. P. 1998. "African-American families." In C. H. Mindel, R. W. Habenstein, & R. Wright (Eds.), *Ethnic families in America: Patterns and variations.* Upper Saddle River, NJ: Prentice Hall.

McCall, G. J. 1982. "Becoming unrelated: The management of bond dissolution." In S. Duck (Ed.), *Personal relationships #4: Dissolving personal relationships.* London: Academic Press.

McCarthy, T. 2001. "He makes a village." *Time,* May 14.

McClaurin, I. 1996. *Women of Belize: Gender and change in Central America.* New Brunswick, NJ: Rutgers University Press.

McCoy, E. 1981. "Childhood through the ages." *Parents Magazine,* January, pp. 60–65.

McCrate, E., & Smith, J. 1998. "When work doesn't work: The failure of current welfare reform." *Gender and Society, 12,* 61–80.

McKenry, P. C., & Price, S. J. 1995. "Divorce: A comparative perspective." In B. B. Ingoldsby & S. Smith (Eds.), *Families in multicultural perspective.* New York: Guilford Press.

McKinney, K. D. 1998. "Space, body, and mind: Parental perceptions of children's privacy needs." *Journal of Family Issues, 19,* 75–100.

McLanahan, S., & Booth, K. 1991. "Mother-only families." In A. Booth (Ed.), *Contemporary families: Looking forward, looking back.* Minneapolis: National Council on Family Relations.

McLanahan, S. S., & Sandefur, G. 1994. *Growing up with a single parent.* Cambridge, MA: Harvard University Press.

McLoyd, V. C., Cauce, A. M., Takeuchi, D., & Wilson, L. 2000. "Marital processes and parental socialization in families of color: A decade review of research." *Journal of Marriage and the Family, 62,* 1070–1094.

McManus, P. A., & DiPrete, T. A. 2001. "Losers and winners: The financial consequences of separation and divorce for men." *American Sociological Review, 66,* 246–268.

McNeil, M. 1997. "Neglect conviction of mom overruled by appeals court." *Indianapolis Star,* January 1.

McRoy, R. G., & Zurcher, L. A. 1983. *Transracial and inracial adoptees: The adolescent years.* Springfield, IL: Thomas.

McWhirter, D. P., & Mattison, A. M. 1984. *The male couple: How relationships develop.* Englewood Cliffs, NJ: Prentice Hall.

Mead, M. 1963. *Sex and temperament in three primitive societies.* New York: Morrow.

———. 1978. "The American family: An endangered species?" *TV Guide,* December 30.

Mellot, K. 1997. "Faith-healers get the max." *Tribune-Democrat* (Johnstown, PA).

Meredith, R. 1999. "Truants' parents face crackdown across the U.S." *New York Times,* December 6.

Meyrowitz, J. 1984. "The adultlike child and the childlike adult: Socialization in an electronic age." *Daedalus, 113,* 19–48.

Miall, C. E. 1989. "The stigma of involuntary childlessness." In A. S. Skolnick & J. H. Skolnick (Eds.), *Family in transition* (6th ed.). Boston: Little, Brown.

Michael, R. T., Gagnon, J. H., Laumann, E. O., & Kolata, G. 1994. *Sex in*

America: A definitive survey. Boston: Little, Brown.

Michener, H. A., DeLamater, J. D., & Schwartz, S. H. 1986. *Social psychology.* San Diego: Harcourt Brace Jovanovich.

Milbank, D. 2001. "Bush's proposals mirror belief that government can aid families." *Indianapolis Star,* April 22.

Miller, C. L. 1987. "Qualitative differences among gender-stereotyped toys: Implications for cognitive and social development." *Sex Roles, 16,* 473–488.

Miller, J. A., Jacobsen, R. B., & Bigner, J. J. 1981. "The child's home environment for lesbian vs. heterosexual mothers: A neglected area of research." *Journal of Homosexuality, 7,* 49–56.

Mills, C. W. 1959. *The sociological imagination.* New York: Oxford University Press.

Minow, M. 1993. "Definitions of family: Who's in, who's out and who decides." In M. Minow (Ed.), *Family matters: Readings on family lives and the law.* New York: Free Press.

Minow, M., & Shanley, M. L. 1996. "Relational rights and responsibilities: Revisioning the family in liberal political theory and law." *Hypatia, 11,* 4–29.

Mintz, S. 1989. "Regulating the American family." *Journal of Family History, 14,* 387–408.

Mintz, S., & Kellogg, S. 1988. *Domestic revolutions.* New York: Free Press.

Miranda, M. R. 1992. "Quality of life and the elderly: The continuing disparity between whites and minorities." *Perspectives on Aging, 21,* 4–10.

Mirande, A. 1988. "Chicano fathers: Traditional perceptions and current realities." In P. Bronstein & R. Cowan (Eds.), *Fatherhood today: Men's changing role in the family.* New York: Wiley.

Mirowsky, J., & Ross, C. E. 1999. "Economic hardship across the life course." *American Sociological Review, 64,* 548–569.

Mitchell, B. A., & Gee, E. M. 1996. "'Boomerang kids' and midlife parental marital satisfaction." *Family Relations, 45,* 442–449.

Mitford, J. 1993. *The American way of birth.* New York: Plume.

Moen, P., & Schorr, A. L. 1987. "Families and social policy." In M. B. Sussman & S. K. Steinmetz (Eds.), *Handbook of*

marriage and the family. New York: Plenum.

Moen, P., & Yu, Y. 2000. "Effective work/life strategies: Working couples, work conditions, gender and life quality." *Social Problems, 47,* 291–326.

Mogelonsky, M. 1996. "The rocky road to adulthood." *American Demographics,* May, 26–34.

———. 1998. "Teens' working dreams." *American Demographics, 20,* p. 14.

Mohr, J. C. 1978. *Abortion in America: The origins and evolution of national policy, 1800–1900.* New York: Oxford University Press.

Molloy, B. L., & Herzberger, S. D. 1998. "Body image and self-esteem: A comparison of African-American and Caucasian women." *Sex Roles, 38,* 631–643.

"Mom's market value." 1998. *Utne Reader,* March–April.

Moore, D. W. 1999. "Americans support teaching creationism as well as evolution in public schools." Gallup News Service Poll Release. Available at www.gallup.com/poll/releases/pr990830.asp. Accessed August 30, 1999.

Moore, K., Manlove, J., Glei, D., & Morrison, D. R. 1998. "Nonmarital school-age motherhood: Family, individual, and school characteristics." *Journal of Adolescent Research, 13,* 433–457.

Moore, M. L. 1992. "The family as portrayed on prime-time television, 1947–1990: Structure and characteristics." *Sex Roles, 26,* 41–61.

Morgan, L., & Kunkel, S. 1998. *Aging and society.* Thousand Oaks, CA: Pine Forge Press.

Mottl, T. L. 1980. "The analysis of countermovements." *Social Problems, 27,* 620–635.

Moynihan, D. P. 1965. *The Negro family: The case for national action.* Washington, DC: Office of Planning and Research, Department of Labor.

Murdock, G. P. 1949. *Social structure.* New York: Free Press.

———. 1957. "World ethnography sample." *American Anthropologist, 59,* 664–687.

Murray, C. 1994. "Does welfare bring more babies?" *American Enterprise, 5,* 53–59.

Murstein, B. I. 1974. *Love, sex, and marriage through the ages.* New York: Springer.

———. 1987. "A clarification and extension of the SVR theory of dyadic pairing." *Journal of Marriage and the Family, 49,* 929–933.

Nack, W., & Munson, L. 1995. "Sports' dirty secret." *Sports Illustrated,* July 31.

Nanda, S. 1990. *Neither man nor woman: The hijras of India.* Belmont, CA: Wadsworth.

———. 1994. *Cultural anthropology.* Belmont, CA: Wadsworth.

Naoi, M., & Schooler, C. 1990. "Psychological consequences of occupational conditions among Japanese wives." *Social Psychology Quarterly, 53,* 100–116.

National Adoption Information Clearinghouse. 2001. Available at www.calib.com/naic/. Accessed May 1, 2001.

National Center for Education Statistics. 2000. "Education indicators: An international perspective." http://nces.ed.gov/pubs/eiip/eiipid24.html. Accessed December 28, 2000.

National Center on Elder Abuse. 2001. "What are the major types of elder abuse?" Available at www.elderabusecenter.org. Accessed May 5, 2001.

National Committee on Pay Equity. 1995. "The wage gap: Myths and facts." In P. S. Rothenberg (Ed.), *Race, class and gender in the United States.* New York: St. Martin's Press.

———. 1999. "The wage gap: 1998." Available at www.feminist.com/fairpay. Accessed July 1, 2000.

National Institute of Population and Social Security Research. 2001. "Selected demographic indicators for Japan." Available at www.ipss.go.jp/English/S_D_I/Indip.html. Accessed July 20, 2001.

National Low Income Housing Coalition. 1999. "Out of reach: The gap between housing costs and income of poor people in the United States." Available at www.nlihc.org/OOR99/index.htm. Accessed June 20, 2000.

National Marriage Project. 2001. "Mission, goals and organization." http://marriage.rutgers.edu/about.htm. Accessed July 7, 2001.

National Opinion Research Center. 1996. *General Social Survey.* Available at www.icpsr.umich.edu/GSS/. Accessed June 1, 2001.

———. 1998. *General Social Survey, 1972–1998.* Available at www.icpsr.umich.edu/GSS/. Accessed June 1, 2001.

National Partnership for Women and Families. 1998. "Balancing acts: Work/family issues on prime-time TV." Available at www.nationalpartnership.org/publications/contenanalysis.htm. Accessed May 8, 2001.

National Women's Law Center. 2001. "Cuts in child care funding would harm women and their families, says NWLC." Available at www.nwlc.org/details.cfm?id=654&section=newsroom. Accessed August 10, 2001.

Navarro, V. 1992. "The middle class—a useful myth?" *The Nation,* March 23.

Neal, A. G., Groat, H. T., & Wicks, J. W. 1989. "Attitudes about having children: A study of 600 couples in the early years of marriage." *Journal of Marriage and the Family, 59,* 313–328.

Nelkin, D., & Lindee, M. S. 1995. *The DNA mystique: The gene as a cultural icon.* New York: Freeman.

Nemy, E. 1995. "No children, and no apologies." *New York Times,* April 6.

Neugarten, B. L. 1980. "Grow old along with me! The best is yet to be." In B. Hess (Ed.), *Growing old in America.* New Brunswick, NJ: Transaction Books.

"New kit can help parents detect their kids' drug use." 1995. *JET Magazine,* April 17.

"The new 'parental rights' crusade." 1996. *The Humanist,* March–April.

Newman, K. 1993. *Declining fortunes: The withering of the American dream.* New York: HarperCollins.

———. 1999a. *Falling from grace: Downward mobility in the Age of Affluence.* Berkeley: University of California Press.

———. 1999b. *No shame in my game: The working poor in the inner city.* New York: Knopf.

Niebuhr, G. 1996. "An interfaith-marriage vote has reform Judaism divided." *New York Times,* December 14.

———. 1998. "Southern Baptist vote puts men first." *Indianapolis Star,* June 10.

———. 2000. "Marriage issue splits Jews, poll finds." *New York Times,* October 31.

Nock, S. L. 1987. "The symbolic meaning of child bearing." *Journal of Family Issues, 8,* 373–393.

———. 1995. "A comparison of marriages and cohabiting relationships." *Journal of Family Issues, 16,* 53–76.

———. 1998a. "The consequences of premarital fatherhood." *American Sociological Review, 63,* 250–263.

———. 1998b. "Too much privacy?" *Journal of Family Issues, 19,* 101–118.

———. 1999. "The problem with marriage." *Society, 36,* 20–27.

Nock, S. L., & Kingston, P. W. 1988. "Time with children: The impact of couples' work-time commitments." *Social Forces, 67,* 59–85.

Noller, P. 1993. "Gender and emotional communication in marriage: Different cultures or differential social power?" *Journal of Language and Social Psychology, 12,* 132–152.

Oaks, D. H. 1995. "Rights and responsibilities." In A. Etzioni (Ed.), *Rights and the common good.* New York: St. Martin's Press.

O'Brien, M., & Huston, A. C. 1985. "Development of sex-typed play behavior in toddlers." *Developmental Psychology, 21,* 866–871.

Ogawa, N., & Retherford, R. D. 1993. "Care of the elderly in Japan: Changing norms and expectations." *Journal of Marriage and the Family, 55,* 585–597.

"Ohio court removes child from parents because of her gender." 2000. Available at http://www.gpac.org. Accessed August 26, 2000.

Ojito, M. 1997. "Culture clash: Foreign parents, American child rearing." *New York Times,* June 29.

Oliker, S. J. 1995. "Work commitment and constraint among mothers on welfare." *Journal of Contemporary Ethnography, 24,* 165–194.

Olsen, F. 1993. "The myth of state intervention in the family." In M. Minow (Ed.), *Family matters.* New York: New Press.

Olson, E. 1981. "Socioeconomic and psychocultural contexts of child abuse and neglect in Turkey." In J. Kobrin

(Ed.), *Child abuse and neglect: Cross-cultural perspectives.* Berkeley: University of California Press.

———. 1998. "U.N. surveys paid leave for mothers." *New York Times,* February 16.

———. 2000. "Study reports 5.3 million new HIV/AIDS infections this year." *Indianapolis Star,* November 25.

Ordover, N. 1996. "Eugenics, the gay gene, and the science of backlash." *Socialist Review, 26,* 125–144.

Orenstein, P. 1994. *School girls: Young women, self-esteem, and the confidence gap.* New York: Anchor.

Orthner, D. K. 1990. "The family in transition." In D. Blankenhorn, S. Bayne, & J. B. Elshtain (Eds.), *Rebuilding the nest: A new commitment to the American family.* Milwaukee, WI: Family Service America.

Ostrander, S. 1984. *Women of the upper class.* Philadelphia: Temple University Press.

O'Sullivan, L. F., & Gaines, M. E. 1998. "Decision-making in college students' heterosexual dating relationships: ambivalence about engaging in sexual activity." *Journal of Social and Personal Relationships, 15,* 347–363.

Owen, M. 1996. *A world of widows.* London: Zed Books.

Pader, E. 1997. "Redefining the home." *New York Times,* May 7.

Palmore, E. 1975. *The honorable elders: A cross-cultural analysis of aging in Japan.* Durham, NC: Duke University Press.

Pampel, F. C. 1998. *Aging, social inequality, and public policy.* Thousand Oaks, CA: Pine Forge Press.

Parcel, T. L., & Menaghan, E. G., 1990. "Maternal working conditions and children's verbal facility: Studying the intergenerational transmission of inequality from mothers to young children." *Social Psychology Quarterly, 53,* 132–147.

———. 1994. "Early parental work, family social capital, and early childhood outcomes." *American Journal of Sociology, 99,* 972–1009.

Parke, R. D., & Buriel, R. 2002. "Socialization concerns in African American, American Indian, Asian American, and Latino Families." In N. V. Benokraitis (Ed.), *Contemporary ethnic families in the United States: Characteristics,* *variations, and dynamics.* Upper Saddle River, NJ: Prentice Hall.

Parlee, M. B. 1989. "Conversational politics." In L. Richardson & V. Taylor (Eds.), *Feminist frontiers.* New York: Random House.

Parsons, T., & Bales, R. F. 1955. *Family socialization and interaction process.* Glencoe, IL: Free Press.

Patterson, C. J. 1992. "Children of lesbian and gay parents." *Child Development, 63,* 1025–1042.

Patterson, C. J., & Chan, R. W. 1999. "Families headed by lesbian and gay parents." In M. E. Lamb (Ed.), *Parenting and child development in "nontraditional" families.* Mahwah, NJ: Erlbaum.

Pattillo-McCoy, M. 1999. *Black picket fences: Privilege and peril among the Black middle class.* Chicago: University of Chicago Press.

Patton, W., & Mannison, M. 1995. "Sexual coercion in high school dating." *Sex Roles, 33,* 447–457.

Payne, R. K. 1998. *Poverty: A Framework for understanding and working with students and adults from poverty.* Baytown, TX: RFT Pub.

Pear, R. 1997. "U.S. inaugurating a vast database of all new hires." *New York Times,* September 22.

———. 2000. "A million parents lost Medicaid, study says." *New York Times,* June 20.

Pearce, D. 1978. "Feminization of poverty—women, work and welfare." *Urban & Social Change Review, 11,* 28–36.

Pearce, L. D., & Axinn, W. G. 1998. "The impact of family religious life on the quality of mother–child relations." *American Sociological Review, 63,* 810–828.

Penner, D. 1995. "Aid recipients defy stereotypes, seek a better way." *Indianapolis Star,* April 16.

Penton-Voak, I. S., Perrett, D. I., Castles, D. L., Kobayashi, T., Burt, D. M., Murray, L. K., & Minamisawa, R. 1999. "Menstrual cycles alter face preference." *Nature, 399,* 741–742.

Perkins, H. W., & DeMeis, D. K. 1996. "Gender and family effects on the 'second shift' domestic activities of college-educated young adults." *Gender and Society, 10,* 78–93.

"Perpetual groom plots 28th wedding." 1990. *Lafayette Journal and Courier,* July 11.

Peterson, I. 1992. "For absent fathers, a ray of hope." *New York Times,* September 29.

Peterson, L. R. 1986. "Interfaith marriage and religious commitment among Catholics." *Journal of Marriage and the Family, 48,* 725–735.

Peterson, R. R. 1996. "A re-evaluation of the economic consequences of divorce." *American Sociological Review, 61,* 528–536.

Peterson, W. C. 1994. *The silent depression: The fate of the American dream.* New York: Norton.

Pfohl, S. J. 1977. "The discovery of child abuse." *Social Problems, 24,* 310–323.

Philipson, I. 2000. "Work as family: The workplace as repository of women's unmet emotional needs." Working paper, Center for Working Families. University of California, Berkeley.

Pillemer, K. A. 1993. "Abuse is caused by the deviance and dependence of abusive caregivers." In R. J. Gelbs & D. R. Loeske (Eds.), *Current controversies in family violence.* Newbury Park, CA: Sage.

Pittman, J. F., & Blanchard, D. 1996. "The effects of work history and timing of marriage on the division of household labor: A life-course perspective." *Journal of Marriage and the Family, 58,* 78–90.

Pleck, E. 1987. *Domestic tyranny.* New York: Oxford University Press.

Pollitt, K. 1991. "Fetal rights: A new assault on feminism." In J. H. Skolnick & E. Currie (Eds.), *Crisis in American institutions.* New York: HarperCollins.

Ponticelli, C. M. 1999. "Crafting stories of sexual identity reconstruction." *Social Psychology Quarterly, 62,* 157–172.

Popenoe, D. 1988. *Disturbing the nest.* New York: Aldine de Gruyter.

———. 1993. "American family decline, 1960–1990: A review and appraisal." *Journal of Marriage and the Family, 55,* 527–555.

———. 1995. "Family values: A communitarian position." In D. Sciulli (Ed.), *Macro-socioeconomics: From theory to activism.* Armonk, NY: M. E. Sharpe.

———. 1996. "Where's Papa?" *Utne Reader,* September–October, pp. 63–66.

———. 1999. "Can the nuclear family be revived?" *Society, 36,* 28–30.

Population Reference Bureau. 2000. "How do children spend their time? Children's activities, school achievement, and well-being." *Today's Issues,* No. 11. Available at http://156.40.88.3/about/cpr/dbs/pubs/ti11.pdf. Accessed October 3, 2001.

Potuchek, J. L. 1997. *Who supports the family? Gender and breadwinning in dual-earner marriages.* Stanford, CA: Stanford University Press.

Powell, B., & Downey, D. B. 1997. "Living in single-parent households: An investigation of the same-sex hypothesis." *American Sociological Review, 62,* 521–539.

"President tells mothers to either name fathers or lose welfare." 1996. *Jet,* July 8.

Presser, H. 1994. "Employment schedules among dual-earner spouses and the division of household labor by gender." *American Sociological Review, 59,* 348–364.

Preston, S. H. 1976. *Mortality patterns in national population: With special references to recorded causes of death.* New York: Academic Press.

"The Promise Keepettes." 1997. *New York Times Magazine,* April 27.

Pyke, K. 1994. "Women's employment as a gift or burden? Marital power across marriage, divorce, and remarriage." *Gender and Society, 8,* 73–91.

———. 1996. "Class-based masculinities: The interdependence of gender, class, and interpersonal power." *Gender and Society, 10,* 527–549.

Quayle, D. 1992. "Restoring basic values: Strengthening the family." *Vital Speeches of the Day, 58,* 517–520.

———. 2001. "Why I think I'm still right." *Newsweek,* May 28.

Queen, S. A., & Habenstein, R. W. 1974. *The family in various cultures.* Philadelphia: Lippincott.

Radin, N. 1988. "Primary caregiving fathers of long duration." In P. Bronstein & C. P. Cowan (Eds.), *Fatherhood today: Men's changing role in the family.* New York: Wiley.

Rafferty, Y., & Rollins, N. 1989. *Learning in limbo: The educational deprivation of homeless children.* New York: Advocates for Children.

Raley, R. K. 1995. "Black–white differences in kin contact and exchange among never married adults." *Journal of Family Issues, 16,* 77–103.

———. 1996. "A shortage of marriageable men? A note on the role of cohabitation in black–white differences in marriage rates." *American Sociological Review, 61,* 973–983.

Ramey, S. L., Ramey, C. T., Phillips, M. M., Lanzi, R. G., Brezausek, C., Katholi, C. R., Snyder, S., & Lawrence, F. 2000. "Head Start children's entry into public school: A report on the National Head Start/Public School Early Children Transition Demonstration Study." Available at http://www2.acf.dhhs.gov/programs/hsb/exesummary/summary.htm. Accessed July 14, 2001.

Rank, M. 1994. *Life on the edge: The realities of welfare in America.* New York: Columbia University Press.

Rank, M. R., & Hirschl, T. A. 1999. "The economic risk of childhood in America: Estimating the probability of poverty across the formative years." *Journal of Marriage and the Family, 61,* 1058–1067.

Raphael, B. 1995. "The death of a child." In J. B. Williamson & E. S. Schneidman (Eds.), *Death: Current perspectives.* Mountain View, CA: Mayfield.

Rapp, R. 1999. "Family and class in contemporary America: Notes toward an understanding of ideology." In S. Coontz (Ed.), *American families: A multicultural reader.* New York: Routledge.

Rasekh, Z., Bauer, H. M., Manos, M. M., & Iacopino, V. 1998. "Women's health and human rights in Afghanistan." *Journal of the American Medical Association, 280,* 449–455.

Recer, P. 2000a. "Gene mutation may extend human life." *Lafayette Journal and Courier,* December 15.

———. 2000b. "Study: Kids are better off, but. . . ." *Lafayette Journal and Courier,* July 14.

Reddy, M. T. 1994. *Crossing the color line.* New Brunswick, NJ: Rutgers University Press.

Reich, R. B. 1996. "My family leave act." *New York Times,* November 8.

Reiman, J. 1998. *The rich get richer and the poor get prison.* New York: Macmillan.

Reinharz, S. 1992. *Feminist methods in social research.* New York: Oxford University Press.

Reinholtz, R. K., Muehlenhard, C. L., Phelps, J. L., & Satterfield, A. T. 1995. "Sexual discourse and sexual intercourse: How the way we communicate affects the way we think about sexual coercion." In P. J. Kalfleisch & M. J. Cody (Eds.), *Gender, power and communication in human relationships.* Hillsdale, NJ: Erlbaum.

Reiss, I. L. 1960. "Toward a sociology of the heterosexual love relationship." *Marriage and Family Living, 22,* 139–145.

Reiss, I. L., & Lee, G. R. 1988. *Family systems in America.* New York: Holt, Rinehart & Winston.

Rennison, C. A., & Welchans, S. 2000. *Intimate partner violence,* Table 2. Available at www.ojp.usdoj.gov/bjs/pub/pdf/ipv.pdf. Accessed October 3, 2001.

Renzetti, C. 1992. *Violent betrayal: Partner abuse in lesbian relationships.* Newbury Park, CA: Sage.

Renzetti, C., & Curran, D. J. 1989. *Women, men and society: The sociology of gender.* Boston: Allyn & Bacon.

"Report on Black America finds college gender gap." 2000. *New York Times,* July 26.

Reskin, B., & Hartmann, H. 1986. *Women's work, men's work: Sex segregation on the job.* Washington, DC: National Academy Press.

Reskin, B., & Padavic, I. 1994. *Women and men at work.* Thousand Oaks, CA: Pine Forge Press.

Ribbens, J. 1994. *Mothers and their children.* London: Sage.

Rico, B. R., & Mano, S. 1991. *American mosaic: Multicultural readings in context.* Boston: Houghton Mifflin.

Ridgeway, C. L. 1997. "Interaction and the conservation of gender inequality: Considering employment." *American Sociological Review, 62,* 218–235.

Riley, G. 1991. *Divorce: An American tradition.* New York: Oxford University Press.

Riley, M. W. 1971. "Social gerontology and the age stratification of society." *The Gerontologist, 11,* 79–87.

———. 1983. "The family in an aging society: A matrix of latent relationships." *Journal of Family Issues, 4,* 439–454.

Riley, M. W., Foner, A., & Waring, J. 1988. "Sociology of age." In N. J. Smelser (Ed.), *Handbook of sociology.* Newbury Park, CA: Sage.

Rimer, S. 1998a. "As centenarians thrive, 'old' is redefined." *New York Times,* June 22.

———. 1998b. "Tradition of care thrives in Black families." *New York Times,* March 15.

———. 1999. "Caring for elderly kin is costly, study finds." *New York Times,* November 27.

Risman, B. J. 1989. "Can men mother? Life as a single father." In B. J. Risman & P. Schwartz (Eds.), *Gender in intimate relationships.* Belmont, CA: Wadsworth.

Risman, B., & Myers, K. 1997. "As the twig is bent: Children reared in feminist households." *Qualitative Sociology, 20,* 229–252.

Rivera, L. 2000. "Welfare to what? Barriers to adult literacy for homeless women in Massachusetts." Paper presented at the Society for the Study of Social Problems, August, Washington, DC.

Roberts, A. R. 1996. "Battered women who kill: A comparative study of incarcerated participants with a community sample of battered women." *Journal of Family Violence, 11,* 291–304.

Roberts, D. E. 1991. "Punishing drug addicts who have babies: Women of color, equality and the right of privacy." *Harvard Law Review, 104,* 1419–1482.

Robinson, C. 1993. "Surrogate motherhood: Implications for the mother–fetus relationship." *Women and Politics, 13,* 203–224.

Robinson, L. 1994. "Religious orientation in enduring marriage: An exploratory study." *Review of Religious Research, 35,* 207–218.

Rodman, H., Pratto, D. J., & Nelson, R. S. 1985. "Child care arrangements and children's functioning: A comparison of self-care and adult care children." *Developmental Psychology, 21,* 413–418.

Rogers, S. 1975. "Female forms of power and the myth of male dominance." *American Ethnologist, 2,* 727-756.

Roland, A. 1988. *In search of self in India and Japan.* Princeton, NJ: Princeton University Press.

Roof, W. C. 1989. "Multiple religious switching: A research note." *Journal for the Scientific Study of Religion, 28,* 530–535.

———. 1999. *Spiritual marketplace: Baby boomers and the remaking of American religion.* Princeton, NJ: Princeton University Press.

Rosaldo, M. Z. 1974. "Woman, culture, and society: A theoretical overview." In M. Z. Rosaldo & L. Lamphere (Eds.), *Woman, culture and society.* Stanford, CA: Stanford University Press.

Roscigno, V. J. 2000. "Family/school inequality and African-American/ Hispanic achievement." *Social Problems, 47,* 266–290.

Rose, A. 1996. "How I became a single woman." *The New Yorker,* April 8.

Rose, S., & Frieze, I. H. 1989. "Young singles' scripts for a first date." *Gender & Society, 3,* 258–268.

Rosellini, L. 1992. "Sexual desire." *U.S. News and World Report,* July 6, pp. 60–66.

Rosen, J. 1997. "Abraham's drifting children." *New York Times Book Review,* March 30.

Ross, C. E., & Van Willigen, M. 1996. "Gender, parenthood, and anger." *Journal of Marriage and the Family, 58,* 572–584.

Rossi, A. 1968. "Transition to parenthood." *Journal of Marriage and the Family, 30,* 26–39.

———. 1977. "A bio-social perspective on parenting." *Daedalus, 106,* 1–31.

Rossi, A. S. & Rossi, P. H. 1990. *On human bonding: Parent–child relations across the life-course.* New York: Aldine de Gruyter.

Roth, R. 1993. "At women's expense: The costs of fetal rights." *Women and Politics, 13,* 117–135.

Rothman, B. K. 1987. "Reproduction." In B. B. Hess & M. M. Ferree (Eds.), *Analyzing gender: A handbook of social science research.* Newbury Park, CA: Sage.

Rothman, E. K. 1984. *Hands and hearts: A history of courtship in America.* New York: Basic Books.

Rowland, R. 1990. "Technology and motherhood: Reproductive choice reconsidered." In C. Carlson (Ed.), *Perspectives on the family: History, class and feminism.* Belmont, CA: Wadsworth.

Rubin, J. Z., Provenzano, F. J., & Luria, Z. 1974. "The eye of the beholder: Parents' views on sex of newborns." *American Journal of Orthopsychiatry, 44,* 512–519.

Rubin, L. 1976. *Worlds of pain.* New York: Basic Books.

———. 1990. *Erotic wars: What happened to the sexual revolution?* New York: Harper Perennial.

———. 1992. "The empty nest." In J. M. Heaslin (Ed.), *Marriage and family in a changing society.* New York: Free Press.

———. 1995. *Families on the fault line.* New York: Harper Perennial.

Rubin, Z. 1973. *Liking and loving.* New York: Holt, Rinehart & Winston.

Rusbult, C. E. 1983. "A longitudinal test of the investment model: The development (and deterioration) of satisfaction and commitment in heterosexual involvement." *Journal of Personality and Social Psychology, 45,* 101–117.

Russell, D. E. H. 1998. "Wife rape and the law." In M. E. Odem & J. Clay-Warner (Eds.), *Confronting rape and sexual assault.* Wilmington, DE: SR Books.

Russell, G. 1999. "Primary caregiving fathers." In M. E. Lamb (Ed.), *Parenting and child development in "nontraditional" families.* Mahwah, NJ: Erlbaum.

Rutter, V. 1995. "Adolescence: Whose hell is it?" *Psychology Today,* January–February.

———. 1997. "Lessons from stepfamilies." In K. R. Gilbert (Ed.), *Annual editions: Marriage and family 97/98.* Guilford, CT: Dushkin.

Ryun, J., & Ryun, A. 1997. "A date with the family." *Harpers Magazine,* January.

Saenz, R., Hwang, S. S., Aguirre, B. E., & Anderson, R. N. 1995. "Persistence and change in Asian identity among children of intermarried couples." *Sociological Perspectives, 38,* 175–194.

Safilios-Rothschild, C. 1976. "A macro- and micro-examination of family power and love: An exchange model." *Journal of Marriage and the Family, 38,* 355–362.

Safire, W. 1995. "News about Jews." *New York Times,* July 17.

Salmon, J. L. 2000. "Study sees no change in mothering time." http://cjonline.com/stories/032800/new_mothering.shtml. Accessed May 1, 2001.

Sanchez, L. 1994. "Gender, labor allocations, and the psychology of entitlement within the home." *Social Forces, 73,* 533–553.

Sanchez-Ayendez, M. 1998. "The Puerto Rican family." In C. H. Mindel, R. W. Habenstein, & R. Wright (Eds.), *Ethnic families in America.* Upper Saddle River, NJ: Prentice Hall.

Sandefur, G. 1996. "Welfare doesn't cause illegitimacy and single parenthood." *Chronicle of Higher Education,* October 4.

Savin-Williams, R. C., & Esterberg, K. G. 2000. "Lesbian, gay, and bisexual families." In D. H. Demo, K. R. Allen, & M. A. Fine (Eds.), *Handbook of family diversity.* New York: Oxford University Press.

Saul, L. 1972. "Personal and social psychopathology and the primary prevention of violence." *American Journal of Psychiatry, 128,* 1578–1581.

Scanzoni, J. 1983. *Shaping tomorrow's family: Theory and policy for the twenty-first century.* Newbury Park, CA: Sage.

———. 1991. "Balancing the policy interests of children and adults." In E. A. Anderson & R. C. Hula (Eds.), *The reconstruction of family policy.* Westport, CT: Greenwood Press.

———. 2000. *Designing families: The search for self and community in the Information Age.* Thousand Oaks, CA: Pine Forge Press.

Scanzoni, J., & Marsiglio, W. 1991. "Wider families as primary relationships." In T. Marciano & M. B. Sussman (Eds.), *Wider families: New traditional family forms.* New York: Haworth Press.

Scanzoni, J., Polonko, K., Teachman, J. & Thompson, L. 1989. *The sexual bond: Rethinking families and close relationships.* Newbury Park, CA: Sage.

Scheper-Hughes, N. 1989. "Lifeboat ethics: Mother love and child death in northeast Brazil." *National History, 98,* 8–16.

Schmitt, E. 1998. "Day-care quandary: A nation at war with itself." *New York Times,* January 11.

———. 2001a. "For 7 million people in census, one race category is not enough." *New York Times,* March 13.

———. 2001b. "New census shows Hispanics now even with Blacks in U.S." *New York Times,* March 8.

Schnaiberg, A., & Goldenberg, S. 1989. "From empty nest to crowded nest: The dynamics of incompletely launched young adults." *Social Problems, 36,* 251–269.

Schneider, D. M. 1980. *American kinship: A cultural account.* Chicago: University of Chicago Press.

Schneider, M. B. 1996. "A campaign truth: Values matter." *Indianapolis Star,* September 29.

Schodolski, V. J. 1993. "Funeral industry, pitching videos, 2-for-1 specials to baby boomers." *Indianapolis Star,* December 26.

Scholinski, D. 1997. "The last time I wore a dress." *Utne Reader,* November–December.

Schopler, J. & Bateson, N. 1965. "The power of dependence." *Journal of Personality and Social Psychology, 2,* 247–254.

Schuller, R. A., & Vidmar, N. 1992. "Battered woman syndrome evidence in the courtroom." *Law and Human Behavior, 16,* 273–291.

Schur, E. 1988. *The Americanization of sex.* Philadelphia: Temple University Press.

Schwartz, F. N. 1989. "Management women and the new facts of life." *Harvard Business Review, 67,* 65–76.

Schwartz, P. 1987. "The family as a changed institution." *Journal of Family Issues, 8,* 455–459.

———. 1994. *Love between equals.* New York: Free Press.

———. 2000. "Creating sexual pleasure and sexual justice in the twenty-first century." *Contemporary Sociology, 29,* 213–219.

Schwartz, P., & Rutter, V. 1998. *The gender of sexuality.* Thousand Oaks, CA: Sage.

Scott, A. O. 2001. "'The wedding planner': Some things just can't be planned." *New York Times,* January 26.

Scritchfield, S. A. 1995. "The social construction of infertility: From private matter to social concern." In J. Best (Ed.), *Images of issues: Typifying contemporary social problems.* New York: Aldine de Gruyter.

Scull, A., & Favreau, D. 1986. "A chance to cut is a chance to cure: Sexual surgery for psychosis in three nineteenth century societies." In S. Spitzer & A. T. Scull (Eds.), *Research in law, deviance and social control* (Vol. 8). Greenwich, CT: JAI Press.

Sedlak, A. J., & Broadhurst, D. D. 1996. *Third national incidence study of child abuse and neglect.* Washington, DC: U.S. Department of Health and Human Services.

Sedney, M. A. 1987. "Development of androgyny: Parental influences." *Psychology of Women Quarterly, 11,* 311–326.

Seelye, K. Q. 1997a. "Future U.S.: Grayer and more Hispanic." *New York Times,* March 27.

———. 1997b. "President is set to approve sweeping shift in adoption." *New York Times,* November 17.

Seff, M. A. 1995. "Cohabitation and the law." *Marriage and Family Review, 21,* 141–168.

Seigel, J. S. 1993. *A generation of change: A profile of America's older population.* New York: Russell Sage Foundation.

Seltser, B. J., & Miller, D. E. 1993. *Homeless families: The struggle for dignity.* Urbana: University of Illinois Press.

Seltzer, J. A. 1994. "Consequences of marital dissolution for children." *Annual Review of Sociology, 20,* 235–266.

Senate Judiciary Committee. 1993. "The response to rape: Detours on the road to equal justice." Available at www.inform.umd.edu/EdRes/Topic/WomensStudies/GenderIssues/Violence+Women/ResponsetoRape/full-text. Accessed January 18, 2001.

Sennett, R. 1984. *Families against the city: Middle-class homes in industrial Chicago.* Cambridge, MA: Harvard University Press.

Sennett, R., & Cobb, J. 1972. *Hidden injuries of class.* New York: Vintage.

Settles, B. H. 1987. "A perspective on tomorrow's families." In M. B. Sussman & S. K. Steinmetz (Eds.), *Handbook of marriage and the family.* New York: Plenum.

"Sexual activity among U.S. youths is declining, a report shows." 1997. *New York Times,* May 2.

Shanahan, M. J. 2000. "Pathways to adulthood in changing societies: Variability and mechanisms in life course perspective." *Annual Review of Sociology, 26,* 667–692.

Sheets, V. L., & Braver, S. L. 1996. "Gender differences in satisfaction with divorce settlements." *Family Relations, 45,* 336–342.

Sheffield, C. J. 1987. "Sexual terrorism: The social control of women." In B. B. Hess & M. M. Ferree (Eds.), *Analyzing gender: A handbook of social science research.* Newbury Park, CA: Sage.

Shelton, B. A. 1992. *Women, men, time.* New York: Greenwood.

Shelton, B. A., & John, D. 1993. "Ethnicity, race, and difference: A comparison of white, black, and Hispanic men's household labor time." In J. C. Hood (Ed.), *Men, work, and family.* Newbury Park, CA: Sage.

Shenk, D. 1997. "Biocapitalism: What price the genetic revolution?" *Harper's Magazine,* December.

Shenon, P. 1995. "Bitter aborigines are suing for stolen childhoods." *New York Times,* July 20.

Sheridan, M. B. 2000. "In Mexico, women take a siesta from housework." *Los Angeles Times,* July 23.

Sherkat, D. E., & Ellison, C. G. 1999. "Recent developments and current controversies in the sociology of religion." *Annual Review of Sociology, 25,* 363–394.

Sherman, S. 1992. *Lesbian and gay marriage: Private commitments, public ceremonies.* Philadelphia: Temple University Press.

Sherman, S. R., Ward, R. A., & LaGory, M. 1988. "Women as caregivers of the elderly: Instrumental and expressive support." *Social Work,* March–April, pp. 164–167.

Shorter, E. 1975. *The making of the modern family.* New York: Basic Books.

Shorto, R. 1997. "Belief by the numbers." *New York Times Magazine,* December 7.

Shotland, R. L., & Straw, M. K. 1976. "Bystander response to an assault: When a man attacks a woman." *Journal of Personality and Social Psychology, 34,* 990–999.

Shweder, R. A. 1997. "It's called poor health for a reason." *New York Times,* March 9.

Sidel, R. 1990. *On her own: Growing up in the shadow of the American dream.* New York: Penguin.

Siegel, J. M. 1995. "Looking for Mr. Right? Older single women who become mothers." *Journal of Family Issues, 16,* 194–211.

Siegel, L. J. 1995. *Criminology: Theories, patterns and typologies.* Minneapolis: West.

Siegel, R. B. 1996. "The rule of love: Wife beating as prerogative and privacy." *Yale Law Journal, 105,* 2116–2207.

Silverman, J. G., Raj, A., Mucci, L. A., & Hathaway, J. E. 2001. "Dating violence against adolescent girls and associated substance use, unhealthy weight control, sexual risk behavior, pregnancy, and suicidality." *Journal of the American Medical Association, 286,* 572–579.

Simmons, T. and O'Neill, G. 2001. *Households and Families: 2000. Census 2000 Brief.* Available at www.census.gov/prod/2001pubs/c2kbr01-8.pdf. Accessed November 30, 2001.

Simon, R., Alstein, H., & Melli, M. S. 1994. *The case for transracial adoption.* Washington, DC: American University Press.

Simon, R. W., Eder, D., & Evans, C. 1992. "The development of feeling norms underlying romantic love among adolescent females." *Social Psychology Quarterly, 55,* 29–46.

Simon, R. W., & Marcussen, K. 1999. "Marital transitions, marital beliefs, and mental health." *Journal of Health and Social Behavior, 40,* 111–125.

Simpson, L. A. 1991. "A critique of 'the mommy track' as organizational intervention." Paper presented at the Annual Meetings of the American Sociological Association. Cincinnati, Ohio.

Sims, C. 1997. "Justice in Peru: Rape victim is pressed to marry attacker." *New York Times,* March 12.

———. 1998. "Using gifts as bait, Peru sterilizes poor women." *New York Times,* February 15.

———. 2000. "Japan's employers are giving bonuses for having babies." *New York Times,* May 30.

Singh, S., & Darroch, J. E. 2000. "Adolescent pregnancy and childbearing: Levels and trends in developed countries." *Family Planning Perspectives, 32,* 14–23.

Singleton, R., Straits, B. C., & Straits, M. M. 1993. *Approaches to social research.* New York: Oxford University Press.

Sink, M. 1999. "Family of one Columbine victim files lawsuit against parents of gunmen." *New York Times,* May 28.

Sjoberg, G., Williams, N., Gill, E., & Himmel, K. F. 1995. "Family life and racial and ethnic diversity: An assessment of communitarianism, liberalism, and conservatism." *Journal of Family Issues, 16,* 246–274.

Skolnick, A. S. 1979. "Public images, private realities: The American family in popular culture and social science." In V. Tufte & B. Myerhoff (Eds.), *Changing images of the family.* New Haven, CT: Yale University Press.

———. 1987. *The intimate environment: Exploring marriage and the family* (4th ed.). Boston: Little, Brown.

———. 1991. *Embattled paradise.* New York: Basic Books.

———. 1996. *The intimate environment: Exploring marriage and the family* (6th ed.). New York: HarperCollins.

Smiley, J. 2000. "Why do we marry?" *Utne Reader,* September–October.

Smith, A. 1996. "Making unpaid labor count." *Ms. Magazine,* September–October.

Smith, K. 2000. *Who's minding the kids? child care arrangements: Fall 1995,* Table 12. *Current Population Reports,* P70-70. Washington, DC: U.S. Bureau of the Census.

Smock, P. J. 2000. "Cohabitation in the United States: An appraisal of research themes, findings, and implications." *Annual Review of Sociology, 26,* 1–20.

Smock, P. J., Manning, W. D., & Gupta, S. 1999. "The effect of marriage and divorce on women's economic well-being." *American Sociological Review, 64,* 794–812.

Smolowe, J. 1994. "When violence hits home." *Time,* July 4.

Snow, E. A. 1997. *Inside Bruegel: The play of images in children's games.* San Francisco: North Point Press.

Snyder, H. N. 2000. "Sexual assault of young children as reported to law enforcement: Victim, incident, and offender characteristics." Table 1. NCJ 182990. Available at www.ojp.usdoj.gov/bjs/pub/pdf/ saycrle.pdf. Accessed October 4, 2001.

Somers, M. D. 1993. "A comparison of voluntarily childfree adults and parents." *Journal of Marriage and the Family, 55,* 643–650.

Sontag, D. 1997. "For some battered women, aid is only a promise." *New York Times,* February 14.

South, S. J. 1991. "Sociodemographic differentials in mate selection processes." *Journal of Marriage and the Family, 53,* 928–940.

———. 1992. "For love or money? Sociodemographic determinants of the expected benefits from marriage." In S. J. South & S. E. Tolnay (Eds.), *The changing American family: Sociological and demographic perspectives.* Boulder, CO: Westview Press.

South, S. J., & Lloyd, K. M. 1992. "Marriage opportunities and family formation: Further implications of imbalanced sex ratios." *Journal of Marriage and the Family, 54,* 440–451.

———. 1995. "Spousal alternatives and marital dissolution." *American Sociological Review, 60,* 21–35.

South, S. J., & Spitze, G. D. 1994. "Housework in marital and nonmarital households." *American Sociological Review, 59,* 327–347.

Spickard, P. R. 1989. *Mixed blood: Intermarriage and ethnic identity in twentieth century America.* Madison: University of Wisconsin Press.

Spitze, G. 1988. "Women's employment and family relations: A review." *Journal of Marriage and the Family, 50,* 595–618.

Sprecher, S., McKinney, K., & Orbuch, T. L. 1987. "Has the double standard disappeared? An experimental test." *Social Psychology Quarterly, 50,* 24–31.

Stacey, J. 1994. "Dan Quayle's revenge: The new family values crusaders." *The Nation,* July 25–August 1, pp. 119–122.

———. 1996a. "The father fixation." *Utne Reader,* September–October, pp. 72–73.

———. 1996b. *In the name of the family.* Boston: Beacon Press.

———. 2001. "Gay and lesbian families are here." In S. J. Ferguson (Ed.), *Shifting the center: Understanding contemporary families.* Mountain View, CA: Mayfield.

Stacey, J., & Biblarz, T. J. 2001. "(How) does the sexual orientation of parents matter?" *American Sociological Review, 66,* 159–183.

Stack, B. W. 2000. "Gay and lesbian couples' adoptions suspended." Available at www.post-gazette.com.regionstate/ 20001110adoption3.asp. Accessed May 1, 2001.

Stack, C. 1974. *All our kin: Strategies for survival in a black community.* New York: Harper & Row.

Staggenborg, S. 1998. *Gender, family and social movements.* Thousand Oaks, CA: Pine Forge Press.

Stammer, L. B. 2000. "Presbyterians' highest court OKs blessing of same-sex unions." *Lafayette Journal and Courier,* May 25, p. A4.

Stanford, E. P., Peddecord, M., & Lockery, S. 1990. "Variations among the elderly in black, Hispanic and white families." In T. Brubaker (Ed.), *Family relations in later life.* Newbury Park, CA: Sage.

Stanley, S. M., & Markman, H. J. 1992. "Assessing commitment in personal relationships." *Journal of Marriage and the Family, 54,* 595-609.

Stapinski, H. 1999. "Y not love." *American Demographics, 21,* 62–68.

Staples, B. 1999. "The final showdown on interracial marriage." *New York Times,* July 6.

Staples, R. 1992. "African American families." In J. M. Henslin (Ed.), *Marriage and family in a changing society.* New York: Free Press.

Steen, S., & Schwartz, P. 1995. "Communication, gender, and power: Homosexual couples as a case study." In M. A. Fitzpatrick & A. L. Vangelisti (Eds.), *Explaining family interactions.* Thousand Oaks, CA: Sage.

Steinberg, S. R., & Kincheloe, J. L. 1997. "Introduction: No more secrets— Kinderculture information saturation and the postmodern childhood." In S. R. Steinberg & J. L. Kincheloe (Eds.), *Kinderculture: The corporate construction of childhood.* Boulder, CO: Westview.

Steinmetz, S. K., Clavan, S., & Stein, K. F. 1990. *Marriage and family realities: Historical and contemporary perspectives.* New York: Harper & Row.

Stephan, C. W., & Stephan, W. G. 1989. "After intermarriage: Ethnic identity among mixed-heritage Japanese-Americans and Hispanics." *Journal of Marriage and the Family, 51,* 507–519.

Stephens, L. S. 1996. "Will Johnny see Daddy this week? An empirical test of three theoretical perspectives on post-divorce contact." *Journal of Family Issues, 17,* 466–494.

Stephens, W. N. 1963. *The family in cross-cultural perspective.* New York: University Press of America.

Stets, J. 1992. "Interactive processes in dating aggression: A national study." *Journal of Marriage and the Family, 54,* 165–177.

Stets, J., & Straus, M. A. 1990. "The marriage license as a hitting license: A comparison of assaults in dating, cohabiting, and married couples." In M. A. Straus & R. J. Gelles (Eds.), *Physical violence in American families.* New Brunswick, NJ: Transaction.

Stewart, A. J., Copeland, A. P., Chester, A. L., Malley, J. E., & Barenbaum, N. B. 1997. *Separating together: How divorce transforms families.* New York: Guilford Press.

Stoddard, T. B. 1992. "Why gay people should seek the right to marry." In S. Sherman (Ed.), *Lesbian and gay marriage.* Philadelphia: Temple University Press.

Stolberg, S. G. 1997. "The better half got the worse end." *New York Times,* July 20.

———. 1998a. "Eyes shut, black America is being ravaged by AIDS." *New York Times,* June 29.

———. 1998b. "Random drug testing comes home." *New York Times,* November 17.

———. 2001. "Science, studies and motherhood." *New York Times,* April 22.

Stoller, E. P., & Gibson, R. C. 1994. *Worlds of difference: Inequality in the aging experience.* Thousand Oaks, CA: Pine Forge Press.

Stolzenberg, R. M., Blair-Loy, M. & Waite, L. J. 1995. "Religious participation in early adulthood: Age and family life cycle effects on church membership." *American Sociological Review, 60,* 84–103.

Stone, L. 1979. *The family, sex and marriage in England 1500–1800.* New York: Harper Torch Books.

"The strange world of JonBenet." 1997. *Newsweek,* January 20.

Straus, M. A. 1990. "Ordinary violence, child abuse, and wife beating: What do they have in common?" In M. A. Straus & R. J. Gelles (Eds.), *Physical violence in American families.* New Brunswick, NJ: Transaction.

———. 1994. *Beating the devil out of them.* New York: Lexington Books.

Straus, M. A., & Gelles, R. J. 1986. "Societal change in family violence from 1975 to 1985 as revealed by two national surveys." *Journal of Marriage and the Family, 48,* 465–479.

———. 1990. "How violent are American families? Estimates from the National Family Violence Resurvey and other studies." In M. A. Straus & R. J. Gelles (Eds.), *Physical violence in American families.* New Brunswick, NJ: Transaction.

Straus, M. A., Gelles, R. J., & Steinmetz, S. K. 1980. *Behind closed doors: Violence in the American family.* New York: Doubleday/Anchor.

Strom, R., Collinsworth, P., Strom, P., & Griswold, D. 1992–1993. "Strengths and needs of black grandparents." *International Journal of Aging and Human Development, 36,* 255–268.

Strom, S. 2001. "On the wane in Japan: Slavish daughters-in-law." *New York Times,* April 22.

Stromberg, L. 1999. "Boy in blue tutu." *Utne Reader,* July–August.

Strube, M. J., & Barbour, L. S. 1983. "The decision to leave an abusive relationship: Economic dependence and psychological commitment." *Journal of Marriage and the Family, 45,* 785–793.

"Study of poor children shows powerful choice: Heat over food." 1992. *New York Times,* September 9.

Suarez, Z. 1998. "The Cuban-American family." In C. H. Mindel, R. W.

Habenstein, & R. Wright (Eds.), *Ethnic families in America: Patterns and variations.* Upper Saddle River, NJ: Prentice Hall.

Sullivan, A. 1996. "When plagues end: Notes on the twilight of an epidemic." *New York Times Magazine,* November 10.

Sullivan, O. 1997. "The division of housework among 'remarried' couples." *Journal of Family Issues, 18,* 205–223.

Sung, K. 1993. "Filial piety and care of the old in Korea." In L. Tepperman & S. J. Wilson (Eds.), *Next of kin.* Englewood Cliffs, NJ: Prentice Hall.

Swarns, R. L. 1997. "In a policy shift, more parents are arrested for child neglect." *New York Times,* October 25.

Sweet, J. A., & Bumpass, L. L. 1987. *American families and households.* New York: Russell Sage.

———. 1992. "Young adults' views of marriage, cohabitation, and family." In S. J. South & S. E. Tolnay (Eds.), *The changing American family: Sociological and demographic perspectives.* Boulder, CO: Westview Press.

Szinovacz, M. E., & Egley, L. C. 1995. "Comparing one-partner and couple data on sensitive marital behaviors: The case of marital violence." *Journal of Marriage and the Family, 57,* 995–1010.

Takagi, D. Y. 1994. "Japanese American families." In R. L. Taylor (Ed.), *Minority families in the United States.* Englewood Cliffs, NJ: Prentice Hall.

Talbot, M. 1997. "Dial-a-wife." *The New Yorker,* October 20 & 27.

———. 2000. "A mighty fortress." *New York Times Magazine,* February 27.

Tauber, M. A. 1979. "Parental socialization techniques and sex differences in children's play." *Child Development, 50,* 225–234.

Tavris, C. 1992. *Mismeasure of women.* New York: Touchstone.

———. 1996. "Goodbye, Ozzie and Harriet." *New York Times Book Review,* September 22.

Taylor, R. J., Chatters, L. M., Tucker, M. B., & Lewis, E. 1990. "Developments in research on black families: A decade review." *Journal of Marriage and the Family, 52,* 993–1014.

Teachman, J. D. 1991. "Contributions to children by divorced fathers." *Social Problems, 38,* 358–371.

Teachman, J. D., Tedrow, L. M., & Crowder, K. D. 2000. "The changing demography of America's families." *Journal of Marriage and the Family, 62,* 1234–1247.

"Ten facts about women workers." 1997. *World Almanac.* Mahwah, NJ: World Almanac Books.

Terman, L. 1938. *Psychological factors in marital happiness.* New York: McGraw-Hill.

Terry, D. 1996. "In Wisconsin, a rarity of a fetal-harm case." *New York Times,* August 17.

Testa, M., & Krogh, M. 1995. "The effect of employment on marriage among black males in inner-city Chicago." In M. B. Tucker & C. Mitchell-Kernan (Eds.), *The decline in marriage among African Americans.* New York: Russell Sage.

Thibaut, J., & Kelley, H. 1959. *The social psychology of groups.* New York: Wiley.

Thompson, L., & Walker, A. J. 1989. "Gender in families: Women and men in marriage, work, and parenthood." *Journal of Marriage and the Family, 51,* 845–871.

Thoresen, J. H. 1991. "Sociolegal definitions of family." *Clinical Sociology Review, 9,* 59–70.

Thorne, B., & Yalom, M. 1982. *Rethinking the family: Some feminist questions.* New York: Longman.

Thornton, A., Axinn, W. G., & Hill, D. H. 1992. "Reciprocal effects of religiosity, cohabitation, and marriage." *American Journal of Sociology, 98,* 628–651.

Thornton, A., & Camburn, D. 1989. "Religious participation and adolescent sexual behavior and attitudes." *Journal of Marriage and the Family, 51,* 641–653.

Tiano, S. 1987. "Gender, work and world capitalism: Third world women's role in development." In B. B. Hess & M. M. Ferree (Eds.), *Analyzing gender: A handbook of social science research.* Newbury Park, CA: Sage.

Tolnay, S. E., & Crowder, K. D. 1999. "Regional origin and family stability in Northern cities: The role of context." *American Sociological Review, 64,* 97–112.

Toner, R. 1999. "As parents age, the personal becomes the political." *New York Times,* July 26.

"Tough love index." 1996. *New York Times,* December 8.

Tran, T. V. 1998. "The Vietnamese-American family." In C. H. Mindel, R. W. Habenstein, & R. Wright (Eds.), *Ethnic families in America: Patterns and variations.* Upper Saddle River, NJ: Prentice Hall.

Treas, J., & Bengtson, V. L. 1982. "The demography of mid- and late-life transitions." *Annals of the American Academy of Political and Social Science, 464,* 11–21.

Trent, K., & South, S. J. 1989. "Structural determinant of the divorce rate: A cross-societal analysis." *Journal of Marriage and the Family, 51,* 391–404.

"Trip home to stand up for their community." 2000. *New York Times,* June 18.

Trost, J. 1988. "Conceptualising the family." *International Sociology, 3,* 301–308.

Tucker, M. B., & Mitchell-Kernan, C. 1990. "New trends in Black American interracial marriage: The social structural context." *Journal of Marriage and the Family, 46,* 279–290.

———. 1995. "Trends in African American family formation: A theoretical and statistical overview." In M. B. Tucker & C. Mitchell-Kernan (Eds.), *The decline in marriage among African Americans.* New York: Russell Sage.

"Tune in to adoption myths." 1988. *Psychology Today,* November, p. 12.

Turner, J. H. 1972. *Patterns of social organization.* New York: McGraw-Hill.

Turner, R. W., & Killian, L. M. 1987. *Collective behavior.* Englewood Cliffs, NJ: Prentice Hall.

Tuttle, W. 1993. *Daddy's gone to war: The Second World War in the lives of America's children.* New York: Oxford University Press.

Twigg, J., & Grand, A. 1998. "Contrasting legal conceptions of family obligation and financial reciprocity in the support of older people: France and England." *Ageing and Society, 18,* 131–146.

Uchitelle, L. 1993. "Use of temporary workers is on rise in manufacturing." *New York Times,* July 6.

———. 1997. "Welfare recipients taking jobs often held by the working poor." *New York Times,* April 1.

Uhlenberg, P. 1980. "Death and the family." *Journal of Family History, 5,* 313–320.

———. 1996. "Mutual attraction: Demography and life-course analysis." *The Gerontologist, 36,* 226–229.

Ulrich, L. T. 1990. *A midwife's tale: The life of Martha Ballard, based on her diary, 1785–1812.* New York: Knopf.

Umberson, D., & Chen, M. D. 1994. "Effects of a parent's death on adult children: Relationship salience and reaction to loss." *American Sociological Review, 59,* 152–168.

Umberson, D., Chen, M. D., House, J. S., Hopkins, K., & Slaten, E. 1996. "The effect of social relationships on psychological well-being: Are men and women really so different?" *American Sociological Review, 61,* 837–857.

Umberson, D., Wortman, C. B., & Kessler, R. C. 1992. "Widowhood and depression: Explaining long-term gender differences in vulnerability." *Journal of Health and Social Behavior, 33,* 10–24.

UNICEF. 2000. *Domestic violence against women and girls.* Innocenti Digest 6. Available at www.unicef-icdc.org. Accessed July 16, 2001.

———. 2001. *Early marriage: Child spouses.* Innocenti Digest 7. Available at www.unicef-icdc.org. Accessed March 8, 2001.

United Nations Statistics Division. 2000. *The world's women 2000: Trends and statistics.* Available at www.un.org/depts/unsd/ww2000/table4a.htm. Accessed October 4, 2001.

U.S. Bureau of Justice Statistics. 1995. *Violence against women: Estimates from the redesigned survey.* Washington, DC: U.S. Government Printing Office.

———. 2000. *Intimate partner violence.* Special Report NCJ 178247. Washington, DC: U.S. Government Printing Office.

———. 2001. "The sexual victimization of college women." BJS Press release. Available at www.ojp.usdoj.gov/bjs/pub/press/svcw.pr. Accessed January 28, 2001.

U.S. Bureau of Labor Statistics. 1999. "Median weekly earnings of full-time wage and salary workers by detailed occupation and sex." *Current Population Statistics.* Available at http://ferret.bls.census.gov/macro/171996/empearn/aat39.txt. Accessed October 4, 2001.

———. 2000. "Employment characteristics of families." Available at www.bls.gov. Accessed December 20, 2000.

U.S. Bureau of the Census. 1975. *Historical statistics of the United States: Colonial times to 1970.* Series B 216–220. Washington, DC: U.S. Government Printing Office.

———. 1992. *Statistical abstract of the United States.* Washington, DC: U.S. Government Printing Office.

———. 1993. *We the American . . . Asians.* Washington, DC: U.S. Government Printing Office.

———. 1997a. *Census and you,* May, p. 8.

———. 1997b. "Half of all mothers with infants return to labor force after giving birth, says Census Bureau report." Press release CB97-192. Available at www.census.gov. Accessed August 4, 2000.

———. 1997c. *Poverty in the United States: 1995, series p. 60–194.* Washington, DC: U.S. Government Printing Office.

———. 1997d. *Statistical abstract of the United States.* Washington, DC: U.S. Government Printing Office.

———. 1997e. *America's children at risk.* Census Brief, CENBR/97-2. Washington, DC: U.S. Government Printing Office.

———. 1998a. *All persons 15 years old and over by median and mean income and sex: 1974–1996.* Table P–9. U.S. Bureau of the Census Web Site. Available at www.census.gov. Accessed June 1, 2001.

———. 1998b. *Statistical abstract of the United States.* Washington, DC: U.S. Government Printing Office.

———. 1998c. "While moms work, dads or other relatives provide primary care for pre-schoolers." *Census and You,* April.

———. 1998d. "Unpublished tables—marital status and living arrangements: March 1998 (update)," Table 2. P20-514. Available at http://www.census.gov/prod/99pubs/p20-514u.pdf. Accessed June 1, 2001.

———. 1999a. *Statistical abstract of the United States.* Washington, DC: U.S. Government Printing Office.

———. 1999b. Internet release, Table MS-2. Available at www.census.gov/population/socdemo/ms-la/tabms-2.txt. Accessed June 1, 2001.

———. 2000a. "Poverty in the United States: 1999." *Current Population Reports,* P60-210. Washington, DC: U.S. Government Printing Office.

———. 2000b. *Statistical abstract of the United States.* Washington, DC: U.S. Government Printing Office.

———. 2001a. "Nation's median age highest ever, but 65-and-over population's growth lags, census 2000 shows." Available at www.census.gov/Press-Release/www/2001/cb01cn67.html. Accessed June 28, 2001.

———. 2001b. "The 'nuclear family' rebounds, Census Bureau reports." Report #CB01-69. Available at www.census.gov/Press-Release/www/2001/cb01-69.html. Accessed April 14, 2001.

———. 2001c. "Overview of race and Hispanic origin." Census 2000 Brief. Available at www.census.gov. Accessed September 1, 2001.

———. 2001d. "Profile of general demographic characteristics for the United States: 2000." Table DP-1. Available at www.census.gov/Press-Release/www/2001/tables/dp_us_2000.pdf. Accessed May 15, 2001.

———. 2001e. "Profile of selected social characteristics: 2000." Quick Table-02. Available at http://factfinder.census.gov/home/en/c2ss.html. Accessed August 6, 2001.

U.S. Department of Agriculture. 1999. "Expenditures on children by families." Center for Nutrition Policy and Promotion. Publication 1528-1999. Washington, DC: U.S. Government Printing Office.

U.S. Department of Health and Human Services. 2001. "Welfare reform: Implementing the Personal Responsibility and Work Opportunity Reconciliation Act of 1996." HHS Fact Sheet. Available at www.hhs.gov/news/press/2001pres/01fswelreform.html. Accessed May 26, 2001.

U.S. Department of Justice. 1998. "Violence by intimates: Analysis of data on crimes by current or former spouses, boyfriends, and girlfriends." NCJ-167237. Available at www.ojp.usdoj.gov/bjs/pub/pdf/vi.pdf. Accessed May 1, 2001.

———. 2000. "Violent crime levels declined between 1998 and 1999, rates for men and women are getting closer." Available at www.ojp.usdoj.gov/bjs/glance/vsx2.htm. Accessed May 1, 2001.

———. 2001a. "Criminal victimization in the United States, 1999 statistical tables." NCJ 184938. Available at www.ojp.usdoj.gov/bjs/pub/pdf/cvus99.pdf. Accessed January 28, 2001.

———. 2001b. *Homicide trends in the U.S.: Infanticide.* Available at www.ojp.usdoj.gov/bjs/. Accessed May 1, 2001.

———. 2001c. "Homicide trends in the U.S.: Intimate homicide." Available at www.ojp.usdoj.gov/bjs/. Accessed May 1, 2001.

U.S. Department of Labor. 2000. *FMLA Survey.* Available at www.dol.gov/dol/asp/public/fmla/toc.htm. Accessed April 9, 2001.

Utne, M. K., Hatfield, E., Traupmann, J., & Greenberger, D. 1984. "Equity, marital satisfaction, and stability." *Journal of Social and Personal Relationships, 1,* 323–332.

Uttal, L. 1999. "Using kin for child care: Embedment in the socioeconomic networks of extended families." *Journal of Marriage and the Family, 61,* 845–857.

Vandell, D. L., & Wolfe, B. 2000. "Child care quality: Does it matter and does it need to be improved?" NICHD Study of Early Child Care Research Network. Available at http://aspe.hhs.gov/hsp/ccquality00/index.htm. Accessed May 1, 2001.

van den Berghe, P. 1979. *Human family systems.* New York: Elsevier.

Vanek, J. 1980. "Work, leisure and family roles: Farm households in the United States: 1920–1955." *Journal of Family History, 5,* 422–431.

Van Willigen, J., & Channa, V. C. 1991. "Law, custom and crimes against women: The problem of dowry death in India." *Human Organization, 50,* 369–377.

Vartanian, T. P., & McNamara, J. M. 2000. "Work and economic outcomes after welfare." *Journal of Sociology and Social Welfare, 27,* 41–77.

Vaughan, D. 1986. *Uncoupling.* New York: Vintage.

Veevers, J. 1980. *Childless by choice.* Toronto: Butterworth.

Vela, D. G. 1996. *The role of religion/spirituality in building strong families: Respondents' perceptions: A qualitative grounded theory.* Dissertation, University of Nebraska. UMI Dissertation Services.

Ventura, S. J., Martin, J. A., Curtin, S. C., Menacker, F., & Hamilton, B. E. 2001. "Births: Final data for 1999." *National Vital Statistics Reports, 49*(1), Table A. Available at www.cdc.gov/nchs/data/nvsr/nvsr49/nvsr49_01.pdf. Accessed October 1, 2001.

Vincent, J. P., Weiss, R. L., & Birchler, G. R. 1975. "Dyadic problem solving behavior as a function of marital distress and spousal vs. stranger interactions." *Behavior Therapy, 6,* 475–487.

Vobejda, B. 1996. "Study rebuts 'danger' of day care." *Indianapolis Star,* April 21.

Vorauer, J. D., & Ratner, R. K. 1996. "Who's going to make the first move? Pluralistic ignorance as an impediment to relationship formation." *Journal of Social and Personal Relationships, 13,* 483–506.

Voyandoff, P. 1990. "Economic distress and family relations: A review of the eighties." *Journal of Marriage and the Family, 52,* 1099–1115.

Vroegh, K. S. 1997. "Transracial adoptees: Developmental status after 17 years." *American Journal of Orthopsychiatry, 67,* 568–575.

Waite, L. J. 1995. "Does marriage matter?" *Demography, 32,* 483–507.

———. 2000. "Social science finds: 'Marriage matters.'" In N. V. Benokraitis (Ed.), *Feuds about families.* Upper Saddle River, NJ: Prentice Hall.

Waite, L. J., & Gallagher, M. 2000. *The case for marriage: Why married people are happier, healthier, and better off financially.* New York: Doubleday.

Waldfogel, J. 1997. "The effect of children on women's wages." *American Sociological Review, 62,* 209–217.

Walker, A., & Parmar, P. 1993. *Warrior marks: Female genital mutilation and the sexual blinding of women.* New York: Harcourt Brace.

Waller, W. 1937. "The rating and dating complex." *American Sociological Review, 2,* 727–737.

Wallis, C. 1989. "Onward, women!" *Time,* December 4.

Walsh, A., & Gordon, R. A. 1995. *Biosociology: An emerging paradigm.* Westport, CT: Praeger.

Walsh, F. 1998. *Strengthening family resilience.* New York: Guilford Press.

Walton, J. 1990. *Sociology and critical inquiry.* Belmont, CA: Wadsworth.

Warren, C. A. B. 1987. *Madwives: Schizophrenic women in the 1950's.* New Brunswick, NJ: Rutgers University Press.

Watson, T. 1987. "Women athletes and athletic women: The dilemmas and contradictions of managing incongruent identities." *Sociological Inquiry, 57,* 431–446.

Wattenberg, E. 1986. "The fate of baby boomers and their children." *Social Work, 31,* 20–28.

Webb, E. J., Campbell, D. T., Schwartz, R. D., & Sechrest, L. 1966. *Unobtrusive measures: Nonreactive research in the social sciences.* Chicago: Rand McNally.

Weibel-Orlando, J. 1997. "Grandparenting styles: Native American perspectives." In M. Hutter (Ed.), *The family experience.* Boston: Allyn & Bacon.

Weigel-Garrey, C. J., Cook, C. C., & Brotherson, M. J. 1998. "Children and privacy: Choice, control, and access in home environments." *Journal of Family Issues, 19,* 43–64.

Weiss, J. 2000. *To have and to hold: Marriage, the Baby Boom and social change.* Chicago: University of Chicago Press.

Weitz, R. 1990. "Living with the stigma of AIDS." *Qualitative Sociology, 13,* 23–38.

Weitzman, L. J. 1985. *The divorce revolution: The unexpected consequences for women and children in America.* New York: Free Press.

West, C., & Zimmerman, D. H. 1987. "Doing gender." *Gender & Society, 1,* 125–151.

Westin, A. 1984. "The origins of modern claims to privacy." In F. D. Schoeman (Ed.), *Philosophical dimensions of privacy: An anthology.* New York: Cambridge University Press.

Westman, J. C. 1996. "The rationale and feasibility of licensing parents." *Society, 34,* 46–52.

Westoff, C. F., & Jones, E. F. 1977. "The secularization of U.S. Catholic birth control practices." *Family Planning Perspectives,* September–October, pp. 203–207.

Weston, K. 1991. *Families we choose: Lesbians, gays and kinship.* New York: Columbia University Press.

White, J. E. 1997. "Multiracialism: The melding of America." *Time,* May 5.

White, L., & Brinkerhoff, D. 1981. "The sexual division of labor: Evidence from childhood." *Social Forces, 60,* 170–181.

White, L., & Edwards, J. N. 1990. "Emptying the nest and parental well-being: An analysis of national panel data." *American Sociological Review, 55,* 235–242.

White, L., & Gilbreth, J. G. 2001. "When children have two fathers: Effects of relationships with stepfathers and noncustodial fathers on adolescent outcomes." *Journal of Marriage and the Family, 63,* 155–167.

White, L., & Keith, B. 1990. "The effect of shift work on the quality and stability of marital relations." *Journal of Marriage and the Family, 52,* 453–462.

White, L., & Riedmann, A. 1992. "When the Brady Bunch grows up: Step/half- and full sibling relationships in adulthood." *Journal of Marriage and the Family, 54,* 197–208.

Whiteford, L. M., & Gonzalez, L. 1995. "Stigma: The hidden burden of infertility." *Social Science and Medicine, 40,* 27–36.

Whitehead, B. D. 1993a. "Dan Quayle was right." *The Atlantic Monthly,* April, pp. 47–84.

———. 1993b. "The new family values." *Utne Reader,* May–June, pp. 61–66.

———. 1997. *The divorce culture.* New York: Knopf.

Whyte, M. K. 1990. *Dating, mating and marriage.* New York: Aldine de Gruyter.

———. 1992. "Choosing mates—the American way." *Society,* March–April, pp. 71–77.

Widom, C. S., & Maxfield, M. G. 2001. "An update on the 'cycle of violence.' "

National Institute of Justice Research in Brief. Available at www.ojp.usdoj. gov/nij/pubs-sum/184894.htm. Accessed July 15, 2001.

Wierzbicki, M. 1993. "Psychological adjustment of adoptees: A meta-analysis." *Journal of Clinical Child Psychology, 22,* 447–454.

Wilcox, W. B. 1998. "Conservative Protestant childrearing: Authoritarian or authoritative?" *American Sociological Review, 63,* 796–809.

———. 2000. "Conservative Protestant child discipline: The case of parental yelling." *Social Forces, 79,* 865–891

Wilgoren, J. 1999. "Quality daycare, early, is tied to achievements as an adult." *New York Times,* October 22.

———. 2000. "The bell rings and students stay." *New York Times,* January 24.

Wilkerson, I. 1990. "Clemency granted to 25 women convicted for assault or murder." *New York Times,* December 22.

———. 1991. "As interracial marriage rises, acceptance lags." *New York Times,* December 12.

Will, J., Self, P., & Datan, N. 1976. "Maternal behavior and perceived sex of infant." *American Journal of Ortho Psychiatry, 46,* 135–139.

Williams, G. H. 1995. *Life on the color line: The true story of a white boy who discovered he was black.* New York: Dutton.

Williams, G. I., & Williams, R. H. 1995. "'All we want is equality': Rhetorical framing in the fathers' rights movement." In J. Best (Ed.), *Images of issues.* New York: Aldine de Gruyter.

Williams, J. 2000. *Unbending gender: Why family and work conflict and what to do about it.* New York: Oxford University Press.

Willie, C. V. 1981. *A new look at the black family.* Bayside, NY: General Hall.

Wilmoth, J., & Koso, G. 1997. "Does marital history matter? The effect of marital status on wealth outcomes among pre-retirement age adults." Paper presented at the annual meetings of the North Central Sociological Association, Cincinnati, Ohio, April.

Wilson, J., & Musick, M. 1996. "Religion and marital dependency." *Journal for the Scientific Study of Religion, 35,* 30–40.

Wilson, W. J. 1987. *The truly disadvantaged: The inner city, the underclass and public policy.* Chicago: University of Chicago Press.

Winkler, A. E. 1998. "Earnings of husbands and wives in dual-earner families." *Monthly Labor Review Online.* Available at http://stats.bls.gov/opub/mlr/1998/04/art4abs.htm. Accessed July 1, 2001.

Winton, C. A. 1995. *Frameworks for studying families.* Guilford, CT: Dushkin.

Winton, M. A., & Mara, B. A. 2001. *Child abuse & neglect: Multidisciplinary approaches.* Needham Heights, MA: Allyn & Bacon.

Wolfe, A. 1998. *One nation, after all: What middle-class Americans really think about.* New York: Penguin.

Wolff, E. N. 1995. "How the pie is sliced: American's growing concentration of wealth." *American Prospect, 22,* 58–64.

Wong, E. 2001. "New rules for soccer parents: 1) No yelling. 2) No hitting ref." *New York Times,* May 6.

Wong, M. G. 1998. "The Chinese-American family." In C. H. Mindel, R. W. Habenstein, & R. Wright (Eds.), *Ethnic families in America: Patterns and variations.* Upper Saddle River, NJ: Prentice Hall.

Woodward, K. L., Quade, V., & Kantrowitz, B. 1995. "Q: When is a marriage not a marriage?" *Newsweek,* March 13.

"Working women's woes." 1994. *US News & World Report,* October 24.

"Workplace experts say more men are taking time off to care for children." 1997. *CNN On-Line,* June 13. Available at www.CNN.com. Accessed April 23, 2000.

Wright, E. O., Baxter, J., & Birkelund, G. E. 1995. "The gender gap in workplace authority: A cross-national study." *American Sociological Review, 60,* 407–435.

Wright, E. O., Costello, C., Hachen, D., & Sprague, J. 1982. "The American class structure." *American Sociological Review, 47,* 709–726.

Wright, E. O., Shire, K., Hwang, S. L., Dolan, M., & Baxter, J. 1992. "The non-effects of class on the gendered division of labor in the home: A comparative study of Sweden and the United States." *Gender and Society, 6,* 252–282.

Wu, L. L. 1996. "Effects of family instability, income, and income instability on the risk of a premarital birth." *American Sociological Review, 61,* 386–406.

Wu, L. L., & Martinson, B. C. 1993. "Family structure and the risk of premarital birth." *American Sociological Review, 58,* 210–232.

Wu, Z., & Penning, M. 1997. "Marital instability after midlife." *Journal of Family Issues, 13,* 459–478.

WuDunn, S. 1996. "A taboo creates a land of Romeos and Juliets." *New York Times,* September 11.

Wuthnow, R. 1998. *After heaven: Spirituality in America since the 1950s.* Berkeley: University of California Press.

Yardley, J. 2000. "Unmarried and living together, till the sheriff do us part." *New York Times,* March 25.

Ybarra, L. 1982. "When wives work: The impact on the Chicano family." *Journal of Marriage and the Family, 44,* 169–178.

Yee, B. W. K. 1992. "Elders in Southeast Asian refugee families." *Generations,* Summer, pp. 24–27.

Yi, Z., & Deqing, W. 2000. "Regional analysis of divorce in China since 1980." *Demography, 37,* 215–219.

Yllo, K. 1993. "Through a feminist lens: Gender, power and violence." In R. J. Gelles & D. R. Loeske (Eds.), *Current controversies on family violence.* Newbury Park, CA: Sage.

Yllo, K., & Straus, M. A. 1990. "Patriarchy and violence against wives: The impact of structural and normative factors." In M. A. Straus & R. J. Gelles (Eds.), *Physical violence in American families.* New Brunswick, NJ: Transaction.

Yoest, C. C. 1997. "Fountain of youth, spring of wealth." In H. A. Widdison (Ed.), *Social problems 1997/1998.* Guilford, CT: Dushkin/McGraw-Hill.

Young, M. E. 1995. "Reproductive technologies and the law: Norplant and the bad mother." *Marriage and the Family Review, 21,* 259–281.

Zelizer, V. 1985. *Pricing the priceless child.* New York: Basic Books.

Zhang, S. D., & Odenwald, W. F. 1995. "Misexpression of the white gene triggers male–male courtship in Drosphilia." *Proceedings of the National Academy of Sciences, 92,* 5525–5529.

Zimmerman, S. L. 1992. *Family policies and family well-being: The role of political culture.* Newbury Park, CA: Sage.

Zurcher, L. A., & Snow, D. A. 1981. "Collective behavior: Social movements." In M. Rosenberg & R. H. Turner (Eds.), *Social psychology: Sociological perspectives.* New York: Basic Books.

Zvonkovic, A. M., Greaves, K. M., Schmiege, C. J., & Hall, L. D. 1996. "The marital construction of gender through work and family decisions: A qualitative analysis." *Journal of Marriage and the Family, 58,* 91–100.

Zweig, M. 2000. *The working class majority: America's best kept secret.* Ithaca, NY: Cornell University Press.

Credits

Glossary/Index

A

abortion issues, 347, 530–531

absent fathers, 470–472

abusive relationships, 416–422. *See also* intimate violence

adolescence The gut-wrenching, noisy, awkward, tumultuous, ill-defined but recognizable stage of life that marks the transition between childhood and adulthood; varies in different eras and different cultures, 373–378

  history and culture of, 375–378

  media portrayal of, 393–394

  onset of puberty and, 219–220

  pregnancy and childbirth in, 25, 220–222

  privacy rights in, 48–49

  risk factors in, 377–378

  sexuality in, 218–220, 222–224, 374–375, 376

  social construction of, 374–375

  study assignment on, 393–394

  summary points on, 393

  See also childhood

adoption

  genetic parenthood vs., 329–331

  kinship ties and, 10

  transracial, 385–386

adulthood transitions, 488–497

  empty nest syndrome, 492–494

  entering adulthood, 489–491

  grandparenthood, 494–497

  old age, 497

Adult Protective Services, 433

Afghanistan, 75

African-American families, 150–154

  child rearing in, 383, 384–385

  class stratification and, 173

  diversity of, 153–154

  divorce in, 446

  domestic division of labor in, 314

  economic factors and, 152

  educational opportunities and, 152

  elder care in, 507

  family patterns in, 153–154, 161–163

  grandparents in, 496

  interracial marriage and, 252–253

  racial discrimination and, 152

  slavery and, 150–151

  transracial adoption and, 385–386

  U.S. population trends and, 545

age

  elderly population trends and, 501–503

  infertility treatments and, 331, 335

  living arrangements and, 489–491, 503–505

  marital patterns and, 248, 249, 255

  social expectations based on, 486

Age Discrimination in Employment Act (1967), 501

age norms Social expectations about how individuals should act based on their age, 486

agents of socialization Sources of socialization such as family, school, peers, friends, and television, which provide children with cultural information concerning behaviors and beliefs, 379

AIDS epidemic, 512, 537–538

Aid to Families and Dependent Children (AFDC), 419

alcohol abuse

  pregnant women and, 347–348

  spousal violence and, 412

Alliance for Marriage, 15

All Our Kin (Stack), 12

Almonte, Danny, 362

Amato, Paul, 458–459

ambiguous genitalia, 116–117

America. *See* United States

American Association of Retired Persons, 507, 508

American Association of University Women, 376

American Home Economics Association (AHEA), 11

American Psychiatric Association (APA), 135, 211

American Public Welfare Association, 429–431

Ammerman, Nancy Tatom, 73

analysis

  content, 98

  historical, 98–99

  units of, 99–100

androgynous socialization Bringing up children to develop both male and female traits and behaviors, 122–123

Annie Hall (film), 211

antinatalism, 328

Arendell, Terry, 470

Aron, Arthur, 95

arranged marriage, 55, 205–206

Asante people, 375

Asian-American families, 154–156

  contemporary changes in, 156

  divorce in, 446

  elderly members of, 56, 500

  ethnic identity in, 148

  internment of Japanese, 155–156

  interracial marriage and, 156, 252

  prejudice and discrimination against, 154–156

  U.S. population trends and, 545

assimilation The process by which members of minority groups change their ways to conform to those of the dominant culture, 160–161

Associate, The (film), 282–283

attraction

  relationship formation and, 234

  sociobiological model of, 232–233

Atwood, Margaret, 522–523

autonomy, 40, 43

Avicolli, Tommy, 124

B

Baby and Child Care (Spock), 431

baby boomers, 29–31, 62, 487–488, 525–526

backstage behavior, 42–43

Baird, Zoe, 311